CIVILIZATION IN THE WEST

VOLUME B 1350 TO 1815

CIVILIZATION IN THE WEST

VOLUME B 1350 TO 1815

MARK KISHLANSKY
University of Chicago

PATRICK GEARY
University of Florida

PATRICIA O'BRIEN
University of California, Irvine

HarperCollins*Publishers*

Executive Editor: Bruce Borland
Development Editor: Betty Slack
Project Coordination: The Wheetley Company, Inc.
Cover Design: Lucy Lesiak Design, Inc.: Lucy Lesiak
Text Design: Debbie Costello
Photo Research: Sandy Schneider
Cartographer: Paul Yatabe. Maps produced by Mapping Specialists, Inc.
Production: Michael Weinstein
Compositor: Dayton Typographic Services
Printer and Binder: R.R. Donnelley & Sons Company
Cover Printer: The Lehigh Press, Inc.

Cover: (background) Detail from the cycle of frescos depicting *The Legend of the True Cross* by Piero della Francesca, c. 1450s. In the church of San Francesco, Arezzo. Scala/Art; (inset) Detail, *The Doge Leonardo Loredan* by Giovanni Bellini, c. 1501. Bridgeman/Art Resource, NY.

Civilization in the West, Volume B 1350 to 1815

Library of Congress Cataloging-in-Publication Data
Kishlansky, Mark A.
    Civilization in the West / Mark Kishlansky, Patrick Geary,
Patricia O'Brien.
        p.   cm.
    Includes bibliographical references and index.
    Contents: v. A. To 1500 -- v. B. 1350-1815 -- v. C. Since 1789.
    ISBN 0-673-46386-9 (v. A). -- ISBN 0-673-46387-7 (v. B). --
ISBN 0-673-46388-5 (v. C)
    1. Civilization, Occidental--History.   I. Geary, Patrick J.,
1948-   . II. O'Brien, Patricia, 1945-   . III. Title.
CB245.K546   1991c
909'.09821--dc20   90-23788
                                                          CIP

91 92 93   9 8 7 6 5 4 3 2

Contents

Maps

Charts, Tables, and Figures

Preface

We have tried to write a book that students would *want* to read. Throughout three years of planning, writing, revising, rewriting, and numerous meetings together, this was our constant overriding concern. Would students read this? Would it be effective in conveying information while stimulating imagination? Would it work across the variety of Western civilization courses, with the different levels and formats that make up this fundamental course? It was not easy to keep this concern in the forefront through the long months of composition, but it was easy to receive the reactions of scores of reviewers to this single questions: "Would students *want* to read these chapters?" Whenever we received a resounding "no!" we began again—not just rewriting, but rethinking how to present material that might be complex in argument or detail or that might simply seem too remote to engage the contemporary student. Though all three of us were putting in long hours in front of word processors, we quickly learned that we were engaged in a teaching rather than a writing exercise. And though the work was demanding, it was not unrewarding. We hope that you will recognize and come to share with us the excitement and enthusiasm we experienced in creating this text. We have enjoyed writing this book, and we want students to enjoy reading it.

Approach

We made a number of decisions early in the project that we feel contributed to our goal. First, we were *not* writing an encyclopedia of Western civilization. Information was not to be included in a chapter unless it fit within the themes of that chapter. There was to be no information for information's sake, and each of us was called upon to defend the inclusion of names, dates, and events whenever we met to critique our chapters. We found, to our surprise, that by adhering to the principle that information included must contribute to or illustrate a particular point or dominating theme, we provided as much, if not more, material than books that habitually list names, places, and dates without any other context.

Secondly, we were committed to integrating the history of ordinary men and women into our narrative. We believe that isolated sections, placed at the end of chapters, that deal with the experiences of women or minority groups in a particular era profoundly distort historical experience. We called this technique *caboosing*, and whenever we found ourselves segregating women or families or the masses, we stepped back and asked how we might recast our treatment of historical events to account for a diversity of actors. How did ordinary men, women, and children affect the course of world historical events? How did world historical events affect the fabric of daily life for men and women and children from all walks of life? We tried to rethink critical historical problems of civilization as gendered phenomena. To assist us in this endeavor, we engaged two reviewers whose sole responsibility was to evaluate our chapters for the integration of these social groups into the themes of our chapters.

We took the same approach to the coverage of central and eastern Europe that we did to women and minorities. Even before the epochal events of 1989 that returned this region to the forefront of international attention, we realized that in too many textbooks the Slavic world was treated as "marginal" to the history of Western civilization. Thus, with the help of a specialist reviewer, we worked to integrate more of the history of eastern Europe into our text than is found in most others, and to do so in a way that presented these regions, their cultures and their institutions, as integral rather than peripheral to Western civilization.

To construct a book that students would *want* to read, we needed to develop fresh ideas about how to involve them with the material, how to transform them from passive recipients to active participants. We borrowed from computer science both the language and the concept of "user-friendly." We wanted to find ways to stimulate the imagination of the student, and the more we experimented with different techniques, the more we realized that the most effective way to do this was visually. It is not true that contemporary students cannot be taught effectively by the written word; it is only true that they cannot be taught *as* effectively as they can by the combination of words and images. From the beginning, we realized that a text produced in full color was essential to the features we most wanted to use: the pictorial chapter openers; the large number of maps, some inset directly into the text for maximum effectiveness; the geographical tours of Europe with their specially designed maps; and the two-page special feature in each chapter, each with its own illustration.

Features

It is hard to have a new idea when writing a textbook—so many authors have come before, each attempting to do something more effective, more innovative than his or her predecessor. It is probably the case that somewhere there has been a text that has used a chapter-opening feature similar to the one we use here. What we can say with certainty is that nothing else we experimented with, no other technique we attempted, has had such an immediate and positive impact on our readers or has so fulfilled our goal of involving the students in learning as our **pictorial chapter openers**. An illustration—a painting, a photograph, a picture, an artifact, an edifice—appears at the beginning of each chapter, accompanied by text through which we explore the picture, guiding students across a canvas or helping them see in an artifact or a piece of architecture details that are not immediately apparent. It is the direct combination of text and image that allows us to achieve this effect, to "unfold" both an illustration and a theme. In some chapters we highlight details, pulling out a section of the original picture to take a closer look. In others we attempt to shock the viewer into the recognition of horror, or of beauty. Some chapter-opener images are designed to transport students back into time, to make them ask the question, "What was it like to be there?" All of the opening images have been chosen to illustrate a dominant theme within the chapter, and the dramatic and lingering impression they make helps reinforce that theme.

We have taken a similar image-based approach to our **presentation of geography**. When teachers of Western civilization courses are surveyed, no single area of need is cited more often that geographical knowledge. Students simply have no mental image of Europe, no familiarity with those geophysical features that are a fundamental part of the geopolitical realities of Western history. We realized that maps, carefully planned and skillfully executed, would be an important component of our text. To complement the standard map program of the text, we have added a special geographical feature. Six times throughout the book, we pause in the narrative to take a tour of Europe. Sometimes we follow an emperor as he tours his realm; sometimes we examine the impact of a peace treaty; sometimes we follow the travels of a merchant. Whatever the thematic occasion, our intention is to guide the student around the changing contours of the geography of Western history. In order to do this effectively, we have worked with our cartographer to develop small inset, or thumbnail, maps to complement the overview map that appears at the beginning of each tour section. We know that only the most motivated students will turn back several pages to locate on a map a place mentioned in the text. Using the small inset map allows us to integrate the map directly into the relevant text, thus relieving the student of the sometimes frustrating experience of attempting to locate not only a specific place on a map but perhaps even the relevant map itself. The great number of maps throughout the text, the specially designed tour-of-Europe geographical feature, and the ancillary programs of map transparencies and workbook exercises combine to provide the strongest possible program for teaching historical geography.

The third technique we have employed to engage students with historical subjects is the two-page **special feature** that appears in each chapter. These special features focus on a single event or personality chosen to enhance the student's sense that history is something that is real and alive. These features are written more dramatically or sympathetically or with a greater sense of wonder than would be appropriate in the body of the text. The prose style and the accompanying illustration are designed to captivate the reader. Three of the features concern utopias (Plato's *Republic*, More's *Utopia*, and Orwell's *Animal Farm*), posing questions about the ways in which different societies dream. Three of the features focus on Paris at various points in its history (the medieval period, the early modern age, and the modern era), tracing the development of the quintessential European city over a millennium. Accounts of the discovery of King Tut's tomb, of the fall of Constantinople, or of tsarist cavalry trampling women protesters place the student squarely in the middle of a historical event.

There are many new features in our text, and much that is out of the ordinary. But there are important traditional aspects of the narrative itself that also require mention. **Civilization in the West** is a mainstream text in which most energies have been placed in developing a solid, readable narrative of Western civilization that integrates coverage of women and minorities into the discussion. We have highlighted personalities while identifying trends. We have spotlighted social history, both in sections of chapters and in separate chapters, while maintaining a firm grip on political developments. We hope that there are many things in this book that teachers of Western civilization will find valuable. But we also hope that there are things here with which you will disagree, themes that you can develop better, arguments and ideas that will stimulate you. A textbook is only one part of a course, and it is always less important than a teacher. What we hope is that by doing our job successfully, we have made the teacher's job easier and the student's job more enjoyable.

Mark Kishlansky
Patrick Geary
Patricia O'Brien

Acknowledgments

We want to thank the many conscientious historians who reviewed our manuscript and gave generously of their time and knowledge. Their valuable critiques and suggestions have contributed greatly to the final product. We are grateful to the following:

Meredith L. Adams, *Southwest Missouri State University*

John W. Barker, *University of Wisconsin*

William H. Beik, *Northern Illinois* University

Lenard R. Berlanstein, *University of Virginia*

Raymond Birn, *University of Oregon*

Donna Bohanan, *Auburn University*

Werner Braatz, *University of Wisconsin at Oshkosh*

Thomas A. Brady, Jr., *University of Oregon*

Anthony M. Brescia, *Nassau Community College*

Elaine G. Breslaw, *Morgan State University*

Daniel Patrick Brown, *Moorpark College*

Ronald A. Brown, *Charles County Community College*

Edward J. Champlin, *Princeton University*

Stephanie Evans Christelow, *Western Washington University*

Gary B. Cohen, *University of Oklahoma*

John J. Contreni, *Purdue University*

Samuel E. Dicks, *Emporia State University*

Frederick Dumin, *Washington State University*

Margot C. Finn, *Emory University*

Allan W. Fletcher, *Boise State University*

Elizabeth L. Furdell, *University of North Florida*

Thomas W. Gallant, *University of Florida*

Joseph J. Godson, *Hudson Valley Community College*

Eric Haines, *Bellevue Community College*

David A. Harnett, *University of San Francisco*

Paul B. Harvey, Jr., *Pennsylvania State University*

Daniel W. Hollis, *Jacksonville State University*

Kenneth G. Holum, *University of Maryland*

Charles Ingrao, *Purdue University*

George F. Jewsbury, *Oklahoma State University*

Donald G. Jones, *University of Central Arkansas*

William R. Jones, *University of New Hampshire*

Richard W. Kaeuper, *University of Rochester*

David Kaiser, *Carnegie-Mellon University*

William R. Keylor, *Boston University*

Joseph Kicklighter, *Auburn University*

Charles L. Killinger, III, *Valencia Community College*

David C. Large, *Montana State University*

Roberta T. Manning, *Boston College*

Lyle McAlister, *University of Florida*

Therese M. McBride, *College of the Holy Cross*

Robert Moeller, *University of California at Irvine*

Pierce C. Mullen, *Montana State University*

Thomas F. X. Noble, *University of Virginia*

Dennis H. O'Brien, *West Virginia University*

Peter E. Piccillo, *Rhode Island College*

Marlette Rebhorn, *Austin Community College*

John P. Ryan, *Kansas City Kansas Community College*

Steven Schroeder, *Indiana University of Pennsylvania*

Bonnie Smith, *University of Rochester*

Peter N. Stearns, *Carnegie-Mellon University*

Darryl R. Sycher, *Columbus State Community College*

Steven Vincent, *North Carolina State University*

Richard A. Voeltz, *Cameron University*

Eric Weissman, *Golden West College*

Each author also received invaluable assistance and encouragement from many colleagues, friends, and family members over the years of research, reflection, writing, and revising that went into the making of this text.

Mark Kishlansky wishes to thank Ann Adams, Robert Bartlett, Ray Birn, David Buisseret, Ted Cook, Frank Conaway, Constantine Fasolt, Katherine Haskins, Richard Hellie, Matthew Kishlansky, Donna Marder, Mary Beth Rose, Jeanne Thiel, The Staff of the Joseph Regenstein Library and the Newberry Library.

Patrick Geary wishes to thank Mary Geary, Catherine Geary, and Anne Geary for their patience, support, and encouragement as well as Anne Picard and Dale Scofield for their able assistance throughout the project.

Patricia O'Brien thanks Jon Jacobson for his constant support and for sharing his specialized knowledge and his historical sense. She also wishes to thank Elizabeth Bryant for her encouragement and enthusiasm throughout the project; Robert Moeller for his keen eye for organization and his suggestions for writing a gendered history; and Katherine Turley for her unflagging assistance with bibliographic issues.

All the authors would also like to thank, though words are but a poor expression of our gratitude, Barbara Muller, Bruce Borland, and Betty Slack, the editors of our project. If ever authors have had more felicitous experiences with their editors than we have had with ours, they have been lucky indeed. The authors also extend sincere appreciation to Michael Weinstein, Elizabeth Gabbard, Susan Ritchey, Lucy Lesiak, Sandy Schneider, and Paul Yatabe, who contributed their skills and expertise to the editorial, design, photo research, and cartographic processes involved in the production of this book.

Supplements

The following supplements are available for use in conjunction with this book:

For the Student

Student Study Guide in two volumes. Volume 1 (chapters 1-16) prepared by Steven Schroeder, Indiana University of Pennsylvania, and Volume 2 (chapters 15-30) prepared by Werner Braatz, University of Wisconsin at Oshkosh. Includes learning objectives, an overview of each chapter, glossary terms, and sample study exercises, including identification questions, chronology exercises, multiple-choice questions, and historical thinking/essay questions. Each volume also contains the essay, "Writing About History," a brief guide to writing a history research paper.

Mapping Western Civilization: Student Activities workbook by Gerald Danzer, University of Illinois at Chicago. Features numerous map skill exercises written to enhance students' basic geographical literacy. The exercises provide ample opportunities for interpreting maps and analyzing cartographic materials as historical documents. The instructor is entitled to one free copy of **Mapping Western Civilization: Student Activities** for each copy of the text purchased from HarperCollins.

Sources of the West by Mark Kishlansky, a collection of primary source documents available in two volumes, features a well-balanced selection of constitutional documents, political theory, intellectual history, philosophy, literature, and social description. Review questions follow each selection. Each volume includes the introductory essay, "How to Read a Document," which leads students step by step through the experience of using historical documents.

SuperShell Computerized Tutorial, an interactive program for computer-assisted learning, prepared by Paul A. Bischoff, Oklahoma State University. Features multiple-choice, true-false, and completion quizzes, comprehensive chapter outlines, "Flash Cards" for key terms and concepts, and diagnostic feedback capabilities. Available for IBM computers.

Historical Geography for Western Civilization: Computerized Atlas by William Hamblin, Brigham Young University. Computerized atlas and historical geography tutorial for the Macintosh.

For the Instructor

Instructor's Resource Manual by Margot C. Finn of Emory University. Includes units on Teaching the Western Civilization Course, Teaching with Primary Sources, Teaching Through Film, and Teaching Through Maps as well as a chapter-by-chapter guide to each chapter of the text. The chapter-by-chapter guides contain a chapter synopsis, a list of key terms, and sample questions for class discussion or writing assignments.

Test Bank prepared by Daniel Patrick Brown, Moorpark College, Paul A. Bischoff, Oklahoma State University, and Darryl R. Sycher, Columbus State

Community College. A total of 1500 questions, 50 per text chapter, including both objective and essay questions. Each test item is referenced by topic, type, and text page number. Available in print and computerized format.

TestMaster Computerized Testing System, test-generation software package available for the IBM, Apple, and Macintosh. Allows users to add, edit, and create graphics. Test questions are translatable to word processing software. Available free to adopters.

Visual Archives of Western Civilization—Video Laser Disc includes a "Portrait Gallery" of fine art and photos, over 300 still images and 29 minutes of full-motion film clips. Crisp detail and remote-control access make this supplement especially useful in large lecture halls. An accompanying **Instructor's Guide** contains fully referenced user's notes keyed to the text, a frame-by-frame list of images, and a brief tutorial on using the laser disc in the classroom.

Discovering Western Civilization Through

Maps and Views by Gerald Danzer, University of Illinois at Chicago, and David Buisseret, Newberry Library, Chicago. This set of 100 four-color transparencies from selected sources is bound in a three-ring binder and available free to adopters. Also contains an introduction on teaching history with maps and a detailed commentary on each transparency. The collection includes cartographic and pictorial maps, views, and photos, urban plans, building diagrams, classic maps, and works of art.

The Winner's Circle Video Program, a collection of ten prize-winning films and videos for Western Civilization. Available for loan exclusively to adopters of the text.

The Integrator, a cross-referencing guide to all print, software, and media supplements accompanying the text.

Grades, a grade-keeping and classroom management system maintains date for up to 200 students.

About the Authors

Mark Kishlansky
Recently appointed to the Committee on Social Thought at the University of Chicago, Mark Kishlansky is among today's leading young scholars. After receiving his Ph.D. at Brown University, Professor Kishlansky joined the University of Chicago faculty where he has taught since. A Fellow of the Royal Historical Society, his primary area of expertise is seventeenth-century English political history. Among his main publications are *Parliamentary Selection: Social and Political Choice in Early Modern England* and *The Rise of the New Model Army*. He is the editor of the *Journal of British Studies* and the recipient of the 1989 Most Distinguished Alumnus Award from SUNY Stony Brook.

Patrick Geary
Holding a Ph.D. in Medieval Studies from Yale University, Patrick Geary is both a noted scholar and teacher. Named outstanding undergraduate history teacher for the 1986-87 year at the University of Florida, where he currently teaches, Professor Geary

has also held academic positions at the Ecole des hautes etudes en sciences sociales, Paris, the Universitat Wien, and Princeton University. A member of the Institute for Advanced Study, his many publications include *Readings in Medieval History, Before France and Germany: The Creation and Transformation of the Merovingian World, Aristocracy in Provence: The Rhone Basin at the Dawn of the Carolingian Age*, and *Furta Sacra: Medieval Narratives of Stolen Relics*.

Patricia O'Brien
An Associate Professor at the University of California, Irvine, and Assistant Vice Chancellor in the Office of Research and Graduate Studies, Professor O'Brien holds a Ph.D. from Columbia University in modern European history. Among her many publications are *The Promise of Punishment: Prisons in 19th Century France, l'Embastillement de Paris: The Fortification of Paris During the July Monarchy, Crime and Punishment as Historical Problem*, and Michel Foucault's *History of Culture*.

11

The Italian Revival

$\mathcal{A}$ Civic Procession

It is 25 April 1444. On this day each year the city of Venice celebrates its patron, Saint Mark, with a procession around the square that bears his name. Processions are a common form of civic ritual through which a community defines itself. The special features that identify Venice for its citizens are all on display. Flags and emblems of the city are mounted on poles, and clothes bear the insignia of various orders and groups. The procession re-creates all forms of communal life. Here are the religious orders (the white-clad brothers of the Confraternity of Saint John are passing before

us now), and the civic leaders can be seen just behind them. Musicians entertain both marchers and onlookers. An entire band files by on the right. The procession is orderly, but it is by no means contrived. It is not staged, as would be a modern ceremony, and this difference is evident in the relaxed attitude of the ordinary citizens who stand in groups in the middle of the square. There is no apparent drama to observe, and they walk and talk quite naturally. So, too, do the participants. In the lower left-hand corner, some friars are reading music; at the lower right, members of the confraternity carry their candles negligently.

Yet the painting, *The Procession of the Relic of the Holy Cross* (1496) by Gentile Bellini (ca. 1429–

the line of brothers breaks. The next day, the boy revived and his injury healed.

The Brothers of Saint John commissioned Bellini to commemorate this event. Bellini came from the most distinguished family of painters in Venice. His father Jacopo had studied in Florence and had brought both of his sons into his workshop when they were young boys. Until the age of thirty Gentile and his younger and more famous brother, Giovanni, worked on their father's commissions, learning the difficult craft of painting. Art was very much a family business in fifteenth-century Italy. The large workshops with their master and hordes of apprentices turned out vast canvasses with almost assembly-line precision. The master created the composition and sketched it out; his skilled assistants, like the Bellini brothers, worked on the more complex parts; and young apprentices painted backgrounds and indistinct faces. The master was first and foremost a businessman, gaining commissions to sustain his family and his workers. The Bellinis were well connected to the Confraternity of Saint John, and it was only natural that Gentile would receive this lucrative contract.

Though *The Procession of the Relic of the Holy Cross* was designed to re-create a central moment in the history of the confraternity, it is not the confraternity that dominates the picture. Miracles were part of civic life, and each town took pride in the special manifestations of heavenly care that had taken place within it. And it is very much Venice that is the centerpiece of Bellini's canvas. Dominating the painting is the Basilica of San Marco, with its four great horses over the center portico and the winged lion, the city's symbol, on the canopy above the horses. The procession emanates from the duke's palace to the right of the church, and the great flags of the city are seen everywhere. By the end of the fifteenth century, Venice was one of the greatest powers on earth, the center for international trade and finance. Home to the largest concentration of wealthy families anywhere in Europe, it could well afford the pomp and splendor of its processions. The achievements of God and the achievements of humans blend together in this painting as they blended together in that era of remarkable accomplishments that historians call the Renaissance.

1507), was commissioned to commemorate a miracle rather than a civic procession. On the evening before Saint Mark's day, a visiting merchant and his son were touring the square when the boy accidentally fell and cracked his skull. The doctors who were called to treat him regarded the case as hopeless and advised the father to prepare for his son's death. The next morning, the Brothers of the Confraternity of Saint John carried the relic of a piece of the true cross beneath an embroidered canopy. The merchant approached the golden altarpiece that contained the relic, dropped to his knees, and prayed that Saint Mark would miraculously cure his son. He is the red-clad figure kneeling just to the right of center where

Renaissance Society

Perhaps the most surprising result of the Black Death was the way in which European society revived itself in the succeeding centuries. Even at the height of the plague a spirit of revitalization was evident in the works of artists and writers. Petrarch (1304–74), the great humanist poet and scholar, was among the first to differentiate the new age in which he was living from two earlier ones: the classical world of Greece and Rome, which he admired, and the subsequent Dark Ages, which he detested. This spirit of self-awareness is one of the defining characteristics of the Renaissance. "It is but in our own day that men dare boast that they see the dawn of better things," wrote Matteo Palmieri (1406–75). Like many others, Marsilio Ficino (1433–99), a Florentine physician and philosopher who translated Plato and dabbled in astrology, dubbed his times a golden age. "This century, like a golden age, has restored to light the liberal arts, which were almost extinct: grammar, poetry, rhetoric, painting, sculpture, architecture, and music." The Renaissance was a new age by self-assertion. In that self-assertion wave after wave of artistic celebration of the human spirit found its wellspring and created a legacy that is still vibrant five hundred years later.

What was the Renaissance? A French word for an Italian phenomenon, *Renaissance* literally means "rebirth." The word captures both the emphasis on humanity that characterized Renaissance thinking and the renewed fascination with the classical world. But the Renaissance was an age rather than an event. There is no moment at which the Middle Ages ended and, as we have seen, late medieval society was artistically creative, socially well developed, and economically diverse. Early Renaissance and late medieval are all but indistinguishable. Yet eventually the pace of change accelerated, and it is best to think of the Renaissance as an era of rapid transitions. Encompassing the two centuries between 1350 and 1550, it passed through three distinct phases. The first, from 1350 to 1400, was characterized by a declining population, the uncovering of classical texts, and experimentation in a variety of art forms. The creation of a set of cultural values and artistic and literary achievements that defined Renaissance style distinguished the second phase, from 1400 to 1500. The large Italian city-states developed stable and coherent forms of government and the warfare between them gradually ended. In the final period, from 1500 to 1550, invasions from France and Spain transformed Italian political life, and the ideas and techniques of Italian writers and artists radiated to all points of the Continent. Though Renaissance ideas and achievements did spread throughout western Europe, they are best studied where they first developed, on the Italian peninsula.

The Environment

The Italian peninsula differed sharply from other areas of Europe in the extent to which it was urban. By the late Middle Ages nearly one in four Italians lived in a town, in contrast to one in ten elsewhere. Not even the plague did much to change this ratio. There were more Italian cities and more people in them. By 1500 seven of the ten largest cities in the West were in Italy. Naples, Venice, and Milan, each with a population of more than one hundred thousand, led the rest. But not every city was a great metropolis, and it was the numerous smaller towns, with populations nearer to one thousand, that gave the Italian peninsula its urban character. Cities were still the wonder of the world, dominating their regions economically, politically, and culturally. The diversified economic activities in which the inhabitants engaged created vast concentrations of wealth. Cities also served as convenient centers of judicial and ecclesiastical power. Moreover, they attracted to their regions the novelties of life, whether new products or new ideas.

Though cities served as regional centers, they cannot be viewed in isolation from their rural surroundings. Cities acted as central places around which a cluster of large and small villages was organized. Urban areas, especially the small towns, provided markets for the agricultural produce of the countryside and for the manufactured goods of the urban craftsmen. It was in the cities that goods and services changed hands. This allowed for the specialization in agricultural and industrial life that increased both productivity and wages. Cities also caught the runoff of rural population, especially the shower of younger sons

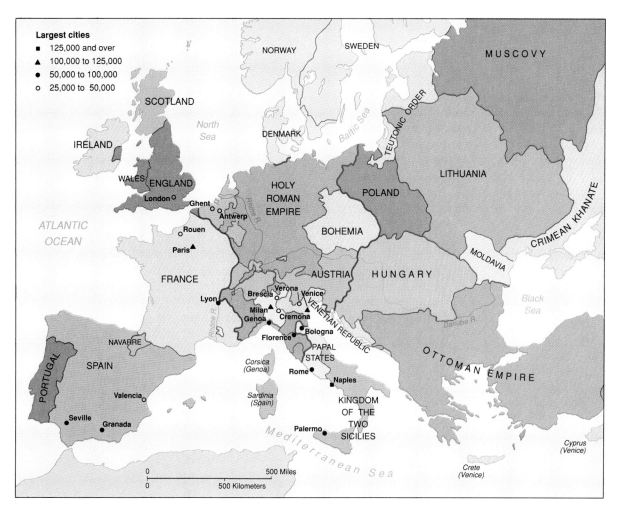

Europe, ca. 1500

and daughters who could not be accommodated on the farms. Cities grew by migration rather than by natural increase, and immigrants flooded into them. Thus the areas surrounding a city were critical to its prosperity and survival. The urban system was a network of cities encompassed by towns encircled by rural villages. Florence, the dominant city in the region of Tuscany, exemplifies this relationship. Though it possessed two-thirds of its region's wealth, Florence contained only 14 percent of the regional population. The surrounding countryside was agriculturally rich, for marketing costs were low and demand for foodstuffs high. A number of smaller cities like Prato and Pistoia to the north and Pisa to the west channeled their local produce and trade to Florence.

Though cities may have dominated Renaissance Italy, by present standards they were small in both area and population. Despite the city's wealth, great banks, magnificent palaces and piazzas, a person could walk across fifteenth-century Florence in less than half an hour. In 1427 its population was thirty-seven thousand, only half its pre-plague size. Most Italian cities contained large fields for agricultural production, and within the outer walls of Florence were gardens and grain fields. Inside the inner city walls the people crowded together into tightly packed quarters. Streets were narrow and dark, with an incredible jumble of buildings in all sizes, shapes, and states of repair, though with the exception of churches and the "towers" of the rich, few were taller than three stories. The intensity of the stench from raw sewage, rotting foodstuffs, and animals being brought to slaughter was equaled only by the din made by hoofs and wooden cartwheels on paving stones and roaring open fires around which people plied their crafts, cooked their food, or huddled for warmth.

Urban populations were organized far differently from rural ones. On the farms the central distinctions involved ownership of land. Some farmers owned their estates outright and left them intact to their heirs. Others were involved in a sharecropping system by which absentee owners of land supplied working capital in return for half of the farm's produce. A great gulf in wealth separated owners from sharecroppers. Those who owned their land normally lived with surplus, those who sharecropped always lived on the margin of subsistence. But within the groups the gaps were not as great. There were gradations, but these were ordinarily temporary conditions that bad harvests, generous dowries, or divided inheritances balanced out over time.

Sheltering Pilgrims, by Francisco Hubertini Bacchiacca. Oil on wood. Pilgrims are looking for lodging on a street in Florence. All public inns in Florence were on a single street, and their management was strictly regulated.

In the city, however, distinctions were based first on occupation, which largely corresponded to social position and wealth. Cities began as markets and it was the privilege to participate in the market that defined citizens. As the trades and crafts expanded, city governments provided protection for consumers and producers by creating monopolies through which standards for craftsmanship were maintained and profits for craftsmen were guaranteed. These monopolies were called guilds or companies. Each large city had its own hierarchy of guilds, and membership in a major guild ensured a successful career. At the top were the important manufacturing groups—clothiers, metalworkers, and the like. Just below them were bankers, merchants, and the administrators of civic and Church holdings. At the bottom were grocers, masons, and other skilled workers. Roughly speaking, all of those within the guild structure, from bottom to top, lived comfortably, though throughout their life-cycle they might experience want as well as plenty. Yet the majority of urban inhabitants were not members of guilds. Many managed to eke out a living as wage laborers; many more were simply destitute. As a group these poor constituted as much as half of the entire population. Most were dependent upon civic and private charity for their very survival, but the continued migration of the destitute into cities suggests that opportunities were greater there than in the countryside.

The disparities between rich and poor were overwhelming. The concentration of wealth in the hands of an ever narrowing group of families and favored guilds characterized every large city. One reason for this was the extreme instability of economic life. Prices and wages fluctuated wildly in response to local circumstance. After an epidemic of plague, wages climbed and the prices of consumer goods tumbled. A bad harvest sent food prices skyrocketing. Only those able to even out these extreme swings by stockpiling goods in times of plenty and consuming them in times of want were safe. Capital, however initially accumulated, was the key to continued wealth. Monopolies ensured the profitability of trade and manufacturing, but only those with sufficient capital could engage in either. In Florence, for example, 10 percent of the families controlled 90 percent of the wealth, with an even more extreme

Cloth making was a major contributor to European economic growth during the Middle Ages. In this 1470 portrait of Cloth Merchants' Street, Bologna, a tailor (center) measures a prospective client.

concentration at the top. The combined wealth of the richest one hundred Florentine families was greater than the combined wealth of 87 percent of the city's population.

Production and Consumption

This concentration of wealth and the way in which it was used defined Renaissance economy. Economic life is bound up in the relationship between resources and desires, or, as economists would have it, supply and demand. The late medieval economy, despite the development of international banking and long-distance trade, was still an economy of primary producers: between 70 and 90 percent of Europe's population was involved in subsistence agriculture. Even in Italy, which contained the greatest concentration of urban areas in the world, agriculture predominated. The manufacture of clothing was the only other significant economic activity, and it was dwarfed in comparison to farming. Moreover, most of what was produced was for local consumption rather than for the marketplace. The relationship between supply and demand was precisely measured by the full or empty stomach. Even in good times more than 80 percent of the population lived at subsistence level with food, clothing, and shelter their only expenses. Thus when we discuss the market economy of the Renaissance, we are discussing the circumstances of the few rather than the many.

The defining characteristic of the early Renaissance economy was change in population. Recurring waves of plague kept population levels low for more than a century. The first shocks of the 1340s and 1350s carried away between one-third and one-half of the European population. Tremors, which curtailed recovery, followed. For example, Florence lost well over one-half of its citizens in the mid-fourteenth century. Population growth began immediately after the first series of plagues, but an epidemic in 1400, which carried away one-fourth of the city's residents, arrested it. Thereafter the population stabilized and recurrences of infectious disease checked each tiny spurt of growth. In the century between 1350 and 1450 one in every six years was characterized by an unusually high mortality rate. At the end of this period Florence's population was only a quarter of what it had been at the beginning.

This dramatic reduction in population depressed economic growth. Until 1460 the major sectors of the economy were stagnant. The general economy did not revive until the sustained population increase toward the end of the fifteenth century. Until then, in both agriculture and manufacturing, supply outstripped demand. On the farms overabundance resulted from two related developments, the concentration of surviving farmers on the best land and the enlargement of their holdings. In the shops finished products outnumbered the consumers who survived the epidemics. Overproduction meant lower prices for basic commodities, and the decline in population meant higher wages for labor. The result was that at the lowest levels of society survivors found it easier to earn their living and even to create a surplus than had their parents. For a time the lot of the masses improved.

But for investors, such economic conditions meant that neither agriculture nor cloth making were particularly attractive. Expensive investments in land or equipment for sharecropping were paid off in inexpensive grain; high wages for the few surviving skilled workers brought a return in cheap cloth. In such circumstances, consumption was more attractive than investment and luxury became more alluring than ever. It was not merely the perceived shortage in profitable investments that brought on the increase in conspicuous consumption during the fifteenth century. In the psychological atmosphere created by unpredictable, swift, and deadly epidemics, people who were interested in life on earth became more concerned with the present than the future. Secondly, in order to pay for wars, both offensive and defensive, rates of taxation increased. Since both houses and personal property were normally exempt from the calculations of wealth upon which taxation was based, the richest members of the community could escape this additional burden by purchasing luxury goods. Even those at the lowest levels of society eagerly purchased whatever their meager means permitted.

For whatever reasons, the production and consumption of luxuries soared. By the middle of the fourteenth century Florence was known for its silks and jewelry as much as for its cloth. Venice became a European center for the glass industry, especially for the finely ground glass that was used in eyeglasses. Production of specialty crops like sugar, saffron, fruits, and high-quality wine expanded. International trade centered more than ever on bringing into western Europe the exotic goods of the East, resulting in the serious outflow of gold and silver that enriched first the Byzantine and then the Ottoman emperors. Both public and private building projects increased, spurring the demand for architects, sculptors, and painters. Centers of government, even in the so-called republican cities, were richly appointed in a new style of conspicuous display. At the courts of the hereditary nobility and of the pope the

Scene From the Life of Saint Nicholas of Bari, *by Fra Angelico (Angelic Brother). The workmen in the foreground are unloading wheat. Fra Angelico, a Dominican monk, helped to pioneer the Renaissance methods of art in Florence.*

ceremonies of state were lavish beyond compare. The rise in the consumption of luxuries was everywhere apparent, taken by some as a sign of the vitality of the age, by others as an indication of its decay.

The Experience of Life

Luxury helped improve a life that for rich and poor alike was short and uncertain. Nature was still people's most potent enemy. Renaissance children who survived infancy found their lives governed by parentage and by sex. In parentage the great divide was between those who lived with surplus and those who lived at subsistence. The first category encompassed the wealthiest bankers and merchants down to those who owned their own farms or engaged in small urban crafts. The vast majority of urban and rural dwellers comprised the second category. About the children of the poor we know very little other than that their survival was unlikely. If they did not die at birth or shortly afterward, they might be abandoned—especially if female—to the growing number of orphanages in the cities, waste away from lack of nutrition, or fall prey to ordinary childhood diseases for which there were no treatments. Eldest sons were favored, younger daughters were disadvantaged. But in poor families this favoritism meant little more than early apprenticeship to day labor in the city or farm labor in the countryside. Girls were frequently sent out as domestic servants far from the family home. The economic necessities of family survival dictated this course of childhood, which made it difficult for Renaissance parents to develop a strong emotional attachment to individual children.

Children of the wealthy had better chances for survival than did children of the poor. For the better off, childhood might begin with "milk parents," life in the home of the family of a wet nurse who would breast-feed the baby through infancy. Only the very wealthy could afford a live-in wet nurse, which would increase the child's chances of survival. Again, daughters were more likely to be sent far from home and least likely to have their nursing supervised. The use of wet nurses not only emancipated parents from the daily care of infants, it also allowed them to resume sexual relations. Nursing women refrained from sex in the belief that it affected their milk, and wet nurses were hired with the stipulation that they remain celibate during their employment.

During the period between weaning and apprenticeship Renaissance children lived with their families. There was no typical Renaissance family. Nuclear families—that is, parents and their children under one roof—were probably more common than extended families, which might include grandparents and other relatives. But the composition of the family changed over the course of the life-cycle and included times in which married children or grandparents were present and others when a single parent and small children were the only members. Moreover, even nuclear families commonly contained stepparents and stepchildren as well as domestic servants or apprentices. Thus a child returning to the parental household was as likely to form emotional bonds with older siblings as with parents.

The family was an economic unit as well as a grouping of relatives. Decisions to abandon children, to send them away from the household when very young, or to take in domestic servants were based on economic calculations. In the competition for scarce resources, the way in which children were managed might determine the survival of the family unit. Sons could expect to be apprenticed to a trade probably between the ages of ten and thirteen. Most, of course, learned the

crafts of their fathers, but not necessarily in their father's shop. By adolescence these fortunate boys, who might have had some rudimentary schooling, were earning token wages that contributed to family income. Sons inherited the family business and its most important possessions, tools of the trade or beasts of labor for the farm. Inheritance customs varied. In some places only the eldest son received the equipment of the family occupation; in others, like Tuscany, all the sons shared it. Still, in the first fifteen years of life, these most favored children would have spent between one-third and one-half of their time outside the household in which they had been born.

Expectations for daughters centered on their chances of marriage. For a girl, dowry was everything. If a girl's father could provide a handsome one, her future was secure; if not, the alternatives were a convent, which would take a small bequest, or a match lower down the social scale, where the quality of life deteriorated rapidly. Daughters of poor families entered domestic service in order to have a dowry provided by their masters. The dowry was taken to the household of their husband. There the couple resided until they established their own separate family. If the husband died, it was to his parental household that the widow returned. After marriage the Renaissance woman was permanently separated from her childhood home.

Women married in late adolescence, usually around the age of twenty. Among the wealthy, marriages were perceived as familial alliances and business transactions rather than love matches. The dowry was an investment on which fathers expected a return, and while the bride might have some choice, it was severely limited. Compatibility was not a central feature in matchmaking. Husbands were, on average, ten years older than their wives and likely to leave them widows. In the early fifteenth century about one-fourth of all adult women in Florence were widows, many without prospects of remarriage.

Married women lived in a state of nearly constant pregnancy. Alessandra Strozzi, whose father was one of the wealthiest citizens of Florence, married at the age of sixteen, gave birth to eight children in ten years, and was widowed at the age of twenty-five. Not all pregnancies produced children. The rates of miscarriages and stillbirths were very high, and abortions and infanticide were not unknown. Only among the families who hovered between surplus and subsistence is there any evidence of attempts to control pregnancies. These efforts, which relied upon techniques like the rhythm method and withdrawal, were not particularly effective. The rhythm method was especially futile because of the misunderstanding of the role of women in conception. It was not yet known that the woman contained an egg that was fertilized during conception. Without this knowledge it was impossible to understand the cycle of ovulation. Practically speaking, family size was limited on the one end by late marriages and on the other by early deaths.

Life experiences differed for males. Men married later, near the age of twenty-five on the farms, nearer thirty in the cities because of the cost of setting up in trade or on the land. Late marriage meant long supervision under the watchful eye of father or master, an extended period between adolescence and adulthood. The reputation that Renaissance cities gained for homosexuality and licentiousness must be viewed in light of the advanced age at which males married. The level of sexual frustration was high and its outlet in ritual violence and rape was also high.

The establishment of one's own household through marriage was a late rite of passage considering the expectations of early death. Many men, even with families, never succeeded in setting up separately from their fathers or elder brothers. Men came of age at thirty but were thought to be old by fifty. Thus for men marriage and parenthood took place in middle age rather than in youth. Valued all their lives more highly than their sisters, male heads of households were the source of all power in their domicile, in their shops, and in the state. They were responsible for overseeing every aspect of the upbringing of their children, even choosing wet nurses for their infants and spouses for their daughters. But their wives were essential partners who governed domestic life. Women labored not only at the hearth, but in the fields and shops as well. Their economic contribution to the well-being of the family was critical, both in the dowry they brought at marriage and in the labor they contributed to the household. If their wives died, men with young children remarried quickly. While there were many bachelors in Renaissance society, there were few widowers.

In most cases death came suddenly. Epidemic diseases, of which plague was the most virulent, struck fifteenth-century Italians with fearful regularity. Even in the absence of a serious outbreak, there were always deaths in town and country attributable to the plague. Epidemics struck harder at the young—children and adolescents who were the majority of the population—and hardest in the summer months when other viruses and bacteria weakened the population. Influenza must have been the second largest cause of death, though in the absence of proper records we can only guess. Medical treatment was more likely to hasten death than to prolong life. Lorenzo de Medici's physician prescribed powdered pearls for the Florentine ruler's gout. After that Lorenzo complained more of stomach pains than of gout. Marsilio Ficino, in his popular medical tract "How to Prolong Your Life," recommended drinking liquefied gold during certain phases of the moon. Such remedies revealed a belief in the harmony of nature and the healing power of rare substances. They were not silly or superstitious; but they were not effective either. Starvation was rare, less because of food shortage than because the seriously undernourished were more likely to succumb to disease than to famine. In urban areas, the government would intervene to provide grain from public storehouses at times of extreme shortage; in the countryside large landholders commonly exercised the same function.

The Quality of Life

Though life may have been difficult during the Renaissance, it was not unfulfilling. Despite constant toil and frequent hardship, people of the Renaissance had reason to believe that their lives were better than those of their ancestors and that their children's lives would be better still. On the most basic level, health improved and, for those who survived plague, life expectancy increased. Better health was related to better diet. Improvement came from two sources, the relative surplus of grain throughout the fifteenth century and the wider variety of foods consumed. Bread remained the most widely consumed foodstuff, but even subsistence consumers were beginning to supplement their diet with meat and dairy products. There was more pork and lamb in the diet of ordinary people in the fifteenth century than there would be for the next four hundred years. At the upper levels of society, sweet wine and citrus fruits helped offset the lack of vegetables. This diversification of diet resulted from improvements in transportation and communication, which brought more goods and services to a growing number of towns in the chain that linked the regional centers to the rural countryside.

But the towns and cities contributed more than consumer goods to Renaissance society. They also introduced a new sense of social and political cohesiveness. The city was something to which people belonged. In urban areas they could join social groups of their own choosing and develop networks of support not possible in rural environments. Blood relations remained the primary social group. Kin were the most likely source of aid in times of need, and charity began at home. Kin groups extended well beyond the immediate family, with both cousins and in-laws laying claim to the privileges of blood. The urban family could also depend upon the connections of neighborhood. In some Italian cities wealth or occupation determined housing patterns. In others, like Florence, rich and poor lived side by side and identified themselves with their small administrative unit and with their local church. Thus they could participate in relationships with others both above and below them in the social scale. From their superiors they gained connections that helped their families; from their inferiors they gained devoted clients. The use of both in such important functions as godparenting demonstrates how the urban family built a complex set of social relations.

As in the Middle Ages, the Church remained the spatial, spiritual, and social center of people's lives. Though the Renaissance is singled out as a time when people became more worldly in their outlook, this worldliness took place within the context of an absorbing devotional life. There was not yet any separation between faith and reason. The Church provided explanations for both the mysterious and the mundane. It offered comfort in this life and in the life to come. In it were performed the rituals of baptism, marriage, and burial that measured the passage of life. The Church was also the source of the key symbols of urban society. The flags of militia troops, the emblems of guilds, the regalia of the city itself were all adorned by recognizably religious symbols. The Church preserved holy relics, like the piece of the true cross in Venice, that were venerated for their power to protect the city or to endow it with particular skills and resources. Churches were the most prominent sites of the urban area, towering above all other buildings. They provided the spatial reference points for where people lived or worked and even the formal geographical divisions into which the city might be divided. Through its holy days, as much as through its rituals, the Church helped channel leisure activities into community celebrations.

A growing sense of civic pride and individual accomplishment were underlying characteristics of the Italian Renaissance, enhanced by the development of social cohesion and community solidarity that both Church and city-state fostered. It is commonly held that the Renaissance was both elitist and male dominated, that it was an experience separate from that of the society at large. There can be no question that it was the rich who commissioned works of art or that it was the highly skilled male craftsmen who executed them. But neither lived in a social vacuum. The Renaissance was not an event whose causes were the result of the efforts of the few or whose consequences were limited to the privileged. In fact, the Renaissance was not an event at all. Family values that permitted early apprenticeships in surrogate households and that emphasized the continuity of crafts from one generation to the next made possible the skilled artists of the Renaissance cities. The stress on the production of luxury goods placed higher value upon individual skills and therefore upon excellence in workmanship. Church and state sought to express social values through representational art. One of the chief purposes of wall murals was to instruct the unlettered in religion, to help them visualize the central episodes in Christian history and thus increase the pleasure they derived from their faith. The grandiose architecture and statuary that adorned central places was designed to enhance civic pride and communicate the protective power of public institutions.

Renaissance Art

In every age, artistic achievement represents a combination of individual talent and predominant social ideals. Artists may be at the leading edge of the society in which they live, but it is the spirit of that society that they capture in word or song or image. Artistic disciplines also have their own technical development. Individually, Renaissance artists were attempting to solve problems about perspective and three-dimensionality that had defeated their predecessors. But the particular techniques or experiments that interested them owed as much to the social context as they did to the artistic one. For example, the urban character of Italian government led to the need for civic architecture, public buildings on a grand scale. The celebration of individual achievement led to the explosive growth of portraiture. Not surprisingly, major technological breakthroughs were achieved in both areas. Nor should we underestimate the brilliance of the artists themselves. To deny genius is to deprecate humanity. What we need to explain is not the existence of a Leonardo or a Michelangelo but their co-existence.

This relationship between artist and social context was all the more important in the Renaissance, when artists were closely tied to the crafts and trades of urban society and to the demands of clients who commissioned their work. Although it was the elite who patronized art, it was skilled tradesmen who produced it. Artists normally followed the pattern of any craftsman, an apprenticeship begun as a teenager and a long period of training and work in a master's shop. This form of education gave the aspiring artist a practical rather than a theoretical bent and a keen appreciation for the business side of art. Studios were identified with particular styles and competed for commissions from clients, especially the Church. Wealthy individuals commissioned art as investments, as marks of personal distinction, and as displays of public piety. They got what they paid for, usually entering into detailed contracts that stipulated the quality of materials and the amount of work done by the master himself. Isabella d'Este (1474–1539), one of the great patrons of Renaissance artists, wrote hundreds of letters specifying the details of the works she commissioned. She once sent an artist a thread of the exact dimensions of the pictures she had ordered. Demand for art was high. The vast public-works projects needed buildings, the new piazzas (public squares) and palazzos (private houses) needed statuary, and the long walls of churches needed murals.

The survival of so many Renaissance masterpieces allows us to reconstruct the stages by which the remarkable artistic achievements of this era took place. Although advances were made in a variety of fields during the Renaissance, the three outstanding areas were architecture, sculpture, and painting. While modern artists would consider each a separate discipline, Renaissance artists crossed their boundaries without hesitation. Not only could these artists work with a variety of materials, their intensive and varied apprenticeships taught them to apply the technical solutions of one field to the problems of another. Few Renaissance artists confined themselves to one area of artistic expression, and many created works of enduring beauty in more than one medium. Was the greatest achievement of Michelangelo his sculpture of David, his paintings on the ceiling of the Sistine Chapel, or his design for the dome of Saint Peter's? Only a century of interdisciplinary cross-fertilization could have prepared the artistic world for such a feat.

Three Masters

That century began with the work of three Florentine masters who deeply influenced one another's development, Brunelleschi (1377–1446), Donatello (1386–1466), and Masaccio (1401–28). In the Renaissance the dominant artistic discipline was architecture. Buildings were the most expensive investment patrons could make and the technical knowledge necessary for their successful construction was immense. The architect not only designed a building, he served as its general contractor, its construction supervisor, and its inspector. Moreover, the architect's design determined the amount and the scale of the statuary and decorative paintings to be incorporated. By 1400 the Gothic style of building had dominated western Europe for over two centuries. Its characteristic pointed arches, vaulted ceilings, and slender spires had simplified building by removing the heavy walls formerly thought necessary to support great structures. Gothic construction permitted greater height, a characteristic especially desirable in cathedrals, which stretched toward the heavens. The thinner walls did not have to support the structure, so they could be pierced by more and larger windows, admitting more light and air. But though the buildings themselves were simplified, the techniques for erecting them became more complex. By the fifteenth century architects had turned their techniques into an intricate style. They became obsessed by angular arches, elaborate vaultings and buttresses, and long, pointed spires. Each element competed with the others for prominence.

It was Brunelleschi who decisively challenged the principles of Gothic architecture by recombining its basic elements with those of classical structures. His achievement was less an innovation than a radical synthesis of old and new. Basing his designs on geometric principles, Brunelleschi reintroduced planes and spheres as dominant motifs. His greatest work was the dome on the cathedral in Florence, begun in 1420. He won the commission by challenging his competitors to make an egg stand on a flat piece of marble, a feat, he claimed, as difficult as designing the dome. When they all failed, Brunelleschi "taking the egg graciously, cracked its bottom on the marble and made it stay upright." The solution was simple but bold. So was his design for the dome. The windows at the base of the dome of the cathedral illustrate the simplicity of Brunelleschi's geometric technique. Circular windows are set inside a square of panels, which in turn are set inside a rectangle. The facades are dominated by columns and rounded arches, proportionally spaced from a central perspective. Brunelleschi is generally credited with having been the first Renaissance artist to have understood and made use of perspective, though it was immediately put to more dramatic effect in sculpture and painting.

The sculptor's study was the human form in all of its three-dimensional complexity. The survival of Roman and Hellenistic pieces, mostly bold and muscular torsos, meant that the influence of

Florence Cathedral. The cathedral was begun by Arnolfo di Cambio in 1296. This view shows the dome and the apse end of the cathedral. The free-standing campanile, or bell tower, at the left recalls early Christian church architecture.

classical art was most direct in sculpture. Donatello translated these classical styles into more naturalistic forms. His technique is evident in the long flowing robes that form the bulk of most of his works. Donatello sculpted the cloth, not in the stylized angularity of the past in which the creases were as sharp as sword blades, but in the natural fashion in which cloth hung. Donatello also revived the free-standing statue, which demanded greater attention to human anatomy because it was viewed from many angles. *Judith Slaying Holofernes* (1455) is an outstanding example of Donatello's use of geometric proportion and perspective. Each side of the piece captures a different vision of Judith in action. In addition Donatello led the revival of the equestrian statue, sculpting the Venetian captain-general *Gattamelata* (1445–50) for a public square in Padua. This enormous bronze horse and rider borrowed from surviving first- and second-century Roman models but relied upon the standpoint of the viewer to achieve its overpowering effect. This use of linear perspective was also a characteristic of Donatello's dramatic works, like the breathtaking altar scenes of the miracles of Saint Anthony in Padua, which resemble nothing so much as a canvas cast in bronze.

These altar scenes clearly evince the unmistakable influence of the paintings of Masaccio. Although he lived less than thirty years, Masaccio created an enduring legacy. His frescoes in the Brancacci Chapel in Florence were studied and sketched by all of the great artists of the next generation, who unreservedly praised his naturalism. What most claims the attention of the modern viewer is Masaccio's shading of light and shadow and his brilliant use of linear perspective to create the illusion that a flat surface has three dimensions. Masaccio's work was on standard Christian themes, but he brought an entirely novel approach to them all. In an adoration scene he portrayed a middle-aged Madonna and a dwarfish baby Jesus; in a painting of Saint Peter paying tribute money, he used his own likeness as the face of one of the Apostles. His two best known works are the *Expulsion of Adam and Eve*

In this fresco, called The Expulsion of Adam and Eve, *Masacchio's mastery of perspective helps create the illusion of movement, as an angel drives the grieving Adam and Eve into the world.*

(ca. 1427) and the *Holy Trinity* (1425). In the *Expulsion of Adam and Eve*, Masaccio has left an unforgettable image of the fall from grace in Eve's primeval anguish. Her deep eyes and hollow mouth are accentuated by casting the source of light downward and shading what otherwise would be lit. In the *Holy Trinity*, Masaccio provides the classic example of the use of linear perspective in painting. The ceiling of a Brunelleschi-designed temple recedes to a vanishing point beyond the head of God, creating the simultaneous illusion of height and depth.

Renaissance Style

By the middle of the fifteenth century a recognizable Renaissance style had triumphed. Florence continued to lead the way although ideas, techniques, and influences had spread throughout the Italian peninsula and even to the north and west. The outstanding architect of this period was Leon Battista Alberti (1404–72), whose treatise *On Building* (1452) remained the most influential work on the subject until the eighteenth century. Alberti consecrated the geometric principles laid down by Brunelleschi and infused them with a humanist spirit. He revived the classical dictum that a building, like a body, should have an even number of supports and, like a head, an odd number of openings. This furthered precise geometric calculations in scale and design. To Brunelleschi's circles and squares Alberti added triangles, reviving another of the classical forms of construction. But it was in civic architecture that Alberti made his most significant contributions. Here he demonstrated how classical forms could be applied to traditional living space by being made purely decorative. His facade of the Palazzo Rucellai uses columns and arches not as building supports, but as embellishments that give geometric harmony to the building's appearance.

No sculptor challenged the preeminence of Donatello for another fifty years, but in painting there were many contenders for the garlands worn by Masaccio. The first was Piero della Francesca (ca. 1420–92) who, though trained in the tradition of Masaccio, broke new ground in his concern for the visual unity of his paintings. From portraits to processions to his stunning

Boticelli's Primavera (Spring), *also called* Garden of Venus. *Venus, in the center, is attended by the three Graces and by Cupid, Flora, Chloris, and Zephyr. With its lack of attention to perspective and elongated figures, the style has more in common with medieval tapestries than with Renaissance art.*

fresco *The Resurrection* (ca. 1463) Piero concentrated upon the most technical aspects of composition. He was influenced by Alberti's ideas about the geometry of form and it is said that his measurements and calculations for various parts of *The Resurrection* took more time than the painting itself. Another challenger was Sandro Botticelli (1445–1510), whose classical themes, sensitive portraits, and bright colors set him apart from the line of Florentine painters with whom he studied. His mythologies of the *Birth of Venus* and *Spring* (ca. 1478) depart markedly from the naturalism inspired by Masaccio. Botticelli's paintings have a dreamlike quality, an unreality highlighted by the beautiful faces and lithe figures of his characters.

Botticelli's concern with beauty and personality is also seen in the paintings of Leonardo da Vinci (1452–1519), whose creative genius embodied the Renaissance ideal of the "universal man."

Leonardo's achievements in scientific, technical, and artistic endeavors read like a list of all of the subjects known during the Renaissance. His detailed anatomical drawings and the method he devised for rendering them, his botanical observations, and his engineering inventions (including models for the tank and the airplane) testify to his unrestrained curiosity. His paintings reveal a continuation of the scientific application of mathematics to matters of proportion and perspective. The dramatic fresco *The Last Supper* (ca. 1495–98), for example, takes the traditional scene of Christ and his disciples at a long table and divides it into four groups of three, each with its own separate action, leaving Jesus to dominate the center of the picture by balancing its two sides. Leonardo's psychological portrait *La Gioconda* (1503–06), popularly called the Mona Lisa, is quite possibly the best-known picture in the Western world.

Michelangelo

The artistic achievements of the Renaissance culminated in the creative outpourings of Michelangelo Buonarroti (1475–1564). It is almost as if the age itself had produced a summation of how it wished to be remembered. Poet, sculptor, painter, and architect, Michelangelo imparted his genius to everything he touched. He was the first Renaissance artist to be publicly recognized as the master he was. His works drew vast crowds and were studied and copied by his competitors. Unlike the early fifteenth-century artists who enjoyed fruitful cooperation, Michelangelo detested his rivals, especially Bramante, the leading architect of Rome, and Raphael, one of its leading painters.

Uncharacteristically, Michelangelo came from a family of standing in Florentine society and gained his apprenticeship over the opposition of his father. He claimed to have imbibed his love of sculpture from the milk of his wet nurse, who was the wife of a stonecutter. At the age of fourteen he was apprenticed to a leading painter, Ghirlandaio, and spent his spare time in Florentine churches copying the works of Masaccio among others. In 1490 Michelangelo gained a place in the household of Lorenzo de' Medici, which was adorned by the presence of a number of gifted artists and philosophers. There he studied art and architecture under a student of Donatello. During this two-year period he claimed to have taught himself sculpturing, a remarkable feat considering the skills required. In fact, what was unusual about Michelangelo's early development was that he avoided the long years of apprenticeship during which someone else's style was implanted upon the young artist. He may well have learned more about philosophy than art in the Medici household, for there he came into contact with leading Neoplatonists, who taught that man was on an ascending journey of perfectability toward God. The human capacity for self-improvement was one of the central ideas of Renaissance thinkers and one that the Neoplatonists forcefully emphasized. Whether these ideas did anything other than fortify Michelangelo's own temperament is questionable, but they can be seen as one source of the heroic concept of humanity that he brought to his work.

In 1496 Michelangelo moved to Rome. There his abilities as a sculptor quickly brought him to the attention of Jacopo Galli, a Roman banker who was interested in art and learning. Galli commissioned a classical work for himself and procured another for a French cardinal, which became the *Pietà*. Although this was his first attempt at sculpting a work of religious art, Michelangelo would never surpass it in beauty or composition. The *Pietà* created a sensation in Rome and by the time that Michelangelo returned to Florence in 1501, at the age of twenty-six, he was already acknowledged as one of the great sculptors of his day. He was immediately commissioned to work on an enormous block of marble that had been quarried nearly a half-century before and had defeated the talents of a series of carvers. He worked continuously for three years on his *David* (1501–04), a piece that completed the union between classical and Renaissance styles. Michelangelo's giant nude gives eloquent expression to his belief that the human body is the "mortal veil" of the soul. The *David* replaced Donatello's *Judith* outside the Palazzo Vecchio.

Though Michelangelo always believed himself to be primarily a sculptor, his next outstanding work was in the field of painting. In 1508 Pope Julius II summoned Michelangelo to Rome and commissioned him to decorate the small ceremonial chapel that had been built next to the new papal residence. The initial plan called for figures of the twelve apostles to adorn the ceiling, but Michelangelo soon launched a more ambitious scheme: to portray, in an extended narrative, man's creation and those Old Testament events that foreshadowed the birth of the Savior. Everything about the execution of the Sistine Chapel paintings was extraordinary. First Michelangelo framed his scenes within the architecture of a massive classical temple. In this way he was able to give the impression of having flattened the rounded surface on which he worked. Then, on the two sides of the central panels, he represented figures of Hebrew prophets and pagan Sybils as sculptured marble statues. Finally, within the center panels came his fresco scenes of the events of the creation and of human history from the Fall to the Flood. His representations were simple and compelling: the fingers of God and Adam nearly touching; Eve with one leg still emerging from

Adam's side; the half-human snake in the temptation are all majestically evocative.

The *Pietà*, the *David*, and the paintings of the Sistine Chapel were the work of youth. Michelangelo's crowning achievement, the building of Saint Peter's, was the work of age. The intervening years saw the production of masterpiece after masterpiece, enough completed and unfinished work to have established his genius. Yet at the age of seventy-one Michelangelo undertook to finish a project that, like the marble block that had become the *David*, had defeated others for decades. The purpose of the church was to provide a suitable monument for the grave of Saint Peter. The basework had already been laid and drawings for its completion had been made thirty years earlier by Bramante. Michelangelo altered these plans in an effort to bring more light within the church and provide a more majestic facade outside. His main contribution, however, was the design of the great dome, which centered the interior of the church on Saint Peter's grave. He integrated the exterior of the dome so that its facade completed the themes of the building itself. The paired ribs on the dome imitate the paired columns on its base and the paired mock columns on the face of the building. More than the height, it is the harmony of Michelangelo's design that creates the sense of the building thrusting upward like a Gothic cathedral of old. The dome on Saint Peter's was the largest then known and provided the model, in succeeding generations, for Saint Paul's Cathedral in London and the U.S. Capitol building in Washington, D.C. Michelangelo did not live to see the dome of Saint Peter's completed.

Renaissance art served Renaissance society. It reflected both its concrete achievements and its visionary ideals. It was a synthesis of old and new, building upon classical models, particularly in sculpture and architecture, but adding newly discovered techniques and skills. Demanding patrons, like Pope Julius II, who commonly interrupted Michelangelo's work on the Sistine Chapel with criticisms and suggestions, fueled the remarkable growth in both the quantity and quality of Renaissance art. When Giorgio Vasari (1511–74) came to write his *Lives of the Great Painters, Sculptors, and Architects* (1550) he found over two hundred artists worthy of distinction. But Renaissance artists did more than construct and adorn buildings or celebrate and beautify spiritual life. Inevitably their work expressed the ideals and aspirations of the society in which they lived, the new emphasis upon learning and knowledge; upon the here and now rather than the hereafter; and most importantly, upon humanity and its capacity for growth and perfection.

The creation of Adam and Eve. Detail from Michelangelo's frescoes on the ceiling of the Sistine Chapel. The Michelangelo frescoes had become obscured by dirt and layers of varnish and glue applied at various times over the years. In the 1980s they were cleaned to reveal their original colors.

Renaissance Ideals

Renaissance thought went hand in glove with Renaissance art. Scholars and philosophers searched the works of the ancients to find the principles on which to build a better life. They scoured monastic libraries for forgotten manuscripts, discovering among other things, Greek poetry, history, the works of Homer and Plato, and Aristotle's *Poetics*. Their rigorous application of scholarly procedures for the collection and collation of these texts was one of the most important contributions of those Renaissance intellectuals who came to be known as humanists. Humanism developed in reaction to an intellectual world that was centered on the Church and dominated by otherworldly concerns. Humanism was secular in outlook, though by no means was it antireligious.

Humanists celebrated worldly achievements. Pico della Mirandola's *Oration on the Dignity of Man* (1486) is the best known of a multitude of Renaissance writings influenced by the discovery of the works of Plato. Pico believed that people could perfect their existence on earth because God had endowed humans with the capacity to determine their own fate. "O highest and most marvelous felicity of man! To him it is granted to have whatever he chooses, to be whatever he wills." A century later Shakespeare echoed these same themes in *Hamlet* (1603): "What a piece of work is a man. How noble in reason, how infinite in faculties, in form and moving how express and admirable, in action how like an angel, in apprehension how like a God! The beauty of the world, the paragon of animals!" This emphasis on human potential finds expression in the celebration of human achievement. Autobiographers like the artist Benvenuto Cellini (1500–71) marveled at their own accomplishments and held them up as a mirror to others. With the symbols of human achievement everywhere apparent, from public art and architecture to the vast accumulations of private riches, the Renaissance emphasized the significance of worldly attainments.

Humanism was neither a set of philosophical principles nor a program for social action. There were no antihumanists to give it form and whatever coherence Italian humanism may have had, it was quickly diluted as it rapidly spread across Europe. Quite simply, humanists studied and taught the humanities, the skills of disciplines like philology, the art of language, and rhetoric, the art of expression. Though they were mostly laymen, humanists applied their learning to both religious and secular studies. We must not think of humanists as antireligious. Although they reacted strongly against Scholasticism, they were heavily indebted to the work of medieval churchmen. Nor were they hostile to the Church. Petrarch, Bruni, and Alberti were all employed by the papal court at some time in their careers, as was Lorenzo Valla, the most influential of the humanists. Their interest in human achievement and human potential must be set beside their religious beliefs. As Petrarch stated quite succinctly: "Christ is my God; Cicero is the prince of the language I use."

The Humanists

The most important achievements of humanist scholars centered upon ancient texts. It was the humanists' goal to discover as much as had survived from the ancient world and to provide as full and accurate as possible texts of classical authors. Though much was already known of the Latin classics, few of the central works of ancient Greece had been uncovered. Humanists preserved this heritage by reviving the study of the Greek language and by translating Greek authors into Latin. After the fall of Constantinople in 1453, Italy became the center for Greek studies as scholars fled the Ottoman conquerors. Humanists also introduced historical methods in studying texts, establishing principles for determining which of many manuscript copies of an ancient text was the oldest and which had been least corrupted by their copyists. This was of immense importance in studying the writings of the ancient Fathers of the Church, many of whose manuscripts had not been examined for centuries. Humanists even introduced a new form of handwriting, the italic that we still use today, which made transcription easier. Their emphasis upon the humanistic disciplines fostered new educational ideals. Along with the study of theology, logic, and natural philosophy which had dominated the medieval university, humanist scholars stressed the importance of grammar, rhetoric, moral philosophy,

A miniature portrait of Petrarch is seen within the illuminated initial A in a manuscript of the poet's treatise De remediis utriusque fortunae *(Remedies Against Fortune).*

and history. They believed that the study of these "liberal arts" should be undertaken for its own sake. This gave a powerful boost to the ideal of the perfectability of the individual that appeared in so many other aspects of Renaissance culture.

Humanists furthered the secularization of Renaissance society through their emphasis on the study of the classical world. The rediscovery of Latin texts during the late Middle Ages spurred interest in all things ancient. Petrarch, who is rightly called the father of humanism, revered the great Roman rhetorician Cicero above all others. "If to admire Cicero means to be a Ciceronian, I am a Ciceronian. I admire him so much that I wonder at people who do not admire him." Petrarch imitated Cicero's style in long imaginary letters to ancient Romans and early Fathers of the Church. For Petrarch, Cicero's legacy was eloquence. He stressed this in his correspondence with the leading scholars of his day and taught it to those who would succeed him. From 1350 to 1450 Cicero was the dominant model for Renaissance poets and orators. Petrarch's emphasis upon language led to efforts to recapture the purity of ancient Latin and Greek, languages that had become corrupted over the centuries. Philology became one of the most celebrated humanist skills and the study of ancient manuscripts one of the most common humanist activities. The leading humanist in the generation after Petrarch was Leonardo Bruni (1370–1444), who was reputed to be the greatest Greek scholar of his day. He translated both Plato and Aristotle and laid the foundation for the Florentine Platonic Academy, which did so much to advance mastery of classical Greek and foster the ideas of Plato in the late fifteenth century.

The study of the origins of words, their meaning, and their proper grammatical usage may seem an unusual foundation for one of the most vital of all European intellectual movements. But philology was the humanists' chief concern. This can best be illustrated by the work of Lorenzo Valla (1407–57). Valla was brought up in Rome, where he was largely self-educated, though according to the prescriptions of the Florentine humanists. After failing to obtain a post at the papal court, he took a job as a lecturer in rhetoric at the university of Pavia. He was forced to leave the city when the supporters of a scholar he had criticized threatened to murder him. Soon he entered the service of Alfonso I, king of Naples, and applied his humanistic training to affairs of state. The kingdom of Naples bordered on the Papal States, and its kings were in continual conflict with the papacy. The pope asserted the right to withhold recognition of the king, a right that was based upon the jurisdictional authority supposedly ceded to the papacy by the Emperor Constantine in the fourth century. This so-called Donation of Constantine had long been a matter of dispute and its authenticity had been challenged frequently in the Middle Ages. But those challenges were made on political grounds and the arguments of papal supporters were as strenuous as those of papal opponents. Valla settled the matter definitively. Applying historical and philological critiques to the text of the Donation, Valla proved that it could not have been written earlier than the eighth century, four hundred years after Constantine's death. He mercilessly exposed words and terms that had not existed in Roman times, like *fief* and *satrap*, and thus proved beyond doubt that the Donation was a forgery and papal claims based upon it were without merit. Interestingly, Valla finally did receive an appointment as a papal secretary and his reputation as the outstanding humanist of his generation was secured.

Valla's career demonstrates the impact of humanist values on practical affairs. Although humanists were scholars, they made no distinction between an active and a contemplative life. A life of scholarship was a life of public service. They saw their studies as means of improving themselves and their society—"man is born in order to be useful to man." Many, like Valla, were active as political councillors. Others like Bruni, who served as Chancellor of Florence, accepted high office. This civic humanism is best expressed in the writings of Leon Battista Alberti (1404–72), whose treatise *On the Family* (1443) is a classic study of the new urban values, especially prudence and thrift. Alberti extolled the virtues of "the fatherland, the public good, and the benefit of all citizens." An architect, a mathematician, a poet, a playwright, a musician, and an inventor, Alberti was one of the great virtuosi of the Renaissance.

Alberti's own life might have served as a model for the most influential of all Renaissance tracts, Castiglione's *The Courtier* (1528). While Alberti directed his lessons to the private lives of successful urban families, Baldesar Castiglione (1478–1529) directed his to the public life of the aspiring elite. It was Castiglione's purpose to prescribe those characteristics that would make the ideal courtier, a man of such charm and accomplishment that he would be able to influence the good government of his state. In Castiglione's view the perfect courtier was as much born as made: "Besides his noble birth I would have the Courtier endowed by nature not only with talent and beauty of person and feature, but with a certain grace and air that shall make him at first sight pleasing." Everything that the courtier did was to maintain his pleasing grace and his public reputation. *The Courtier* was an etiquette book, and in it Castiglione prescribed every detail of the education necessary for the ideal state servant from table manners to artistic attainments. Though each talent was to be acquired through careful study and application, it was to be manifested with *sprezzatura*, a natural ease and superiority that was the essence of the gentleman. Castiglione's perfect courtier was an amalgam of all that the elite of Renaissance society held dear. He was to be educated as a scholar, he was to be occupied as a soldier, and he was to serve his state as an advisor.

Machiavelli

At the same time that Castiglione was drafting a blueprint for the idealized courtier, Niccolo Machiavelli (1469–1527) was laying the foundation for the realistic sixteenth-century ruler. No Renaissance work has been more important or more controversial than Machiavelli's *The Prince* (1513). Its vivid prose, its epigrammatic advice— "men must either be pampered or crushed"— and its clinical dissection of power politics have attracted generation after generation of readers. With Machiavelli, for better or worse, begins the science of politics. Machiavellianism has passed into the language as a label for the ruthless, amoral pursuit of power, though the fact that subsequent generations needed a word to describe such behavior is as interesting as the one they chose. Machiavelli himself has been depicted as everything from an evil genius to a champion of republicanism. He could hardly have imagined himself one or the other.

Machiavelli's early life gave no promise of his distinguished career or his far-reaching and long-lasting reputation. Though he came from an established Florentine family, his father was a struggling lawyer who could provide his son with little more than a good humanist education, especially in the Latin classics. Machiavelli entered state service as an assistant to one of his teachers and unexpectedly rode those coattails into the relatively important office of secretary to the Council of Ten, the organ of Florentine government that had responsibility for war and diplomacy. Here Machiavelli received his education in practical affairs. His special interest was in the militia, and he was an early advocate of organizing and training Florentine citizens to defend the city rather than hiring Swiss or French mercenaries. He drafted position papers on the tense international situation that followed the French invasion of Italy in 1494 and was soon used as an envoy in diplomatic missions. He was an emissary to Cesare Borgia during his consolidation of the Papal States at the turn of the century and carefully studied Borgia's methods. Clearly Machiavelli devoted all his energies and his entire intellect to his career. He was a tireless correspondent and he began to collect materials for various tracts on military matters. He also planned out a prospective history in which to celebrate the greatness of the Florentine republic that he served.

But as suddenly as he rose to his position of power and influence he fell from it. The militia that he had advocated and in part organized was soundly defeated by the Spaniards, and the Florentine republic fell. Machiavelli was summarily dismissed from office in 1512 and was imprisoned and tortured the following year. Released and banished from the city, he retired to a small country estate and turned his restless energies to writing. Immediately he began writing what became his two greatest works, *The Prince* (1513) and *The Discourses on Livy* (1519). He followed these with the comic play *Mandragola* (1518), the treatise *The Art of War* (1520), and the massive *History of Florence* (1525). He died in 1527.

Machiavelli has left a haunting portrait of his life in exile, and it is important to understand how intertwined his studies of ancient and modern politics were.

> On the coming of evening, I return to my house and enter my study; and at the door I take off the day's clothing, covered with mud and dust, and put on garments regal and courtly; and reclothed appropriately, I enter the ancient courts of ancient men, where, received by them with affection, I feed on that food which only is mine and which I was born for. For four hours of time I do not feel boredom, I forget every trouble, I do not dread poverty, I am not frightened by death; entirely I give myself over to them.

In this state of mind *The Prince* was composed.

The Prince is a handbook for a ruler who would establish a lasting government. It attempts to set down principles culled from historical examples and contemporary events to aid the prince in attaining and maintaining power. By study of these precepts and by their swift and forceful application Machiavelli believed that the prince might even control fortune itself. *The Prince* is purely secular in content and philosophy. Where the medieval writer of a manual for princes would stress the divine foundations of the state, Machiavelli asserted the human bases: "The chief foundations on which all states rest are good laws and good arms." What made *The Prince* so remarkable in its day, and what continues to enliven debate over it, is that Machiavelli was able to separate all ethical considerations from his analysis. Whether this resulted from cynicism or from his own expressed desire for realism, Machiavelli uncompromisingly instructed the would-be ruler to be half man and half beast—to conquer neighbors, to murder enemies, and to deceive friends. Nothing better illustrates the principle that humanists were not necessarily humanitarians.

Terra-cotta bust of Niccolò Machiavelli by an unknown artist. Because of the ideas set forth in The Prince, *the name of Machiavelli has long stood for treachery, duplicity, and bad faith in statesmanship.*

Machiavelli combines admiration for the ancient world with the duty of the humanist citizen to perfect the present. Unlike most Renaissance thinkers, Machiavelli preferred change to stability. The great princes were all innovators rather than conservators. They joined with the warrior citizens to make their own fortune and that of their state. Taken as a whole, Machiavelli's writings aspire to the restoration of the glory of Rome, the establishment of an empire that is a good in itself. "I believe that the finest deed man can achieve, and the one most precious to God, is what he does for his Fatherland." A life bounded by a half-century of destructive warfare might have taught no other lesson than the sweetness of peace. But Machiavelli's thought transcended the immediacy of his historical context. Steeped in the humanist ideals of fame and *virtù*—a combination of virtue and virtuosity, of valor, character, and ability—he sought to reestablish Italian rule and place government upon a stable, scientific basis that would end the perpetual conflict among the Italian city-states.

The Politics of the Italian City-States

Like studs on a leather boot, city-states dotted the Italian peninsula. They differed in size, shape, and form. Some were large seaports, others small inland villages; some cut wide swaths across the plains, others were tiny islands. The absence of a unifying central authority in Italy, resulting from the collapse of the Holy Roman Empire and the papal schism, allowed ancient guilds and confraternities to transform themselves into self-governing societies. By the beginning of the fifteenth century the Italian city-states were the center of power, wealth, and culture in the Christian world.

This dominion rested on several conditions. First, their geographical position favored the exchange of resources and goods between East and West. Until the fifteenth century, and despite the crusading efforts of medieval popes, East and West fortified each other. A great circular trade had developed, encompassing the Byzantine Empire, the North African coastal states, and the Mediterranean nations of western Europe. The Italian peninsula dominated the circumference of that circle. Its port cities, Genoa and Venice especially, became great maritime powers through their trade in spices and minerals. Second, just beyond the peninsula to the north lay the vast and populous territories of the Holy Roman Empire. There the continuous need for manufactured goods, especially cloths and metals, was filled by long caravans that traveled from Italy through the Alps. Milan specialized in metal crafts and was, for a time, the armory of Europe. Florence, which originally founded its wealth on the woolen cloth trade, was now a financial capital as well as a center for the manufacture of fine luxury goods. Finally, the city-states and their surrounding areas were agriculturally self-sufficient. This is all the more remarkable in that most were entirely urban and held large concentrations of people who were not engaged in growing food. But in the south were great breadbaskets, like Naples and Sicily, which could feed not only Italians, but northern and eastern Europeans as well.

Because of their accomplishments we tend to think of these Italian city-states as small nations.

Even the term *city-state* implies national identity. Inhabitants, like the Roman citizens of old, identified themselves with their city, as Milanese or Florentines or Venetians. Each city-state governed itself according to its own rules and customs and each defined itself in isolation from the larger regional or tribal associations that once prevailed. Indeed, their struggles against one another speak eloquently of their local self-identification. Italy was neither a nation nor a people.

The Five Powers

Although there were dozens of Italian city-states, by the early fifteenth century five had emerged to dominate the politics of the peninsula. In the south was the kingdom of Naples, the only city-state governed by a hereditary monarchy. Its politics were mired by conflicts over its succession. During the fourteenth century Naples was successively ruled by French and Hungarian princes. The fifteenth century began with civil warfare between rival claimants of both nations and it was not until the Spaniard Alfonso I of Aragon (1442–58) secured the throne in 1443 that peace was restored and Naples and Sicily were reunited. Bordering Naples were the Papal States, whose capital was Rome but whose territories stretched far to the north and lay on both sides of the spiny Apennine mountain chain that extends down the center of the peninsula. Throughout the fourteenth and early fifteenth centuries, the territories under the nominal control of the Church were largely independent and included such thriving city-states as Bologna, Ferrara, and Urbino. Even in Rome the weakened papacy had to contend with noble families for control of the city.

The three remaining dominant city-states were bunched together in the north. Florence, center of Renaissance culture, was one of the wealthiest cities of Europe before the devastations of the plague and the sustained economic downturn of the late fourteenth century. The city itself was inland and its main waterway, the Arno, ran to the sea through Pisa, whose subjugation in 1406 was a turning point in Florentine history. Nominally Florence was a republic, but during the fifteenth century it was ruled in effect by its principal banking family, the Medici.

To the north of Florence was the duchy of Milan, the major city in Lombardy. It too was landlocked, cut off from the sea by Genoa. But Milan's economic life was oriented northward to the Swiss and German towns beyond the Alps, and its major concern was preventing foreign invasions. The most warlike of the Italian cities, Milan was a despotism, ruled for nearly two centuries by the Visconti family.

The last of the five powers was the republic of Venice. Ideally situated at the head of the Adriatic Sea, Venice became the leading maritime power of the age. Until the fifteenth century, Venice was less interested in securing a landed empire than in dominating a seaborne one. Its outposts along the Grecian and Dalmatian coasts, and its favored position in Constantinople, were the source of vast mercantile wealth. The republic was ruled by a hereditary elite, headed by an elected doge, who was the chief magistrate of Venice, and a variety of small elected councils.

The political history of the peninsula during the late fourteenth and early fifteenth centuries is one of unrelieved turmoil. Wherever we look, the governments of the city-states were threatened by foreign invaders, internal conspiracies, or popular revolts. In the 1370s the Genoese and Venetians fought their fourth war in little more than a century, this one so bitter that the Genoese risked much of their fleet in an unsuccessful effort to conquer Venice itself. At the turn of the century, the Hungarian occupant of the throne of Naples invaded both Rome and Florence. Florence and Milan were constantly at war with each other. Nor were foreign threats the only dangers. In Milan three Visconti brothers inherited power. Two murdered the third, and then the son of one murdered the other to reunite the inheritance. The Venetians executed one of their military leaders who was plotting treachery. One or another Florentine family usually faced exile when governments there changed hands. Popular revolts channeled social and economic discontent against the ruling elites in Rome, Milan, and Florence. The revolt of the "Ciompi" (the wooden shoes) in Florence in 1378 was an attempt by poorly paid wool workers to reform the city's exclusive guild system and give guild protection to the wage laborers lower down the social scale. In Milan an abortive republic was established in reaction against strong-arm Visconti rule.

By the middle of the fifteenth century, however, two trends were apparent amid this political chaos. The first was the consolidation of strong centralized governments within the large city-states. These took different forms but yielded a similar result—internal political stability. The return of the popes to Rome after the Great Schism restored the pope to the head of his temporal estates and began a long period of papal dominance over Rome and its satellite territories. In Milan, one of the great military leaders of the day, Francesco Sforza (1401–66), seized the reins of power after the failure of the Visconti line. The succession of King Alfonso I in Naples ended a half-century of civil war. In both Florence and Venice the grip that the political elite held over high offices was tightened by placing greater power in small advisory councils and, in Florence, by the ascent to power of the Medici family. In sum, this process is known as the rise of signorial rule. Whether the signories usurped power or had it thrust upon them in the hope that they might relieve the sustained economic and political crises is difficult to determine. But their rise made possible the second development of this period, the establishment of a balance of power within the peninsula.

It was the leaders of the Italian city-states who first perfected the art of diplomacy. Constant warfare necessitated continual alliances, and by the end of the fourteenth century the large city-states had begun the practice of keeping resident ambassadors at the major seats of power. This enhanced communication, a principal challenge in Renaissance diplomacy, and also provided leaders with accurate information about the conditions of potential allies and enemies. Diplomacy was both an offensive and defensive weapon. This was especially so because the city-states hired their soldiers as contract labor. These mercenary armies, whose leaders were known as *condottieri* from the name of their contract, were both expensive and dangerous to maintain. If they did not bankrupt their employers, they might desert them or, even worse, turn on them. Thus Francesco Sforza, the greatest *condottiere* of the fifteenth century, gained power in Milan. Before serving the Milanese, Sforza had been in the pay of the Florentines in a war against Milan. Sforza's consolidation of power in Milan initially led to warfare, but ultimately it formed the basis of the

Peace of Lodi (1454). This established two balanced alliances, one between Florence and Milan, the other between Venice and Naples. These states, along with the papacy, pledged mutual nonaggression, a policy that lasted for nearly forty years.

The Peace of Lodi did not bring peace. It only halted the long period in which the major city-states struggled against one another. Under cover of the peace, the large states continued the process of swallowing up their smaller neighbors and creating quasi-empires. This was a policy of imperialism as aggressive as that of any in the modern era. Civilian populations were overrun, local leaders exiled or exterminated, tribute money taken, and taxes levied. Each of the five states either increased its mainland territories or strengthened its hold upon them. Venice and Florence especially prospered.

Venice

Water was the source of the prosperity of Venice. Located at the head of the Adriatic Sea, the city is formed by a web of lagoons. Through its center snakes the Grand Canal, whose banks were lined with large and small buildings that celebrated its civic and mercantile power. At the Piazza San Marco stood the vast palace of the doge, elected leader of the republic, and the Basilica of Saint Mark, a domed church built in the Byzantine style. At the Rialto were the stalls of the bankers and moneylenders, less grand perhaps but no less important. Here, too, were the auction blocks for the profitable trade in European slaves, east European serfs, and battlefield captives who were sold into service to Egypt or Byzantium. On the eastern edge of the island city was the Arsenal, erected in the twelfth century to house the shipbuilding and arms manufacturing industries. Three centuries later it was the industrial marvel of the world, where the Venetian great galleys were constructed with assembly-line precision.

Its prosperity based on trade rather than conquest, Venice enjoyed many natural advantages. Its position at the head of the Adriatic permitted access to the raw materials of both East and West. The rich Alpine timberland behind the city provided the hardwoods necessary for shipbuilding. The hinterland population were steady consumers of grain, cloth, and the new manufactured goods—glass, silk, jewelry, and cottons—that came pouring onto the market in the late Middle Ages. The winged lion of Saint Mark, the city's emblem, could be seen up and down the Italian and Dalmatian coasts, on the Greek islands, and in the ports of the Black Sea.

But the success of Venice owed more to its own achievements than to these rich inheritances. "It is the most triumphant city I have ever seen," wrote the Frenchman Philippe de Commynes at the end of the fifteenth century. The triumph of the Venetian state was the triumph of dedicated efficiency. The heart of its success lay in the way in which it organized its trade and its government. The key to Venetian trade was its privileged position with the Byzantine Empire. Venice had exchanged with the Byzantines military support for tax concessions that gave Venetian traders a competitive edge in the spice trade with the East. Venetians were the largest group of resident Europeans in Constantinople, and their personal contacts with eastern traders were an important part of their success. The spice trade was so lucrative that special ships were built to accommodate it. These galleys were constructed at public expense and doubled as the Venetian navy in times of war. By controlling these ships, the government strictly regulated the spice trade. Goods imported into or exported from Venice had to be carried in Venetian ships and be consigned by Venetian merchants. The trade in spices was carefully organized in other ways as well. Rather than allow the wealthiest merchants to dominate it, as they did in other cities, Venice specified the number of annual voyages and sold shares in them at auction based on a fixed price. This practice allowed big and small merchants to gain from the trade and encouraged all merchants to find other trading outlets. In the fourteenth century the Venetian empire included all of the most important trading ports on the coast of Dalmatia and in the Aegean Sea.

Like its trade, Venetian government was also designed to disperse power. Although it was known as "the most serene republic," Venice was not a republic in the sense that we use the word; it was rather an oligarchy—a government by a restricted group. Political power was vested in a Great Council whose membership had been fixed at the end of the thirteenth century. All males whose fathers enjoyed the privilege of membership in the Great Council were registered at birth in the Book of Gold and became members of the Great Council when adults. There were no further distinctions of rank within this nobility, whose members varied widely in wealth and intermarried freely with other groups in the society. From the body of the Great Council, which numbered about twenty-five hundred at the end of the fifteenth century, was chosen the Senate, a council about one-tenth the size, whose members served a one-year term. It was from the Senate that the true officers of government were selected: the doge, who was chosen for life, and members of a number of small councils, who administered affairs and advised the doge. Members of these councils were chosen by secret ballot in an elaborate process by which nominators were selected at random. Terms of office on the councils were extremely short in order to limit factionalism and to prevent any individual from gaining too much power. Though small groups exercised more power in practice than they should have in theory, the Venetian oligarchy was never troubled by either civil war or popular rebellion. "Venice governs itself with the greatest wisdom," Commynes declared, and Venetian-style republicanism was much admired throughout Europe.

With its mercantile families firmly in control of government and trade, Venice created a vast overseas empire in the East during the thirteenth and fourteenth centuries. Naval supremacy, based largely on technological advances that made long-distance and winter voyages possible, allowed the Venetians to offer protection to strategic outposts in return for either privileges or tribute. But in the fifteenth century Venice turned west. In a dramatic reversal of its centuries-old policy, it began a process of conquest in Italy itself, an empire on "terra firma," as Venetian islanders called it. There were several reasons for this new policy. First, the Venetian navy was no longer the unsurpassed power that it once had been. The Genoese wars had drained resources, and the revival of

the Ottoman Turks in the east posed a growing threat that ultimately resulted in the fall of Constantinople (1453) and the end of Venetian trading privileges. Outposts in Dalmatia and the Aegean came under assault from both the Turks and the king of Hungary, cutting heavily into the complicated system by which goods were circulated by Venetian merchants. Additionally, the trade in both sweet wine and sugar that the Venetians dominated through control of the Greek islands was now challenged by the Portuguese. It was not long before Portuguese competition affected the most lucrative of all the commodities traded by the Venetians—pepper. Perhaps most importantly, mainland expansion offered new opportunities for Venice. Not all Venetians were traders, and the new industries that were being developed in the city could readily benefit from control of mainland markets. So could those Venetian nobles employed to administer the conquered lands. They argued persuasively that the supply of raw materials and foodstuffs on which Venetian trade ultimately depended should be secured by the republic itself. Most decisively of all, opportunity was knocking. In Milan Visconti rule was weakening and the Milanese territories were ripe for picking.

Venice reaped a rich harvest. From the beginning of the fifteenth century to the Peace of Lodi, the Most Serene Republic engaged in unremitting warfare. Its successes were remarkable. It pushed out to the north to occupy all the lands between the city and the Habsburg territories; it pushed to the east until it straddled the entire head of the Adriatic; and it pushed to the west almost as far as Milan itself. Venetian victories resulted from both the traditional use of hired mercenaries and from the Venetians' own ingenuity at naval warfare. Although Venice was creating a landed empire, the course of expansion, especially in Lombardy, was along river routes. At the Arsenal were built new oared vessels armed with artillery for river sieges. Soon the captured territories were paying for continued expansion. The western conquests in particular brought large populations under Venetian control which, along with their potential as a market, provided a ready source of taxation. By the end of the fifteenth century the mainland dominions of Venice were contributing nearly 40 percent of the city's revenue at a cost far smaller than that of the naval empire a century earlier. Venice had become the most powerful city-state in Italy.

Florence

"What city, not merely in Italy, but in all the world ... is more proud in its palazzi, more bedecked with churches, more beautiful in its architecture, more imposing in its gates, richer in piazzas, happier in its wide streets, greater in its people, more glorious in its citizenry, more inexhaustible in wealth, more fertile in its fields?" So boasted the humanist Coluccio Salutati (1331–1406) in 1403 during one of the most calamitous periods in Florentine history. Salutati's boastings were not unusual; the Florentines' mythical view of their homeland, as savior of Christianity and as heir to the republican greatness of Rome, was everywhere apparent. And it seemed to be most vigorously expressed in the city's darkest moments. There is much in the belief that the artistic genius of Florence flowed from the turmoil of its economic and political life.

Florentine prosperity was built on two foundations: money and wool. Beginning in the thirteenth century, Florentine bankers were among the wealthiest and most powerful in the world. Initially their position was established through support of the papacy in its long struggle with the Holy Roman Empire. Florentine financiers established banks in all the capitals of Europe and the East, though their seats in Rome and Naples were probably most important. In the Middle Ages, bankers served more functions than simply handling and exchanging money. Most were also tied to mercantile adventures and underwrote industrial activity. So it was in Florence where international bankers purchased high-quality wool to be manufactured into the world's finest woven cloth. At its height before the plague, the cloth industry employed nearly thirty thousand workers, providing jobs at all levels of society, from the rural women who spun the wool into yarn at piecework wages, to the highly paid weavers and dyers whose skills made Florentine cloth so highly prized.

The activities of both commerce and cloth manufacture depended on external conditions, and thus the wealth of Florence was potentially unstable. In the mid-fourteenth century instability came with the plague that devastated the city. Nearly 40 percent of the entire population was lost in the single year 1348, and recurring outbreaks continued to ravage the already weakened survivors. Loss of workers and loss of markets seriously disrupted manufacturing. By 1380 cloth production had fallen to less than a quarter of preplague levels. On the heels of plague came wars. The property of Florentine bankers and merchants abroad was an easy target, and in this respect the wars with Naples at the end of the fourteenth century were particularly disastrous. Thirty years of warfare with Milan, interrupted by only a single decade of peace (1413–23), resulted in total bankruptcy for many of the city's leading commercial families. More significantly, the costs of warfare, offensive and defensive, created a massive public debt. Every Florentine of means owned shares in this debt, and the republic was continually devising new methods for borrowing and staving off crises of repayment. Small wonder that the republic turned for aid to the wealthiest banking family in Europe, the Medici.

As befitted a city whose prosperity was based on manufacturing, Florence had a strong guild tradition. The most important guilds were associated with banking and cloth manufacture but they included the crafts and food-processing trades as well. Only guild members could participate in government, electing the nine *Signoria* who administered laws, set tax rates, and directed foreign and domestic policy. Like that of Venice, Florentine government was a republican oligarchy and like Venice, it depended upon rotated short periods in office and selections by lot to avoid factionalism. But Florence had a history of factionalism longer than its history of republican government. Its formal structures were occasionally altered so that powerful families could gain control of the real centers of political power, the small councils and emergency assemblies through which the *Signoria* governed. This was especially the case following the revolt of the Ciompi (1378) in which the workers in the severely depressed cloth industry rioted and briefly gained control of the city. After that the merchant elite gripped the reins of government tightly, even establishing a kind of secret police to quash conspiracies. Conservative leadership drawn from the upper ranks of Florentine society guided the city through the wars of the early fourteenth century. But soon afterward the leaders of its greatest families, the Albizzi, the Pazzi, and the Medici, again divided Florentine politics into factions.

The ability of the Medici to secure a century-long dynasty in a government that did not have a head of state is just one of the mysteries surrounding the history of this remarkable family. Cosimo de' Medici (1389–1464) was one of the richest men in Christendom when he returned to the city in 1434 after a brief exile. His leading position in government rested upon supporters who were able to gain a controlling influence on the *Signoria*. Cosimo built his party carefully, banishing his Albizzi enemies, recruiting followers among the craftsmen whom he employed, and even paying delinquent taxes to maintain the eligibility of his voters. Most importantly, emergency powers were invoked to reduce the number of citizens qualified to vote for the *Signoria* until the majority were Medici backers.

Cosimo was a practical man. He raised his children along humanist principles and was a great patron of artists and intellectuals. He collected books and paintings, endowed libraries, and spent lavishly on his own palace, the Palazzo Medici, which after his death was transformed into the very center of Florentine cultural life. Cosimo's position as an international banker brought him into contact with the heads of other Italian city-states and it was his personal relationship with Francesco Sforza that finally ended the Milanese wars and brought about the Peace of Lodi.

It was Cosimo's grandson, Lorenzo (1449–92), who linked the family's name to that of the age. Lorenzo was trained to office as if he had been a prince rather than a citizen of a republic. His own father ruled for five years and used his son as a diplomat in order to acquaint him with the leaders of Europe. Diplomacy was Lorenzo's greatest achievement. He held strong humanist values instilled in him by his mother, Lucrezia Tornabuoni, who organized his education. He wrote poetry and drama and even entered competitions for architectural designs. But Lorenzo's chief contri-

bution to artistic life as it reached its height in Florence was to facilitate its production. He brought Michelangelo and other leading artists to his garden; he brought Pico della Mirandola and other leading humanists to his table. He secured commissions for Florentine artists throughout the peninsula, ensuring the spread of their influence and the continued regeneration of artistic creativity in Florence itself.

Lorenzo was generally regarded as the leading citizen of Florence and this was true both in terms of his wealth and his influence. He did not rule from high office, though he maintained the party that his grandfather had built and even extended it through wartime emergency measures. His power was based on his personality and reputation, a charisma enhanced when he survived an assassination attempt in which his brother was killed. His diplomatic abilities were the key to his survival. Almost immediately after Lorenzo came to power, Naples and the papacy began a war with Florence, a war that was costly to the Florentines in both taxation and lost territory. In 1479 Lorenzo traveled to Naples and personally convinced the Neapolitan king to sign a separate treaty. This restored the Italian balance of power and ensured continued Medici rule in Florence. Soon Lorenzo even had a treaty with the pope that allowed for the recovery of lost territories and the expansion of Florentine influence.

There is some doubt whether Lorenzo should be remembered by the title "the Magnificent" that was bestowed upon him. His absorption in politics came at the expense of the family's commercial enterprises, which were nearly ruined during his lifetime. Branch after branch of the Medici bank closed as conditions for international finance deteriorated. Though his children were all to enjoy successful careers, one as ruler of Florence, one as Pope Leo X, and the third as duke of Nemours, to whom Machiavelli originally dedicated *The Prince*, the family fortune was dwindling. Moreover, the emergency powers that Lorenzo invoked to restrict participation in government changed forever the character of Florentine republicanism, irredeemably corrupting it. There is no reason to accept the judgment of his enemies that Lorenzo was a tyrant, but the negative consequences of his rule cannot be ignored. Yet Lorenzo was celebrated because he stood for all that Florentines believed about their city during the last moments that its splendor was unquestionable. It was the city more than the man that was being dubbed "magnificent." In 1494, two years after Lorenzo's death, the peninsula was plunged into those wars that turned it from the center of European civilization into one of its lesser satellites.

The End of Italian Hegemony

In the course of the Renaissance western Europe was Italianized. For a century the city-states dominated the trade routes that connected East and West. Venetian and Genoese merchants exchanged spices and minerals from the Black Sea to the North Sea, enriching the material life of three continents. They brought wool from England and Spain to the skilled craftsmen in the Low Countries and Florence. Italian manufactures, such as Milanese artillery, Florentine silk, and Venetian glass, were prized above all others. The ducat and the florin, two Italian coins, were universally accepted in an age when every petty prince minted his own. The peninsula exported culture in the same way that it exported goods. Humanism quickly spread across the Alps, aided by the recent invention of printing (which the Venetians soon dominated), while Renaissance standards of artistic achievement were known worldwide and everywhere imitated. The city-states shared their technology as well. The compass and the navigational chart, projection maps, double-entry bookkeeping, eyeglasses, the telescope—all profoundly influenced what could be achieved and what could be hoped for. In this spirit Christopher Columbus, a Genoese seaman, successfully crossed the Atlantic under the Spanish flag, and Amerigo Vespucci, a Florentine merchant, gave his name to the newly discovered continents.

But it was not in Italy that the rewards of innovation or the satisfactions of achievement were enjoyed. There the seeds of political turmoil and military imperialism, combined with the rise of the Ottoman Turks, were to reap a not-unexpected harvest. Under the cover of the Peace of Lodi, the major city-states had scrambled to enlarge their mainland empires. By the end of the fifteenth century they eyed one another greedily and warily. Each expected the others to begin a

Italy, 1494

peninsula-wide war for hegemony and took the steps that ultimately ensured the contest. Perhaps the most unusual aspect of the imperialism of the city-states was that it had been restricted to the peninsula itself. Each of the major powers shared the dream of recapturing the glory that was Rome. Though the Venetians had expanded abroad, their acquisitions had not come through conquest or occupation. In their Greek and Dalmatian territories local law and custom continued to govern under the benevolent eye of Venetian administrators. But in their mainland territories the Venetians were as ruthless as were the Florentines in Pisa or as was Cesare Borgia in Romagna when he consolidated the Papal States by fire and sword. Long years of siege and occupation had militarized the Italian city-states. Venice and Florence balanced their budgets on the backs of their captured territories. Milan had been engaged in constant war for decades and even the papacy was militarily aggressive.

And the Italians were no longer alone. The most remarkable military leader of the age was not a Renaissance *condottiere* but an Ottoman prince, Mehmed II (1451–81), who conquered Constantinople and Athens and threatened

Rome itself. The rise of the Ottomans, whose name is derived from Osman, their original tribal leader, is one of the most compelling stories in world history. Little more than a warrior tribe at the beginning of the fourteenth century, a hundred and fifty years later the Ottomans had replaced stagnant Byzantine rule with a virile and potent empire. First they gobbled up the towns and cities in a wide arc around Constantinople. Then they fed upon the Balkans and the eastern kingdoms of Hungary and Poland. By 1400 they were a presence in all the territory that stretched from the Black Sea to the Aegean. By 1450 they were its master. (See Special Feature, "The Fall of Constantinople," pp. 350–351.)

Venice was most directly affected by the Ottoman advance. Not only was its favored position in eastern trade threatened, but during a prolonged war at the end of the fifteenth century the Venetians lost many of their most important commercial outposts. Ottoman might closed off the markets of eastern Europe. Islands in the Aegean and seaports along the Dalmatian coast fell to the Turks in alarming succession. By 1480 Venetian naval supremacy was a thing of the past.

The Italian city-states might have met this challenge from the east had they been able to unite in opposing it. Successive popes pleaded for holy wars to halt the advance of the Turks, which was compared in officially inspired propaganda to an outbreak of plague. The fall of Constantinople in 1453 was an event of epochal proportions for Europeans, many believing that it foreshadowed the end of the world. "A thing terrible to relate and to be deplored by all who have in them any spark of humanity. The splendor and glory of the East has been captured, despoiled, ravaged and completely sacked by the most inhuman barbarians," the Venetian doge was informed. Yet it was Italians rather than Ottomans who plunged the peninsula into those wars from which it never recovered.

The Wars of Italy (1494–1529) began when Naples, Florence, and the Papal States united against Milan. At first this alliance seemed little more than another shift in the balance of power. But rather than call upon Venice to redress the situation, the Milanese leader, Ludovico il Moro, sought help from the French. An army of French cavalry and Swiss mercenaries, led by Charles VIII of France (1483–98) invaded the peninsula in 1494. With Milanese support the French swept all before them. Florence was forced to surrender Pisa, a humiliation that led to the overthrow of the Medici and the establishment of French sovereignty. The Papal States were next to be occupied, and within a year Charles had conquered Naples without engaging the Italians in a single significant battle. Unfortunately, the Milanese were not the only ones who could play at the game of foreign alliances. Next it was the turn of the Venetians and the pope to unite and call upon the services of King Ferdinand of Aragon and the Holy Roman Emperor. Italy was now a battleground in what became a total European war for dynastic supremacy. The city-states used their foreign allies to settle old scores and to extend their own mainland empires. At the turn of the century Naples was dismembered. In 1509 the pope conspired to organize the most powerful combination of forces yet known against Venice. All of the "terra firma" possessions of the Most Serene Republic were lost, but by a combination of good fortune and skilled diplomacy Venice itself survived. Florence was less fortunate, becoming a pawn first of the French and then of the Spanish. The final blow to Italian hegemony was the sack of Rome in 1527, when German mercenaries fulfilled the fears of what the "infidels" would do to the Holy City.

Surveying the wreckage of the Italian wars Machiavelli ended *The Prince* with a plea for a leader to emerge to restore Italian freedom and re-create the unity of the ancient Roman republic. He concluded with these lines from Petrarch:

> Then virtue boldly shall engage
> And swiftly vanquish barbarous rage,
> Proving that ancient and heroic pride
> In true Italian hearts had never died.

The revival of "ancient and heroic pride" fueled the Italian revival. The sense of living in a new age, the spirit of human achievement, and the curiosity and wonderment of writers and artists all characterized the Renaissance. The desire to re-create the glories of Rome was not Machiavelli's alone. It could be seen in the palaces of the Italian aristocracy; in the papal rebuilding of the Holy City; and in the military ambitions of princes. But the legacy of empire, of "ancient and heroic pride," had passed out of Italian hands.

The Fall of Constantinople

The prayers of the devout were more fervent than ever on Easter Sunday, 1453. The Christians of Constantinople knew that it was only a matter of time before the last remaining stronghold of the Byzantine Empire came under siege. For decades the ring of Ottoman conquests had narrowed around this holy city until it alone stood out against the Turkish sultan. Constantinople, the bridge between Europe and Asia, was tottering. The once teeming center of Eastern Christianity had never recovered from the epidemics of the fourteenth century. Dwindling revenues matched the dwindling population. Concessions to Venetian and Genoese traders reduced customs while Ottoman conquests eliminated tribute money.

Perhaps it was this impoverishment that had kept the Turks at bay. Constantinople was still the best-fortified city in the world. Two of its three sides faced the sea, and the third was protected by two stout rings of walls and a trench lined with stones. No cannon forged in the West could dent these battlements and no navy could hope to force its way through the narrow mouth of the Golden Horn. A siege of Constantinople hardly seemed worthwhile as long as there were conquests to be made in eastern Europe and Asia Minor. Thus an uneasy peace existed between sultan and emperor. It

was shattered in 1451 when a new sultan, the nineteen-year-old Mehmed II, came to the throne. Mehmed's imagination was fired by the ancient prophecies that a Muslim would rule in all of the territories of the east. Only Constantinople was a fitting capital for such an empire, and Mehmed immediately began preparations for its conquest.

In 1452 Mehmed had constructed a fortress at the narrow mouth of the Bosporus and demanded tribute from all ships that entered the Golden Horn. The Byzantine emperor sent ambassadors to Mehmed to protest this aggression. Mehmed returned their severed heads. When the first Venetian convoy refused to lower its sails, Mehmed's artillery efficiently sank one of the galleys with a single shot. The Turks now controlled access to the city for trade and supplies. An attack the following spring seemed certain.

The emperor appealed far and wide for aid for his beleaguered city. Many had reasons for preserving Constantinople—the Venetians and Genoese to protect their trade; the pope to defend Christianity. Reluctantly, they agreed to act. But the Europeans were in no hurry to pledge their support, as it was inconceivable that the Ottomans could assemble the army necessary to besiege Constantinople before summer. By then, the Europeans assumed, an Italian armada could easily dislodge the Ottoman fortress and reinforce the city with trained fighting men.

But in this they reckoned

without Mehmed. While the Italians bickered over their share of the expedition and Christians everywhere made ready to celebrate Holy Week, the Ottomans assembled a vast army of fighters and laborers and a huge train of weapons and supplies. Among this was the largest cannon ever cast, with a twenty-six-foot barrel that shot a twelve-hundred-pound ball. Fifty teams of oxen and two hundred men took two months to pull it in place.

Mehmed's forces, which eventually numbered more than 150,000, of which 60,000 were soldiers, assembled around the walls of Constantinople on April 5. During the next week a great flotilla sailed up the Bosporus and anchored just out of reach of the Byzantine warships in the Golden Horn. A census taken inside the city revealed that there were only 7,000 able-bodied defenders, about 5,000 Greek residents and 2,000 foreigners, mostly Genoese and Venetians. The Italians were the only true soldiers among them.

Though the defenders were vastly outnumbered, they still held the military advantage. As long as their ships controlled the entrance to the Golden Horn, they could limit the Ottoman attack to only one side, where all of the best defenders could be massed. The Byzantines cast a boom—an iron chain supported by wooden floats—across the mouth of the bay to forestall a naval attack. By the middle of April the Turks had begun their land assault. Each day great guns pounded the walls of the city and each night residents worked frantically to repair the damage. Everyone contributed. Old women wove baskets in which children carried stones, monks and nuns packed mud and cut branches to shore up the breaches in the wall. The Turks suffered heavily for each attempt to follow a cannon shot with a massed charge. But the attack took its toll among the defenders as well. No one was safe from the flaming arrows and catapulted stones flung over the city's walls. Choking black smoke filled the air as the huge cannon shook the foundations of the city and treated its stout stone walls as if they were plaster. Nevertheless, in the first month of siege the defenders held their own.

The vigorous defense of the city infuriated Mehmed. As long as there was only one point of attack, the defenders could resist indefinitely. The line of assault had to be extended, and this could only be done by sea. With the boom effectively impregnable and with Italian

seamen superior to the Turks, the prospects seemed dim. But what could not be achieved by force might be achieved by cunning. A plan was devised to carry a number of smaller ships across land and then to float them behind the Christian fleet. Protected by land forces, the ships could be used as a staging point for another line of attack. Thousands of workmen were set the task of building huge wooden rollers, which were greased with animal fat. Under cover of darkness and the smoke of cannon fire, seventy-two ships were pulled up the steep hills and pushed down into the sea. Once they were safely anchored, a pontoon bridge was built and cannon were trained on the seaward walls of the city.

The crafty plan succeeded, but moving ships across dry land was not the only engineering feat that sapped the defenders. One night a tower higher than the city's battlements was assembled in front of the landward walls. From there archers pelted the city and sorties of attackers sallied forth. In May, the defenders discovered the tunnels the Turks had built underneath the city, one of which had reached beyond the second ring of protective walls. The attacks and bombardments were now relentless. The city had withstood siege for nearly six weeks without any significant reinforcement. At the end of the month there was a sudden lull. A messenger from the sultan arrived to demand surrender. The choice was clear. If the city was taken by force the customary three days of unrestricted pillage would be allowed, but if it yielded, the

sultan pledged to protect the property of all who desired to remain under his rule. The emperor replied feebly that no one who had ever laid siege to Constantinople had enjoyed a long life. He was ready to die in defense of the city.

On May 30 the final assault began. Mehmed knew that his advantage lay in numbers. First he sent in waves of irregular troops, mostly captured slaves and Christians, who suffered great losses and were finally driven back by the weakened defenders. Next, better-trained warriors attacked and widened the breaches made by the irregulars. Finally came the crack Janissaries, the sultan's elite warriors, disciplined from birth to fight. It was the Janissaries who found a small door left open at the base of the wall. In they rushed, quickly overwhelming the first line of defenders and battering their way through the weaker second walls. By dawn the Ottoman flag was raised over the battlements and the sack of Constantinople had begun.

There was no need for the customary three days of pillage. By the end of the first day there was nothing left worth taking. The churches and monasteries had been looted and defaced, the priests and nuns murdered or defiled, and thousands of civilians had been captured to be sold into slavery. Large areas of the city smoldered from countless fires. The desolation was so complete that not even Mehmed could take joy in the ceremonial procession into the new capital of his empire. The bastion of Eastern Christendom was no more.

Suggestions for Further Reading

General Reading

Ernst Breisach, *Renaissance Europe 1300–1517* (New York: Macmillan, 1973). A solid survey of the political history of the age.

* Denys Hay, *The Italian Renaissance* (Cambridge: Cambridge University Press, 1977). An elegant interpretive essay. The best first book to read.

* J. R. Hale, ed., *A Concise Encyclopedia of the Italian Renaissance* (Oxford: Oxford University Press, 1981). A treasure trove of facts about the major figures and events of the era.

* P. Burke, *Culture and Society in Renaissance Italy* (Princeton, NJ: Princeton University Press, 1987). A good introduction to social and intellectual developments.

Renaissance Society

* M. Aston, *The Fifteenth Century: The Prospect of Europe* (London: Thames and Hudson, 1968). A concise survey of Continental history; well written and illustrated.

* J. R. Hale, *Renaissance Europe: The Individual and Society* (Berkeley, CA: University of California Press, 1978). A lively study that places the great figures of the Renaissance in their social context.

* Carlo Cipolla, *Before the Industrial Revolution: European Society and Economy, 1000–1700* (New York: Norton, 1976). A sweeping survey of social and economic developments across the centuries.

* Harry Miskimin, *The Economy of Early Renaissance Europe 1300–1460* (Englewood Cliffs, NJ: Prentice Hall, 1969). A detailed scholarly study of economic development.

D. Herlihy and C. Klapiche-Zuber, *The Tuscans and Their Families* (New Haven, CT: Yale University Press, 1985). Difficult but rewarding study of the social and demographic history of Florence and its environs.

* Christiane Klapiche-Zuber, *Women, Family, and Ritual in Renaissance Italy* (Chicago: University of Chicago Press, 1985). A sparkling collection of essays on diverse topics in social history from wet-nursing to family life.

Renaissance Art

* Michael Baxandall, *Painting and Experience in Fifteenth Century Italy* (Oxford: Oxford University Press, 1972). A study of the relationship between painters and their patrons, of how and why art was produced.

Frederick Hartt, *History of Italian Renaissance Art* (Englewood Cliffs, NJ: Prentice Hall, 1974). The most comprehensive survey, with hundreds of plates.

* Michael Levey, *Early Renaissance* (London: Penguin Books, 1967). A concise survey of art; clearly written and authoritative.

* Rudolph Wittkower, *Architectural Principles in the Age of Humanism* (New York: Norton, 1971). A difficult but rewarding study of Renaissance architecture.

John Pope-Hennessy, *Introduction to Italian Sculpture* (New York: Phaidon, 1972). A thorough analysis of the development of sculpture; carefully illustrated.

* Linda Murray, *High Renaissance and Mannerism* (London: Thames and Hudson, 1985). The best introduction to late Renaissance art.

* Howard Hibbard, *Michelangelo* (New York: Harper & Row, 1974). A compelling biography of an obsessed genius.

Renaissance Ideals

* Hans Baron, *The Crisis of the Early Italian Renaissance* (Princeton, NJ: Princeton University Press, 1966). One of the most influential intellectual histories of the period.

* Ernst Cassirer, ed., *The Renaissance Philosophy of Man* (Chicago: University of Chicago Press, 1948). Translations of the works of Petrarch, Valla, and Pico della Mirandola, among others, with excellent introductions.

George Holmes, *The Florentine Enlightenment* (New York: Pegasus, 1969). The best work on the successive generations of Florentine humanists.

Albert Rabil, ed., *Renaissance Humanism* (Philadelphia: University of Pennsylvania Press, 1988). A multi-authored, multi-volume collection of essays on humanism, with all of the latest scholarship.

* Quentin Skinner, *Machiavelli* (Oxford: Oxford University Press, 1981). A brief but brilliant life.

The Politics of the Italian City-States

* Lauro Martines, *Power and Imagination: City-States in Renaissance Italy* (New York: Alfred A. Knopf, 1979). An important interpretation of the politics of the Italian powers.

* Frederic C. Lane, *Venice: A Maritime Republic* (Baltimore: Johns Hopkins University Press, 1973). A complete history of Venice, which stresses its naval and mercantile developments.

* Gene Brucker, *Renaissance Florence*, 2d ed. (Berkeley, CA: University of California Press, 1983). The best single volume introduction to Florentine history.

* J. R. Hale, *Florence and the Medici* (London: Thames and Hudson, 1977). A compelling account of the relationship between a city and its most powerful citizens.

* Eugene F. Rice, Jr., *The Foundations of Early Modern Europe 1460–1559* (New York: Norton, 1970). The best short, synthetic work.

*Indicates paperback edition available.

12

The European Empires

Ptolemy's World

For over a thousand years, educated Europeans thought of the world as it had been described by Ptolemy in the second century. Most of their knowledge came from guesswork rather than observation. The world was a big place when you had to cross it on foot or by four-legged beast or in small rickety vessels that hugged the shoreline as they sailed. Those without education lived in a world bounded by their farm and their village and thought of neighboring cities as faraway places. There were few experiences to pass from generation to generation, and those that were handed down changed from fact to fancy in the retelling. The people of the Renaissance probably knew less for certain about the planet they inhabited than had the Greeks, and the Greeks knew precious little. But lack of knowledge did not cause confusion. People who lived at the end of the fifteenth century knew enough to conduct their affairs and to dream their dreams. Ptolemy's earth was as real then as the astronaut's solar system is now.

The map on the facing page depicts the image of the world that Ptolemy bequeathed, the world that the Renaissance inherited with his calculations and writings. The first thing to notice is that it is shaped as a sphere. Though popular myth, confirmed by common sense, held that the world was flat and that one could theoretically fall off its edges, educated Europeans understood that it was spherical. Ptolemy had shown the earth as an irregular semicircle divided into degrees of longitude, beginning with 0° in the west, where Europe was situated, and progressing to 180° in the east. His construction of latitude was less certain, for less was known (then as now) about the extreme north and south. But Ptolemy did locate an equator, somewhat off center, and he portrayed as accurately as he could what was known of the European landmass. Scandinavia in the north and England and Ireland, set off from the Continent and from each other, are readily visible. The contours of Spain in the southwest are clear, though distorted. As the ancient world centered on the Mediterranean—literally "sea in the middle of the earth"—it was most accurately reconstructed. Italy, Greece, and Asia Minor are easily recognizable, while France and Spain stretch out of shape like taffy. The size of the Mediterranean is grossly overestimated, its coastline occupying nearly a quarter of the map.

Africa, too, is swollen. It spans the too-wide Mediterranean and then balloons out to cover the entire southern hemisphere. Its eastern portions stretch into Asia, though so little is certain that they are labeled *terra incognita*—unknown lands. Europe, Africa, and Asia are the only continents. They are watered by a single ocean whose name changes with the languages of its neighboring inhabitants. Most remarkable of all is the division of the earth's surface. Land covers three-quarters of it. This was the world as it was known in 1400, and this was why the ensuing century would be called the age of discovery.

The European Discoveries

There were many reasons why this map of the world changed in the early sixteenth century. It was an age of discovery in many ways. Knowledge bequeathed from the past created curiosity about the present. Technological change made long sea voyages possible, and the demands of commerce provided incentives. Ottoman expansion on the southern and eastern frontiers of the Continent threatened access to the goods of the East on which Europeans had come to rely. Spices were rare and expensive, but they were not merely luxuries. While nobles and rich merchants consumed them lavishly to enhance their reputations for wealth and generosity, spices had many practical uses. Some acted as preservatives, others as flavorings to make palatable the rotting foodstuffs that were the fare of even the wealthiest Europeans. Some spices were used as perfumes to battle the noxious gases that rose from urban streets and invaded homes and workplaces. The drugs of the East, the nature of which we can only guess at, helped soothe chronic ill health. The demand for all of these "spices" continued to rise at a greater rate than their supply. There was more than a fortune to be made by anyone who could participate in the trade.

Eastern spices were expensive. Most European manufactured goods had little utility in the East. Woven wool, which was the staple of western industry, was too heavy to be worn in eastern climes. Both silk and cotton came from the East and were more expertly spun there. Even western jewelry relied upon imported stones. While metalwork was an attractive commodity for export, the dilemma of the arms trade was as acute then as it is now. Providing Ottomans or other Muslims with weapons to wage holy wars against Christian Europe posed problems of policy and morality. And once the Turks began to cast great bronze cannon of their own, European arms were less eagerly sought. Western gold and silver flowed steadily east. As supplies of precious metals dwindled, economic growth in Europe slowed. Throughout the fifteenth century ever larger amounts of western specie were necessary to purchase ever smaller amounts of eastern commodities. Europe faced a severe shortage of gold and silver, a shortage that threatened its standard

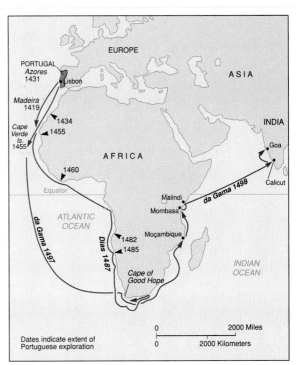

Portuguese Explorations

of living and its prospects for economic growth. The search was on to discover new sources of gold.

A Passage to India

It was the Portuguese who made the first dramatic breakthroughs in exploration and colonization. Perched on the southwestern tip of Europe, Portugal was an agriculturally poor and sparsely populated nation. Among its few marketable commodities were fish and wine, which it traded with Genoese and Venetian galleys making their voyages to northern Europe. Portugal's North African trade was more lucrative, but extended warfare between Christians and Muslims had made it unreliable. The Portuguese had long been sea explorers, especially in the Atlantic Ocean, where they had established bases in the Azores and Madeira islands. Their small ships, known as caravels, were ideal for ocean travel and their navigators were among the most skillful in the world. Yet they were unable to participate in the lucrative Mediterranean trade in bullion and spices until the expanding power of the Ottomans threatened the traditional eastern sea routes.

In the early fifteenth century, the Portuguese gained a foothold in northern Africa and used it to stage voyages along the continent's unexplored western coast. Like most explorers, the Portuguese were motivated by an unselfconscious mixture of faith and greed. Establishing southern bases would enable them to surround their Muslim enemies while also giving them access to the African bullion trade. The Portuguese navigator Bartolomeu Dias (ca. 1450–1500) summarized these goals succinctly: "To give light to those who are in darkness and to grow rich." Under the energetic leadership of Prince Henry the Navigator (1394–1460), the Portuguese pushed steadily southward. Prince Henry studied navigational techniques, accumulated detailed accounts of voyages, and encouraged the creation of accurate maps of the African coastline. Great stone columns were erected to mark the southern progress of each voyage. What was learned on one trip was applied to the next. Soon the Portuguese were a power in the West African trade in slaves and gold ore. Black slaves became a staple of the African voyages, with nearly 150,000 slaves imported in the first fifty years of exploration. Portugal became the first European nation in which black slavery was common. Most slaves were used as domestics and laborers in Portugal; others were sent to work the lucrative sugar plantations that Prince Henry had established on the island of Madeira.

Prince Henry's systematic program paid off in the next generation. By the 1480s Portuguese outposts had reached almost to the equator, and in 1487 Bartolomeu Dias rounded the tip of Africa and opened the eastern African shores to Portuguese traders. The aim of these enterprises was access to Asia rather than Africa. Dias might have reached India if his crew had not mutinied and forced him to return home. A decade later Vasco da Gama (ca. 1460–1524) rounded the Cape of Good Hope and crossed into the Indian Ocean. His journey took two years, but when he returned to Lisbon in 1499 laden with the most valuable spices of the East, Portuguese ambitions were achieved. Larger expeditions followed, one of which, blown off course, touched the South American coast of Brazil, which was soon subsumed within the Portuguese dominions.

The Portuguese came to the East as traders rather than as conquerors. Building on their expe-rience in West Africa, they developed a policy of establishing military outposts to protect their investments and subduing native populations only when necessary. Their achievements resulted more from determination than from technological superiority, though their initial displays of force, like da Gama's attack on Calicut in 1503, terrified the Asian rulers who controlled the spice trade. Throughout the East the Portuguese took advantage of local feuds to gain allies, and they established trading compounds that were easily defensible. The great Portuguese general Alfonso de Albuquerque (1453–1515) understood the need for strategically placed garrisons and conquered the vital ports of the Middle East and India. By the first decade of the sixteenth century the Portuguese were masters of a vast empire, which spanned both the eastern and western coasts of Africa and the western shores of India. Most importantly, the Portuguese controlled Ceylon and Indonesia, the precious Spice Islands from

Vasco da Gama. After his 1498 voyage to India, Da Gama was given the title Admiral of the Sea of the Indies by the Portuguese king. This portrait was made in 1524, when Da Gama was appointed Portugal's viceroy in India.

which came cloves, cinnamon, and pepper. Almost overnight, Lisbon became one of the trading capitals of the world, tripling in population between 1500 and 1550.

It was northern Europe that was to harvest what Portugal had sown. The long voyages around Africa were costly and dangerous. Portugal produced no valuable commodities and had to exchange bullion for spices. Moreover, the expense of maintaining a far-flung empire ate into the profits of trade at the same time that the increased volume necessary to make the voyages worthwhile drove down spice prices. Between 1501 and 1505 over eighty ships and seven thousand men sailed from Portugal to the East. This vast commitment was underwritten by Flemish, German, and Italian bankers. Soon Antwerp replaced Lisbon as the marketplace for Asian spices. Ironically, it was in the accidental discovery of Brazil rather than in Asia that the Portuguese were rewarded for the enterprise of their explorers.

Mundus Novus

While the bulk of Portuguese resources were devoted to the Asian trade, those of the Spanish kingdom came to be concentrated in the New World. Though larger and richer than its eastern neighbor, Spain had been segmented into a number of small kingdoms and principalities and divided between Christians and Muslims. Not until the end of the fifteenth century, when the crowns of Aragon and Castile were united and the Muslims expelled from Granada, could the Spanish concentrate their resources. By then they were far behind in establishing commercial enterprises. With Portugal dominating the African route to India, Queen Isabella of Castile was persuaded to take an interest in a western route by a Genoese adventurer, Christopher Columbus (ca. 1446–1506). That interest resulted in one of the greatest accidents of history. (See Special Feature, "Christopher Columbus," pp. 360–361.)

Initially, Columbus' discovery of a Mundus Novus, a New World, was a disappointment. He had gone in search of a western passage to the Indies and he had failed to return to Spain laden with eastern spices. Despite his own belief that the islands he had discovered lay just off the coast of Japan, it was soon apparent that he had found an altogether unknown landmass. Columbus' own explorations and those of his successors continued to focus on discovering a route to the Indies. This was all the more imperative once the Portuguese succeeded in finding the passage around Africa. Rivalry between the two nations intensified after 1500 when the Portuguese began exploring the coast of Brazil. In 1494 the Treaty of Tordesillas had confined Portugal's right to the eastern route to the Indies as well as to any undiscovered lands east of an imaginary line fixed west of the Cape Verde Islands. This entitled Portugal to Brazil. The Spanish received whatever lay west of the line. At the time few doubted that Portugal had the better of the bargain.

But Spanish-backed explorations soon proved the value of the newly discovered lands. Using the Caribbean islands as a staging ground, successive explorers uncovered the vast coastline of Central and South America. In 1513 Vasco Núñez de Balboa (1475–1517) crossed the land passage in Panama and became the first European to view the Pacific Ocean. The discovery of this ocean refueled Spanish ambitions to find a western passage to the Indies.

In 1519 Ferdinand Magellan (ca. 1480–1521), a Portuguese mariner in the service of Spain, set sail in pursuit of Columbus' goal of reaching the Spice Islands by sailing westward. His voyage, which he did not live to complete, remains the most astounding of the age. After making the Atlantic crossing, Magellan resupplied his fleet in Brazil. Then his ships began the long southerly run toward the tip of South America, though he had no idea of the length of the continent. Suppressing mutinies and overcoming shipwrecks and desertions, Magellan finally found the straits that still bear his name. This crossing was the most difficult of all; the three hundred miles took thirty-eight terrifying days to navigate. By the time Magellan entered the Pacific Ocean he had already lost two of his ships and much of his crew.

The Pacific voyage was equally remarkable. The sailors went nearly four months without taking on fresh food or water. Survival was miraculous. "We drank yellow water and often ate sawdust. Rats were sold for half a ducat a piece." When they finally did reach land, first in the Marianas, and then in the Philippines, they fell prey to natives more aggressive than those they had met in South America. Theft and murder further reduced provisions and their ranks. Magellan's foolhardy decision to become involved in a local war cost him his life. It was left to his navigator, Sebastián Elcano (ca. 1476–1526), to complete the journey. In 1522, three years and one month after setting out, Elcano returned to Spain with a single ship and 18 survivors of the crew of 280. But in his hold were spices of greater value than the cost of the expedition, and in his return was practical proof that the world was round.

The circumnavigation of Magellan and Elcano brought to an end the first stage of the Spanish exploration of the new world. Columbus' dreams were realized, but the vastness of the Pacific Ocean made a western passage to the Indies uneconomical. While the Portuguese could secure their cargoes through a series of fortresses along the Indian Ocean, the Spanish had to face the dangers of the difficult Pacific crossing. In 1529 the Spanish crown relinquished its claims to the Spice Islands to the Portuguese for a cash settlement. By then trading spices was less alluring than mining gold and silver.

The Spanish Conquests

At the same moment that Magellan's voyage closed one stage of Spanish discovery, the exploits of Hernando Cortés (1485–1547) opened another. The Spanish colonized the New World along the model of their reconquest of Spain. Individuals were given control over land and the people on it in return for military service. The interests of the crown were threefold: to convert the natives to Christianity; to extend sovereignty over new dominions; and to gain some measure of profit from the venture. The colonial entrepreneurs had a singular interest—to grow rich. By and large the colonizers came from the lower orders of Spanish society. Even the original captains and governors were drawn from groups, like younger sons of the nobility, that would have had little opportunity for rule in Castile. They undertook great risks in expectation of great rewards. Ruthlessness and greed were their universal qualities.

Thus many of the protective measures taken by the crown to ensure orderly colonization and fair treatment of the natives were ineffective in

practice. The *requiremiento* was a case in point. When conquering new lands, Spanish captains had to offer the natives the opportunity to live in peace and security if they would acknowledge the supremacy of the pope and the queen of Castile. Not surprisingly, few natives accepted this generous offer, read to them in Latin or Castilian. During the first decades of the sixteenth century, Spanish captains and their followers subdued the Indian populations of the Caribbean Islands and put them to work on the agricultural haciendas that they had carved out for themselves. As early as 1498 Castilian women began arriving in the New World. Their presence helped change the character of the settlement towns from wild frontier garrisons to civilized settlements. Younger daughters of the lesser nobility, guided and guarded by chaperones, came to find husbands among the successful *conquistadores*. Some of these women ultimately inherited huge estates and participated fully in the forging of Spanish America.

Life on the hacienda, even in relative ease with a Castilian wife and family, did not always satisfy the ambitions of the Spanish colonizers. Hernando Cortés was one such *conquistador*. Having participated in the conquest of Cuba, Cortés sought an independent command to lead an expedition into the hinterland of Central America, where a fabulous empire was rumored to exist. Gathering a force of six hundred men, Cortés sailed across the Gulf of Mexico in 1519, established a fort at Vera Cruz, where he garrisoned two hundred men, and then sank his boats so that none of his company could turn back. With four hundred soldiers, he began his quest. The company marched two hundred fifty miles through steamy jungles and over rugged mountains before glimpsing the first signs of the great Aztec civilization. The Aztec empire was a loose confederation of native tribes that the Aztecs had conquered during the previous century. They were ruled by the emperor Montezuma II (1502–20) from his capital at Tenochtitlán, a marvelous city built of stone and baked clay in the middle of a lake. Invited to an audience with the Aztec emperor, Cortés and his men saw vast stores of gold and silver.

The conquest of the Aztecs took nearly a year and remains an overwhelming feat of arms. Cortés' success depended upon three factors. First

Christopher Columbus

Christopher Columbus, the eldest son of a wool weaver, was born in Genoa in 1451. His father was sufficiently prosperous to own a shop and employ other laborers. In the normal course of affairs, Christopher would have entered the weavers' guild and inherited his father's business. We shall never know why he turned to the sea rather than to the loom. Perhaps his father had visions of expanding his trade by purchasing raw materials in bulk, or perhaps Christopher had ambitions of becoming a Genoese merchant. For whatever reasons, Columbus spent his adolescence at sea, first on routine trading runs, then as a sailor on a Genoese warship.

When Columbus first became obsessed with the idea of traveling to the Indies is unknown, but obsessed he became. From the time he was thirty he could think and talk about little else. He avidly read the geographies of the ancients and the travelers' tales of the moderns. He was especially impressed by the descriptions of Marco Polo. Like all well-informed people of his day, Columbus believed that the world was round and that it contained three continents set inside one ocean. Following the Bible, he also believed that six-sevenths of the earth was land and only one-seventh water. By carefully calculating routes and distances, he concluded that a western track would be shorter and less expensive than the path that the Portuguese were breaking around Africa. He assumed, logically enough, that on the route to Japan lay other islands that might contain riches of their own and that could be used as staging points for the long journey.

Columbus' conclusions were based partly on conventional knowledge and partly on his own self-assurance. All were wholly erroneous. He misjudged the size of the globe by a quarter and the distance of the journey by 400 percent. And, of course, he knew nothing of the vast continents that lay in the middle of his route. His first proposal for support from the king of Portugal in 1484 was rejected on the basis of estimates vastly superior to his own. It was not ignorance that Columbus encountered, but practicality. The Portuguese had invested heavily in the African route and each new voyage was more promising than the last. Expeditions were expensive and it was hardly surprising that the king and his council decided against diluting their resources. Still the refusal was a disappointment. Years of study and planning now seemed wasted and another bitter blow awaited him. In the following year his wife Felipa died.

Her death severed his strongest tie to Portugal, and Columbus decided to go to Spain to seek support for his venture. But he had no concrete plan of action, no patrons to approach for aid, and little more than his dream to sustain him. Again accident intervened. Looking for a place to board his young son, he made the connection that led him first to an important Spanish shipowner and eventually to Queen Isabella. It took Columbus six agonizing years to persuade the queen and her advisors to sponsor his voyage and to grant him high honors should he succeed. By then, Bartolomeu Dias had rounded the Cape of Good Hope for Portugal and the fever of exploration had spread throughout Europe.

Columbus discovered the New World for three reasons: because he could build upon the Portuguese achievements in exploration, including his own practical experience on the sea; because the skills and equipment of ordinary seafarers had advanced so dramatically during the fifteenth century that long ocean voyages were technically possible; and because he willed it. Of these, the most important was the force of his own personality. That an obscure Genoese seaman could marry into one of the leading families of Lisbon, could raise himself into the elite of Portuguese master mariners, and could gain audience with the monarchs of Portugal and Spain all testify to his indomitable self-confidence. That he could spend the best years of his life single-mindedly pursuing a plan for a western voyage to the Indies testifies to his perseverance. That he could demand high honor and rich reward for his unproven services testifies to his ambition. A devout religious faith sustained his other qualities. All these elements of his personality would come into play as his ships sailed from the south of Spain in the summer of 1492.

There was nothing special about the expedition Columbus led. The ninety men who signed on for the voyage came mostly from local seafaring families and the ships were traditional ocean-faring vessels. Their square mainsails allowed them to run at great speed before the strong Atlantic winds. Logically, western exploration would set off from the Azores, the westernmost known islands in the Atlantic, but Columbus' experience in the African trade led him to believe that better winds prevailed to the south. Thus he used the Canary Islands to jump off into the Atlantic, a decision that led him to the Caribbean rather than to the northern Atlantic coast of North America.

For over a month the three ships sailed without sight of land. Favorable trade winds alternated with calm, flat sea. Each was equally alarming. The stiff breezes blew the ships at a rate of nearly a hundred miles a day, carrying them far beyond the point at which Columbus expected to find land. When the winds dropped, their pace was quartered and the sailors began to doubt whether they could go forward or back. Columbus carefully calculated the distances that the ships had traveled, but he was equally careful to misrepresent them to his sailors. By the end of September he was convinced that he had overshot Japan and was making directly for China. Early in October he had to quell the first serious dissension on board. The fresh water and provisions that had been taken on at the Canaries were running low for a return journey.

In the midst of so much uncertainty, there was also some reassurance. Vegetation was found floating on the ocean surface. On October 6 an enormous flock of migrating birds passed overhead, and Columbus wisely decided to follow the birds rather than the course on which he was set and which he had steadfastly refused to alter. Five days later the birds led him to land. The island of San Salvador—Holy Savior, as Columbus christened it—was a far cry from the images of China and Japan that had been conjured by Marco Polo. Instead of domed palaces, grave noblemen, and richly attired ladies of the court of the khan, they found grass huts and smiling, naked natives. Columbus could only conclude that he had struck a chain of islands off of the Chinese coast. With native guides, he began further exploration. Each new island whetted his appetite, for the natives were adorned with golden jewelry, which they happily bartered for the most insignificant European trinkets. After several weeks of island hopping, Columbus decided to return to Spain, bringing back with him native islanders, exotic plants and animals, and the belief that Japan and China were just off to the west.

Columbus made four journeys across the ocean. He continued to believe that the Caribbean islands that he explored were off the Chinese coast and for a time even contended that Cuba was part of the Asiatic mainland. While other explorers soon found the North and South American continents, Columbus continued to search for a western passage to India. Though his accomplishments were among the most significant in the history of the world, he died with his own dream unrealized.

was his ability to recruit allies. Nearly one hundred thousand natives from the tribes that the Aztecs had conquered supported the Spanish assault. Second was the superiority of European technology. Artillery and small arms were important, but it was Cortés' cavalry that was so terrifying to the Aztecs. They had never seen either horses or iron armaments. For a time the Aztecs believed that horse and armored rider were one beast. Finally, Cortés benefited from Aztec religion. It is impossible to know if Montezuma believed that Cortés was the ancient god Quetzalcoatl or what effect such a belief might have had on the conquest. What is easier to measure was the impact of the Aztec practice of taking battlefield captives to be used in religious sacrifices. This allowed many Spanish soldiers who would otherwise have been killed to be rescued and to fight again.

By 1522 Cortés was master of an area larger than all of Spain. But the cost in native lives was staggering. In thirty years a population of approximately 25 million had been reduced to less than 2 million. Most of the loss was due to exposure to European diseases like smallpox, typhoid, and measles, against which the natives were helpless. Their labor-intensive system of agriculture could not survive the rapid decrease in population, and famine followed pestilence.

This tragic sequence was repeated everywhere the Europeans appeared. In 1531 Francisco Pizarro (ca. 1475–1541) matched Cortés' feat when he conquered the Peruvian empire of the Incas. This conquest vastly extended the territory under Spanish control and became the true source of profit for the crown, when a huge silver mine was discovered in 1545 at Potosí in what is now southern Bolivia. The gold and silver that poured into Spain in the next quarter century helped support Spanish dynastic ambitions in Europe. The New World also provided Spain with an outlet for its surplus population. During the course of the sixteenth century over 200,000 Spaniards migrated across the ocean. Perhaps one in ten were women, who married and set up families in the New World. In succeeding generations these settlers created huge haciendas built on the forced labor of black African slaves, who proved better able to endure the rigors of mining and farming than did the natives.

The Legacy of the Discoverers

Gold, God, and glory neatly summarized the motives of the European explorers. Perhaps it is not necessary to delve any further. The gold of Africa and the silver of South America enriched the western nations. Christian missions arose wherever the European empires touched down: among Africans, Asians, and Amerindians. And glory there was in plenty. The feats of the great discoverers were recounted in story and song. *The Lusiads* (1572) by Luíz de Camões (ca. 1524–80), one of the greatest works of Portuguese literature, celebrated the new age. "They were men of no ordinary stature, equally at home in war and in dangers of every kind: they founded a new kingdom among distant peoples, and made it great." In the achievement of exploration and discovery the modern world had finally surpassed the ancients. "Let us hear no more then of Ulysses and Aeneas and their long journeyings, no more of Alexander and Trajan and their famous victories. My theme is the daring and renown of the Portuguese, to whom Neptune and Mars alike give homage."

The feats were worthy of celebration. In less than fifty years tenacious European seafarers found passages to the east and continents to the west. In doing so they overcame terrors both real and imagined. Hazardous journeys in uncharted waters took their toll in men and ships. The odds of surviving a voyage of discovery were no better than those of surviving an epidemic of plague. Nearly two-thirds of da Gama's crew perished on the passage to India. The forty men that Columbus left on Hispaniola, almost half his company, disappeared without trace. Only one of the five ships that set out with Magellan in 1519 returned to Spain. "If you want to learn how to pray, go to sea" was a Portuguese proverb that needed no explanation.

However harsh was reality, fantasy was more terrifying still. Out of sight of land for three months, da Gama's crew brooded over the folk wisdom of the sea: that the earth was flat and the ships would fall off its edge; that the green ocean was populated by giant monsters. As they approached the equator they feared that the water would become so hot it would boil them alive and the sun so powerful it would turn their

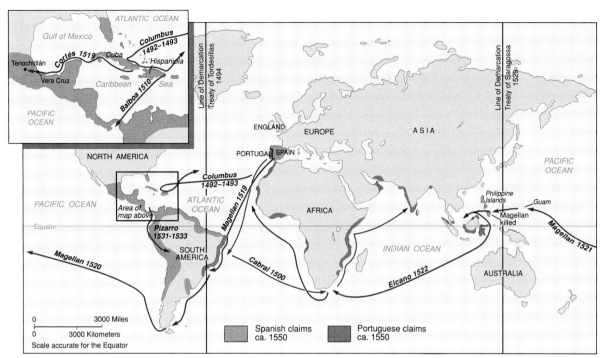

Voyages of Discovery and World Empires, 1550

skin black. Sailors to the New World expected to find all manner of horrible creations. Cyclopes and headless, one-legged torsos were popularized in drawings, while cannibals and giants were described in realistic detail by the earliest voyagers. No wonder mutiny was a constant companion of discovery.

Yet all of these inhibitions were overcome. So too were those over which the discoverers had more control. The expansion of Europe was a feat of technology and a feat of arms. Advances in navigational skills, especially in dead reckoning and later in calculating latitude from the position of the sun, were essential preconditions for covering the distances that were to be traveled. So were the more sophisticated ship designs. The magnetic compass and the astrolabe were indispensable tools. New methods for the making of maps and charts, and the popular interest in them, fueled both ambitions and abilities. It was a mapmaker who named the newly found continents after Amerigo Vespucci (1451–1512), the Italian explorer who voyaged to Brazil for the Portuguese. It may have been an accident that Columbus·

found the New World, but it was no coincidence that he was able to land in the same place three more times.

Nor was it happenstance that European forces conquered the peoples they encountered in both east and west. Generations of warfare against Muslims had honed the skills of Christian warriors. European ships were sturdily built and armed with cannon that could be used on land or at sea. Soldiers were well equipped and battle-tested. Generals were trained and experienced in the arts of siege. Both Albuquerque and Cortés practiced the tactics of divide and conquer, cleverly building alliances and taking advantage of local warfare. Spain and Portugal maintained empires thousands of miles from their homelands, empires greater than any Europe had ever known.

Riches and converts, power and glory, all came in the wake of discovery. But in the process of discovering new lands and new cultures, Europe also discovered itself. It learned something of its own aspirations. Early Portuguese voyagers went in quest of the mythical Prester

John, a saintly figure who was said to rule a heaven on earth in the middle of Africa. The first children born on Madeira were named Adam and Eve, though this slave plantation of sugar and wine was an unlikely Garden of Eden. The optimism of those who searched for the fountain of youth in the Florida swamps was not only that they would find it there, but that a long life was worth living.

Contact with the cultures of the New World also forced a different kind of thinking about life in the old one. The French essayist Michel de Montaigne (1533–92) was less interested in the perceptions of Native Americans than he was of his own countrymen when he recorded this encounter: "They have a way in their language of thinking of men as halves of one another. They noticed among us some men gorged to the full with things of every sort while their other halves were beggars at their doors. They found it strange that these poverty stricken halves should suffer such injustice." The supposed customs of strange lands also provided the setting for one of the great works of English social criticism, Sir Thomas More's *Utopia* (1516).

Europe also discovered and revealed a darker side of itself in the age of exploration. Accompanying the boundless optimism and assertive self-confidence that made so much possible was a tragic arrogance and callous disregard toward native races. Portuguese travelers described Africans as "dog-faced, dog-toothed people, satyrs, wild men, and cannibals." Such attitudes helped justify enslavement. It is not the brutality of the European conquests that should give us pause—each age sets its own standards in that regard—but the wastefulness. The Dominican priest Bartolomé de Las Casas (1474–1566) championed the cause of the native inhabitants at the court of the Spanish kings. His *Apologetic History of the Indies* (1550) highlighted the complexity of native society even as he witnessed its destruction. The German artist Albrecht Dürer (1471–1528) marveled at the "subtle ingenuity of the men in those distant lands," after viewing a display of Aztec art. But few Europeans were so enlightened.

Though they encountered heritages that were in some ways richer than their own, only the most farsighted westerners could see that there was

The Spanish attitude toward the Indians is demonstrated in this sixteenth-century drawing of a Spaniard kicking an Indian. Spanish colonial society was divided into classes on the basis of birthplace and race.

more value in their preservation than in their demolition. The Portuguese spice trade did not depend upon da Gama's indiscriminate bombardment of Calicut. The obliteration of millions of Aztecs and Incas was not a necessary result of the fever for gold and silver. The destruction was wanton. It revealed the rapaciousness, greed, and cruelty of the Portuguese and Spanish conquerors. These were the impulses of the Crusades rather than of the Renaissance. The Iberian *reconquista*, the holy war against the Muslims by which the peninsula was won back into Christian hands, was replayed throughout South America with tragic results. The consequences of black slavery and the destruction of native populations have as much to do with the shape of the modern world as the discoveries themselves.

Europe in 1500

Just as the map of the world was changing as a result of the voyages of discovery, so the map of Europe was changing as a result of the activities of princes. The early sixteenth century was the age of the prince, the first great stage of nation building that would last for the next three hundred years. The New Monarchies, as they are sometimes called, consolidated territories that were divided culturally, linguistically, and historically. The states of Europe are political units and they were forged by political means: by diplomacy, by marriage, and most commonly by war. The national system that we take for granted when thinking about Europe is a relatively recent development. Before we can observe its begin-

nings we must first have a picture of Europe as it existed in 1500. At that time it was composed of nearly five hundred distinct political units; today it is composed of only thirty.

Europe is a concept, like all concepts it is difficult to define. The vast plain that stretches from the Netherlands to the steppes of Russia presents few natural barriers to migration. Tribes had been wandering across this plain for thousands of years, slowly settling into the more fertile lands to practice their agriculture. Only in the south did geographical forces stem the flow of humanity. The Carpathian Mountains created a basin for the settlement of Slavic peoples that ran down to the Black Sea. The Alps provided a boundary for French, Germanic, and Italian settlements. The Pyrenees defined the Iberian peninsula with a mixture of African and European peoples.

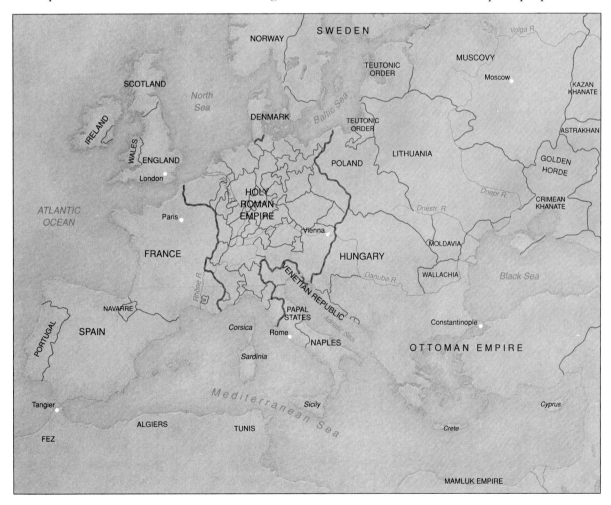

Eastern Boundaries

In the east, three great empires had created the political geography that could be said to define a European boundary: the Mongol, the Ottoman, and the Russian. During the early Middle Ages, Mongol warriors had swept across the Asian steppes and conquered most of central and southern Russia. By the sixteenth century the Mongol empire was disintegrating, its lands divided into a number of separate states called khanates. The khanate of the Crimea, with lands around the northern shores of the Black Sea, created the southeastern border of Europe.

The Ottoman territories defined the southern boundary. The ceaseless march of Ottoman conquests in the fourteenth and fifteenth centuries advanced across the southern shores of east Europe. By 1450 the Ottomans controlled all of Byzantium and Greece, dominating from the Black Sea to the Aegean. Fifty years later they had conquered nearly all the lands between the Aegean and the Adriatic seas. A perilous frontier was established on the Balkan peninsula. There the principalities of Moldavia, Wallachia, Transylvania, and Hungary held out against the Ottomans for another quarter century before being overrun.

The Russian state defined the eastern boundary of Europe. Russia too had been a great territorial unit of the Middle Ages, centered at Kiev in the west and stretching eastward into Asia. The advance of the Mongols in the thirteenth century had contracted the eastern part of Russia. Its western domains had disintegrated under the practice of dividing the ruling prince's inheritance among his sons. In 1500 Europe reached as far east as the principality of Muscovy. There the heritage of East and West mingled. In some periods of history Russia's ties with the West were most important; at other times Russia retreated into isolation from Europe.

The northern borders of eastern Europe centered on the Baltic Sea, one of the most important trading routes of the early modern era. On the northern coasts lay the Scandinavian nations of Sweden, Norway, and Denmark. These loosely confederated nations had a single king throughout the fifteenth century. Denmark, the southernmost of the three, was also the richest and most powerful. It enjoyed a favorable trading position on both the North and Baltic seas and social and economic integration with the Germanic states on its border. On the southern side of the Baltic lay the dominions of the Teutonic Knights, physically divided by the large state of Poland-Lithuania. The Teutonic territories, which encompassed the valuable Baltic region of Prussia, had been colonized by German crusaders in the thirteenth century. Since that time the territories had continued to expand, especially into Livonia in the east, where they came into conflict with the kingdom of Poland-Lithuania.

Poland-Lithuania comprised an enormous territory that covered the length of Europe from the Baltic to the Black Sea. The crowns of these two nations had been joined at the end of the fourteenth century and their dynastic history was tied up with the nations of Bohemia and Hungary to their west and south. While Bohemia was increasingly drawn into the affairs of central Europe, Hungary remained more eastern in orientation. This was partly because the Bohemians gave nominal allegiance to the Holy Roman Emperor and partly because the Ottoman conquests had engulfed a large part of the Hungarian territories. At the end of the fifteenth century Poland, Lithuania, Bohemia, and Hungary were all ruled by the same family, the Jagiellons.

Mongols and Ottomans to the south, Russians in the east, Scandinavia in the north, Poland-Lithuania in the center, and Hungary in the west:

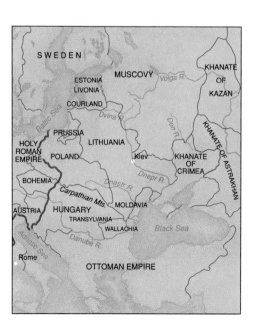

such were the contours of the eastern portion of Europe. Its lands were, on the whole, less fertile than those farther west, and its climate was more severe. It was a sparsely populated region. Its wealth lay in the Baltic fisheries, especially the herring schools off the Danish coasts, in the Hungarian and Bohemian silver mines, and in the enormous Russian forests where wood and its byproducts were plentiful. Except in the southern portions of Poland and central Bohemia, the region was agriculturally poor. Most Europeans who lived in the eastern part of the continent eked out a livelihood from a grudging and forbidding landscape. Their territories had been resettled during the population crisis of the early fourteenth century. Then native Slavs were joined by German colonizers from the west and Asian conquerors from the east. This clash of races did much to define the political history of eastern Europe.

Central Europe

The middle of the continent was defined by the Holy Roman Empire and occupied almost entirely by Germanic peoples. In length the empire covered the territory from the North and Baltic seas to the Adriatic and the Mediterranean, where the Italian city-states were located. In width it stretched from Bohemia to Burgundy. Politically, central Europe comprised a bewildering array of principalities, Church lands, and free towns. By the end of the fifteenth century, the Holy Roman Empire was an empire in name only. The large states of Brandenburg, Bohemia, and Bavaria resembled the political units of the east. In the south, the Alps provided an effective physical boundary, which allowed the Archduchy of Austria and the Swiss Confederation to follow their own separate paths. Stretching across the center of the empire, from the Elbe River to the North Sea, were a jumble of petty states. Great cities like Nuremberg and Ulm in the south, Bremen and Hamburg in the north, and Frankfurt and Cologne in the west were free municipalities. Large sections of the northwestern part of the empire were governed by the Church through resident bishops. Further to the west were the prosperous Low Countries, Holland and its port of Amsterdam, Brabant and its port of

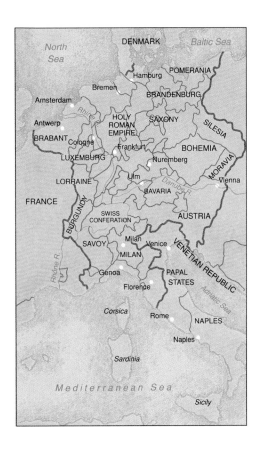

Antwerp. The Low Countries were among the wealthiest and most densely populated areas of Europe. In the southwest, the empire extended in some places as far as the Rhône River and included the rich estates of Luxembourg, Lorraine, and Burgundy.

The riches of the empire made it the focal point of Europe. Nearly 15 million people lived within its borders. Its agriculture varied from the olive- and wine-producing areas in the southwest to the great granaries in its center. Rich mineral deposits and large reserves of timber made the German lands industrially advanced. The European iron industry was centered here and the empire was the arms manufacturer for the western world. The empire was also a great commercial center, heir to the Hanseatic League of the Middle Ages. Its northern and western ports teemed with trade, and its merchants were replacing the Italians as the leading international bankers.

Like the empire, the Italian peninsula was divided into a diverse collection of small city-states. During the course of the fifteenth century five of these had emerged as most powerful (see chapter 11). In the north, the Duchy of Milan was an imperial territory despite its close ties to its southern neighbors. Florence in the northwest and Venice in the northeast were republics with elaborate constitutional arrangements to preserve the power of their ruling mercantile families. Both were among the richest and most powerful cities in Europe, home of the greatest artistic and literary talents of the age and center for the world's banking and commerce. In the south was Rome, spiritual center of Catholicism and residence of the pope. Though Roman and papal government were separate jurisdictions, in fact their fates were bound together. Roman citizens benefited from the presence of the Church bureaucracy in their city and from the thousands of faithful pilgrims who visited each year. Papal lands stretched far to the north of Rome, and wars to defend or expand them were Roman as well as papal ventures. The kingdom of Naples occupied the southernmost part of Italy and included the agriculturally rich island of Sicily. Naples was the breadbasket of the Mediterranean and a kingdom that was vigorously contested for throughout the fifteenth and early sixteenth centuries.

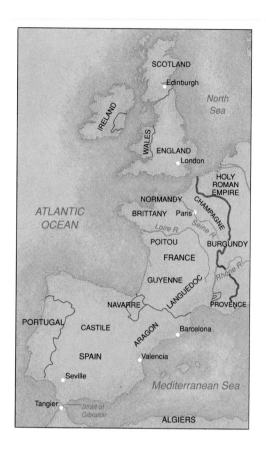

The West

The Iberian peninsula, the French territories, and the British Isles formed the westernmost borders of Europe. The Iberian peninsula is situated on the southwestern corner of the continent. Separated from France in the north by the Pyrenees, it is surrounded by the Atlantic Ocean and the Mediterranean Sea on the west and east. But neither its protective mountain barrier nor its ample coastlines was its most significant geographical feature during its formative period. Rather it was the fact that Iberia is separated from North Africa only by the easily navigable Strait of Gibraltar. During the Middle Ages the peninsula was overrun by North African Muslims, whom the Spanish called Moors. From the eighth to the fifteenth centuries, Iberian history was dominated by the *reconquista*, the recapture and re-Christianization of the conquered territories. This reconquest was finally completed in 1492, when the Moors were pushed out of Granada and the Jews were expelled from Spain. At

the end of the fifteenth century, the Iberian peninsula contained several separate kingdoms. The most important were Portugal on the western coast—the only Continental nation to have the same borders in 1500 as it does today—Aragon, with its Mediterranean ports of Barcelona and Valencia, and Castile, the largest of the Iberian states. The marriage of King Ferdinand of Aragon and Queen Isabella of Castile in 1469 had joined the crowns of Aragon and Castile, but the two kingdoms remained separate.

The remnants of ancient Gaul were also favored by a maritime location. Like Iberia, French coasts let out onto the Mediterranean and the Atlantic. To the northwest, France was less than thirty miles from Britain across the English Channel. Its eastern boundaries touched the empire, its southern mountain border touched Spain. Toward the end of the fifteenth century, France was still divided into many smaller fiefs. The royal domain centered on Paris and extended to Champagne in the east and Normandy in the west. South of this area, however, from Orleans to Brittany, were principalities that had long been contested between England and France. Nor was the rich central plain yet integrated into the royal domain. Agriculturally, French lands were the richest in Europe. "This Kingdom is, thanks to God, so opulent and fertile in all human necessities that it can do without all the other Kingdoms, but our neighbors cannot do without us," proclaimed a chauvinistic Frenchman at the beginning of the sixteenth century. France enjoyed both Mediterranean and Atlantic climates, which suited the growing of the widest variety of foodstuffs. Its population of approximately 13 million was second only to that of the empire.

Across the Channel lay Britain (comprising England, Scotland, and Wales) and Ireland. Britain had been settled by an array of European colonizers—Romans, Danes, Angles, and Saxons—before being conquered in the eleventh century by the French Normans. From that time, it was protected by the rough waters of the English Channel and the North Sea and allowed to develop a distinct cultural and political heritage. The southern and central portions of England were the most suitable for agricultural and commercial development, while the wet climate and rolling terrain of western England provided ideal conditions for the development of a woolen industry. Wales to the west and Scotland to the north were still separate nations at the beginning of the sixteenth century. Both were mountainous lands with harsh climates and few natural advantages. They were sparsely populated. Ireland, though farther west than Wales and farther north than most of England, was better insulated from the rough weather. Though it too was sparsely populated, it contained several rich agricultural areas especially suited for dairying and grazing.

In 1500 Europe exhibited a remarkable diversity of political and geographical forms. Huge states in the east, tiny principalities in the center, emerging nations in the west, seemingly had little in common. There was as yet no state system and no clear group of dominant powers. The western migration of the Germanic peoples appeared to be over, but their consolidation was as yet unimagined. The Iberians struggled to expel the Moors, the Hungarians to hold back the Ottomans. Everywhere one looked there was fragmentation and disarray. Yet in less than half a century the largest empire yet known in the west would be formed. States would come to be con-

solidated and dynasties established all over the continent. And with the rise of the state would come the dream of dominion, an empire over all of Europe. In the early sixteenth century the struggle for European mastery had entered a new phase.

The Formation of States

It was Machiavelli who identified the prince as the agent of change in the process of state formation. He believed that the successful prince could bring unity to his lands, security to his borders, and prosperity to his subjects. The unsuccessful prince brought nothing but ruin. It did, of course, serve Machiavelli's purposes to stress the overriding importance of the ruler. He was writing to a prince in hope of employment, and he was writing about the destructive warfare that had engulfed Italy and threatened the independence of the Italian city-states. He could be forgiven his enthusiasm for the power of princes.

A process as long and as complex as the formation of nations is not subject to the will of individuals. Factors as diverse as geography, population, and natural resources are all decisive. So too are the structures through which human activity is channeled. The ways in which families are organized and wealth is transmitted from generation to generation can result in large estates with similar customs or small estates with varying ones. The manner in which social groups are formed and controlled can mean that power is centralized or dispersed. The beliefs of ordinary people and the way they practice them can define who is a part of a community and who is apart from it. All these elements and many others have much to do with the way in which European states began to take shape at the end of the fifteenth century. Despite these complexities, we should not lose sight of the simple truth of Machiavelli's observations. In the first stages of the consolidation of European nations the role of the prince was crucial.

Indeed, in the middle of the fifteenth century there were many factors working against the formation of large states in Europe. The most obvious involved simple things like transportation and communication. The distance that could

A delegation of Russian boyars bearing gifts visited the Holy Roman Emperor Maximilian II in 1576 to seek his aid against Poland-Lithuania.

be covered quickly was very small. In wet and cold seasons travel was nearly impossible. The emperor Charles V sat in Burgundy for two months awaiting a favorable wind to take him to his newly inherited kingdom of Spain. Similarly, directives from the center to the localities were slow to arrive and slower still to be adopted. Large areas were difficult to control and to defend. Communication was not only subject to the hazards of travel. Distinct languages or dialects were one of the principal features of small states. Only the most educated could use Latin as a common written language. Separate languages contributed to separate cultures. Customary practices, common ancestry, and shared experiences helped define a sense of community through which small states defined themselves.

To these natural forces that acted to maintain the existence of small units of government were added invented ones. To succeed, a prince had to establish supremacy over a number of rivals. For the most part, states were inherited. In some places it was customary to follow the rule of primogeniture, inheritance by the eldest son. In others, estates were split among sons, or among children of both sexes. Some traditions, like the French, excluded inheritance through women; others, like the Castilian, treated women's claims as equal to men's. Short lives meant prolonged disputes about inheritance. Rulers had to defend their thrones from any number of rivals with strong claims to legitimacy.

So, too, did rulers have to defend themselves from the ambitions of their mightiest subjects. Dukes could dream only one dream. The constant warfare of the European nobility was one of the central features of the later Middle Ages. "Uneasy lies the head that wears a crown" was a fact of life in the fifteenth century. To avoid resort to arms, princes and peers entered into all manner of alliances, using their children as pawns and the marriage bed as the chessboard. Rulers also faced independent institutions within their states, powerful organizations that had to be won over or crushed. The long process of taming the Church was well advanced by the end of the fifteenth century and about to enter a new stage. Fortified towns presented a different problem. They possessed both the manpower and wealth necessary to raise and maintain armies. They also jealously guarded their privileges. Rulers who could not tax their towns could not rule their state. Finally, most kingdoms had assemblies that represented the propertied classes, especially in matters of taxation. Some, like the English Parliament and the Spanish Cortes, were strong; others, like the Imperial Diet and the French Estates-General, were weak. But everywhere they posed an obstacle to the extension of the power of princes.

In combination, these factors slowed and shaped the process of state formation. But neither separately nor together were they powerful enough to overcome it. The fragmentation of Europe into so many small units of government made some consolidation inevitable. There were always stronger and weaker neighbors, always broken successions and failed lines. The practice of dynastic marriage meant that smaller states were continually being inherited by the rulers of larger ones. If the larger state was stable, it absorbed the smaller one. If not, the smaller state would split off again to await its next predator or protector. As the first large states took shape, the position of smaller neighbors grew ever more precarious.

This was especially true by the end of the fifteenth century because of the increase in the destructive power of warfare. Technological advances in cannonry and in the skills of gunners and engineers made medieval fortifications untenable. The fall of Constantinople was as much a military watershed as it was a political one. Gunpowder decisively changed battlefield tactics. It made heavy armor obsolete. This lowered the cost of equipping skilled fighters, but more importantly, it allowed for the development of a different type of warfare. Lightly armored horses and riders could not only inflict more damage upon one another, but they were now mobile enough to be used against infantry. Infantry armed with long pikes or small muskets became the crucial components of armies that were growing ever larger. Systems of supply were better, sources of small arms were more available, and the rewards of conquest were more tangible. What could not be inherited, or married, could be conquered.

Eastern Configurations

The interplay of factors that encouraged and inhibited the formation of states is most easily observed in the eastern parts of Europe. There the different paths taken by Muscovy and Poland-Lithuania stand in contrast. At the beginning of the sixteenth century, the principality of Muscovy was the largest European political unit. Muscovy had established itself as the heir to the ancient state of Russia through conquest, shrewd political alliances, and the good fortune of its princes to be blessed with long reigns. Muscovy's growth was phenomenal. Under Ivan III, "the Great" (1462–1505), Muscovy expanded to the north and west. During a long series of wars it annexed Novgorod and large parts of Livonia and Lithuania. Its military successes were almost unbroken, but so too were its diplomatic triumphs. Ivan the Great preferred pacification to conquest, though when necessary he could conquer with great brutality. Between 1460 and 1530, Muscovy increased its landed territory by 1.5 million square miles.

A number of factors led to the rise of Muscovy. External threats had diminished. The deterioration of the Mongol empire that had dominated south central Russia allowed Ivan to escape the yoke of Mongol rule that the Russian princes had worn for centuries. Not only did he refuse to pay tribute money, but in 1480 his armies repelled the Mongols when they attempted to collect it by force. Secondly, the fall of Constantinople made Muscovy the heir to eastern Christendom, successor to the Roman and Byzantine empires. Ivan's

marriage to Sophia, niece of the last emperor of Byzantium, cemented this connection. Sophia brought both Italian craftsmen and Byzantine customs to the Russian court, helping Ivan open his contacts with the wider world. Though it would be some time before the princes of Muscovy would transform themselves into the tsars of Russia, the heritage of Byzantium held great political value among the eastern nobility that preferred Orthodox Christianity to Roman Catholicism.

Territorial conquests and the decline of Byzantium were not the only important features of the consolidation of the Muscovite state. Ivan the Great was fortunate in having no competitors for his throne. He was able to use other social groups to help administer the new Muscovite territories without fear of setting up a rival to power. Ivan extended the privileges of his nobility and organized a military class who received land as a reward for their fidelity. He also developed a new theory of sovereignty that rested on divine rather than temporal power. Traditionally, Russian princes ruled their lands by patrimony. They owned both estates and occupants. Ivan the Great extended this principle to cover all lands to which there was an ancient Russian claim and combined it with the religious authority of the Orthodox church. Both he and his successors ruled with the aid of able Church leaders who were normally part of the prince's council.

Ivan the Great's achievements were both military and political. In the history of the struggles among the Russian princes there had been many occasions when one house or another had gained an upper hand. What made the expansion of Muscovy so impressive is that land once gained was never lost. The achievements of Ivan the Great were furthered by his son Vasili and his more famous grandson Ivan IV, "the Terrible" (1533–84). Ivan IV continued the quest to reconstitute the old Russian state. He defeated the Mongols on his southeastern border and incorporated the entire Volga basin into Muscovy. Ivan resettled noble families there to ensure that it would remain securely under Muscovite dominion. But his greatest ambition was to gain a port on the Baltic Sea and establish a northern outlet for commerce. His objective was to conquer Livonia. Nearly three decades of warfare between Muscovy and Poland-Lithuania, with whom Livonia had allied itself, resulted in large territorial gains, but Muscovy always fell short of the real prize. And Ivan's northern campaigns seriously weakened the defense of the south. In 1571 the Crimean Tartars advanced from their territories on Muscovy's southwestern border and inflicted a powerful psychological blow when they burned the city of Moscow. Although the Tartars were eventually driven off Muscovite soil, expansion in both north and south was at an end for the next seventy-five years.

By the reign of Ivan IV, Muscovite society was divided roughly into three groups: the hereditary nobility known as the boyars, the military service class, and the peasantry who were bound to the land. There was no large mercantile presence in Muscovy and its urban component remained small. The boyars, who were powerful landlords of great estates, owed little to the tsar. They inherited their lands and did not necessarily benefit from expansion and conquest. Members of the military service class, on the other hand, were bound to the success of the crown. Their military service was a requirement for the possession of their estates, which were granted out of lands gained through territorial expansion. Gradually the new military service class grew in power and prestige, largely at the expense of the older boyars. Ivan IV used members of the military service class as legislative advisors and elevated them in his parliamentary council (the Zemsky Sobor), which also contained representatives of the nobility, clergy, and towns.

Unlike his grandfather, Ivan IV had an abiding mistrust of the boyars. They had held power when he was a child and it was rumored that his mother had been poisoned by them. It was in his treatment of the boyars that he earned the nickname "the Terrible." During his brutal suppression of supposed conspiracies, several thousand families were massacred by Ivan's own orders and thousands more by the violent excesses of his agents. Ivan constantly imagined plots against himself and many of the men who served him met horrible deaths. He also forcibly relocated boyar families, stripping them of their lands in one place but granting them new lands elsewhere. This practice made their situation similar to that of the military service class, who owed their fortunes to the tsar. Indeed, for the first time the boyars were required to perform military service to the tsar.

All of these measures contributed to the breakdown of local networks of influence and power and to a disruption of local governance. But they also made possible a system of central administration, one of Ivan IV's most important achievements. He created departments of state to deal with the various tasks of administration, and this resulted in more efficient management of revenues and of the military. Ivan IV promoted the interests of the military service class over those of the boyars but he did not destroy the nobility. New boyars were created, especially in conquered territories, and these new families owed their positions and loyalty to the prince. Both boyars and the military benefited from Ivan's policy of binding the great mass of people to the land. Russian peasants had few political or economic rights in comparison to western peasants, but during the early sixteenth century even the meager rights Russian peasants had were curtailed. The right of peasants to move from the estate of one lord to that of another was suspended, all but binding the peasantry to the land. This serfdom made possible the prolonged absence of military leaders from their estates and contributed to the creation of the military service class. But it also made imperative the costly system of coercing agricultural and industrial labor. In the long term, serfdom retarded the development of the Muscovite economy by removing incentive from large landholders to make investments in commerce or to improve agricultural production.

The growth of an enlarged and centralized Muscovy stands in contrast to the experiences of Poland-Lithuania during the same period. At the end of the fifteenth century Casimir IV (1447–92) ruled the kingdom of Poland and the grand duchy of Lithuania. His son Vladislav II ruled Bohemia (1471–1516) and Hungary (1490–1516). Had the four states been permanently consolidated they could have become an effective barrier to Ottoman expansion in the south and Russian expansion in the east. But the union of crowns had never been the union of states. The union of crowns had taken place over the previous century by political alliances, diplomatic marriages, and the consent of the nobility. Such arrangements kept peace among the four neighbors, but it kept any one of them from becoming a dominant partner.

While the Polish-Lithuanian monarchs enjoyed longevity similar to that of the Muscovites, those who ruled Hungary and Bohemia were not so fortunate. By the sixteenth century a number of claimants to both crowns existed and the competition was handled by diplomacy rather than war. The accession of Vladislav II, for example, was accompanied by large concessions first to the Bohemian towns and later to the Hungarian nobility. The formal union of the Polish and Lithuanian crowns in 1569 also involved the decentralization of power and the strengthening of the rights of the nobility in both countries. In the end, the states split apart. The Russians took much of Lithuania, the Ottomans much of Hungary. Bohemia, which in the fifteenth century had been ruled more by its nobles than its king, was absorbed into the Habsburg territories after 1526.

There were many reasons why a unified state did not appear in east central Europe. In the first place, external forces disrupted territorial and political arrangements. Wars with the Ottomans and the Russians absorbed resources. Second, the princes faced rivals to their crowns. Though Casimir IV was able to place his son on the thrones of both Bohemia and Hungary, he managed to do so against the powerful claims of the Habsburg princes, who continued to intrigue against the Jagiellons. These contests for power necessitated concessions to leading citizens, which decreased the ability of the princes to centralize their kingdoms or to effect real unification among them. The nobility of Hungary, Bohemia, and Poland-Lithuania all developed strong local interests that increased over time. In Bohemia, Vladislav II was king in name only, and even in Poland the nobility won confirmation of its rights and privileges from the monarchy. War, rivalries for power, and a strong nobility prevented any one prince from dominating this area as the princes of Muscovy dominated theirs.

The Western Powers

Just as in the east, there was no single pattern to the consolidation of the large western European states. They, too, were internally fragmented and externally imperiled. While England had to overcome the ruin of decades of civil war, France and Spain faced the challenges of invasion and occupation. Western European princes struggled against powerful institutions and individuals within their states. Some they conquered, others they absorbed. Each nation formed its state differently: England by administrative centralization, France by good fortune, and Spain by dynastic marriage. Yet in 1450 few imagined that any one of these states would succeed.

The Taming of England. Alone among European states, England suffered no threat of foreign invasion during the fifteenth century. This island fortress might easily have become the first consolidated European state were it not for the ambitions of the nobility and the weakness of the crown. For thirty years the English aristocracy fought over the spoils of a helpless monarch. The Wars of the Roses (1455–85), as they came to be called, were as much a free-for-all among the English peerage as they were a contest for the throne between the houses of Lancaster and York. At their center was an attempt by the dukes of York to wrest the crown from the mad and ineffective Lancastrian king Henry VI (1422–61). All around the edges was the continuation of local and family feuds that had little connection to the dynastic struggle.

Three decades of intermittent warfare had predictable results. The houses of Lancaster and York were both destroyed. Edward IV (1461–83) succeeded in gaining the crown for the House of York, but he was never able to wear it securely. When he died, his children, including his heir, Edward V (1483), were placed in the protection of their uncle Richard III (1483–85). It was protection that they did not survive. The two boys disappeared, reputedly murdered in the Tower of London, and Richard declared himself king. Richard's usurpation led to civil war, and he was killed by the forces of Henry Tudor at the battle of Bosworth Field in 1485. By the end of the Wars of the Roses the monarchy had lost both revenue and prestige, and the aristocracy had stored up bitter memories for the future.

It was left to Henry Tudor to pick up the pieces of the kingdom as legend has it he picked up the crown off a bramble bush. The two chief obstacles to his determination to consolidate the English state were the power of the nobility and the poverty of the monarchy. No English monarch had held secure title to the throne for over a century. Henry Tudor, as Henry VII (1485–1509), put an end to this dynastic instability at once. He married Elizabeth of York, in whose heirs would rest the legitimate claim to the throne. Their children were indisputable successors to the crown. He also began the long process of taming his overmighty subjects. Traitors were hung and turncoats rewarded. Henry's strategy befit his power. He was not strong enough to rule without the aid of many peers who had proven themselves disloyal to their monarch, but he was not so weak that he could not choose his companions. He and his son Henry VIII (1509–47) adroitly created a new peerage, which soon was as numerous as the old feudal aristocracy. These new nobles owed their titles and loyalty to the Tudors. They were favored with offices and spoils and were relied upon to suppress both popular and aristocratic rebellions. Henry VIII was even more ruthless than his father. He preferred the chopping block to the peace treaty. In 1450 there were nine English dukes; by 1525 there were only two. With both carrot and stick the Tudors tamed the peerage.

The financial problems of the English monarchy were not so easily overcome. In theory and practice an English king was supposed to live "of his own," that is off the revenues from his own estates. This was practical only when royal lands were large and rental income was high, a situation that had not existed for well over a century. The other important source of money for the crown was the duties imposed on the export of wool, the main commodity produced in England. Together, rentals from land and customs from wool made up over 80 percent of the king's revenues. In normal circumstances, royal revenue did not come from the king's subjects. The English landed classes had established the principle that only on extraordinary occasions were they to be required to contribute to the maintenance of government. This principle was defended through their representative institution, the Parliament. When the kings of England wanted to tax their subjects, they had first to gain the assent of Parliament. Though Parliaments did grant requests for extraordinary revenue, especially for national defense, they did so grudgingly. The English landed elites were not exempt from taxation, but they were able to control the amount of taxes they paid. Not surprisingly, they were among the least taxed landholders in Europe.

The inability of the crown to extract its living from its subjects made it more dependent upon the efficient management of its own estates. Thus English state building depended upon the growth of centralized institutions that could oversee royal lands and collect royal customs. Gradually, medieval institutions like the Exchequer were supplanted by newer organs that were better able to adjust to modern methods of accounting, record keeping, and enforcement. English landowners and tenants had basked in the glow of the lax royal administration that was practiced during the Wars of the Roses. The reign of Henry VII was like a splash of cold water. Henry sent ministers to view and value royal lands. He ordered the cataloging and collection of feudal obligations. Ship cargoes were inspected thoroughly and every last penny of customs charged. Whether Henry's reputation for greed and rapacity was warranted, it was undeniable that he squeezed as much as could be taken from a not very juicy inheritance. His financial problems limited both domestic and foreign policy.

It was not until the middle of the next reign that the English monarchy was again solvent. As a result of his dispute with the papacy, Henry VIII confiscated the enormous wealth of the Catholic church, and with one stroke solved the crown's monetary problems (see chapter 13). But the real contribution that Henry and his chief minister, Thomas Cromwell (ca. 1485–1540), made to forming an English state was the way in which this windfall was administered. Cromwell accelerated the process of centralizing government that had begun under Edward IV. He divided administration according to its functions by creating separate departments of state, modeled upon courts. These new departments were responsible for record keeping, revenue collection, and law enforcement. Each had a distinct jurisdiction and a permanent, trained staff. Cromwell coordinated the work of these distinct departments by expanding of the power of the Privy Council, which included the heads of these administrative bodies. Through a long evolution, the Privy Council came to serve as the king's executive. Cromwell also saw the importance of Parliament as a legislative body. Through Parliament, royal policy could be turned into statutes that had the assent of the political nation. If Parliament was well managed, issues that were potentially controver-

Holbein's last portrait of Henry VIII, 1542. Henry made England into one of the world's greatest naval powers but embroiled the kingdom in a series of costly foreign wars. He married six times in an effort to produce a legitimate male heir.

sial could be defused. Laws passed by Parliament were more easily enforced locally than were proclamations issued by the king. By the end of Henry VIII's reign the English monarchy was strong enough to withstand the succession of a child king, precisely the circumstance that had plunged the nation into civil war a century earlier.

The Unification of France. Perhaps the most remarkable thing about the unification of France is that it took place at all. The forces working against the consolidation of a French state were formidable. France was surrounded by aggressive and powerful neighbors with whom it was frequently at war. Its greatest nobles were semi-independent princes who were constant rivals for the throne. They ruled vast territories through their own local institutions. They were also consistent opponents of the extension of royal power.

French people were primarily loyal to their province. Great and small viewed the pretensions of the monarchy with deep suspicion. Provincialism was not simply a negative; it was a fierce pride and loyalty toward local customs and institutions that had deep roots within communities. And France was splintered by profound regional differences. The north and south were divided by culture and by language (the *langue d'oc* in the south and the *langue d'oïl* in the north). As late as the fifteenth century, a French king needed a translator to communicate with officials from his southern lands.

The first obstacles that were overcome were the external threats to French security. For over a century the throne of France had been contested by the kings of England. The so-called Hundred Years' War, which was fought intermittently between 1337 and 1453, originated in a dispute over the inheritance of the French crown and English possessions in Gascony in southern France (see chapter 10). The war was fought on French soil, and by the early fifteenth century English conquests in north central France extended from Normandy to the borders of the Holy Roman Empire. Two of the largest French cities, Paris and Bordeaux, were in English hands.

The problems posed by the Hundred Years' War were not just in victory and defeat. The struggle between the kings of England and the kings of France allowed French princes and dukes, who were nominally vassals of the king, to enhance their autonomy by making their own alliances with the highest bidder. And the kings of France had little with which to bid. The French victory was miraculous, resulting from the combination of an ineffectual English king, Henry VI, and a visionary French maiden, Joan of Arc. But when the English were finally driven out of France in the middle of the fifteenth century, the kings of France came into a weakened and divided inheritance.

Nor was England the only threat to the security of the French monarchy. On France's eastern border, in a long arching semicircle, were the estates of the dukes of Burgundy. The dukes of Burgundy and the kings of France shared a common ancestry; both were of the House of Valois. Still, the sons of brothers in one generation were only cousins in the next, and the two branches of the family grew apart. The original Burgundian inheritance was in the southeast, centered at

Dijon. A good marriage and good fortune brought to the first duke the rich northern province of Flanders. For the next hundred years the aim of the dukes of Burgundy was to unite their divided estates. While England and France were locked in deadly embrace, Burgundy systematically grew. It absorbed territory from both the Holy Roman Empire and France. To little pieces gained through marriages were added little pieces taken through force. As the second half of the fifteenth century began, the court of the duke of Burgundy was the glittering jewel of Europe, the heir of the Italian Renaissance. Wealthy and powerful, it stood poised to achieve what had once only been dreamed: the unification of the Burgundian lands. The conquest of Lorraine finally connected the ducal estates in one long unbroken string.

But it was a string stretched taut. The power of Burgundy threatened its neighbors in all directions. Both France and the empire were too weak to resist its expansion, but the confederation of Swiss towns to the southwest of Burgundy was not. Fearing a Burgundian advance against them, a number of independent Swiss towns pooled their resources to raise a large army. In a series of stunning military victories Swiss forces repelled the Burgundians from their lands and demolished their armies. Charles the Bold, the last Valois duke of Burgundy, fell at the Battle of Nancy in 1477. Like his body, his estates were quickly dismembered. The Swiss had fought a defensive war and had no desire for territorial expansion, but the French were not so high-minded. France recovered its ancestral territories, including Burgundy itself, and through no effort of its own was now secure on its eastern border.

Peace brought many blessings to the kings of France. Not only were they secure in their own patrimony, they now held the upper hand in dealing with their nobility. And that hand frequently held a sword. The king most associated with the consolidation of France was Louis XI (1461–83). He inherited an estate exhausted by warfare and civil strife. More by chance than by plan he vastly extended the territories under the dominion of the French crown and, more importantly, subdued the nobility. Louis XI was as cunning as he was peculiar. In an age in which royalty was expressed through magnificence, Louis sported an old felt hat and a well-worn coat. His enemies constantly underestimated his abilities, which

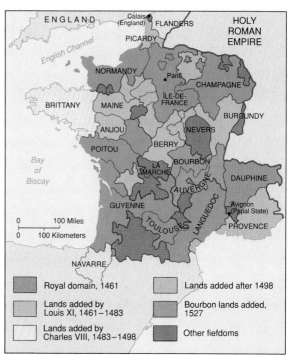

Unification of France

earned him the nickname "the Spider." Early in his reign Louis met the threat of a full-scale aristocratic rebellion with a crafty series of concessions that ensured that those who had rebelled against him would fall out among themselves.

The middle of the fifteenth century was one of the lowest points for the fortunes of the French monarchy in its ageless struggle with the princes and dukes who were its vassals. But gradually during the course of his reign, Louis XI won back what he had been forced to give away. Years of fighting both the English and each other left the ranks of the French aristocracy depleted. As blood spilled on the battlefields, the stocks of fathers and sons ran low. Estates to which no male heirs existed fell forfeit to the king. In this manner the crown absorbed Anjou and Maine in the northwest and Provence in the south. More importantly, Louis XI ultimately obtained control of the two greatest independent fiefs, Brittany and Orléans. He managed this feat by arranging the marriage of his son Charles to the heiress of Brittany and of his daughter Jeanne to the heir of Orléans. When in 1527 the lands of the duke of Bourbon fell to the crown, the French monarch ruled a unified state.

The consolidation of France was not simply the result of the incorporation of diverse pieces of territory into the domain of the king. More than in any other state the experience in France demonstrated how a state could be formed without the designs of a great leader. Neither Louis XI nor his son Charles VIII (1483–98) were nation builders. Louis' main objective was always to preserve his estate. He was as likely to outsmart himself as his enemies, and he frequently blundered either into conceding too much or demanding too much. His good fortune saved him from the consequences of many ill-conceived policies. But no amount of luck could make up for Louis' failure to obtain the Burgundian Low Countries for France after the death of Charles the Bold in 1477. The marriage of Mary of Burgundy to Maximilian of Habsburg was one of the great turning points in European history. It initiated the struggle for control of the Low Countries that endured for over two centuries.

These long years of war established the principle of royal taxation, which was so essential to the process of state building in France. This enabled the monarchy to raise money for defense and for consolidation. Because of the strength of the nobles, most taxation fell only on the commoners, the so-called third estate. The nobility and the clergy were exempted from much taxation. The *taille* was a direct tax on property from which the nobility and clergy were exempt. The *gabelle* was a consumption tax on the purchase of salt in most parts of the kingdom, and the *aide* was a tax on a variety of commodities including meat and wine. These consumption taxes were paid by all members of the third estate no matter how poor they might be. Though there was much complaint about taxation, it remains one of the distinctive features of the French monarchy that it established a broad base for taxation and a high degree of compliance long before any other European nation.

Along with money went soldiers, fighting men necessary to repel the English and to defend the crown against rebels and traitors. Again the French monarchy was the first to establish the principle of a national army, raised and directed from the center but quartered and equipped regionally. From the nobility were recruited the cavalry, from the towns and countryside the massive infantry. Fortified towns received privileges in return for military service to the king. Originally towns were required to provide artillery, but constant troubles with the nobility had led the kings of France to establish their own store of heavy guns. The towns supplied small arms, pikes, and swords and later pistols and muskets. By the beginning of the sixteenth century the French monarch could raise and equip an army of his own.

Taxation and military obligation demanded the creation and expansion of centralized institutions of government. This was the most difficult development in the period of state formation in France. The powers of royal agents were constantly challenged by the powers of regional nobles. It is easy to exaggerate the extent of the growth of central control and to underestimate the enduring hold of regional and provincial loyalties. Even the crown's absorption of estates did not always end local privileges and customs. France was not a nation and was hardly a state by the opening of the sixteenth century. But despite continued regional autonomy, a beginning had been made. Chance, good fortune, and military necessity all played their part in centralizing French government.

The Marriages of Spain. Before the sixteenth century there was little prospect of a single nation emerging on the Iberian peninsula. North African Muslims called Moors occupied the province of Granada in the south while the stable kingdom of Portugal dominated the western coast. The Spanish peoples were divided among a number of separate states. The two most important were Castile, the largest and wealthiest kingdom, and Aragon, which was composed of a number of quasi-independent regions, each of which maintained its own laws and institutions. Three religions and four languages (not including dialects) widened these political divisions. And the different states had different outlooks. Castile was, above all, determined to rid itself of the Moors in Granada and to convert to Christianity its large Jewish population. Aragon played in the high-stakes game for power in the Mediterranean. It claimed sovereignty over Sicily and Naples and exercised it whenever it could.

A happy teenage marriage brought together the unhappy kingdoms of Castile and Aragon. When Ferdinand of Aragon and Isabella of Castile secretly exchanged wedding vows in 1469, both their homelands were rent by civil war. In Castile, Isabella's brother Henry IV (1454–74) struggled unsuccessfully against the powerful Castilian nobility. In Aragon, Ferdinand's father, John II (1458–79), faced a revolt by the rich province of Catalonia on one side and the territorial ambitions of Louis XI of France on the other. Joining the heirs together increased the resources of both kingdoms. Ferdinand took an active role in the pacification of Castile, while Castilian riches allowed him to defend Aragon from invasion. In 1479 the two crowns were united and the Catholic monarchs, as they were called, ruled the two kingdoms jointly. But the unification of the crowns of Castile and Aragon was not the same as the formation of a single state between them. Local privileges were zealously guarded, especially in Aragon, where the representative institutions of the towns, the Cortes, were aggressively independent. Their attitude is best expressed in the oath of the townsmen of Saragossa: "We accept you as our king provided you observe all our liberties and laws; and if not, not." The powerful Castilian nobility never accepted Ferdinand as their king and refused him the crown after Isabella's death.

But Ferdinand and Isabella (1479–1516) took the first steps toward forging a Spanish state. Their most notable achievement was the final recovery of the lands that had been conquered by the Moors. For centuries the Spanish kingdoms had fought against the North African Muslims who had conquered large areas of the southern peninsula. The *reconquista* was characterized by short bursts of warfare followed by long periods of wary coexistence. By the middle of the fifteenth century, the Moorish territory had been reduced to the province of Granada, but civil strife in Castile heightened the possibility of a new Moorish offensive. "We no longer mint gold, only steel," was how a Moorish ruler replied to Isabella's demand for the traditional payment of tribute money. The final stages of the *reconquista* began in 1482 and lasted for a decade. It was waged as a holy war and was financed in part by grants from the pope and the Christian princes of Europe. It was a bloody undertaking. The Moorish population of nearly half a million was reduced to one hundred thousand before the town of Granada

finally fell and the province was absorbed into Castile.

The *reconquista* played an important part in creating a national identity for the Christian peoples of Spain. In order to raise men and money for the war effort, Ferdinand and Isabella mobilized their nobility and town governments and created a central organization to oversee the invasion. Ferdinand himself was actively involved in the warfare, gaining the respect of the hostile Castilian nobles in the process. The conquered territories were used to reward those who had aided the effort, though the crown maintained control and jurisdiction over most of the province. But the idea of the holy war also had a darker side and an unanticipated consequence. The Jewish population that had lived peacefully in both Castile and Aragon became another object of hostility. Many Jews had risen to prominence in government and in skilled professions. Others, who had accepted conversion to Christianity and were known as *conversos*, had become among the most powerful figures in Church and state.

Both groups were now attacked. The *conversos* fell prey to a special Church tribunal created to examine their sincere devotion to Catholicism. This was the Spanish Inquisition which, though it used traditional judicial practices— torture to gain confessions, public humiliation to show contrition, and burnings at the stake to maintain purity—used them on a scale never before seen. Thousands of *conversos* were killed and many more families had their wealth confiscated to be used for the *reconquista*. In 1492 the Jews themselves were expelled from Spain. Though the *reconquista* and the expulsion of the Jews inflicted great suffering upon victims and incalculable loss to the Castilian economy, both events enhanced the prestige of the Catholic monarchs.

In many ways, Ferdinand and Isabella tread the paths of the medieval monarchy. They relied upon personal contact with their people more than upon the use of a centralized administration. They frequently dispensed justice personally, sitting in court and accepting petitions from their subjects. Quite remarkably, they had no permanent residence and traveled the length and breadth of their kingdoms. Isabella is said to have visited every town in Castile, and it is entirely possible that a majority of the population of both

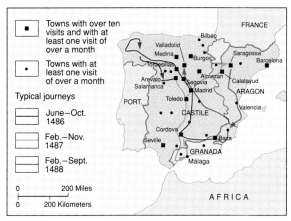

Travels of Ferdinand and Isabella

kingdoms actually saw their monarchs at one time or another. Queen Isabella was venerated in Castile, where womens' rights to inheritance remained strong. Ferdinand's absences from Aragon were always a source of contention between him and the Cortes of the towns. Yet he was careful to provide regents to preside in his absence and regularly returned to visit his native kingdom. He was not an absentee monarch.

The joint presence of Ferdinand and Isabella in the provinces of Spain was symbolic of the unity that they wished to achieve. Despite the great obstacles, they were consciously concerned to bring about a more permanent blending. Ferdinand made Castilian the official language of government in Aragon and even appointed Castilians to Aragonese posts. He and Isabella actively encouraged the intermarriage of the two aristocracies and the expansion of the number of wealthy nobles who held land in both kingdoms. A single coinage was established for both kingdoms, stamped with the heads of both monarchs. Nevertheless, these measures did not unify Spain or erase the centuries' long tradition of hostility among the diverse Iberian peoples.

It was left to the heirs of Ferdinand and Isabella to forge together the Spanish kingdoms, and the process was a painful one. The hostility to a foreign monarch that both the Castilian nobility and the Aragonese towns had shown to Ferdinand and Isabella increased dramatically at the accession of their grandson Charles V (1516–56), who had been born and raised in the Low Countries, where he ruled over Burgundy and the Netherlands. Through a series of dynastic accidents, Charles was heir to the Spanish crown with its possessions in the New World and to the vast Habsburg estates that included Austria. The Castilian nobles were especially hostile to Charles and plotted to place his younger brother on their throne. Charles established his rule in Spain gradually. For a time he was forced to share power in Castile and to suppress a disorganized aristocratic rebellion.

Because of his foreign obligations, Charles was frequently absent from Spain. During those periods he governed through regents and royal councils that did much to centralize administration. Though Castile and Aragon had separate councils, they were organized similarly and had greater contact than before. Charles V realized the importance of Spain, especially of Castile, in his empire. He learned Castilian and spent more time there than in any other part of his empire, calling it "the head of all the rest." Like Ferdinand and Isabella he traveled throughout Castile and Aragon, but unlike them he established a more permanent bureaucratic court, modeled on that of Burgundy, and placed able Spaniards at the head of its departments. This smoothed over the long periods when Charles was abroad, especially the thirteen years between 1543 and 1556.

Yet neither his personal efforts to rule as a Spanish monarch, nor those of his able administrators were the most important factor in uniting the Spanish kingdoms of Iberia. Rather it was the fact that Charles V brought Spain to the forefront of European affairs in the sixteenth century. Spanish prowess, whether in arms or in culture, became a source of national pride that helped erode regional identity. Gold and silver from the New World helped finance Charles' great empire. Whether or not he dreamed of uniting all of Europe under his rule, Charles V fulfilled nearly all of the ancient territorial ambitions of the Spanish kingdoms. In Italy he prosecuted Aragonese claims to Sicily and Naples; in the north he held on firmly to the kingdom of Navarre, which had been annexed by Ferdinand and which secured Spain's border with France. In the south he blocked off Ottoman and Muslim expansion. The reign of Charles V ushered in the dawn of Spain's golden age.

The Dynastic Struggles

The formation of large states throughout Europe led inevitably to conflicts among them. Long chains of marriages among the families of the European princes meant that sooner or later the larger powers would lay claim to the same inheritances and test the matter by force. Thus the sixteenth century was a period of almost unrelieved general warfare that took the whole of the Continent as its theater. Advances in technology made war more efficient and more expensive. They also made it more horrible. The use of artillery against infantry increased the number of deaths and maiming injuries, as did the replacement of the arrow by the bullet. As the size of armies increased, so did casualties. Nearly sixty thousand men met at Marignano in 1515, where it took thirty French cavalry charges and twenty-eight consecutive hours of battle before the Swiss infantry was driven from the field. The slaughter of French nobility at Pavia in 1525 was the largest in a century, while the Turkish sultan, Suleiman the Magnificent, recorded the burial of twenty-four thousand Hungarian soldiers after the battle of Mohács in 1526. Civilians fared little better than combatants. Plunder was a soldier's salary. What was most shocking about the sack of Rome in 1527 was that the property of churches was treated with no greater respect than that of private persons.

Power and Glory

The frequency with which offensive war was waged in the sixteenth century raises a number of questions about the militaristic values of the age. Valor remained greatly prized—a Renaissance virtue inherited from the crusading zeal and chivalric ideals of the Middle Ages. Wars were fought "for the desire for glory, the hope of booty, and the fear that the strength of others is allowed to increase," as Lorenzo Valla believed. Princes saw valor as a personal attribute and sought to do great deeds. Ferdinand of Aragon and Francis I (1515–47) of France won fame for their exploits in war. Charles the Bold and Louis II of Hungary were less fortunate. Their battlefield deaths led to the breakup of their states. Wars were fought to further the interests of princes rather than the interests of national sovereignty or international Christianity. They were certainly not fought in the interests of their subjects. States were an extension of a prince's heritage; what rulers sought in battle was a part of their historical and familial rights, which defined themselves and their subjects. The wars of the sixteenth century were dynastic wars.

Along with desire came ability. The New Monarchs were capable of waging war. The very definition of their states involved the ability to accumulate territories and to defend them. Internal security depended upon locally raised forces or hired mercenaries. Both required money, which was becoming available in unprecedented quantities as a result of the increasing prosperity of the early sixteenth century and the windfall of gold and silver from the New World. Professional soldiers, of whom the Swiss and Germans were the most noteworthy, sold their services to the highest bidders. Developments in transport and supply enabled campaigns to take place far from the center of a state. Charles VIII was able to advance the length of Italy with his French troops in the 1490s, while the Ottomans stretched their lines of supply from Asia to the walls of Vienna. Finally, communications were improving. The need for knowledge about potential rivals or allies had the effect of expanding the European system of diplomacy. Resident agents were established in all the European capitals and they had a decisive impact upon war and peace. Their dispatches formed the most reliable source of information about the strengths of armies or the weaknesses of governments, about the birth of heirs or the death of princes.

Personality also played a part in the international warfare of the early sixteenth century. The three most consistent protagonists, Charles V, Francis I, and Henry VIII, were of similar age and outlook. Each came unexpectedly to his throne in the full flush of youth, eager for combat and glory. The three were self-consciously rivals, each jealous of the other's successes, each triumphant in the other's failures. Henry VIII and Francis I held wrestling bouts when they met in 1520. Francis I challenged Charles V to single combat after the French king's humiliating imprisonment in Madrid in 1526. All three were figures larger than life whose exploits, whether military or amorous, were popularized throughout Europe. As they aged together, their youthful wars of conquest matured into strategic warfare designed to maintain a Continental balance of power. Until their deaths they pursued a rivalry that was intensely emotional and competitive.

The Italian Wars

The struggle for supremacy in Europe in the sixteenth century pitted the French House of Valois against the far-flung estates of the Habsburg empire. Yet the wars took place in Italy. The rivalries among the larger Italian city-states proved fertile ground for the newly consolidated European monarchies. Both French and Spanish monarchs had remote but legitimate claims to the kingdom of Naples in southern Italy. In 1494 the French king, Charles VIII, took up an invitation from the ruler of Milan to intervene in Italian affairs. His campaign was an unqualified, if fleeting, success. He marched the length of the peninsula, overthrew the Medici in Florence, forced the pope to open the gates of Rome, and finally seized the crown of Naples. The occupation was accomplished without a single great battle and lasted until the warring Italian city-states realized that they had more to fear from the French than from one another. Once that happened, Charles VIII beat a hasty retreat. But the French appetite for Italian territory was not sated. Soon a deal was struck with Ferdinand of Aragon to divide the kingdom of Naples in two. All went according to plan until these thieves fell out among themselves. In the end, Spain wound up with all of Naples and France was left with nothing but debts and grievances.

Thus when Francis I came to the French throne and Charles V to the Spanish, Naples was just one of several potential sources of friction. Not only had Ferdinand betrayed the French in Naples, he had also broken a long-standing peace on the Franco-Spanish border by conquering the independent but French-speaking kingdom of Navarre. Francis could be expected to avenge both slights. Charles, on the other hand, was the direct heir of the dukes of Burgundy. From his childhood he longed for the restoration of his ancestral

lands, including Burgundy itself, which had been gobbled up by Louis XI after the death of Charles the Bold. Competition between Francis and Charles became all the more ferocious when Charles' grandfather, the Holy Roman Emperor Maximilian I (1486–1519), died in 1519. Both monarchs launched a vigorous campaign for the honor of succeeding him.

For nearly a century the Holy Roman Emperor had come from the Austrian ruling family, and there was little reason to believe that Charles V, who now inherited the Habsburg lands in Austria and Germany, would not also succeed to this eminent but empty dignity. Nevertheless, the electors were willing to be bribed by French agents who supported Francis' candidacy and even English agents who supported Henry VIII. Charles spent the most of all, and his eventual election not only aggravated the personal animosity among the monarchs, but added another source of conflict in Italy. When Louis XII (1498–1515) succeeded Charles VIII as king of France, he had laid claim to the duchy of Milan through an interest of his wife's, though he was unable to

The Italian Wars

The Field of the Cloth of Gold, the lavish setting for the meeting between Henry VIII and Francis I in June 1520. The fountain in the foreground provides free wine for all.

enforce it. Francis I proved more capable. In 1515 he stunned all of Europe by crushing the vaunted Swiss mercenaries at the battle of Marignano. As one of the terms of peace, Francis extracted an agreement that in the future the Swiss would fight only for France. But the duchy of Milan was a territory under the protection of the Holy Roman Emperor and it soon appealed for Imperial troops to help repel the French invaders. Milan was strategically important to Charles V as it was the vital link between his Austrian and Burgundian possessions. Almost as soon as he took up the imperial mantle, Charles V was determined to challenge Francis I in Italy.

The key to such a challenge was the construction of alliances among the various Italian city-states and most especially with England, whose aid both Charles and Francis sought to enlist in the early 1520s. Henry VII had found foreign alliances a ready source of cash, and he was always eager to enter into them as long as they did not involve raising armies and fighting wars. He gladly accepted pensions from France and Spain and happily married his daughter to a French king and his son to a Spanish princess, in return for promises of neutrality. Henry VIII was made of sterner stuff. He longed to reconquer France and to cut a figure on the European scene. Despite the fact that his initial Continental adventures had emptied his treasury without fulfilling his dreams, Henry remained eager for war. He was also flattered to find himself the object of attention by both Valois and Habsburg emissaries. Charles V made two separate trips to

London, while Henry crossed the Channel in 1520 to meet Francis I in one of the gaudiest displays of conspicuous consumption that the century would witness, appropriately known as the Field of the Cloth of Gold.

The result of these diplomatic intrigues was an alliance between England and the Holy Roman Empire. English and Burgundian forces would stage an invasion of northern France while Spanish and German troops would again attempt to dislodge the French and their Swiss mercenaries from Italy. The strategy worked better than anyone could have imagined. In 1523 Charles' forces gained a foothold in Milan by taking the heavily fortified town of Pavia. Two years later Francis was ready to strike back. At the head of his own royal guards, he massed Swiss mercenaries and French infantry outside Pavia and made ready for a swift assault. Instead, a large imperial army arrived to relieve the town, and in the subsequent battle the French suffered a shattering defeat. Thousands were killed, including many of the king's noble attendants. Francis I was captured.

The victory at Pavia, which occurred on Charles V's twenty-fifth birthday, seemingly made him master of all of Europe. His ally Henry VIII urged an immediate invasion and dismemberment of France and began raising an army to spearhead the attack. But Charles' position was much less secure than it appeared. The Ottomans threatened his Hungarian territories, and the Protestants threatened his German lands. He could not afford a war of conquest in France. His hope now was to reach an agreement with Francis I for a lasting European peace, and for this purpose the French king was brought in captivity to Madrid.

It is doubtful that there was ever any real chance for peace between Habsburg and Valois after the battle of Pavia. Francis' personal humiliation and Charles' military position were both too strong to allow for a permanent settlement in which Habsburgs ruled in Milan and Naples. But it was neither political nor personal considerations that were the source of another thirty years of continuous European warfare. Rather it was Charles' demand that Burgundy be returned to him. Though Francis was hardly in a position to bargain, he held out on this issue for as long as possible and he secretly prepared a disavowal of the final agreement before it was made. By the Treaty of Madrid in 1526, Francis I yielded Burgundy and recognized the Spanish conquest of Navarre and Spanish rule in Naples. The agreement was sealed by the marriage of Francis to Charles' sister, Eleanor of Portugal. But marriage was not sufficient security for such a complete capitulation. To secure his release from Spain, Francis was required to leave behind as hostages his seven- and eight-year-old sons until the treaty was fulfilled. For three years the children languished in Spanish captivity.

No sooner had he set foot upon French soil than Francis I renounced the Treaty of Madrid. Despite the threat that this posed to his children, Francis argued that the terms had been extracted against his will, and he even gained the sanction of the pope for violating his oath. Setting France on a war footing, he began seeking new allies. Henry VIII, disappointed with the meager spoils of his last venture, switched sides. So too did a number of Italian city-states, including Rome. Most importantly, Francis I entered into an alliance with the Ottoman sultan, Suleiman the Magnificent (1520–66), whose armies were pressing against the southeastern borders of the Holy Roman Empire. In the year following Pavia, the Ottomans secured an equally decisive triumph at Mohács, which cut Hungary in two, and threatened Vienna, the eastern capital of the Habsburg lands. Almost overnight Charles V had been turned from hunter into hunted. The Ottoman threat demanded immediate attention in Germany, the French and English were preparing to strike in the Low Countries, and the Italian wars

continued. In 1527 Charles' unpaid German mercenaries stormed through Rome, sacked the papal capital, and captured the pope. Christian Europe was mortified.

The struggle for European mastery ground on for decades. The Treaty of Cateau-Cambrésis in 1559 brought to a close sixty years of conflict. In the end the French were no more capable of dislodging the Habsburgs from Italy than were the Habsburgs of forcing the Ottomans out of Hungary. The great stores of silver that poured into Castile from the New World were consumed in the fires of Continental warfare. In 1557 both France and Spain declared bankruptcy to avoid foreclosures by their creditors. For the French, the Italian wars were disastrous. They seriously undermined the state's financial base, eroded confidence in the monarchy, and thinned the ranks of the ruling nobility. The adventure begun by Charles VIII in search of glory brought France nearly to ruin. It ended with fitting irony. After the death of Francis I, his son Henry II (1547–59) continued the struggle. Henry never forgave his father for abandoning him in Spain, and he sought revenge on Charles V, who had been his jailer. He regarded the Treaty of Cateau-Cambrésis as a victory and celebrated it with great pomp and pageantry. Among the feasts and festivities were athletic competitions for the king's courtiers and attendants. Henry II entered the jousting tournament and there was killed.

Charles V died in his bed. The long years of war made clear that the dream to dominate Europe could only be a dream. He split apart his empire and granted to his brother, Ferdinand I (1558–64), the Austrian and German lands and the mantle of the Holy Roman Empire. To his son, Philip II (1556–98), he ceded the Low Countries, Spain and the New World, Naples, and his Italian conquests. In 1555 Charles abdicated all of his titles and retired to a monastery to live out his final days. The cares of an empire that once stretched from Peru to Vienna were lifted from his shoulders. Beginning with his voyage to Castile in 1517 he had made ten trips to the Netherlands, nine to Germany, seven to Italy, six to Spain, four to France, two to England, and two to Africa. "My life has been one long journey," he told those who witnessed him relinquish his crowns. On 21 September 1558, he finally rested forever.

Suggestions for Further Reading

General Reading

* G. R. Potter, ed., *The New Cambridge Modern History, Vol. I The Renaissance 1493–1520* (Cambridge: Cambridge University Press, 1957). Comprehensive survey of political history written by renowned scholars.

* Denys Hay, *Europe in the Fourteenth and Fifteenth Centuries* (London: Longman, 1966). A good first survey of political history.

* Eugene Rice, *The Foundations of Early Modern Europe 1460–1559* (New York: Norton, 1970). An outstanding synthesis.

The European Discoveries

C. R. Boxer, *The Portuguese Seaborne Empire 1415–1825* (London: Hutchinson, 1968). The best history of the first of the explorer nations.

* Samuel Morrison, *Christopher Columbus, Mariner* (New York: New American Library, 1985). A biography by a historian who repeated the Columbian voyages.

* Dan O'Sullivan, *Age of Discovery 1400–1550* (London: Longman, 1984). A short, synthetic work.

* Lyle McAlister, *Spain and Portugal in the New World 1492–1700* (Minneapolis: University of Minnesota Press, 1984). An up-to-date history of the great South American empires.

* J. H. Parry, *The Age of Reconnaissance* (New York: New American Library, 1963). A survey of technological and technical changes that made possible the European discovery of America.

* J. H. Elliot, *The Old World and the New 1492–1650* (Cambridge: Cambridge University Press, 1970). A brilliant look at the reception of knowledge about the new world by Europeans.

* A. W. Crosby, *The Columbian Exchange: Biological and Cultural Consequences of 1492* (Westport, CT: Greenwood Press, 1972). An argument about the medical consequences of the transatlantic encounter.

Europe in 1500

N. J. G. Pounds, *An Historical Geography of Europe 1500–1800* (Cambridge: Cambridge University Press, 1979). A remarkable survey of the relationship between geography and history.

* Daniel Waley, *Later Medieval Europe* (London: Longman, 1985). A good, brief account.

The Formation of States

J. H. Shennan, *The Origins of the Modern European State 1450–1725* (London: Hutchinson, 1974). An analytic account of the rise of the state.

Bernard Guenée, *States and Rulers in Later Medieval Europe* (London: Basil Blackwell, 1985). An engaging argument about the forces that helped shape the state system in Europe.

* Norman Davies, *God's Playground: A History of Poland, Vol. 1. The Origins to 1795* (New York: Columbia University Press, 1982). The best treatment in English of a complex history.

* Richard Pipes, *Russia Under the Old Regime* (London: Widenfeld and Nicolson, 1974). A majesterial account.

Robert O. Crummey, *The Formation of Muscovy 1304–1613* (London: Longman, 1987). The best one-volume history.

* J. R. Lander, *Government and Community, England 1450–1509* (Cambridge, MA: Harvard University Press, 1980). A comprehensive survey of the late fifteenth century.

* S. B. Chrimes, *Henry VII* (Berkeley, CA: University of California Press, 1972). A traditional biography of the first Tudor king.

* C. D. Ross, *The Wars of the Roses* (London: Thames and Hudson, 1976). The best one-volume account.

* G. R. Elton, *Reform and Reformation, England 1509–1558* (Cambridge, MA: Harvard University Press, 1977). An up-to-date survey by the dean of Tudor historians.

Richard Vaughan, *Valois Burgundy* (Hampden, CT: Shoe String Press, 1975). An engaging history of a vanished state.

* Paul M. Kendall, *Louis XI: The Universal Spider* (New York: Norton, 1971). A highly entertaining account of an unusual monarch.

* R. J. Knecht, *French Renaissance Monarchy* (London: Longman, 1984). A study of the nature of the French monarchy and the way it was transformed in the early sixteenth century.

* Henry Kamen, *Spain 1469–1714* (London: Longman, 1983). The most up-to-date survey.

* J. H. Elliot, *Imperial Spain 1469–1716* (New York: Mentor, 1963). Still worth reading for its insights and examples.

The Dynastic Struggles

* J. R. Hale, *War and Society in Renaissance Europe* (Baltimore: Johns Hopkins University Press, 1986). Assesses the impact of war on the political and social history of early modern Europe.

M. F. Alvarez, *Charles V* (London: Thames and Hudson, 1975). An accessible biography of the most remarkable man of the age.

* R. J. Knecht, *Francis I* (Cambridge: Cambridge University Press, 1982). A compelling study by the leading scholar of sixteenth-century France.

* J. J. Scarisbrick, *Henry VIII* (Berkeley, CA: University of California Press, 1968). The definitive biography.

* Indicates paperback edition available.

13

The Reform
of
Religion

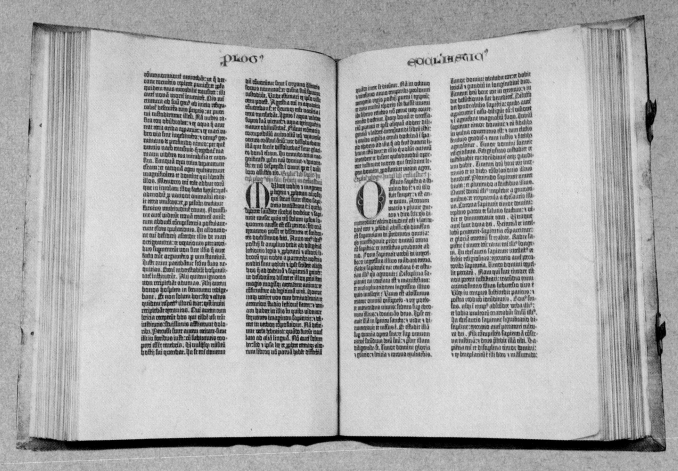

Sola Scriptura

"In the beginning was the word, and the word was with God, and the word was God." In no other period of European history was this text of the apostle John so appropriate. Men and women shared a consuming desire to hear and to read the Word of God as set down in the Bible. In the early sixteenth century, Europeans developed an insatiable appetite for the Bible. Scriptures rolled off printing presses in every shape and form, from the great vellum tomes of Gutenberg, pictured here, to pocket Bibles that soldiers carried into battle. They came in every imaginable language. Before 1500 there were fourteen complete Bibles printed in German, four each in Italian, French, and Spanish, one in Czech, and even one in Flemish. There were hundreds more editions in Latin, the official Vulgate Bible first translated by Saint Jerome in the fourth century. Whole translations and editions of the Bible were only part of the story. Separate sections, especially the Psalms and the first books of the Old Testament, were printed by the thousands. There were twenty-four French editions of the Old Testament before an entirely new translation appeared in 1530. When Martin Luther began his own

German translation of the Bible in 1522, it immediately became an international best-seller. In twenty-five years it went into 430 editions. It is estimated that one million German Bibles were printed in the first half of the sixteenth century—a time when Europe had a German-speaking population of about 15 million people, 90 percent of whom were illiterate.

Bible owning was no fad. It was but one element in a new devotional outlook that was sweeping the Continent and that would have far-reaching consequences for European society during the next 150 years. A renewed spirituality was everywhere to be seen. It was expressed in a desire to change the traditional practices and structures of the Roman church. It was expressed in a desire to have learned and responsible ministers to tend to the needs of their parishioners. It was expressed in a desire to establish godly families and godly cities and godly kingdoms. Sometimes it took the form of sarcasm and bitter denunciations; sometimes it took the form of quiet devotion and pious living. The need for reform was everywhere felt; the demand for reform was everywhere heard. It came from within the Roman church as much as from without.

The inspiration for reform was based on the Word of God. Scholars, following humanist principles, worked on biblical translations in an attempt to bring a purer text to light. Biblical commentary dominated the writings of churchmen as never before. Woodcut pictures, depicting scenes from the life of Jesus or from the Old Testament, were printed in untold quantities for the edification of the unlettered. For the first time common people could, in their own dwellings, contemplate representations of the lives of the saints. Many of the Bibles that were printed in vernacular—that is, in the languages spoken in the various European states rather than in Latin—were interleaved with illustrations of the central events of Christian history. Preachers spoke to newly aware audiences and relied on biblical texts to draw out their message. Study groups, especially in urban areas, proliferated so that the literate could read and learn together. Bible reading became a part of family life, one which mothers and fathers could share with their children and their servants. *Sola Scriptura*—by the word alone—became the battle cry of religious reform.

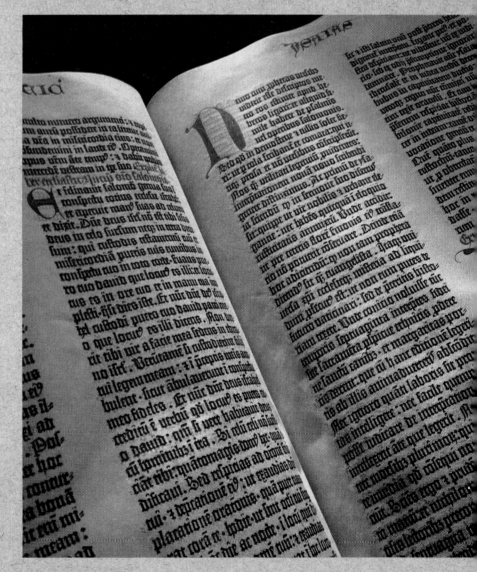

The Intellectual Reformation

There is nothing as powerful as an idea whose time has come. But the coming of ideas has a history as complex as the ideas themselves. In the early sixteenth century reformers throughout western Europe preached new ideas about religious doctrine and religious practice. At first these ideas took the form of a sustained critique of the Roman Catholic church, but soon they developed a momentum of their own. Some reformers remained within traditional Catholicism; others moved outside and founded new Protestant churches. Wherever this movement for religious reform, whether Catholic or Protestant, appeared it was fed by new ideas. But if new ideas were to supplant old ones they had to be communicated, not only heard and repeated but accurately recorded and understood. This was made possible by the development of the technology of printing, which appeared in Germany in the late fifteenth century and rapidly spread across Europe in the succeeding decades. Yet printing was as much a result as it was a cause of the spread of ideas. The humanist call for a return to the study of the classics and for the creation of accurate texts, first heard in Italy, aroused scholars and leaders in all of the European states. Their appetite for manuscripts exhausted the abilities of the scribes and booksellers who reproduced texts. Printing responded to that demand.

The Print Revolution

The development of printing did not cause religious reform, but it is difficult to see how reform would have progressed in its absence. The campaign to change the doctrine and practice of Catholicism was waged through the press, with millions of flyers and pamphlets distributed across Europe to spread the new ideas. Martin Luther was an international celebrity whose face appeared on hundreds of different works that flowed like a river from the presses. A third of all books sold in Germany between 1518 and 1525 were written by Luther. But the ways in which printing came to be used by religious reformers could hardly have been foreseen by the artisans, bankers, and booksellers who together created one of the true technological revolutions in Western history.

Printing was not invented. It developed as a result of progress made in a number of allied industries, of which papermaking and goldsmithing were the most important. Scholars and university students needed copies of manuscripts. Their need led to the development of a trade in bookselling that flourished in almost every university town. To avoid corruption through the repetition of error, professional scribes were required to make their hand copies directly from the original texts held by the universities. Hand copying naturally slowed the process of reproduction. So did difficulties in obtaining the sheep- and calfskins on which the manuscripts were written. It took the skins of three hundred sheep to produce a single Bible. In the early fifteenth century, copyists began to substitute paper made from linen rags for the expensive vellum skins. A number of German craftsmen experimented with using movable metal type to make exact reproductions of manuscripts on paper. Paper took a better impression and provided an absolutely smooth surface, which was essential for pressing the image. In the 1450s in Mainz, Johannes

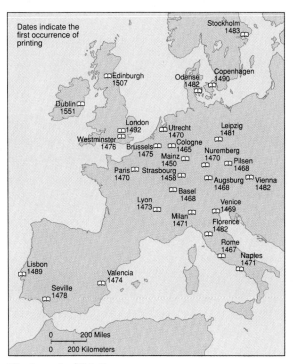

The Spread of Printing

Gutenberg (ca. 1400–1468) and his partners succeeded and published their famous Bibles.

Printing was a business and an expensive one at that. The association of early printing with goldsmithing resulted from the high level of technical skill that was necessary to create the hard metal stamps from which the softer metal type was produced. The investment in type and in paper was considerable. Only the press itself was cheap. Any corn or wine press could be used to bring the long flat sheets of paper down upon a wooden frame filled with ink-coated metal type. Booksellers had the most to gain from the new technique and initially put up the capital needed to cast the stamps, mold the type, and buy the paper. They bound the printed pages and found the markets to distribute them. At first sales were slow. Printed books were considered inferior to manuscripts despite the fact that all books in an edition were exact replicas. Nor at first were printed books less expensive than handwritten manuscripts. Bibles, like those printed by Gutenberg, were major investments, equivalent to purchasing a house today. Many early printing shops quickly went bankrupt as they misjudged their markets and were unable to pay back their loans. Gutenberg himself lost his precious stock of type to his creditors. He died penniless.

Still, once it was begun, printing spread like wildfire. Many of the early craftsmen had been apprentices trained in Gutenberg's shop, and they set out to found presses of their own. By 1480 over 110 towns had established presses, most in Italy and Germany. After that the pace quickened. By the beginning of the sixteenth century Venice and Paris were the centers of the industry, with the Paris presses producing over three hundred new titles annually. Most of the early printed works were either religious or classical. Bibles, church service books, and the commentaries of the Church Fathers were most common. Cicero topped the list of classical authors. Over three hundred separate editions of his works were produced before the end of the fifteenth century.

What is most amazing about the printing revolution is how rapidly printing came to be a basic part of life. In the first forty years after the presses began, perhaps as many as twenty million books were produced and distributed. Printing changed the habits of teachers and students and therefore the possibilities of education. It altered the methods by which the state conducted its business. It affected both legal training and legal proceedings. Compilations of laws could now be widely distributed and more uniformly enforced. Printing had a similar effect on the development of scientific study. The printing press popularized the discoveries of the New World and contributed to the reproduction of more accurate charts and maps, which in turn facilitated further discovery. Printing also helped standardize language, both Latin and vernacular, by frequent repetition of preferred usage and spelling. With the introduction of the octavo, the so-called pocketbook, printing also changed leisure habits. Travelers on horseback or on ship could now carry with them books to help pass their time. Perhaps most importantly printing created an international intellectual community whose ideas could be dispersed the length and breadth of the Continent. The printing press enhanced the value of ideas and of thinking. Nothing could be more central to the reform of religion.

Christian Humanism

Many of the ideas that spread across Europe as the result of the printing revolution originated in Italian humanism (see chapter 11). The revival of classical literature, with its concern for purity in language and eloquence in style, was one of the most admired achievements of the Renaissance. Students from all over Europe who descended upon Italian universities to study medicine and law came away with a strong dose of philology, rhetoric, moral philosophy, and the other liberal arts. Their heads were filled with the new learning. By the beginning of the sixteenth century, the force of humanism was felt strongly in northern and western Europe, where it was grafted to the dominant strains of traditional theological teaching. The combination was a new and powerful intellectual movement known as Christian humanism.

Though the humanism of the north differed from that of the Italian city-states, this is not to say that northern humanists were Christians and Italian humanists were not. But Italian intellectual interests were in secular subjects, especially in mastering classical languages and in translating classical texts. Italian humanists had established techniques for the recovery of accurate texts and had developed principles for compiling the scholarly editions that now poured forth from the printing presses. Christian humanists applied these techniques to the study of the authorities and texts of the Church. Most of the new humanists had been trained in Italy, where they devoted themselves to the mastery of Greek and Latin. They had imbibed the idea that scholars, using their own critical faculties, could establish the authority of texts and the meaning of words. Building upon the patient work of their predecessors and the advantages offered by printing, this new generation of humanists brought learning to educated men and women throughout Europe.

Christian humanism was a program of reform rather than a philosophy. It aimed to make better Christians through better education. Humanists were especially interested in the education of women. "For what is more fruitful than the good education and order of women, the one half of all mankind," wrote Thomas More (1478–1535). They helped found schools for girls and advocated that they be trained in the same subjects as boys. Thomas More raised his daughters to be among the educated elite of England and they enjoyed international renown. The Spanish humanist Juan Luis Vives (1492–1540) wrote *The Instruction of a Christian Woman* (1523), a handbook for women of the elite orders commissioned by Catherine of Aragon. Renowned women scholars even held places at Italian universities. Humanist educational principles posed an implicit challenge to Roman Catholicism. Schools had once been the monopoly of the Church, which used them to train clergymen. The Church had founded them and kept them afloat in good times and in bad. Literacy itself had been preserved over the centuries so that the gospel could be propagated.

By the sixteenth century these purposes had been transformed. Schools now trained many who were not destined for careers in the Church, and literacy served the needs of the state, the aristocracy, and the merchant classes. More importantly, as the humanists perfected their techniques of scholarship, the Church continued to rely upon traditional methods of training and traditional texts. The dominant manner of teaching at the schools and universities was known as Scholasticism. Passages of biblical texts were studied through the commentaries of generations of Church Fathers. Rote memorization of the opinions of others was more highly valued than critical thinking. Argument took place by formal disputation of questions on which the Fathers of the Church disagreed. Disputed questions became more and more obscure. Even if Scholastics did not debate the question, "How many angels can dance on the head of a pin?" it seemed to many humanists that they might as well have. The Vulgate Bible was used throughout Western Christendom. It was now a thousand years old.

The Humanist Movement

Many humanist criticisms of Church teaching focused on its failure to inspire individuals to live a Christian life. Humanist writers were especially scathing about popular practices that bordered on superstition, like pilgrimages to holy places or the worship of relics from the early history of the Church. Shrines established to preserve a vial of the milk of the Virgin Mary or a piece of the cross on which Christ had been crucified became the butt of popular humor. "She has left us so much of her milk that it's scarcely credible a woman with only one child could have so much, even if the child had drunk none of it. The same thing is said about the Lord's Cross. If the fragments were joined together they would seem a full load for a freighter. And yet the Lord carried his whole cross." This ironic strain in humanist writing is most closely associated with the great Dutch humanist, Desiderius Erasmus, but it is also visible in the humanist social criticism of Sir Thomas More's *Utopia* (See Special Feature, "Utopia," pp. 392–393). Christian humanists wanted to inspire Christians. As Erasmus observed, "to be learned is the lot of only a few; but no one is unable to be a Christian, no one is unable to be pious."

Christian humanism was an international movement. Not only did the humanists share the objectives of reforming education and providing up-to-date texts from which to teach, but they were commonly in contact with one another, either through correspondence or travel. They formed the elite of the intellectual world of the sixteenth century, and their services were sought by princes and peers as well as by the most distinguished universities. In fact, the New Monarchs supported the humanists and protected them from their critics. Marguerite of Navarre, sister of Francis I, was an accomplished writer who frequently interceded on behalf of the leading French humanists. Ferdinand of Aragon, Henry VIII, and the Holy Roman Emperors Maximilian I and Charles V all brought humanists to their courts and aided their projects. Maria of Hungary and Mary and Elizabeth Tudor were trained in humanist principles and participated in humanist literary achievements. This support was especially important for educational reforms. Under the influence of the French humanist Jacques Lefèvre d'Etaples (ca. 1455–1536), Francis I established the Collège de France; under the direction of Cardinal Jiménez de Cisneros, the University of Alcalà was founded in Spain. Throughout northern Europe professorships in Greek and Latin were endowed at universities to help further the study of classical languages.

The centerpiece of humanist reforms was the

Engraving of Erasmus by the German master Albrecht Dürer. The title, date, and signature appear behind the philosopher. The Greek inscription reads "His writings depict him even better."

translation of Christian texts. Armed with skills in Greek and Latin, informed by scholars of Hebrew and Aramaic, humanist writers prepared new editions of the books of the Bible and of the writings of the early Church Fathers. Their favorite method was the side-by-side translation. Thus Lefèvre produced a new edition of the Book of Psalms in which five different versions of the texts were reproduced. The Polyglot Bible—literally "many languages"—that was produced in 1522 at Jiménez de Cisneros' University of Alcalà took a team of scholars fifteen years to complete. They gathered together copies of all known biblical manuscripts and rigorously compared their texts. They established the principle that inconsistencies among Latin manuscripts were to be resolved by reference to Greek texts and difficulties in Greek texts by reference to Hebrew texts. The result was six elegantly printed volumes that allowed scholars to compare the texts. The Old Testament was printed in three parallel columns of Hebrew, Latin Vulgate, and Greek. The New Testament was printed in double columns with the Greek text on one side and the Vulgate on the other. The Greek edition of the Bible and its establishment as a text superior to the Vulgate caused an immediate sensation throughout humanist and Church circles.

The Wit of Erasmus

Though the Polyglot Bible contained the first completed Greek edition of the New Testament, it was not the first published one. That distinction belongs to the man whose name is most closely associated with the idea of Christian humanism, Desiderius Erasmus of Rotterdam (ca. 1466–1536). Erasmus' career was that of the humanist par excellence. Orphaned at an early age, Erasmus was educated by the Brothers of the Common Life, a lay brotherhood that specialized in schooling children and preparing them for a monastic life. Marked out early by his quick wit, pleasant though strong personality, and extraordinary intellectual gifts, Erasmus entered a monastery and was then allowed to travel to pursue his studies, first in France and then in England.

In England Erasmus learned of new techniques for instructing children both in classical knowledge and in Christian morals, and he became particularly interested in the education

Utopia

"It is a general rule that the more different anything is from what people are used to, the harder it is to accept." So warned the imaginary traveler, Raphael Hythloday as he described Utopia, a fabulous society he had visited in the New World. Utopian society was different indeed. In Utopia, all property was held in common; there were no social classes; families were extended to include grandparents, in-laws, and flocks of children; and all work and most social activities were regulated by the state. Utopians were rarely tempted to sin. Everyone wore the same practical clothes to abolish vanity. "No matter how delicate the thread, they say a sheep wore it once and still was nothing but a sheep." Everyone ate the same food in large common halls to abolish jealousy. "A man would be stupid to take the trouble to prepare a worse meal at home when he had a sumptuous one near at hand in the hall." To abolish greed, Utopians scorned gold and silver. "Criminals who are to bear through life the mark of some disgraceful act are forced to wear golden rings on their ears, golden bands on their

fingers, golden chains around their necks, and even golden crowns on their heads." Utopians lived harmoniously in planned cities, honored their elders, cared for their sick, and brought up their children to love learning and respect hard work. They "lead a life as free of anxiety and as full of joy as possible."

There were many ways in which Christian humanists attempted to instruct their contemporaries to lead a joyful life. None has proved more enduring than the imaginary community Sir Thomas More created in *Utopia*, a social satire so convincing that a Catholic priest sought to become its bishop and sea travelers tried to learn its location. More's creation has

proven so compelling that it has given its name to the entire genre of dreamworlds that followed in its wake. His vision of a carefully planned and permanently contented society has passed into our language, but in a way that would not have pleased the author. Now, *utopian* has a wistful ring. It is a label for impractical ideals that will never come to pass, a name for well-meaning but misguided daydreams. For More, as for his generation of humanists, the goal of teaching Christians to lead a Christian life was neither wistful nor impractical.

Sir Thomas More was a London lawyer by vocation but a humanist scholar by avocation. His father practiced law and planned a similar career for his son. But Thomas' stay at Oxford University coincided with the first flush of humanist enthusiasm there, especially in the study of Greek. More proved so exceptionally able that his father removed him to London in fear that reading Greek would turn him away from Catholicism. More proved as able at law school as he had at the university, and he was soon singled out as one of the best lawyers of his day. But in his spare time he continued to study the classics and became part of the growing humanist circle in London. There he met Erasmus, who was to become his lifelong friend.

Erasmus left a vivid portrait of More. "His complexion is fair, his face being rather blond than pale; his hair is auburn inclining to black, his eyes a bluish grey. It is a face more expressive of pleasantry than of gravity or dignity. He seems to be born and made for friendship, his extraordinary kindness and sweetness of temper are such as to cheer the dullest spirit."

More wrote *Utopia* in 1516, before he embarked upon the public career that would result in his becoming Chancellor of England, Speaker of the House of Commons, Privy Councilor and companion to Henry VIII, and finally a victim of the king's divorce and assumption of the title Supreme Head of the Church of England. More ended his life on the chopping block, and his death was mourned by humanists throughout Europe.

The community that More described in *Utopia* combined Plato's republic with a Christian monastery and was wrapped about by travelers' tales of the New World. But More's Utopia resembled nothing so much as England. The real and the imaginary, the serious and the absurd intermingle to disguise the author's point of view. *Utopia* is written in the form of a dialogue in which the author pretends to be one of the characters. On a visit to Antwerp, the character More is introduced to an imaginary traveler named Raphael Hythloday. During a long evening, Hythloday related a tale of a remarkable society that he encountered on his voyages. Utopia was a self-sufficient island, protected from invasion by the sea and thus able to develop its social customs without interference.

Hythloday contrasted the practices of the Utopians with those of contemporary Europeans and confounded the character More's objections that such arrangements were impractical. For example, where European peasants or craftsmen worked for fourteen hours a day, Utopians worked for only six. But *all* Utopians worked. There were no idle aristocrats with their marauding retainers, no priests and monks and nuns, no beggars unable to find jobs. Moreover, there was no surplus of workers in one field and shortage in another. For two years, each Utopian worked on the farm. After that, Utopians worked at a craft according to the needs of the city. Both males and females were educated to be of service to their community. Women were trained in less strenuous but no less essential trades like weaving or spinning. The population of cities was strictly controlled so that there was neither poverty nor homelessness. In their spare time Utopians engaged in uplifting activities like music, gardening, or artistic pursuits. Severe punishment awaited transgressors, but in contrast to the European practice of executing thieves, Utopian criminals were enslaved so that they could work for the restitution of the wrongs that they committed. Even as slaves they lived well, with good food and much leisure. Though they had not the benefit of Christian religion, the Utopians believed in a single divinity as well as an afterlife and their worship was simple and natural.

More's *Utopia* was written in Latin, but the name of the island and its central places were all Greek words. For More's humanist friends the joke was plain. *Utopia* meant "nowhere" in Greek and *Hythloday* meant "peddler of nonsense." Humanist interest in the New World and in the strange native customs of the Amerindians made it a logical setting for an idealized community. But *Utopia* was a model for a Christian community, one in which the seven deadly sins had all been abolished and replaced by a life led according to the Golden Rule, where people did attempt to do to others what they wished done to themselves. By ironic contrast with the unfulfilling life led by Europeans, grasping for riches, dominated by vanity, motivated by pride, the peaceful and simple life of the Utopians held great attraction. By contrasting the success of heathen Utopians with the failure of Christian Europeans, More called upon his contemporaries to reform their own lives. The purpose of *Utopia* was not to advocate the abolition of wealth and property or the intervention of the state in the affairs of the individual but to demonstrate that a society founded upon good principles would become a good society. A society that dedicated itself to Christian principles would become truly Christian.

of women. He dedicated a number of his later writings to women patrons who were accomplished humanist scholars. While in England, Erasmus decided to compose a short satire on the lines of his conversations with Thomas More, extolling what was silly and condemning what was wise. The result was *In Praise of Folly* (1509), a work that became one of the first best-sellers in publishing history. This along with his famous *Adages*, pithy quotations taken from the writings of the ancients, made Erasmus an overnight sensation. Princes and humanist groups throughout Europe eagerly sought his company.

Before his visit to England, Erasmus had worked solely on Latin translations, but he came to realize the importance of recovering the texts of the early Church Fathers. At the age of thirty he began the arduous task of learning ancient Greek and devoted his energies to a study of the writings of Saint Jerome, the principal compiler of the Vulgate, and to preparing an edition of the Greek texts of the Bible. Erasmus' translation of the New Testament and his edition of the writings of Saint Jerome both appeared in 1516. Coming from the pen of the most renowned intellectual in Europe, they were an immediate success. Erasmus followed his Greek edition with a new Latin translation of the New Testament and began a series of commentaries on biblical texts that enabled other humanist writers to prepare vernacular editions based upon the most up-to-date texts.

Erasmus devoted his life to restoring the direct connection between the individual Christian and the textual basis of Christian doctrine. Although he is called the father of biblical criticism, Erasmus was not a theologian. He was more interested in the practical impact of ideas than in the ideas themselves. His scathing attacks upon the Scholastics, popular superstition, and the pretensions of the traditionalists in the Church and the universities all aimed at the same goal: to restore the experiences of Christ to the center of Christianity. Many of his popular writings were how-to books—how to improve one's manners, how to speak Latin properly, how to write letters—he even propounded twenty-two rules on how to lead a Christian life. Though his patrons were the rich and his language was Latin, Erasmus also hoped to reach men and women lower down the social order, those whom he believed the Church had failed to educate. "The doctrine of Christ casts aside no age, no sex, no fortune or position in life. It keeps no one at a distance." He hoped that his biblical translations would comfort others in the same way that they had comforted him. "I would to God that the plowman would sing a text of the Scripture at his plow and that the weaver would hum them to the tune of his shuttle. I wish that the traveler would expel the weariness of his journey with this pastime. I wish that all communication of the Christian would be of the Scriptures."

The Lutheran Reformation

On the surface the Roman Catholic church appeared as strong as ever at the end of the fifteenth century. The growth of universities and the spread of the new learning had helped create a better-educated clergy. The printing press proved an even greater boon to the Church than it had to the humanists by making widely available both instructional manuals for priests and up-to-date service books for congregations. The prosperity of European societies enhanced the prosperity of the Church. As an institution it seemed as powerful as ever. In Rome successive late medieval popes had managed to protect Church interests in the wake of the disintegration of the autonomous power of the Italian city-states. This was a remarkable feat. Popes had become first diplomats and then warriors in order to repel French and Spanish invaders. Though Rome was invaded, it was never conquered. And it was more beautiful than ever as the greatest artists and craftsmen of the Renaissance built and adorned its churches. Pilgrims came in the hundreds of thousands to bask in its glory. On the surface all was calm.

Yet everywhere in Europe the cry was for reform. Reform the venal papacy and its money-sucking bishops. Reform the ignorant clergy and the sacrilegious priests. Raise up the fallen nuns and the wayward friars. Wherever one turned one saw abuses. Parish livings were sold to the highest bidder to raise money. This was simony. Rich appointments were given to the kinsmen of powerful Church leaders rather than to those most qualified. This was nepotism. Individual clergymen accumulated numerous positions whose responsibilities they could not fulfill. This was pluralism. Some priests who took the vow of chastity lived openly with their concubines. Some mendicants who took the vow of poverty dressed in silk and ate from golden plates.

Yet the cry for reform that pierced the states of Europe at the beginning of the sixteenth century was a cry not so much of anguish as of hope. It came at a moment when people from all walks of life demanded greater spiritual fulfillment and held those whose vocation it was to provide such fulfillment to higher standards of achievement. It was expectation rather than experience that powered the demands for reform.

The Spark of Reform

Europe was becoming more religious. The signs of religious fervor were everywhere. Cities hired preachers to expound the gospel. Pilgrims to the shrines of saints clogged the roadways every spring and summer. It is estimated that 140,000 people visited the relics at Aachen on one day in 1496. Rome remained the greatest attraction, but pilgrims covered the Continent. The shrine of the apostle Saint James at Compostela in Spain was believed to cure the ill. Minor saints were petitioned for the special protections they offered. With so many journeying to shrines it is perhaps not surprising that Saint Christopher became the patron saint of travelers. Endowments of masses for the dead increased. Henry VII of England provided money for ten thousand masses to be said for his soul. Even moderately well-to-do city merchants might bequeath funds for several hundred. The chantries, where such services were performed, became overburdened by this "arithmetical piety" as there were neither enough priests nor enough altars to supply the demand. At one church in Breslau 122 priests worked 47 altars in shifts to fulfill their obligations.

People wanted more from the Church than the Church could possibly give them. Humanists condemned visits to the shrines as superstitious; pilgrims demanded that the relics be made more accessible. Reformers complained of pluralism; the clergy complained that they could not live on the salary of a single office. In one English diocese 60 percent of all parish incomes were inadequate to live on. Civic authorities demanded that the established Church take greater responsibility for good works; the pope demanded that civic authorities help pay for them.

Contradiction and paradox dominated the movements for reform. Though the most vocal critics of the Church complained that its discipline was too lax, for many ordinary people its demands were too rigorous. The obligations of penance and confession weighed heavily upon them. Church doctrine held that sins had to be washed away before the souls of the dead could enter heaven. Until then they suffered in purgatory. Sins were cleansed through penance, the performance of acts of contrition assigned after confession. Despite the rule that confession must be made at least annually, it is doubtful if many Catholics entered the confessional for years on end. This is not to say that they were unconcerned about their sins or did not desire to do penance for them. Rather, it was the ordeal of the confession itself that kept many people away. "Have you skipped mass? Have you dressed proudly? Have you thought of committing adultery? Have you insulted or cursed your parents? Have you failed to offer prayers, give alms, and endow masses for departed parents?" These were just a few of the uncomfortable questions that priests were instructed to pose in confession. In towns merchants were asked about their trading practices, shopkeepers about the quality of their goods. Magistrates were questioned about their attitudes to the clergy, intellectuals about their attitudes to the pope.

Thus it is hardly surprising that the sale of indulgences became a popular substitute for penance and confession. An indulgence was a portion of the treasury of good works performed by righteous Christians throughout the ages. They could be granted to those who desired to atone for their sins. Strictly speaking, an indulgence supplemented penance rather than substituted for it. It was effective only for the contrite—for sinners who repented of their sins. But as the practice of granting indulgences spread, this subtle distinction largely disappeared. Indulgences came to be viewed as pardons and the gift given to the Church in return as payment. "So soon as coin in coffer rings, the soul from purgatory springs." Indulgences were bought by the living to cleanse the sins of the dead, and some people even bought indulgences in anticipation of sins they had not yet committed.

An anonymous caricature of Johann Tetzel, whose preaching of an indulgence inspired Martin Luther's ninety-five theses. Tetzel answered with 122 theses of his own, but was rebuked and disowned by the Catholics.

By the sixteenth century, to limit abuses by local Church authorities, only the pope, through his agents, could grant indulgences. And their sale had become big business. Indulgences were one of the first items printed on Gutenberg's press. Popes used special occasions to offer an indulgence for pilgrimages to Rome or for contributions to special papal projects. Other indulgences were licensed locally, usually at the shrines of saints or at churches that contained relics. This was one reason why pilgrimages became increasingly popular. Frederick III, the Wise (1463–1525), ruler of Saxony, was one of the largest collectors of relics in Europe. At its height, his collection contained 17,000 different items, including a branch of Moses' burning bush, straw from Christ's manger, and 35 fragments of the true cross. Together, his relics carried remission for sins that would otherwise have taken over a quarter of a million years in purgatory to be cleansed.

It was the sale of indulgences that brought to a head the various movements for the reform of religion. The indulgence controversy was a symptom rather than a cause of the explosion of feelings that erupted in the small German town of Wittenberg in the year 1517. In that year the pope was offering an indulgence to help finance the rebuilding of Saint Peter's Basilica in Rome. The pope chose Prince Albert of Brandenburg (1490–1545) to distribute the indulgence in Germany, and Albert hired the Dominican friar Johann Tetzel (ca. 1465–1519) to preach its benefits. Tetzel was an aggressive salesman and he did a brisk business. He offered little warning about the theological niceties of indulgences to those who paid to mitigate their own sins or alleviate the suffering of their ancestors whose souls resided in purgatory.

Enthusiasm for the indulgence spread to the neighboring state of Saxony, where Frederick banned its sale. His great collection of relics carried their own indulgences and Tetzel offered unwelcome competition. But Saxons flocked into Brandenburg to make their purchases. By the end of October, Tetzel was not very far from Wittenberg Castle, where Frederick's relics were housed. On All Saints' Day the relics would be opened to view and, with the harvest done, one of the largest crowds of the year would gather to see them. On the night before, Martin Luther (1483–1546), a professor of theology at Wittenberg University, posted on the door of the castle church ninety-five theses attacking indulgences and their sale.

Other than the timing of Luther's action, there was nothing unusual about the posting of theses. In the Scholastic tradition of disputation, scholars presented propositions, or theses, for debate and challenged all comers to argue with them in a public forum. Luther's theses were controversial, but as that was the whole point of offering them for discussion, they were meant to be. Only circumstance moved Luther's theses from the academic to the public sphere. Already there was growing concern about Tetzel's blatant sale of indulgences. Clergy and theologians watched with mounting horror as hordes of ordinary people made purchases in the belief that they were buying unconditional remission of sin. In the late summer and early fall of 1517 the frenzy to buy indulgences had reached gold-rush proportions, and individual priests and monks began to sound the alarm. An indulgence without contrition was worthless.

Luther's theses focused this concern and finally communicated it beyond the walls of the church and university. The theses were immediately translated into German and spread throughout the Holy Roman Empire by humanists who had long criticized such practices as the sale of indulgences as superstitious. Prospective buyers became wary, past purchasers became angry. They had been duped again by the Church, by the priests who took their money, by the Italian pope who cared nothing for honest hard-working Germans. But Prince Albert and the pope needed the income. They could not stand by while sales collapsed and anticlerical and antipapal sentiment grew. Luther and his theses would have to be challenged.

The Faith of Martin Luther

Martin Luther was not a man to challenge lightly. Although he was only an obscure German professor, he had already marked himself out to all who knew him. In his youth Luther was an

Martin Luther

exceptionally able student whose father sent him to the best schools in preparation for a career in law. But Martin had his own ideas about his future, which were made more vivid when he was nearly struck by lightning. Against the wishes of his father he entered an Augustinian monastery, wholeheartedly followed the strict program of his order, and was ordained a priest in 1507. Intellectually gifted, he went on to study at the university, first at Erfurt and then at Wittenberg, where he received his doctorate and was appointed to the theology faculty in 1512.

A professor at the age of twenty-nine, he also served as priest at the castle church, where he preached each week. He attracted powerful patrons in the university and gained a reputation as an outstanding teacher. He began to be picked for administrative posts and became overseer of eleven Augustinian monasteries. His skills in disputation were so widely recognized that he was sent to Rome to argue a case on behalf of his order. Each task he was given he fulfilled beyond expectation; at every step he proved himself ready to go

higher. In all outward appearances Luther was successful and contented.

But beneath this tranquil exterior lay a soul in torment. As he rose in others' estimation, he sank in his own. Through beating and fasting he mortified his flesh. Through vigil and prayer he nourished his soul. Through study and contemplation he honed his intellect. Still he could find no peace. Despite his devotion, he could not erase his sense of sin; he could not convince himself that the righteousness God demanded of him was a righteousness he could achieve. "I was one who terribly feared the last judgment and who nevertheless with all my heart wished to be saved."

Salvation came to Luther through study. His internal agonies led him to ponder over and over again the biblical passages that described the righteousness of God. In the intellectual tradition in which he had been trained, that righteousness was equated with law. The righteous person either followed God's law or was punished by God's wrath. It was this understanding that tormented him. "I thought that I had to perform good works till at last through them Jesus would become a friend and gracious to me." But no amount of good works could overcome Luther's feelings of guilt for his sins. Like a man caught in a net, the more he struggled the more entangled he became. For years he wrestled with his problem. Almost from the moment he began lecturing in 1512 he searched for the key to the freedom of his own soul.

It is impossible to know precisely at what moment the door was unlocked. Even before he wrote his Ninety-five Theses, Luther had made the first breakthrough by a unique reading of the writings of Saint Paul. "I pondered night and day until I understood the connection between the righteousness of God and the sentence 'The just shall live by faith.' Then I grasped that the justice of God is the righteousness by which through grace and pure mercy, God justifies us through faith. Immediately I felt that I had been reborn and that I had passed through wide open doors into paradise!" Finally he realized that the righteousness of God was not a burden that humans carried, but a gift that God bestowed. It could not be earned by good works but was freely given to the faithful. To receive God's righteousness one only had to believe in God's infinite mercy. It was this belief that fortified Luther during his years of struggle with both civil and Church powers.

Over the next several years, Luther refined his spiritual philosophy and drew out the implications of his newfound beliefs. His religion was shaped by three interconnected tenets. First came justification by faith alone—*sola fide*. An individual's everlasting salvation came from faith in God's goodness rather than from the performance of good works. Sin was ever present and inescapable. It could not be washed away by penance, and it could not be forgiven by indulgence. Second, faith came only through the knowledge and contemplation of the Word of God—*sola scriptura*. All that was needed to understand the justice and mercy of God was contained in the Bible, the sole authority in all things spiritual. Reading the Word, hearing the Word, expounding upon and studying the Word, this was the path to faith and through faith to salvation. Finally, all who believed in God's righteousness and had achieved their faith through the study of the Bible were equal in God's eyes. No longer was it necessary for men and women to renounce their worldly existence and take up a life consumed by spiritual works. Neither pope nor priest, neither monk nor nun could achieve a higher level of spirituality than the most ordinary citizen. The priesthood was of all believers. Each followed his or her own calling in life and found his or her own faith through Scripture. Ministers and preachers were valuable because they could help others learn God's Word. But they could not confer faith.

Luther's spiritual rebirth and the theology that developed from it posed a fundamental challenge to the Roman Catholic Church. The doctrine of justification by faith alone called into question the Church's emphasis upon the primacy of works—that is, receiving the sacraments administered by the priests and performing acts of charity and devotion. The doctrine that faith was achieved through Scripture weakened the mediating power of the Church by making salvation an individual rather than a collective event. The doctrine of the equality of all believers struck at the vast establishment of religious houses as well as the spiritual hierarchy of the Church from the lowest priest to the pope. Though for centuries the Roman Catholic Church had met doctrinal challenges and had absorbed many seemingly unorthodox ideas, Luther's theology could not be among them. It struck too deeply at the roots of belief, practice, and structure. If Luther was right, then the Roman Catholic Church must be wrong.

Yet for all of the transforming power of these apparently simple ideas, it was not Luther alone who initiated the reform of religion. His obsession with salvation was based on the same impulse that had made indulgences so popular. Before Luther, countless thousands strove for salvation. Justification by faith alone provided an alternative to the combination of works and faith that many Roman Catholics found too difficult to fulfill. Luther's insistence that faith comes only through the study of the Word of God was facilitated by the new learning and the invention of printing. The printing press prepared the ground for the dissemination of his thought as much as it disseminated it. This was a contribution of the Renaissance. Luther's hope for the creation of a spiritual elite, confirmed in their faith and confident of their salvation, readily appealed to the citizens of hundreds of German towns who had already made of themselves a social and economic elite. This was a contribution of the growth of towns. The idea of the equality of all believers meant that all were equally responsible for fulfilling God's commandments. This set secular rulers on an equal footing with the pope at a moment in Western history when they were already challenging papal power in matters of both Church and state. This was a contribution of the formation of states. For all of the painful soul-searching by which he came to his shattering insight, there was embodied in Luther the culmination of changes of which he was only dimly aware.

Lutheranism

The first to feel the seriousness of Luther's challenge to the established order was the reformer himself. The head of his order, a papal legate, and finally the Emperor Charles V all called for Luther to recant his views on indulgences. To all he gave the same infuriating reply that he made to the emperor at the Diet of Worms in 1521: if he could be shown the places in the Bible that contradicted his views he would gladly change them. "I cannot and I will not retract anything since it is neither safe nor right to go against conscience. I cannot do otherwise." In fact, during the three years between the posting of his theses and his appearance before the emperor, Luther came to conclusions much more radical than his initial attack on indulgences. Preparing to contend with papal representatives about the pope's right to issue indulgences, Luther came to believe that the papacy was a human rather than a divine invention. Therefore he denounced both the papacy and the general councils of the Church. In his *Address to the Christian Nobility of the German Nation* (1520) he called upon the princes to take the reform of religion into their own hands. No longer was there hope of compromise. In 1521 the pope excommunicated him and Charles V declared him an enemy of the empire. In both Church and state he was now an outlaw.

But Luther had attracted powerful supporters as well as powerful enemies. Prince Frederick III of Saxony consistently intervened on his behalf, and the delicate international situation forced Luther's chief antagonists to move more slowly than they might have wished. The pope hoped first to keep Charles V off the imperial throne and then to maintain a united front with the German princes against him. Charles V, already locked in his lifelong struggle with the French, needed German military support and peace in his German territories. These factors consistently played into Luther's hands.

While pope and emperor were otherwise occupied, Luther refined his ideas and thus was able to hold his own in the theological debates in which he won important converts. More importantly, as time passed Luther's reputation grew, not only in Germany, but all over Europe. Between 1517 and 1520 he published thirty works, all of which achieved massive sales. Perhaps 300,000 copies of these writings, with the various editions of the Ninety-five Theses leading the way, reached the reading public. His image, with cherubic face and deep-set eyes, became the best known in the world. It was no longer possible to silence him in any traditional fashion. Friends hid him and princes protected him. While in hiding in 1522 he translated Erasmus' New Testament into German. He began writing hymns and alternative services for the mass. In everything he wrote Luther combined a fierce, passionate prose with a simple and direct style that was often powerful enough to make converts.

Yet Luther alone could not sustain what came

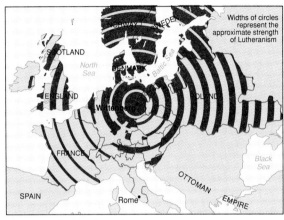

The Spread of Lutheranism

to be called Lutheranism. The Roman Catholic Church had met heresy before and knew how to deal with it. What turned Luther's theology into a movement, which after 1529 came to be known as Protestantism, was the support he received among German princes and within German cities. While Luther's writings had the power to convert, they did not have the power to protect.

There were many reasons that individual princes turned to Luther's theology. First and foremost was sincere religious conviction. Matters of the hereafter were a pressing concern in a world in which the average life span was thirty years and nearly all natural phenomena were inexplicable. And they were more pressing still among the educated elites infected by the new learning and self-confident of their power to reason critically. Yet there were secular reasons as well. The formation of large states had provided a model for civil government, even for the fragmented units of the Holy Roman Empire. On a smaller scale, German princes worked to centralize their administration, protect themselves from predatory neighbors, and increase their revenues. They had long suffered under the burden of papal exactions. Taxes and gifts flowed south to a papacy dominated by Italians. Luther's call for civil rulers to lead their own churches meant that civil rulers could keep their own revenues.

The reformation spread particularly well in

the German cities, especially those that the emperor had granted the status of freedom from the rule of any prince. There the communal aspects of life were strong, and once Protestant ideas were established entire towns adopted them. The cities had long struggled with the tension of the separate jurisdictions of state and Church. Much urban property was owned by the Church, and thus exempt from taxation and law enforcement, and the clergy constituted a significant proportion of urban populations. Reformed religion stressed the equality of clergy and laity and thus the indisputable power of civil authorities. Paradoxically, it was because the cities contained large numbers of priests that Luther's ideas reached them quickly. Many of his earliest students saw towns as fertile ground for preaching the Word. They served urban congregations and began to develop doctrines and practices that, though based on Luther's ideas, were adapted to the circumstances of city life. The reform clergy became integrated into the life of the city in a way that the Catholic clergy had not. They married the daughters of citizens, became citizens themselves, and trained their children in the guilds. Moreover, the imperial free cities were also the center of the printing trade and home to many of the most noted humanists who were initially important in spreading Luther's ideas.

Luther's message held great appeal for the middle orders in the towns. While it was necessary for the leader of a state to support reform if it was to survive, in the cities it was rare for more than a small proportion of the wealthiest citizens to become early adherents to Luther's ideas. Rather it was the petty burghers, lesser merchants, tradesmen, and artisans who led the movements that ultimately gained the approval of city governments. These groups resented the privileges given to priests and members of religious orders who paid no taxes and were exempt from the obligations of citizenship. The level of anticlericalism, always high in Germany, was especially acute in cities that were suffering economic difficulties. In general, the reformation of the cities was a process in which all social classes took part. Pressure from ordinary people and petty traders forced town leaders into action. The evangelism of reforming ministers created converts and an atmosphere of reform. Support from members of the ruling oligarchy both mobilized these pressures and capitalized upon them. Town governments secured their own autonomy over the church, tightening their grip upon the institutions of social control and enhancing the social and economic authority of their members. Once Protestant, city governments took over many of the functions of the religious houses, often converting them into schools or hostels for the poor. Former monks were allowed to enter trades and to become citizens. Former nuns were encouraged to marry. Luther himself married an ex-nun after the dissolution of her convent.

Religious reform appealed to women as well as men, but it affected them differently. Noblewomen were among the most important defenders of Protestant reformers, especially in states in which the prince opposed it. Marguerite of Navarre (1492–1549), sister of Francis I, frequently intervened with her brother on behalf of individual Lutherans who fell afoul of Church authorities. She created her own court in the south of France and stocked it with both humanists and Protestants. Her devotional poem, *Mirror of the Sinful Soul* (1533), inspired women reformers and was translated into English by Elizabeth I. Mary of Hungary (1505–58) served a similar role in the Holy Roman Empire. Sister of both Charles V and Ferdinand I, queen of Hungary and later regent of the

Marguerite of Navarre

Netherlands, she acted as patron to Hungarian reformers. Though Mary was more humanist than Protestant, Luther dedicated an edition of Psalms to her, and she read a number of his works. Her independent religious views infuriated both of her brothers. Bona, wife of Sigismund I of Poland, was especially important in eastern reform. An Italian by birth, Bona (1493–1558) was a central figure in spreading both Renaissance art and humanist learning into Poland. She became one of the largest independent landowners in the state and initiated widespread agricultural and economic reforms. Her private confessor was one of Poland's leading Protestants.

Luther's reforms also offered much to women who were not so highly placed in society. The doctrine of the equality of all believers put men and women on an equal spiritual footing even if it did nothing to break the male monopoly of the ministry. Some Protestant groups saw this as a contradiction and allowed women preachers. But the most important difference that Protestantism made to ordinary women was in the private rather than the public sphere. Family life became the center of faith when salvation was removed from the control of the Church. Luther's marriage led him to a deeper appreciation of the importance of the wife and mother in the family's spirituality. "Next to God's word there is no more precious treasure than holy matrimony."

By following humanist teaching on the importance of educating women of the upper orders and by encouraging literacy, the reformers did much that was uplifting. Girls' schools were founded in a number of German cities and towns-women could use their newly acquired skills in their roles as shopkeepers, family accountants, and teachers of their children. But there were losses as well as gains. The attack upon the worship of saints and especially of the Virgin Mary removed female images from religion. Protestantism was male dominated in a way that Catholicism was not. Moreover, the emphasis upon reading the Bible tended to reinforce the image of women as weak and inherently sinful. This was especially true in the writings of Saint Paul, which were favorite texts of the early reformers. The dissolution of the convents took away from women the one institution that valued their gender and allowed them to pursue a spiritual life outside marriage.

The Spread of Lutheranism

By the end of the 1520s the empire was divided between cities and states that accepted reformed religion and those that adhered to Roman Catholicism. Luther's call for religious reform was sweeping the Continent. Printing presses, traveling merchants, and hordes of students who claimed—not always accurately—to have attended Luther's lectures or sermons spread the message. Large German communities across northern Europe, mostly founded as trading outposts, became focal points for the penetration of reformist ideas. In Livonia the Teutonic Knights

established a Lutheran form of worship that soon took hold all along the shores of the Baltic. Lutheran-inspired reformers seized control of the Polish port city of Gdánsk, which they held for a short time, while neighboring Prussia officially established a Lutheran church. The University of Koenigsberg, founded there in 1545, became a center for Lutheran education. Polish translations of Luther's writings were disseminated into Poland-Lithuania, and Protestant communities were established as far south as Kraków.

Merchants and students carried Luther's ideas into Scandinavia, but there the importance of political leaders was crucial. Christian III (1534–59) of Denmark had been present at the Diet of Worms when Luther made his famous reply to Charles V. Christian was deeply impressed by the reformer and after a ruinous civil war, he confiscated the property of the Catholic church in Denmark and created a reformed religion under Luther's direct supervision. The first Danish translation of the Bible appeared in 1550, and a Danish church service replaced the Latin mass.

Paradoxically, Lutheranism came to Sweden as part of an effort to throw off the yoke of Danish dominance. Here, too, direct connection with Luther provided the first impulses. Olaus Petri (1493–1552) had studied at Wittenberg and returned to preach Lutheran doctrine among the large German merchant community in Stockholm. He was a trained humanist who used both Erasmus' Greek New Testament and Luther's German one to prepare his Swedish translation (1526). When Gustav I Vasa (1523–60) led a successful uprising against the Danes and became king of Sweden, he immediately saw the advantages of breaking the strength of the Catholic church, which had long supported Danish hegemony in Sweden. He encouraged the spread of Protestant ideas and allowed Petri to continue his Swedish translations of the mass and the Lutheran service. Under the protection of the monarchy Lutheranism flourished in Scandinavia, where it remains the dominant religion to this day.

Luther's impact extended into central Europe. There the feebleness of the prince, rather than his strength, aided reform. Ferdinand I was the titular ruler of Hungary and Bohemia. In Hungary, Ottoman military victories and a rival to his throne weakened Ferdinand. He could not afford to alienate either the nobles or the towns that adopted reformed religion. Luther's ideas were quickly imported into the German areas of Hungary, but surprisingly, they also spread rapidly within the Magyar areas. János Sylvester, a Hungarian humanist, translated the New Testament into Magyar and Mátyás Bíró, who had studied under Luther at Wittenberg, became the leading Protestant theologian in Transylvania.

Neighboring Bohemia had had a reforming tradition of its own that antedated Luther. Though the teachings of Jan Hus (1373–1415) had been condemned by the Catholic church, Hussitism was in fact the all but established religion in most parts of Bohemia. Ferdinand was bound by law to allow its moderate practice. Hussites had already initiated many of the reforms insisted upon by Luther: the mass was said in Czech, and the Bible had been translated into the vernacular. Most importantly, the laity took the wine as well as the bread at communion. Hussites believed that communion in both forms was mandated by the Bible. This was the real issue that separated them from Roman Catholics, for the Hussites refused to accept the traditional view that the authority of either the pope or the general council of the Church could alter God's command. On all these issues, Hussites and Lutherans shared a common program. But the Hussites were conservative in almost everything else. Having walked so far down the path themselves, they refused to go any further with Luther. While the German communities in Bohemia accepted the core of Lutheran doctrine, most Czechs rejected justification by faith alone and maintained their own practices. This split within Bohemian reformed religion weakened both groups.

As important as Protestant ideas were in northern and central Europe, it was in the Swiss towns of the empire that they proved most fertile. Here was planted the second generation of reformers, theologians who drew from Luther's insights radical new conclusions. In the east, Huldrych Zwingli (1484–1531) brought reformed religion to the town of Zurich. Although Zwingli was born within weeks of Luther, he developed his brand of reformed theology in a different context. Educated at the University of Basel and deeply influenced by humanist thought early in his career, Zwingli was a preacher among the Swiss mercenary troops that fought for the empire. He survived the dreadful battle of Marig-

nano (1515), where the charging French horsemen slaughtered the Swiss infantry, and he developed a lifelong opposition to selling "blood for money." He was thus a Swiss patriot not in the national sense, but in opposition to the demands of the emperor on one hand and of the pope on the other. In 1516 he met Erasmus in Basel and under his influence began a study of the Greek writings of the Church Fathers and of the New Testament. Zwingli was also influenced by reports of Luther's defiance of the pope, for his own antipapal views were already developing. Perhaps most decisively for his early development, in 1519 Zwingli was stricken by plague. In his life-and-death struggle he came to a profoundly personal realization of the power of God's mercy.

These experiences became the basis for the reform theology Zwingli preached in Zurich. He believed that the Church had to recover its earlier purity and to reject the innovations in practices brought in by successive popes and general councils. In 1522 he preached against fasting during Lent. This led to a controversy with the local bishop and ultimately to a formal disputation in 1523 in which Zwingli expounded his faith. He stressed the equality of believers, justification by faith alone, and the sufficiency of the gospel as authority for church practice. He attacked indulgences, penance, clerical celibacy, prayers to the Virgin, statues and images in churches, and a long list of other abuses. He also stressed that the mass was to be viewed as a commemorative event rather than one which involved the real presence of Christ. He preferred to call the service the Lord's Supper. His arguments were so effective that the town council adopted them as the basis for a reform of religion and encouraged Zwingli to develop a new church service to be used in Zurich's churches.

The principles Zwingli preached quickly spread to neighboring Swiss states. He participated in formal religious disputations in both Bern and Basel. In both places his plea for a simple, unadorned religious practice met widespread approval. Practical as well as theological, Zwingli's reforms were carried out by the civil government with which he allied himself. This was not the same as the protection that princes had given to Lutherans. Rather, in the places that came under Zwingli's influence, there was an important integration of church and state.

Zwingli organized a formal military alliance of the Protestant Swiss towns. For him, the Bible carried a social message and it is fitting that he died on the battlefield defending the state. He stressed the divine origins of civil government and the importance of the magistrate as an agent of Christian reform. "A church without the magistrate is mutilated and incomplete." This theocratic idea—that the leaders of the state and the leaders of the church were linked together—became the basis for further social and political reform.

The Protestant Reformation

By the middle of the 1530s Protestant reform had entered a new stage. Luther did not intend to form a new religion; his struggle had been with Rome. Before he could build he had to tear down—his religion was one of protest. Most of his energy was expended in attack and counterattack. The second generation of reformers faced a different task. The new reformers were the church builders who had to systematize doctrine for a generation that had already accepted religious reform. Their challenge was to draw out the logic of reformed ideas and to create enduring structures for reformed churches. The problems they faced were as much institutional as doctrinal. How was the new church to be governed in the absence of the traditional hierarchy? How could discipline be enforced when members of the reformed community went astray? What was the proper relationship between the community of believers and civil authority? Whatever the failings of the Roman Catholic Church, it had ready answers to these critical questions. The first generation of reformers had thrown out the stagnant bathwater of ecclesiastical abuses; it was left to the second generation to discover if they had thrown out the baby and the bathtub as well.

Geneva and Calvin

The Reformation came late to Geneva. In the sixteenth century Geneva was under the dual government of the Duchy of Savoy, which owned most of the surrounding rural areas, and the Catholic bishop of the town, who was frequently a Savoy client. The Genevans also had their own town council, which traditionally struggled for power against the bishop. By the 1530s the council had gained the upper hand. The council confiscated Church lands and institutions, secularized the Church's legal powers, and forced the bishop and most of his administrators to flee the city. War with Savoy inevitably followed and Geneva would certainly have been crushed into submission except for its alliance with neighboring Bern, a potent military power among the Swiss towns.

Geneva was saved and was free to follow its own course in religious matters. Under Zwingli's influence, Bern had become Protestant, and it might have been expected that Geneva would adopt this model even though French rather than German was the predominant language of the city. Some Protestant preachers arrived in Geneva to propagate reformed religion and after a public disputation the town council abolished the mass. In 1536 the adult male citizens of the city voted to become Protestant. But as yet there was no reformer in Geneva to establish a Protestant program and no clear definition of what that program might be.

Martin Luther had started out to become a lawyer and ended up a priest. John Calvin started out to become a priest and ended up a lawyer. The difference tells much about each man. Calvin (1509–64) was born in France, the son of a bishop's secretary. His education was based on humanist principles, and he learned Greek and Hebrew, studied theology, and received a legal degree from the University of Orléans. Around the age of twenty he converted to Lutheranism. He described the experience as "unexpected," but it had predictable results. Francis I had determined to root Protestants out of France and Calvin fled Paris. Persecution of Protestants continued in France and one of Calvin's close friends was burned for heresy. These events left an indelible impression upon him. In 1535 he left France for Basel, where he wrote and published the first edition of his *Institutes of the Christian Religion* (1536), a defense of French Protestants against persecution. Directed to Francis I, it set out "the whole sum of godliness and whatever it is necessary to know of the doctrine of salvation." Calvin returned briefly to France to wind up his personal affairs, and then decided to settle in Strasbourg, where he could retire from public affairs and live out his days as a scholar.

To Calvin, providence guided all human action. He could have no better evidence for this belief than what happened next. War between France and the empire clogged the major highways to Strasbourg. Soldiers constantly menaced travelers and Protestants could expect the worst from both sides. Thus Calvin and his companions detoured around the armies and passed through Geneva. How Calvin's presence there came to be known remains a mystery, but when Guillaume Farel (1489–1565), one of Geneva's leading Protestant reformers, heard of it, he quickly made his way to the inn where Calvin was staying. Farel implored Calvin to remain in Geneva and lead its reformation. Calvin was not interested. Farel tried every means of persuasion he knew until, in exasperation, Farel declared "that God would curse my retirement if I should withdraw and refuse to help when the necessity was so urgent. By this imprecation I was so terror-struck that I gave up the journey that I had undertaken." For a quarter of a century, Calvin labored to bring order to the Genevan church.

Calvin's greatest contributions to religious reform came in church structure and discipline. He had studied the writings of the first generation of reformers and accepted without question justification by faith alone and the biblical foundation of religious authority. Like Luther and Zwingli he believed that salvation came from God's grace. But more strongly than his predecessors he believed that the gift of faith was granted only to some and that each individual's salvation or damnation was predestined before birth. "We call predestination God's eternal decree. For all are not created in equal condition; rather, eternal life is foreordained for some, eternal damnation for others." The doctrine of predestination was a traditional one, but Calvin emphasized it differently and brought it to the center of the problem of faith. "Many are called but few are chosen," Calvin quoted from the Bible. Those who were predestined to salvation were obliged to govern; those who were predestined to damnation were obliged to be governed. Thus for the church that Calvin erected, discipline was the central concern.

Calvin structured the institution of the Genevan church in four parts. First were the pastors who preached the Word to their congregations. There were fewer than ten pastors in Geneva in the early 1540s, fewer than twenty by the time of Calvin's death, a far cry from the five hundred priests who administered the sacraments there under Catholicism. While the pastors preached, the doctors, the second element in Calvin's church, studied and wrote. The doctors were scholars who mastered the difficult portions of the Bible and who increased the stock of learned pastors by their teaching. In the beginning, Calvin was the only Genevan doctor, but after he helped to establish the University of Geneva in 1559, there was a ready supply of learned theologians.

Pastors and doctors made up the top tier of the official church; deacons and elders the lower. Deacons, the third element in Calvin's four-part structure, were laymen chosen by the congregation to oversee the institutions of social welfare run by the church. These included the hospitals and schools that cared for the sick and the poor and instructed the young. The last element were the elders of the church, who were its governors in all moral matters. They were the most controversial part of Calvin's establishment and the most fundamental. They had the power to discipline. Chosen from among the elite of the city, the twelve elders enforced the strict Calvinist moral code that extended into all aspects of private life. The elders and the pastors met each week in a body known as the consistory to examine violations of God's laws; for them was reserved the ultimate sanction of excommunication. Offenses ranged from trivial superstitions—a woman wrapping a walnut containing a spider around the neck of her sick husband—to cases of blasphemy. Sexual offenses were the most common. Adultery and fornication were vigorously suppressed and prostitutes, who had nearly become a recognized guild in the early sixteenth century, were expelled from Geneva.

The structure that Calvin gave to the Genevan church soon became the basis for reforms throughout the Continent. The Calvinist church was self-governing, independent of the state, and therefore capable of surviving and even flourishing in a hostile environment. Expanded in several subsequent editions, *The Institutes of the Christian Religion* became the most influential work of Protestant theology. It had begun as an effort to extend Protestantism to France, and Calvin never abandoned hope that his homeland would be converted. Waves of Calvinist-educated pastors returned to France in the mid-sixteenth century and established churches along Calvinist lines. Calvinism spread north to the Low Countries, where it became the basis for Dutch Protestantism, and east to Poland, where it flourished in Lithuania. It reached places untouched by Luther and revitalized reform where Lutheranism had been suppressed. Perhaps its greatest impact was in Britain, where the reformation took place not once but twice.

The English Reformation

The king of England wanted a divorce. Henry VIII had been married to Catherine of Aragon (1485–1536) as long as he had been king and she had borne him no male heir to carry on his line. Catherine of Aragon had done her duty: in ten years she had given birth to six children and endured several miscarriages. Yet only one daughter, Mary, survived. Nothing so important as the lack of a male heir could happen by accident, and Henry came to believe that it was God's punishment for his marriage. Catherine had been mar-

ried first to Henry's older brother, who had died as a teenager, and there was at least one scriptural prohibition against marrying a brother's wife. A papal dispensation had been provided for the marriage, and now Henry wanted a papal dispensation for an annulment. For three years his case ground its way through the papal courts. Catherine of Aragon was the aunt of the Emperor Charles V, and the emperor had taken her side in the controversy. With imperial power in Italy at its height, the pope was content to hear all of the complex legal and biblical precedents argued at leisure.

By 1533 Henry could wait no longer. He had already impregnated Anne Boleyn (ca. 1507–36), one of the ladies-in-waiting at his court, and if the child—which Henry was certain would be a boy—was to be legitimate a marriage would have to take place at once. Legislation was prepared in Parliament to prevent papal interference in the decisions of England's courts, and Thomas Cranmer (1489–1556), archbishop of Canterbury, England's highest ecclesiastical officer, agreed to annul Henry's first marriage and celebrate his second. This was the first step in a complete break with Rome. Under the guidance of Thomas Cromwell (ca. 1485–1540), the English Parliament passed statute after statute that made Henry supreme head of the church in England and owner of its vast wealth. Monasteries were dissolved and a Lutheran service was introduced. England's first reformation came as a result of the "King's Great Matter." On 7 September 1533, Anne Boleyn gave birth not to the expected son, but to a daughter, the future Queen Elizabeth I.

Henry's reformation was an act of state, but the English Reformation was not. There was an English tradition of dissent from the Roman church that stretched back to the fourteenth century and that had survived even the most determined efforts to suppress it. Anticlericalism was especially virulent in the towns, where citizens refused to pay fees to priests for performing services like burial. And humanist ideas flourished in England, where Thomas More, John Colet, and a host of others supported both the new learning and its efforts to reform spiritual life. The English were as susceptible as other Europeans to Luther's ideas, which crossed the Channel with German merchants and English travelers. Luther's attack on ritual and the mass and his emphasis on Scripture and faith echoed the lost

This painting shows a Calvinist service in Lyon, France, in 1564. The sexes are segregated and the worshipers are seated according to rank. An hourglass times the preacher's sermon.

Lollard program and found many recruits in London and the northern port towns.

Protestantism grew slowly in England because it was vigorously repressed. Like Francis I and Charles V, Henry VIII viewed actual attacks on the established church as potential attacks on the established state. The consolidation of the Tudor monarchy was too recent for him not to be concerned with its stability. Henry had earned the title Defender of the Faith from the pope in 1521 for authoring an attack on Luther. Bonfires of Lutheran books lit the English skies. Small groups of Protestants at Cambridge and Oxford universities were sniffed out and hunted down by Henry's agents. Some made public recantations, some fled to the Continent, one—Thomas Bilney—went to the stake. The first published English translation of the New Testament, made by William Tyndale in 1525, had to be smuggled into England. As sensitivity to the abuses of the Church grew and Lutheran ideas spread, official censorship and persecution sharpened.

Pope Clement VIII's confirmation of the title Defender of the Faith, given to Henry VIII by Pope Leo X in recognition of Henry's attack on Luther and his defense of the teachings of the Church.

Henry's divorce unleashed a groundswell of support for religious change. The king's own religious beliefs remained a secret, but Anne Boleyn and Thomas Cromwell sponsored Lutheran reforms and Thomas Cranmer put them into practice. Religion was legislated through Parliament and the valuable estates of the Church were sold to the gentry. These practices found favor with both the legal profession and the landed elites and made Protestantism more palatable among these conservative groups. It was in the reign of Edward VI (1547–53), Henry's son by his third wife, that the central doctrinal and devotional changes were made.

Though they were Protestant in tenor, there remained compromises and deliberate ambiguities. The chantries were abolished and with them masses for the dead. Church service was now conducted in English and the first two English Prayer Books were created. The mass was reinterpreted along Zwinglian lines and became the Lord's Supper, the altar became the communion table, and the priest became the minister. Preaching became the center of the church service and concern over the education of learned ministers resulted in commissions to examine and reform the clergy.

Beginning in the 1530s, state repression turned against Catholics. Those who would not swear the new oaths of allegiance or recognize the legality of Henry VIII's marriage suffered for their beliefs as the early Protestants had suffered for theirs. Thomas More and over forty others paid with their lives for their opposition. Others took up arms against the government, marrying economic and political grievances to religious ones. An uprising in the north in 1536, known as the Pilgrimage of Grace, posed the most serious threat to the English Crown since the Wars of the Roses. Gentry and common people opposed the dissolution of the monasteries and feared for provision for their spiritual needs. Henry's ability to suppress the Pilgrimage of Grace owed more to his political power than to the conversion of his governing classes to Protestantism. Edward VI's government faced a similar rising in 1549 when it attempted to introduce a new and more Protestant prayer book. Catholicism continued to flourish in England, surviving underground during the reigns of Henry and Edward, and reemerging under Mary I (1553–58).

Mary Tudor was her mother's child. The first woman to rule England, she held to the Catholic beliefs in which Catherine of Aragon had raised her, and she vowed to bring the nation back to her mother's church. When Edward VI died, the English ruling elite opted for political legitimacy rather than religious ideology in supporting Mary against a Protestant pretender to the throne. The new queen was as good as her word. She reestablished papal sovereignty, abolished Protestant worship, and introduced a crash program of education in the universities to train a new generation of priests. The one thing that Mary could not achieve was restoration of monastic properties and Church lands. They had been scattered irretrievably and any attempt at confiscation from the landed elite would surely have been met with insurrection. Mary had to be content with reestablishing orthodoxy. She fought fire with fire. Catholic retribution for the blood of their martyrs was not long in coming. Cranmer and three other bishops were burned for heresy, and over 270 others, mostly commoners, were consigned to the flames.

Nearly 800 Protestants fled the country rather than suffer a similar fate. These Marian exiles, as they came to be called, settled in a number of reformed communities, Zurich, Frankfurt, and Geneva among them. There they imbibed the second generation of Protestant ideas, especially Calvinism, and from there they began a propaganda campaign to keep reformed religion alive in England. It was the Marian exiles who were chiefly responsible for the second English reformation, which began in 1558 when Mary died and her half-sister, Elizabeth I (1558–1603), came to the throne.

Under Elizabeth England returned to Protestantism. The rapid reversals of established religion were more than disconcerting to laity and clergy alike. Imagine the experience of ordinary churchgoers. For all their lives they had prayed to the Virgin Mary for aid and comfort. One day all images of the Virgin disappeared from the church. The Latin mass was replaced by a whole new English service. Then the Latin mass returned and back came the images of the Virgin. Five years later the Virgin was gone again and the English service was restored. Imagine the plight of a clergyman who questioned the vow of chastity in the 1540s. Prohibited from marrying under Henry VIII, he was encouraged to marry under Edward VI. When Mary came to the throne he had to put his wife aside and deny the legitimacy of his children. At Elizabeth's accession he was married again—if he could find his wife and if she had not taken another husband. The Elizabethan reforms put an end to these uncertainties.

But what was reestablished was not what had come before. Even the most advanced reforms during Edward's reign now seemed too moderate for the returning exiles. Against Elizabeth's wishes the English church adopted the Calvinist doctrine of predestination and the simplification (but not wholesale reorganization) of the structure of the church. But it did not become a model of thoroughgoing reformation. The Thirty-nine Articles (1563) continued the English tradition of compromising points of disputed doctrine and of maintaining traditional practices wherever possible. The Calvinism that the exiles learned abroad was more demanding than the Calvinism than the queen practiced at home.

The Reformation of the Radicals

Schism breeds schism. That was the stick with which Catholic church and civil authorities beat Luther from the beginning. By attacking the authority of the established church and flouting the authority of the established state he was fomenting social upheaval. It was a charge to which he was particularly sensitive. He insisted that his own ideas buttressed rather than subverted authority, especially civil authority under whose protection he had placed the Church. As early as 1525 peasants in Swabia appealed to Luther for support in their social rebellion. They based some of their most controversial demands, such as the abolition of tithes and labor service, on biblical authority. Luther offered them no comfort. "Let every person be subject to the governing authorities with fear and reverence," he quoted from the Bible while instructing rebels to lay down their arms and await their just rewards in heaven.

But Luther's ideas had a life of their own. He clashed with Erasmus over free will and with Zwingli over the mass. Toward the end of his life he felt he was holding back the floodgates against the second generation of Protestant thinkers. Time and again serious reformers wanted to take one or another of his doctrines further than he was willing to go himself. The water was seeping in everywhere.

The most dangerous threat to the establishment of an orthodox Protestantism came from groups who were described, not very precisely, as Anabaptists. *Anabaptist* was a term of abuse. Though it identified people who practiced adult baptism—literally "baptism again"—the label was mainly used to tar religious opponents with the brush of extremism. For over a hundred years it defined the outcast from the Protestant fold. New ideas were branded Anabaptist to discredit them, religious enthusiasts were labeled Anabaptists to expel them. Catholics and Protestants both used the term to describe what they were not and thereby defined what they were.

Anabaptists appeared in a number of German and Swiss towns in the 1520s. Taking seriously the doctrine of justification by faith, Anabaptists argued that only believers could be members of the true church of God. Those who were not of God could not be members of his church. While Catholics, Lutherans, and Calvinists incorporated all members of society into the church, Anabaptists excluded all but true believers. As baptism was the sacrament through which entry into the church took place, Anabaptists reasoned that it was a sacrament for adults rather than infants. Though this practice was as much symbolic as substantive, it was a practice that horrified others. Infant baptism was a core doctrine for both Catholics and Protestants. It was one of only two sacraments that remained in reformed religion. It symbolized the acceptance of Christ and without it eternal salvation was impossible. Luther, Zwingli, and Calvin agreed that infant baptism was biblical in origin and all wrote vigorously in its defense. It was a doctrine with practical import. Unbaptized infants who died could not be accepted in heaven, and infant mortality was appallingly common.

Thus the doctrine of Anabaptism posed a psychological as well as a doctrinal threat to the reformers. But the practice of adult baptism paled in significance to many of the other conclusions that religious radicals derived from the principle of *sola scriptura*—by the Word alone. Some groups argued the case that since true Christians were only those who had faith, all others must be cast out of the church. These true Christians formed small separate sects. Many believed that their lives were guided by the Holy Spirit who directed them from within. Both men and women could give testimony of revelations that appeared to them or of mystical experiences. Some went further and denied the power of civil authority over true believers. They would have nothing to do with the state, refusing to pay taxes, perform military obligations, or give oaths. "The Sword must not be used by Christians even in self-defense. Neither should Christians go to law or undertake magisterial duties." Some argued for the community of goods among believers and rejected private property. Others literally followed

passages in the Old Testament that suggested polygamy and promiscuity.

Wherever they settled, these small bands of believers were persecuted to the brutal extent of the laws of heresy. Catholics burned them, Protestants drowned them, and they were stoned and clubbed out of their communities. Though Anabaptists were never a large group within the context of the Protestant churches, they represented an alternative to mainstream views, whether Lutheran or Calvinist, that was both attractive and persistent. There was enough substance in their ideas and enough sincerity in their patient sufferings that they continued to recruit followers as they were driven from town to town, from Germany into the Swiss cities, from Switzerland into Bohemia and Hungary.

There on the eastern edges of the empire the largest groups of Anabaptists finally settled. Though all practiced adult baptism, only some held goods in common or remained pacifist. Charismatic leaders such as Balthasar Hubmaier (1485–1528) and Jacob Hutter (d. 1536) spread Anabaptism to Moravia in southern Bohemia, where they converted a number of the nobility to their views. They procured land for their communities, which came to be known as the Moravian Brethren. The Moravian Anabaptists ultimately split on the question of pacifism when the advancing Turkish armies posed the problem starkly. Anabaptists remained a target of official persecution and Hubmaier, Hutter, and a number of other leaders met violent deaths. But the Moravian communities were able to survive and to spread their movement throughout Hungary and Poland. Independent groups existed in England and throughout northwest Europe, where Menno Simons (1496–1561), a Dutch Anabaptist, spent his life organizing bands of followers who came to be known as Mennonites.

The Catholic Reformation

Like a rolling wave Protestant reform slapped up across the face of Europe, but the rock of the Roman Catholic Church endured. Though pieces of the universal church crumbled away, in northern Germany, Switzerland, Bohemia, Scandinavia, England, and Scotland, the dense mass remained in southern Germany, Italy, Poland-Lithuania, Spain, France, and Ireland. Catholics felt the same impulses toward a more fulfilling religious life as did Protestants and complained of the same abuses of clerical, state, and papal powers. But the Catholic response was to reform the Church from within. A new personal piety was stressed, which led to the founding of additional spiritual orders. The ecclesiastical hierarchy became more concerned with pastoral care and initiated reforms of the clergy at the parish level. The challenge of converting other races, Asians and Amerindians especially, led to the formation of missionary orders and to a new emphasis on preaching and education. Protestantism itself revitalized Catholicism. Pope and emperor met the challenge of religious reform with all of the resources at their disposal. If anything, Roman Catholicism was stronger at the end of the era of religious reformation than it had been at the beginning.

The Catholic Revival

The quest for individual spiritual fulfillment dominated later medieval Roman Catholicism. Erasmus, Luther, and Zwingli were all influenced by a Catholic spiritual movement known as the New Piety. It was propagated in Germany by the Brethren of the Common Life, a lay organization that stressed the importance of personal meditation upon the life of Christ. The *Imitation of Christ* (1427) the central text of the New Piety, commonly attributed to Thomas à Kempis (1379–1471), was among the most influential works of the later Middle Ages with seventy editions printed before 1500. The Brethren taught that a Christian life should be lived according to Christ's dictates as expressed in the Sermon on the Mount. They instructed their pupils to lead a simple ascetic life with personal devotion at its core. These were the lessons that the young Erasmus found so liberating and the young Luther so stifling.

The New Piety with its emphasis on a simple personal form of religious practice was a central influence upon Christian humanism. It is important to realize that humanism developed within the context of Catholic education and that many churchmen embraced the new learning and supported educational reform or patronized works of humanist scholarship. The Polyglot Bible, the

first new translation project of the sixteenth century, was organized by Cardinal Jiménez de Cisneros (1436–1517), Archbishop of Toledo and Primate of Spain. The greatest educational reformer in England, John Colet (1467–1519) was dean of Saint Paul's, London's cathedral church. Without any of his famed irony, Erasmus dedicated his Greek Bible to the pope. Though they set out to reform education and to provide better texts through which Christian learning could be accomplished, the leading Christian humanists remained within the Catholic Church even after many of their criticisms formed the basis of Protestant reforms.

This combination of piety and humanism imbued the ecclesiastical reforms initiated by Church leaders. Archbishop Jiménez de Cisneros, who also served as Inquistor-General of the Spanish Inquisition, undertook a wide-ranging reorganization of Spanish religious life in the late fifteenth century. He tackled the Herculean task of reforming the parish clergy in his diocese. He emphasized the need for priests to explain the gospel to their congregations and to instruct children in Church doctrine. Jiménez de Cisneros also initiated reforms in the religious houses, especially within his own Franciscan order. Though not every project was successful, Jiménez de Cisneros' program took much of the sting out of Protestant attacks on clerical abuse, and there was never a serious Protestant movement in Spain.

The most influential reforming bishop was Gian Matteo Giberti (1495–1543) of Verona. Like Jiménez de Cisneros, Giberti believed that a bishop must be a pastor rather than an administrator. After a period of service in Rome, Giberti returned to live in his diocese and made regular visits to all of its parishes. Using his own frugal life as an example, Giberti rigorously enforced vows, residency, and the pastoral duties of the clergy. "The priests in this diocese are marked men; the unworthy are removed from their offices; the jails are full of their concubines; sermons for the people are preached incessantly and study is encouraged," came the report after one of his tours. He founded almshouses to aid the poor and orphanages to house the homeless. In Verona Giberti established a printing press, which turned out editions of the central works of Roman Catholicism, especially the writings of Augustine.

The most important indication of the

reforming spirit within the Roman church was the foundation of new religious orders in the early sixteenth century. Devotion to a spiritual life of sacrifice was the chief characteristic of the lay and clerical orders that had flourished throughout the Middle Ages. In one French diocese, the number of clergy quadrupled in the last half of the fifteenth century, and while entrants to the traditional orders of Franciscans and Dominicans did not rise as quickly, the growth of lay communities like the Brethren of the Common Life attested to the continuing appeal of Catholic devotionalism.

Devotionalism was particularly strong in Italy where a number of new orders received papal charters. The Capuchins were founded by the Italian peasant Matteo de Bascio (ca. 1495–1552). He sought to follow the strictest rule of the life of Saint Francis of Assisi, a path that even the so-called Observant Franciscans had found too arduous. Bascio won admiration for his charitable works among the poor and the victims of the plague in the late 1520s and ultimately secured approval for the establishment of a small community devoted to penance and good works. In contrast, the Theatines were established by a group of well-to-do Italian priests who also wished to lead a more austere devotional existence than was to be found in the traditional orders. Like the Capuchins they accepted a life of extreme poverty, in which even begging was only a last resort. Their small house in Rome became a center for intellectual spirituality that nurtured two subsequent popes. Throughout Italy spiritual groups coalesced, some to become permanent orders like the Capuchins and Theatines, some to remain loose affiliations.

This spiritual revival spread all over Catholic Europe and was not limited to male orders. In Spain, Saint Teresa of Ávila (1515–82) led the reform of the Carmelites. From an early age she had had mystical visions and had entered a convent near her home. But her real spiritual awakening came when she was forty. She believed that women had to withdraw totally from the world around them in order to achieve true devotion. Against the wishes of the male superiors of her order she founded a convent to put her beliefs into practice and began writing devotional tracts like *The Way of Perfection* (1583). Teresa was ultimately granted the right to establish convents throughout Castile, and she supervised the organization of sixteen religious houses for women. In 1535 Angela Merici (ca. 1474–1540) established another female order. The Ursulines were one of the most original of the new foundations, composed of young unmarried girls who remained with their families but lived chaste lives devoted to the instruction of other women. The group met together monthly and submitted to the discipline of a superior, but otherwise they rejected both the cloistered monastic life and vows. The Ursuline movement, begun in northern Italy, spread into France and helped provide women with education and with moral role models.

Loyola's Pilgrimage

At first sight Saint Ignatius Loyola (1491–1556) appears an unlikely candidate to lead one of the most vital movements for religious reform in the sixteenth century. The thirteenth child of a Spanish noble family, Loyola trained for a military life in the service of Castile. He began his career as an administrative official and then became a soldier. In 1521 he was one of the garrison defenders when the French besieged Pamplona. A cannonball shattered his leg and he was carried home for a long enforced convalescence. There he slowly and carefully read the only books in the castle, a life of Christ and a history of the saints. His reading inspired him. Before he had sought glory and renown in battle. But when he compared the truly heroic deeds of the saints to his own vainglorious exploits, he decided to give his life over to spirituality.

Loyola was not a man to do things by halves. He resolved to model his life on the sufferings of the saints about whom he had read. He renounced his worldly goods and endured a year-long regimen of physical abstinence and spiritual nourishment in the town of Manresa. He deprived himself of food and sleep for long periods and underwent a regimen of seven hours of daily prayer, supplemented by nearly continuous religious contemplation. "But when he went to bed great enlightenment, great spiritual consolations often came to him, so that he lost much of the time he had intended for sleeping." During this period of intense concentration he first began to have visions, which later culminated in a mystical experience in which Christ called him directly to his service.

Like Luther, Loyola was tormented by his inability to achieve grace through penance, but unlike Luther he redoubled his efforts. At Manresa Loyola encountered the *Imitation of Christ*, which profoundly influenced his conversion. He recorded the techniques he used during this vigil in *The Spiritual Exercises*, which became a handbook for Catholic devotion. In 1523, crippled and barefoot, he made a pilgrimage to Jerusalem, where he intended to stay and battle the infidel. But he was dissuaded from this course and returned to Spain intent upon becoming a priest.

By this time Loyola had taken on a distinctive appearance that attracted both followers and suspicion. Twice the Spanish ecclesiastical authorities summoned him to be examined for heresy. In 1528 he decided to complete his studies in France. Education in France brought with it a broadening of horizons that was so important in the movement that Loyola was to found. He entered the same college that Calvin had just left, and it is more than likely that he came into contact with the Protestant and humanist ideas that were then in vogue. Given his own devotional experiences, Protestantism held little attraction. While in France, Loyola and a small group of his friends decided to form a brotherhood after they became priests. They devoted themselves to the cure of souls and took personal vows of poverty, chastity, and obedience to the pope. On a pilgrimage to Rome, Loyola and his followers again attracted the attention of ecclesiastical authorities. Loyola explained his mission to them and in 1540 won the approval of Pope Paul III to establish a new holy order, the Society of Jesus.

Loyola's Society was founded at a time when the spiritual needs of the church were being extended beyond the confines of Europe. Loyola volunteered his followers, who came to be known as Jesuits, to serve in the remotest parts of the world, and this offer was soon accepted. One disciple, Francis Xavier (1506–52), was sent to Portugal, where he embarked with an expedition to the East. For ten years Xavier made converts to Catholicism in the Portuguese port cities in the East and then in India and Japan. Other Jesuits became missionaries to the New World, where they offered Christian consolation to the Amerindian communities. By 1556 the Society of Jesus had grown from ten to a thousand and Loyola had become a full-time administrator in Rome.

Loyola never abandoned the military images that had dominated his youth. He thought of the world as an all-consuming struggle between the forces of God and Satan. "It is my will to conquer the whole world and all of my enemies." He enlisted his followers in military terms. The Jesuits were "soldiers of God" who served " beneath the banner of the Cross." Loyola's most fundamental innovation in these years was the founding of schools to train recruits for his order. Jesuit training was rigorous. The period of the novitiate was extended and a second period of secular education was added. Since they were being prepared for an active rather than a contemplative life, Jesuits were not cloistered during their training. At first Loyola wanted to train only those who wished to be missionaries. When this proved impractical, Jesuit schools were opened to the laity and lay education became one of the Jesuits' most important functions. Loyola lived to see the establishment of nearly a hundred colleges and seminaries and the spread of his order throughout the world. He died while at prayer.

The Counter-Reformation

The Jesuits were both the culmination of one wave of Catholic reform and the advance guard of another. They combined the piety and devotion that stretched from medieval mysticism through humanism, diocesan reforms, and the foundations of new spiritual orders. But they also represented an aggressive Catholic response that was determined to meet Protestantism head on and repel it. This was the Church militant. Old instruments like the Inquisition were revived, and new weapons like the Index of prohibited books were forged. But the problems of fighting Protestantism were not only those of combating Protestant ideas. Like oil and water, politics and religion failed to combine. The emperor and the hierarchy of the German church, where Protestantism was strong, demanded thoroughgoing reform of the Catholic church; the pope and the hierarchy of the Italian church, where Protestantism was weak, resisted the call. As head of the Catholic church, the pope was distressed by the spread of heresy in the lands of the empire. As head of a large Italian city-state the pope was consoled by the weakening of the power of his Spanish rival. Brothers in Christ, pope and emperor were mor-

The Council of Trent, painted by Titian in 1586. Despite interruptions and delays, the Council arrived at a definitive restatement of Catholic doctrine, even though it failed at the original goal of reconciliation with the Protestants.

tal enemies in everything else. Throughout the Catholic states of Germany came the urgent cry for a reforming council of the Church. But the voices were muffled as they crossed the Alps and made their way down the Italian peninsula.

At the instigation of the emperor, the first serious preparations for a general council of the Church were made in the 1530s. The papacy warded it off. The complexities of international diplomacy were one factor—the French king was even less anxious to bring peace to the empire than was the pope—and the complexities of papal politics were another. The powers of a general council in relation to the powers of the papacy had never been clarified. Councils were usually the product of crises and crises were never the best times to settle constitutional matters. Hard cases make bad law. After the advent and spread of Protestantism, successive popes had little reason to believe that in this gravest crisis of all a council would be mindful of papal prerogatives. In fact, Catholic reformers were as bitter in their denunciations of papal abuses as were Protestants. The second attempt to arrange a general council of the Church occurred in the early 1540s. Again the papacy warded it off.

These factors ensured that when a general council of the Church did finally meet, its task would not be an easy one. The emperor wanted the council in Germany, the pope wanted it in Italy. The northern churches, French and German alike, wanted reforms of the papacy; the papacy wanted a restatement of orthodox doctrine. The Spanish church wanted reform along the principles set down by Jiménez de Cisneros; for exam-

ple, that bishops must be made resident in their dioceses. The papacy needed bishops to serve as administrators in Rome. Many princes whose states were divided among Catholics and Protestants wanted compromises that might accommodate both. Ferdinand I, King of Bohemia, saw the council as an opportunity to bring the Hussites back into the fold. He wanted to allow the laity to take communion in both kinds and the clergy to marry. Charles V and the German bishops wanted the leading Protestant church authorities to offer their own compromises on doctrine that might form a basis for reuniting the empire. The papacy wanted traditional Church doctrine reasserted.

The general council of the Church that finally met in Trent from 1545 to 1563 thus had nearly unlimited potential for disaster. It began in compromise—Trent was an Italian town under the government of the emperor—but ended in total victory for the views of the papacy. For all of the papacy's seeming weaknesses—the defections of England and the rich north German territories cut into papal revenues and Italy was under Spanish occupation—an Italian pope always held the upper hand at the council. Fewer than a third of the delegates came from outside Italy. The French looked upon the council suspiciously and played only a minor role, and the emperor forbade his bishops to attend after the council moved to Bologna. While 270 bishops attended one or another of the council's sessions, 187 of them were Italians.

Yet for all of these difficulties, the councillors at Trent made some real progress. They corrected a number of abuses, of which the sale of indulgences was the most substantive. They formulated rules for the better regulation of parish priests and stressed the obligation of priests and bishops to preach to their congregations. Following the work of Jiménez de Cisneros and Giberti, they emphasized the pastoral function of the clergy. On the heels of the success of the Jesuits, they ordered seminaries to be founded in all dioceses where there was not already a university so that priests could receive sufficient education to perform their duties. They prepared a new modern and uniform Catholic service and centralized and updated the Index of prohibited books to include Protestant writings from all over the Continent.

The Council of Trent made no concessions to Protestants, moderate or radical. The councillors attempted to turn back every doctrinal innovation of the previous forty years. Though Protestant theologians attended one of the council's sessions, their views were totally repudiated and efforts at compromise, which were supported by a number of Catholics on the council, were rejected. The councillors upheld justification by faith and works over justification by faith alone. They confirmed the truth of Scripture and the traditions of the Church against Scripture alone. They declared the Vulgate the only acceptable text of the Bible and encouraged vast bonfires of Greek and Hebrew Scriptures in an effort to undo the great scholarly achievements of the humanists. They reaffirmed the seven sacraments and the doctrine of the miracle of the Eucharist. They upheld clerical celibacy. The redefinition of traditional Roman Catholicism drew the doctrinal lines clearly and ended decades of confusion. But it also meant that the differences between Catholics and Protestants could now be settled only by the sword.

The Empire Strikes Back

Warfare dominated the reform of religion almost from its beginning. The burnings, drownings, and executions by which both Catholics and Protestants attempted to maintain religious purity were but raindrops compared to the sea of blood that was shed in sieges and on battlefields beginning in the 1530s. Neither side was capable of waging an all-out war against the other, but

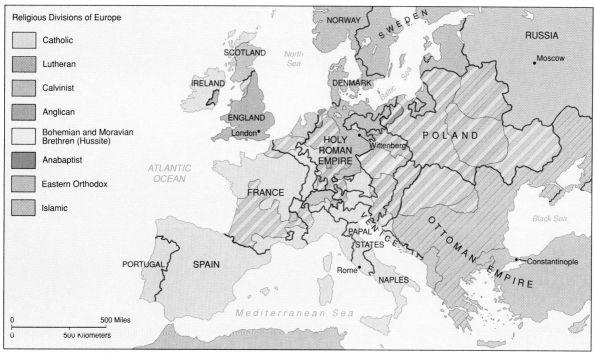

Religious Divisions of Europe, ca. 1555

they fought intermittently for twenty-five years. The Catholic divisions were clear. The empire continued to be engaged in the west with its archenemy France, and in the south with the ever expanding Ottoman Empire. Charles V needed not only peace within his own German realms, but positive support for his offensive and defensive campaigns. He could never devote his full resources to suppressing Protestant dissent.

Yet there was never a united Protestant front to suppress. The north German towns and principalities that accepted Lutheranism in the 1520s had had a long history of warfare among themselves. Princes stored up grievances from past wars and contested inheritances, cities stored up jealousies from commercial rivalries and special privileges. Added to this was the division between Luther and Zwingli over doctrinal issues that effectively separated the German and Swiss components of the reformation from each other. Each formed its own political league and their division almost certainly cost Zwingli his life in 1531, when Zurich was left to stand by itself against imperial allies.

Though both the Protestant and the Catholic sides were internally weak, it was the greater responsibilities of Charles V that allowed for the uneasy periods of peace. Each pause gave the Protestant reformers new life. Lutheranism continued to spread in the northern part of the empire, Zwinglian reform in the south. Charles V asked the papacy to convoke a general council and the Protestants to stop evangelizing in new territories. But Protestant leaders were no more capable of halting the spread of the reformation than were Catholics. Thus each violation of each uneasy truce seemed to prove treachery. In 1546, just after Luther's death, both sides raised armies in preparation for renewed fighting. In the first stage of war Charles V scored a decisive victory, capturing the two leading Protestant princes and conquering Saxony and Thuringia, the homeland of Lutheran reform.

Charles V's greatest victories were always preludes to his gravest defeats. The remaining Protestant princes were driven into the arms of the French, who placed dynastic interests above religious concerns. Again Europe was plunged into

Fishing for Souls, by Adriaen Van De Velde, 1614. This allegorical painting shows Protestants (on the left) and Catholics (on the right) vying for the souls of Christians. In the water, parties from both banks try to drag naked men and women into their boats. Overhead, uniting them all, shines the unheeded rainbow of God.

The Reformation and the Counter-Reformation

1517   Luther writes his Ninety-five Theses

1521   Luther is excommunicated and declared an enemy of the empire; Henry VIII receives title Defender of the Faith

1523   Zwingli expounds his faith in formal disputation

1533   Henry VIII divorces Catherine of Aragon, marries Anne Boleyn, and breaks with the church of Rome.

1536   Calvin publishes *Institutes of the Christian Religion*

1540   Loyola receives papal approval for Society of Jesus

1545–63 Council of Trent

1553   Mary I restores Catholicism in England

1563   Elizabeth I enacts the Thirty-nine articles, which restores Protestantism to England

general conflict, with the French invading the German states from the west, the Turks from the south, and the Protestant princes from the north. Charles V, now an old and broken man, was forced to flee through the Alps in the dead of winter and was brought to the bargaining table soon after. By the Peace of Augsburg in 1555 the emperor agreed to allow the princes of Germany to establish the religion of their people. Protestant princes would govern Protestant states, Catholic princes Catholic states. The Peace of Augsburg ended forty years of religious struggle in Germany.

In 1547 the then-victorious Charles V stood at the grave of Martin Luther. He had been buried in the shadow of the church in which he had been baptized, and now other shadows darkened his plot. Imperial troops were masters of all Saxony and were preparing to turn back the religious clock in Luther's homeland. The emperor was advised to have the body exhumed and burned, to carry out twenty-five years too late the Edict of Worms that had made Luther an outlaw from church and state. But Charles V was no longer the self-confident young emperor who had been faced down by the Saxon monk on that long-ago day. Popes had come and gone, and his warrior rivals Francis I and Henry VIII were both dead. He alone survived. He had little stomach for the petty revenge that he might now exact upon the man who more than any other had ruined whatever hope there might have been for a united empire dominant over all of Europe. "I do not make war on dead men," Charles declared as he turned away from the reformer's grave. But the ghosts of Luther and Zwingli, of Calvin and Ignatius of Loyola were not so easily laid to rest. For another century they would haunt a Europe that could do nothing else but make war on dead men.

Suggestions for Further Reading

General Reading

* G. R. Elton, ed., *The New Cambridge Modern History*, Vol. II, *The Reformation 1520–1559* (Cambridge: Cambridge University Press, 1958). A multi-authored study of the Protestant movement with sections on social and political life.

* Owen Chadwick, *The Reformation* (London: Penguin Books, 1972). An elegant and disarmingly simple history of religious change.

Harold J. Grimm, *The Reformation Era 1500–1650* (New York: Macmillan, 1973). A comprehensive textbook.

* Lewis Spitz, *The Protestant Reformation 1517–1559* (New York: Harper & Row, 1985). A recent synthesis by a distinguished Reformation scholar.

* Steven Ozment, *The Age of Reform 1250–1550* (New Haven, CT: Yale University Press, 1980). An important interpretation of an epoch of religious change.

The Intellectual Reformation

Lucien Febvre and Henri Martin, *The Coming of the Book* (Atlantic Highlands, NJ: Humanities Press, 1976). A study of the early history of bookmaking.

* E. Eisenstein, *The Printing Revolution in Early Modern Europe* (Cambridge: Cambridge University Press, 1983). An abridged edition of a larger work that examines the impact of printing upon European society.

* Indicates paperback edition available

R. W. Scribner, *For the Sake of Simple Folk* (Cambridge: Cambridge University Press, 1981). A study of the impact of the Reformation on common people. Especially good on the iconography of reform.

Jerry H. Bentley, *Humanists and Holy Writ* (Princeton, NJ: Princeton University Press, 1983). An important though challenging work on the contributions of humanists to the spread of biblical studies.

Maria Dowling, *Humanism in the Age of Henry VIII* (London: Basil Blackwell, 1986). A detailed study of English humanism.

Richard Marius, *Thomas More* (New York: Knopf, 1984). A recent reinterpretation of the complex personality of England's greatest humanist.

* Philip Hughes, *Lefèvre: Pioneer of Ecclesiastical Renewal in France* (Grand Rapids, MI: Eerdmans, 1984). French humanism through the career of its central proponent.

Roland Bainton, *Erasmus of Christendom* (New York: Charles Scribner's Sons, 1969). Still the best starting point and the most compelling biography.

Richard L. DeMolen, *Erasmus* (New York: St. Martin's Press, 1974). Selections from Erasmus' writings.

The Lutheran Reformation

* Francis Oakley, *The Western Church in the Later Middle Ages* (Ithaca, NY: Cornell University Press, 1979). A study of the spiritual and intellectual state of the Roman Catholic Church on the eve of the Reformation.

* Hajo Holborn, *A History of Modern Germany, Vol. I, The Reformation* (New York: Knopf, 1964). A widely respected account in a multivolume history of Germany. Especially strong on politics.

* Roland Bainton, *Here I Stand* (New York: New American Library, 1968). The single most absorbing biography of Luther.

* John Dillenberger, *Martin Luther: Selections From His Writings* (New York: Doubleday, 1961). A comprehensive selection from Luther's vast writings.

Eric Erikson, *Young Man Luther* (New York: Norton, 1958). A classic psychoanalytic study of Luther's personality.

Mark U. Edwards, *Luther's Last Battles* (Ithaca, NY: Cornell University Press, 1983). A sophisticated study of Luther's later years.

* Bernd Moeller, *Imperial Cities and the Reformation* (Durham, NC: The Labyrinth Press, 1982). A central work that defines the connection between Protestantism and urban reform.

* Steven Ozment, *The Reformation in the Cities* (New Haven, CT: Yale University Press, 1975). A study of the social and intellectual basis of urban Protestantism.

Thomas Brady, *Turning Swiss* (Cambridge: Cambridge University Press, 1985). A complex study of the Reformation in the imperial cities of South Germany.

R. Po-chia Hsia, ed., *The German People and the Reformation* (Ithaca, NY: Cornell University Press, 1988). A collection of essays exploring the social origins of the Reformation.

G. R. Potter, *Huldrych Zwingli* (New York: St. Martin's Press, 1977). A difficult but important study of the great Swiss reformer.

The Protestant Reformation

E. William Monter, *Calvin's Geneva* (London: John Wiley & Sons, 1967). A social and political history of the birthplace of Calvinism.

T. H. L. Parker, *John Calvin: A Biography* (Philadelphia: Westminster Press, 1975). The classic study.

William Bousma, *John Calvin* (Oxford: Oxford University Press, 1987). A study that places Calvin within the context of the social and intellectual movements of the sixteenth century.

* John Dillenberger, *John Calvin: Selections From His Writings* (New York: Doubleday, 1971). A comprehensive collection.

* J. J. Scarisbrick, *Henry VIII* (Berkeley: University of California Press, 1968). The classic biography of the larger-than-life monarch.

* A. G. Dickens, *The English Reformation* (New York: Schocken Books, 1964). An important interpretation of the underlying causes of the English Reformation.

* Rosemary O'Day, *The Debate on the English Reformation* (London: Methuen, 1986). A survey of conflicting views by eminent scholars.

George H. Williams, *The Radical Reformation* (Philadelphia: Westminster Press, 1962). A comprehensive synthesis of the first generation of radical Protestants.

Claus-Peter Clasen, *Anabaptism, A Social History 1525–1618* (Ithaca, NY: Cornell University Press, 1972). A study of the Anabaptist movement.

The Catholic Reformation

* H. Outram Evennett, *The Spirit of the Counter-Reformation* (Cambridge: Cambridge University Press, 1968). A valuable essay on the intellectual roots of revived Catholicism.

Jean Delumeau, *Catholicism Between Luther and Voltaire* (Philadelphia: Westminster Press, 1977). A reinterpretation of the Counter-Reformation.

* John C. Olin, *The Autobiography of St. Ignatius Loyola* (New York: Harper & Row, 1974). The best introduction to the founder of the Jesuits.

* A. D. Wright, *The Counter-Reformation* (New York: St. Martin's Press, 1984). A comprehensive survey.

* A. G. Dickens, *The Counter Reformation* (London: Thames and Hudson, 1968). An excellent introduction, handsomely illustrated.

* Indicates paperback edition available

14

The Experiences of Life in Sixteenth-Century Europe

Haymaking

It is summer in the Low Countries. The trees are full, the meadows green, flowers rise in clumps, and bushes hang heavy with fruit. The day has dawned brightly for haymaking. Yesterday the long meadow was mowed and today the hay will be gathered and the first fruits and vegetables of the season harvested. From throughout the village families come together in labor. Twice each summer the grass is cut, dried, and stacked. Some of it will be left in the fields for the animals until autumn, some will be carried into large lofts and stored for the winter.

This scene of communal farming is one that is repeated with little variation throughout Europe in the sixteenth century. The village we are viewing is fairly prosperous. We can see at least three horses and a large wheeled cart. Horses are still a luxury for farmers; they can be used for transportation as well as labor, making it possible to market goods at greater distances. But horses are weaker than oxen, prone to injury, and they must be fed on grain rather than grass. The houses of the village also suggest comfort. The one at the far right is typical. It contains one floor for living and a loft for storage. The chimney separates a kitchen in the back from the long hall where the family works, sleeps, and entertains itself. The bed—it is not uncommon for there to be only one for the whole family—would be located near the fireplace. It will be restuffed with straw after the harvest. The spinning wheel and whatever other machines the family possesses would be situated nearest the single window that lets in light and air on good days and cold and rain on bad ones. It is covered by oiled animal skin since glass is still much too expensive for use in rural housing. The long end of the hall, farthest from heat and light, will be home to the family's animals once winter sets in. But now, in summer, it is luxurious space where children can play or parents claim a little privacy.

The church is easily distinguished by its steeple and arched doorway and is made of brick. The steeple has sixteen windows, probably all set with expensive glass and some even stained. The church would have been built over several generations at considerable cost to the villagers. Even the most prosperous houses in the far meadow are all made of timber and thatch and only the village well, in the middle of the picture, and the chimneys of the houses show any other sign of brick. The layout of the buildings shows us how the village must have grown. The original settlement was all on the rise above the church, where there appears to be another large meadow and, at the base of the craggy rocks, several planted fields. The houses nearer the center of the picture were undoubtedly added later, perhaps to allow the sons of the more

laborers. Four men with pitchforks load the cart while two women sweep the hay that falls back into new piles. Throughout the field, men and women, distinguished only by their clothing, rake hay into large stacks for successive loadings of the cart. At least twenty-five individuals work at these tasks. Men perform the heaviest work of loading the haycart and hammering the scythes while men and women share all the other work. Though no children appear in the scene, some are undoubtedly at work picking berries and beans.

The three faces in the detail are of the women returning to work. Perhaps they are of the same family, a young girl flanked by her grandmother and mother. The expression of the eldest woman tells a tale of lifelong exertion as she holds her rake loosely and balances it carefully on her shoulder to lessen its weight. The woman on the other end has a look of determination. She is holding her hat rather than wearing it, and her thick muscular shoulders suggest a regimen of heavy labor. She had made this journey many times before. The young girl seems almost serene, still invigorated rather than ground down by the day's exercise.

As a trio they remind us that the life of ordinary people in the sixteenth century was neither romantic nor despondent, neither quaint nor primitive. It had its own joys and sorrows, its own triumphs and failures, its own measures of progress and decay. Inevitably, we compare it to our experiences and contrast it to our comforts. By our standards, a sixteenth-century prince endured greater material hardships than a twentieth-century welfare recipient. There was no running water, no central heating, no lavatories, no electricity. There was no relief for toothache, headache, or numbing pain. Travel was dangerous and exhausting. There was no protection from the open air and many nights were spent on the bare ground. Waiting for winds to sail was more tedious than waiting for planes to fly. Entertainment was sparse and the court jester was no match for stereo and video. But though we cannot help but be struck by these differences, we will not understand very much about the experiences of life in sixteenth-century Europe if we judge it by our own standard of living. We must exercise our historical imagination if we are to appreciate the conditions of European society in the sixteenth century.

prosperous village farmers to begin their own families before their parents' death. The larger setting of the community gives us an idea of the isolation of rural communities. A windmill, down the hill from the original settlement, marks the end of the village. Then as far as one can see there are no other habitations for miles until, in the upper right-hand quadrant, a town appears to be situated on the banks of the river.

The haymaking progresses rhythmically. The high road leads into the field and back through the village. At the extreme left of the picture sits the smith repairing one of the scythes that the men have used for mowing. The long wooden handles and sharp curved blades allow the work to be done upright in rows but this design restricts it to the strongest male villagers. Coming toward the smith are three women striding resolutely to the field. They carry wooden rakes, toothed on both ends to sweep the cut hay into stacks to be loaded on the cart. Behind them pass others who have been gathering berries. Men and women together carry the laden wicker baskets, while the horse, ridden by either an elderly or a pregnant woman, pulls a sled loaded with beans. Their procession passes a wooden post on which is mounted an icon of the Virgin Mary and the baby Jesus.

In the center of the scene are a large number of

Economic Life

There was no typical sixteenth-century European. Travelers' accounts and ambassadors' reports indicate that contemporaries were constantly surprised by the habits and possessions of other Europeans. Language, custom, geography, and material conditions separated peoples in one place from those in another. Contrasts between social groups were more striking still. A Muscovite boyar had more in common with an English nobleman than either had with his country's peasants. A Spanish goldsmith and a German brass maker lived remarkably similar lives when compared to that of a shepherd anywhere in Europe. No matter how carefully historians attempt to distinguish between country and town life, between social or occupational groups, or between men and women, they are still smoothing out edges that are very rough, still turning individuals into aggregates, still sacrificing the particular for the general. No French peasant family ever had 3.5 children even if, on average, they all did. There was no typical sixteenth-century European.

But there were experiences that most Europeans shared and common structures through which their activities were channeled that separated them from their predecessors and their successors. There was a distinctive sixteenth-century experience that we can easily discern and that they could dimly perceive. Much of it was a natural progression in which one generation improved upon the situation of another. Agriculture increased; more land was cleared, more crops were grown, and better tools were crafted. Some of the experience was natural regression. Irreplaceable resources were lost; more trees were felled, more soil was eroded, and more fresh water was polluted. But some of what was distinctive about sixteenth-century life resulted from dynamic changes in economic and social conditions. The century-long population explosion and increase in commodity prices fundamentally altered people's lives. Not since the Black Death had Europe experienced so thorough a transformation in its economic development and its social organization. Change and reactions to change became dominant themes of everyday life.

This picture, painted in 1530, shows farmworkers threshing grain. The figure at the door seems to be an overseer. He has just sold a sack of grain, indicating the transition from a system of self-sufficient manors to a market economy.

Rural Life

In the sixteenth century as much as 90 percent of the European population lived on farms or in small towns in which farming was the principal occupation. Villages were small and relatively isolated, even in densely populated regions like Italy and the Low Countries. They might range in size from a hundred families, as was common in France and Spain, to less than twenty families, which was the average size of Hungarian villages. It was these villages, large or small, prosperous or poor, that were the bedrock of the sixteenth-century state. Surplus peasant population fed the insatiable appetite of towns for laborers and crowns for soldiers. The manor, the parish, and the rural administrative district were the institutional infrastructures of Europe. Each organized the peasantry for its own purposes. Manorial rents supported the life-style of the nobility; parish tithes supported the works of the Church; local taxes supported the power of the state. Rents, tithes, and taxes easily absorbed more than half of the wealth produced by the land. From the remaining half the peasant had to make provision for the present and the future.

To survive, the village community had to be self-sufficient. In good times there was enough to eat and some to save for the future. Hard times meant hunger and starvation. Both conditions were accepted as part of the natural order and both occurred regularly. One in every three harvests was bad, one in every five disastrous. Bad harvests came in bunches. Depending upon the soil and crop, between one-fifth and one-half of the grain harvested had to be saved as seed for the next planting season. When hunger was worst, people faced the agonizing choice of eating or saving their "seed corn."

Hunger and cold were the constant companions of the average European. In Scandinavia and in Muscovy, winter posed as great a threat to survival as did starvation. There the stove and garments made from animal fur were essential requirements as were the hearth and the woolen tunic in the south. Everywhere in Europe homes were inadequate shelter against the cold and damp. Most were built of wood and roofed in thatch, which was an excellent but dangerous insulation material. Thatched houses were a constant fire hazard, and the use of thatch was banned in most densely populated villages. Inside walls were patched with dried mud. They were sometimes covered with bark or animal skins, but most were bare. Windows were few and narrow. They were essential to let in light and to let out smoke, but the animal skins used to seal them often came loose. Piled leaves or straw which could be easily replaced covered the ground and acted as insulation. The typical house was one long room with a stone hearth at the end. The hearth provided both heat and light and belched forth soot and smoke through a brick chimney. Wood and peat were the dominant fuels in the sixteenth century, and both were in short supply except in mountainous regions and in the east. Poland-Lithuania and Muscovy actually exported wood.

People had relatively few household possessions. The essential piece of furniture was the wooden chest, which was used for storage. A typical family could keep all of its belongings in the chest, which could then be buried or carried away in times of danger. The chest had other uses as well. Its flat top served as a table or bench or a raised surface on which food could be placed.

Tables and stools were becoming more common during the sixteenth century, though chairs were still a great luxury. Most domestic activities, of which cooking, eating, and sleeping were dominant, took place close to the ground and squatting, kneeling, and sitting were the usual postures of family members. In areas in which spinning, weaving, or other domestic skills were an important part of the family's economy, a long bench was propped against the wall, usually beneath a window. Bedsteads were also becoming more common as the century wore on. They raised the straw mattresses off the ground, keeping them warmer and drier. All other family possessions related to food production. Iron spits and pots, or at least metal rings and clamps for wooden ones, were treasured goods that were passed from generation to generation. Most other implements were wooden. Long-handled spoons, boards known as trenchers, which were used for cutting and eating, and one large cup and bowl were the basic stock of the kitchen. The family ate from the long trencher and passed the bowl and cup. Knives were essential farm tools that doubled for kitchen and mealtime duty, but forks were still a curiosity.

This picture, The Old Woman Frying Eggs, *was painted in 1618 by the Spanish master Diego Velázquez. This is a superior example of a* bogedón *painting, in which ordinary people are shown in association with food.*

The scale of life was small and its pace was controlled by the limits that nature imposed. It was a civilization of daylight—up at dawn, asleep at dusk, long working hours in summer, short ones in winter. For most people, the world was bounded by the distance that could be traveled on foot. Those who stayed all their lives in their rural villages may never have seen more than a hundred other people at once or have heard any noise louder than a human voice and terrifying thunder. Their wisdom—hard won and carefully preserved—was of the practical experience necessary to survive the struggle with nature. This was the most important legacy that parents left their children.

Peasant life centered on agriculture. Technology and technique varied little across the continent, but there were significant differences depending upon climate and soil. The lives of those who grew crops contrasted with the experiences of those who raised animals. Across the great plain, the breadbasket that stretched from the Low Countries to Poland-Lithuania, the most common form of crop growing was still the three-field rotation system. In this method, winter crops like wheat or rye were planted in one field, spring crops like barley, peas, or beans were planted in another, and the third field was left fallow. Over 80 percent of what was grown on the farm was consumed on the farm. In most parts of Europe, wheat was a luxury crop, sold at market rather than eaten at home. Wheat bread was prized for its taste, its texture, and its white color. Much could be told about people from the color of the bread they ate. The bread the invading Spanish found in the Low Countries was so black that it could not have been sold in Spain. Rye and barley were the staples for peasants. These grains were cheaper to grow, had higher yields, and could be brewed as well as baked. Most was baked into the coarse black bread that was the monotonous fare of the peasant diet. Two to three pounds a day for an adult male was an average allotment when grain was readily available. Beer and gruels of grain and skimmed milk or water flavored with fruit juice supplemented peasant fare. In one form or another grain provided over 75 percent of the calories in a typical diet.

The warm climate and dry weather of Mediterranean Europe favored a two-crop rotation system. With less water and stronger sunlight, half the land had to be left fallow each year to restore its nutrients. Here fruit, especially grapes and olives, was an essential supplement to diet. With smaller cereal crops, wine replaced beer as a beverage, though water was more common than both. The fermentation of grapes and grain into wine and beer also provided convenient ways of storing foodstuffs, a constant problem during the winter and early spring. Wine and olive oil were also luxury products and were most commonly exchanged for meat, which was less plentiful on southern European farms. In Spain, the mule replaced the ox as a work animal, and neither beef cattle nor pigs flourished in the hotter climate.

Animal husbandry was the main occupation in the third agricultural area of Europe, the mountainous and hilly regions that were best suited for dairying and sheep grazing. Sheep were the most common animal that Europeans raised. Sheep provided the raw material for almost all clothing, their skins were used for parchment and as window coverings, and they were a ready source of inexpensive meat. They were bred in hundreds of thousands, migrating across large areas of grazing land, especially in western Europe, where their wool was the main export of both England and Spain. Sheep could graze on land that was unsuitable for grain growing, and they could be sheared twice a year to provide a surplus of wool. Pigs were domestic animals prevalent in woodland settlements. They foraged for food and were kept, like poultry, for slaughter. Cattle, on the other hand, were essential farm animals. "The fundamentals of the home," wrote the Spanish poet Luís de Leon (1527–91), "are the woman and the ox, the ox to plow and the woman to manage things." In the dairying areas of Europe cattle produced milk, cheese, and butter; in Hungary and Bohemia, the great breeding center of the continent, they were raised for export; and most everywhere else they were used as beasts of burden.

Because agriculture was the principal occupation of Europeans, land was the principal resource. Most land was owned not by those who worked it, but by lords who let it out in various ways. The land was still divided into manors, and the manor lord or seigneur was still responsible for maintaining order, administering justice, and arbitrating disputes. Though the personal bonds between lords and tenants were gradually loosen-

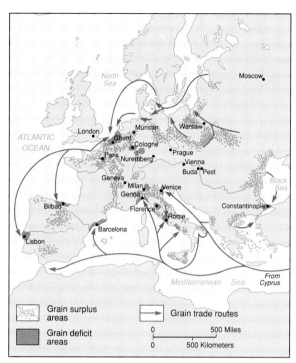

Grain Supply and Trade in 16th-Century Europe

ing, political and economic ties were as strong as ever. Lords were not necessarily individual members of the nobility; in fact, they were more commonly the church or the state. In western Europe peasants generally owned between a third and a half of the land they worked, while eastern European peasants owned little if any land. But by the sixteenth century almost all peasants enjoyed security of tenure on the land they worked. In return for various forms of rents, they used the land as they saw fit and could hand it down to their children. Rents were only occasionally paid in coin, though money rents became more common as the century progressed. More frequently, the lord received a fixed proportion of the yield of the land or received labor from the peasant. Labor service was being replaced by monetary payments in northern and western Europe, but it continued in the east, where it was known as the *robot*. German and Hungarian peasants normally owed two or three days' labor on the lord's estate each week, while Polish peasants might owe as much as four days. Labor service tied the peasants to the land they worked. Eastern European peasants were less mobile than peasants in the west and, as a result, towns were fewer and smaller in the east.

Though the land in each village was set out in large fields so that crops could be rotated, families owned their own pieces within the field, usually in scattered strips that they plowed, manured, and planted individually. There were also large common fields used as pasture, as well as common woodlands where animals foraged, fuel was gathered, and game hunted. Even the common fields and woodlands were not shared equally. Those who held the most land in the fields possessed greater shares of the commons. Villagers disputed frequently over rights to sticks and branches of trees and over the number of sheep or cows that could be grazed in the meadows, especially when resources were scarce.

Farm work was ceaseless toil. Daily bread was earned by the sweat of one's brow. Six or seven times a year farmers tilled the fields to spread animal manure below the surface of the soil. While most villages possessed metal plows, the team of draught animals was the single essential component for farming. The births of foals and calves were more-celebrated events than the births of children—and brought more prosperity—while the death of an ox or horse was a catastrophe that could drive a family into debt or from the land entirely. Calamities lurked everywhere, from rain and drought to locusts and crows. Long-term success depended as much upon good fortune as upon the amount of land or common rights that a family possessed. Most farms could support only one family at subsistence level, and excess sons and daughters had to fend for themselves, either through marriage in the village or by migration to a town.

Town Life

If nature governed rural life, human invention governed urban life. The rooster and the bell symbolize the difference. In the country men and women worked to the natural rhythm of the day, up at the cock's crow, at work in the cooler hours, at rest in the hotter ones. Rain and cold kept them idle, sunlight kept them busy. Each season brought its own activity. In the town the bell tolled every hour. In the summer the laborers gathered at the town gates at four in the morning, in the winter at seven. The bell signaled the time for morning and afternoon meals as well as the hour to lay down tools and return home. Wages were paid for hours worked, seven in winter, as many as sixteen in June and July.

The work was always the same. The bell governed the day, but the town council governed everything else. In all towns there was an official guild structure that organized and regulated labor. Rules laid down the requirements for training, the standards for quality, and the conditions for exchange. Only those officially sanctioned could work in trades and each trade could perform only specified tasks. In the German town of Nuremberg a swordmaker could not make knives nor could a pinmaker make thimbles. Specialization went even further in London, Paris, and other large cities.

While the life of the peasant community turned on self-sufficiency, that of the town turned on interdependence. Exchange was the medium that transformed labor and skill into food and shelter. The town was one large marketplace in which the circulation of goods dictated the survival of the residents. Men and women in towns worked as hard as did those on farms, but town dwellers received a more varied and more comfortable life in return. This is not to suggest that hunger and hardship were unknown in towns. Urban poverty was endemic and grew worse as the century wore on. In most towns as much as a quarter of the entire population might be destitute, living from casual day labor, charity, or crime. But even for these people food was more readily available in greater varieties than in the countryside and the institutional network of support for the poor and homeless was stronger. In Lyon the overseers of the poor distributed a daily ration of a pound and a half of bread, more than half of what a farm laborer would consume. The urban poor fell victim more often to disease than to starvation.

Towns were distinguished by the variety of occupations that existed within them. The preparation and exchange of food dominated small market towns. Peasants would bring in their finest produce for sale and exchange it for vital manufactured goods like iron spits or pots for cooking, or metal and leather tools for farm work. In smaller towns there was as much barter as sale; in larger places money was exchanged for commodities. Women dominated the food trades in most market towns, trading, buying, and sell-ing in the shop fronts that occupied the bottom story of their houses. Because of their skills in food preparation they were better able to obtain the best prices and advantageously display the best goods. In these small towns, men divided their time between traditional agricultural pursuits—there were always garden plots and even substantial fields attached to towns—and manufacturing. Half of the households in the Spanish town of Ciudad Real derived their income entirely from farming. Almost every town made and distributed to the surrounding area some special product that drew to the town the wealth of the countryside.

In larger towns the specialization of labor was more intense and wage earning more essential. Large traders dominated the major occupations like baking, brewing, or cloth manufacture, leaving distribution in the hands of the family economy, where there might still be a significant element of bartering. Piecework handicrafts became the staple for less prosperous town families, who prepared raw materials for the large manufacturers or finished products before their sale. Occupations were normally organized geographically, with metal- or glassworking taking place in one quarter of the town, brewing or baking in another. There was a strong family and kin network to these occupations, as each craft required long years of technical training, which was handed down from parents to children.

In large towns there were also specialized trades performed by women. Most related to their gender. In the sixteenth century, midwives were always female as, of course, were wet nurses. There were fifty-five midwives in Nuremberg in the middle of the sixteenth century, and a board of women chosen from among the leading families of the town supervised their work. Nursing the sick was a logical extension of these services and also appears to have been an exclusively female occupation. So, too, was prostitution, which was an officially sanctioned occupation in most large towns in the early sixteenth century. There were official brothels, situated in specified districts, subject to taxation and government control. Public bathhouses, which employed skilled women workers, served as unofficial brothels for the upper ranks of urban society. They too were regulated, especially after the first great epidemic of venereal disease in the early sixteenth century.

Most town dwellers, however, lived by unskilled labor. The most lucrative occupations were strictly controlled, so those who flocked to towns in search of employment usually hired themselves out as day laborers, hauling and lifting goods onto carts or boats, stacking materials at building sites, or delivering water and food. These tasks were in constant demand, but after the first decades of the century the supply of laborers exceeded the amount of work to occupy them. Town authorities were constantly attempting to expel the throngs of casual workers, especially in the winter when the shorter working hours made it impossible for them to earn a living wage. The most fortunate of the casual laborers might succeed in becoming servants.

Domestic service was a critical source of household labor. Even families on the margins of subsistence employed servants to undertake the innumerable household tasks, which allowed parents to pursue their primary occupations. Everything was done by hand and on foot and extra pairs of each were essential. In Münster at mid-century there were four hundred servants for a thousand households. Domestics were not apprentices, though they might aspire to become apprentices to the trade followed in the family with whom they lived. If they had kinship bonds in the town, apprenticeship was a likely outcome. But more commonly, domestics remained household servants, frequently changing employers in hope of more comfortable housing and better food. Their lives were always precarious. Any number of circumstances, from the death of their employer to allegations of misconduct, could cost them their places. Male servants were scapegoats for missing household items, female servants were vulnerable to sexual assaults.

Just as towns grew by the influx of surplus rural population, they sustained themselves by the import of surplus agricultural production. Most towns owned vast tracts of land, which they leased to peasants or farmed by hired labor. The town of Nuremberg controlled twenty-five square miles of forest and farmlands, while the region around Toledo was inhabited by thousands of peasants who paid taxes and rents to city landlords. Agriculture was the fourth largest occupation in the Spanish city of Barcelona, which had a population of over 35,000 in the early sixteenth century. All towns had municipal storehouses of grain to preserve their inhabitants from famine during harvest failures. Grain prices were strictly regulated and frequently subsidized to ensure that laborers were adequately fed. The diet of even a casual laborer would have been envied by an average peasant. Male grape pickers in Stuttgart received meat, soup, vegetables, wine, and beer; females got soup, vegetables, milk, and bread. In addition they received their wages. It is hardly surprising that towns were enclosed by thick walls and defended by armed guards.

A bathhouse in Leuk, Switzerland, is shown in this 1597 painting by Hans Bloch the Elder. The various amusements depicted gave bathhouses a somewhat scandalous reputation.

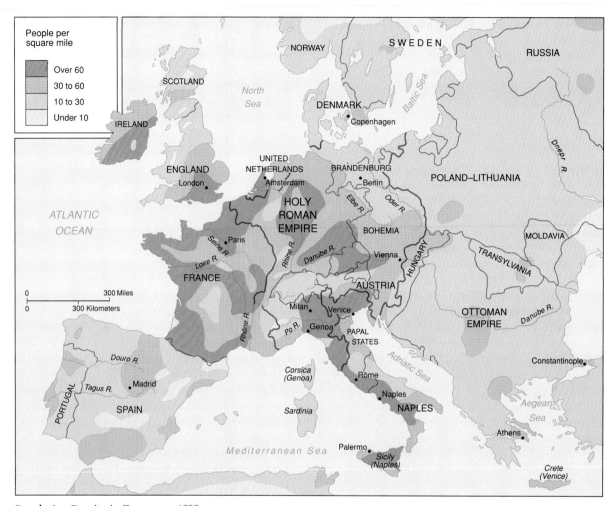

Population Density in Europe, ca. 1600

Economic Change

The basic fact of sixteenth-century life was that there were more people living it. Over the course of the century the European population increased by about a third, with much of the growth taking place in the first fifty years. Rough estimates suggest the rise to have been from about 80 to 105 million. Patterns of growth varied by region. The population of the eastern part of Europe seems to have increased more steadily across the century, while in western Europe there was a population explosion in the early decades. The population of France may have doubled between 1450 and 1550, from 10 to 20 million, before the wars of religion reversed the trend at the end of the century. The population of England nearly doubled between 1500 and 1600 from over

2 million to over 4 million. Castile, the largest of the regions in Spain, grew 50 percent in fifty years. Europe had finally recovered from the devastation of the Black Death and by 1600 its population was greater than it had ever been. Demographic growth was even more dramatic in the cities. In 1500 only four cities had populations greater than 100,000; in 1600 there were eight. Naples had grown from 150,000 to 280,000 and both Paris and London to more than 200,000 inhabitants. (See Special Feature, "Paris in the Sixteenth Century," pp. 428–429.) Fifteen large cities more than doubled their populations, with London experiencing a phenomenal 400 percent increase.

The rise in population dramatically affected the lives of ordinary Europeans. In the early part of the century the first phase of growth brought prosperity. The land was still not farmed to capacity and extra hands meant increased productivity. As there was uncultivated land that could be plowed, convenient room for new housing, and enough commons and woodlands to be shared, population increase was a welcome development. Even when rural communities began to reach their natural limits as people's needs pressed against nature's resources, opportunity still existed in the burgeoning towns and cities. At first the cycle was beneficial. Surplus on the farms led to economic growth in the towns. Growth in the towns meant more opportunities for those on the farms. More food supported more workers, and more workers produced more goods and services, which were exchanged for more food.

The first waves of migrants to the towns found opportunity everywhere. Even the most lucrative textile and provisioning trades were recruiting new members and apprenticeships were easy to find. A shortage of casual labor kept wages at a decent rate. Successful migrants encouraged kin from their villages to move to the towns and sponsored their start in trade or service. For a short while, rural families did not have to make elaborate preparations to provide for their younger sons and daughters. They could be sent to the towns. Instead of saving every extra penny to give their children some start in life, farmers could purchase some luxury goods or expand their landholdings.

Such a window of opportunity could not remain open forever. With more mouths to feed, more crops had to be planted. Since the most productive land was already under the plow, new fields were carved from less fertile areas. In some villages land was taken from the common waste, the wood or scrub lands that were used for animal forage and domestic fuel. It was less suitable for crops and it diminished other important resources. In Spain, for example, the land that was reclaimed came at the expense of land used for sheep grazing. This reduced the size of the sheep flocks and damaged both the domestic and the foreign wool trade. It also reduced the amount of fertilizer available for enriching the soil. In England and the Low Countries large drainage projects were undertaken to reclaim land for crops. In the east so-called forest colonies sprang up, clearing space in the midst of woodlands for new farms. Colonization of the eastern areas of Poland-Lithuania and Muscovy can be compared with the overseas ventures of Spain and Portugal. The settlement of the Ukraine, in the face of formidable obstacles, brought large tracts of land under cultivation.

By mid-century the window of opportunity shut more firmly on those who were attempting to enter the urban economy. There was a natural limit to the number of workers who could profitably engage in any given trade. Those safely in were eager to pull the ladder up behind them. Town governments came under pressure from the guilds to enforce apprenticeship requirements that had been relaxed during the period of growth. Guilds raised fees for new entrants and designated only a small number of places where their goods could be purchased. Most apprenticeships were limited to patrimony; one son for each full member. Such restrictions meant that newly arrived immigrants could enter only into the less profitable small crafts or, more commonly, find work as domestics or as casual laborers.

As workers continued to flood into the towns, real wages began to fall, not only among the unskilled but throughout the work force. A black market in labor developed to take advantage of the surplus population. In terms of purchasing power, the wages of a craftsman in the building trade in England fell by half during the sixteenth century. A French stonemason, a highly paid skilled laborer, could buy 33 pounds of bread with his daily wage in 1480; by 1550 he could buy less than 10. From Poland to England the decline was precipitous. Peasants in the French region of Languedoc who hired out for farm labor lost 56 percent of their purchasing power during the century. Only reapers, who were the physically strongest agricultural laborers, appear to have kept pace with inflation; grape pickers, among the least skilled, endured declines up to 300 or 400 percent.

The fall in real wages took place against a backdrop of inflation that has come to be called the Price Revolution. Over the course of the century, cereal prices increased between five- and sixfold, manufactured goods between two- and threefold. Most of the rapid increase came in the second half of the century, a result of both population growth and the import of precious metals from the New World. Sixteenth-century govern-

Paris in the Sixteenth Century

By the sixteenth century Paris was bursting at the seams. From every part of France people streamed to the city, one of the largest urban areas in Europe. Most came in search of opportunity, the opportunity for riches, the opportunity for creative expression, the opportunity for survival. While many were poor people who came in hope of finding occasional labor or constant charity, others were among the most able and skilled craftsmen of the day.

Paris was the center of the legal profession, and lawyers, jurists, and theoreticians made it their home. It was also the center of learning, where Francis I had recently founded the Collège de France to set alongside the Sorbonne, one of the greatest centers of European learning. Students from all parts of France and from all countries in Europe crowded the left bank of the river Seine. Highly skilled artisans came to ply their specialized crafts. There was always work in Paris for stonecutters, masons, and carpenters who knew their trades and were willing to work. Architects, sculptors, and painters could always find commissions. Paris was constantly under construction; every age was the age of the great rebuilding of Paris.

Perhaps most importantly, Paris had finally become home to the monarch and his ever-growing entourage of state servants. As the state became more unified, it was less important that the monarch be constantly on the move. Governors could rule the king's territories by directive from a single capital and the great expense and other complications of a mobile court could be curtailed. With the monarch came the court, the hundreds of officers and hangers-on who served the king while they served themselves. At the beginning of the century Francis I began the reconstruction of the Louvre, a vast royal residence in the western part of the right bank of the river. In mid-century, Catherine de Médicis commissioned the even larger residence of the Tuileries, west of the Louvre, so that she could be near her son Charles IX. Together the palaces took generations to complete, after which the Louvre was turned into a museum and the Tuileries was burned down.

To match its speculator growth in population, Paris had expanded its boundaries. By the sixteenth century a second set of walls had been constructed with towers at the critical points overlooking the Seine from which great chains could be strung to block off the river. The fortifications served Paris well during the devastating wars of religion at the end of the century. In 1590 the city withstood a three-month siege. To the north and the east the boundaries pressed up against marshy lowlands unsuitable for either building or habitation. The greatest amount of new construction took place in the southern and the western portions of the city, although some of the most notable rebuilding projects were still in the fashionable aristocratic quarters of the east.

With its expansion Paris took on its characteristic shape. The Right Bank was formed like a section from a large grapefruit; the Left like a section from an orange. Between the two floated the Seine with the Île de la Cité, the seed from which the halves had grown. This island was still the city's administrative center with the expansive Palais, the old medieval royal palace, now occupied by an array of law courts. It was also the religious center of Paris. The majestic cathedral of Notre-Dame with its immense rose windows dominated the skyline. Nearby stood Sainte-Chapelle, originally the king's private chapel, now housing one of Europe's largest and most important collections of relics. Four bridges, two on each side, connected the island to the two banks. The bridges were overgrown with shops and houses and overburdened by the weight of the traffic that crossed them daily. Twice in the sixteenth century the Pont St.-Michel came dislodged from its moorings by the ice floes that clogged the Seine in the winter. In 1499 the Pont Notre-Dame collapsed, spilling into the river its ramshackle buildings and the stores of countless merchants and vendors. It took thirteen years before this vital link to the Right Bank was reforged. But the reconstruction was a great success. The houses that lined the rebuilt bridge were of uniform design and were the first in the city to be numbered, odd

on one side, even on the other. At the end of the century an even more ambitious project was undertaken: the construction of the Pont Neuf, which spanned the Seine and allowed for direct travel between the two banks. It took twenty-six years to complete and was financed by a tax on wine.

Sixteenth-century building introduced the Renaissance style to Parisian architecture. Traditional buildings, especially aristocratic and bourgeois mansions, which were known as hôtels, were in the form of a courtyard. Walls on all sides surrounded the property and small gates permitted entry into the courtyard. Inside the residential buildings were domiciles not only for the owner of the hôtel, but also for a large and varied group of renters. Residence was structured vertically. The wealthiest inhabitants occupied the ground floors, which looked out on the paved court in front and the grassed garden behind. On the next floors up were the prosperous traders or craftsmen, and as the staircases mounted, the circumstances of those that climbed them declined.

At the end of the sixteenth century, Henry IV supervised the building of the first residential squares in Paris. The Place Royal was built as a public square like those in Venice or Florence. The buildings on the three sides of the square were uniform and the large concourse, which soon became a center for Parisian society, was surrounded by symmetrical archways. Leading European architects designed and executed the many public building projects that Henry IV initiated. By the end of the sixteenth century the old Paris was giving way to a new. Central planning and architectural innovation would make Paris one of the most beautiful cities in the world.

ments understood little about the relationship between money supply and prices. Gold and silver from America flooded the international economy, raising commodity prices. As prices rose so did the deficits of the state, which was the largest purchaser of both agricultural and manufactured goods. With huge deficits, states began to devalue their coins in the mistaken belief that this would lower their debt. But debased coinage resulted in still higher prices and higher prices resulted in greater debt. The Price Revolution was felt throughout the Continent and played havoc with government finances, international trade, and the lives of ordinary people.

A 500-percent inflation in agricultural products over a century is not much by modern standards. Compounded, the rate averages less than 2 percent a year. But the Price Revolution did not take place in a modern society or within a modern market economy. In the sixteenth century this level of rising prices disrupted everything. In the Spanish town of Seville almost all buildings were rented on 99-year leases to the families who lived and worked in them. This was a fairly common practice throughout Europe. It meant that a landlord who rented a butcher shop and living quarters in 1501 could not raise the rent until 1600! In England, a common form of agricultural landholding was known as three lives. Land was rented for a payment that was fixed until the last of three persons named in the contract died. Three-life leases averaged around 35 years but if one of the persons named was a young child who survived into adulthood, the rents were fixed for much longer periods. Similarly, lords frequently held the right to purchase agricultural produce at specified prices. This system, similar to today's commodity market, helped both lords and peasants plan ahead. It assured the lord a steady supply and the peasant a steady market. But it assumed steady prices. Until the seventeenth century, the king of England had the right to purchase wheat at prices set 300 years earlier.

Thus an enduring increase of prices created profound social dislocation and threw into turmoil all groups and sections of the European economy. Some people became destitute, others became rich beyond their dreams. The towns were particularly hard hit, for they exchanged

The new money economy inspired this satirical portrait by Quentin Massys. It shows a moneylender counting his receipts while his wife is distracted from her Bible by the pile of coins. Many such merchants won fame and power and even titles.

manufactured goods for food and thus suffered when grain prices rose faster than other commodities. Landholders who derived their income from rents were squeezed; those who received payment in kind reaped a windfall of more-valuable agricultural goods. Ordinary peasants were largely protected from the rise in food prices, but they were not insulated from its consequences. As long as they consumed what they raised, the nominal value of commodities was of no great matter. But if some part of their subsistence had to be obtained by labor they were in grave peril.

There was now an enormous incentive to produce a surplus for market and to begin to specialize in particular grains that were in high demand. Every small scrap of land that individual peasant families could bring under cultivation would now yield foodstuffs that could be exchanged for manufactured goods that had been unimaginable luxuries a generation earlier. The tendency for all peasants to hold roughly equivalent amounts of land abruptly ceased. The fortunate could now become prosperous by selling their surplus. The unfortunate found ready purchasers for their strips and common rights. Villagers began to be divided into those who held large amounts of land and sold their surplus at a profit and those who held small amounts of land and hired out as laborers to their more fortunate neighbors.

The beneficial cycle now turned vicious. Those who had sold out and left the land looking for prosperity in the towns were forced to return to the land as agrarian laborers. In western Europe they became the landless poor, seasonal migrants without the safety net of rooted communal life. In eastern Europe, labor service enriched the landed nobility, who were able to sell vast stores of grain in the export market. They used the law to tie the peasants to the land to ensure that grain would be cultivated for the market. Poland-Lithuania became a major supplier of cereals to northern Europe, and Gdansk became the most important agricultural seaport in the world. But agricultural surplus from the east could not make up for the great shortfall in the west. By the end of the sixteenth century the western European states faced a crisis of subsistence. Everyone was hungry; many were starving.

Social Life

The ways in which societies are organized is a mysterious process. Social organization combines elements of tradition, belief, and function, but these elements are so fused together that it is impossible to determine where one ends and the other begins. Society is a human construct, subject to the strengths and frailties of its creators. The basic assumption of sixteenth-century European society was inequality, and its basic form of social organization was stratification. The group, rather than the individual, was the predominant unit in society. The first level of the social order was the family and the household, then came the village or town community, and finally the gradations of ranks and orders of society at large. Elaborate rituals helped define membership in all of these groups, from the marriage ceremony to the initiation rites of citizens, to the processions and ceremonial displays of the nobility. All stressed the significance of the rights and obligations of different levels of society. Each group had its own place in the social order and

Children's Games, by Pieter Bruegel, 1560. In this picture, the whole town becomes a playground. Most of the games—more than eighty have been identified—are still popular today.

each performed its own essential function. Society was the sum of its parts.

This traditional social organization was severely tested over the course of the sixteenth century. Economic change reshaped ideas of mobility and drew sharper distinctions between rural and urban life. The growth of towns and their domination of the countryside around them challenged beliefs about the primacy of agricultural production and the subordinate nature of trade and commerce. The rise to new wealth and prominence of some social groups challenged traditional elites' hold upon power and prestige. The transformation of landholding patterns in the villages challenged the stability of rural communities. The rising numbers of both urban and rural poor challenged the institutions of charitable relief and posed the threat of crime and disorder. Eventually these developments led to bloody confrontations between social groups.

Social Constructs

Hierarchy was the dominant principle of social organization in the sixteenth century. Hierarchy existed at every level, from the basic distinction of lords and commoners to the fastidious complexity of the ranks of the nobility. The hierarchy of masters, journeymen, and apprentices dominated trades; trades themselves existed in a hierarchy. Urban dwellers lived under the hierarchy of civic government in which each official held a place in an ascending order up to the elite of councilors and mayors. On the land was the hierarchy of freeholder, laborer, and leaseholder among the peasants, as well as the more flexible social hierarchy among the ancient and prosperous families and the newer and struggling ones. The family itself was hierarchically organized, with the wife subordinate to her husband, the children to their parents, and the apprentices and servants to their master and mistress. "All things observe degree, priority and place," Shakespeare wrote of both natural and human order in *Troilus and Cressida* (1601–02). "Take but degree away, untune that string, and hark what discord follows."

Hierarchy was a principle of orderliness that helped govern social relations. It is alien to the modern mind, hard to understand, and impossible to accept. It is tempting to approach hierarchy through wealth, to divide groups and individuals into rich and poor. Many gradations in the sixteenth-century social hierarchy corresponded to levels of wealth, but they were threshold levels rather than absolute levels. Lords, by definition, did not engage in manual labor. They were wealthier than peasants. The governing elites of towns needed sufficient wealth to neglect their own affairs while occupied in public service. They were wealthier than wage earners. But the ranks of the nobility cannot be explained by gradations of wealth among nobles and there were many rich town dwellers who were not members of the governing elite.

Status rather than wealth determined the social hierarchy of the sixteenth century. It conferred privileges and exacted responsibilities according to rank. Status was everywhere apparent. It was confirmed in social conventions like bowing and hat doffing. In towns and cities the clothing that people were allowed to wear, even the foods that they were allowed to eat reflected status. It was signified in titles, not just in the ranks of the nobility or between nobles and commoners, but even in ordinary communities of masters and mistresses, goodmen and goodwives, squires and ladies, to adopt the English equivalents of a wide variety of European titles. The acceptance of status was an everyday, uncomplicated, unreflective act—like stopping at a red light. Inequality was a fact of European social life that was as unquestioned as it was unquestionable.

Images that people used to describe both the natural world and their social world reinforced the functional nature of hierarchy. The first, and most elaborate image, was that of the Great Chain of Being. The Great Chain was a description of the universe in which everything had a place, from God at the top of the chain to inanimate objects like rocks and stones at the bottom. Complex accounts of the Chain listed the seven orders of angels, the multiple ranks of humans, even the degrees of animals and plants from which lions emerged as kings of the jungle. Spanish botanists were dispatched to the New World to help identify the unknown flora and fauna in terms of their places in the Chain. Native Americans were first thought to be the lost tribes of Israel, as these were the only humans missing from traditional accounts of the Chain. For ordinary people, the Great Chain of Being expressed the belief that all life was interconnected, that every link was a part of a divinely ordered universe and was as necessary as every other.

The second metaphor used to describe society stressed this notion of interdependency even more strongly. This was the image of the Body Politic. In the Body Politic, the head ruled, the arms protected, the stomach nourished, and the feet labored. The image described a small community as well as a large state. In the state the king was the head, the church the soul, the nobles the arms, the artisans the hands, and the peasants the feet. Each performed its own function and each function was essential to the health of the body. The Body Politic was an organic unity of separate parts working harmoniously for a common goal. Like the Chain of Being, it was a profoundly conservative concept of social organization. Taken literally, it precluded the idea of social mobility, of people rising or falling from one group to another. The foot could not perform the functions of the stomach or the hands any more than in the Great Chain of Being a rock could become a tree.

Social Structure

The Great Chain of Being and the Body Politic were static concepts of social organization. But in the sixteenth century, European society was in a state of dynamic change. Fundamentally, all European societies were divided between nobles and commoners. This was a basic distinction that existed throughout the Continent, though relationships between the two orders differed from place to place. Nobility was a legal status that conferred certain privileges upon its holders. The first was rank and title, a well defined place at the top of the social order that was passed from one generation to the next. Each rank had its own privileges and each was clearly demarcated from the next by behavior, dress, and title. The escutcheon—the coat of arms—was a universally recognized symbol of rank and family connection. The coat of arms was woven in garments, emblazoned on windows, carriages, and household

goods, and displayed on banners during formal processions. Though there were various systems of title in use across the Continent and the nobility of one state could not claim noble privileges in another state, the hierarchy of prince, duke, earl, count, and baron was roughly standard.

Because rulers conferred these titles on individuals, elevating some to higher ranks and others from commoner to noble, the nobility was a political order as well as a social one. Political privileges were among the nobility's most important attributes. In many countries, the highest offices of the state and the military were reserved for members of the nobility. In Poland, for example, all offices were held by noblemen. This was a privilege that could work both ways, either restricting officeholders to those already ennobled or, as in town councils in France and Spain, ennobling those who achieved certain offices. The nobility was also granted rights of political participation in the deliberative bodies of the state. In England, the peerage was defined as all those who were summoned to the House of Lords. In most parts of central Europe the nobility alone composed the diets that advised the monarch. In the empire, the rank of imperial free knights allowed the nobility to separate itself entirely from the jurisdiction of towns or individual principalities.

Finally, members of the nobility held economic privileges, a result both of their rank and of their role as lords on the lands they owned. In almost every state, the nobility was exempt from most kinds of taxation. This was an area in which the interests of the nobles conflicted directly with those of the ruler. The larger the number of tax exemptions for the nobility, the stronger was its power in relation to the monarch. Tax exemptions of the nobility were most extensive in eastern and central Europe. There the crowns were elective rather than hereditary, allowing the nobles to bargain their support. The Polish nobility was exempt from the salt tax, the alcohol tax, and all internal tolls and customs. As Polish agriculture developed into an export industry, exemption from tolls gave the nobility a competitive advantage over merchants in the marketing of goods. The Hungarian nobility was exempt from all direct taxes, most importantly from the land tax. The nobility in western Europe enjoyed fewer immunities but not necessarily less valuable ones. French nobles were exempt from the *taille*, Spanish nobles from the hearth tax. As French nobles had vast incomes and Spanish nobles' houses had many hearths, both were important exclusions. The English nobility enjoyed no exemptions from direct taxation, but then there was little direct taxation from which to be exempted. The most important English taxes were on exports of wool and cloth and thus fell on merchants rather than landholders.

Privileges implied obligations. Initially the nobility was the warrior caste of the state and its primary obligations were to raise, equip, and lead troops into battle. Much of the great wealth that nobles possessed was at the service of the ruler during times of war, and war was a perpetual activity. By the sixteenth century, the military needs of the state had far surpassed the military power of its nobility. Warfare had become a national enterprise that required central coordination. Nobles became administrators as much as warriors, though it is fair to say that many did both. The French nobility came to be divided into the nobility of the sword and the nobility of the robe—that is warriors and officeholders. The old military nobility could hardly understand the new service nobility. "I have continually been astounded," one of them remarked, "that so many young men could thus amuse themselves in a law court, since ordinarily youthful blood is boiling." A glorious battlefield death was still an ideal for most of Europe's noblemen.

Nobles also had the obligation of governing at both the national and the local level. At the discretion of the ruler, they could be called to engage in any necessary occupation, no matter how disruptive to their economic or family affairs. On their land, they administered their estates and settled the disputes of their tenants. In times of want they were expected to provide for the needy, in times of dearth for the hungry. There was an obligation of good lordship which was implicitly understood, if not always explicitly carried out, between lord and peasant.

The principal distinction in sixteenth-century society was between lord and commoners, but it was not the only one. In both town and countryside a new social group was emerging. It had neither the legal nor the social privileges of nobility but it performed many of the same functions. Over the course of the century this group carved out a place that was clearly distinct from the commoners even if it was not clearly identical to the lords. It is easiest to describe in the towns, for the towns remained a separate unit of social organization in most states. Towns enjoyed many of the same political and economic privileges as did the nobility. In many states the towns sent representatives to meet with the nobles and the king and were the most important part of the national deliberative assemblies, like the English Parliament, the French estates, or the Spanish Cortes. Towns were granted legal rights to govern their own citizens, to engage in trade, and to defend themselves by raising and storing arms. Though they paid a large share of most taxes, towns also received large tax concessions.

Yet as individuals, members of the town elite held no special status in society at large. Some were among the richest people in the state, great bankers and merchants wealthier than dukes, but they had to devise their own systems of honor and prestige. In Venice the Book of Gold distinguished the local elite from the ranks of ordinary citizens. Members of the "Old Families," who monopolized the highest civic offices ruled Nuremberg. In France and Spain, some of the highest officers of leading towns were granted noble status, like the "honored citizens" of Barcelona who were ennobled by King Ferdinand of Aragon. In England wealthy guild members could become knights, a rank just below noble status. German burghers, as prosperous townsmen were called, remained caught between noble and common, despised from above because they worked with their hands, envied from below for their wealth and comfort. In Münster, many withdrew from urban affairs and sought the privileges of the lower nobility. In Würtenberg the nobility withdrew from the towns and sought the status of free knights.

In the rural society the transformation of agricultural holdings in many places also created a group that fit uncomfortably between lords and commoners. The accumulation of larger and larger estates, by purchase from the nobility, the state, or the Church, made lords—in the sense of landowners with tenants—out of many who were not lords in rank. They received rents and dues from their tenants, administered their estates, and preserved the so-called moral economy that sustained the peasants during hard times. In England this group came to be known as the gentry, and there were parallel groups in Spain, France, and the empire. The gentry aspired to the privileges of the nobility. In England members of the gentry had the right to have a coat of arms and could be knighted. But knighthoods were not hereditary and did not confer membership in the House of Lords. In Spain, the caballeros and hidalgos gained noble privileges but were still of lower status than the grandees. The gentry aped the habits of the nobility, often outdoing nobles in lavish displays of wealth and spending. In France, members of the gentry sought the educational and cultural attributes that distinguished the nobility, founding schools and patronizing artists in an effort to ascend the social ladder.

Social stratification did not only apply to the wealthy groups within European societies. Though it is more difficult to reconstruct the principles upon which rural communities based their complicated systems of status and order, there can be no doubt that orders existed and that they helped create the bonds that tied communities together. In many German villages a principal distinction was between those who held land in the ancient part of the settlement—the *Esch*—and those who held land in those areas into which the village had expanded. The *Esch* was normally the best land, and thus the distinction was likely to correlate with the relative wealth of the two groups. But interestingly, the holders of the *Esch* were tied to the lord of the estate while holders of the less desirable lands were free peasants. Here freedom to move from place to place was less valued than the right to live in the heart of the village.

Just the opposite set of values prevailed in English villages, where freeholders were in the most enviable position. They led the movements to break up the common fields for planting and were able to initiate legal actions against their lord. They might not have the best lands in the village but whenever village land was converted to freehold, unfree tenants would go into debt to buy it. Increasingly, French peasants came to own the land that they farmed. They protested against the very title of *villein*, claiming that its older association with serfdom discouraged others from trading with those so labeled. The relationship of free and unfree went even further in Muscovy, where

thousands of starving laborers sold themselves into slavery. Perhaps as much as 10 percent of the population of Muscovy accepted their loss of freedom and became domestic slaves of the military and noble orders.

In towns, the order of rank below the elite pertained as much to the kind of work that one performed as it did to the level at which it was undertaken. The critical division in town life was between those who had the freedom of the city—citizens—and those who did not. Citizenship was restricted to membership in certain occupations and was closely regulated. It could be purchased, especially by members of learned professions whose services were becoming vital in the sixteenth century. But most citizenship was earned by becoming a master in one of the guilds after a long period of apprenticeship and training. Only males could be citizens. In Germany, the feminine equivalent for the word used to denote a male citizen in good standing meant prostitute! But women who were married to citizens enjoyed their privileges and widows of citizens could pass the privileges to their new husbands when they remarried. In both town and countryside the privileges and obligations of each social group was the glue that held communities together.

Social Change

Plus ça change, plus c'est la même chose, "the more things change, the more they remain the same" is a French adage that points to the evolutionary nature of most alterations in human affairs. But in the sixteenth century, social commentators believed that change was transforming the world in which they lived. In 1600 a Spanish observer blamed the rise of the rich commoners for the ills of the world: "they have obtained a particular status, that of a self-made group; and since they belong neither to the rich nor to the poor nor to the middle, they have thrown the state into the confusion we now see it in." An Englishman commenting upon the rise of the gentry could give no better definition of its status than to say that a gentleman was one who lived like a gentleman. The challenge that the new nobility of the robe posed to the old nobility of the sword poisoned relations between these two segments of the French ruling elite. The military service class in Muscovy, who were of more use to the Muscovite princes than were the traditional landed nobility, posed an even greater threat to the privileges of the boyars.

Pressures on the ruling elites of European society came from above as well as below. The expansion of the state and the power of the prince frequently came as a result of direct conflict with the nobility. Only in east central Europe, in Hungary, Bohemia, and Poland-Lithuania did the consolidation of the state actually enhance the privileges of the traditional noble orders, and these were areas in which towns were small and urban elites weak.

There were many reasons why the traditional European social hierarchy was transformed during the course of the sixteenth century. In the first place, population increase necessitated an expansion of the ruling orders. With more people to govern there had to be more governors who could perform the military, political, and social functions of the state. The traditional nobility grew slowly as titles could be passed to only one son and intermarriage within the group was very high. Secondly, opportunities to accumulate wealth expanded dramatically with the Price Revolution. Traditionally wealth was calculated in land and tenants rather than in the possession of liquid assets like gold and silver. But with the increase in commodity prices, surplus producers could rapidly improve their economic position. What might previously have taken a generation or two of good fortune to amass might now be gathered seemingly overnight. Moreover, state service became a source of unlimited riches. The profits to be made from tax collecting, officeholding, or the law could easily surpass those to be made from landholding, especially after the economic downturn at the end of the century. The newly rich clamored for privileges, and many were in a position to lobby rulers effectively for them. Across European society the nobility grew, fed from fortunes made on the land, in trade, and in office. The inflation of honors matched the inflation of prices.

Social change was equally apparent at the bottom of the social scale, but here it could not be so easily absorbed. The continuous growth of population created a group of landless poor who squatted in villages and clogged the streets of towns and cities. Although poverty was not a new development of the sixteenth century, its growth created new problems. Rough estimates suggest that as many as a quarter of all Europeans were destitute. This was a staggering figure in great cities, tens of thousands in London or Paris, where it was observed "the crowds of poor were so great that one could not pass through the streets."

Traditionally, local communities cared for their poor. Widows, orphans, and the handicapped, who would normally constitute over half of the poor in a village or town, were viewed as the "deserving poor," worthy of the care of the community through the Church or through private almsgiving. Catholic communities like Venice created a system of private charity that paralleled the institutions of the Church. Though Protestant communities took charity out of the control of the church, they were no less concerned about the plight of the deserving poor. In England a special tax, the poor rate, supported the poor and provided them with subsistence until they remarried or found employment. Perhaps the most elaborate system of all existed in the French town of Lyon. There all the poor were registered and given identity cards. Each Sunday they would receive a week's worth of food and money. Young girls were provided with dowries, young boys were taught crafts. Vagrants from the surrounding countryside were given one week's allotment to enable them to travel on. But this enlightened system was for the deserving poor only and as the century progressed it was overwhelmed.

Charity began at home—it was an obligation of the community. But as the sixteenth century wore on, the number of people who lived on the margins of subsistence grew beyond the ability of the local community to care for them. Perhaps more importantly, many of those who now begged for alms fell outside the traditional categories of the deserving poor. In England they were called the sturdy beggars, men and women capable of working but incapable of finding more than occasional labor. To support themselves and their families, they left their native communities in search of employment and thus forfeited their claims on local charity. Most wound up in the towns and cities, where they slept and begged in the streets. Some disfigured themselves to enhance their abilities as beggars. As strangers they had no claim on local charity, as able-bodied workers they had no claim on local sympathy.

Feeding the Hungry, *by Cornelius Buys, 1504. A maidservant is doling out small loaves to the poor and the lame at the door of a wealthy person's home. The poor who flocked to the towns were often forced to rely on charity to survive.*

Poor mothers abandoned their newborn infants on the steps of foundling hospitals or the houses of the rich—in the Spanish city of Valladolid it is estimated that 10 percent of all newborn babies were abandoned.

The problem of crime complicated the problems of poverty and vagrancy. Increasing population and increasing wealth equaled increasing crime; the addition of the poor to the equation aggravated the situation. The poor, destitute, outsiders to the community, without visible means of support, were the easiest targets of official retribution. Throughout the century numerous European states passed vagrancy laws in an effort to alleviate the problem of the wandering poor. In England the poor were whipped from village to village until they were returned home. The sturdy beggars were branded with a letter V on their chests to identify them as vagrants and therefore as potential criminals. Both Venetian and Dutch

vagrants were regularly rounded up for galley service, while vagrants in Hungary were sold into slavery. Punishments for theft and robbery, already harsh enough, were extended. Whipping, branding, and other forms of physical mutilation were used in an ineffective effort at deterrence. Thieves had fingers chopped off which, of course, made it impossible for them to perform manual labor and thus likely to steal again. Sexual offenses were criminalized, especially bastardy, since the birth of illegitimate children placed an immediate burden on the community. Prostitutes, who had long been tolerated and regulated in towns, were now persecuted. Rape increased. Capital punishment was reserved for the worst crimes—murder, incest, and grand larceny being most common—but not surprisingly, executions were carried out mostly on outsiders to the community—single women, the poor, and the vagrant being the most frequent victims.

Peasant Revolts

The economic and social changes of the sixteenth century bore serious consequences. Most telling was the upswing of violent confrontations between peasants and their lords. There was more than one difference between rich and poor in sixteenth-century society, but when conflict arose between them the difference that mattered was that the wealthy orders controlled the means of coercion: the military and the law. Across Europe and with alarming regularity peasants took up arms to defend themselves from what they saw as violations of traditional rights and obligations. Peasant revolts were not hunger riots. Though they frequently occurred in periods of want, after bad harvests or marauding armies had impoverished villages, peasant revolts were not desperate attacks against warehouses or grain silos. Nor did those who took part in them form an undisciplined mob. Most revolts chose leaders, drew up petitions of grievances, and organized the rank and file into a semblance of military order. Leaders were literate—drawn more commonly from among the lower clergy or minor gentry than from the peasantry—political demands were moderate, and tactics were sophisticated. But peasant revolts so profoundly threatened the social order that they were met with the severest repression. Confronted with the execution of their estate agents, rent strikes, and confiscation of their property, lords responded as if they were at war. Veteran soldiers and trained mercenaries were called out to fight peasant armies composed mostly of raw recruits. The results were horrifying.

It is essential to realize that while peasants revolted against their lords, at bottom their anger and frustration were products of agrarian changes that could be neither controlled nor understood. As population increased and market production expanded, many of the traditional rights and obligations of lords and peasants became oppressive. One example is that of forest rights. On most estates, the forests surrounding a village belonged to the lord. Commonly the village had its own woodlands in which animals foraged and fuel and building material were available. As population increased, more farms came into existence. New land was put under the plow and grain fields pressed up against the forest. Berries and nuts that grew wild in the forest were gathered in greater amounts to feed the increased population. There were more animals in the village and some of them were let loose to consume the young sprouts and saplings. Soon there was not enough food for the wild game that was among the lord's most valuable property. So the game began to feed on the peasants' crops, which were now placed so appetizingly close to the forests. It was a capital crime for a peasant to kill wild game, but neither could the peasants allow the game to consume their crops. Gaming rights had always been a source of conflict between lords and peasants, but the conflict had been intermittent. Now it was becoming acute.

A similar conflict arose over enclosing crop fields. An enclosure was a device—normally a fence or hedge that surrounded an area—to keep a parcel of land separate from the planted strips of land owned by the villagers. It could be used for grazing animals or raising a specialty crop for the market. But an enclosure destroyed the traditional form of village agriculture whereby decisions on which crops to plant were made communally. It became one of the chief grievances of the English peasants. It was even satirized by Sir Thomas More in his *Utopia* (1516) when he observed that the sheep that replaced grain in the enclosed fields "are becoming so greedy and wild that they devour men themselves." But while enclosures broke up the old field system in many villages, they were a logical response to the transformation of land ownership that had already taken place. As more and more land was accumulated by fewer and fewer families, it made less and less sense for them to work widely scattered strips all over the village. If a family could consolidate its holdings by swaps and sales, it could gain an estate large enough to be used for both crops and grazing. An enclosed estate allowed wealthy farmers to grow more luxury crops for market or to raise only sheep on a field that had once been used for grain.

Enclosure was a process that both lord and rich peasant undertook, but it was a process that drove the smallholders from the land and was thus a source of bitter resentment for the poorer peasants. It was easy to protest the greed of the lords who, owning the most land, were the most successful enclosers: "living in idleness and luxury no longer satisfies them; they have to do positive evil. For they leave no land free for the plow, they have to enclose every acre," wrote Sir Thomas More. But enclosures resulted more from the process whereby villages came to be characterized by a very small elite of large landholders and a very large mass of smallholders and landless poor. It was an effect rather than a cause.

From Hungary to England peasant revolts brought social and economic change into sharp relief. A call for a crusade against Ottoman advances in 1514 provided the opportunity for Hungarian peasants to revolt against their noble landlords. Thousands dropped their plowshares and grasped the sword of a holy war. But, in fact, war against the Ottomans did not materialize. Instead the mobilized peasants, under the leadership of disaffected army officers and clergymen, issued grievances against the labor service that they owed to their lords as well as numerous violations of customary agricultural practices. Their revolt turned into a civil war and was crushed with great brutality. In England, severe economic conditions led to a series of revolts in 1549. Participants in the Western Rising, who succeeded in storming the town of Exeter, also combined religious and economic grievances. Cornish rebels added a social dimension with their slogan "kill the gentlemen." In eastern England Ket's Rebellion centered on peasant opposition to enclosure. The rebels occupied Norwich, the second largest city in the realm, but their aspirations were for reform rather than revolution. They, too, were crushed by well-trained forces.

The complexity of these problems is perhaps best revealed in the series of uprisings that are known collectively as the German Peasants' War. It was by far the most widespread peasant revolt of the sixteenth century, involving tens of thousands of peasants, and it combined a whole series of agrarian grievances with an awareness of the new religious spirit preached by Martin Luther. Luther condemned both lords and peasants, the lords for their rapaciousness, the peasants for their rebelliousness. Though he had a large following among the peasants, his advice that earthly oppressions be passively accepted was not followed. The Peasants' War was directed against secular and ecclesiastical lords, and the rebels attacked both economic and religious abuses. The combination of demands, such as the community's right to select its own minister and the community's right to cut wood freely, attracted a wide following in the villages and small towns of southern and central Germany. The printed demands of the peasantry, the most famous of which was the Twelve Articles of the Peasants of Swabia (1525), helped spread the movement far beyond its original bounds. The peasants organized themselves into large armies led by experienced soldiers. Initially they were able to besiege castles and abbeys and plunder lords' estates. Ultimately, those movements that refused compromise were ruthlessly crushed. By conservative estimates over one hundred thousand peasants were slaughtered during and after the wars, many to serve as warning against future uprisings.

At base the demands of the peasantry addressed the agrarian changes that were transforming German villages. Population growth was creating more poor villagers who could only hire out as laborers but who demanded a share of common grazing and woodlands. Because the presence of these poor increased the taxable wealth of the village, they were advantageous to the lord. But the strain they placed on resources was felt by both the subsistence and the surplus farmers. Tensions within the village were all the greater in that the landless members were the kin of the landed—sons and daughters, brothers and sisters. If they were properly to be settled on the land, then the lord would have to let the village expand. If they were to be kept on the margins of subsistence, then the more prosperous villagers would have to be able to control their numbers and their conduct. In either case, the peasants needed more direct responsibility for governing the village than existed in their traditional relationship with their lord. Thus the grievances of the peasants of Swabia demanded release of the village peasantry from the status of serfs. They wanted to be allowed to move off the land, to marry out of the village without penalty, and to be free of the death taxes that further impoverished their children. These concessions would make it easier for the excess population to adjust to new conditions. They also wanted stable rents fixed at fair rates, a limit placed on labor service, and a return to the ancient customs that governed relations between lords and peasants. All of these proposals were backed by an appeal to Christian principles of love and charity. They were profoundly conservative.

The demands of the German peasants reflected a traditional order that no longer existed. In many places the rents and tithes that the peasants wanted to control no longer belonged to the lords of the estates. They had been sold to town corporations or wealthy individuals who purchased them as an investment and expected to realize a fair return. Most tenants did enjoy stable and fixed rents, but only on their traditional lands. As they increased their holdings, perhaps to keep another son in the village or to expand production for the market, they were faced with the fact that rents were higher and land more expensive than it had been before. Marriage fines, death duties, and labor service were oppressive, but then they balanced the fact that traditional rents were very low. In many east German villages, peasants willingly increased their labor service for a reduction in their money rents. It was hardly likely that they could have both. If the peasants were being squeezed, and there can be little doubt that they were, it was not only the lords who were doing the squeezing. The Church took its tenth, the state increased its exactions, and the competition for survival and prosperity among the peasants themselves was ferocious. Peasants were caught between the jaws of an expanding state and a changing economy. When they rebelled, the jaws snapped shut.

Private Life

The great events of the sixteenth century—the discovery of the New World, the consolidation of states, the increasing incidence and ferocity of war, the reform of religion—all had profound impact on the lives of ordinary people. There could be no private life separate from these developments. However slowly they penetrated to isolated village communities, however intermittent their effect, they were inextricably bound up with the experiences and the world view of all Europeans. The states offered more protection and demanded more resources. Taxes increased and tax collecting became more efficient. Wars took village boys and made them soldiers. Armies brought devastation to thousands of communities. The New World offered new opportunities, brought new products, and increased the wealth of the Continent. Religious reform, both Protestant and Catholic, penetrated into popular beliefs and personal piety. All these sweeping changes blurred the distinction between public and private life.

Still the transformations wrought by political and intellectual developments were not necessarily the most important ones in people's lives. Nor was change the benchmark of experience. In private life, long-term continuities in the family, in the community, and in daily customs and beliefs preserved a sense of orderliness and control of the natural environment. The lives of most Europeans, whose primary concern was with survival, centered on births and deaths, on the harvest, and on the social relations in their communities. For them, great events were the successful crop, the marriage of their heir, or the festivals that marked the progress of the year. Their beliefs were based as much on the customs they learned as children as on the religion they learned at church. Their strongest loyalties were to family and community rather than to church or state.

The Family

Sixteenth-century life centered on the family. Blood was still thicker than any other substance that bound people together. The family was a crucial organizing principle for Europeans of all social ranks and it served a variety of functions. In the most obvious sense, the family was the primary kin group. European families were predominantly nuclear, composed of a married couple and their children. Some families contained an elderly grandparent, but this was a small number given the life cycle of late marriages and early deaths. In western Europe, an even smaller number of families contained the adult siblings of the family head, uncles and aunts who had not yet established their own families. This pattern was more common in the east, especially in Hungary and Muscovy, where taxation was based on households and thus encouraged extended families. There several nuclear families might live under the same roof. Yet however families were composed, kinship had a wider orbit than just parents and children. In-laws, step-relations, and cousins were considered part of the kin group and could be called upon for support in a variety of contexts from charity to employment and business partnerships. In towns, such family connections created large and powerful clans.

In a different sense, family was lineage, the connections between preceding and succeeding generations. This was an important concept among the upper ranks of society where ancient lineage, genuine or fabricated, was a valued component of nobility. Family insignia were placed on coats of arms and an elaborate system of heraldry was devised to celebrate the interconnection of lineages. This concept of family imparted a sense of stability and longevity in a world in which individual life was short. Even in peasant communities, however, lineage existed in the form of the family farm, that is, the strips in the field that were passed from generation to generation and named for the family that owned them. The village's fields and landmarks also bore the names of individual families, and membership in one of the ancient families of the village was a mark of social distinction.

The family was also an economic unit. Here family overlapped with the household, that is, all those members who lived under the same roof, including servants and apprentices. In its economic functions, the family was the basic unit for the production, accumulation, and transmission of wealth. Occupation determined the organization of the economic family. Every member of the household had his or her own functions that were essential to the survival of the unit. Tasks were divided by gender and by age, but there was far more intermixture than is traditionally assumed. On farms, women worked at nearly every occupation with the exception of mowing and plowing. In towns they were vital to the success of shops and trades, though they were denied training in the skilled crafts. As laborers, they worked in the town fields—for little more than half the wages of men performing the same tasks—and in carrying and delivering goods and materials. Children contributed to the economic vitality of the household from an early age. Many domestics and apprentices took their first jobs before they were teenagers.

Finally, the family was the primary unit of social organization. It was in the family that children were educated and the social values of hierarchy and discipline were taught. Authority in the family was strictly organized in a set of three overlapping categories. At the top was the husband, head of the household, who ruled over his wife, children, and servants. All members of the family owed obedience to the head. The family was like "a little commonwealth," as English writers put it, in which the adult male was the governor and all others the governed. But two other categories of relationships in the family dispersed this authority. Children owed obedience to their parents, male or female. In this role the wife and mother was governor as well as

In an age of high infant mortality and short life expectancy, women were expected to bear many children to ensure family continuity. This embroidery depicts a mother with her thirteen daughters.

governed. Similarly, servants owed obedience to both master and mistress. Male apprentices were under the authority of the wife, mother, and mistress of the household. The importance of the family as a social unit was underscored by the fact that people unattached to families attracted suspicion in sixteenth-century society. Single men were often viewed as potential criminals, single women as potential prostitutes. Both lived outside the discipline and social control of families.

Though the population of Europe was increasing in the sixteenth century, families were not large. Throughout northern and western Europe, the size of the typical family was two adults and three or four children. Late marriages and breast-feeding helped control family size. The first restricted the number of child bearing years, the second increased the space between pregnancies. Women married around age twenty-five, men slightly later. Most women could expect about fifteen fertile years and seven or eight pregnancies if neither they nor their husband died in the interim. As the rates of infant and child mortality were still over 40 percent and the rate of miscarriages probably higher than it is today, only three or four children were likely to survive beyond the age of ten. In her fertile years, a woman was constantly occupied with infants. She was either about to give birth or about to become pregnant. If she used a wet nurse rather than fed her own babies, as many women in the upper ranks of society did, then she was likely to have ten or twelve pregnancies during her fertile years and correspondingly more surviving children.

Constant pregnancy and child care may help explain some of the gender roles that men and women assumed in the sixteenth century. Biblical injunctions and traditional stereotypes help explain others. Pregnant or not, women's labor was a vital part of the domestic economy, especially until the first surviving children were strong enough to assume their share. Women continued their normal working patterns until the final months of pregnancy and resumed them shortly after their deliveries. The woman's sphere was the household. On the farm she was in charge of the preparation of food, the care of domestic animals, the care and education of children, and the manufacture and cleaning of the family's clothing. In towns, women supervised the shop that was part of the household. They sold goods, kept accounts, and directed the work of domestics or apprentices. Mothers trained their daughters to perform these tasks in the same way that fathers trained their sons to work the fields or ply their craft.

The man's sphere was the public one, the fields in rural areas, the streets in towns. Men plowed, planted, and did the heavy reaping work of farming. They made and maintained essential farm equipment and had charge of the large farm animals that helped them in the fields. They marketed surplus produce and made the few purchases of equipment or luxury goods. Men performed the labor service that was normally due the lord of the estate, attended the local courts in various capacities, and organized the affairs of the village. In towns, men engaged in heavy labor, procured materials for craft work, and marketed their product if it was not sold in the household shop. Only men could be citizens of the towns or full members of most craft guilds, and only men were involved in civic government.

This separation of men and women into the public and the domestic spheres meant that marriage was a blending of complementary skills. Each partner brought to the marriage essential knowledge and abilities that were fundamental to the economic success of the union. Except in the largest towns, nearly everyone was married for at least a part of his or her life. Remarriage was more common for men than women, however, because men continued to control the family's property after the death of their wife, whereas a widow might have only a share of it after bequests to children or provisions for apprentices. In the French town of Nantes a quarter of the annual weddings were remarriages.

While male roles were constant throughout the life cycle, as men trained for and performed the same occupations from childhood to death, female roles varied greatly depending upon the situation. While under the care of fathers, masters, or husbands, women worked in the domestic sphere; once widowed, they assumed the public functions of head of household. Many women inherited shops or farmland; most became responsible for the placement and training of their children. But because of the division of labor upon which the family depended and because of the inherent social and economic prejudices that segregated public and domestic roles, widows were particularly disadvantaged. The most fortunate among them remarried—"the widow weeps with one eye and casts glances with the other," an English proverb held. Their financial and personal independence from men, prized today, was a millstone in the sixteenth century.

Community

Despite its central place in all aspects of sixteenth-century life, the family was a fragile and impermanent institution. Even without divorce—which though permitted in Protestant communities never became very common—marriages were short. The early death of one of the partners abbreviated the life of the natural family. New marriage partners or social welfare to aid the indigent were sought from within the wider community of which families were a part. On the farm this community was the rural village, in the town it was the ward, quarter, or parish in which the family lived. Community life must not be romanticized. Interpersonal violence, law suits, and feuds were extraordinarily common in both rural and urban communities. The community was not an idyllic haven of charity and love, where everyone knew and respected neighbors and worked toward a common goal. Like every other aspect of society, the community was socially and economically stratified, gender roles were segregated, and resources were inequitably divided. But the community was the place where people found their social identity. It provided marriage partners for its families, charity for its poor, and a local culture for all of its inhabitants. The community bound people together by incorporating its members and isolating outsiders.

The two basic forces that tied the rural community together were the lord and the priest. The lord set conditions for work and property ownership that necessitated common decision making on the part of the village farmers. The lord's presence, commonly in the form of an agent, could be both a positive and a negative force for community solidarity. Use of the common lands, the rotation of labor service, the form in which rents in kind were paid were all decisions that had to be made collectively. Village leadership remained informal, though in some villages headmen or elders bargained with the lord's agent or resolved petty disputes among the villagers. Communal agreement was also expressed in communal resistance to violations of custom or threats to the moral economy. All these forms of negotiation fused individual families into a community. So, too, in a different way did the presence of the parish priest or minister, who attended all the pivotal events of life—birth, marriage, and death. The church was the only common building of the community; it was the only space that was not owned outright by the lord or an individual family. The scene of village meetings and ceremonies, it was the center of both spiritual and social life. The parish priest served as a conduit for all the news of the community and the focal point for the village's festive life. In rural communities the church was the only organization to which people belonged.

Communities were bound together by the authorities that ruled them and by their common activities. But they were also bound together by their own social customs. Sixteenth-century communities used a number of ceremonial occasions as opportunities for expressing solidarity and confirming, in one way or another, the values to which they adhered. In rural parishes there was the annual perambulation, a walk around the village fields that usually occurred before planting began. It was led by the priest, who carried with him any particularly sacred objects that the parish possessed. Behind him followed the village farmers, in some places all members of the village who were capable of walking the distance. The perambulation had many purposes. The priest blessed the fields and prayed for a bountiful crop; the farmers surveyed their own strips and any damage that had been done to the fields during the winter; the community defined its geographical space in distinction to the space of others; and all the individuals who took part reaffirmed their shared identity with others in the village.

In towns, ceremonial processions were far more elaborate. Processions might take place on saints' days in Catholic communities, on anniversaries of town liberties, or on special civic occasions. The order of the march, the clothing worn by the participants, and the objects displayed reflected the strict hierarchies of the town's local organizations. Each rank and occupation carried banners and wore identifying emblems. In Catholic towns the religious orders led the town governors in their robes of office. Following the governors were the members of guilds, each guild placed according to its rank of importance and each organized by masters, journeymen, and apprentices. In some towns the wives of citizens marched in procession, in others they were accorded special places from which to view the ceremony. Village and civic ceremonies normally ended with communal feasting and dancing, which were the most popular forms of recreation.

Not all ceremonial occasions were so formal. The most common ceremony was the wedding, a rite of passage that was simultaneously significant to the individual, the family, and the community. The wedding was a public event that combined a religious ceremony and a community procession with feasting and festivity. It took different forms in different parts of Europe and in different social groups. But whether eastern or western, noble or common, the wedding was celebrated as the moment when the couple entered fully into the community. Marriage involved more than just the uniting of bride and groom. Parents were a central feature in the event, both in arranging the economic aspects of the union—dowry and inheritance—and in approving the occasion. Many couples were engaged long before they were married, and in many places it was the engagement that was most important to the individuals and the wedding that was most important to the community. One German townsman described how he "had taken a wife but they have not held the wedding yet."

Traditional weddings involved the formal transfer of property, an important event in rural communities where the ownership of strips of land or common rights concerned everyone. The bridal dowry and the groom's inheritance were formally exchanged during the wedding, even if both were small. The public procession, "the marriage in the streets" as it was sometimes called in towns, proclaimed the union throughout the community and was considered to be as important as the religious ceremony. It was followed by a feast as abundant as the families of bride and groom could afford. In peasant communities gifts of food for the feast were as common as were gifts to the couple. There were always provisions made that excess food should be sent to the poor or unfortunate after the wedding. Weddings also legitimated sexual relations.

Carnivals were occasions for games and feasting. A Carnival on the Feast Day of Saint George in a Village Near Antwerp, *painted around 1605 by Abel Grimmer, shows the revels of the villagers presided over by the religious figure on the banner at the right.*

Many of the dances and ceremonies that followed the feast symbolized the sexual congress. Among German burghers it was traditional for the bride to bring the bed to her new home and bridal beds were passed from mothers to daughters. Among the nobility, the consummation of the marriage was a vital part of the wedding, for without it the union could be annulled. Finally, the marriage inaugurated both bride and groom into new roles in the community. Their place at the wedding table next to their parents elevated them to the status of adults.

Other ceremonies were equally important in creating a shared sense of identity within the community. In both town and countryside the year was divided by a number of festivals that defined the rhythm of toil and rest. They coincided with both the seasonal divisions of agricultural life and with the central events of the Christian calendar. There was no essential difference between the popular and Christian elements in festivals, however hard the official church insisted upon one. Christmas and Easter were probably the most widely observed Christian holidays, but Carnival, which preceded Lent, was a frenzied round of feasts and parties that resulted in a disproportionate number of births nine months later. The twelve days of Christmas, which inaugurated the slow, short days of winter,

were only loosely attached to the birth of Jesus and were even abolished by some Protestant churches. The rites of May, which celebrated the rebirth of spring, were filled with sexual play among the young adults of the community. Youth groups went "a-Maying" by placing flowers at the homes of marriageable girls, electing a Queen of the May, and dancing and reveling before the hard work of planting. All Hallows' Eve was a celebration for the community's dead. Their spirits wandered the village on that night, visiting kin and neighbors.

Festivals helped maintain the sense of community that might be weakened during the long months of increased work or enforced indoor activity. They were first and foremost celebrations in which feasting, dancing, and play were central. But they also served as safety valves for the pressures and conflicts that built up over the year. There were frequently group and individual sports, like soccer or wrestling, which served to channel aggressions. Parishes would compete with their neighbors—not always in friendly play—village elders would arbitrate disputes, and marriage alliances or property transactions would be arranged.

Festivals further cemented the political cohesion of the community. Seating arrangements signaled the hierarchy of the community, and public punishment of offenders reinforced deference and social and sexual mores. Youth groups, or even the village women, might band together to shame a promiscuous woman or to place horns on the head of a cuckolded husband. Sometimes a man who had been beaten or abused by his wife, or who had simply failed to enforce obedience from her, was forced to ride backward on a horse or donkey to symbolize the misrule in his family. At such processions, which the French called charivaris and the English skimmingtons, rough music was played and the offense of the individual or couple was elaborately re-created. These forms of community ritual worked not only to punish offenders but also to reinforce the social and sexual values of the village as a whole.

Popular Beliefs

Ceremony and festival are reminders that sixteenth-century Europe was still a preliterate society. Despite the introduction of printing and the millions of books that were produced during the period, the vast majority of Europeans conducted their affairs without the benefit of literacy. Their culture was oral and visual. They had need of an exact memory and they developed a shorthand of adages, charms, and spells that helped them organize their activities and pass down their knowledge. It is difficult for us to re-create this mental world in which almost all natural events were unpredictable and in which there was little certainty. Outside a small circle of intellectuals, there was little effective knowledge about either human or celestial bodies. The mysteries of the sun, moon, and stars were as deep as those of health and sickness. But this does not mean that ordinary people lived in a constant state of terror and anxiety. They used the knowledge they did have to form a view of the universe that conformed to their experiences and that responded to their hopes. Though many of their beliefs seem mere superstitions, in fact they allowed people to form a coherent explanation of the natural world and of their relationship to it.

These beliefs blended Christian teaching and folk wisdom with a strong strain of magic. Popular belief in magic could be found everywhere in Europe, and it operated in much the same way as science does today. Only skilled practitioners could perform magic. It was a technical subject that combined expertise in the properties of plants and animals with theories about the composition of human and heavenly bodies. It had its own language, a mixture of ancient words and sounds with significant numbers and catch phrases. Magicians specialized. Some concentrated on herbs and plants, others on the diseases of the body. Alchemists worked with rocks and minerals, astrologers with the movement of the stars. Witches were thought to understand the properties of animals especially well. The witches of Shakespeare's *Macbeth* chanted their exotic recipe for witch's gruel: "Eye of newt and toe of frog,/ Wool of bat and tongue of dog,/ Adder's fork and blindworm's sting,/ Lizard's leg and howlet's wing,/ For a charm of powerful trouble,/ Like a hell-broth boil and bubble."

Magical practices appealed to people at all levels of society. The wealthy favored astrology and paid handsomely to discover which days and months were the most auspicious for marriages and investments. So-called cunning men predicted the future for those of the lower orders who would not be able to give an astrologer such vital information as the date of their birth or to pay such exorbitant fees. The poorest villagers sought the aid of herbalists to help control the constant aches and pains of daily life. Sorcerers and wizards were called upon in more extreme circumstances, such as a threatened harvest or matters of life and death. These magicians competed with the remedies offered by the Church. Special prayers and visits to the shrines of particular saints were believed to have similar curative value. Magical and Christian beliefs did not oppose each other; they existed on a spectrum and were practiced simultaneously. In some French villages, for example, four-leaf clovers were considered especially powerful if they were found on a particular saint's day. It was not until the end of the century when Protestant and Catholic leaders condemned magical practices and began a campaign to root them out that magic and religion came into conflict.

Magical practices served a variety of purposes. Healing was the most common and many "magical" brews were effective remedies to the minor ailments for which they were prescribed.

Most village magicians were women because it was believed that women had unique knowledge and understanding of the body. This may well be why women also dominated nursing and midwifery. Women were also familiar with the properties of the herbs from which most remedies were derived. Magic was also used for predictive purposes. Certain charms and rituals were believed to have the power to affect the weather, the crops, and even human events. As always, affairs of the heart were as important as those of the stomach. Magicians advised the lovesick on potions and spells that would gain them the object of their desires. Cats were particularly associated with love spells as were the petals of certain flowers. "He loves me, he loves me not" was more than a child's game. Finally it was believed that magic had the power to alter the course of nature and could be used for both good and evil purposes.

Magic for evil was black magic, or witchcraft, which utilized beliefs in the presence of spiritual forces in nature. Witches were believed to possess special powers that put them into contact with the devil and the forces of evil which they could then use for their own purposes. Belief in the prevalence of good and evil spirits was Christian as well as magical. But the Church had gradually consigned the operation of the devil to the afterlife and removed his direct agency from earthly affairs. Beginning in the late fifteenth century, Church authorities began to prosecute large numbers of suspected witches. By the end of the sixteenth century there was a continent-wide witch craze. Unexplained misfortune or simple malice could set off accusations that might include dozens or even hundreds of suspected witches. Confessions were obtained under torture as were further accusations. In the period from 1550 to 1650 there were more than thirty thousand prosecutions in Germany alone.

Witches were usually women, most often those unmarried or widowed. Though male sorcerers and wizards were thought to have powers over evil spirits, by the sixteenth century it was females who served as the mediators between humans and the diabolical. In a sample of more than seven thousand cases of witchcraft prosecuted in early modern Europe, over 80 percent of the defendants were women. There is no clear explanation for why women fulfilled this important and powerful role. Belief in women's special powers over the body through their singular ability to give birth is certainly one part of the explanation, for many stories about the origins of witches suggest that they were children fathered by the devil and left to be raised by women. This sexual element of union with the devil and the common belief that older women were sexually aggressive combined to threaten male sexual dominance. Witches were also believed to have peculiar physical characteristics. A group of Italian witches, male and female, were distinguished by having been born with a caul, that is, a membrane around their heads that was removed after birth. Accused witches were strip-searched to find the devil's mark, which might be any bodily blemish. Another strand of explanation lies in the fact that single women existed on the fringes of society, isolated and exploited by the community at large. Their occult abilities thus became a protective mechanism that gave them a function within the community while they remained outside it.

It is difficult to know how important black magical beliefs were in ordinary communities.

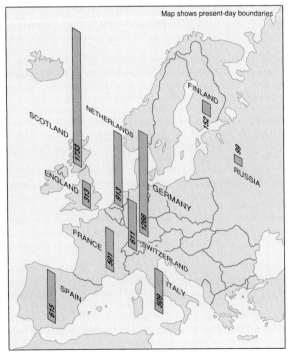

Witchcraft persecutions

A reluctant witch rides off to hell with the devil while indifferent peasants go about their business. This woodcut is from the Historia de gentibus septentrionalibus (History of the Northern Folk), *by Olaus Magnus, published at Rome in 1555.*

Most of the daily magic that was practiced was the mixture of charms, potions, and prayers that mingled magical, medical, and Christian beliefs. But as the century progressed, more and more notice was taken of black magic. Misfortunes that befell particular families or social groups were blamed upon the activities of witches. The campaign of the established churches to root out magic was largely directed against witches. The churches transposed witches' supposed abilities to communicate with the devil into the charge that they worshiped the devil. Because there was such widespread belief in the presence of diabolical spirits and in the capabilities of witches to control them, Protestant and Catholic church courts could easily find witnesses to testify in support of the charges against individual witches. Yet wherever sufficient evidence exists to understand the circumstances of witchcraft prosecutions, it is clear that the community itself was under some form of social or economic stress rather than that there was any increase in the presence or use of witches. Sacrificing a marginal member of the community might be the means to restore village solidarity.

Population growth, economic diversification, and social change characterized life in sixteenth-century Europe. It was a century of extremes. The poor were getting poorer and the rich were getting richer. The early part of the century has been called the golden age of the peasantry; the later part has been called the crisis of subsistence. At all levels of the social scale the lives of grandparents and grandchildren were dramatically different. For surplus producers, the quality of life improved throughout the century. The market economy expanded. Agricultural surplus was exchanged for more land and a wider variety of consumer goods. Children could be provided with an education, and domestic and agricultural labor was cheap and plentiful. For subsistence producers, the quality of life eroded. In the first half of the century their diet contained more meat than it would for the next three hundred years. Their children could be absorbed on new farms or sent to towns where there was a shortage of both skilled and unskilled labor. But gradually the outlook turned bleak. The land could support no more new families, and the towns needed no more labor. As wages fell and prices rose, peasants in western Europe were caught between the crushing burdens of taxation from lord, state, and church, and the all too frequent catastrophes of poor harvests, epidemic disease, and warfare. In eastern Europe the peasantry was tied to the land in a new serfdom, which provided minimum subsistence in return for the loss of freedom and opportunity. When peasants anywhere rose up against these conditions, they were cut down and swept away like new-mown hay.

Suggestions for Further Reading

General Reading

Henry Kamen, *European Society 1500–1700* (London: Hutchinson, 1984). A general survey of European social history.

* Robert Mandrou, *Introduction to Modern France* (New York: Harper & Row, 1977). Explores a variety of subjects in French social history from the mental to the material world.

* Peter Laslett, *The World We Have Lost: Further Explored* (New York: Scribners, 1984). One of the pioneering works in the family and population history of England.

George Huppert, *After the Black Death* (Bloomington, IN: Indiana University Press, 1986). An up-to-date and detailed study of social history in all parts of the Continent.

Economic Life

* Fernand Braudel, *Civilization and Capitalism: The Structures of Everyday Life* (New York: Harper & Row, 1981). Part of a larger work filled with fascinating detail about people's social behavior during the early modern period.

Le Roy Ladurie, Emmanuel, *The French Peasantry 1450–1660*, (London: Scholar Press, 1987). A complex study of the lives of the French peasantry.

Gerald Strauss, *Nuremberg in the Sixteenth Century* (New York: John Wiley and Sons, 1966). A political and social history of a typical German town.

David Palliser, *Tudor York* (Oxford: Oxford University Press, 1979). A study of the second largest English urban area and its decline in the sixteenth century.

* Natalie Z. Davis, *Society and Culture in Early Modern France* (Stanford, CA: Stanford University Press, 1975). A collection of compelling essays drawn from the author's research on the French town of Lyon.

* Carlo Cipolla, ed., *Fontana Economic History of Europe, Vol. II, The Sixteenth and Seventeenth Centuries* (London: Harvester Press, 1977). A multi-authored compendium of information and analysis on all aspects of European economic life.

* Peter Kriedte, *Peasants, Landlords and Merchant Capitalists* (Cambridge: Cambridge University Press, 1983). A Marxist interpretation of the transformations of the European economy.

Hermann Kellenbenz, *The Rise of the European Economy* (London: Weidenfeld and Nicolson, 1976). A general survey of economic life with good material from Scandinavian and German sources.

Social Life

* E. M. W. Tillyard, *The Elizabethan World Picture* (New York: Harper & Row, 1960). The classic account of the social constructs of English society.

* Arthur Lovejoy, *The Great Chain of Being* (New York: Random House, 1959). An intellectual history of an idea through its centuries of development.

Michael Bush, *Noble Privilege* (New York: Holmes & Meier, 1983). An analytic account of the types of privileges enjoyed by the European nobility, based on wide reading.

Antoni Maczak, Henryk Samsonowicz, and Peter Burke, eds., *East Central Europe in Transition* (Cambridge: Cambridge University Press, 1985). Essays by leading historians of eastern Europe, most of which focus upon economic development.

Michael Weisser, *The Peasants of the Montes* (Chicago: University of Chicago Press, 1972). A study of the lives of the Spanish peasantry who lived in the shadow of Toledo.

* Margaret Spufford, *Contrasting Communities* (Cambridge: Cambridge University Press, 1974). A detailed reconstruction of three English villages, which explores social, economic, and religious life in the late sixteenth and early seventeenth centuries.

* R. Scribner and G. Benecke, *The German Peasant War 1525* (London: George Allen & Unwin, 1979). Essays by leading scholars on different aspects of the most important of all peasant revolts.

* Peter Blickle, *The Revolution of 1525* (Baltimore, MD: Johns Hopkins University Press, 1981). A provocative interpretation of the causes and meaning of the German Peasants' War.

Yves-Marie Bercé, *Revolt and Revolution in Early Modern Europe* (New York: St. Martin's Press, 1987). A study of the structure of uprisings throughout Europe by a leading French historian.

Private Life

* Michael Mitterauer and Reinhard Sieder, *The European Family* (Chicago: University of Chicago Press, 1982). A sociological survey that presents the varying ways in which European families were structured.

* Ralph Houlbrooke, *The English Family 1450–1700* (London: Longmans, 1984). A thorough survey of family history for the society that has been most carefully studied.

* Jean-Louis Flandrin, *Families in Former Times* (Cambridge: Cambridge University Press, 1976). Studies of kinship, household, and sexuality by one of the leading French family historians.

Merry Wiesner, *Working Women in Renaissance Germany* (New Brunswick, NJ: Rutgers University Press, 1986). A survey of women's work in Germany and the ways in which it changed during the sixteenth century.

Brian Pullan, *Rich and Poor in Renaissance Venice* (Cambridge, MA: Harvard University Press, 1971). A massive history of social classes in Venice with a detailed account of poverty and vagrancy.

* Peter Burke, *Popular Culture in Early Modern Europe* (New York: Harper & Row, 1978). A lively survey of cultural activities among the European populace.

R. Muchembled, *Popular Culture and Elite Culture in France 1400–1750* (Baton Rouge: Louisiana State University Press, 1985). A detailed treatment of the practices of two conflicting cultures.

* Keith Thomas, *Religion and the Decline of Magic* (New York: Scribners, 1971). A gargantuan descriptive and anecdotal account of the forms of religious and magical practice in England.

* Brian Levack, *The Witch-Hunt in Early Modern Europe* (London: Longmans, 1987). A study of the causes and meaning of the persecution of European witches in the sixteenth and seventeenth centuries.

* Indicates paperback edition available

15

Europe at War, 1555–1648

The Massacre of the Innocents

"War is one of the scourges with which it has pleased God to afflict men," wrote Cardinal Richelieu (1585–1642), the French minister who played no small part in spreading the scourge. War was a constant of European society and penetrated to its very core. It dominated all aspects of life. It enhanced the power of the state, it defined gender roles, it consumed lives and treasure and commodities ravenously. War affected every member of society from combatants to civilians. There were no innocent bystanders. Grain in the fields was destroyed because it was food for soldiers; houses were burned because they provided shelter for soldiers. Civilians were killed for aiding the enemy or holding out against demands for their treasure and supplies. Able-bodied men were taken forcibly to serve as conscripts, leaving women to plant and harvest as best as they could.

There was nothing new about war in the middle of the sixteenth century. The early part of the century had witnessed the dynastic struggle between the Habsburgs and the House of Valois as well as the beginnings of the religious struggle between Catholics and Protestants. But the wars that dominated Europe from 1555 to 1648 brought together the worst of both of these conflicts. War was fought on a larger scale, it was more brutal and more expensive, and it claimed more victims, civilians and combatants alike. During this century war extended throughout the Continent. Dynastic strife, rebellion, and international rivalries joined together with the ongoing struggle over religion. Ambition and faith were an explosive mixture. The French endured forty years of civil war; the Spanish eighty years of fighting with the Dutch. The battle for hegemony in the east led to dynastic strife for decades on end, as Poles, Russians, and Swedes pressed their rival claims to each other's crowns. Finally, in 1618 these separate theaters of war came together in one of the most brutal and terrifying episodes of destruction in European history, the Thirty Years' War.

Neither the ancient temple nor the Roman costume can conceal the immediacy of the picture on the facing page. It is as painful to look at now as it was when it was created over 350 years ago. Painted by Nicolas Poussin (1594–1665) at the height of the Thirty Years' War, the *Massacre of the Innocents* remains a horrifying composition of power, terror, and despair. The cruel and senseless slaughter of the innocent baby which is about to take place is echoed throughout the canvas. Between the executioner's legs can be seen a mother clasping her own child tightly and anticipating the fall of the sword. In the background on the right another mother turns away from the scene and carries her infant to safety. In the foreground strides a mother holding her dead child. She tears at her hair and cries in anguish. To a culture in which the image of mother and child—of Mary and Jesus—was one of sublime peacefulness and inexpressible joy, the contrast could hardly be more shocking.

The picture graphically displays the cruelty of the soldier, the helplessness of the child, and the horror of the mother. By his grip on the mother's hair and his foot on the baby's throat, the warrior shows his brute power. The mother's futile effort to stop the sword illustrates her powerlessness. She scratches uselessly at the soldier's back. Naked, the baby boy raises his hands as if to surrender to the inevitable, as if to reinforce his innocence.

To study Europe at war, we must enter into a world of politics and diplomacy, of issues and principles, of judgment and error. We must talk about armies in terms of their cost and numbers, of generals in terms of their strategy and tactics, of battles in terms of winners and losers. There can be no doubt that the future of Europe was decisively shaped by this century of wholesale slaughter during which dynastic and religious fervor finally ran its course. The survival of Protestantism, the disintegration of the Spanish empire, the rise of Holland and Sweden, the collapse of Poland and Muscovy, the fragmentation of Germany—these were all vital transformations whose consequences would be felt for centuries. We cannot avoid telling this story, untangling its causes, narrating its course, revealing its outcome. But neither should we avoid facing its reality. Look again at the painting by Poussin.

The Crises of the Western States

"*Un roi, une foi, une loi*"—one king, one faith, one law. This was a prescription that members of all European states accepted without question in the sixteenth century. Society was an integrated whole, equally dependent upon monarchical, ecclesiastical, and civil authority for its effective survival. A European state could no more tolerate the presence of two churches than it could the presence of two kings. But the Reformation had created two churches. The coexistence of both Catholics and Protestants in a single realm posed a stark challenge to accepted theory and traditional practice.

In Germany, where the problem first arose, the Peace of Augsburg (1555) enacted the most logical solution. The religion of the ruler was to be the religion of the subjects. Princes, town governments, or bishops would determine faith. Not surprisingly, this was a policy more convenient for rulers than for the ruled. Sudden conversions of princes, a hallmark of Protestantism, threw the state into disarray. Those closely identified with Catholicism as well as those who firmly believed in its doctrines had no choice but to move to a neighboring Catholic community and begin again. Given the dependence of ordinary people upon networks of kin and neighbors, enforced migration was devastating. Protestant minorities in Catholic states suffered the same fate. The enmity between the two groups came as much from bitter experience as from differences of belief.

The problem proved intractable because it admitted only one solution: total victory. There could be no compromise for several reasons. Religious beliefs were profoundly held. Religious controversy was a life-and-death struggle, but it was a struggle between everlasting life and eternal damnation. What happened on earth was of less consequence than what happened in the hereafter. Both Catholics and Protestants revered their martyrs, and in the sixteenth century each religion obliged the other by making new ones. The willingness to die for one's religious beliefs was extremism only to those who did not believe in the extreme importance of religion. Thus compromises that might have brought Protestants back into a reformed Catholic church were doomed from the start.

Doomed too was the practical solution of toleration. To the modern mind, toleration seems so logical that it is difficult to understand why it took over a century of bloodshed before it came to be grudgingly accepted by those countries most bitterly divided. But toleration was not a practical solution in a society that admitted no principle of organization other than one king, one faith. In such a world, toleration was more threatening than warfare. Pope Clement VIII (1592–1605) described liberty of conscience as "the worst thing in the world." Those who advocated limited forms of toleration were universally despised. Those occasions during which toleration was a reluctant basis for a cease-fire were moments for catching breath before resuming the struggle for total victory. Only Poland-Lithuania, Hungary, and a few German states experimented with religious toleration during the sixteenth century.

The crises of the western European states that stretched from the middle of the sixteenth century to the middle of the seventeenth were as much internal and domestic as they were external and international. In France, a half-century of religious warfare sapped the strength of both the monarchy and the nation. In Spain, the protracted revolt of the Netherlands drained men, money, and spirit from the most powerful nation in Europe. Decades of intermittent warfare turned the golden age of Spain to lead and hastened the decline of the Spanish empire. Each crisis had its own causes and its own history. Yet it was no coincidence that they occurred together or that they starkly posed the conflict between the authority of the state and the conscience of the individual. The century between the Peace of Augsburg (1555) and the Peace of Westphalia (1648) was the century of total war.

The French Wars of Religion

No wars are more terrible than civil wars. They tear at the very fabric of society, rending its institutions and destroying the delicate web of relationships that underlie all communal life. The nation is divided; communities break into factions; families are destroyed. At every level of organization the glue that binds society together comes unstuck. Civil wars are wars of passion. The issues that bring them on are not easily resolved because they can rarely be compromised. Something so fundamental is at stake that neither side can yield, something important enough to be worth risking all. Issues become elevated into causes, into principles that form the rallying cry of heroic self-sacrifice or wanton destruction. Civil wars feed on themselves. Each act of war becomes an outrage to be revenged, each act of revenge a new outrage. Passions run deep and, however primitive, the rules for the civilized conduct of war are quickly broken. The loss of lives and property is staggering but the loss of communal identity is greater still. Generations pass before societies recover from their civil wars.

Such was the case with the French wars of religion. For nearly half a century civil war tore France apart. Massacres of Catholic congregations matched massacres of Protestant ones. Assassinations of Catholic leaders followed assassinations of Protestant ones. Kings of France died at the hands of their subjects. Leaders of Protestant and Catholic movements died by the order of the king. Aristocratic armies roamed the country wreaking havoc on friend and foe alike. Indeed, the religious causes that brought the wars about were soon forgotten.

Protestantism came late to France. The unyielding hostility of the monarchy had prevented Lutheran reforms from making much headway there. Through a series of concessions made by the papacy in the fifteenth century, and codified in the Concordat of Bologna (1516), the French kings had gained the right to make ecclesiastical appointments and thus controlled much of the wealth of the Church. Lutheranism held little attraction for Francis I (1515–47) and he rigorously suppressed it, sending John Calvin, among others, into exile. The Catholic church directed by the monarchy proved even more resistant to reform than had the Catholic church directed by the papacy. It was not until after Calvin reformed the church in Geneva and began to export his brand of Protestantism that French society began to divide along religious lines. Calvinist pastors received a warm reception in many French towns. They soon found that they could hardly meet the demand for preaching and instruction from newly formed congregations. By

Religious Divisions in France

1560 there were over two thousand Protestant congregations in France, whose membership totaled nearly 10 percent of the French population. Calvin and his successors concentrated their efforts on large provincial towns and had their greatest success among the middle ranks of urban society, merchants, traders, and craftsmen. They also found a receptive audience among aristocratic women, whose conversions were a turning point in the movement. These women sheltered the fledgling Calvinist congregations before they were able to fend for themselves. Eventually, they also converted their husbands and their sons. By 1560 between one third and one half of the French lesser nobility professed Calvinism.

The wars of religion, however, were brought on by more than the rapid spread of Calvinism. Equally important was the vacuum of power that had been created when Henry II (1547–59) died in a jousting tournament. Surviving Henry were his extraordinary widow, Catherine de Médicis, three daughters, and four sons, the oldest of whom, Francis II (1559–60), was only fifteen. At the best of times the leaders of the French nobility played a high-stakes game for influence with the king. A strong monarch balanced the aristocratic factions at court and made sure that each raked in an occasional pot. Now the accession of a malleable and sickly teenager intensified the competition. Though the aristocracy no longer contested for the throne, it remained inherently dangerous to the crown. High offices were found for all of the leaders of the greatest families and all were kept at court under the watchful eyes of the monarch.

It had taken four kings of France nearly a century to quell the ambitions of the aristocracy. It took Francis II less than a year to revive them. Under the influence of his beautiful young wife, Mary, Queen of Scots, Francis II allowed the Guise family to dominate the great offices of state and to exclude their rivals from power. The Guises controlled the two most powerful institutions of the state, the army and the Church. Two of the Guises were cardinals, and Francis, Duc de Guise, was France's greatest general. The Guises were staunchly Catholic and among their enemies were the Bourbons, princes of the blood with a direct claim to the French throne but also a family with powerful Protestant members. The revelation of a Protestant plot to remove the king from Paris provided the Guises with an opportunity to eliminate their most potent rivals. The Bourbon Duc de Condé, the leading Protestant peer of the realm, was sentenced to death. But five days before Condé's execution, Francis II died and Guise power evaporated. The new king, Charles IX (1560–74) was only ten years old and firmly under the grip of his mother, Catherine de Médicis, who now declared herself regent of France. (See Special Feature, "The Monstrous Regiment of Women," pp. 456–457.)

The diverse elements of Calvinist zeal, monarchical weakness, and aristocratic ambition now combined. Condé's death sentence convinced him that the Guises would stop at nothing to gain their ambitions. Force would have to be met with force. Protestants and Catholics alike raised armies and in 1562 civil war ensued. As was to be the case for nearly four decades, the initial battles were indecisive. Protestant strength lay in the south and west of France, Catholic strength in Paris and the northern portions of the country. Though destructive, aristocratic armies were too weak to wage an offensive war. At best, they could fortify the towns that were under their control and retreat to them in times of danger. In holding Paris, the Catholics held the monarch and this was their ultimate advantage. But like the Protestant leaders, Catherine de Médicis feared the power of the Guises. Throughout the wars she followed only one principle, to protect the succession of her sons and the authority of the monarchy. However duplicitous were her policies, her purpose was singular.

Because of the tangle of motives among the participants, each side in the struggles had different objectives. Catherine wanted peace and was willing to accept almost any strategy for securing it. War weakened the state and weakened loyalty to the monarch. At first she negotiated with the Bourbons, but she was ultimately forced to accept the fact that the Guises were more powerful. The Guises wanted to suppress Protestantism and eliminate Protestant influence at court. They were willing to undertake the task with or without the king's express support. Once the wars began, the leading Protestant peers had fled the court, but the position of the Guises was not altogether secure. Henry Bourbon, king of Navarre, was the next in line to the throne should Charles IX and his two brothers die without male heirs. Henry had been raised in the Protestant faith by his mother, Jeanne d'Albret, whose own mother, Marguerite of Navarre, was among the earliest protectors of the French Protestants. The objectives of the Huguenots, as the French Calvinists came to be called, were less clear-cut. The townsmen wanted the right to practice their faith, the clergy wanted the right to preach and make converts, and the nobility wanted their rightful place in local government. Almost from the beginning, the Huguenots were on the defensive, fighting to preserve what they already had and to avoid annihilation.

The inconclusive nature of the early battles might have allowed for the pragmatic solution sought by Catherine de Médicis had it not been for the assassination of the Duc de Guise in 1563 by a Protestant fanatic. This act added a personal vendetta to the religious passions of the Catholic leaders. When Charles IX issued the Edict of Amboise (1563), which allowed free worship for Protestant noblemen and restricted worship for all other Huguenots, Catholic leaders deliberately undermined royal policy. They encouraged the slaughter of Huguenot congregations and openly planned the murder of Huguenot leaders. Protestants gave as good as they got, though their movement was limited to a number of fortified towns. Catherine de Médicis looked with horror upon the warfare that physically divided the country and made mockery of the power of the monarchy. In open defiance of Valois dynastic interests, the Guises courted support from Spain, while the Huguenots imported Swiss and German mercenaries to fight in France. Noble factions and irreconcilable religious differences were together pulling the government apart.

By 1570 Catherine was ready to attempt another reconciliation. She blamed the Guises for the failure of the Edict of Amboise and informed Protestant leaders that they would be welcomed back to court and would be placed in positions of trust in the government. Charles IX was nearly twenty years old, and if he lacked the substance of a great monarch, now at least he could make the show of one. Through him Catherine announced her plans for a marriage between her daughter Margaret and Henry of Navarre, a marriage that would symbolize the spirit of conciliation between the crown and the Huguenots. The marriage was to take place in Paris during August 1572, and preparations that befit a royal wedding were under way all that summer. Huguenot lead-

The scene below depicts the mistreatment of French Catholics by the Protestants in the town of Angoulême. They were deprived of all nourishment, dragged over a taut rope, and then slowly roasted at the stake.

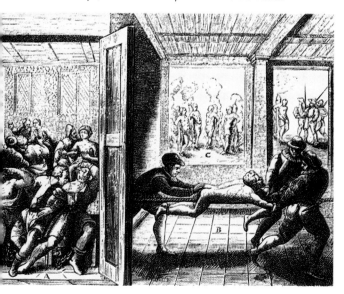

ers who had not seen the capital for years came to celebrate the union of Valois and Bourbon as well as the dawn of a new era of peace.

But preparations for the wedding festival were not the only plans being made that summer. The arrival of Huguenot leaders from all over France presented an opportunity of a different kind to the Guises and their supporters. If leading Huguenots could be assassinated in Paris, the Protestant cause might collapse and the truce that the wedding signified might be turned instead into a Catholic triumph. It is not altogether clear how Catherine de Médicis and Charles IX were persuaded to support this reckless plan. The murder of Huguenot leaders had been discussed before, both as an effective policy and as revenge for the killing of the Duc de Guise. What Catherine undoubtedly did know was that her plans to bring a halt to open warfare and to give her son the opportunity to establish his authority depended upon Catholic cooperation. After ten years of civil war it was clear that the Huguenots could not win and the Guises would not accept toleration. Catherine may actually have believed that the death of a few Huguenot leaders might satiate the Catholics. Desperate problems called for desperate solutions.

Saint Bartholomew was the apostle that Jesus described as a man without guile. Ironically it was on his feast day that the Huguenots who had innocently come to celebrate Henry's marriage were led like lambs to the slaughter. The attempt on the life of the first Huguenot leader failed; he was merely wounded by a musket shot. When news of the Guise plot spread, the Huguenots threatened retaliation. These threats were used to justify the subsequent massacre. "Kill them all, the King commands it," was the order given by the young Duc de Guise, intent on revenge for the murder of his father. On 24 August 1572 the streets of Paris ran red with Huguenot blood. Though frenzied, the slaughter was inefficient. Henry of Navarre and a number of other important Huguenots escaped the carnage and returned to their urban strongholds. In the following weeks the violence spread from Paris to the countryside and thousands of Protestants paid for their beliefs with their lives. Until the French Revolution, no event in French history would evoke as much passion as the memory of the Saint Bartholomew's Day massacre.

The Monstrous Regiment of Women

"To promote a woman to bear rule, superiority, dominion or empire above any realm, nation, or city is repugnant to nature, contumely to God, and the subversion of good order, of all equity and justice." So wrote the Scottish theologian John Knox (1513–72) in *The First Blast of the Trumpet Against the Monstrous Regiment of Women* (1558). Though he made his points more emphatically than many others, Knox was only repeating the commonplace notions of his day. He could quote Aristotle and Aquinas as well as a host of secular authorities to demonstrate female inadequacies: "Nature, I say, doth paint them forth to be weak, frail, impatient, feeble, and foolish." He could quote Saint Paul along with the ancient Fathers of the Church to demonstrate the "proper" place of women—"Man is not of the woman, but the woman of the man."

But no stacking up of authorities, no matter how numerous or revered, could erase the fact that all over Europe in the sixteenth century women could and did rule. In the Netherlands Mary, Queen of Hungary (1531–52) and Margaret of Parma (1559–67) were successful regents. Jeanne d'Albret (1562–72) was queen of the tiny state of Navarre, territory claimed by both France and Spain but kept independent by this remarkable woman. Catherine de Médicis (1560–89), wife of one king of France and mother of three others, was the effective ruler of that nation for nearly thirty years. Mary, Queen of Scots (1542–87) was the nominal ruler of Scotland almost from her birth. England was ruled by two very different women, the Catholic Mary I (1553–58) and her Protestant half-sister Elizabeth I (1558–1603).

The problems faced by this long list of queens and regents were more than just the ordinary cares of government. The belief that women were inherently inferior in intelligence, strength, and character was so pervasive that for men like Knox, a woman ruler was almost a contradiction in terms.

Yet this was not the view taken by everyone, and female rule had its defenders as well as its detractors. One set of objections was overcome by the traditional medieval theory of the two bodies of the monarch. This argument was developed to reconcile the divine origins and functions of monarchs with their very real human frailties. In the theory of the two bodies, there was the body natural and the body politic. Both were joined together in the person of the ruler but the attributes of each could be separated. Rule of a woman did nothing to disrupt this notion. In fact, it made it easier to argue that the frailties of the body natural of a woman were in no way related to the strengths of the body politic of a monarch.

While such ideas might help a female ruler win the acceptance of her subjects, they did little to invigorate her own sense of her role. Female rulers often strained against the straitjacket that definitions of gender placed them in. When angered, Elizabeth I would proclaim that she had more courage than her father, Henry VIII, "though I am only a woman." Mary, Queen of Scots, once revealed that her only regret was that she "was not a man to know what life it was to lie all night in the fields or to walk with a buckler and a broadsword." Some queens assumed masculine traits, riding in armor or leading forces to battle. Elizabeth's presence in armor at the threat of the landing of the Spanish Armada was viewed as one of the heroic moments of her reign. Other women rulers mixed together characteristics that were usually separated by gender definitions. Margaret of Parma was considered one of the most accomplished horse riders of her day. After leading her courtiers through woods and fields at breakneck speed, she would then attend council meetings and work on her needlepoint. Mary, Queen of Scots, loved hawking, a traditional kingly sport in the Scottish wilds. After relishing the hawk's destruction of its prey, she liked to negotiate matters of state by beginning with tears and entreaties and ending with accusations and threats. The effect was more than discomforting.

Women were no more nor less successful as rulers than were men. Women's achievements, like men's, depended upon strength of character and the circumstances of the times. All the women rulers of the sixteenth century had received

outstanding educations. Whether raised Catholic or Protestant, each was trained in Latin as well as modern languages, in the liberal arts, and in fine arts. Mary and Elizabeth Tudor of England wrote poetry and played musical instruments with considerable accomplishment. Mary, Queen of Scots, who was raised at the court of France, was considered particularly apt at learning, praise not often accorded a foreigner by the French. Catherine de Médicis, orphaned as an infant, was raised in convents and instructed in the new learning by Italian nuns. It was said that her political instincts were in her blood. Machiavelli had dedicated *The Prince* to her father. Marguerite of Navarre chose one of the leading French humanists to supervise the training of her daughter, Jeanne d'Albret.

Mary, Queen of Scots, was the only one of these female rulers born to rule. She was the sole survivor of her father, who died shortly after her birth. Mary and Elizabeth Tudor came to their thrones after the death of their younger brother

Edward VI; Mary of Hungary and Margaret of Parma came to theirs as princesses of the House of Habsburg. The rule of Catherine de Médicis was the most unexpected of all. Her vigorous husband, Henry II, died during a jousting tournament and her eldest son, Francis II, husband of Mary, Queen of Scots, died the following year. Instead of retirement as a respected queen dowager—the widow of a previous king— Catherine de Médicis was forced into the vortex of French politics to protect the rights of her ten-year-old son, Charles IX.

Unfortunately, the accomplishments of women rulers did little to dispel prejudices against women as a whole or to alter the definition of gender roles. Except for Mary, Queen of Scots, whose principal achievement was to provide an heir to the English throne, all the queens and regents of the sixteenth century were successful rulers. Margaret of Parma steered the careful middle course in the conflict between Spain and the Netherlands. She opposed the intervention of the Duke of Alba, and had her advice been followed, the eighty years of war between Spain and the Netherlands might have been avoided. Catherine de Médicis held the crown of France on the heads of her sons, navigated the treacherous waters of civil war, and provided the model for religious toleration that finally was adopted in the Edict of Nantes. Elizabeth I of England became one of the most beloved rulers

in that nation's history. A crafty politician who learned to balance the factions at her court and who turned the aristocracy into a service class for the crown, she brought nearly a half-century of stability to England at a time when the rest of Europe was in flames.

For most of these queens and regents, marriage was of central importance to their position. Both Mary, Queen of Hungary, and Mary, Queen of Scots, married kings whose reigns were exceedingly brief. Lewis of Hungary died at the battle of Mohács in 1526, just four years after Mary had become his queen. Mary, Queen of Scots, was widowed even sooner and throughout the rest of her remarkable career schemed for remarriage. To strengthen her claim to the throne of England, she married the Scottish Lord Darnley. When he proved unsatisfactory to her plans, she plotted his murder and then married one of his assassins. When this husband died, she sought a match with a powerful English lord who might help her capture Elizabeth's throne. These intrigues finally led to her execution in England in 1587. Mary Tudor married Philip II of Spain in hope of reestablishing Catholicism in England through a permanent alliance with the most powerful Catholic state in Europe. Her dreams went unfulfilled when she failed to produce an heir and the throne passed to her sister Elizabeth who, alone among the women rulers of the period, did not marry.

One King, Two Faiths

The Saint Bartholomew's Day massacre was a transforming event in many ways. In the first place it prolonged the wars. A whole new generation of Huguenots now had an emotional attachment to the continuation of warfare. Their fathers and brothers had been mercilessly slaughtered. By itself the event was shocking enough. But in the atmosphere of anticipated reconciliation created by the wedding, it screamed out for revenge. And the target for retaliation was no longer limited to the Guises and their followers. By accepting its results, the monarchy sanctioned the massacre and spilled Huguenot blood on itself. For over a decade Catherine de Médicis had maintained a distance between the crown and the leaders of the Catholic movement. That distance no longer existed.

Nor could the Huguenots continue to maintain the fiction that they were fighting against the king's evil advisors rather than against the king. After Saint Bartholomew's Day, Huguenot theorists began to develop the idea that resistance to a monarch whose actions violated divine commandments or civil rights was lawful. For the first time, Huguenot writers provided a justification for rebellion. Perhaps most importantly, a genuine revulsion against the massacres swept the nation. A number of Catholic peers now joined with the Huguenots to protest the excesses of the crown and the Guises. These Catholics came to be called the *politiques* from their desire for a practical settlement of the wars. They were led by the duc d'Anjou, next in line to the throne when Charles IX died in 1574 and Henry III (1574–89) became king.

There can be no doubt that whatever strategy had led to the massacres, it had backfired. The defection of important Catholic noblemen from the court further weakened the monarchy. Joining forces with the Huguenots, Anjou inflicted a humiliating defeat upon the new king in 1576, and the authority of the crown was openly flouted. The extreme Catholic party again organized its strength, but it no longer made any pretense of being led by the king. In Paris and a number of other towns the Catholic League was formed, a society that pledged its first allegiance to religion. The League took up where the Saint Bartholomew's Day massacre left off, and the slaughter of ordinary people who unluckily professed the wrong religion continued. Matters grew worse in 1584 when Anjou died. With each passing year it was becoming apparent that Henry III would produce no male heir. After Anjou's death, Henry of Navarre was the next in line for the throne, and he was a Huguenot. The leaders of the Catholic League had little interest in the niceties of the lawful succession. They were

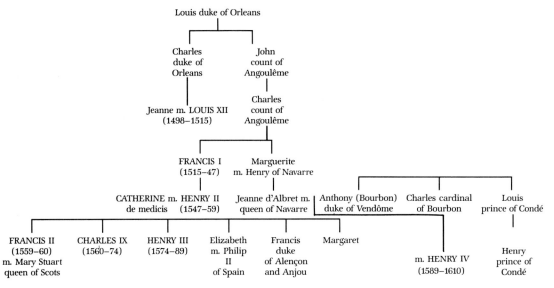

THE HOUSES OF VALOIS AND BOURBON OF FRANCE (to 1610)

interested only in ensuring that the crown of France rested on a Catholic head.

The bolder the League became, the more desperate was the position of the crown. Though Catherine de Médicis had frequently advocated a policy similar to that supported by the *politiques*, after the Saint Bartholomew's Day massacre she had little credit with the Huguenots. Catholic Leaguers talked openly of altering the royal succession and began to develop their own theories of lawful resistance to monarchical power. By 1585, when the final civil war began—the war of the three Henrys, named for Henry III, Henry Guise, and Henry of Navarre—the crown was in the weakest possible position. Paris and the Catholic towns were controlled by the League, the Protestant strongholds by Henry of Navarre. The king could not abandon his capital or his religion, but neither could he gain control of the Catholic party. The extremism of the Leaguers kept the *politiques* away from court, and without the *politiques*, there could be no settlement. To make matters worse, Henry III's military forays against the Huguenots always ended in humiliation while those of Henry Guise ended in triumph. Desperate problems demanded desperate solutions.

In December 1588 Henry III summoned Henry Guise and Guise's brother to a meeting in the royal bedchamber. There they were murdered by the king's order. But the elimination of the leaders of the League did not secure Catholic support for the king. A tactic that might have worked a decade earlier, when the Guises still claimed to represent the crown, now served only to invigorate the League. The *politiques* were blamed for the murders—revenge was taken on a number of them—and Henry III was forced to flee his capital. Paris was still firmly in the hands of the League and Henry was in danger of becoming a king without a country. He made a pact with Henry of Navarre and together royalist and Huguenot forces besieged Paris. All supplies were cut off from the city and only the arrival of a Spanish army prevented its fall. In 1589 Catherine de Médicis died, her ambition to reestablish the authority of the monarchy in shambles, and in the same year a fanatic priest gained revenge for the murder of the Guises by assassinating Henry III.

Finally, Henry of Navarre came into his inheritance. After nearly thirty years of continuous civil war it was certain that a Huguenot could never rule France. The League had already proclaimed a Catholic rival as king, and the pope excommunicated Henry of Navarre and absolved France from loyalty to him. If Henry was to become king of all France, he would have to become a Catholic king. It is not clear when Henry made the decision to accept the Catholic faith—"Paris is worth a mass," he reportedly declared—but he did not announce his decision at once. Rather he strengthened his forces, tightened his bonds with the *politiques*, and urged his countrymen to expel the Spanish invaders. He finally made his conversion public and in 1594 was crowned Henry IV (1589–1610). A war-weary nation was willing to accept the sincerity of its new king rather than endure a seemingly endless struggle. Even the Leaguers were exhausted. Their claimant to the throne had died, and they were now seen as rebels rather than patriots. War had sapped both their treasuries and their spirit. Most of the leading peers on both sides were nearly bankrupt, and Henry IV was willing to pay large cash settlements to all those who would return to their estates and pledge allegiance to him.

Resistance to the reestablishment of the monarchy continued for several years, but Henry IV was a strong and capable ruler. He declared war on Spain to unite his nation against foreign aggression, and he carefully reestablished the balance of aristocratic factions at his court. The league collapsed and moderate Catholics rallied around the king. Though Huguenots and Calvinists everywhere were shocked by Henry's conversion, they were hardly in a position to wage a successful war against their former leader. Henry's accession gave them their first real hope for an enduring settlement with the crown.

In 1598 Henry proclaimed the Edict of Nantes, which granted limited toleration to the Huguenots. It was the culmination of decades of attempts to find a solution to the existence of two religions in one state. It was a compromise that satisfied no one, but it was a compromise that everyone could accept. One king, two faiths was as apt a description of Henry IV as it was of the settlement. Yet neither Henry's conversion nor the Edict of Nantes stilled the passions that had spawned and sustained the French wars of religion. Sporadic fighting between Catholics and Huguenots continued and fanatics on both sides fanned the flames of religious hatred. Henry IV

The French Wars of Religion

1559   Death of Henry II

1560   Protestant Duc de Condé sentenced to death

1562   First battle of wars of religion

1563   Catholic Duc de Guise assassinated

Edict of Amboise grants limited Protestant worship

1572   Saint Bartholomew's Day massacre

1574   Accession of Henry III

1576   Formation of Catholic League

1584   Death of Duc d'Anjou makes Henry of Navarre heir to throne

1585   War of the three Henrys

1588   Duc de Guise murdered by order of Henry III

1589   Catherine de Médicis dies; Henry III assassinated

1594   Henry IV crowned

1598   Edict of Nantes

survived eighteen attempts on his life before he was finally felled by an assassin's knife in 1610. But by then he had reestablished the monarchy and brought a semblance of peace to France.

The World of Philip II

By the middle of the sixteenth century Spain was the greatest power in Europe. The dominions of Philip II (1556–98) of Spain stretched from the Atlantic to the Pacific: his continental territories included the Netherlands in the north and Milan and Naples in Italy. In 1580 Philip became king of Portugal, uniting all the states of the Iberian peninsula. With the addition of Portugal's Atlantic ports and its sizable fleet, Spanish maritime power was now unsurpassed. Spain was also a great cultural and intellectual center. The fashions and tastes of its golden age dominated all the courts of Europe. The expansion of Spanish dominion and the increase in Spain's wealth and prestige was reflected in a self-conscious spirit of national pride that could be seen even in the story of *Don Quixote*, the knight who tilted at windmills in search of greatness in the novel published by Miguel de Cervantes (1547–1616) between 1605 and 1615.

Great power meant great responsibilities, and few monarchs took their tasks more seriously than did Philip II. Trained from childhood for the cares of office, he exceeded all expectations. Philip II earned his reputation as "King of Paper" by maintaining a grueling work schedule. Up at eight and at mass soon afterwards, he met with his advisers and visitors on official business until noon. After a brief lunch, he began the real business of the day, the study of the mountains of papers that his empire generated. Though summaries were prepared of the hundreds of documents he handled each day, Philip II frequently read and annotated the longer originals. No detail was too small to escape his attention. His work day often lasted ten hours or longer. Even when he was traveling, his secretaries carried huge chests of state papers that Philip studied in his carriage and annotated on a portable desk that always accompanied him.

There was good reason why this slightly stooped king appeared as if he had the weight of the world on his shoulders. In the Mediterranean, Spain alone stood out against the expansion of Ottoman power. The sultan's navy continually threatened to turn the Mediterranean into a Turkish lake, while his armies attempted to capture and hold Italian soil. All Europe shuddered at the news of each Ottoman advance. Popes called for holy wars against the Turks but only Philip heeded the cry. From nearly the moment that he inherited the Spanish crown he took up the challenge of defending European Christianity. For over a decade Philip maintained costly coastal garrisons in North Africa and Italy and assembled large fleets and larger armies to discourage or repel Turkish invasions. This sparring could not go on indefinitely, and in 1571 both sides prepared for a decisive battle. A combined Spanish and Italian force of over three hundred ships and eighty thousand men met an even larger Ottoman flotilla off the coast of Greece. The Spanish naval victory at Lepanto was considered one of the great events of the sixteenth century, celebrated in story and song for the next three hundred years. Though the Turks continued to menace the Mediterranean islands, Lepanto marked the end of Ottoman advances.

If Philip II saw himself as a Christian monarch fending off the advance of the infidel, he also saw himself as a Catholic monarch fending off the spread of heresy. There can be no doubt of Philip's personal devotion to Catholicism or of his oft-expressed conviction that "I would prefer to lose all my dominions and a hundred lives if I had them [rather] than be lord over heretics." The lives that were to be lost in battling heretics were numbered not in hundreds, but in hundreds of thousands. Philip II came to the throne at just the moment that Calvinism began its rapid growth in northern Europe. He supported the Catholic cause in France throughout the civil wars, sending money, advisers, and ultimately an army to relieve Paris. His ambassadors urged Catherine de Médicis and her sons to take the most repressive measures against the Huguenots, including the Saint Bartholomew's Day massacre.

Philip was equally aggressive against English Protestants. For a brief time he had been king in England through his marriage to Mary I (1553–58). He encouraged Mary's efforts to restore the Catholic church in England and supported her policies of repression. When Mary died and Elizabeth I (1558–1603) rejected his marriage proposal, his limited rule in England came to an end. From then on England and Spain entered a long period of hostility. English pirates raided Spanish treasure ships returning to Europe and Elizabeth covertly aided both French and Dutch Protestants. Finally in 1588 Philip decided upon invasion. A great fleet set sail from the Portuguese coast to the Netherlands, where a large Spanish army stood waiting to be conveyed to England.

The Spanish Armada comprised over 130 ships, many of them the pride of the Spanish and Portuguese navies. They were bigger and stronger than anything possessed by the English, whose forces were largely merchant vessels hastily converted for battle. But the English ships were faster and more easily maneuverable in the unpredictable winds of the English Channel. They also contained guns that could easily be reloaded for multiple firings, while the Spanish guns were designed to discharge only one broadside before hand-to-hand combat ensued. With these advantages the English were able to prevent the Armada from reaching port in the Netherlands and to destroy many individual ships as they were blown off course. The defeat of the Spanish Armada was less a military than a psychological blow to Philip II. He could more easily replace ships than restore confidence in Spanish power.

The Burgundian Inheritance

This confidence was all the more necessary when Philip II faced the gravest crisis of his reign: the revolt of the Netherlands. Though Philip's father, Charles V, amassed a great empire, he had begun only as the Duke of Burgundy. Charles' Burgundian inheritance encompassed a diverse territory in the northwestern corner of Europe. The seventeen separate provinces of this territory were called the Netherlands or the Low Countries because of the flooding that kept large portions of them under water. The Netherlands was one of the richest and most populous regions of Europe, an international leader in manufacturing, banking, and above all, commerce. Antwerp and Amsterdam were bustling port cities with access to the North Sea; inland were the prosperous industrial towns of Ghent and Brussels. The preeminence of the Netherlands was all the more remarkable because the provinces themselves were divided geographically, culturally, and linguistically. Rivers, lakes, and flooded plains separated the southern provinces, where French was the background and language of the inhabitants, from the northern ones where Germans had settled and Dutch was spoken. Charles V attempted to unify the provinces by removing them from the

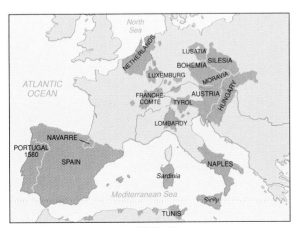

Habsburg Empire Under Philip II

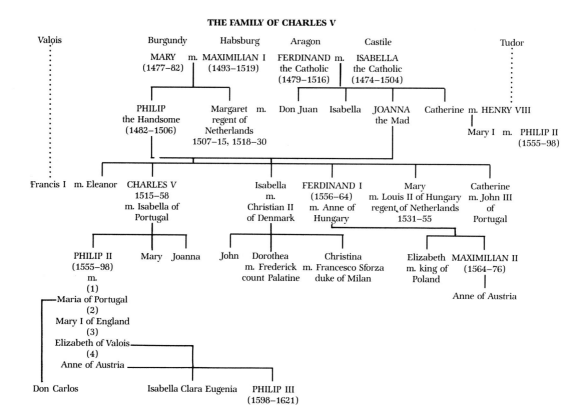

THE FAMILY OF CHARLES V

Valois — Burgundy — Habsburg — Aragon — Castile — Tudor

MARY (1477–82) m. MAXIMILIAN I (1493–1519) — FERDINAND the Catholic (1479–1516) m. ISABELLA the Catholic (1474–1504)

PHILIP the Handsome (1482–1506) — Margaret m. regent of Netherlands 1507–15, 1518–30 — Don Juan — Isabella — JOANNA the Mad — Catherine m. HENRY VIII

Mary I m. PHILIP II (1555–98)

Francis I m. Eleanor — CHARLES V 1515–58 m. Isabella of Portugal — Isabella m. Christian II of Denmark — FERDINAND I (1556–64) m. Anne of Hungary — Mary m. Louis II of Hungary regent of Netherlands 1531–55 — Catherine m. John III of Portugal

PHILIP II (1555–98) m. — Mary — Joanna — John — Dorothea m. Frederick count Palatine — Christina m. Francesco Sforza duke of Milan — Elizabeth m. king of Poland — MAXIMILIAN II (1564–76)

Anne of Austria

(1) Maria of Portugal
(2) Mary I of England
(3) Elizabeth of Valois
(4) Anne of Austria

Don Carlos — Isabella Clara Eugenia — PHILIP III (1598–1621)

jurisdiction of the Holy Roman Empire and establishing a separate regency under his eldest son, Philip II. Thus the future of the Netherlands was tied to Spain and the New World when Philip II set sail for Castile in 1559 to claim the crown of Spain.

Though Philip II had every intention of returning to the Low Countries, in fact the Netherlands had seen the last of their king. Philip left his half-sister, Margaret of Parma, as regent and provided her with a talented group of Spanish administrators to carry out policies that were to be formulated in Madrid. As Philip's own grasp on the affairs of the Netherlands loosened, so did the loyalty of the native nobility to the absent monarch. The resentments that built up were the traditional ones—hostility to foreigners, distrust of royal advisors, and contempt for policies that lacked understanding of local conditions. All of these discontents came together over Philip's religious policies. The Low Countries had accepted the Peace of Augsburg in a spirit of conciliation in which it was never intended. Here Catholics, Lutherans, Anabaptists, and Calvinists peaceably coexisted. Though the laws against

heresy promulgated by Charles V and Philip II ostensibly pertained to the Low Countries, local magistrates rarely enforced them.

As in France, this situation changed dramatically with the spread of Calvinism. In their cat-and-mouse game with Catholic authorities, French Calvinists crossed back and forth along the borders of the provinces. The heavy concentration of urban populations in the Low Countries provided the natural habitat for Calvinist preachers, who made converts across the entire social spectrum. While in France Calvinism survived as a religion of the nobility and middle classes, in the Netherlands it attracted peasants, laborers, and artisans as well. As Holy Roman Emperor, Charles V may have made his peace with Protestants, but as king of Spain he had not. Charles V had maintained the purity of the Spanish Catholic church through a sensible combination of reform and repression. Philip II intended to pursue a similar policy in the Low Countries. With papal approval he initiated a scheme to reform the hierarchy of the Church by expanding the numbers of bishops, and he invited the Jesuits to establish schools for orthodox learning. Simultaneously, he strengthened the power of the Inquisition and ordered the enforcement of the decrees of the Council of Trent.

Philip's intended reforms ran into immediate difficulties. In the first place there were the Protestants, not only aggressive Calvinists, but also settled Lutherans and Anabaptists who lived quietly in their own communities. They sought the protection of their local nobility who, Catholic or Protestant, had their own reasons for opposing the strict enforcement of heresy laws. Philip's harsh dictates threatened the uneasy peace that kept religious extremists from each other's throats. Moreover, the imposition of the Inquisition robbed local governors of their long-established powers. Provincial nobility and magistrates resented both the policies that were being pursued and the fact that they disregarded local autonomy. Town governors and noblemen refused to cooperate in implementing the new laws. Leading Protestants like Prince William of Orange, one of the largest landholders in the Netherlands, and Count Egmont, an outstanding military leader, urged Margaret to adopt a policy of toleration along the lines of the Peace of Augsburg and made clear that they would resign from office rather than support anything else.

The Revolt of the Netherlands

The passive resistance of nobles and magistrates was soon matched by the active resistance of the Calvinists. Unable to enforce Philip's policy, Margaret and her advisers agreed to a limited toleration. But in the summer of 1566, before it could be put into effect, bands of Calvinists unleashed a storm of iconoclasm in the provinces, breaking stained glass windows and statues of the Virgin and the saints, which they claimed were idolatrous. Catholic churches were stormed and turned into Calvinist meeting houses. Local authorities were helpless in the face of determined Calvinists and apathetic Catholics; they could not protect Church property. Iconoclasm gave way to open revolt. Fearing social rebellion, even the leading Protestant noblemen took part in suppressing these riots. But they could not escape blame for having encouraged the weakening of royal resolve. Many found it prudent to retire to estates outside the Netherlands. It was a prudence that saved their lives.

In Spain, the events in the Netherlands were treated for what they were: open rebellion. Despite the fact that Margaret had already restored order, Philip II was determined to punish the rebels and enforce the heresy laws. A large military force under the command of the Duke of Alba (1507–82), Philip's ablest general, whose record of success was matched only by his record of brutality, was sent from Spain as an army of occupation. As befit a warrior who had made his reputation leading imperial troops against the Lutherans, Alba gave no quarter to the Protestants of the Netherlands. Like Machiavelli, he believed that terror was more effective than mercy: "Everyone must be made to live in constant fear of the roof breaking down over his head," he wrote.

Alba lured Count Egmont and other Protestant noblemen to Brussels, where he publicly executed them in 1568. He also established a military court to punish participants in the rebellion, a court that came to be called the Council of Blood. The Council handed down over nine thousand convictions, a thousand of which carried the death penalty. As many as sixty thousand Protestants fled beyond Alba's jurisdiction, swelling the Protestant population of France and the northern provinces. Alba next made an example of several small towns that had been implicated in the iconoclasm. He allowed his soldiers to pillage the towns at will before slaughtering their entire populations and razing them to the ground. By the end of 1568 royal policy had gained a sullen acceptance in the Netherlands, but the hostilities did not end. For the next eighty years, with only occasional truces, Spain and the Netherlands were at war.

Like the French civil wars, the Dutch revolts fed upon themselves. Alba's policies drove Protestants into rebellion. This forced the Spanish government to maintain its army by raising taxes from those provinces that had remained loyal. Soon the loyal provinces too were in revolt, not over religion, but over taxation and local autonomy. In 1571 a number of southern provinces staged a tax strike against Alba's plan to collect the "tenth penny," a 10 percent levy on trade. Tax resistance and fear of an invasion from France left Alba unprepared for the series of successful assaults Protestants launched in the northern provinces during 1572. Though their forces were never a match for Alba's battle-tested veterans, the Protestant generals were able to take advantage of the geography of the provinces to capture coastal towns and establish a permanent base in the northwestern provinces of Holland and Zeeland. By 1575 the Protestants had gained a stronghold that they would never relinquish. Prince William of Orange assumed the leadership of the two provinces that were now united against the tyranny of Philip's rule. Though neither province had been predominantly Calvinist at the beginning of the revolts, both became progressively so as exiles from the south fled Spanish persecution. Spanish persecution of Protestants in the south was matched by Calvinist persecution of Catholics in the north. Despite sincere efforts by William—who himself had been Catholic, Lutheran, and Calvinist—the newly united provinces were no more tolerant of religious differences than was the old Habsburg one.

Spanish government was collapsing all over the Netherlands. William ruled in the north, and the States-General, a parliamentary body composed of representatives from the separate provinces, ruled in the south. Margaret of Parma had resigned in disgust at Alba's tactics, and Alba had been relieved of his command when his tactics had failed. No one was in control of the Spanish army. The soldiers, who had gone years with only partial pay, now roamed the southern provinces looking for plunder. Brussels and Ghent both had been targets, and in 1576 the worst atrocities of all occurred when mutinous Spanish troops sacked Antwerp. One of the wealthiest cities in Europe, home to the most important mercantile and banking establishments in the world, Antwerp was torn apart like a roasted pig. The rampage lasted for days. When it ended over seven thousand people had been slaughtered and nearly a third of the city burned to the ground.

The "Spanish fury" in Antwerp effectively ended Philip's rule over his Burgundian inheritance. The Protestants had established a permanent home in the north—whose borders would shift continually over the next thirty years. The States-General had established its ability to rule in the south, and Spanish policy had been totally discredited. To achieve a settlement, the Pacification of Ghent of 1576, the Spanish government conceded local autonomy in taxation, the central

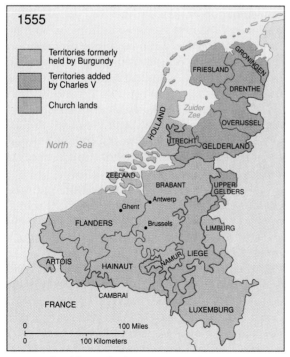

The Revolt of the Netherlands

Revolt of the Netherlands

1559 Margaret of Parma named regent of the Netherlands

1566 Calvinist iconoclasm begins revolt

1567 Duke of Alba arrives in Netherlands and establishes Council of Blood

1568 Protestant Count Egmont executed

1571 "Ten Penny" revolt begins

1572 Protestants capture Holland and Zeland

1573 Alba relieved of his command

1576 Sack of Antwerp

Pacification of Ghent

1581 Catholic and Protestant provinces split

1585 Spanish forces under Alexander Farnese take Brussels and Antwerp

1609 Twelve Years' Truce

role of the States-General in legislation, and the immediate withdrawal of all Spanish troops from the Low Countries. Five southern provinces pledged to remain Catholic and to accept the authority of the king's regent. This rift among the provinces was soon followed by a permanent split. In 1581 one group of provinces voted to depose Philip II while a second group decided to remain loyal to him.

The cost of the revolts was staggering. Commerce and agriculture throughout the Low Countries had been permanently disrupted and vast movements of population had occurred. All this tore at the fabric of Burgundian society. For Spain the price was reckoned in gold—pounds and pounds of South American specie went to finance year after year of indecisive military campaigns. Though as early as the 1570s it was clear that the war could not be won, decade after decade it continued. Philip II refused to accept the dismemberment of his inheritance and refused to recognize the independent Dutch state that now existed in Holland. Throughout the 1580s and 1590s military expeditions attempted to reunite

the southern provinces and to conquer the northern ones. Appointed commander of Spanish forces in 1578, Alexander Farnese, Margaret of Parma's son, brought the southern and eastern provinces back under Spanish control. He took Ghent in 1584, Brussels and Antwerp in 1585. But Spanish military successes in the south were outweighed by the long-term failure of their objectives in the north. In 1609 Spain and the Netherlands concluded the Twelve Years' Truce, which tacitly recognized the existence of the state of Holland. By the beginning of the seventeenth century Holland was not only an independent state, it was one of the greatest rivals of Spain and Portugal for the fruits of empire.

The Reorganization of Northeastern Europe

In eastern Europe dynastic struggles outweighed the problems created by religious reform. Muscovy remained the bulwark of Eastern Orthodox Christianity, immune from the struggles over the Roman faith. Protestantism did spread into Poland-Lithuania, but unlike in the west, the Polish state tolerated its presence. The spread of dissent was checked not by repression, but by a vigorous Catholic reformation led by the Jesuits. The domestic crises in the east were crises of state rather than of church. The biological failure of the Jagiellon monarchy in Poland ended that nation's most successful line of kings. Without a natural heir, the Polish nobility and gentry, who officially elected the monarch, had to peddle their throne among the princes of Europe. In Muscovy, the disputed succession that followed the death of Ivan the Terrible plunged the state into anarchy and civil war. Centuries of conflict between Poland-Lithuania and Muscovy came to a head with the Poles' desperate gamble to seize control of their massive eastern neighbor. War between Poland-Lithuania and Muscovy inevitably dominated the politics of the entire region. The Baltic states, of which Sweden was to become the most important, had their own ambitions for territory and economic gain. They soon joined the fray, making alliances in return for concessions and conquering small pieces of the mainland.

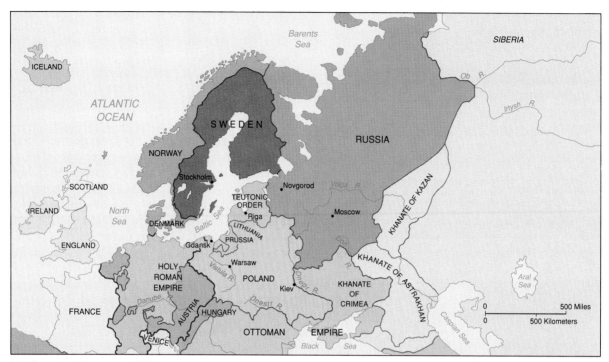

Northeastern Europe, ca. 1550

Religious conflict may not have been a national problem in eastern Europe, but it was an international one. The persistent warfare between the Roman-dominated Christianity of Poland-Lithuania and the Eastern Orthodox Christianity of Muscovy always had a religious tinge to it. Along the Baltic Sea, the Roman Catholic settlements of the Knights of the Teutonic Order crusaded for religious converts. Adherents of both Roman and Eastern Christianity belonged to the Lithuanian aristocracy. Sometimes these nobles were subject to Polish rule, at other times to Muscovite. Poland had a large minority of Eastern Christians. The Poles saw themselves as the bulwark of Roman Catholicism in Europe and justified their offensive wars against Muscovy as efforts to defend and to spread the true faith.

But the most important source of religious conflict in northeastern Europe resulted from the rise to prominence of the Lutheran state of Sweden. Before religious reformation swept Sweden, the country's traditional enemies had been the Danes and the Russians, who kept the Swedes hemmed in by the Baltic Sea. Security rather than religion motivated these hostilities. In 1587 the heir to the Swedish crown, Sigismund Vasa, was elected king of Poland. Though he lived in a Lutheran land, Sigismund had a Jesuit upbringing and strongly supported Jesuit reforms in Poland. When Sigismund inherited the Swedish crown in 1592, the Lutheran nobility faced a new threat to its religious and national independence. To protect both, the Swedes were forced into an active role in European affairs, a role that propelled their tiny nation into one of the greatest powers of the seventeenth century.

The Struggles in the East

In 1572 Sigismund II (1548–72) of Poland died without an heir. Though the Polish monarchy was elective rather than hereditary, during the centuries of rule by the Jagiellon family the electoral process had more form than substance. Sons succeeded their fathers to the throne and the Jagiellons regarded the Polish and Lithuanian crowns as their rightful inheritance. But now there were no heirs and the nobility and gentry of Poland-Lithuania had to select their king from among the princes of Europe. In fact, the next three Polish kings were so chosen, giving the Polish crown successively to a prince of France, a prince of Transylvania, and finally a prince of Sweden. Each was bound more tightly than his predecessor to a set of constitutional and religious restrictions that protected the power and privileges of the nobility and gentry. Matters of war and peace, of taxation, and of reform were placed under the strict supervision of the Polish Diet, a parliamentary body that represented the Polish landed elite. The Diet also carefully controlled religious policy. Roman Catholicism was the principal religion in Poland but the state tolerated numerous Protestant and Eastern creeds. In the Warsaw Confederation of 1573 the Polish gentry vowed "that we who differ in matters of religion will keep the peace among ourselves," a remarkable pledge that was honored by kings and subjects for over a half of a century. Poland was the only state in Europe where religious toleration was practiced as well as preached.

Until the end of the sixteenth century, Poland-Lithuania was the dominant power in the eastern part of Europe. It was economically healthy and militarily strong. Through its Baltic ports, especially Gdansk, Poland played a central role in international commerce and a dominant role in the northern grain trade. Poland's agricultural surplus nourished the Netherlands during the long years of civil war. The vast size of the Polish state made defense difficult, and during the course of the sixteenth century it had lost lands to Muscovy in the east and to the Crimean Tartars in

An assembly of the Polish Diet, the parliamentary body composed of the landed elite. On the throne is Sigismund III. Rivalry among the magnates weakened the Diet, and conflicts with the elected monarchs were frequent.

the south. But the permanent union with Lithuania in 1569 and the gradual absorption of the Baltic region of Livonia more than compensated for these losses. The Poles were able to raise and maintain large armies, and when the Polish Diet thought that the prize was worth fighting for, it could finance long and costly campaigns.

When Sigismund III (1587–1632) was elected to the Polish throne in 1587, he was also heir to the crown of Sweden. His Jesuit upbringing, under the direction of his Polish mother, was an ideal background for extending the Catholic reformation in Poland. Sigismund accepted the prohibitions against religious repression outlined in the Warsaw Confederation, but he actively encouraged the establishment of Jesuit schools, the expansion of monastic orders, and the strengthening of the Roman Catholic church. During his reign the numbers and importance of Protestant gentry declined significantly.

All of these policies enjoyed the approval of the Polish ruling classes. But the Diet would not support Sigismund's efforts to gain control of the Swedish crown, which he inherited in 1592 but from which he was deposed three years later. The Polish gentry had little to gain and much to lose from their king's success in Sweden. They were uninterested in the spoils to be taken from Sweden's poor agrarian economy and unimpressed by the prospect of converting the Swedes to Roman Catholicism. If Sigismund triumphed in Sweden, all Poland would get was a part-time monarch. The Polish Diet consistently refused to give the king the funds necessary to invade Sweden successfully. Nevertheless, Sigismund mounted several unsuccessful campaigns against the Swedes, campaigns that sapped Polish money and manpower.

If their king was to be militarily aggressive, the leaders of the Diet preferred that he look east rather than north. Before the seventeenth century there was little history of hostility between Poland and Sweden; between Poland and Muscovy there was no history of anything else. The wars of Ivan the Great and Ivan the Terrible in the fifteenth and sixteenth centuries were waged to secure agricultural territory in the west and a Baltic port in the north. Both objectives came at the expense of Poland-Lithuania. But following the death of Ivan the Terrible in 1584, the Muscovite state began to disintegrate. For years it had been held together only by conquest and fear—the military service class received prizes of captured territory; the boyars, or hereditary nobility, were cowed by Ivan's brutal policies. Ivan's conflicts with the boyars created an aristocracy unwilling and unable to come to the aid of his successors. Landowners and merchants retreated eastward beyond Ivan's grasp, leaving the center of the country depopulated. Siberia was colonized and its riches discovered by those who preferred the Arctic's frigid winters to Ivan's torrid temper. Near-anarchy prevailed in the south as Tartars raided Russian settlements for slaves and bands of Cossacks pillaged them for food. Peasant revolts followed harvest failures as the fragile agrarian economy broke down.

By 1601 the crown was plunged into a crisis of legitimacy known as the Time of Troubles. Ivan had murdered his heir in a fit of anger and left his half-witted son to inherit the throne. This led to a vacuum of power at the center as well as a struggle for the spoils of government. Private armies ruled great swaths of the state and pretenders to the crown—all claiming to be Dimitri, the lost brother of the last legitimate tsar—appeared everywhere. Ambitious groups of boyars backed their own claimants to the throne. So, too, did ambitious foreigners who eagerly sought to carve up Muscovite possessions.

Muscovy's Time of Troubles was Poland's moment of opportunity. While anarchy and civil war raged—perhaps as many as two and a half million people perished in one decade—Poland looked to regain the territory that it had lost to Muscovy over the previous century. Sigismund abandoned war with Sweden in order to intervene in the struggle for the Russian crown. Polish forces crossed into Muscovy and Sigismund's generals backed one of the strongest of the false Dimitris. They provided him with Jesuits for religious instruction and a Polish princess for a wife. Their plan to put him on the throne failed when he was assassinated. Sigismund used the death of the last false Dimitri as a pretext to assert his own claim to the Muscovite crown. More Polish forces poured across the frontier. In 1610 they took Moscow and Sigismund proclaimed himself tsar, intending to unite the two massive states.

The Russian boyars, so long divided, now rose against the Polish enemy. The Polish garrison in Moscow was starved into submission and a native Russian, Michael Romanov (1613–45) was chosen tsar by an assembly of landholders, the Zemsky Sobor. He made a humiliating peace with the Swedes—who had also taken advantage of the Time of Troubles to invade Muscovy's Baltic provinces—in return for Swedish assistance against the Poles. Intermittent fighting continued for another twenty years. In the end, Poland agreed to peace and a separate Muscovite state, but only in exchange for large territorial concessions. Peace allowed Tsar Michael to establish the legitimacy of his rule, rebuild his shattered state and to plot his revenge.

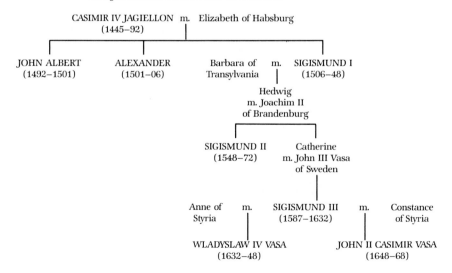

THE JAGIELLON MONARCHY OF POLAND

CASIMIR IV JAGIELLON m. Elizabeth of Habsburg
(1445–92)

JOHN ALBERT   ALEXANDER   Barbara of   m.   SIGISMUND I
(1492–1501)   (1501–06)   Transylvania   (1506–48)

Hedwig
m. Joachim II
of Brandenburg

SIGISMUND II   Catherine
(1548–72)   m. John III Vasa
                   of Sweden

Anne of   m.   SIGISMUND III   m.   Constance
Styria   (1587–1632)   of Styria

WLADYSLAW IV VASA   JOHN II CASIMIR VASA
(1632–48)   (1648–68)

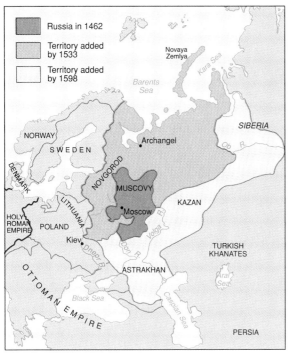

The Rise of Russia

The Rise of Sweden

Sweden's rise to power during the seventeenth century was as startling as it was swift. Until the Reformation, Sweden had been part of the Scandinavian confederation ruled by the Danes. Although the Swedes had a measure of autonomy, they were very much a junior partner in Baltic affairs. Denmark controlled the narrow sound that linked the Baltic with the North Sea, and its prosperity derived from the tolls it collected on imports and exports. When, in 1523, Gustav I Vasa led the uprising of the Swedish aristocracy that ended Danish domination, he won the right to rule over a poor, sparsely populated state with few towns or developed seaports. Its internal economy was based almost entirely on barter and most of its vast territory, which included Lapland in the north and Finland in the east, was uninhabitable.

The Vasas ruled Sweden in conjunction with the aristocracy. Although the throne was hereditary, the part played by the nobility in elevating Gustav I Vasa (1523–60) gave the nobles a powerful voice in Swedish affairs. Through the council of state, known as the Rad, the Swedish nobility exerted a strong check on the monarch. Still, the active engagement of the nobility in civil government meant that the king could count on their resources in times of crisis. This became increasingly important as Sweden took a greater interest in Baltic affairs.

Sweden's aggressive foreign policy began accidentally. When in the 1550s the Teutonic Knights found themselves no longer capable of ruling in Livonia, the Baltic seaports that had been under their dominion scrambled for new alliances. Muscovy and Poland-Lithuania were the logical choices, but the town of Reval, an important outlet for Russian trade near the mouth of the Gulf of Finland, asked Sweden for protection. After some hesitation, since the occupation of territory on the southern shores of the Baltic would involve great expense, Sweden fortified Reval in 1560. A decade later, Swedish forces captured Narva, farther to the east, and consolidated their hold on the Livonian coast. By occupying the most important ports on the Gulf of Finland, Sweden could control a sizable portion of the Muscovite trade.

Having gained so much so soon, the Swedes yearned to gain more. Only two obstacles prevented them from dominating trade with Muscovy: Archangel in the north and Riga in the south. In the 1580s, as the Muscovites pushed eastward across their immense territories, they established a port at Archangel on the White Sea. With this new port they opened a trading route to the west, around northern Scandinavia. There were two advantages of the Arctic route; it made direct trade between Muscovy and the west possible and it avoided the Danish tolls in the Baltic. In the west, England and the Low Countries benefited from the White Sea trade, being directly in its route. In the east, Sweden benefited by claiming the northern portions of the Scandinavian peninsula necessary to make the trade secure. In all of their dealings with Muscovy the Swedes sought further privileges at Archangel while laying plans for its conquest. Riga was a problem of a different sort. It was the most important port in Livonia, providing easy access to the Lithuanian and Russian hinterland. Under Polish domination it was the center for Poland's eastern trade. As the Swedes secured the northern Livonian ports, more of the Muscovy trade moved to the south and passed through Riga. It, too, would have to be captured or blockaded if the Swedes were to control commerce in the eastern Baltic.

Surprisingly, it was not Swedish belligerence that initiated the near continuous warfare of the next half-century. Though the ambition may have been to control the Muscovy trade, Sweden had very little prospect of actually doing so. Poland was far too strong to be challenged over Livonia, and Denmark also laid claim to the northern Scandinavian coast. But the fact that Sweden aspired to power in the Baltic made Livonia a more attractive target than ever before. Because Sigismund III, king of Poland, was also heir to the Swedish crown, it became possible that a combination of Swedish and Polish forces would challenge Danish dominion in the Baltic. Yet it soon became clear that the Swedes were far more interested in their religious liberty and national freedom than they were in the spoils of commerce. Sigismund's aggressive alliance with the Polish Jesuits persuaded the Swedish nobility that he would undermine their Lutheran church. Sigismund was deposed in favor of his uncle Charles IX (1604–11). Soon Sweden was fighting simultaneously with the Poles and the Danes.

Both conflicts were initially disastrous. War with Poland resulted from Sigismund's efforts to regain the Swedish crown. The Swedes used the opportunity to blockade Riga and to occupy more Livonian territory. The Swedish navy was far superior to any force that the Poles could assemble, but on land Polish forces were masters. The Swedish invasion force suffered a crushing defeat and had to retreat to its coastal enclaves. The Poles now had an opportunity to retake all of Livonia but, as always, the Polish Diet was reluctant to finance Sigismund's wars. Furthermore, Sigismund had his eyes on a bigger prize. Rather than follow up its Swedish victory, Poland invaded Muscovy.

Meanwhile, the blockade of Riga and the assembly of a large Swedish fleet in the Baltic threatened Denmark. The Danes continued to claim sovereignty over Sweden and took the opportunity of the Polish-Swedish conflict to reassert it. In 1611, under the energetic leadership of the Danish king Christian IV (1588–1648), Denmark invaded Sweden from both the east and the west. The Danes captured the towns of Kalmar and Alvsborg and threatened to take Stockholm. The loss of Alvsborg was of critical importance. A large part of the Swedish fleet was anchored there, and it was the only Swedish port that let out

A Livonian peasant. Livonia was conquered by Ivan the Terrible in his campaign of 1563, but was soon reclaimed by the Poles. In 1660 Livonia became part of the Swedish empire. Livonia was originally inhabited by the Livs, a Finnish people.

directly on the North Sea. To end the Danish war, Sweden accepted humiliating terms in 1613. Not only did Sweden renounce all claims to the northern coasts and recognize Danish control of the Arctic trading route, but Alvsborg remained in Danish possession for six years until a huge ransom had been paid.

Paradoxically, these setbacks became the springboard for Swedish success. Fear of the Danes led both the English and the Dutch into alliances with Sweden. The countries all shared Protestant interests, and the English were heavily committed to the Muscovy trade, which was still an important part of Swedish commerce. It was the Dutch who financed the ransom of Alvsborg. In exchange for Swedish iron and copper, the Dutch provided credit to meet the stiff annual payments. Fear of the Poles had a similar effect upon Muscovy. In 1609 the Swedes agreed to send five thousand troops to Muscovy to help repel the Polish invasion. In return, Muscovy agreed to cede to Sweden its Baltic possessions. This was accomplished in 1617 and gave Sweden complete control of the Gulf of Finland.

In 1611, during the middle of the Danish war, Charles IX died and was succeeded by his son Gustavus Adolphus (1611–32). Unlike his father and cousin before him, who had come by chance to the Swedish throne, Gustavus Adolphus was raised to be king. Gruff and affable by turns, he was one of the leading Protestant princes of his day, in every way a match for Christian IV of Denmark. Gustavus' greatest skills were military. He inherited an ample navy and an effective army. Unlike nearly every other European state, Sweden raised its forces from its own citizens. Gustavus' predecessors had made important innovations in the training of soldiers and in their battlefield tactics. These the new king improved upon. He introduced new weapons like the light mobile gun and reshaped his army into standard-size squadrons and regiments, which were easier to administer and deploy.

The calamitous wars inherited from his father occupied Gustavus during the early years of his reign. He was forced to conclude the humiliating peace with the Danes in 1613 and to go to war with the Russians in 1614 to secure the Baltic coastal estates that had been promised in 1609. Gustavus' first military initiative was to resume war with Poland in order to force Sigismund to renounce his claim to the Swedish throne. In 1621 Gustavus landed in Livonia and in two weeks captured Riga, the capstone of Sweden's Baltic ambitions. Occupation of Riga increased Swedish control of the Muscovy trade and it deprived Den-

The Rise of Sweden

mark of a significant portion of its customs duties. Gustavus now claimed Riga as a Swedish port and successfully demanded that ships sailing from there pay tolls to Sweden rather than Denmark. The capture of Riga firmly established Sweden as a co-equal Baltic power.

By the mid-seventeenth century, the Sweden of Gustavus Adolphus was well on its way to international prominence. The capture of Riga gave Sweden complete control of the eastern Baltic and ended Polish pretensions to the Swedish

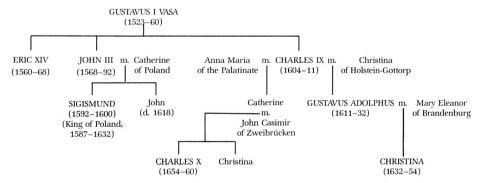

throne. In 1619 Alvsborg returned to Swedish hands and immediately began a prosperous trade with the Dutch. A negotiated settlement with the Danes over the collection of tolls enhanced Swedish prestige and increased Sweden's commercial prosperity. Moreover, Gustavus' marriage into the family of the Protestant rulers of Prussia gave Sweden a presence in Germany as well. For the time being Sweden faced east. But the storm clouds of religious warfare were already bursting over the Holy Roman Empire. Gustavus Adolphus now took his place among the Protestant princes of Europe, and Sweden ranked among the leading Protestant powers.

The Thirty Years' War

Perhaps it was just a matter of time before the isolated conflicts that dotted the corners of Europe were joined together. At the beginning of the seventeenth century the battle lines were clearly drawn. Two great forces swelled against each other: the religious struggle between Catholics and Protestants and the dynastic struggle between the Habsburgs and their enemies. At times they intersected, as in the revolt of the Netherlands, where Protestantism could be defended and the Habsburgs attacked. Other times they diverged, as in the support that Catholic France provided to the Protestant enemies of Spain and the Holy Roman Empire. This mixture of religion and politics was extremely volatile. Some princes hid their dynastic ambitions beneath the cloak of religious conviction. Others pursued holy war without regard for the well-being of their state. In this battle for the glory of God and the glory of man there could be no end, only occasional interruptions.

It was one such interruption that claimed the attention of the European powers at the beginning of the seventeenth century. In 1609 Spain and the Dutch Republic had signed a truce that was to last until 1621. In over forty years of nearly continuous fighting the Dutch had carved out a state in the northern Netherlands. They used the truce to consolidate their position and increase their prosperity. A maritime state, Holland expanded overseas, largely at the expense of Spain and Portugal.

Gustavus Adolphus of Sweden, shown at the Battle of Breitenfeld in 1631. The battle was the first important Protestant victory of the Thirty Years' War. Gustavus died on the battlefield at Lützen in the following year.

Thus to the insult of rebellion was added the injury of commercial competition. Spain had reluctantly accepted Dutch independence, but Philip III (1598–1621), like his father before him, never abandoned the objective of recovering his Burgundian inheritance. By the opening of the seventeenth century Philip had good reasons for hope. Beginning in the 1580s, Spanish forces had reconquered the southern provinces of the Netherlands. The prosperous towns of Brussels, Antwerp, and Ghent were again under Spanish control, and they provided a springboard for another invasion.

The Twelve Years' Truce gave Spain time to prepare for the final assault. During this time Philip III attempted to resolve all of Spain's other European conflicts so that he could then give full attention to a resumption of the Dutch war. Circumstance smiled upon his efforts. In 1603 the pacific James I (1603–25) came to the English throne. Secure in his island state, James I desired peace among all Christian princes. He quickly concluded the war with Spain that had begun with the invasion of the Spanish Armada, and he entered into negotiations to marry his heir to a Spanish princess. In 1610 the bellicose Henry IV of France was felled by an assassin's knife. French plans to renew war with Spain were abandoned with the accession of the eight-year-old Louis XIII (1610–43). As the sands of the Twelve Years' Truce ran out, Spain and the Netherlands readied for war. Towns were fortified and cannons were cast. Mercenaries offered their services to the highest bidder. But not even the greatest empire in Europe could control its own destiny. War was in the air all over the Continent, and not everyone could wait until 1621.

The Bohemian Revolt

The Peace of Augsburg had served the German states well. The principle that the religion of the ruler was the religion of the state complicated the political life of the Holy Roman Empire, but it also pacified it. Though rulers had the right to enforce uniformity on their subjects, in practice many of the larger states tolerated more than one religion. By the beginning of the seventeenth century Catholicism and Protestantism had achieved a rough equality within the German states, symbolized by the fact that of the seven electors who chose the Holy Roman Emperor, three were Catholic, three Protestant, and the seventh was the emperor himself, acting as king of Bohemia. This situation was not unwelcome to the leaders of the Austrian Habsburg family who succeeded Emperor Charles V. By necessity, the eastern Habsburgs were more tolerant than their Spanish kinfolk. Protestants fought the Ottomans with as much zeal as did Catholics, and the Ottomans were the empire's more potent enemy. The unofficial policy of toleration not only helped the Austrian Habsburgs defend their state, it allowed them to expand it. The head of their house was elected king of Bohemia and king of Hungary, both states with large Protestant populations.

But the delicate religious balance in central Europe presented difficulties as well as advantages. The appearance of Calvinism in Germany led to more Protestant converts, the appearance of the Counter-Reformation to more Catholic reconversions. Each change heightened anxieties. Every diplomatic marriage or contested inheritance threatened to upset the balance. Protestant and Catholic states, fearful of the power of their rivals, formed separate defensive alliances. The arming of one camp incited the arming of the other. The military temperature rose along with the religious and the political.

Matters came to a head in 1617 when Mathias, the childless Holy Roman Emperor, began making plans for his cousin, Ferdinand Habsburg, to succeed him. In order to ensure a Catholic majority among the electors, the emperor relinquished his Bohemian title and pressed for Ferdinand's election as the new king of Bohemia. Ferdinand was Catholic, very devout and very committed. He had been educated by Jesuits and practiced what had been preached to him. On his own estates, Ferdinand abandoned the policy of toleration. Jesuit schools were founded and the precepts of the Council of Trent were enforced. Protestant preachers were barred from their offices, Protestant books were publicly burned, and thousands of common people were forced to flee, many into nearby Bohemia, where Protestants constituted the majority of the population.

Thus Ferdinand's election as king of Bohemia was no foregone conclusion. Though in the end the Protestant nobles of Bohemia could not prevent his election, they forced the new king to accept the strictest limitations upon his political and religious powers. But once elected Ferdinand had not the slightest intention of honoring the provisions that had been thrust upon him. His opponents were equally strong willed. When Ferdinand violated Protestant religious liberties, a group of noblemen marched to the royal palace in Prague in May 1618, found two of the king's chief advisers, and hurled them out of an upper-story window. The officials' lives, if not their dignity, were preserved by the pile of manure in which they landed.

The Defenestration of Prague, as this incident came to be known, initiated a Protestant counteroffensive throughout the Habsburg lands. Fear of Ferdinand's policies led to Protestant uprisings in Hungary as well as Bohemia. Those who seized control of the government declared Ferdinand deposed and the throne vacant. But they had no candidate to accept their crown. The stakes were extremely high. Whatever their religion, princes were always uneasy about the overthrow of a lawful ruler. There had been nothing improper about Ferdinand's election. His policies may have been impolitic, but they were not illegal. Whoever came to be called king of Bohemia in place of

Ferdinand would also be called rebel of the empire. And his rebellion would have to face the combined might of the Habsburgs. Philip III of Spain saw with great clarity that a successful Protestant revolt in central Europe would threaten his plans to resume the war in the Netherlands. A successful Protestant revolt would win the Dutch new allies and might sever the vital supply lines through the Alps. Spain again would be forced to fight a war on two fronts. Suppression of the Bohemian revolt would have to precede resumption of the Dutch war.

These considerations weighed heavily upon the Protestant princes of Germany who, one by one, declined the offer of the Bohemian crown. When Emperor Mathias died in 1619, the stalemate was broken. Ferdinand succeeded to the imperial title as Ferdinand II (1619–37) and Frederick V, one of the Protestant electors, accepted the Bohemian crown. Frederick was a sincere but weak Calvinist whose credentials were much stronger than his abilities. His mother was a daughter of Prince William of Orange and his wife, Elizabeth, a daughter of James I of England. It was widely believed that it was Elizabeth's resolution that she would "rather eat sauerkraut with a King than roast meat with an Elector," that decided the issue. No decision could have been more disastrous for the fate of Europe. Frederick ruled a geographically divided German state known as the Palatinate. One hundred miles separated the two segments of his lands, but both were strategically important. The Lower Palatinate bordered on the Catholic Spanish Netherlands and the Upper Palatinate on Catholic Bavaria.

Once Frederick accepted the Bohemian crown, he was faced with a war on three fronts. It was over almost before it began. Ferdinand II had no difficulty enlisting allies to recover the Bohemian crown, since he could pay them with the spoils of Frederick's lands. Spanish troops from the Netherlands occupied the Lower Palatinate, and Bavarian troops occupied the Upper Palatinate. Frederick, on the other hand, met rejection wherever he turned. Neither the Dutch nor the English would send more than token aid—both had advised him against breaking the imperial peace. The Lutheran princes of Germany would not enter into a war between Calvinists and Catholics, especially after Ferdinand II promised to protect the Bohemian Lutherans.

At the battle of the White Mountain in 1620, Ferdinand's Catholic forces annihilated Frederick's army. Frederick and Elizabeth fled north, first to Denmark and then to Holland. Bohemia was left to face the wrath of Ferdinand, the victorious king and emperor. The retribution was horrible. Mercenaries who had fought for Ferdinand II were allowed to sack Prague for a week. Elective monarchy was abolished and Bohemia became part of the hereditary Habsburg lands. Free peasants were enserfed and subjected to imperial law. Those nobles who had supported Frederick lost their lands and their privileges. Calvinism was repressed and thoroughly rooted out, consolidating forever the Catholic character of Bohemia. Frederick's estates were carved up and his rights as elector transferred to the Catholic duke of Bavaria. The battle of the White Mountain was a turning point in the history of central Europe.

The War Widens

Yet the Catholic triumph may have been too complete. For the Habsburgs, religious and dynastic interests were inseparable. Ferdinand II and Philip III of Spain fought for their beliefs and for their patrimony. Their victory gave them more than they could have expected. Ferdinand swallowed up Bohemia and strengthened his position in the empire. Philip gained possession of a vital link in his supply route between Italy and the Netherlands. The Habsburgs were now more dangerous than ever. Ferdinand's aggressive Catholicism threatened the Protestant princes of Germany, who prudently began to seek allies outside the empire. Spanish expansion threatened France. The occupation of the Lower Palatinate placed a ring of Spanish armies around the French borders from the Pyrenees to the Low Countries. The French too searched for allies; in one diplomatic maneuver Louis XIII's sister, Henrietta Maria, was married to the heir to the English throne. But French opinion remained divided over which was the greater evil: Spain or Protestantism.

Frederick, now in Holland, refused to accept the judgment of battle. He lobbied for a grand alliance to repel the Spaniards from the Lower Palatinate and to restore the religious balance in the empire. Though his personal cause met with little sympathy, his political logic was impeccable, especially after Spain again declared war upon the Dutch. A grand Protestant alliance—secretly supported by the French—brought together England, Holland, a number of German states, and Denmark. It was the Danes who led this potentially powerful coalition. In 1626 a large Danish army under the command of King Christian IV engaged imperial forces on German soil.

But the Danes received little effective support from their allies. For three years they were the chief hope of Protestant Europe, and each year that hope grew dimmer. Danish forces could not match the superior numbers and the superior leadership of the Catholic mercenary forces under the command of the ruthless and brilliant Count Albrecht von Wallenstein (1583–1634). In each successive campaign Wallenstein inflicted heavy defeats upon the Danish armies and exacted even heavier retribution from the German population that stood in his path. In 1629 the Danes withdrew from the empire and sued for peace. Their grand Protestant alliance fell apart and Danish ambitions to lead international Protestantism were crushed.

If the Catholic victory at the White Mountain in 1620 threatened the well-being of German Protestantism, the Catholic triumph over the Danes threatened its survival. More powerful than ever, Ferdinand II determined to turn the religious clock back to the state of affairs that had existed when the Peace of Augsburg was concluded in 1555. He demanded that all lands that had then been Catholic but had since become Protestant must now be returned to the fold. He also proclaimed that as the Peace of Augsburg made no provision for the toleration of Calvinists, they would no longer be tolerated in the empire. These policies together constituted a virtual revolution in the religious affairs of the German states, and they proved impossible to impose. Ferdinand succeeded in only one thing—he united Lutherans and Calvinists against him. As long as the main Protestant creeds had been divided, Ferdinand had had little difficulty in undermining their alliances and defeating their armies. He also had little need to compromise with his own German allies, whose leaders were increasingly nervous about Spanish occupation of the Lower Palatinate and Ferdinand's confrontational policies. By demanding the restitution of Catholic lands and the suppression of Calvinism, Ferdinand II strengthened every position but his own.

This direct challenge to the survival of Protestantism was met from an unexpected quarter. Twelve years of fighting had devastated much of the empire. Marauding armies cared little for the distinctions of friend and foe, but it was the Protestant north that had borne the brunt of the destruction. After the defeat of the Danes, Catholic policy was to secure a beachhead on the Baltic from which a fleet could be built that would disrupt Protestant, and especially Dutch, shipping. Though these efforts were unsuccessful, they threatened the security of Sweden, which had recently concluded a long war with the Poles for control of the Baltic. In 1630 King Gustavus Adolphus of Sweden decided to enter the German conflict. To protect Swedish interests, he reasoned, he must defend the Protestant states of northern Germany. Moreover, France was willing to pay much of the cost of a war against Ferdinand. The French too felt the pressure of increasing imperial and Spanish power.

Gustavus Adolphus had more success gaining the support of Catholic France than he did gaining the support of the Protestant German princes. Saxony and Brandenburg, the two largest states, feared the consequences of renewed war. Though both suffered under Ferdinand's policies, they were fearful of his wrath. It was hard to forget what had happened to Frederick. Nor did they think that the Swedes would succeed where the Danes had failed. But in fact the situation in 1630 was far different than it had been five years earlier. Ferdinand's alliances were coming unraveled, both for fear of his power and dislike of his policies. The costs of the war were heavy even for the victors. Wallenstein, who had over 130,000 men in arms, would no longer take orders from anyone, and Ferdinand II was forced to dismiss him from service. The loss of Wallenstein reduced imperial military might just at the moment that the empire was to face its greatest challenge.

Moreover, the Swedes were not the Danes. The Swedish army was composed of battle-tested veterans used to the conditions of land war. Their king and commander, Gustavus Adolphus, was a military leader of considerable talent and verve. He had continued Swedish innovations in military tactics and he had already proven himself an able strategist. Gustavus believed that he could defend the north German states from Ferdinand's aggression and by doing so protect Sweden's Baltic empire. "I seek not my own advantage in this war, nor any gain save the security of my Kingdom," he lectured the reluctant Germans. It was a far-sighted strategy. In fact, the only thing he could not foresee when he landed in Germany early in 1630 was how successful his intervention would be.

While Gustavus Adolphus struggled to construct his alliance, imperial forces continued their triumphant progress. In 1631 they besieged, captured, and put to the torch the town of Magdeburg. In a war noted for cruelty between combatants and atrocities against civilians, the destruction of Magdeburg set new standards. Perhaps three-fourths of the forty thousand inhabitants of the town were slaughtered—"in the midst of a horrible din of heart-rending shrieks and cries they were tortured and put to death in so cruel a manner that no words would suffice to describe nor no tears to bewail it," was the report in one pamphlet. The sack of Magdeburg marked a turning point in Protestant fortunes. It gave the international Protestant community a unifying symbol that enhanced Gustavus' military efforts. Hundreds of pamphlets, woodcuts, and news-paper accounts brought the horror of Magdeburg home to Protestants throughout the Continent. Brandenburg and Saxony joined Gustavus Adolphus, not only enlarging his forces, but allowing him to open a second front in Bohemia. He would soon have 140,000 men under his command, only 13,000 of whom were Swedish. In the autumn of 1631 this combination overwhelmed the imperial armies. Gustavus won a decisive triumph at Breitenfeld, while the Saxons occupied Prague. For the first time since 1618, Protestant forces were ascendant, and they brought the war into the Catholic heartland of the empire.

Gustavus Adolphus lost no time in pressing his advantage. While Ferdinand II pleaded with Wallenstein to resume his command, the Swedes marched west to the Rhine, easily conquering the richest of the Catholic cities and retaking the Lower Palatinate. In early 1632 Protestant forces plundered Bavaria. It was the Bavarian ruler Maximilian who had gained most from the years of war. His troops had occupied the Upper Palatinate, and he had received Frederick's rights as imperial elector in return for support of Ferdinand. It was Maximilian who had insisted on the dismissal of Wallenstein and Maximilian who had played a double game of negotiating with the French for neutrality and with the emperor for the spoils of victory. So there was poetic justice when Maximilian's state was invaded, his castles looted, and his lands plundered. There was poetic justice, too, when Wallenstein resumed his com-

The siege of Magdeburg, 1631. The sack of the city by the Imperial troops of Tilly's army was one of the most barbarous incidents of a brutal war.

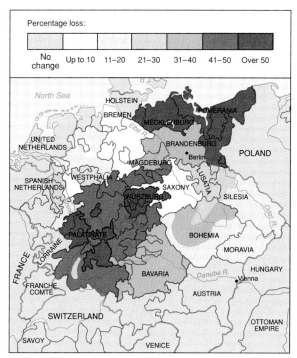

*Population Loss in Germany During the Thirty Years'
War*

mand and chose to chase the Saxons from
Bohemia rather than the Swedes from Bavaria.
But there was no justice at all for the wretched
inhabitants of this stronghold of German Catholicism. Town and countryside were laid waste. Not
until the winter of 1632 did the armies of Gustavus and Wallenstein finally meet. At the battle
of Lutzen the Swedes won the field but lost their
beloved king. Wounded in the leg, the back, and
the head, Gustavus Adolphus died. In less than
two years he had decisively transformed the
course of the war and the course of Europe's
future. Protestant forces now occupied most of
central and northern Germany. Ferdinand's ability to redraw the religious map of the empire was
at an end.

The Long Quest for Peace

The Thirty Years' War was barely half over
when Gustavus Adolphus fell at Lutzen. But from
that time forward its central European phase
receded in importance. The final stages of the war
involved the resumption of the century old struggle between France and Spain. When the Twelve
Years' Truce expired in 1621, Spain again declared

war upon the Dutch. Philip III's hopes of concentrating all his resources against Holland had
been disappointed by the outbreak of war in central Europe. Not until after the Bohemian revolt
had been repressed did the Spanish army begin
the long, laborious process of besieging the well-
fortified and well-defended towns of the
Netherlands. There were successes and failures.
But now Dutch strategy was not only to protect
the homeland. Dutch naval power was considerable and the Dutch took the war to the far reaches
of the globe, attacking Portuguese settlements in
Brazil and in the East and harassing Spanish
shipping on the high seas. In 1628 the Dutch
captured the entire Spanish treasure fleet as it
sailed from the New World. Not since the defeat of
the Armada in 1588 had Spain suffered such a
blow to its prestige. But the dent in its pride was
nothing compared to the dent in its pocketbook.
Spain had declared bankruptcy in 1627, and the
loss of the whole of the next year's treasure from
America exacerbated an already catastrophic situation. The golden age of Spain had melted away.

These reversals, combined with the continued successes of Habsburg forces in central
Europe, convinced Louis XIII and his chief minister, Cardinal Richelieu, that the time for active
involvement in European affairs was now at
hand. Throughout the early stages of the war,
France had secretly aided anti-Habsburg forces.
From 1624 it had provided a subsidy to the Dutch
and from 1630 one to the Swedes. French support
for princes in a number of small states situated in
the passages of the Alps continually threatened
the Spanish supply route to the Netherlands and
had more than once nearly led to open warfare.
Gustavus Adolphus' unexpected success dramatically altered French calculations. Now it was evident that the Habsburgs could no longer combine
their might, and Spanish energies would be
drained off in the Netherlands and in central
Europe. The time had come to take an open stand.
In 1635 France declared war on Spain.

Neither country was prepared for large-scale
military action, and neither could afford it. The
war resembled nothing so much as two punch-
drunk fighters pounding each other, both receiving as much punishment as they inflicted. France
took the offensive first, invading the Spanish
Netherlands. In 1636 a Spanish army struck back,
pushing to within twenty-five miles of Paris before

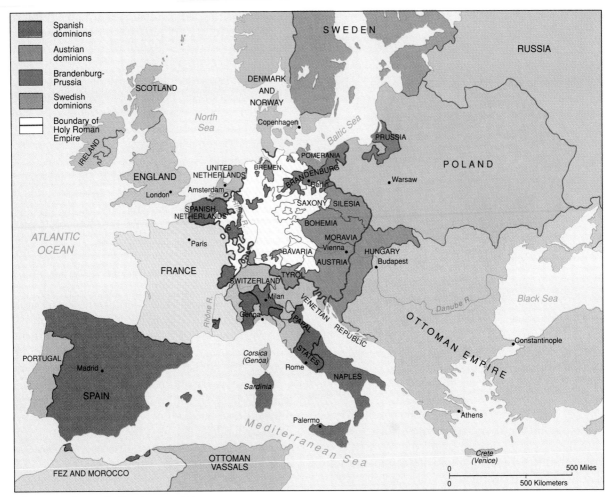

The Peace of Westphalia, Europe 1648

it was repelled. Both sides soon began to search for a settlement, but pride prevented them from laying down their gloves. Spain toppled first. Its economy in shambles and its citizens in revolt over high prices and higher taxes, it could no longer maintain its many-fronted war. The Swedes again defeated imperial forces in Germany, the Dutch destroyed much of Spain's Atlantic fleet in 1639, and the Portuguese rose up against the union of crowns that had brought them nothing but expense and the loss of crucial portions of their empire. In 1640 the Portuguese regained their independence. In 1643 Spain gambled once more on a knockout blow against the French. But at the battle of Rocroi, exhausted French troops held out and the Spanish invasion failed.

By now the desire for peace was universal. Most of the main combatants had long since per-ished: Philip III, ever optimistic, in 1621; Frederick V, an exile to the end, in 1632; Gustavus Adolphus, killed at Lutzen in the same year; Wallenstein, murdered by order of Ferdinand II in 1634; Ferdinand himself in 1637; and Louis XIII in 1643, five days before the French triumph at Rocroi. Those who succeeded them had not the same passions, and after so many decades the longing for peace was the strongest emotion on the Continent. But the tangle of wars and alliances was not easily unsnarled, and those who saw themselves as victors at one stage or another still sought desperately for their spoils. Some wanted to reconstruct the political world as it had existed in 1618, others to reestablish it as it was after the first round of Catholic victories in 1627. The Swedes, who had gained most from the struggle—they now occupied much of northern Germany and, after a brief war with Denmark, much territory in the western Baltic as well—wished to settle things largely as they stood. Fighting persisted as each effort to reach a universal peace failed. Finally, at the beginning of 1648 Spain and the Netherlands concluded their eighty years of fighting. This bilateral agreement broke the log jam. One by one the combatants agreed to end their hostilities with one another, and soon the stage was set for a Continent-wide settlement.

A series of agreements, collectively known as the Peace of Westphalia, established the outlines of the political geography of Europe for the next century. Its focus was on the Holy Roman Empire and it reflected Protestant successes in the final two decades of war. It was the powers who had been brought into the war in central Europe that benefited most from the peace. Sweden gained further territories on the Baltic, making it master of the north German ports. Along with the territorial concessions it had won from Denmark, Sweden was now an international power. France, too, gained in territory and prestige. It kept the vital towns in the Lower Palatinate through which Spanish men and material had moved and, though it did not agree to come to terms with Spain immediately, France's fear of encirclement was at an end. The Dutch gained statehood through official recognition by Spain and through the power they had displayed in building and maintaining an overseas empire.

Settlement in the empire also reflected Protestant successes. Territorial boundaries were reestablished as they had existed in 1624, giving the Habsburgs control of both Bohemia and Hungary. But the independence of the Swiss cantons was now officially recognized as were the rights of Calvinists to the protection of the Peace of Augsburg, which again was to govern the religious affairs of the empire. Two of the larger German states were strengthened as a counterweight to the emperor's power. Bavaria was allowed to retain the Upper Palatinate, and Brandenburg, which ceded some of its coastal territory to Sweden, gained extensive territories in the east. The emperor's political control over the German states was also weakened. German rulers were given independent authority over their states and the imperial diet, rather than the emperor, was empowered to settle disputes. Thus weakened, future emperors ruled in the Habsburg territorial

The Thirty Years' War

1618 Defenestration of Prague
1619 Ferdinand Habsburg elected Holy Roman Emperor
      Frederick of the Palatinate accepts the crown of Bohemia
1620 Catholic victory at battle of White Mountain
1621 End of Twelve Years' Truce; war between Spain and Netherlands
1626 Danes form Protestant alliance under Christian IV
1627 Spain declares bankruptcy
1630 Gustavus Adolphus leads Swedish forces into Germany
1631 Sack of Magdeburg
      Protestant victory at Breitenfeld
1632 Protestant victory at Lutzen; death of Gustavus Adolphus
1635 France declares war on Spain
1640 Portugal secedes from Spain
1643 Battle of Rocroi; French forces repel Spaniards
1648 Peace of Westphalia

lands with little ability to control, or influence, or even arbitrate German affairs. The judgment that the Holy Roman Empire was neither holy, Roman, nor an empire was now irrevocably true.

The Peace of Westphalia put the pieces of the map of European states back together. Protestantism and Catholicism now coexisted and there was to be little further change in the geography of religion. The northwest of Europe—England, Holland, Scandinavia, and the north German states—was Protestant, the south was Catholic. The empire of the German peoples was now at an end, the Austro-Hungarian empire at a beginning. Holland and Sweden had become international powers, Spain and Denmark faded from prominence. Muscovy began a long period of isolation from the west, attempting to restore a semblance of government to its people. But if the negotiators at Westphalia could resolve the political and religious ambitions that gave rise to a century of nearly continuous warfare, they could do nothing to eradicate the effects of war itself. The devastation of humanity in the name of God with which the reform of religion had begun was now exhausted. The costs were horrific. The population of Germany fell from 15 million in 1600 to 11 million in 1650. The armies brought destruction of all kinds in their wake. Plague again raged in Europe—the town of Augsburg lost eighteen thousand inhabitants in the early 1630s. Famine, too, returned to a continent that fifty years earlier had been self-sufficient in grain. The war played havoc with all of the economies that it touched. Inflation, devaluation of coinage, huge public and private debts were all directly attributable to the years of fighting. And the toll taken on the spirit of those generations that never knew peace is incalculable.

Suggestions for Further Reading

General Reading

* J. H. Elliott, *Europe Divided 1559–1598* (New York: Harper & Row, 1968). An outstanding synthesis of European politics in the second half of the sixteenth century.

* Geoffrey Parker, *Europe in Crisis 1598–1648* (London: William Collins and Sons, 1979). An up-to-date study of European states in the early seventeenth century.

* Richard Dunn, *The Age of Religious Wars 1559–1715* (New York: Norton, 1979). A well-written survey of early modern society.

* H. G. Koenigsberger, *Early Modern Europe* (London: Longmans, 1987). A general overview designed for beginning students.

The Crises of the Western States

J. H. M. Salmon, *Society in Crisis* (New York: St. Martin's Press, 1975). The best single-volume account of the French civil wars; difficult but rewarding.

N. M. Sutherland, *The Massacre of St. Bartholomew and the European Conflict* (London: Macmillan, 1973). Argues the case for the importance of Spanish influence on the massacre and the course of the wars of religion.

Robert Kingdon, *Myths About the St. Bartholomew's Day Massacres 1572–76* (Cambridge, MA: Harvard University Press, 1988). A study of the impact of a central event in the history of France.

David Buisseret, *Henry IV* (London: George Allen & Unwin, 1984). A stylish biography of a problematic personality.

* Mark Greengrass, *France in the Age of Henri IV* (London: Longmans, 1984). An important synthesis of French history in the early seventeenth century.

Geoffrey Parker, *Philip II* (Boston: Little, Brown, 1978). The best introduction.

* Garrett Mattingly, *The Armada* (Boston: Houghton Mifflin, 1959). Still the classic account despite recent reinterpretations.

Colin Martin and N. G. Parker, *The Spanish Armada* (London: Hamilton Press, 1988). A recent study based on archaeological finds and a fresh look at the evidence.

John Lynch, *Spain Under the Hapsburgs, Vol. II. Spain and America* (Oxford: Oxford University Press, 1969). A full treatment of Spanish history with sections on society and culture as well as politics.

* Henry Kamen, *Spain 1469–1714* (London: Longmans, 1983). A recent survey with up-to-date interpretations.

* Geoffrey Parker, *The Dutch Revolt* (London: Penguin Books, 1977). An outstanding account of the tangle of events that comprised the revolts of the Netherlands.

* Pieter Geyl, *The Revolt of the Netherlands* (London: Ernest Benn, 1962). Still worth reading for its passion and enthusiasm.

The Reorganization of Northeastern Europe

W. F. Reddaway, et al., eds., *The Cambridge History of Poland to 1696* (Cambridge: Cambridge University Press, 1950). A difficult but thorough narrative of Polish history.

S. F. Platonov, *The Time of Troubles* (Lawrence, KS: University Press of Kansas, 1970). A good narrative of the disintegration of the Muscovite state.

Michael Roberts, *Gustavus Adolphus and the Rise of Sweden* (London: English Universities Press, 1973). A highly readable account of Sweden's rise to power.

Michael Roberts, *The Swedish Imperial Experience* (Cambridge: Cambridge University Press, 1979). Reflections on Swedish history by the preeminent historian of early modern Sweden.

The Thirty Years' War

* C. V. Wedgwood, *The Thirty Years' War* (New York: Doubleday, 1961). A heroic account; the best narrative history.

Geoffrey Parker, *The Thirty Years' War* (London: Routledge and Kegan Paul, 1984). A multi-authored account that views the war from a variety of vantage points.

* Peter Limm, *The Thirty Years' War* (London: Longmans, 1984). An excellent brief survey with documents.

J. H. Elliott, *Richelieu and Olivares* (Cambridge: Cambridge University Press, 1984). A comparison of statesmen and statesmanship in the early seventeenth century.

* Indicates paperback edition available

16

The
Royal State

Fit for a King

Behold Versailles: the greatest palace of the greatest king of the greatest state in seventeenth-century Europe. Everything about it was stupendous, a reflection of the grandeur of Louis XIV and of France. Sculptured gardens in dazzling geometric forms stretched for acres, scenting the air with exotic perfumes. Nearly as beautiful as the grounds were the 1,400 fountains, especially the circular basins of Apollo and Latona, the sun god and his mother. The hundreds of water jets that sprayed at Versailles defied nature as well as the senses, for the locale was not well irrigated and water had to be pumped through elaborate mechanical works all the way from the Seine. Gardens and fountains provided the setting for the enormous palace with its hundreds of rooms for both use and show. Five thousand people, a tenth of whom served the king alone, inhabited the palace. Thousands of others flocked there daily. Most lived in the adjacent town, which had grown from a few hundred to over forty thousand in a single generation. The royal stables quartered twelve thousand horses and hundreds of carriages. The cost of all of this magnificence was equally astounding. Fragmentary accounts indicate that construction costs were over 100 million French pounds. Louis XIV ordered the official receipts burned.

Like the marble of the palace, nature itself was chiseled to the requirements of the king. Forests were pared to make leafy avenues or trimmed to conform to the geometric patterns of the gardens. In spring and summer groves of orange trees grown in tubs were every-

where; in winter and fall they were housed indoors at great expense. Life-size statues and giant carved urns lined the carefully planned walkways that led out to breathtaking views or into sheltered grottoes. A cross-shaped artificial canal, over a mile long, dominated the western end of the park. Italian gondolas skimmed along its surface, carrying visitors to the zoo and aviary on one side or to the king's private château on the other.

But this great pile of bricks and stone, of marble and precious metals expressed the contradictions of its age as well as its grandeur. The seventeenth century was an era when the rich got richer and the poor got poorer. It was a time when the monarchical state expanded its power and prestige even as it faced grave challenges to its very existence. It was an epoch of unrelenting war amid a nearly universal desire for lasting peace. Thus it was fitting that this prodigious monument was uncomfortable to live in, so unpleasant that Louis had a separate château built on the grounds as a quiet retreat. His wife and his mistresses com-

plained constantly of accommodations in which all interior comforts had been subordinated to the external facade of the building. Versailles was a seat of state as well as the home of the monarch, and it is revealing that the private was sacrificed to the public.

The duc de Saint-Simon, who passed much of his time at Versailles, was well aware of the contradictions. "The beautiful and the ugly were sown together, the vast and the constricted." Soldiers, tradesmen, and the merely curious clogged the three great avenues that led from Paris to the palace. When the king dined in public, hordes of Parisians drove out for the spectacle, filing past the monarch as if he were an exhibit at a museum. The site itself was poorly drained. "Its mud is black and stinking with a stench so penetrating that you can smell it for several leagues around." The orange groves and the stone urns filled with flower petals were more practical than beautiful: they masked the stench of sewage that was particularly noxious in the heat and the rain. Even the gardens were too vast to be enjoyed. In the planted areas, the smell of flowers was over-powering while the acres of mown lawn proved unattractive to an aristocracy little given to physical exercise. "The gardens were admired and avoided," Saint-Simon observed acidly. In these contrasts of failure amid achievement Versailles stands as an apt symbol of its age: a gaudy mask to hide the wrinkles of the royal state.

The Rise of the Royal State

The religious and dynastic wars that dominated the early part of the seventeenth century had a profound impact upon the western European states. Not only did they cause terrible suffering and deprivation but they also demanded efficient and better-centralized states to conduct them. War was both a product of the European state system and a cause of its continued development. As armies grew in size, the resources necessary to maintain them grew in volume. As the battlefield spread from state to state, defense became government's most important function. More and more power was absorbed by the monarch and his chief advisers, more and more of the traditional privileges of aristocracy and of towns were eroded. At the center of these rising states, particularly in western Europe, were the king and his court. In the provinces were tax collectors and military recruiters.

Divine Kings

"There is a divinity that doth hedge a king," wrote Shakespeare. Never was that hedge more luxuriant than in the seventeenth century. In the early sixteenth century, monarchs treated their states and their subjects as personal property. Correspondingly, rulers were praised in personal terms, for their virtue, their wisdom, or their strength. By the early seventeenth century, the monarchy had been transformed into an office of state. Now rulers embodied their nation and, no matter what their personal characteristics, they were held in awe because they were monarchs.

Thus as rulers lost direct personal control over their patrimony, they gained indirect symbolic control over their nation. This symbolic power was everywhere to be seen. By the beginning of the seventeenth century, monarchs had set permanent seats of government attended by vast courts of officials, place seekers, and servants. The idea of the capital city emerged, with Madrid, London, and Paris as the models. Here, the grandiose style of the ruler stood proxy for the wealth and glory of the nation. Great display bespoke great pride, and great pride was translated into great strength.

Portraits of rulers in action and in repose conveyed the central message. Elizabeth I was depicted bestriding a map of England or clutching a rainbow and wearing a gown woven of eyes and ears to signify her power to see and hear her subjects. The Flemish painter Sir Anthony Van Dyck (1599–1641) created powerful images of three generations of Stuart kings of England. He was court painter to Charles I, whose qualities he portrayed with great sympathy and not a little exaggeration. Diego Velázquez (1599–1660) was court painter to Philip IV of Spain. His series of equestrian portraits of the Habsburgs—kings, queens, princes, and princesses—exude the spirit of the seventeenth-century monarchy, the grandeur and pomp, the power and self-assurance. Peter Paul Rubens (1577–1640) represented twenty-one separate episodes in the life of Marie de Médicis, queen regent of France.

The themes of artists were no different than those of writers. Monarchy was glorified in a variety of forms of literary representation. National history, particularly of recent events, enjoyed wide popularity. Its avowed purpose was to draw the connection between the past and the present glories of the state. One of the most popular French histories of the period was entitled *On the Excellence of the Kings and the Kingdom of France.* Francis Bacon (1561–1626), who is remembered more as a philosopher and scientist, wrote a laudatory history of Henry VII, founder of the Tudor dynasty. Artistic enterprise flourished across the Continent. The century between 1550 and 1650 was one of the richest periods of high culture in European history.

In England it was a period of renaissance. Poets, playwrights, historians, and philosophers by the dozens gravitated to the English court. One of the most remarkable of them was Ben Jonson (1572–1637). He began life as a bricklayer, fought against the Spanish in Flanders, and then turned to acting and writing. His wit and talent brought him to court, where he made his mark by writing and staging masques, light entertainment that included music, dance, pantomime, and acting. Jonson's masques were distinguished by their lavish productions and exotic costumes and the inventive set designs of the great architect Inigo

Queen Elizabeth I of England. This portrait was commissioned by Sir Henry Lee to commemorate the Queen's visit to his estate at Ditchley. Here the queen is the very image of Gloriana—ageless and indomitable.

Jones (1573–1652). They were frequently staged at Christmastime and starred members of the court as players. The masques took the grandeur of England and its rulers for their themes.

The role of William Shakespeare (1564–1616) in the celebration of monarchy was more ambiguous. Like Jonson, Shakespeare came from an ordinary family, had little formal education, and began his astonishing career as an actor and producer of theater. He soon began to write as well as direct his plays and his company, the King's Players, received royal patronage. He set many of his plays at the courts of princes and even comedies like the *Tempest* (1611) and *Measure for Measure* (1604) centered on the power of the ruler to dispense justice and to bring peace to his subjects. Both were staged at court. His history plays focused entirely on the character of kings. In *Richard II* (1597) and *Henry VI* (3 parts, 1591–94) Shakespeare exposed the harm that weak rulers inflicted on their states, while in *Henry IV* (2 parts, 1598–1600) and *Henry V* (1599) he highlighted the

benefits to be derived from strong rulers. Shakespeare's tragedies made this point in a different way. The tragic flaw in the personality of rulers exposed the world around them to ruin. In *Macbeth* (1606) this flaw was ambition. Macbeth killed to become a king and had to keep on killing to remain one. In *Hamlet* (1602) the tragic flaw was irresolution. The inability of the "Prince of Denmark" to act decisively and reclaim the crown that was his by right brought his state to the brink of collapse. Shakespeare's plays were viewed in London theaters by members of all social classes, and his concentration on the affairs of rulers helped reinforce their dominating importance in the lives of all of their subjects.

The political theory of the divine right of kings further enhanced the importance of monarchs. This theory held that the institution of monarchy had been created by God, and the monarch functioned as God's representative on earth. One clear statement of divine right theory was actually written by a king, James VI of Scotland, who later became James I of England (1603–25). In *The True Law of Free Monarchies* (1598) James instructed the leaders of the Scottish nobility and the Scottish church on their duties to their king. He recalled the Old Testament story of how the Israelites begged the Lord to create a king to rule over them. Thus, James reasoned, God had placed kings on earth to rule, and he would judge them in heaven for their transgressions.

The idea of the divine origin of monarchy was uncontroversial, and it was espoused not only by kings. One of the few things that the French Estates-General actually agreed upon during its meeting in 1614—the last for over 175 years—was the statement that "the king is sovereign in France and holds his crown from God only." This sentiment echoed the commonplace view of French political theorists. The greatest writer on the subject, Jean Bodin (1530–96), called the king "God's image on earth." In *The Six Books of the Commonwealth* (1576), Bodin defined the essence of the monarch's power: "The principal mark of sovereign majesty is essentially the right to impose laws on subjects generally without their consent."

Though at first glance the theory of the divine right of kings appears to be a blueprint for arbitrary rule, in fact it was yoked together with a number of principles that restrained the conduct of the monarch. As James I pointed out, God had charged kings with the obligations "to minister justice; to establish good laws; and to procure peace." By these standards would kings ultimately be judged; failure would be met with the wrath of God. For a king who viewed himself as father of his nation, or as head of the body politic, there was no contradiction between his power and his subjects' welfare. *Rex est Lex; Lex est Rex*: "the king is the law and the law is the king." Kings were bound by the law of nature and the law of nations. They could not deprive their subjects of their lives, their liberties, or their property without due cause established by law. As one French theorist held, "while the kingdom belongs to the king, the king also belongs to the kingdom."

Wherever they turned, kings were instructed in the duties of kingship. In tracts, in letters, and in literature they were lectured on the obligations of their office. "A true king should be first in government, first in council, and first in all the offices of state." If such advice appealed to strong personalities like Philip II of Spain, Henry IV of France, or Elizabeth I of England, it burdened their weaker successors. Louis XIII (1610–43) loved nothing more than to hunt in the French countryside and hated nothing more than the daily burdens of affairs of state. James I may have embraced the theory of his divine office, but he recoiled from the London crowds that jostled for a glimpse of him whenever he set foot outside his palace. Both kings had speech impediments that led them to shy away from public ceremonies. They nervously endured obligations like the "royal touch," during which people afflicted with certain diseases hoped for a miraculous cure from the hands of the king. The nine-year-old Louis XIII touched over nine hundred supplicants following his coronation in 1610 and remarked with great pride that he had sickened only slightly and "never let it show."

The Court and the Courtiers

For all of the bravura of divine-right theory, far more was expected of kings than they could possibly deliver. They were to be soldiers in times of war and statesmen in times of peace. They were to administer the affairs of society, legislate the affairs of state, and adjudicate the affairs of jus-

tice. "I am neither a god nor an angel but a man like any other," James I proclaimed in a moment when he wasn't thinking about his divine right. Small wonder that seventeenth-century kings built palaces in which to hide.

The increase in the power of the monarchy required an increase in the effectiveness of the monarch. The day-to-day affairs of government had grown beyond the capacity of any monarch to handle them. The expansion in the powers of the western states absorbed more officials than ever. At the beginning of the sixteenth century the court of Francis I employed 622 officers; at the beginning of the seventeenth century the court of Henry IV employed over 1,500. Yet the difference was not only in size. Members of the seventeenth-century court were becoming servants of the state as well as of the monarch.

Expanding the court was one of the ways in which monarchs co-opted potential rivals within the aristocracy. In return, those who were favored enhanced their power by royal grants of titles, lands, and income. As the court expanded so did the political power of courtiers. Royal councils—a small group of leading officeholders who advised the monarch on state business—grew in significance. Not only did the council assume the management of government, it also began to advocate policies for the monarch to adopt.

Yet, like everything else in seventeenth-century government, the court revolved around the monarch. The monarch appointed, promoted, and dismissed officeholders at will. As befit this type of personal government, most monarchs chose a single individual to act as a funnel for private and public business. This was the "favorite," whose role combined varying proportions of best friend, right-hand man, and hired gun. Some favorites, like the French Cardinal Richelieu and the Spanish Count-Duke Olivares, were able to transform themselves into chief ministers with a political philosophy and a vision of government. Others, like the English Duke of Buckingham, simply remained royal companions. Favorites walked a not very tight rope. They could retain their balance only as long as they retained their influence with the monarch. Richelieu claimed that it was "more difficult to dominate the four square feet of the king's study than the affairs of Europe." Ministers acted as a safety valve for the monarchy. When royal policy suc-

This portrait of Richelieu by Philippe de Champaigne shows the cardinal's intellectual power and controlled determination.

ceeded it was the king's success; when royal policy failed it was the minister's failure. Critics could attack the influence of "evil advisers" without attacking the king. The parallel careers of Richelieu, Olivares, and Buckingham neatly illustrate the dangers and opportunities of the office.

Cardinal Richelieu (1585–1642) was born into a noble family of minor importance. A younger son, he trained for the law and then for a position that his family owned in the Church. After skillful participation in the meeting of the Estates-General of 1614, Richelieu was given a court post through the patronage of Queen Marie de Médicis, mother of Louis XIII. He gradually established his own relationship with the king. Richelieu was sixteen years older than Louis XIII and he often acted toward him as a parent to a child, roles to which neither the celibate cardinal nor the fatherless monarch were well suited. Still the two men made a good match. Louis XIII hated the work of ruling and Richelieu loved little else. Though Richelieu received great favor from the king—he became a duke and amassed the largest private fortune in France—his position rested upon his managerial abilities. Richelieu never enjoyed a close personal relationship with his monarch, and he never felt that his position was secure. In 1630, Marie de Médicis turned against him and he was very nearly ousted from office. His last years were filled with suppressing plots to undermine his power or to take his life. Yet in 1642 he died in the arms of the king whom he had served with near total devotion for almost two decades.

The Count-Duke Olivares (1587–1645) was a younger son of a lesser branch of a great Spanish noble family. Though Olivares trained for a career in the Church, by the time he was twenty he had outlived his father and two elder brothers. He was thus able to become a courtier with a title, a large fortune, and most unusually, a university education. Olivares was soon the favorite courtier of the prince, and when Philip III suddenly died in 1621, Olivares became the favorite of the new king, Philip IV (1621–65. He was elevated to the highest rank of the nobility and lost no time consolidating his position. He moved into rooms directly adjoining those of the monarch and served personally as one of the grooms of the chamber who helped the king to dress.

Olivares used his closeness to the monarch to gain court appointments for his relatives and political supporters, but he was more interested in establishing political policy than in building a court faction. His objective was to maintain the greatness of Spain, whose fortunes, like the Count-Duke's moods, waxed and waned. Like Richelieu, Olivares attempted to further the process of centralizing royal power, which was not very advanced in Spain. And like his French counterpart, he was unable to overcome entrenched opposition. Olivares' plans for a nationally recruited and financed army ended in disaster. His efforts at tax reform went unrewarded. He advocated the aggressive foreign policy that mired Spain in the Thirty Years' War in Europe and the eighty years of war in the Netherlands. As domestic and foreign crises mounted, Philip IV could not resist the pressure to dismiss his chief minister. In 1643 Olivares was removed from office and two years later, physically exhausted and mentally deranged, he died.

The Spanish master Diego Velázquez painted this portrait of the Count-Duke Olivares.

George Villiers, duke of Buckingham. The royal favorite virtually ruled the country between 1618 and 1628. The general rejoicing at his death embittered the king and helped bring about the eleven years' rule without Parliament.

The Duke of Buckingham (1592–1628) was also a younger son, but not of the nobility. He received the aimless education of a country gentleman, spending several years in France learning the graces of fashion and dancing. Reputedly one of the most handsome men in Europe, Buckingham hung about the fringes of the English court until his looks and charm brought him to the attention of Queen Anne, James I's wife. She recommended him for the office of cupbearer, a minor official who carried drinks to the royal table. Frequently in the king's presence, Buckingham quickly caught the eye of James I. Soon

James would have no one else at his side, and Buckingham's rise was meteoric. In less than seven years he went from commoner to duke, the highest rank of the English nobility.

Along with his titles, Buckingham acquired political power. He assumed a large number of royal offices, among them Admiral of the Navy, and placed his relatives and dependents in many others. Buckingham took his obligations seriously. He began a reform of naval administration, for example, but his rise to power was so sudden that he found enemies at every turn. These increased dramatically when James I died in 1625. There was to be no new broom to sweep away the duke and his supporters. He succeeded where so many others had failed by becoming the favorite and chief minister of the new king, Charles I (1625–49). His accumulation of power and patronage proceeded unabated, as did the enmity he aroused. Buckingham became the symbol of everything that was wrong with the nation. But Charles I stood firmly behind him. A discontented naval officer finally accomplished what the most powerful men in England could not. In 1628 Buckingham was assassinated. While Charles I wept inconsolably at the news, ordinary Londoners drank to the health of his killer.

The Drive to Govern

Richelieu, Olivares, and Buckingham met very different ends. Yet in their own ways they shared a common goal, to extend the authority and control of the monarch over his state.

One of the chief means by which kings and councilors attempted to expand the authority of the state was through the legal system. Administering justice was one of the sacred duties of the monarchy. The complexities of ecclesiastical, civil, and customary law gave trained lawyers an essential role in government. As legal experts and the demands for legal services increased, royal law courts multiplied and expanded. In France, the Parlement of Paris, the main law court of the state, became a powerful institution that contested with courtiers for the right to advise the monarch. The number of regional parlements increased, bringing royal justice to the farthest reaches of the realm. Members of the Parlement of Paris and of the expanding provincial parlements were known as nobility of the robe, from the long gowns worn by lawyers and judges. In Spain the *letrados*—university-trained lawyers who were normally members of the nobility—were the backbone of royal government. Formal legal training was a requirement for many of the administrative posts in the state. In Castile members of all social classes frequently used the royal courts to settle personal disputes. The expansion of a centralized system of justice thus joined the interests of subjects and the monarchy.

In England the legal system expanded differently. Central courts situated in the royal palace of Westminster grew and the lawyers and judges who practiced in them became a powerful profession. They were especially active in the House of Commons of the English Parliament, which along with the House of Lords had extensive advisory and legislative powers. More important than the rise of the central courts, however, was the rise of the local ones. The English Crown extended royal justice to the counties by granting legal authority to members of the local social elite. These justices of the peace, as they were known, became agents of the Crown in their own localities. Justices were given power to hear and settle minor cases and to imprison those who had committed serious offenses until the assizes, the semiannual sessions of the county court.

Assizes combined the ceremony of rule with its process. Royal authority was displayed in a great procession to the courthouse that was led by the judge and the county justices, followed by the grand and petty juries of local citizens who would hear the cases, and finally by the carts carrying the prisoners to trial. Along with the legal business that was performed, assizes were occasions for edifying sermons, typically on the theme of obedience. Their solemnity, marked by the black robes of the judge, the Latin of the legal proceedings, and the public executions with which assizes invariably ended, all served to instill a sense of the power of the state in the throngs of ordinary people who witnessed them.

Efforts to integrate center and locality extended to more than the exercise of justice. The monarch also needed officials who could enforce royal policy in those localities where the special privileges of groups and individuals remained strong. The best strategy was to appoint local leaders to royal office. But with so much of the aristocracy resident at court, this was not always an effective course. In France, the provincial governors were traditionally members of the ancient nobility who enjoyed wide powers in matters of military recruitment, revenue collection, and judicial administration. But many governors spent far more time in Paris than in the locality that they were to administer and often opposed the exactions demanded by the monarch. By the beginning of the seventeenth century, the French monarchy began to rely on new central officials known as *intendants* to perform many of the tasks of the provincial governors. Cardinal Richelieu expanded the use of the intendants and by the middle of the century they had become a vital part of royal government.

The Lords Lieutenant were a parallel institution created in England. Unlike every other European state, England had no national army. Every English county was required to raise, equip, and train its own militia. Lords Lieutenant were in charge of these trained bands. Since the aristocracy was the ancient military class in the state, the lieutenants were chosen from the greatest nobles of the realm. But they delegated their work to members of the gentry, large local landholders who took on their tasks as a matter of prestige rather than profit. Perhaps not surprisingly, the English military was among the weakest in Europe and nearly all its foreign adventures ended in disaster.

Efforts to centralize the affairs of the Spanish monarchy could not proceed so easily. The separate regions over which the king ruled maintained their own laws and privileges. Attempts to apply Castilian rules or implant Castilian officials always drew opposition from other regions. Olivares frequently complained that Philip IV was the king of Castile only and nothing but a thorough plan of unification would make him the king of Spain. This he proposed in 1625 to attempt to solve the dual problems of military manpower and military finance. After 1621, Spain was again deeply involved in European warfare. Fighting in the Netherlands and in Germany demanded large armies and larger sums of money. Olivares launched a plan for a Union of Arms to which all the separate regions of the empire, including Mexico and Peru in the west, Italy in the east, and the separate regions in Iberia would contribute. He envisioned an army of 140,000 but soon lowered his sights. Not all of the Iberian provinces were persuaded to contribute. Catalonia, stood upon its ancient privileges and refused to grant either troops or funds. But Olivares was able to establish at least the principle of unified cooperation.

Taxing Demands

More than anything else, war propelled the consolidation of the state. Whether offensive or defensive, continuous or intermittent, successful or calamitous, war was the irresistible force of the seventeenth-century monarchy. War taxation was its immovable object. Perhaps half of all revenue of the western states went to finance war. To maintain its armies and navies, its fortresses and outposts, the state had to squeeze every penny from its subjects. Old taxes had to be collected more efficiently, new taxes had to be introduced and enforced. As one Spanish jurist observed in a familiar refrain, "there can be no peace without arms, no arms without money, and no money without taxation." On the other side, the unprecedented demands for money on the part of the state were always resisted. The privileged challenged the legality of levying taxes, the unprivileged did whatever they could to avoid paying them.

The claims and counterclaims were very strong. In the first place, armies were bigger and more expensive. In 1625 Philip IV had nearly three hundred thousand men in arms throughout his empire. The expense of maintaining Spanish fortresses alone had quintupled since the time of Philip II. Not only were there more men to pay, equip, and supply, but the cost of war materials continued to rise with inflation. Similarly, the cost of food and fodder rose. Marauding armies might be able to plunder sufficient grain during the spring and autumn, but they still consumed massive amounts of meat and drink that could not be supplied locally.

The economic hardships caused by the ceaseless military activity touched everyone. Those in the direct path of battle had little left to feed themselves, let alone to provide to the state. The disruption of the delicate cycle of planting and harvesting devastated local communities. Armies plundered ripened grain and trampled seedlings as they moved through fields. The conscription of village men and boys removed vital skills from the community and upset the gender-based division of labor. Peasants were squeezed by the armies for crops, by the lords for rents, and by the state for taxes.

In fact, the inability of the lower orders of European society to finance a century of warfare was clear from the beginning. In Spain and France, the principal problem was that so much of the wealth of the nation was beyond the reach of traditional royal taxation. The nobility and many of the most important towns had long achieved exemption from basic taxes on consumption and wealth. European taxation was regressive, falling most heavily upon those least able to pay. Rulers and subjects alike recognized the inequities of the European system of taxation. Regime after regime began with plans to overhaul the national system of taxation before settling for propping up new emergency levies against the rotting foundations of the old structure. Nevertheless, the fiscal crisis that the European wars provoked did result in an expansion of state taxation.

In France, for example, royal expenditures rose 60 percent during the first two decades of the seventeenth century, while the yield from the *taille*, the crown's basic commodity tax, remained constant. Thus the crown was forced to search for new revenues, the most important of which was the *paulette*, a tax on officeholding. To raise money, especially in emergencies, the crown had been forced to sell government offices, until by the seventeenth century a majority of offices had been obtained by direct purchase. The sale of an office provided a one-time windfall for the crown, but after that the cost of salaries and benefits was a perpetual drain. So, too, were the administrative costs of potentially inefficient officeholders. Many purchased their posts as an investment and treated them as personal property. For an annual payment of 1/60 the value of the office, the *paulette* allowed the current holder to sell or bequeath it as desired. Henry IV instituted the *paulette* in 1604, and it became a vital source of royal revenue as well as an acute source of aristocratic and legal complaint. In the early 1620s, revenue from the sale of offices amounted to one-third of the crown's income. The purchase of office was inherently corrupt, but it was not necessarily inefficient. Sons who were to inherit offices could be trained for their posts, if for no other reason than to operate them profitably. The crown received money from classes in society that were generally beyond the reach of taxation, while members of these classes received power, prestige, and experience in public service. As long as profit and efficiency went hand in hand, both officeholder and monarch might be well served. Unfortunately, it was the king rather than his officers who had the greatest incentive to manipulate the system. The more offices that could be created, the larger the income from the *paulette*. During fiscal emergencies this was a temptation to which all French monarchs succumbed.

Fiscal emergency was just another name for the routine problems of the Spanish monarchy. As the greatest military power in Europe, Spain necessarily had the greatest military budget and thus the most extensive system of taxation. The crown taxed both domestic and imperial trade and took a healthy share of the gold and silver that continued to be mined in America. But all these revenues fell short of the state's needs. In the 1590s Philip II established an important new source of internal taxation. In an agreement with the Cortes of Castile he introduced the *milliones*, a tax on consumption that was to yield millions of ducats a year for war costs. An extremely regressive measure, the *milliones* taxed the sale of meat, wine, and oil, the basic elements of diet. It was a tax that hit urban areas particularly hard and was originally designed to last only six years. But the crises that the crown pleaded in the 1590s were even deeper at the turn of the century. The *milliones* became a permanent tax and a permanent grievance throughout Castile.

By contrast, the English crown was never able to persuade Parliament to grant permanent additional revenues. Though uninvolved in the European conflicts, England was not immune from military spending. War with Ireland in the 1590s and with Spain between 1588 and 1604 depleted the reserves that the crown had obtained when Henry VIII dissolved the monasteries. Disasterous wars against France and Spain in the 1620s provoked fiscal crisis for a monarchy that had few direct sources of revenue. While the great wealth of the kingdom was in land, the chief sources of revenue for the crown were in trade. In the early seventeenth century customs duties, or impositions, became a lucrative source of income when the judges ruled that the king could determine which commodities could be taxed and at what rate. Impositions fell heavily upon the merchant classes and upon urban consumers, but unlike the *milliones*, impositions were placed on luxury import goods rather than basic commodities.

Because so much of the crown's revenues derived from commerce and because foreign invasion could only come from the sea, the most pressing military need of the English monarchy was for naval defense. Even during the Armada crisis, the largest part of the English fleet had been made up of private merchant ships pressed into service through the emergency tax of Ship Money. This was a tax on each port town to hire a merchant ship and fit it out for war. In the 1630s, Charles I revived Ship Money and extended it to all English localities. His innovation aroused much opposition from the gentry, especially after his refusal to call Parliament into session to have the tax confirmed.

War finance was like an all-consuming monster. No matter how much new revenue was fed into it, its appetite grew for more. New taxes and increased rates of traditional taxation created suffering and a sense of grievance throughout the western European states. Opposition to taxation was not based on greed. The state's right to tax was not yet an established principle. Monarchs received certain forms of revenue in return for grants of immunities and privileges to powerful groups in their state. The state's efforts to go beyond these restricted grants was viewed as theft of private property. In the Ship Money case challengers argued that the king had no right to what belonged to his subjects except in a case of national emergency. This was a claim that the king accepted, arguing that such an emergency existed in the presence of pirates who were attacking English shipping. But if Charles I did not make a convincing claim for national emergency, the monarchs of France and Spain, the princes of Germany, and the rulers of the states of eastern Europe all did.

The Crises of the Royal State

The expansion of the functions, duties, and powers of the state in the early seventeenth century was not universally welcomed in European societies. The growth of central government came at the expense of local rights and privileges held by corporate bodies like the Church and the towns or by individuals like provincial officials and aristocrats. The state proved a powerful competitor, especially in the contest for the meager surplus produced on the land. As rents and prices stabilized in the early seventeenth century, after a long period of inflation, taxation increased, slowly at first and then at a pace with the gathering momentum of the Thirty Years' War. State exactions burdened all segments of society. Peasants lost the small benefit that rising prices had conferred upon producers. The surplus that parents had once passed on to children was now taken by the state. Local officials, never altogether popular, came to be seen as parasites and were easy targets for peasant rebellions. Larger landholders, whose prosperity depended upon rents and services from an increasingly impoverished peasantry, suffered along with their tenants. Even the great magnates were appalled by the state's insatiable appetite.

It was not only taxation that aroused opposition. Social and economic regulation meant more laws. More laws meant more lawyers and agents of enforcement. State regulation may have been more efficient—though many believed it was more efficient only for the state—but it was certainly disruptive. It was also expensive at a time when the fragile European economy was in a phase of decline. The early seventeenth century was a time of hunger in most of western Europe. Subtle changes in climate reduced the length of growing seasons and the size of crops. Bad harvests in the 1620s and 1640s left disease and starvation in their wake. And the wars ground on. Armies brought misery to those who were forcibly recruited to fight, those who were taxed into destitution, and those who simply had the misfortune to live in the path of destruction.

By the middle of the seventeenth century, a Europe-wide crisis was taking shape, though its timing and its forms differed from place to place.

Rural protests, like grain riots and mob assaults on local institutions, had a long history in all of the European states. Popular revolt was not the product of mindless despair, but rather the natural form of political action for those who fell outside the institutionalized political process. Bread riots and tax revolts became increasingly common in the early seventeenth century. More importantly, as the focus of discontent moved from local institutions to the state, the forms of revolt changed. So, too, did the participants. Members of the political elite began to formulate their own grievances against the expansion of state power. A theory of resistance, first developed in the French wars of religion, came to be applied to political tyranny and posed a direct challenge to the idea of the divine right of kings. By the 1640s all of these forces converged and rebellion exploded across the Continent. In Spain the ancient kingdoms of Catalonia and Portugal asserted their independence from Castilian rule; in France members of the aristocracy rose against a child monarch and his regent. In Italy, revolts rocked Naples and Sicily. In England, a constitutional crisis gave way to civil war and then to the first political revolution in European history.

The Need to Resist

Europeans lived more precariously in the seventeenth century than in any period since the Black Death. One benchmark of crisis was population decline. In the Mediterranean, Spanish population fell from 8.5 to 7 million and Italian population from 13 to 11 million. The ravages of the Thirty Years' War were most clearly felt in central Europe. Germany lost nearly a third of its people, Bohemia nearly half. Northwestern Europe—

European Population Data (in millions)							
Year	1550	1575	1600	1625	1650	1675	1700
England	3		4	4.5		5.8	5.8
France		20					19.3
Italy	11	13	13	13	12	11.5	12.5
Russia	9		11	8	9.5	13	16
Spain	6.3		7.6		5.2		7
All Europe	85	95	100	100	80	90	100

that is, England, the Netherlands, and France—was hardest hit in the first half of the century and only gradually recovered by 1700. Population decline had many causes and, rather remarkably, direct casualties from warfare were a very small component. The indirect effects of war, the disruption of agriculture, and the spread of disease were far more devastating. Spain alone lost a half million people at the turn of the century and another half million between 1647 and 1652. Severe outbreaks in 1625 and in 1665 hit England, while France endured three consecutive years of epidemics from 1629 to 1631.

All sectors of the European economy from agriculture to trade stagnated or declined in the early seventeenth century. Not surprisingly, peasants were hardest hit. The surplus from good harvests did not remain in rural communities to act as a buffer for bad ones. Tens of thousands died during the two great subsistence crises in the late 1620s and the late 1640s. In England, starvation was most common in the north, where scrubland had been put under the plow to accommodate the expanding population. Northern Italy lost nearly a third of its inhabitants between 1628 and 1630 with the simultaneous appearance of bad harvests, plague, and marauding armies. Even the weather became a scourge. The entire period from 1647 to 1653 was the worst ever in parts of France. Five consecutive bad harvests decimated the countryside. A Spanish official observed: "many places which a few years ago had 500 inhabitants now have barely 100. There are numerous families who go one or two days without a full meal and others live on herbs and roots from the fields."

Predictably, acute economic crisis led to rural revolt. As the French peasants reeled from visitations of plague, frost, and floods, the French state was raising the *taille*, the tax that fell most heavily upon the lower orders. A series of French rural revolts in the late 1630s focused on opposition to tax increases. The Nu-Pieds—the barefooted—rose against changes in the salt tax, others rose against new levies on wine. These revolts began in the same way, with the murder of a local tax official, the organization of a peasant militia, and the recruitment of local clergy and notables. The rebels forced temporary concessions from local authorities, but they never achieved lasting

The Plague in Milan, *a painting by Caspar Crayer of the seventeenth-century Flemish school. The victims of the epidemic are shown being consoled by a priest.*

reforms. Each revolt ended with the reimposition of order by the state. In England the largest rural protests, like the Midland Revolt of 1607, centered upon opposition to the enclosure of grain fields and their conversion to pasture.

The most spectacular popular uprisings occurred in Spanish-occupied Italy. In the spring of 1647 the Sicilian city of Palermo exploded under the pressure of a disastrous harvest, rising food prices, and relentless taxation. A city of 130,000 inhabitants, Palermo imported nearly all of its foodstuffs. As grain prices rose, the city government subsidized the price of bread, running up huge debts in the process. When the town governors could no longer afford the subsidies, they decided to reduce the size of the loaf rather than increase its price. This did not fool the women of the city, who rioted when the first undersized loaves were placed on sale. Soon the entire city was in revolt. "Long live the king and down with taxes," became the rebel slogan. Commoners who were not part of the urban power structure led the revolt in Palermo. For a time they achieved the abolition of Spanish taxes on basic foodstuffs. Their success provided the model for a similar uprising in Naples, the largest city in Europe. The Neapolitan revolt began in 1647 after the Spanish placed a tax on fruit. A crowd gathered to protest the new imposition, burned the customs house, and murdered several local officials. The protesters were led first by a fisherman and then by a blacksmith, and again the rebels achieved the temporary suspension of Spanish taxation. But neither of the Italian urban revolts could attract support from the local governors or the nobility. Both uprisings were eventually crushed.

The Right to Resist

Rural and urban revolts by members of the lower orders of European society were doomed to failure. Not only did the state control vast military resources, but it could count upon the loyalty of the governing classes to suppress local disorder. It was only when local elites rebelled and joined their social and political discontent to the economic grievances of the peasants that the state faced a genuine crisis. Traditionally, aristocratic rebellion centered upon the legitimacy rather than the power of the state. Claimants to the throne initiated civil wars for the prize of the crown. By the early seventeenth century, however, hereditary monarchy was too firmly entrenched to be threatened by aristocratic rebellions. When Elizabeth I of England died without an heir, the throne passed to her cousin, James I, without even a murmur of discontent. The assassination of Henry IV in 1610 left a child on the French throne, yet it provoked little more than intrigue over which aristocratic faction would advise him. The principles of hereditary monarchy and the divine right of kings laid an unshakable foundation for royal legitimacy. But if the monarch's right to rule could no longer be challenged, was the method of rule equally unassailable? Were subjects bound to their sovereign in all cases whatsoever?

Luther and Calvin had preached a doctrine of passive obedience. Magistrates ruled by divine will and must be obeyed in all things, they argued. Both left a tiny crack in the door of absolute submission, however, by recognizing the right of lesser magistrates to resist their superiors if divine law was violated. It was during the French civil wars that a broader theory of resistance began to develop. In attempting to defend themselves from accusations that they were rebels, a number of Huguenot writers responded with an argument that accepted the divine right of kings but that limited royal power. They claimed that kings were placed on earth by God to uphold piety and justice. When they failed to do so, lesser magistrates were obliged to resist them. As God would not institute tyranny, oppressive monarchs could not be acting by divine right. Therefore, the king who violated divine law could be punished. In the most influential of these writings, *A Defense of Liberty Against Tyrants* (1579), Philippe Duplessis-Mornay (1549–1623) took the critical next step and argued that the king who violated the law of the land could also be resisted.

In the writings of both Huguenot and Dutch Protestants there remained strict limits to this right to resist. These authors accepted all the premises of divine right theory and restricted resistance to other divinely ordained magistrates. Obedience tied society together at all levels. Loosening any of the knots might unravel everything. In fact, one crucial binding had already come loose when the arguments used to justify resistance in matters of religion came to be applied to of matters of state. Logic soon drove the argument further. If it was the duty of lesser magistrates to resist monarchical tyranny, why was it not the duty of all citizens to do so? This was a question posed not by a Protestant rebel, but by a Jesuit professor, Juan de Mariana (1536–1624). In *The King and the Education of the King* (1598), Mariana described how human government developed from the need of individuals to have leaders to act for their convenience and well-being. These magistrates were first established by the people and then legitimated by God. Magistrates were nothing other than the people's representatives, and if it was the duty of magistrates to resist the tyranny of monarchs, then it must also be the duty of every individual citizen. "If the sacred fatherland is falling into ruins, he who tries to kill the tyrant will be acting in no ways unjustly."

Mariana was careful to specify that only the most willful and deliberate lawbreakers were actually tyrants. He also advocated the use of national assemblies rather than individual assassins to make the decision to punish them. But there was no escaping the implications of his argument. If anyone could judge the conduct of kings, then there would be no standards of judgment. As Cardinal Richelieu observed succinctly: "tyranny is monarchy misliked." In 1605 a Catholic conspiracy to murder James I of England was foiled by government agents at the last moment. In 1610 a religious fanatic assassinated Henry IV of France. The right of individuals to resist tyrants was rapidly developing into the right of subjects to overthrow their monarchs.

In fact, there remained one more vital link in the chain. This was supplied by the great English poet John Milton (1608–74) in his defense of the English Revolution. Milton built upon traditional resistance theory as it had developed over the previous fifty years. Kings were instituted by the people to uphold piety and justice. Lesser magistrates had the right to resist monarchs. An unjust king forfeited his divine right and was to be punished as any ordinary citizen. In *The Tenure of Kings and Magistrates* (1649), Milton expanded upon the conventional idea that society was formed by a covenant, or contract, between ruler and ruled. The king in his coronation oath promised to uphold the laws of the land and to rule for the benefit of his subjects. The subjects promised to obey. Failure to meet obligations—by either side—broke the contract.

By the middle of the seventeenth century, resistance theory provided the intellectual justification for a number of quite different attacks upon monarchical authority. In 1640 simultaneous rebellions in the ancient kingdoms of Portugal and Catalonia threatened the Spanish monarchy. The Portuguese successfully dissolved the rather artificial bonds that had been created by Philip II and resumed their separate national identity. Catalonia, the easternmost province of Spain, which Ferdinand of Aragon had brought to the union of crowns in the fifteenth century, presented a more serious challenge. Throughout the 1620s, Catalonia, with its rich Mediterranean city of Barcelona, had consistently rebuffed Olivares' attempts to consolidate the Spanish provinces.

The Catalonian Cortes—the representative institution of the towns—refused to make even small contributions to the Union of Arms or to successive appeals for emergency tax increases. Catalonian leaders feared that these demands were only the thin edge of the wedge. They did not want their province to go the way of Castile, where taxation was as much an epidemic as was plague.

Catalonia relied upon its ancient laws to fend off demands for contributions to the Spanish military effort. But soon the province was embroiled in the French war and Olivares was forced to bring troops into Catalonia. The presence of the soldiers and their conduct inflamed the local population. In the spring of 1640 an unconnected series of peasant uprisings took place. Soldiers and royal officials were slain, and the Spanish viceroy of the province was murdered. But the violence was not only directed against outsiders. Attacks upon wealthy citizens raised the specter of social revolt.

It was at this point that a peasant uprising broadened into a provincial rebellion. The political leaders of Barcelona not only decided to sanction the rebellion, they decided to lead it. They declared that Philip IV had violated the fundamental laws of Catalonia and that in consequence their allegiance to the crown of Spain was dissolved. Instead they turned to Louis XIII of France, offering him sovereignty if he would preserve their liberties. In fact, the Catalonians simply exchanged a devil they knew for one they did not. The French happily sent troops into Barcelona to repel a Spanish attempt to crush the rebellion. Now two armies occupied Catalonia. The Catalan rebellion lasted for twelve years. When the Spanish finally took Barcelona in 1652, both rebels and ruler were exhausted from the struggle.

The revolt of the Catalans posed a greater external threat to the Spanish monarchy than it did an internal one. In contrast, the French Fronde, an aristocratic rebellion that began in 1648, was more directly a challenge to the underlying authority of the state. It too began in response to fiscal crises brought on by war. Throughout the 1640s the French state had tottered on the edge of bankruptcy. It had used every means of creative financing that its ministers could devise, mortgaging as much of the future as anyone would buy. Still it was necessary to raise traditional taxes and to institute new ones. The first tactic revived

A episode from the second Fronde, one of the two French civil wars that occurred during the minority of Louis XIV.

peasant revolts, especially in the early years of the decade; the second led to the Fronde.

Louis XIV (1643–1715) was four years old when he inherited the French throne. His mother, Anne of Austria (1601–66), ruled as regent with the help of her Italian advisor, Cardinal Mazarin (1602–61). In the circumstances of war, agricultural crisis, and financial stringency, no regency government was going to be popular, but Anne and Mazarin made the worst of a bad situation. They initiated new taxes on officeholders, Parisian landowners, and the nobility. Soon all three united against them, led by the Parlement of Paris, the highest court in the land, in which new decrees of taxation had to be registered. In 1648 the Parlement refused to register a number of the new taxes proposed by the government and soon insisted upon the right to control the crown's financial policy. When Anne and Mazarin struck back by arresting a number of leading members of the Parlement, barricades went up in Paris, and the court, along with the nine-year-old king, fled the capital. As the in-group of courtiers scurried out of Paris, the out-group hustled into it. Quickly the Fronde—which took its name from the slingshots that children used to hurl stones at carriages—became an aristocratic revolt aimed not at the king, but at his advisers. Demands for Mazarin's resignation, the removal of the new taxes, and greater participation in government by nobles and Parlement were coupled with profuse statements of loyalty to the king. Even the Parisian population, who took the opportunity of the dis-

order to settle old scores with the tax collectors, wanted little more than the stable rule of the boy king.

Had the Fronde taken place during a period of international peace, Mazarin might have succeeded in isolating Paris and starving the rebels into submission. Instead the French got a taste of the medicine they had served up to the Spanish in the Catalonian revolt. The Duc de Condé, leader of the Parisian insurgents, courted Spanish aid against Mazarin's forces, and the cardinal was forced to make concessions to prevent another Spanish invasion of France. The leaders of the Fronde agreed that the crown must overhaul its finances and recognize the rights of the administrative nobility to participate in formulating royal policy. But they had no concrete proposals to accomplish either aim. Nor could they control the deteriorating political situation in Paris and a number of provincial capitals where urban and rural riots followed the upper-class attack upon the state. The catastrophic winter of 1652, with its combination of harvest failure, intense cold, and epidemic disease, brought the crisis to a head. Louis XIV was declared old enough to rule and his forces recaptured Paris, where he was welcomed as a savior. Born of frustration, fear, and greed, the Fronde accomplished little. Like the Catalonian revolt, it revealed the fragility of the absolute state on the one hand, yet its underlying stability on the other. In neither France nor Spain was there ever any real alternative to royal rule.

The English Civil Wars

On the surface, it is difficult to understand why the most profound challenge to monarchical authority took place in England. Among the nations of Europe, England alone enjoyed peace in the early seventeenth century. Except for a brief period around 1620, the English economy sputtered along. The monarchy itself was stable. James I had succeeded his cousin Elizabeth I without challenge and already had as many children as the Tudors had produced in nearly a century.

James I was not a lovable monarch but he was capable, astute, and generous. In the eyes of his critics he had two great faults: he succeeded a legend and he was Scottish. There was little he could do about either. Elizabeth I had ruled England successfully for over forty years. As the economy soured and the state tilted toward bankruptcy in the 1590s, the queen remained above criticism. She sold off royal lands worth thousands of pounds and ran up huge debts at the turn of the century. Yet the gleaming myth of the glorious virgin queen tarnished not the least bit. When she died, the general population wept openly and the governing elite breathed a collective sigh of relief. There was so much to be done to set things right.

At first, James I endeared himself to the English gentry and aristocracy by showering them with the gift of social elevation. On his way to London from Scotland, the first of the Stuart kings knighted thousands of gentlemen who had waited in vain for favor from the queen. He promoted peers and created new titles to meet the pent-up demands of decades of stinginess. But he showered favor equally on his own countrymen, members of his royal Scottish court who accompanied him to England. A strong strain of ethnic prejudice combined with the disappointed hopes of English courtiers to generate immediate hostility to the new regime. If Elizabeth could do no wrong, James could do little right. Though he relied upon Elizabeth's most trusted ministers to guide state business, James was soon plunged into financial and political difficulties. He never escaped from either.

His financial problems resulted directly from the fact that the tax base of the English monarchy was undervalued. For decades the monarchy had staved off a crisis by selling lands that had been confiscated from the Church in the mid-sixteenth century. But this solution reduced the crown's long-term revenues and made it dependent upon extraordinary grants of taxation from Parliament. Royal demands for money were met by parliamentary demands for political reform, and these differing objectives provoked unintentional political controversies in the 1620s. The most significant, in 1628, during the reign of Charles I, led to the formulation of the Petition of Right, which restated the traditional English freedoms from arbitrary arrest and imprisonment (habeas corpus), from nonparliamentary taxation, and from the confiscation of property by martial law.

Religious problems mounted on top of economic and political difficulties. Demands were made for thoroughgoing church reforms by groups and individuals who had little in common other than the name given to them by their detractors: Puritans. One of the most contentious issues raised by Puritans was the survival in the Anglican church of the Catholic hierarchy of archbishops and bishops. They demanded the abolition of this episcopal form of government and its replacement with a presbyterial system similar to that in Scotland, in which congregations nominated their own representatives to a national assembly. As the king was the supreme head of the English church, an attack upon church structure was an attack upon the monarchy. "No bishop, no king," James I declared as he rejected the first formal attempts at reform. But neither James I nor his son, Charles I, opposed religious reform. They too wanted a better educated clergy, a plain and decorous worship service, and godly citizens. But to achieve their reforms they strengthened episcopal power. In the 1620s Archbishop William Laud (1573–1645) rose to power in the English church by espousing a Calvinism so moderate that many denied it was Calvinism at all. Laud preached the beauty of holiness and strove to reintroduce decoration in the church and a formal decorum in the service. One of Laud's first projects after he was appointed archbishop of Canterbury was to establish a consistent divine service in England and Scotland by creating new prayer books.

It fell to the unfortunate dean of St. Giles Cathedral in Edinburgh Cathedral to introduce the new Scottish prayer book in 1637. The reaction was immediate: someone threw a stool at his head and dozens of women screamed that "popery" was being brought to Scotland. There were riots by citizens and resistance to the use of the new prayer book by clergy and the nobility. To Charles I the opposition was rebellion and he began to raise forces to suppress it. But Scottish soldiers were far more determined to preserve their religious practice than were English soldiers to impose the king's. By the end of 1640 a Scottish army had successfully invaded England.

Now the fiscal and political problems of the Stuart monarchs came into play. For eleven years Charles I had managed to do what he was in theory supposed to do, live from his own revenues. He had accomplished this by a combination of economy and the revival of ancient feudal rights that struck hard at the governing classes. He levied fines for unheard-of offenses, expanded traditional taxes, and added a brutal efficiency to the collection of revenue. While these expedients sufficed during peacetime, now that an army had to be raised and a war fought, Charles I was again dependent upon grants from Parliament, which he reluctantly summoned in 1640.

The Long Parliament, which met in November 1640 and sat for thirteen years, saw little urgency in levying taxes to repel the Scots. After all, the Scots were resisting Laud's religious innovations and there were many Englishmen who believed that they should be resisted. More to the point, members of Parliament had a host of political grievances to be redressed before they granted the king his money. Parliament proposed a number of constitutional reforms that Charles I reluctantly accepted. The Long Parliament would not be dismissed without its own consent. In the future Parliaments would be summoned once in every three years. Due process in common law would be observed and the ancient taxes that the crown had revived would be abolished. To show its seriousness of purpose, Parliament, as the highest court in the land, tried and executed Charles' leading political adviser, the Earl of Strafford, and imprisoned Archbishop Laud.

At first Charles I could do nothing but bide his time and accept these assaults upon his power and authority. Once he had crushed the Scots he would be able to bargain from a position of strength. But as the months passed it became clear that Parliament had no intention of providing him with money or forces. Rather, the members sought to negotiate with the Scots themselves and to continue to demand concessions from the king as long as the Scottish threat remained. By the end of 1641 Charles' patience had worn thin. He bungled an attempt to arrest the leaders of the House of Commons, but he successfully spirited his wife and children out of London. Then he too left the capital and headed north where, in the summer of 1642, he raised the royal standard and declared the leaders of Parliament rebels and traitors. England was plunged into civil war.

Parliament had finally pushed too hard and its members now found themselves in the unprecedented situation of having to fight a war against their sovereign, a war that few of them wanted and that hardly anyone believed they could win. One of the Parliament's generals summed up the futility of the situation: "If we defeat the king ninety-nine times, yet still he is king. But if he defeat us once we will all be hanged as traitors." Nevertheless, there were strong passions on both sides. Parliamentarians believed that they were fighting to defend their religion, their liberties, and the rule of law. Royalists believed they were fighting to defend their monarch, their church, and social stability. After nearly three years of inconclusive fighting, in June 1645 Parliament won a decisive victory at Naseby and brought the war to an end the following summer. The king was in captivity, bishops had been abolished, a Presbyterian church had been established, and limitations were placed on royal power. All that remained necessary to end three years of civil war was the king's agreement to abide by the judgment of battle.

But Charles I had no intention of surrendering either his religion or his authority. Despite the rebels' successes, they could not rule without him, and he would concede nothing as long as opportunities to maneuver remained. In 1647 there were opportunities galore. The war had proved ruinously expensive to Parliament. It owed enormous sums to the Scots, to its own soldiers, and to the governors of London. Each of these elements had its own objectives in a final settlement of the war and they were not altogether compatible. London feared the parliamentary army, unpaid

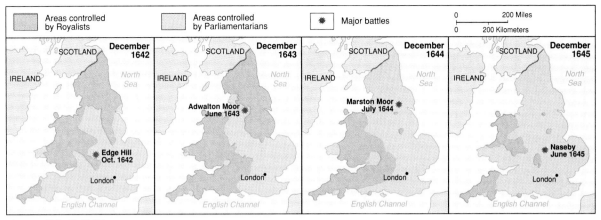

The English Civil War

and camped dangerously close to the capital. The Scots and the English Presbyterians in Parliament feared that the religious settlement already made would be sacrificed by those known as Independents, who desired a more decentralized church. The Independents feared that they would be persecuted just as harshly by the Presbyterians as they had been by the king. In fact, the war had settled nothing.

The English Revolutions

Charles I happily played both ends against the middle until the army decisively ended the game. In June 1647 soldiers kidnaped the king and demanded that Parliament pay their arrears, protect them from legal retribution, and recognize their service to the nation. Those in Parliament who opposed the army's intervention were impeached, and when London Presbyterians rose up against the army's show of force, troops moved in to occupy the city. The civil war, which had come so close to resolution in 1647, had now become a military revolution. Religious and political radicals flocked to the army and encouraged the soldiers to support their programs and to resist disbandment. New fighting broke out in 1648 as Charles encouraged his supporters to resume the war. But forces under the command of Sir Thomas Fairfax (1612–71) and Oliver Cromwell (1599–1658) easily crushed the royalist uprisings in England and Scotland. The army now

demanded that Charles I be brought to justice for his treacherous conduct both before and during the war. When the majority in Parliament refused, still hoping against hope to reach an accommodation with the king, the soldiers again acted decisively. In December 1648 army regiments were sent to London to purge the two houses of Parliament of those who opposed the army's demands. The remaining members, contemptuously called the Rump Parliament, voted to bring the king to trial for his crimes against the liberties of his subjects. On 30 January 1649, Charles I was executed and England was declared to be a commonwealth. (See Special Feature, "King Charles' Head," pp. 500–501.) The monarchy and the House of Lords were abolished and the nation was to be governed by what was left of the membership of the House of Commons.

For four years the members of the Rump Parliament struggled with proposals for a new constitution while balancing the demands of moderate and radical reformers and an increasingly hostile army. It achieved little other than to raise the level of frustration. In 1653 Oliver Cromwell, with the support of the army's senior officers, forcibly dissolved the Rump and became the leader of the revolutionary government. At first he ruled along with a Parliament handpicked from among the supporters of the commonwealth. When Cromwell's Parliament proved no more capable of governing than had the Rump, a written constitution, The Instrument of Government (1653) established a new polity. Cromwell was

King Charles' Head

They could have killed him quietly: the executioners slipping away silently in the night, unauthorized, unknown. It was the quickest way and it would end all doubts. Since June 1647, Charles I had been prisoner of the parliamentary army, and there had been more than one moment in which his elimination would have settled so many vexing problems. They could have let him escape: a small boat, an unlocked door, a guard conveniently asleep. Let him take his chances on the open sea. Let him live out his life in exile. Dangerous, perhaps, but still he would be gone and a new government in the name of the people could get on with creating a new order. They could have done it quietly.

Instead the leaders of Parliament and the army decided on a trial, a public presentation of charges against the king, a public judgment of his guilt. A high court of justice, enforcing the laws of England, would try its king for treason against the state. The logic was simple: if Parliament had fought for the preservation of the liberties of all Englishmen, then they could only proceed against the king by law. If they followed any other course, they were open to the charge that they were usurpers, that they ruled by the power of might rather than by the power of law. But if the logic was simple, everything else was hopelessly complex. English law was a system of precedents, one case stacking upon another to produce the weighty judgments of what was and was not law-

ful. Never had there been a treason case like this one. Indeed, how could the king commit treason, how could he violate his own allegiance? Always before the king acted as prosecutor, the king's judges had rendered decisions, and the king's executioner had carried out sentences. Not one of these precedents was now in the least way useful.

Nor was it clear what court had jurisdiction over this unprecedented case. The royal judges would have no part of it; neither would the House of Lords. The House of Commons was forced to create its own high court of justice, 135 supporters of the parliamentary cause drawn from its own members, from the army, and from among the leading citizens of London. Barely half attended any of the sessions. Judge John Bradshaw, who presided over two provincial royal courts, was chosen to preside at the king's trial after several of his more distinguished col-

leagues tactfully declined the post. Bradshaw took the precaution of lining his hat with lead against the chance that he would be shot at from the galleries rather than the floor.

These shortcomings did not deter the leaders of the parliamentary cause. These were unprecedented times and the ossified procedures of lawyers and law courts could not be allowed to detract from the undeniable justice of their cause. Charles I had committed treason against his nation. He had declared war on his people. He had brought Irish and Scottish armies into England to repress Parliament, and when that had failed he had negotiated with French, Danish, and Dutch troops for the same purpose. Even when he had been defeated in battle, when the judgment of God was clear for all to see, even then he plotted and he tricked. His lies were revealed by his own hand, his captured correspondence detailing how he intended to double-cross those to whom he swore he would be faithful. Cromwell called him "a man against whom the Lord had witnessed," and the prosecution needed no better testimony than that. If there were no precedents, then this trial would set one.

Nevertheless, the makeshift nature of the court provided the king with his line of attack. If there was to be a public display, then Charles I was determined to turn it to his advantage. Even as his royal palace was being converted into a courtroom and an execution platform was being hastily erected on one of its balconies, even now the king could not conceive that the nation could be governed without him. Royal government had guided England for a millennium and for all he could see would do so for another. Rather he feared that he would be deposed and replaced, and against that eventuality he had secured the escape of his two elder sons. They were safe in France and only his youngest child was in the hands of these savage parliamentarians.

About the trial itself, he worried not at all. There could be no court in the land that could try its king, no authority but his own that could determine a charge of treason. When it was read out that he was a tyrant and traitor, he burst out laughing. "Remember, I am your king, your lawful king and what sins you bring upon your heads and the judgment of God upon this land, think well upon it," he told his accusers.

The trial began on Saturday, 20 January 1649. Armed soldiers in battledress cleared the floor of the large chamber. Curious onlookers packed the galleries. Despite the fact that all former royalists had been ordered out of the city before the trial began, the king had more than one supporter well placed to heckle the commissioners. The king wore the enormous golden star of the Order of the Garter on his cloak but was allowed no other symbol of royalty to overawe his accusers.

The charge of "treason and high misdemeanors" had been carefully prepared. The king was accused of making war on his people "whereby much innocent blood of the free people of this nation hath been spilt." When the resounding indictment concluded, all eyes turned toward Charles I. Now he would have to answer the charge, guilty or not guilty, and in answering show the line of his defense. But the king chose a different strategy. Rather than answer the charge, he questioned the authority of the court. "I would know by what power I am called hither, a king cannot be tried by any superior jurisdiction here on earth." This was the weakest point of the parliamentary strategy. Judge Bradshaw could only assert that the court represented the free people of England. But Charles was relentless. He demanded precedents and refused to be silenced by the assertion that his objections were overruled.

The prosecutors had prepared a case against the king and were ready to call their witnesses. They hoped to place the king's evil conduct before the eyes of the nation. But in English law, a defendant who refused to plead was presumed to have pleaded guilty. Thus the king's trial ended as soon as it had begun. After three fruitless sessions, and much behind-the-scenes maneuvering, it was decided that the king should be condemned and sentenced to die. On 27 January, Judge Bradshaw appeared in the scarlet robes of justice and issued the sentence. Charles had prepared a statement for maximum effect and waited patiently to deliver it. Now it was the king's turn to be surprised. After pronouncing sentence, Bradshaw and the commissioners rose from the bench. "Will you not hear me a word, Sir," called a flustered Charles I. "No," replied the judge. "Guards, withdraw your prisoner."

Tuesday, 30 January, dawned cold and clear. It had been a bitter winter. Charles put on two shirts so that if he trembled from the cold it would not be interpreted as fear. In fact he made a very good end. The chopping block had been set very low, and great iron staples were driven in the platform to pin down the king's arms if he attempted to resist his fate. But those who exercised such caution understood little of the man they had opposed for the last seven years. Charles was more than ready to accept his fate. He spoke briefly and to the point, denying that he had acted against the true interests and rights of his subjects. Then he lay down on the platform, placed his head upon the block, and prayed. As the axe fell, one witness recorded "such a groan as I never heard before and hope never to hear again," broke forth from the crowd. The English Revolution had begun.

given the title Lord Protector, and he was to rule along with a freely elected Parliament and an administrative body known as the Council of State.

Cromwell was able to hold the revolutionary cause together through the force of his own personality. A member of the lesser landed elite who had opposed the arbitrary policies of Charles I, he was a devout Puritan who believed in a large measure of religious toleration for Christians. As both a member of Parliament and a senior officer in the army, he had been able to temper the claims of each when they conflicted. Cromwell saw God's hand directing England toward a more glorious future and he believed that his own actions were divinely ordained: "No man climbs higher than he that knows not whither he goes." Though many urged him to accept the crown of England and begin a new monarchy, Cromwell steadfastly held out for a government in which fundamental authority resided in Parliament. Until his death he defended the achievements of the revolution and held its conflicting constituents together.

But a sense that only a single person could effectively rule a state remained too strong for the reforms of the revolutionary regimes to have much chance of success. When Cromwell died in

1658 it was only natural that his eldest son Richard should be proposed as the new Lord Protector despite the fact that Richard had very little experience in either military or civil affairs. Nor did he have the sense of purpose that was his father's greatest source of strength. Without an individual to hold the movement together, the revolution fell apart. In 1659 the army again intervened in civil affairs, dismissing the recently elected Parliament and calling for the restoration of the monarchy, to provide stability to the state. After a period of negotiation in which the king agreed to a general amnesty with only a few exceptions, the Stuarts were restored when Charles II (1649–85) took the throne in 1660.

Twenty years of civil war and revolution had their effect. Parliament became a permanent part of civil government and now had to be managed rather than ignored. Royal power over taxation and religion was curtailed, though in fact Parliament proved more vigorous in suppressing religious dissent than the monarchy ever had. England was to be a reformed Protestant state though there remained much dispute about what constituted reform. Absolute monarchy had become constitutional monarchy with the threat of revolution behind the power of Parliament and

War and Peace in Europe, 1598–1650

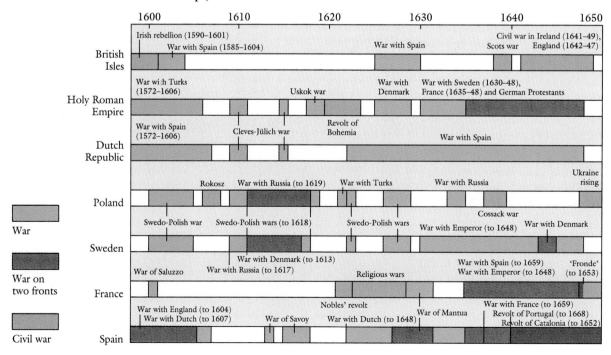

the threat of anarchy behind the power of the crown.

Both threats proved potent in 1685 when James II (1685–88) came to the throne. A declared Catholic, James attempted to use his power of appointment to foil the constraints that Parliament imposed upon him. He elevated Catholics to leading posts in the military and in the central government and began a campaign to pack a new Parliament with his supporters. This proved too much for the governing classes, who entered into negotiations with William, Prince of Orange, husband of Mary Stuart, James' eldest daughter. In 1688 William landed in England with a small force. Without support, James II fled to France, the English throne was declared vacant, and William and Mary were proclaimed king and queen of England. There was little bloodshed in England and little threat of social disorder, and the event soon came to be called the Glorious Revolution. Its achievements were set down in the Declaration of Rights (1689), which was presented to William and Mary before they took the throne. The Declaration reasserted the fundamental principles of constitutional monarchy as they had developed over the previous half-century. Security of property and the regularity of Parliaments were guaranteed. The Toleration Act (1689) granted religious freedom to nearly all groups of Protestants. The liberties of the subject and the rights of the sovereign were to be in balance.

The events of 1688 in England reversed a trend toward increasing power on the part of the Stuarts. This second episode of resistance resulted in the development of a unique form of government which, a century later, would spawn dozens of imitators. John Locke (1632–1704) was the theorist of the Revolution of 1688. He was heir to the century-old debate on resistance and he carried the doctrine to a new plateau. In *Two Treatises on Civil Government* (1690), Locke developed the contract theory of government. Political society was a compact that individuals entered into freely for their own well-being. It was designed to maintain each person's natural rights—life, liberty, and property. Natural rights were inherent in individuals; they could not be given away. The contract between rulers and subjects was an agreement for the protection of natural rights. "Arbitrary power cannot consist with the ends of society and government. Men would not quit the

freedom of the state of nature were it not to preserve their lives, liberties, and fortunes and by stated rules to secure their peace and happiness." When rulers acted arbitrarily, they were to be deposed by their subjects, preferably in the relatively peaceful manner in which James II had been replaced by William III.

The Zenith of the Royal State

The mid-century crises tested the mettle of the royal states. Over the long term, the seventeenth-century crises had two different consequences. First they provided a check to the exercise of royal power. Fear of recurring rebellions had a chilling effect upon policy, especially taxation. Reforms of financial administration, long overdue, were one of the themes of the later seventeenth century. Even as royal government strengthened itself, it remained concerned about the impact of its policies. On the other hand, the memory of rebellion served to control the ambitions of factious noblemen and town oligarches.

If nothing else, these episodes of opposition to the rising royal states made clear the universal desire for stable government, which was seen as the responsibility of both subjects and rulers. By the second half of the seventeenth century, effective government was the byword of the royal state. As Louis XIV proclaimed, rule was a trade that had to be constantly studied and practiced. The natural advantages of monarchy had to be merged with the interests of the citizens of the state and their desires for wealth, safety, and honor. After so much chaos and instability, the monarchy had to be elevated above the fray of day-to-day politics, elevated to become a symbol of the power and glory of the nation. Control no longer meant the greedy grasp of royal officials but their practiced guidance of affairs.

In England, Holland, and Sweden a form of constitutional monarchy developed in which rulers shared power, in varying degrees, with other institutions of state. In England it was Parliament, in Holland the town oligarchies, and in Sweden the nobility. But in most other states in Europe there developed a pure form of royal government known as absolutism. Absolute monarchy revived the divine right theories of kingship and added to them a cult of the personality of the ruler. Absolutism was practiced in states as dissimilar as Denmark, Brandenburg-Prussia, and Russia. It reached its zenith in France under Louis XIV, the most powerful of the seventeenth-century monarchs.

Absolute Monarchy

Locke's theory of contract provided one solution to the central problem of seventeenth-century government: how to balance the monarch's right to command and the subjects' duty to obey. By establishing a constitutional monarchy, in which power was shared between the ruler and a representative assembly of subjects, England found one path out of this thicket. But it was not a path that many others could follow. The English solution was most suited to a state that was largely immune from invasion and land war. Constitutional government required a higher level of political participation of citizens than did an absolute monarchical one. Greater participation in turn meant greater freedom of expression, greater toleration of religious minorities, and greater openness in the institutions of government. All were dangerous. The price that England paid was a half-century of governmental instability.

The alternative to constitutional monarchy was absolute monarchy. It, too, found its greatest theorist in England. Thomas Hobbes (1588–1679) was one of many Englishmen who went into exile in France during the course of the English civil wars. In his greatest work, *Leviathan* (1651), Hobbes argued that before civil society had been formed, humans lived in a savage state of nature, "in a war of every man against every man." This was a ghastly condition without morality or law—"the notions of right and wrong, of justice and injustice have there no place." People came together to form a government for the most basic of all purposes: for self-preservation. Without government they were condemned to a life that was "solitary, poor, nasty, brutish, and short." To escape the state of nature, individuals pooled their power and granted it to a ruler. The terms of the Hobbesian contract were simple. Rulers agreed to rule; subjects agreed to obey. When the contract was intact, people ceased to live in a state

of nature. When it was broken, they returned to it. With revolts, rebellions, and revolutions erupting in all parts of Europe, Hobbes' state of nature never seemed very far away.

For most states of Europe in the later seventeenth century, absolute monarchy became not only a necessity but an ideal. The consolidation of power in the hands of the divinely ordained monarch who, nevertheless, ruled according to principles of law and justice, was seen as the perfect form of government. Absolutism was an expression of control rather than of power. If the state was sometimes pictured as a horse, the absolute monarch gripped the reins rather than the whip most tightly. "Many writers have tried to confound absolute government with arbitrary government. But no two things could be more unlike," wrote Bishop Jacques Bossuet (1627–1704), who extolled absolutism in France. The absolute ruler ruled in the interests of his people:

The title page of the first edition of Thomas Hobbes' Leviathan, *published in 1651. The huge figure composed of many tiny human beings symbolizes the surrender of individual human rights to those of the state.*

"the prince is the public person, the whole state is included in him, the will of all the people is enclosed within his own."

The main features of absolute monarchy were all designed to extend royal control. As in the early seventeenth century, the person of the monarch was revered. Courts grew larger and more lavish in an effort to enhance the glory of the monarchy and thereby of the state. *L'état, c'est moi*—"I am the state"—Louis XIV was supposed to have said. No idea better expresses absolutism's connection between governor and governed. As the king grew in stature, his competitors for power all shrank. Large numbers of nobles were herded together at court under the watchful eye of monarchs who now ruled rather than reigned. The king shed the cloak of his favorites and rolled up his own sleeves to manage state affairs. Representative institutions, especially those that laid claim to control over taxation, were weakened or cast aside for obstructing efficient government and endangering the welfare of the state. Monarchs needed standing armies, permanent forces that could be drilled and trained in the increasingly sophisticated arts of war. Thus the military was expanded and made an integral part of the machinery of government. The military profession developed within nations, gradually replacing mercenary adventurers who had fought for booty rather than for duty.

Yet the absolute state was never as powerful in practice as it was in theory. Nor did it ever exist in its ideal shape. Absolutism was always in the making, never quite made. Its success depended upon a strong monarch who knew his own will and could enforce it. It depended upon unity within the state, upon the absence or ruthless suppression of religious or political minorities. The absolute ruler needed to control information and ideas, to limit criticism of state policy. Ultimately, the absolute state rested upon the will of its citizens to support it. The seventeenth-century state remained a loose confederation of regions, many acquired by conquest and whose loyalty was practical rather than instinctive. There were no state police to control behavior or attitudes, no newspapers or mass communication to spread propaganda. Censorship might restrict the flow of forbidden books, but it could do little to dam up the current of ideas.

Absolutism in the East

Frederick William, the Great Elector of Brandenburg-Prussia (1640–88), was one of the European princes who made the most effective use of the techniques of absolutism. In 1640 he inherited a scattered and ungovernable collection of territories that had been devastated by the Thirty Years' War. Brandenburg, the richest of his possessions, had lost nearly half of its population. The war had a lasting impact upon Frederick William's character. As a child he had hidden in the woods to escape bands of marauding soldiers; as a teenager he had followed to its burial the corpse of Gustavus Adolphus, the man he most admired and wished to emulate. A long stay in Holland during the final stages of the Dutch Revolt impressed upon him the importance of a strong army and a strong base of revenue to support it.

Frederick William had neither. In 1640 his forces totaled no more than 2,500 men, most of them, including the officers, the dregs of German society. Despite the fact that he was surrounded by powerful neighbors—Sweden and Poland both claimed sovereignty over parts of his inheritance—the territories under his control had no tradition of military taxation. The nobility, known as *die Junker*, enjoyed immunity from almost all forms of direct taxation, and the towns had no obligation to furnish either men or supplies for military operations beyond their walls. When Frederick William attempted to introduce an excise—the commodity tax on consumption that had so successfully financed the Dutch Revolt and the English Revolution—he was initially rebuffed. But military emergency overcame legal precedents. By the 1650s Frederick William had established the excise in the towns though not on the land.

With the excise as a steady source of revenue, the Great Elector could now create one of the most capable standing armies of the age. He built his forces in stages, careful not to frighten his powerful eastern neighbors. The geographical scattering of his territory was a benefit. He could raise and train his troops in the west without endangering his security in the east. The strictest discipline was maintained in the new army, and the Prussian army developed into a feared and

TSARS OF RUSSIA

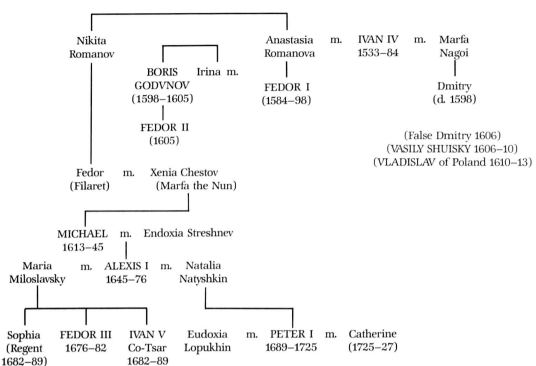

efficient fighting machine. Frederick William organized one of the first departments of war to oversee all of the details of the creation of his army, from housing and supplies to the training of young officer candidates. This department was also responsible for the collection of taxes. By integrating military and civilian government, Frederick William was able to create an efficient state bureaucracy that was particularly responsive in times of crisis. By the time that Frederick William died, the army had grown to over thirty thousand and state revenues had tripled. The creation of the Prussian army was the force that led to the creation of the Prussian state.

The same materials that forged the Prussian state led to the transformation of Russia. Soon after the young tsar Peter I (1682–1725) came to the throne, he realized that he could compete with the western states only by learning to play their game. In 1697 Peter visited the west, ostensibly to build an alliance against the Turks but actually to learn as much as he could about western military technology. He worked as an apprentice shipbuilder in Holland and as a blacksmith in

an arms foundry in England. Everywhere he went he tried to learn about the systems of taxation, the structure of administration, and, above all, the organization of the military. His stay in Germany led him to admire the reforms of the Great Elector and his son, especially the bureaucratic control of the army.

When Peter returned to Russia he attempted to implement at once all that he had learned. It is impossible to describe Peter's various personalities or to do justice to his ever changing character. He was ruthless and brutal in the tradition of Ivan the Terrible but far-sighted and determined in the tradition of Ivan the Great. Despite the fact that he was nearly seven feet tall, Peter attempted to walk the streets of Moscow in disguise so that he could gauge the impact of his reforms. He loved novelty, introducing new agricultural products like wine and potatoes to his subjects. When he determined that Russians should no longer wear beards, he took a hand in cutting them off. When he was persuaded of the benefits of dentistry, he practiced it himself upon his terrified subjects. His campaign to westernize

Russia frequently confused the momentous with the inconsequential, but it had an extraordinary impact at all levels of government and society.

Like those of Frederick William, Peter's greatest reforms were military. Peter realized that if Russia were to flourish in a world dominated by war and commerce it would have to reestablish its hold on the Baltic ports. This meant dislodging the Swedes from the Russian mainland and creating a fleet to protect Russian trade. Neither goal seemed likely. The Swedes were one of the great powers of the age, constant innovators in battlefield tactics and military organization. Peter studied their every campaign. His first wars against the Swedes ended in humiliating defeats, but with each failure came a sharper sense of what was needed to succeed.

First Peter introduced a system of conscription that resulted in the creation of a standing army. Conscripts were branded to inhibit desertion, and a strict discipline was introduced to prepare the soldiers for battle. Peter unified the military command at the top and stratified it in the field. He established promotion based on merit. For the first time Russian officers were given particular responsibilities to fulfill during both training and battle. Peter created military schools to train cadets for the next generation of officers. Finally in 1709 Peter realized his ambitions. At the Battle of Poltava the Russian army routed the Swedes, wounding King Charles XII, annihilating his infantry, and capturing dozens of his leading officers. That night Peter toasted the captured Swedish generals. He claimed that everything he knew about warfare he had learned from them and he congratulated them on their success as teachers. After the Battle of Poltava, Russia gradually replaced Sweden as the dominant power in the Baltic.

Like everything else about him, Peter the Great's absolutism was uniquely his own. In Russia there was little to be made of the distinction between absolute and arbitrary power. Peter consciously borrowed from the west, but he adapted western ideas to Russian conditions. He created a series of regions that were to be controlled from the center by officers similar to the French intendants. He also borrowed from the Prussian example by establishing departments of state, especially to control the organization and finance

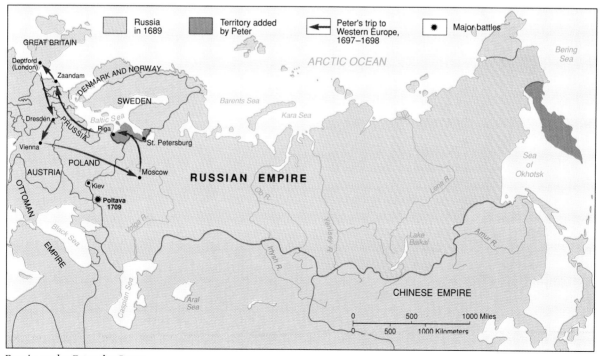

Russia under Peter the Great

of the military. Peter confirmed his intention of establishing a "window to the west" by building a new port city on the Baltic at Saint Petersburg. Here he helped construct the Russian navy, actually working on the docks for a time. Though Peter's power was unlimited, it was not uncontested. He secularized the Russian Orthodox church, subjecting it to the control of state power and confiscating much of its wealth in the process. He broke the old military service class, which attempted a coup d'etat when he was abroad in the 1690s. By the end of his reign, the Russian monarchy was among the strongest in Europe.

The Origins of French Absolutism

Nowhere was absolutism as successfully implanted as in France, and nowhere was it less likely to have grown. Not since Francis I (1515–47) had there been a king who was able to consolidate power, develop a policy of government, and attempt to carry it through. Henry IV (1589–1610) hoped to do all three. He was a vigorous and powerful man who exuded the qualities of a king. He literally bought peace from Catholic and Huguenot competitors, granting enormous sums to those aristocratic leaders willing to lay down arms and give their undivided allegiance to the monarchy. Under the watchful eye of his capable finance minister, the Duc de Sully, he began a program of fiscal reforms, which included taxing the sale of offices. He also looked to secure French interests against the expanding power of the Habsburgs. But the assassin's knife cut short the reinvigoration of the monarchy. Louis XIII (1610–43) was only eight years old when he came to the throne, and he grew slowly into his role under the tutelage of Cardinal Richelieu.

It was Richelieu's vision that stabilized French government. As chief minister, Richelieu saw clearly that the prosperity and even the survival of France depended upon strengthening royal power. He preached a doctrine of *raison d'etat*—reason of state—in which he placed the needs of the nation above the privileges of its most important groups. "One must be inflexible in punishing those who fail to obey," Richelieu wrote in his *Political Testament* (1646). Richelieu saw three threats to stable royal government, "the Huguenots shared the state, the nobles conducted them-

selves as if they were not subjects, and the most powerful governors in the provinces acted as if they were sovereign in their office."

Richelieu took measures to control all three. The power of the nobles was the most difficult to attack. The nobles' long tradition of independence from the crown had been enhanced by the wars of religion. Perhaps more importantly, the ancient aristocracy, the nobility of the sword, felt themselves in a particularly vulnerable position. Their world was changing and their traditional roles were becoming obsolete. Professional soldiers replaced them at war; professional administrators at government. Mercantile wealth threatened their economic superiority, the growth of the nobility of the robe—lawyers and state officials—threatened their social standing. They were hardly likely to take orders from a royal minister like Richelieu, especially when he attacked one of the great symbols of their power, the duel. Dueling was the traditional method of settling affairs of honor. Hand-to-hand combat with large, unwieldy swords provided satisfaction for perceived affronts as much through exhaustion as anything else. But at the same time that the nobility became more self-conscious about its honor, and thus more ready to perceive insults, technology changed the game. The introduction of the rapier made dueling deadly serious. A single thrust with the razorlike blade, skillful or lucky, bled the nation of hundreds of nobles. Richelieu banned the duel and executed the first noblemen to violate the ban.

To limit the power of local officials, Richelieu used intendants to examine their conduct and to reform their administration. He made careful appointments of local governors and brought more regions under direct royal control. Against the Huguenots, Richelieu's policy was more subtle. He was less interested in challenging their religion than their autonomy. In 1627 when the English sent a force to aid the Huguenots against the government, Richelieu and Louis XIII abolished the Huguenots' privileges altogether. They were allowed to maintain their religion but not their special status. They would have no privileges other than to be subjects of the king of France.

Richelieu's program was a vital prelude to the development of absolute monarchy in France. But the cardinal was not a king. While it is clear that Richelieu did not act without the full support of

Louis XIII, and clear that the king initiated many reforms for which the cardinal received credit, there can be no doubt that Richelieu was the power behind the throne. Louis XIII hated the business of government and even neglected his principal responsibility of providing the state with an heir. For years he and his wife slept in separate palaces and only a freak rainstorm in Paris forced him to spend a night with the queen, Anne of Austria, in 1637. It was the night of the conception of Louis XIV. Louis XIII and Richelieu died within six months of each other in 1642–43, and the nation again endured the turmoil of a child king. Richelieu's aggressive policy to curb the nobility as well as his stringent financial program in the 1630s helped precipitate the Fronde. Louis XIV (1643–1715) was never to forget the terror of the aristocratic rebellion in Paris: how he was forced to flee the capital in the dead of night, how he endured the penury of exile, how he suffered the humiliation of being bossed about by the rebels. He would never forget, and he would have a long time to remember.

Louis le Grand

While most seventeenth-century monarchs received a humanist education as preparation for rule, Louis XIV learned statecraft by the seat of his pants. Not quite five years old when he came to the throne, he was tutored by Cardinal Jules Mazarin (1602–61), Richelieu's successor as chief minister. If anything, Mazarin was more ruthless and less popular than his predecessor. An Italian from a modest background, Mazarin won the money to launch his career at the gaming table. Good fortune seemed to follow him everywhere. He gambled with his life and his career and each time he raked in the stakes. He died with the largest private fortune that had ever been accumulated by a French citizen, easily surpassing the fortune of Richelieu. Despite his foreign background and his connections with the papal court at Rome—either of which would normally have been debilitating—Mazarin rose to the pinnacle of French government. Like Richelieu, whom he emulated, Mazarin was an excellent administrator who had learned well the lessons of *raison d'etat*. At the conclusion of the Thirty Years' War, for example, Mazarin refused to make peace with

Spain, believing that the time was ripe to deliver a knockout blow to the Spanish Habsburgs. Even during the Fronde, France fought on, ultimately winning back small pieces of strategic territory. The peace treaty of 1659 was sealed by the marriage of Louis XIV to one of the heirs to the Spanish throne, a match that brought further territorial gains for France. Mazarin taught the boy king many valuable lessons in how to deal from positions of weakness as well as from positions of strength.

In order to pacify the rebellious nobility, who opposed Mazarin's power, Louis XIV was declared to have reached his majority at the age of thirteen. But it was not until Mazarin died ten years later in 1661 that the king began to rule. Then, he astounded his court by announcing that he would be his own chief minister and guide the affairs of state with his own hand. It was a momentous decision that at the time was thought to be catastrophic, but it was a decision that Louis XIV never had cause to regret. In fact, Louis was blessed with able and energetic ministers. The two central props of his state—money and might—were in the hands of dynamic men, Jean-Baptiste Colbert (1619–83) and the Marquis de Louvois (1639–91). Colbert, to whom credit belongs for the building of the French navy, the reform of French legal codes, and the establishment of national academies of culture, was Louis' chief minister for finance. Colbert's fiscal reforms were so successful that in less than six years a debt of 22 million French pounds had become a surplus of 29 million. Colbert achieved this astonishing feat not by raising taxes but by increasing the efficiency of their collection. Until Louis embarked upon his wars, the French state was solvent.

To Louvois, Louis' minister of war, fell the task of reforming the French army. During the Fronde, royal troops were barely capable of defeating the makeshift forces of the nobility. Louis XIV inherited an army of less than 20,000 whose officers were noblemen who had purchased their commissions as much for status as for use. By the end of the reign, the army had grown to 400,000 and its organization had been thoroughly reformed. Louvois introduced new ranks for the field officers who actually led their men into battle, and promotions were distributed by merit rather than purchase. He also solved one of the most serious logistical problems of the age by establishing storehouses of arms and ammunition throughout the realm. The greatest achievements of the reign were built on the backs of fiscal and military reforms, which were themselves a product of the continuing sophistication of French administration.

Louis XIV furthered the practice of relying upon professional administrators to supervise the main departments of state and to offer advice on matters of policy. He created a nearly complete separation between courtiers and officeholders and largely excluded the nobility of the sword from the inner circles of government. These were composed of ministers of departments and small councils that handled routine affairs. These councils were connected to the central advisory body of government, the secret council of the king. Within each department, ministers furthered the process of professionalization that led to the advancement of talented clerks, secretaries, and administrators. Though there still remained a large gulf between the promulgation of policy at Versailles and its enforcement in the provinces, it was now a gulf that could be measured and ultimately bridged. Louis XIV built upon the institution of the intendant that Richelieu had developed with so much success. Intendants were now a permanent part of government, and their duties expanded from their early responsibilities as coordinators and mediators into areas of policing and tax collection. It was through the intendants that the wishes of central government were made known in the provinces.

Though Louis XIV was well served, it was the king himself who set the tone for French absolutism. "If he was not the greatest king, he was the best actor of majesty that ever filled the throne," wrote an English observer. The acting of majesty was central to Louis' rule. His residence at Versailles was the most glittering court of Europe, renowned for its beauty and splendor. It was built on a scale never before seen, and Louis took a personal interest in making sure it was fit for a king. When the court and king moved there permanently in 1682, Versailles became the envy of the Continent. But behind the imposing facade of Versailles stood a well-thought-out plan for domestic and international rule.

Louis XIV attempted to tame the French

This Hyacinthe Rigaud portrait of Louis XIV in his coronation robes shows the splendor of the Roi Soleil (Sun King), who believed himself to be the center of France as the sun is the center of the solar system.

nobles by requiring their attendance at his court. Though not all provincial nobles hurried to Versailles, the more attractive the honey, the more numerous were the flies drawn to it. Louis established a system of court etiquette so complex that constant study was necessary to prevent humiliation. While the nobility studied decorum, they could not plot rebellion. At Versailles one never knocked on a door, one scratched with a fingernail. This insignificant custom had to be learned and remembered—it was useless anywhere else—and practiced if one hoped for the favor of the king. Leading noblemen of France rose at dawn so that they could watch Louis be awakened and hear him speak his first words. Dozens followed him from hall to gallery and from gallery to chamber as he washed, dressed, prayed, and ate. There was no greater concern than the king's health, unless it was the king's mood, which was as changeable as the weather.

This aura of court culture was equally successful in the royal art of diplomacy. For Louis XIV image was everything. In fact, we know very little about his private personality. Even his love letters to his mistresses appear to have been written for effect. "I prefer fame above all else, even life itself," he wrote in his memoirs. It was the fame of Versailles that stamped him with the power to dominate international affairs. During his reign, France replaced Spain as the greatest nation in Europe. Massive royal patronage of art, science, and thought brought French culture to new heights. The French language replaced Latin as the universal European tongue. France was the richest and most populous European state, and Louis' absolute rule finally harnessed these resources to a single purpose. France became a commercial power rivaling the Netherlands, a naval power rivaling England, and a military power without peer. It was not only for effect that Louis took the image of the sun as his own. In court, in the nation, and throughout Europe everything revolved around him.

France's rise to preeminence in Europe was undoubtedly the greatest accomplishment of the absolute monarchy of Louis XIV. But it did not come without costs. The strength of absolutism was that it harnessed the energies of the state to the purpose of the monarch. Its weakness was that it required a level of wisdom and foresight that was not very common among either monarchs or subjects. Louis XIV made his share of mistakes, which were magnified by the awe in which his opinions were held. His aggressive foreign policy ultimately bankrupted the crown. But without doubt, his greatest error was to persecute the Huguenots. As an absolute ruler, Louis believed that it was necessary to have absolute conformity and obedience. The existence of the Huguenots, with their separate communities and distinct forms of worship, seemed an affront to his authority. Almost from the beginning, Louis

allowed the persecution of Protestants, despite the protection provided by the Edict of Nantes. Protestant churches were pulled down, conversions to Catholicism were bought with the lure of immunities from taxation, children were separated from their families to be brought up in Catholic schools. Finally, in 1685 Louis XIV revoked the Edict of Nantes. All forms of Protestant worship were outlawed and the ministers who were not hunted down and killed were forced into exile. Despite a ban on Protestant emigration, over two hundred thousand Huguenots fled the country, many of them carrying irreplaceable skills with them to Holland and England in the west and to Brandenburg in the east.

Supporters of the monarchy celebrated the revocation of the Edict of Nantes as an act of piety. Religious toleration in seventeenth-century Europe was still a policy of expediency rather than of principle. Even the English, who prided themselves on developing the concept, and the Dutch, who welcomed Jews to Amsterdam, would not officially tolerate Catholics. But the persecution of the Huguenots was a social and political disaster for France. Those who fled to other Protestant states spread the stories of atrocities that stiffened European resolve against Louis. Those who remained became an embittered minority who pulled at the fabric of the state at every chance. Nor did the official abolition of Protestantism have much effect upon its existence. Against these policies, the Huguenots held firm to their beliefs. There were well over a million French Protestants, undoubtedly the largest religious minority in any state. Huguenots simply went underground, practicing their religion secretly and gradually replacing their numbers. No absolutism, however powerful, could succeed in eradicating religious beliefs.

Louis XIV gave his name to the age that he and his nation dominated, but he was not its only towering figure. The Great Elector, Peter the Great, Louis the Great: so they were judged by posterity, kings who had forged nations for a new age. Their style of rule showed the royal state at its height, still revolving around the king but more and more dependent upon permanent institutions of government that followed their own imperatives. The absolute state harnessed the economic and intellectual resources of the nation to the political will of the monarch. It did so to ensure survival in a dangerous world. But while monarchs ruled as well as reigned, they did so by incorporating vital elements of the state into the process of government. In England the importance of the landholding classes was recognized in the constitutional powers of Parliament. In Prussia the military power of *die Junker* was asserted through command in the army, the most important institution of the state. In France, Louis XIV co-opted many nobles at his court, while he made use of a talented pool of lawyers, clergymen, and administrators in his government. A delicate balance existed between the will of the king and the will of the state, a balance that would soon lead these continental powers into economic competition and military confrontation.

Suggestions for Further Reading

General Reading

A. L. Moote, *The Seventeenth Century* (Lexington, MA: D. C. Heath, 1970). A comprehensive survey.

* William Doyle, *The Old European Order* (Oxford: Oxford University Press, 1978). An important synthetic essay bristling with ideas.

* Geoffrey Parker, *Europe in Crisis 1598–1648* (London: William Collins and Sons, 1979). The best introduction to the period.

Perry Anderson, *Lineages of the Absolutist State* (London: NLB Books, 1974). A sociological study of the role of absolutism in the development of the western world.

The Rise of the Royal State

* Graham Parry, *The Golden Age Restor'd* (New York: St. Martin's Press, 1981). A study of English court culture in the reigns of James I and Charles I.

J. H. Elliott and Jonathan Brown, *A Palace for a King* (New Haven, CT: Yale University Press, 1980). An outstanding work on the building and decorating of a Spanish palace.

* J. N. Figgis, *The Divine Right of Kings* (Cambridge: Cambridge University Press, 1914). Still the classic study of this central doctrine of political thought.

* J. H. Elliott, *The Count-Duke of Olivares* (New Haven, CT: Yale University Press, 1986). A massive and massively important study of the leading statesman of Spain.

* Roger Lockyer, *Buckingham* (London: Longman, 1984). A stylish biography of the favorite of two monarchs.

The Crises of the Royal State

* Quentin Skinner, *The Foundations of Modern Political Thought*, 2 vols. (Cambridge: Cambridge University Press, 1978). A seminal work on the history of ideas from Machiavelli to Calvin.

* Perez Zagoin, *Rebels and Rulers*, 2 vols. (Cambridge: Cambridge University Press, 1982). A good survey of revolutions, civil war, and popular protests throughout Europe.

* Trevor Aston, ed., *Crisis in Europe 1600–1660* (Garden City, NY: Doubleday, 1967). Essays on the theme of a general crisis in Europe by distinguished historians.

G. Parker and L. Smith, eds., *The General Crisis of the Seventeenth Century* (London: Routledge & Kegan Paul, 1978). A collection of essays on the problem of the general crisis.

* Lawrence Stone, *The Causes of the English Revolution* (New York: Harper & Row, 1972). A vigorously argued explanation of why England experienced a revolution in the mid-seventeenth century.

* J. S. Morrill, *The Revolt of the Provinces* (London: Longman, 1980). An outstanding essay on the importance of the localities in the English civil war.

* D. E. Underdown, *Pride's Purge* (London: Allen and Unwin, 1985). The most important work on the politics of the English Revolution.

The Zenith of the Royal State

* H. W. Koch, *A History of Prussia* (London: Longman, 1978). A comprehensive study of Prussian history with an excellent chapter on the Great Elector.

* Paul Dukes, *The Making of Russian Absolutism* (London: Longman, 1982). A thorough survey of Russian history in the seventeenth and eighteenth centuries.

* Vasili Klyuchevsky, *Peter the Great* (Boston: Beacon Press, 1984). A classic work, still the best study of Peter.

* W. E. Brown, *The First Bourbon Century in France* (London: University of London Press, 1971). A good introduction to French political history.

* William Beik, *Absolutism and Society in Seventeenth Century France* (Cambridge: Cambridge University Press, 1985). The single best study of the government of a French province in the seventeenth century.

Victor Tapié, *France in the Age of Louis XIII and Richelieu* (Cambridge: Cambridge University Press, 1984). A translation of the classic narrative of events in the reign of Louis XIII.

John Wolf, *Louis XIV* (New York: Norton, 1968). An outstanding biography of the Sun King.

* Indicates paperback edition available.

17

Conquering the Material World

Rembrandt's Lessons

By the early seventeenth century interest in scientific investigation had spread out from narrow circles of specialists to embrace educated men and women. One of the more spectacular demonstrations of new knowledge was public dissection, by law performed only on the corpses of criminals. Here the secrets of the human body were revealed both for those who were in training as physicians and for those who had the requisite fee and strong stomach. Curiosity about the human body was becoming a mark of education. New publications, both scientific and popular, spread ancient wisdom as well as the controversial findings of the moderns. Pictures drawn on the basis of dissections filled the new medical texts like the one on the stand at the feet of the corpse in *The Anatomy Lesson of Dr. Nicolaes Tulp* (1632) by Rembrandt van Rijn (1606–69).

Dr. Tulp's anatomy lesson was not meant for the public. In fact, those gathered around him in various poses of concentration were not students at all. They were members of the Amsterdam company of surgeons, the physicians' guild of the early seventeenth century. The sitters had commissioned the picture, which was a celebration of themselves as well as of the noted Professor Tulp. They hired the young Rembrandt to compose the picture with the assurance that each of the sitters (whose names are written on the paper one of them holds in his hand) would appear as if he alone were the subject of a portrait. Rembrandt succeeded beyond expectation. Each individual was given his due. The expressions on their faces as much as their physical characteristics mark each one out from the group. Yet the portraits were only one part of the painting. The scene that Rembrandt depicted unified them. They became a group by their participation in the anatomy lesson. Rembrandt has chosen a moment of drama to stop the action. Dr. Tulp is about to make some point before cutting the tendons of the arm on the gruesome cadaver. The central figures of the group are rapt in attention though only one of them is actually observing the procedure of the anatomy. Each listens to Tulp, comparing his own experience and knowledge to that of the professor and the text that stands open.

The Anatomy Lesson established the twenty-five-year-old Rembrandt as one of the most gifted and fashionable painters in Amsterdam. If any people could be said to be consumers of art in seventeenth-century Europe, it was the Dutch. Artists flourished and pictures abounded. Travelers were struck by the presence of artwork in both public and private places and in the homes of even moderately prosperous people. The group portrait, which Rembrandt brought to new levels of expression, was becoming a favorite genre. It was used to celebrate the leaders of Dutch society who, unlike the leaders of most other European states, were not princes and aristocrats, but rather merchants, guild officials, and professionals. Rembrandt captured a spirit of civic pride in his group portraits. Here it was the surgeons' guild; later it would be the leaders of the cloth merchants' guild, another time a militia company.

Like the leaders of the surgeons' guild who commissioned their own portrait, which hung in their company's hall, the Dutch Republic

swelled with pride in the seventeenth century. Its long war with Spain
was finally drawing to a close and it was time to celebrate the birth of
a new state. The Dutch were a trading people and their trade
flourished as much in times of war as in times of peace. Their ships
traveled to all parts of the globe and they dominated the great luxury
trades of the age. Bankers and merchants were the backbone of the
Dutch Republic. Yet this republic of merchants was also one of the
great cultural centers of the Continent. Intellectual creativity was
cultivated in the same manner as was a trading partner. In the
burgeoning port of Amsterdam, the fastest growing city in Europe,
artists, philosophers, and mathematicians lived cheek by jowl. The
free exchange of ideas made Amsterdam home to those exiled for
their beliefs. The Dutch practiced religious toleration as did no one
else. Catholics, Protestants, and Jews all were welcomed to the
Republic and found that they could pursue their own paths without
persecution. Freedom of thought and freedom of expression helped
develop a new spirit of scientific inquiry, like that portrayed in *The
Anatomy Lesson of Dr. Nicolaes Tulp.*

The New Science

"And new Philosophy calls all in doubt,/ The element of fire is quite put out;/ The sun is lost and the earth, and no man's wit/ Can well direct him where to look for it." So wrote the English poet John Donne (1572–1631) about one of the most astonishing yet perplexing moments in the history of Western thought: the emergence of the new science. It was astonishing because it seemed truly new. The discoveries of the star-gazers, like those of the sea explorers, challenged people's most basic assumptions and beliefs. Men dropping balls from towers or peering at the skies through a glass claimed that they had disproved thousands of years of certainty about the nature of the universe. "And new Philosophy calls all in doubt." But it was perplexing because it seemed to loosen the moorings of everything that educated people thought they knew about their world. Nothing could be more disorienting than to challenge common sense. One needed to do little more than wake up in the morning to know that the sun moved from east to west while the earth stood still. But mathematics, experimentation, and deduction were needed to understand that the earth was in constant motion and that it revolved around the sun. "And no man's wit/ Can well direct him where to look for it."

The scientific revolution was the opening of a new era in European history. After two centuries of classical revival, European thinkers had finally come against the limits of ancient knowledge. Ancient wisdom had served Europeans well, and it was not to be discarded lightly. But one by one, the certainties of the past were being called into question. The explanations of the universe and the natural world that had been advanced by Aristotle and codified by his followers no longer seemed adequate. There were too many contradictions between theory and observation, too many things that did not fit. Yet breaking the hold of Aristotelianism was no easy task. If there is anything as powerful as an idea whose time has come, it is one whose time has gone. A full century was to pass before even learned people would accept the proofs that the earth revolved around the sun. Even then, the most famous of them had to recant these views or be condemned as a heretic.

The two essential characteristics of the new science were that it was materialistic and mathematical. Its materialism was contained in the realization that the universe is composed of matter in motion. This meant that the stars and planets were not made of some perfect ethereal substance but of the same matter that was found on earth. They were thus subject to the same rules of motion as were earthly objects. The mathematics of the new science was contained in the realization that calculation had to replace common sense as the basis for understanding the universe. Mathematics itself was transformed with the invention of logarithms, analytic geometry, and calculus. More importantly, scientific experimentation took the form of measuring repeatable phenomena. When Galileo attempted to develop a theory of acceleration, he rolled a brass ball down an inclined plane and recorded the time and distance of its descent one hundred times before he was satisfied with his results.

The new science was also a Europe-wide movement. The spirit of scientific inquiry flourished everywhere. The main contributors to astronomy were a Pole, a Dane, a German, and an Italian. The founder of medical chemistry was

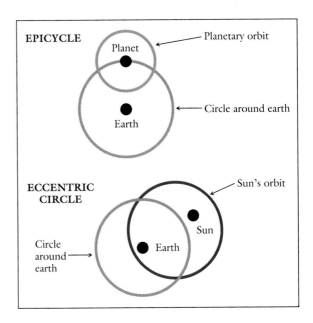

Swiss, the best anatomist was Belgian. England contributed most of all—the founders of modern chemistry, biology, and physics. By and large, these scientists operated outside the traditional seats of learning at the universities. Though most were university trained and not a few taught the traditional Aristotelian subjects, theirs was not an academic movement. Rather it was a public one made possible by the printing press. Once published, findings became building blocks for scientists throughout the Continent and from one generation to the next. Many discoveries were made in the search for practical solutions to ordinary problems, and what was learned fueled advances in technology and the natural sciences. The new science gave seventeenth-century Europeans a sense that they might finally master the forces of nature.

Heavenly Revolutions

There was much to be said for Aristotle's understanding of the world, for his cosmology. For one thing, it was harmonious. It incorporated a view of the physical world that coincided with a view of the spiritual and moral one. The heavens were unchangeable and therefore they were better than the earth. The sun, moon, and planets were all faultless spheres, unblemished and immune from decay. Their motion was circular because the circle was the perfect form of motion. The earth was at the center of the universe because it was the heaviest planet and because it was at the center of the great chain of being, between the underworld of spirits and the upperworld of gods. The second advantage to the Aristotelian world view was that it was easily incorporated into Christianity. Aristotle's description of the heavens as being composed of a closed system of crystalline rings that held the sun, moon, and planets in their circular orbits around the earth left room for God and the angels to reside just beyond the last ring. There were many passages of Scripture that described heaven and earth in just this way. Aristotle was both a philosopher and a scientist, for natural philosophy was the branch of knowledge devoted to understanding the physical world.

There were, of course, problems with Aristotle's explanation of the universe as it was pre-

served in the work of Ptolemy, the greatest of the Greek astronomers. For one thing, if the sun revolved in a perfect circle around the earth, then why were the seasons not perfectly equal? If the planets all revolved around the earth in circles, then why did they look nearer or farther, brighter or darker at different times of year? To solve these problems, a host of ingenious hypotheses were advanced. Perhaps the sun revolved around the earth in an eccentric circle, that is, a circle not centered on the earth. This would account for the differing lengths of seasons. Perhaps the planets revolved in circles that rested on a circle around the earth. Then when the planet revolved within the larger circle, it would seem nearer and brighter, and when it revolved outside it, it would seem farther away and darker. This was the theory of epicycles. Yet in order to account for the observable movement of all the known planets, there had to be fifty-five of these epicycles, of these circles within circles. As ingeniously complex as they were, the modifications of Aristotle's views made by the theories of eccentric circles and epicycles had one great virtue: they accurately predicted the movements of the planets. Though they were completely hypothetical, they answered the most troubling questions about the Aristotelian system.

The Polish University of Kraków had one of the leading mathematical faculties in Europe. There they taught the latest astronomical theories and vigorously debated the existence of eccentric circles and epicycles. In the 1490s, Nicolaus Copernicus (1473–1543) came to Kraków for a liberal arts education before pursuing a degree in Church law. He became fascinated by astronomy and puzzled by the debate over planetary motion. Copernicus believed, like Aristotle, that the simplest explanations were the best. If the sun were at the center of the universe and the earth simply another planet in orbit, then many of the most elaborate explanations of planetary motion were unnecessary. "At rest, in the middle of everything is the sun," Copernicus wrote in *On the Revolutions of the Heavenly Spheres* (1543). "For in this most beautiful temple who would place this lamp in another or better position than that from which it can light up the whole thing at the same time?"

Though Copernicus had discovered the key to

This chart of the heavens was engraved by Andreas Cellarius in 1660. It portrays the heliocentric universe described by Nicolaus Copernicus and accepted by Galileo. Earth and Jupiter are shown with moons orbiting them.

understanding the planetary system, he was never satisfied with his findings. When he was finally persuaded to publish his results at the end of his life, he already knew that he had created more problems than he had solved. Because Copernicus accepted most of the rest of the traditional Aristotelian explanation, especially the belief that the planets moved in circles, his sun-centered universe was only slightly better at predicting the position of the planets than the traditional earth-centered one.

Copernicus' idea stimulated other astronomers to make new calculations. Under the patronage of the king of Denmark, Tycho Brahe (1546–1601) built a large observatory to study planetary motion. In 1572, Brahe discovered a nova, a brightly burning star that was previously unknown. This discovery challenged the idea of an immutable universe composed of crystalline rings. In 1577 the appearance of a comet cutting through the supposedly impenetrable rings punched another hole into the old cosmology. Brahe's own views were a hybrid of old and new. He believed that all planets but the earth revolved around the sun and that the sun and the planets

revolved around a fixed earth. To demonstrate this theory, Brahe and his students compiled the largest and most accurate mathematical tables of planetary motion yet known. From this research, Brahe's pupil, Johannes Kepler (1571–1630), one of the great mathematicians of the age, formulated laws of planetary motion. Kepler discovered that planets orbited the sun in an elliptical rather than a circular path. This accounted for their movements nearer and farther from the earth. More importantly, he demonstrated that there was a precise mathematical relationship between the speed with which a planet revolved and its distance from the sun. Kepler's findings supported the view that the galaxy was heliocentric and that the heavens, like the earth, were made of matter that was subject to physical laws.

What Kepler demonstrated mathematically, the Italian astronomer Galileo (1564–1642) confirmed by observation. Creating a telescope by using magnifying lenses and a long tube, Galileo saw parts of the heavens that had never been dreamt of before. In 1610 he discovered four moons of Jupiter, proving conclusively that all heavenly bodies did not revolve around the earth. He observed the landscape of the earth's moon and described it as full of mountains, valleys, and rivers. It was of the same imperfect form as the earth itself. He even found spots on the sun, which suggested that it, too, was composed of ordinary matter. Through the telescope, Galileo gazed upon an unimaginable universe: "the Galaxy is nothing else but a mass of innumerable stars," he wrote. Galileo's greatest scientific discoveries had to do with motion—he was the first to posit a law of inertia—but his greatest contribution to the new science was his popularization of the Copernican theory. He took the debate over the structure of the universe to the public, popularizing the discoveries of scientists in his vigorous Italian tracts.

As news of his experiments and discoveries spread, Galileo became famous throughout the Continent, and his support for heliocentrism became a celebrated cause. In 1616 the Roman Catholic church cautioned him against promoting his views. In 1633, a year after publishing his *A Dialogue Between the Two Great Systems of the World*, Galileo was tried by the Inquisition and forced specifically to recant the idea that the earth moves. He spent the rest of his life under house arrest, where Europeans of all nations came to pay him homage—both Hobbes and Milton were taken to see him when touring Italy. Galileo insisted that there was nothing in the new science that was anti-Christian. He rejected the view that his discoveries refuted the Bible, arguing that the words of the Bible were often difficult to interpret and that nature was another way in which God revealed himself. In fact, Galileo feared that the Church's opposition to what he deemed as scientific truth could only bring the Church into disrepute. (See Special Feature, "The Trials of Galileo," pp. 520–521.)

The Natural World

The new science originated from a number of traditions that were anything but scientific. Inquiry into nature and the environment grew out of the discipline of natural philosophy and was nurtured by spiritual and mystical traditions. Much of the most useful medical knowledge had come from the studies of herbalists; the most reliable calculations of planetary motion had come from astrologers. Though the first laboratories and observatories were developed in aid of the new science, practice in them was as much magical as experimental. For those attempting to unlock the mysteries of the universe, there was no separation between magic and science. Some of the most characteristic features of modern science, such as the stress on experimentation and empirical observation, developed only gradually. What was new about the new science was the determination to develop systems of thought that could help humans understand and control their environment. Thus there was a greater openness and spirit of cooperation about discoveries than in the past, when experiments were conducted secretly and results were kept hidden away.

Aristotelianism was not the only philosophical system to explain the nature and composition of the universe. During the Renaissance the writings of Plato attracted a number of Italian humanists, most notably Marsilio Ficino (1433–99) and Pico della Mirandola (1463–94). At the Platonic Academy in Florence they taught Plato's theory that the world was composed of ideas and forms, which were hidden by the physical properties of objects. These Neoplatonic humanists believed that the architect of the universe possessed the spirit of a geometrician and that the

perfect disciplines were music and mathematics. These elements of Neoplatonism created an impetus for the mathematically based studies of the new scientists. They were especially important among the astronomers, who used both calculation and geometry in exploring the heavens. But they served as well to bolster the sciences of alchemy and astrology. Alchemy was the use of fire in the study of metals, an effort to find the essence of things through their purification. While medieval alchemists mostly attempted to find gold and silver as the essence of lead and iron, the new experimentation focused on the properties of metals in general. Astrology was the study of the influence of the stars on human behavior, calculated by planetary motion and the harmony of the heavenly spheres. Astrologers made careful calculations based on the movement of the planets and were deeply involved in the new astronomy.

The Neoplatonic emphasis upon mathematics also accorded support for a variety of mystical sciences based on numerology. These were efforts to predict events from the combination of particular numbers. Arcane calculations of ancient prophecies were combined with the years and dates of significant occurrences in the lives of individuals to yield lucky or unlucky numbers. The most influential of these mystical traditions was that associated with Hermes Trismegistus (Thrice Greatest), an Egyptian who was reputed to have lived in the second century A.D. and to have known the secrets of the universe. A body of writings mistakenly attributed to Hermes was discovered during the Renaissance and formed the basis of a Hermetic tradition. The core of Hermetic thinking centered on the idea of a universal spirit that was present in all objects and that spontaneously revealed itself. Kepler was one of many of the new scientists influenced by Hermeticism. His efforts to understand planetary motion derived from his search for a unifying spirit.

A combination of Neoplatonic and Hermetic traditions was central to the work of one of the most curious of the new scientists, the Swiss alchemist Paracelsus (1493–1541). The son of a Zurich doctor, Paracelsus spent some of his youth working in the mines, where he gained knowledge in metallurgy. He studied with a leading German alchemist before following in his father's footsteps by becoming a physician. Paracelsus led an

The Trials of Galileo

For eight years he had held his peace. Since 1616 he had bided his time, waiting for a change in the attitudes of the Catholic authorities or, as he believed, waiting for reason to prevail. For a time he had even abandoned his astronomical investigations for the supposedly safer fields of motion and physics. Even there Aristotle had been wrong. No matter what he touched, his reason showed him that the conclusions of Aristotle, the conclusions adopted and supported by the Roman Catholic Church, were wrong. Now finally, with the accession of Pope Urban VIII, old Cardinal Barbarini, who was himself a mathematician, Galileo felt confident that he could resume his writing and publishing.

Galileo's rebellion began early, when he decided to study mathematics rather than medicine. Galileo was fascinated with the manipulation of numbers and by the age of twenty-five was teaching at the University of Pisa. There he began to conduct experiments to measure rates of motion. Galileo was soon in trouble with his colleagues and was forced to leave Pisa for Padua.

It was in Padua that his real difficulties began. After seeing a small prototype made in Holland, Galileo developed a telescope that could magnify objects to thirty times their size, which made it possible to see clearly the stars and planets that had been only dimly perceptible before. In 1610 Galileo had looked at the moon and discovered that its properties were similar to those of the earth. He had seen four moons of Jupiter, the first conclusive proof that there were heavenly bodies that did not revolve around the earth. Even before he had gazed at the stars, Galileo was persuaded that Copernicus must be right in arguing that the earth revolved around the sun. Now he believed he had irrefutable proof, the proof of his own eyes. From the publication of the *Starry Messenger* in 1610, Galileo became the most active and best known advocate of the Copernican universe.

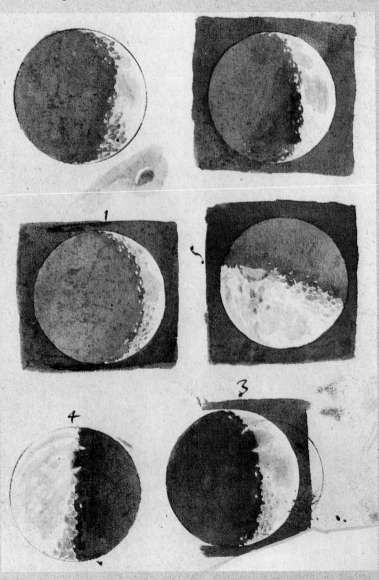

In 1616 he was called to Rome and warned about his opinions. Belief in the theories of Copernicus was heresy, he was told. If Galileo held or maintained them, he would incur a heavy penalty. The Church accepted unequivocally the Ptolemaic explanations of the structure of the universe and could cite innumerable passages in the Bible to support them. It was willful and stubborn to oppose official doctrine, doctrine that had been frequently and fully examined. At first it looked like Galileo would be silenced, but the erudite Cardinal Bellarmine, to whom the case had been assigned, wished only to caution him. Galileo might still examine the Copernican hypotheses; he might still discuss them with his learned colleagues, as long as he did not hold or maintain them to be true.

For eight years he kept his peace. When he decided to write again, it was with the belief that things were changing. He created a dialogue between a Ptolemaist and a Copernican. Let the one challenge the other on the most basic points just as if they were in formal academic dispute. How did each explain the most difficult things that there were to explain, the existence of spots on the sun or the movement of the tides. Especially the tides. If the earth stood still and the sun moved, why were there tides in the seas that moved with such regularity that they could be predicted?

Galileo was no heretic. He had no desire to challenge the Church. He would not print his tract anonymously in a Protes- tant country. Rather he would create a true dialogue, one with which not even the most narrow-minded censor of the Roman church could find fault. He submitted his book to the official censor in Rome for approval, then to the official censor in Florence. The censors struck out passages, changed some words, and deleted others. They demanded a new preface, even a new title: *A Dialogue Between the Two Great Systems of the World*. Finally, in 1632 the book went to press and it was an immediate success.

Indeed it was a success that could not be ignored. The Jesuits, who regarded learning and education as their special mission, demanded that action be taken against Galileo. Their teachings had been held up to ridicule; their official astronomers had been challenged; their doctrines had been repudiated. There was much at stake. Galileo's book had not been the vigorous academic dispute that he promised and it had not concluded with the triumph of Church doctrine over the speculations of Copernicus. No, it had been advocacy. Anyone could see where the author's true sympathies lay. The character chosen to speak the part of Aristotle was not named Simplicio for nothing. Though this was the name of an ancient Aristotelian, it was also a perfect description for the arguments that the speaker advanced. Especially in the matter of the tides, Galileo had reduced the Aristotelian position to nonsense. The Jesuits brought their case directly to the pope and won an investigation, an investigation that they knew would end with Galileo's condemnation.

Though initially Pope Urban VIII was reluctant to prosecute the seventy-year-old astronomer, "the light of Italy," ultimately he had no choice. The great war to stamp out heresy was going badly for the Church. The pope needed the support of the Jesuits in Vienna and in Madrid much more than he needed the support of a scientist who had seen the moons of Jupiter. Nevertheless, when the case was turned over to the Inquisition, it proved weak in law. Galileo had only to present the book itself to show that he had received the official sanction of not one, but two censors of the Roman Catholic Church. If there was still anything in his book that offended, could the fault be his alone? The argument stymied the prosecutors, who were forced to find evidence where none existed. Resurrecting the agreement between Galileo and Bellarmine, they attempted to make it say that Galileo was under an absolute ban from even discussing the Copernican theories. Either Galileo would agree to recant his views, admit his errors, and beg the forgiveness of the Church or he would be tried and burned as a heretic. But though he could be forced to recant his view that the earth orbits the sun, Galileo could not be forced to change his mind.

After his recantation, Galileo was sentenced to live out his days under house arrest. Five years after his death in 1642, his greatest scientific work, *The Two New Sciences*, was smuggled out of Italy and printed anonymously in Holland in 1648.

unsettled life, moving from town to town in the Swiss cantons and German states. His rash temper and unusual behavior marked him wherever he went. Though he worked as a doctor, his true vocation was alchemy, and he conducted innumerable experiments designed to extract the essence of particular metals. After his death stories began to circulate attributing miraculous cures to Paracelsus's secret remedies. Masses of his papers were discovered and published, though most were an entirely incoherent blend of astrology, philosophy, alchemy, and his own unique terms for the substances he had created. Paracelsus taught that all matter was composed of combinations of three principles: salt, sulfur, and mercury. This view replaced the traditional belief in the four elements of earth, water, fire, and air. Paracelsus also believed that the properties of things were contained in their forms. Like the Hermetic magician, he saw inherent properties in the remedies he prescribed. "The Syderica bears the image and form of a snake on each of its leaves, and thus it gives protection against any kind of poisoning."

Though the Paracelsian system was peculiar, it transformed ideas about chemistry and medicine. Paracelsus rejected the theory that disease was caused by an imbalance in the humors of the body, the standard view of Galen, the great Greek physician of the second century A.D. Instead, Paracelsus argued that each disease had its own cause, which could be diagnosed and remedied. Where traditional doctors treated disease by bloodletting or sweating to correct the imbalance of humors, Paracelsus prescribed the ingestion of particular chemicals, especially distilled metals like mercury, arsenic, and antimony, and he favored administering them at propitious astrological moments.

Paracelsus' experimentation with metals and his practice of diagnostic medicine gave a practical turn to the study of alchemy. Efforts to cure new diseases like syphilis led to the continued study of the chemical properties of substances and to a new confidence about medical science. Although established physicians and medical faculties rejected Paracelsian cures and methods, his influence spread among ordinary practitioners. It ultimately had a profound impact on the studies of Robert Boyle (1627–91), an Englishman who helped establish the basis of the science of chem-

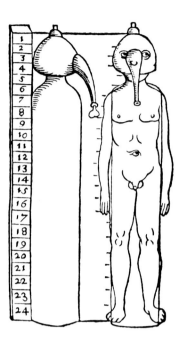

Paracelsus devised this "anatomical furnace" in which a patient's urine was distilled in a measuring cylinder, the parts of which correspond in length and width to those of the human body. Thus the body was "chemically dissected" for the benefit of the patient.

istry. Boyle devoted his energies to raising the study of medical chemistry above that of merely providing recipes for the cure of disease. He worked carefully and recorded each step in his experiments. Boyle's first important work, *The Sceptical Chymist* (1661), attacked both the Aristotelian and Paracelsian views of the basic components of the natural world. Boyle rejected both the four humors and the three principles. Instead he favored an atomic explanation in which matter "consisted of little particles of all sizes and shapes." Changes in these particles, which would later be identified as the chemical elements, resulted in changes in matter. Boyle's most important experiments were with gases—a word invented by Paracelsus. He formulated the relationship between the volume and pressure of a gas (Boyle's Law) and invented the air pump.

The new spirit of scientific inquiry also affected medical studies. The study of anatomy through dissection had helped the new scientists reject many of the descriptive errors in Galen's texts. The Belgian doctor Andreas Vesalius (1514–64), who was physician to the Emperor Charles V, published the first modern set of anatomical drawings in 1543, the same year that Copernicus published his work. But accurate knowledge of the composition of the body did not also mean better understanding of its operation. Dead bodies didn't easily yield the secrets of life. Much of what was known about matters as common as reproduction was a combination of ancient wisdom and practical experiences of midwives and doctors. Both were woefully inadequate.

One of the greatest mysteries was the method by which blood moved through the vital organs. It was generally believed that the blood originated in the liver, traveled to the right side of the heart, and then passed to the left side through invisible pores. Anatomical investigation proved beyond doubt that there was blood in both sides of the heart, but no one could discover the pores through which it passed. William Harvey (1578–1657), an Englishman who had received his medical education in Italy, offered an entirely different explanation. Harvey was employed as royal physi-

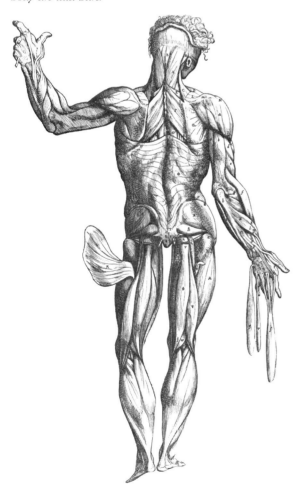

Tenth "Muscle plate" from Adreas Vesalius' De Humani Corporis Fabrica (Concerning the Fabric of the Human Body), published in 1543. The muscles of the back of the body are laid bare.

cian to both James I and Charles I and had one of the most lucrative medical practices in Europe. His real interest, however, was in studying the anatomy of the heart. Harvey examined hearts in more than forty species before concluding that the heart worked like a pump or, as he put it, a water bellows. Harvey observed that the valves of the heart chambers allowed the blood to flow in only one direction. He thus concluded that the blood was pumped by the heart and circulated throughout the entire body.

The greatest of all English scientists was the mathematician and physicist Sir Isaac Newton (1642–1727). It was Newton who brought together the various strands of the new science. He merged the materialists and Hermeticists, the astronomers and astrologers, the chemists and alchemists. He made stunning contributions to the sciences of optics, physics, astronomy, and mathematics, and his magnum opus, *Mathematical Principles of Natural Philosophy* (1687), is one of a handful of the most important scientific works ever composed. Most importantly, Newton solved the single most perplexing problem: if the world was composed of matter in motion, what was motion?

Newton came from a moderately prosperous background and was trained at a local grammar school before entering Cambridge University. There was little in his background or education to suggest his unique talents and in fact his most important discoveries were not appreciated until years after he had made them. Newton was the first to understand the composition of light, the first to develop a calculus, the first to build a reflecting telescope. Though Newton became a professor at Cambridge, he spent much of his time alone. He made a great study of Hermetic writings and from them revived the mystical notions of attraction and repulsion.

Though Galileo had first developed a theory of inertia, the idea that a body at rest stays at rest, most materialists believed that motion was inherent in objects. In contrast, Newton believed that motion was the result of the interaction of objects and that it could be calculated mathematically. From his experiments he formulated the concept of force and his famous laws of motion: (1) that objects at rest or of uniform linear motion remain in such a state unless acted upon by an external force; (2) that changes in motion are proportional to force; and (3) that for every action there is an equal and opposite reaction. From these laws of motion, Newton advanced one step further. If the world was no more than matter in motion and if all motion was subject to the same laws, then the movement of the planets could be explained in the same way as the movement of an apple falling from a tree. There was a mathematical relationship between attraction and repulsion, a universal gravitation as Newton called it, that governed the movement of all objects. Newton's theory of gravity joined together Kepler's astronomy and Galileo's physics. The mathematical, materialistic world of the new science was now complete.

Science Enthroned

By the middle of the seventeenth century, the new science was firmly established throughout Europe. Royal and noble patrons supported the enterprise by paying some of the costs of equipment and experimentation. Royal observatories were created for the astronomers, colleges of physicians for the doctors, laboratories for the chemists. Both England and France established royal societies of learned scientists to meet together and discuss their discoveries. The French Académie des Sciences (1666) was composed of twenty salaried scientists and an equal number of students, divided among the different branches of scientific learning. They met twice weekly throughout the year and each worked on a project of his own devising. The English Royal Society (1662) boasted some of the greatest minds of the age. It was there that Newton first made public his most important discoveries. Scientific bodies were also formed outside the traditional universities. These were the so-called mechanics colleges, like Gresham College in London, where the practical applications of mathematics and physics were studied and taught. Navigation was a particular concern of the college, and the faculty established close ties with the Royal Navy and with London merchants.

The establishment of learned scientific societies and practical colleges fulfilled part of the program advocated by Sir Francis Bacon (1561–1626), one of the leading supporters of scientific research in England. In the *Advancement of Learning* (1605) Bacon proposed a scientific method through inductive, empirical experimentation. Bacon believed that experiments should be carefully recorded so that results were both reliable and repeatable. He advocated the open world of the scientist over the secret world of the magician. In his numerous writings he stressed the practical impact of scientific discovery and even wrote a utopian work in which science appeared as the savior of humanity. Though he was not himself a scientific investigator, Bacon used his considerable influence to support scientific projects in England.

Bacon's support for the new science contrasts markedly with the stance taken by the Roman Catholic church. Embattled by the Reformation and the wars of religion, the Church had taken the offensive in preserving the core of its heritage. By the early seventeenth century the missionary work of the Jesuits had won many reconversions and had halted the advance of Protestantism. Now the new science appeared to be another heresy. Not only did it confound ancient wisdom and contradict Church teachings, but it was also a lay movement that was neither directed nor controlled from Rome. The trial of Galileo slowed the momentum of scientific investigation in Catholic countries and starkly posed the conflict between authority and knowledge. But the stand taken by the Church was based on more than narrow self-interest. Ever since Copernicus had published his views, a new skepticism had emerged among European intellectuals. Every year new theories competed with old ones, and dozens of contradictory explanations for the most common phenomena were advanced and debated. The skeptics concluded that nothing was known and nothing was knowable. Their position led inevitably to the most shocking of all possible views: atheism.

There was no necessary link between the new science and an attack upon established religion. So Galileo had argued all along. Few of the leading scientists ever saw a contradiction between their studies and their faith. Sir Robert Boyle endowed a lectureship for the advancement of Christian doctrine and contributed money for the translation of the New Testament into Turkish. Still by the middle of the century attacks upon the Church were increasing and some blamed the new science for them. Thus it was altogether fitting that one of the leading mathematicians of the day should also provide the method for harmonizing faith and reason.

René Descartes (1596–1650) was the son of a provincial lawyer and judge. He was trained in one of the best Jesuit schools in France before taking a law degree in 1616. While it was his father's intention that his son practice law, it was René's intention that he become educated in "the school of life." He entered military service in the Dutch Republic and after the outbreak of the Thirty Years' War, in the Duke of Bavaria's army. Descartes was keenly interested in mathematics, and during his military travels he met and was tutored by a leading Dutch mathematician. For the first time he learned of the new scientific discoveries and of the advances made in mathematics. In 1619 he dreamt of discovering the scientific principles of universal knowledge. After this dream, Descartes returned to Holland and began to develop his system. He was on the verge of publishing his views when he learned of Galileo's condemnation. Reading Galileo's *Dialogue Between the Two Great Systems of the World* (1632), Descartes discovered that he shared many of the same opinions and had worked out mathematical proofs for them. He refrained from publishing until 1637 when he brought out the *Discourse on Method.*

In the *Discourse on Method*, Descartes demonstrated how skepticism could be used to produce certainty. He began by declaring that he would reject everything that could not be clearly proven beyond doubt. Thus he rejected the material world, the testimony of his senses, all known or imagined opinions. He was left only with doubt. But what was doubt, if not thought, and what was thought, if not the workings of his mind. The only thing of which he could be certain, then, was that he had a mind. Thus, his famous formulation: "I think, therefore I am." From this first certainty came another, the knowledge of perfectibility. He knew that he was imperfect and that a perfect being had to have placed that knowledge within him. Therefore, a perfect being—God—existed.

Descartes' philosophy, known as Cartesianism, rested on the dual existence of matter and mind. Matter was the material world subject to the incontrovertible laws of mathematics. Mind was the spirit of the creator. Descartes was one of the leading mechanistic philosophers, believing that all objects operated in accord with natural laws. He invented analytic geometry and made important contributions to the sciences of optics and physics upon which Newton would later build. Yet it was in his proof that the new science could be harmonized with the old religion that Descartes made his greatest contribution to the advancement of learning. Despite the fact that his later work was condemned by the Catholic church and that he preferred the safety of Protestant Holland to the uncertainty of his Catholic homeland, Cartesianism became the basis for the unification of science and religion.

"I shall attempt to make myself intelligible to everyone," Descartes wrote. Like many of the new scientists, he preferred the use of vernacular languages to elite Latin, hoping that his work would reach beyond the narrow bounds of high culture. Descartes was one of many new scientists who saw the practical import of what they had learned and who hoped to bring that knowledge to the aid of the material well-being of their contemporaries. John Dee (1527–1608) translated the Greek geometrician Euclid into English so that ordinary people might "find out and devise new works, strange engines and instruments for sundry purposes in the commonwealth." Though many of the breakthrough discoveries of the new scientists would not find practical use for centuries, the spirit of discovery was to have great impact in an age of commerce and capital. The quest for mathematical certainty and prime movers led directly to improvements in agriculture, mining, navigation, and industrial activity. It also brought with it a sense of control over the material world, which provided a new optimism for generations of Europeans.

Empires of Goods

"The discovery of America and that of a passage to the East Indies by the Cape of Good Hope, are the two greatest and most important events in the history of mankind." So wrote the great Scottish economist Adam Smith (1723–90) in *The Wealth of Nations* (1776). For Smith and his generation the first great age of commerce was coming to an end. Under the watchful eye of the European states, a worldwide marketplace for the exchange of commodities had been created. First the Dutch and then the English had established monopoly companies to engage in exotic trades in the East. First the Spanish and Portuguese, then the English and French had established colonial dependencies in the Atlantic, which they carefully nurtured in hope of economic gain. Protected trade had flourished beyond the wildest dreams of its promoters. Luxury commodities became staples; new commodities became luxuries. Trade enhanced the material life of all European peoples, though it came at great cost to the Asians, Africans, and Latin Americans whose labor and raw materials were converted into the new crazes of consumption.

Though long-distance trade was never as important to the European economy as was inland and intracontinental trade, its development in the seventeenth and eighteenth centuries

The Geographer by Jan Vermeer van Delft, 1669. A Dutch cartographer, holding dividers, is shown surrounded by charts, a globe, and other paraphernalia of his craft. Such cartographers combined the skills of artist and mathematician.

had a profound impact upon life-styles, economic policy, and ultimately on warfare. It was the Dutch who became the first great commercial power. Their achievements were based on innovative techniques, rational management, and a social and cultural environment that supported mercantile activities. Dutch society was freer than any other, open to new capital, new ventures, and new ideas. The Dutch innovated in the organization of trade by developing the concept of the entrepôt, a place where goods were brought for storage before being exchanged. They pioneered in finance by establishing the Bank of Amsterdam. They led in shipbuilding by developing the flyboat, a long, flat-hulled vessel designed specifically to carry bulky cargoes like grain. They traded around the globe with the largest mercantile fleet yet known. It was not until the end of the seventeenth century that England and France surpassed the Dutch. This reversal owed less to new innovations than it did to restrictions on trade. Because the Dutch dominated the European economy, the French and English began to pass laws to eliminate Dutch competition. The English banned imports carried in Dutch ships; the French banned Dutch products. Both policies cut heavily into the Dutch superiority and both ultimately resulted in commercial warfare.

The Marketplace of the World

By the seventeenth century, long-distance trade had begun to integrate the regions of the world into a single marketplace. Slaves bought in Africa mined silver in South America. The bullion was shipped to Spain, where it was distributed across Europe. Most went to Amsterdam to settle Spanish debts, Dutch bankers having replaced the Italians as the paymasters of Europe. From Holland the silver traveled east to the Baltic Sea, the Dutch lifeline where vital stores of grain and timber were purchased for home consumption. By the 1630s over five hundred Dutch ships a year called at Gdansk, the largest of the Baltic ports. From there the silver was transported to the interior of Poland and Russia, the great storehouses of European raw materials. Even more of this African-mined Spanish silver, traded by the Dutch, was carried to Asia to buy spices in the South Sea Islands, cottons in India, or silk in China. Millions of ounces flowed from America to

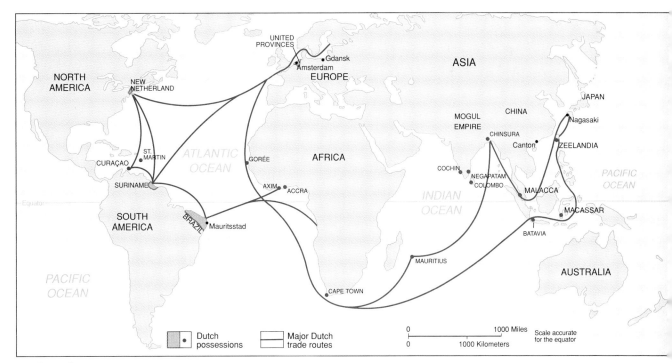

Dutch Trade Routes, ca. 1650

Asia via the European trading routes. On the return voyage, brightly colored Indian cottons were traded in Africa to purchase slaves for the South American silver mines.

The remarkable fact about the expansion of European trade in the seventeenth and eighteenth centuries is that it took place as a result of the ingenuity of traders rather than because of technological or geographical discoveries. By the sixteenth century all the major trading routes had already been opened. The Spanish moved back and forth across the Atlantic; the Dutch and Portuguese sailed around the tip of Africa to the Indian Ocean. The Baltic trade connected the eastern and western parts of Europe as Danes, Swedes, and Dutch exchanged Polish and Russian raw materials for English and French manufactured goods. The Mediterranean, which had dominated world trade for centuries, was still a vital artery of intercontinental trade, but its role was diminishing. In 1600 almost three-quarters of the Asian trade was still land based, much of it carried through the Middle East to the Mediterranean. A century later nearly all Asian trade was carried directly to western Europe by Dutch and English vessels. Commercial power was shifting

to the northern European states just as dramatically as was military and political power.

The technology associated with commerce achieved no breakthroughs to compare with the great transformations of the fifteenth century, when new techniques of navigation made transatlantic travel possible. It is certainly true that there continued to be improvements. The astronomical findings of the new science were a direct aid to navigation as were the recorded experiences of so many practiced sea travelers. The materials used to make and maintain ships improved with the importation of pitch and tar from the east and with the greater availability of iron and copper from Scandinavia. It was the Dutch who made the single most important innovation in shipbuilding. To gain maximum profit from their journeys to the Baltic, the Dutch designed the so-called flyboats. Flyboats sacrificed speed and maneuverability, but they were cheap to build and could be manned by small crews. They carried no heavy armaments and were thus well adapted to the serene Baltic trade.

It was unspectacular developments like the flyboat that had such an impact on seventeenth- and eighteenth-century transcontinental trade.

Innovation, organization, and efficient management were the principal elements of what historians have called the commercial revolution. Concerted efforts to maximize opportunities and advantages accounted for the phenomenal growth in the volume and value of commercial exchange. One of the least spectacular and most effective breakthroughs was the replacement of bilateral with triangular trade. In bilateral trade, the surplus commodities of one community were exchanged for those of another. This method, of course, restricted the range of trading partners to those with mutually desirable surplus production: England and Italy were unlikely to swap woolens or Sicily and Poland to trade grain. For those with few desirable commodities, bilateral trade meant the exchange of precious metals for goods, and throughout much of the sixteenth and early seventeenth centuries bullion was by far the most often traded commodity. Triangular trade created a larger pool of desirable goods. British manufactured goods could be traded to Africa for slaves, the slaves could be traded in the West Indies for sugar, and the sugar could be consumed in Britain. Moreover, the merchants involved in shifting these goods from place to place could achieve profits on each exchange. Indeed their motive in trading could now change from dumping surplus commodities to matching supply and demand.

Equally important were the changes made in the way trade was financed. As states, cities, and even individuals could stamp their own precious metal, there were hundreds of different European coins with different nominal and metallic values. The influx of American silver further destabilized an already unstable system of exchange. The Bank of Amsterdam was created in 1609 to establish a uniform rate of exchange for the various currencies traded in that city. From this useful function a second developed, transfer, or giro, banking, a system that had been invented in Italy. In giro banking, various merchant firms held money on account and issued bills of transfer from one to another. This transfer system meant that merchants in different cities did not have to transport their precious metals or endure long delays in having their accounts settled. Giro banking facilitated exchanges between merchants and allowed money to circulate more often simply by staying in the same place. The Bank of Amsterdam soon became the center of European transfer banking, the number of accounts grew from 700 to 2,700 during the course of the seventeenth century.

Giro banking also aided the development of bills of exchange, an early form of checking. Merchants could conclude trades by depositing money in a given bank or merchant house and then having a bill drawn for the sum they owed. Bills of exchange were especially important in international trade as they made large-scale shipments of precious metals to settle trade deficits unnecessary. By the end of the seventeenth century, bills of exchange had become negotiable, that is, they could pass from one merchant to another without being redeemed. Thus a Dutch merchant could buy French wines in Bordeaux with a bill of exchange drawn on an account in the Bank of Amsterdam. The Bordeaux merchant could then purchase Spanish oranges and use the same bill of exchange as payment. There were two disadvantages to this system: ultimately the bill had to return to Amsterdam for redemption, and when it did the account on which it was drawn might be empty. The establishment of the Bank of England in 1694 overcame these difficulties. The Bank of England was licensed to issue its own bills of exchange, or bank notes, which were backed by the revenue from specific English taxes. This security of payment was widely sought after, and the Bank of England soon became a clearing house for all kinds of bills of exchange. The Bank would buy in bills at a discount, paying less than their face value, and pay out precious metal or their own notes in exchange. Again, the discounting of bills allowed for the rapid turnover of money, while the security offered by the Bank lowered the risks of business.

The effects of these and many other small-scale changes in business practice helped fuel prolonged growth in European commerce. It was the European merchant who made this growth possible, accepting the risks of each individual transaction, building up small pools of capital from which successive transactions could take place. Most mercantile ventures were conducted by individuals or families and were based on the specialized trade of a single commodity. Trade offered high returns because it entailed high risks. The long delays in moving goods and their uncertain arrival; the unreliability of agents and the unscrupulousness of other traders; the inefficiencies in transport and communication all weighed heavily against success. Those who succeeded did so less by luck than by hard work. They used family members to receive shipments. They lowered shipping costs by careful packaging. They lowered protection costs by securing their trade routes. Financial publications lowered the costs of information. Ultimately, lower costs meant lower prices. For centuries luxury goods dominated intercontinental trade. But by the eighteenth century European merchants had created a world marketplace in which the luxuries of the past were the common fare of the present.

Consumption Choices

As long-distance trade became more sophisticated, merchants became more sensitive to consumer tastes. Low-volume, high-quality goods like spices and silks could not support the growing merchant communities in the European states. These goods were the preserve of the largest trading companies and, more importantly, they had reached saturation levels by the early seventeenth century. The price of pepper, the most used of all spices, fell nearly continuously after 1650. Moreover, triangular trade allowed merchants to provide a better match of supplies and demands. The result was the rise to prominence of a vast array of new commodities, which not only continued the expansion of trade but also reshaped diet, life-styles, and patterns of consumption. New products came from both east and west. Dutch and English incursions into the Asian trade provoked competition with the Portuguese and expanded the range of commodities that were shipped back to Europe. An aggressive Asian triangle was created in which European bullion bought Indonesian spices that were exchanged for Persian silk and Chinese and Japanese finished goods. In the Atlantic, the English were quick to develop both home and export markets for a variety of new or newly available products.

The European trade with Asia had always been designed to satisfy consumer demand rather than to exchange surplus goods. Europeans manufactured little that was desired in Asia, and neither merchants nor governments saw fit to attempt to influence Asian tastes in the way they did those of Europeans. The chief commodity imported to the East was bullion, tons of South American silver, perhaps a third of all that was produced. In return came spices, silk, coffee, jewels, jade, porcelain, dyes, and a wide variety of other exotic goods. By the middle of the seventeenth century the Dutch dominated the spice trade, obtaining a virtual monopoly over cinnamon, cloves, nutmeg, and mace and carrying the largest share of pepper. Each year Europeans consumed perhaps a million pounds of the four great spices and 7 million pounds of pepper. Both Dutch and English competed for preeminence in the silk trade. The Dutch concentrated on Chinese silk, which they used mostly in trade with Japan. The English established an interest in lower-quality Indian silk spun in Bengal and even hired Italian silk masters to try to teach European techniques to the Indian spinners.

The most important manufactured articles imported from the East to Europe were the lightweight, brightly colored Indian cottons known as calicoes. It was the Dutch who first realized the potential of the cotton market. Until the middle of the seventeenth century cotton and cotton blended with silk were used in Europe only for wall hangings and table coverings. Colorful Asian chintz contained floral patterns that Europeans still considered exotic. But the material was also soft and smooth to the touch, and it soon replaced linen for use as underwear and close-fitting garments among the well-to-do. The fashion quickly caught on and the Dutch began exporting calicoes throughout the Continent. The English and French followed suit, establishing their own trading houses in India and bringing European patterns and designs with them for the Asians to copy. The calico trade was especially lucrative because the piece goods were easy to pack and ship and, unlike consumables, could be stored indefinitely. When the English finally came to dominate the trade in the middle of the eighteenth century, they were shipping over a million cloths a year into London. The craze for calicoes was so great that both the English and French governments attempted to ban their import to protect their own clothing industries.

Along with the new apparel from the East came new beverages. Coffee, which was first drunk in northern Europe in the early seventeenth century, became a fashionable drink by the end of the century. Coffeehouses sprang up in the

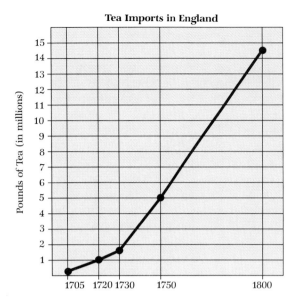

Tea Imports in England

major urban areas of northern Europe. There political and intellectual conversation was as heady as the strong Middle Eastern brew that was served. The Dutch and English both established themselves in the coffee trade, which was centered in the Middle Eastern seaport of Mocha. By the beginning of the eighteenth century the Dutch began to grow their own coffee for export from their island colony of Java and the two different types of coffee competed for favor.

As popular as coffee became among the European elites, it paled in comparison to the importance of tea as both an import commodity and a basic beverage. While coffee drinking remained the preserve of the wealthy, tea consumption spread throughout European society. It was probably most important in England, where the combination of China tea and West Indian sugar created a virtual revolution in nutrition. The growth in tea consumption was phenomenal. In 1706 England imported 100,000 pounds of tea. By the end of the century the number had risen to over 15 million pounds. The English imported most of this tea directly from China, where an open port had been established at Canton. Originally just one of a number of commodities that was carried on an Asian voyage, tea soon became the dominant cargo of the large English merchant

ships. Some manufactured goods would be brought to India on the outward voyage, to fill as much cargo space as possible, but once the ships had loaded the green and black teas, they sailed directly home. Almost all tea was purchased with bullion as the Chinese had even less use for European goods than did other Asians. It was not until the discovery that the Chinese consumed large quantities of opium, which was grown in India and Southeast Asia, that a triangular trade developed.

The success of tea was linked to the explosive growth in the development of sugar in Europe's Atlantic colonies. The Portuguese had attempted to cultivate sugar in the Azores at the end of the fifteenth century, but it was not until the settlement of Brazil, whose hot, humid climate was a natural habitat for the cane plants, that widespread cultivation began. The island of Barbados became the first English sugar colony. Barbados turned to sugar production accidentally when its first attempts to market tobacco failed. The planters modeled their development on Brazil, where African slaves were used to plant, tend, and cut the giant canes from which the sugar was extracted. For reasons that will never be fully understood, the English had an insatiable appetite for sugar's sweetness. It was taken plain, like candy, used in small quantities in almost all types of recipes, and diluted in ever increasing quantities of tea. Hot, sweet tea became a meal for the lower orders of English society, a meal which, unlike beer, provided a quick burst of energy. By 1700 the English were sending home over 50 million pounds of sugar besides what they were shipping directly to the North American colonies. This quantity doubled by 1730 and still there was no slackening of demand. What might have become a valuable raw material in English trade instead became a staple of consumption.

The triangular trade of manufactures—largely reexported calicoes—to Africa for slaves, who were exchanged in the West Indies for sugar, became the dominant form of English overseas trade. Colonial production depended upon the enforced labor of hundreds of thousands of Africans. Gold and silver, tobacco, sugar, rice, and indigo were all slave crops. Africans were enslaved by other Africans and then sold to Europeans to be used in the colonies. Over six million black slaves were imported into the Americas during the course of the eighteenth century. While rum and calicoes were the main commodities exchanged for slaves, the African tribes that dominated the slave trade organized a highly competitive market. Every colonial power participated in this lucrative trade. Over three million slaves were imported into the Portuguese colony of Brazil; by the end of the eighteenth century there were 500,000 slaves and only 35,000 French inhabitants of the sugar island of Saint Domingue. But it was the English with their sugar colonies of Barbados and Jamaica and their tobacco colonies of Virginia and Maryland who ultimately came to control the slave trade. The prosperity of Newport, Rhode Island, in North America and the port of Liverpool in Lancashire were built entirely upon the slave trade as were hundreds of plantation fortunes. The sweet tooth of Europe was fed by the sweat of black Africans.

Sugar was by far the dominant commodity of the colonial trade but it was not the only one. Furs and fish had first driven Europeans toward North America and both remained important commodities. Beaver and rabbit skins were the most common materials for making headgear in an age in which everyone wore a hat. The Canadian cod schools were among the richest in the world and the catch was shipped back either salted or dried. The English established what amounted to a manufacturing industry on the Newfoundland coast, where they dried the tons of fish that they caught. In the eighteenth century, rice was grown for export in the southern American colonies, particularly South Carolina. Rice never achieved great popularity in England, though it was in constant demand in the German states. Tobacco was the first new American product to come into widespread use in Europe, and its popularity—despite various official efforts to ban its use as dirty and unhealthy—grew steadily. American tobacco was grown principally in the colonies of Virginia and Maryland and shipped across the ocean, where it was frequently blended with European varieties. Although the English were the principal importers, it was the Dutch who dominated the European tobacco trade, making the most popular blends.

The new commodities flooded into Europe from all parts of the globe. By the middle of the eighteenth century tea, coffee, cocoa, gin, and rum were among the most popular beverages. These were all products that had been largely unknown a century earlier. Among the wealthy, tea was served from porcelain pots imported from China; among all classes it was drunk with sugar imported from America. Beaver hats and Persian silks were fashionable in the upper reaches of society; rabbit caps and calico prints in the lower. New habits were created as new demands were satisfied. Tea and sugar passed from luxury to staple in little more than a generation and the demand for both products continued to increase. To meet it, the European trading powers needed to create and maintain a powerful and efficient mercantile system.

Dutch Masters

For the nearly eighty years between 1565 and 1648 that the Dutch were at war they grew ever more prosperous. While the economies of most other European nations were sapped by warfare, the Dutch seemed to draw strength from their interminable conflict with the Spanish empire. They did have the advantage of fighting defensively on land and offensively on sea. Land war was terribly costly to the aggressor, who had to raise large armies, transport them to the site of battles or sieges, and feed them while they were there. The defender simply had to fortify strong places, keep its water routes open to secure supplies, and wait for the weather to change. Sea war—or piracy, depending on one's viewpoint—required much smaller outlays for men and material and promised the rewards of captured prizes. The Dutch became expert at attacking the Spanish silver fleets, hunting like a lion against a herd by singling out the slower and smaller vessels for capture. The Dutch also benefited from the massive immigration into their provinces of Protestants who had lived and worked in the southern provinces. They brought with them vital skills in manufacturing and large reserves of capital for investment in Dutch commerce.

The Dutch grounded their prosperity on commerce. Excellent craftsmen, they took the lead in the skilled occupations necessary for finishing cloth, refining raw materials, and decorating consumer goods. They were also successful farmers, especially given the small amounts of land with which they had to work and the difficult ecological conditions in which they worked it. But their greatest abilities were in trade. Like the Venetians they were a water people and they proved to be skillful at moving goods from place to place and in developing the machinery and knowledge to move them efficiently.

Though the Dutch Republic comprised seven separate political entities, with a total population of about two million, the province of Holland was preeminent among them. Holland contained more than a quarter of this population and its trading port of Amsterdam was one of the great cities of Europe. The city had risen dramatically in the seventeenth century, growing from a mid-sized urban community of 65,000 in 1600 to a metropolis of 170,000 fifty years later. The port was one of the busiest in the world, for it was built to be an entrepôt. Vast warehouses and docks lined its canals. Visitors were impressed by the bustle, the cleanliness, and the businesslike appearance of Amsterdam. There were no great public squares and few recognizable monuments. The central buildings were the Bank and the Exchange, testimony to the dominant activities of the residents.

"The Dutch must be understood as they really are, the carriers of the world, the middle persons in trade, the factors and brokers of Europe," wrote the Englishman Daniel Defoe (1660–1731), who was much impressed by their prosperity. The Dutch dominated all types of European trade. They carried more English coal than England, more French wine than France, more Swedish iron than Sweden. Dutch ships outnumbered all others in every important port of Europe. Goods were brought to Amsterdam to be redistributed throughout the world. Dutch prosperity rested first upon the Baltic trade. Even after it ceased to expand in the middle of the seventeenth century, the Baltic trade composed over a quarter of all of Holland's commercial enterprise. The Dutch also were the leaders in the East Indian trade throughout the seventeenth century. They held a virtual monopoly on the sale of exotic spices and the largest share of the pepper trade. Their imports of cottons and especially of porcelain began new consumer fads that soon resulted in the development of European industries. Dutch potteries began to produce china, as lower-quality ceramic goods came to be known. Dutch trade in the Atlantic was of less importance, but the Dutch did have a colonial presence in the New World, controlling a number of small islands and the rapidly growing mainland settlement of New Netherland. Yet the Dutch still dominated the secondary market in tobacco and sugar, becoming the largest processor and refiner of these important commodities.

In all of these activities the Dutch acted as merchants rather than as consumers. Unlike most other Europeans they regarded precious metal as a commodity like any other and took no interest in accumulating it for its own sake. This attitude enabled them to pioneer triangular trading and develop the crucial financial institutions necessary to expand their overseas commerce. The Dutch were not so much innovators as improvers. They saw the practical value in Italian accounting and banking methods and raised them to new levels of efficiency. They made use of marine insurance to help diminish the risks of mercantile activity. Their legal system favored the creation of small trading companies by protecting individual investments. The European stock and commodity markets were centered in Amsterdam. Shares of the Dutch East India Company were traded with the same confidence as gold and silver, and by the 1670s over 500 commodities were traded on the Amsterdam exchange. Even a primitive futures market evolved for those who wished to speculate.

There were many explanations for the unparalleled growth of this small maritime state into one of the greatest of European trading empires. Geography and climate provided one impetus, the lack of sufficient foodstuffs another. Yet there were cultural characteristics as well. One was the openness of Dutch society. Even before the struggle with Spain, the northern provinces had shown a greater inclination toward religious toleration than had most parts of Europe. Amsterdam became a unique center for religious and intellectual exchange. European Jews flocked there, as did Catholic dissidents like Descartes. They brought with them a wide range of skills and knowledge along with capital that could be invested in trade. There was no real social nobility among the Dutch and certainly no set of values that prized investment in land over investment in trade. The French and Spanish nobility looked with scorn upon their mercantile classes and shunned any form of commercial investment, and the English, though more open to industry and trade, sank as much of their capital as possible into landed estates and country houses. The Dutch economic elite invested in trade. By the middle of the seventeenth century the Dutch Republic enjoyed a reputation for cultural creativity that was the envy of the Continent. A truly extraordinary school of Dutch artists led by Rembrandt celebrated this new state born of commerce with vivid portrayals of its people and its prosperity.

Mercantile Organization

Elsewhere in Europe, trade was the king's business. The wealth of the nation was part of the prestige of the monarch and its rise or fall part of the crown's power. Power and prestige were far more important to absolute rulers than was the profit of merchants. Indeed, in all European states except the Dutch Republic, the activities of merchants were scorned by both the landed elite and the salaried bureaucrats. Leisure was valued by the one and royal service by the other. The pursuit of wealth by buying and selling somehow lacked dignity. Yet the activities of the mercantile classes took on increasing importance for the state for two reasons. First, imported goods, especially luxuries, were a noncontroversial target for taxation. Customs duties and excise taxes grew all over Europe. Representative assemblies composed of landed elites were usually happy to grant them to the monarch, and merchants could pass them on to consumers in higher prices. Secondly, the competition for trade was seen as a competition between states rather than individual merchants. Trading privileges involved special arrangements with foreign powers, arrangements that recognized the sovereign power of European monarchs. In this way, trade could bring glory to the state.

The competition for power and glory derived from the theory of mercantilism, a set of assumptions about economic activity that were commonly held throughout Europe and that guided the policies of almost every government. There were two interrelated ideas. One was that the wealth of a nation resided in its stock of precious metal, and the other was that economic activity was a zero-sum game. There was thought to be a fixed amount of money, a fixed amount of commodities, and a fixed amount of consumption. Thus what one country gained, another lost. If England bought wine from France and paid £100,000 in precious metal for it, then England was £100,000 poorer and France £100,000 richer. If one was to trade profitably, it was absolutely necessary to wind up with a surplus of precious metal. Therefore it was imperative that governments regulate trade so that the stocks of precious metal were protected from the greed of the merchants. The first and most obvious measure of protection, then, was to prohibit the export of coin except by license, a prohibition that was absolutely unenforceable and was violated more often by government officials than by merchants.

These ideas about economic activity led to a variety of forms of economic regulation. The most common was the monopoly, a grant of special privileges in return for both financial considerations and an agreement to abide by the rules set out by the state. In the context of the seventeenth-century economy, there were a number of advantages to monopolies. First, of course, were those that accrued to the crown. There were direct and indirect revenues: monopolists usually paid considerable fees for their rights, and their activities were easy to monitor for purposes of taxation. The crown could use the grant of monopoly to reward past favors or to purchase future support from powerful individuals. There were also advantages for the monopolists. They could make capital investments with the expectation of long-term gains. This advantage was especially important in attracting investors for risky and expensive ventures like long-distance trade. Indeed, there were even benefits for the economy as a whole, as monopolies increased productive investment at a time when most capital was being used to purchase land, luxury goods, or offices.

Two monopoly companies, the English and the Dutch East India companies, dominated the Asian trade. The English East India Company, founded in 1600 with a capital of £30,000, was given the exclusive right to the Asian trade and immediately established itself throughout the Indian Ocean. The Dutch East India Company was formed two years later with ten times the capital of its English counterpart. By the end of the century the Dutch company employed over twelve thousand people. Both companies were known as joint-stock companies, an innovation in the way in which businesses were organized. Subscribers owned a percentage of the total value of the company, based on the number of shares they bought, and were entitled to a distribution of profits on the same basis. Initially, the English company determined profits on single voyages and was to distribute all of its assets to its shareholders after a given period. But changes in legal practice gave the company an identity separate from the individuals that held the shares. Now shares could be exchanged without the breakup of the company as a whole. Both Amsterdam and London soon developed stock markets to trade the shares of monopoly companies.

Both East India companies were remarkably good investments. The Dutch East India Company paid an average dividend of 18 percent for over two hundred years. The value of English East India Company shares rose fivefold in the second half of the seventeenth century alone. Few other monopoly companies achieved a record comparable to that of the East India companies. The English Royal African Company, founded in 1672 to provide slaves for the Spanish colonies, barely recouped costs and was soon superseded by private trade. Even the French East Indian and African companies, which were modeled on the Dutch and English, were forced to abandon their monopolies. The Dutch and English companies were successful not because of their special privileges but because they were able to lower the costs of protecting their ships and cargoes.

Monopolies were not the only form of regulation in which seventeenth-century government engaged. For those states with Atlantic colonies, regulation took the form of restricting markets rather than traders. In the 1660s the English government, alarmed at the growth of Dutch mercantile activity in the New World, passed a series of Navigation Acts designed to protect English shipping. Colonial goods—primarily tobacco and sugar—could be shipped to and from England only in English boats. If the French wanted to purchase West Indian sugar, they could not simply send a ship to the English colony of Barbados loaded with French goods and exchange them for sugar. Rather, they had to make their purchases from an English import-export merchant and the goods had to be unloaded in an English port before they could be reloaded to be shipped to France. As a result, the English reexport trade skyrocketed. In the year 1700 reexports amounted to nearly 40 percent of all English commerce.

With such a dramatic increase in trading, all moved in English ships, shipbuilding boomed. English coastal towns enjoyed heightened prosperity as did the great colonial ports of Bristol and Liverpool. For a time, colonial protection proved effective.

French protectionism was as much internal as colonial. The French entered the intercontinental trade later than their north Atlantic rivals, and they were less dependent upon trade for their subsistence. Of all the states of Europe, only France could satisfy its needs from its own resources. But to achieve such self-sufficiency required coordination and leadership. In the 1670s Louis XIV's finance minister, Jean-Baptiste Colbert (1619–83) developed a plan to bolster the French economy by protecting it against European imports. First Colbert followed the English example of restricting the reexport trade by requiring that imports come to France either in French ships or in the ships of the country from which the goods originated. In addition, he used tariffs to make imported goods unattractive in France. He sponsored a drive to increase French manufacturing, especially of textiles, tapestries, linens, glass, and furniture. To protect the investments in French manufacturing, enormous duties were placed on the import of similar goods manufactured elsewhere. The Venetian glass industry, for example, suffered a serious blow from Colbert's tariffs. English woolen manufacturers were also damaged and the English sought retaliatory measures. But in fact, the English had already begun to imitate this form of protection. In the early eighteenth century England attempted to limit the importation of cotton goods from India to prevent the collapse of the domestic clothing industry.

The Navigation Acts and Colbert's program of protective tariffs were directed specifically against Dutch reexporters. The Dutch were the acknowledged leaders in all branches of commerce in the seventeenth century. There were many summers when there were more Dutch vessels in London Harbor than there were English ships. In the 1670s the Dutch merchant fleet was probably larger than the English, French, Spanish, Portuguese, and German fleets combined. Restrictive navigation practices were one way to combat an advantage that the Dutch had built through heavy capital investment and by breaking away from the prevailing theories about the relationship between wealth and precious metals. The English and French Navigation Acts cut heavily into the Dutch trade and ultimately both the English and French overtook them. But protectionism had its price. Just as the dynastic wars were succeeded by the wars of religion, so were the wars of religion succeeded by the wars of commerce.

The Wars of Commerce

It was not inevitable that economic competition would lead to warfare, only that restrictive competition would. This was the lesson that Adam Smith attempted to teach in 1776. He argued that in economic affairs, that government governs best that governs least. Monopolies, special trading privileges, tariffs—all were equally destructive of commerce, wealth, and political stability. Smith advocated a policy of laissez-faire toward all commercial enterprise. Governments should leave commerce to follow its natural path without any legislative interference. This freedom would allow nations to grow, wealth to accumulate, and goods to circulate freely. But Smith's ideas were built upon a century of commercial warfare, which had sapped the strength of even the strongest European states. Hindsight made it easy to see that restrictive economic policies led to political and military confrontations.

The view ahead was much cloudier. For one thing, the belief that there was a fixed amount of trade in the world was still strong in the late seventeenth century. One country's gains in trade were another's losses. Economic rivalry was just that. There was not more than enough to go around and it could not be easily understood how the expansion of one country's trade could benefit all countries. Moreover, trade, like wealth itself, was still viewed as part of the glory of a state and therefore of the glory of the monarch. It was another of the personal attributes of the absolute ruler. Thus competition for trade was the same as competition for territory or subjects, part of the struggle by which the state grew powerful. Louis XIV and his ministers compared Dutch trading superiority in the seventeenth century to Spanish military superiority in the sixteenth. Its very existence posed a national danger. From these ideas followed warfare. Much of the warfare of the century between 1660 and 1763 was explicitly commercial. Wars were fought over protective regulations, access to markets, smuggling, and colonies. Most took place on the high seas or in small colonial outposts. But some of the bloodiest fighting, especially the land wars of the late seventeenth century, demonstrated how commercial interests could become intertwined with dynastic and political concerns.

The Mercantile Wars

Commercial warfare in Europe began between the English and the Dutch in the middle of the seventeenth century. That these two states should find themselves enemies was surprising for they had much in common. Both were maritime peoples with strong seafaring traditions. They were also natural trading partners. For centuries English wool and woolen cloth had been imported into the Low Countries for processing. Both were Protestant states that had resisted the perils of the Counter-Reformation. The English had supported the Dutch in their struggle with Philip II, and Queen Elizabeth called them "our most ancient and familiar neighbors." For a time, when the English rebelled against their king and established a commonwealth, they were even both republics. But for all their natural affinities, the English and Dutch increasingly found themselves rivals for trade. Both had established aggressive overseas trading companies in the Atlantic and in Asia. In the early seventeenth century the Dutch were the undisputed leaders, their carrying capacity and trade monopolies the greatest in the world. But the English were rising quickly. Their Atlantic colonies began to produce valuable new commodities like tobacco and sugar and their Asian trade was expanding decade after decade. Conflict was inevitable.

It began in the east where competition for the establishment of trading outposts at vital geographical points led to small armed confrontations. In the early seventeenth century, the English were forcibly evicted from the Spice Islands and Indonesia, two of the most lucrative trading centers. Matters deteriorated considerably in 1651 when Cromwell's regime passed the first Naviga-

Painter Jan Peter depicts an incident in the naval warfare caused by trade rivalry between the Dutch and the English. The Dutch fleet sailed up the Medway River and destroyed many English vessals, towing away a battleship.

tion Ordinance, which barred the Dutch from transporting the goods of other states into England. This measure struck at the very heart of the Dutch entrepôt system. The result was a series of three naval wars in 1652–54, 1665–67, and 1672–74.

Though the Dutch had by far the larger fleet, few of their ships were fitted for naval warfare. The flyboats, which had given them such an overwhelming advantage in bulk trading, were easy prey for the armed English merchant vessels. It is estimated that in the three wars over 2,500 Dutch ships were captured and placed into English service. By 1675 perhaps as much as half of the English merchant fleet was foreign-built. The Dutch, of course, had their own successes in capturing English cargoes, and their privateers were especially active in the second and third naval wars with England. Naval warfare was by no means limited to battles between heavily armed men-of-war. Equally important was the seizing of richly laden trading vessels on their return voyages from the Atlantic or Asia. The Dutch had made a living from the Spanish treasure fleets during the Eighty Years' War (1568–1648). But the shoe was now on the other foot. There were many more Dutch vessels on the seas than English ones and Dutch cargoes were normally more valuable. There can be no doubt that on balance the wars

were disastrous for Dutch shipping and Dutch commerce.

The principle of restricted navigation ran like a thread through the Anglo-Dutch wars. The English had to protect their burgeoning colonial trade from the superior Dutch carrying capacity if English commerce was to grow. Restricting carrying to English ships provided incentive to merchants, work for the shipbuilding industry, and closer ties between the English and North American economies. The Navigation Act of 1660 not only restricted trade to English ships, it also enumerated certain goods that could not be imported from the Dutch Republic in any circumstances. For the Dutch the principle of "free ships, free goods" lay at the heart of the matter. Because they had few natural resources, they had developed a manufacturing and trading economy. Paying the excess freight charges and extra customs duties would make their finished products uncompetitive in the international marketplace. Closing the English market for certain commodities lowered their value by creating oversupply.

The Dutch had little choice but to strike out against English policy, but they also had little chance of overall success. Their spectacular naval victory in 1667, when the Dutch fleet surprised many English warships at port and burned both ships and docks at Chatham, obscured the fact that Dutch commercial superiority was slipping. In 1664 the English conquered New Netherland on the North American mainland and renamed it New York. With this defeat, the Dutch lost their largest colonial possession and became more dependent than ever on English reexports. Moreover, the wars intensified commercial rivalries between the states. Anti-Dutch sentiment in England and anti-English sentiment in the United Provinces, whipped up by official propaganda in both newspapers and pamphlets, grew during the periods of belligerence. The wars were costly to both states, nearly bankrupting the English crown in 1672. Anglo-Dutch rivalry was finally laid to rest after 1688, when William of Orange, stadtholder of Holland, became William III (1689–1702), king of England.

The Anglo-Dutch commercial wars were just one part of a larger European conflict. Dutch commerce was as threatening to France as it was to England, though in a different way. Under Colbert, France pursued a policy of economic independence. The state supported internal industrial activity through the financing of large workshops and the encouragement of new manufacturing techniques. Dutch imports constantly jeopardized the survival of these new (and inferior) French commodities. Not only could the Dutch buy raw materials cheaply, but the Dutch were also the most skilled artisans in the world. They could produce nearly any commodity of a higher quality and at a lower price than could the French. Colbert decided that only preventive tariffs would stop Dutch trading from ruining French industry. "As we have destroyed Spain on land, we must destroy Holland at sea. The Dutch have no right to seize all trade," Colbert declared. To achieve this aim, Colbert levied a series of punitive tariffs on Dutch imports, which severely depressed both trade and manufacture in Holland. Import of manufactured goods that directly competed with French production was prohibited, as was refined sugar, one of the most important commodities exported from Holland to France. Though the Dutch retaliated with restrictive tariffs of their own—in 1672 they banned the import of all French goods for an entire year—the Dutch economy depended upon free trade. The Dutch had much more to lose than did France in a battle of protective tariffs.

But the battle that Louis XIV had in mind was to be more deadly than one of tariffs. Greedily he eyed the Spanish Netherlands—to which he had a weak claim through his Habsburg wife—and believed that the Dutch stood in the way of his plans. Indeed, he had nothing but contempt for the merchant republic. The Dutch had entered into an alliance with the English and Swedes in 1668 to counter French policy, and Louis was determined to crush them in retaliation. He successfully bought off both of Holland's supposed allies, providing cash pensions to the kings of England and Sweden in return for England's active participation and Sweden's passive neutrality in the impending war. In 1672 Louis' army, over one hundred thousand strong, invaded the Low Countries and swept all before them. Only the opening of the dikes prevented the French from entering the province of Holland itself.

The French invasion coincided with the third Anglo-Dutch war, and the United Provinces found themselves besieged on land and sea. Their international trade was disrupted, their manufacturing industries were in ruins, and their military budget skyrocketed. Only able diplomacy and skillful military leadership prevented total Dutch demise. A separate peace was made with England, and Spain, whose sovereign territory had been invaded, entered the war on the side of the Dutch as did a number of German states. Louis' hope for a lightning victory faded and the war settled into a series of interminable sieges and reliefs of fortified towns. The Dutch finally persuaded France to come to terms in the Treaty of Nijmegen (1678–79). While Louis XIV retained a number of the territories he had taken from Spain, his armies withdrew from the United Provinces and he agreed to lift most of the commercial sanctions against Dutch goods. The first phase of mercantile warfare was over.

The Wars of Louis XIV

Mercantile competition added a new element to European warfare but it did not supplant the old causes of conflict. National security and dynastic ambition provided equally powerful motives for settling differences by might. So too did glory, the driving force behind the foreign policy of Louis XIV. Only on his deathbed did he confess to "having loved glory too much." It was

Louis' ambition to restore the ancient Burgundian territories to the French crown and to provide secure northern and eastern borders for his state. Pursuit of these aims involved him in conflicts with nearly every other European state. Spain had fought for eighty years to preserve the Burgundian inheritance in the Low Countries. By the Peace of Westphalia (1648), the northern portion of this territory became the United Provinces while the southern portion remained loyal to the crown and became the Spanish Netherlands. This territory provided a barrier between Holland and France that both states attempted to strengthen by establishing fortresses and bridgeheads at strategic places. French designs on the Spanish Netherlands were bound to lead to conflict with Spain and the Dutch Republic. In the east, Louis XIV eyed the duchies of Lorraine and Alsace and the large swath of territory further south known as Franche-Comté. The Peace of Westphalia had granted France control of a number of imperial cities in these duchies, and Louis aimed to link them together. All of these territories were ruled by Habsburgs: Alsace and Lorraine by the Austrian Holy Roman Emperor, Franche-Comté by the Spanish king.

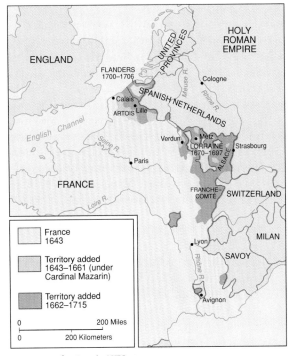

France under Louis XIV

French expansion in either direction not only threatened the other states directly involved but also posed a threat to European security in general. In the late seventeenth century, ambassadors and ministers of state began to develop the theory of a balance of power in Europe. This was a belief that no state or combination of states should be allowed to become so powerful that its existence threatened the peace of the others. Behind this purely political idea of the balance of power lay a theory of collective security that knit together the European state system. Balance of power politics demonstrated clearly that religious considerations had all but disappeared from diplomacy. In the last quarter of the seventeenth century the balance of power was easily practiced. France was as strong as all of the rest of the major states combined, and only their coalition could prevent Louis XIV from getting his way.

Louis showed his hand clearly enough in the Franco-Dutch war that had ended in 1679. Though he withdrew his forces from the United Provinces and evacuated most of the territories he had conquered, by the Treaty of Nijmegen France absorbed Franche-Comté as well as portions of the Spanish Netherlands. Louis began plotting his next adventure almost as soon as the treaty was signed. Over the next several years, French troops advanced steadily into Alsace, ultimately forcing the city of Strasbourg to recognize French sovereignty. A vital bridgehead on the Rhine, Strasbourg was ideal as either an offensive or a defensive position. Expansion into northern Italy was similarly calculated. Everywhere Louis looked, French engineers rushed to construct fortresses and magazines in preparation for another war.

It finally came in 1688 when French troops poured across the Rhine to seize Cologne. A united German empire led by Leopold I, Archduke of Austria, combined with the maritime powers of England and Holland, led by William III, to form the Grand Alliance, the first of the great balance of power coalitions. In fact, the two sides proved so evenly matched that the Nine Years' War (1688–97) settled very little. After his initial aggression, Louis XIV retreated to his fortress positions and withstood attacks in the Rhineland and the Spanish Netherlands. The real importance of the Nine Years' War was that it demonstrated that a successful European coalition could be formed against France. It also signified the permanent shift in alliances that resulted from the Revolution of 1688 in England. Although the English had allied with France against the Dutch in 1672, after William became king he persuaded the English Parliament that the real enemy was France. English naval power and finance were vital to the success of the Grand Alliance. England now aspired to a place as one of the great European powers, an aspiration that was quickly achieved.

The dreary details of these seemingly unending wars would be of little concern were it not for what happened next. The Franco-Dutch war had revealed Louis' appetite for the Spanish Netherlands, the Nine Years' War his hunger for the German Rhineland. Both ambitions were considered too dangerous to be tolerated by the other major European states. Even a conflict as inconclusive as the Nine Years' War might have convinced Louis XIV to be satisfied with his past gains. After all, he was no longer young—he was nearly sixty when the Peace of Ryswick ended the war in 1697—and the French economy suffered terribly from maintaining a standing army of over two hundred thousand soldiers. Louis could not successfully invade the empire, but neither could the combined might of the Grand Alliance successfully invade France. Louis' greatest objective, to secure the borders of his state, had withstood its greatest test. He might have rested satisfied but for the vagaries of births, marriages, and deaths. The great Habsburg dynasty had one last trick to play upon the peoples of Europe.

Like his father, Louis XIV had married a daughter of the king of Spain. Philip IV had married his eldest daughter to Louis XIV and a younger one to Leopold I of Austria, who subsequently became the Holy Roman Emperor (1658–1705). Before he died, Philip finally fathered a son, Charles II (1665–1700), who attained the Spanish crown at the age of four and was mentally and physically incapable of ruling his vast empire. For decades it was apparent that there would be no direct Habsburg successor to an empire which, despite its recent losses, still contained Spain, South America, the Spanish Netherlands, and most of Italy. Louis XIV and Leopold I both had legitimate claims to an inheritance that would have irreversibly tipped the European balance of power.

As Charles II grew increasingly feeble, efforts to find a suitable compromise to the problem of the Spanish succession were led by William III who, as stadtholder of Holland, was vitally interested in the fate of the Spanish Netherlands and, as king of England, in the fate of the Spanish American colonies. In the 1690s two treaties of partition were drawn up. The first achieved near universal agreement but was nullified by the death of the German prince who was to inherit the Spanish crown. The second, which would have given Italy to Louis' son and everything else to Leopold's son, was opposed by Leopold, who had neither naval nor commercial interests and who claimed most of the Italian territories as imperial fiefs. As one of Leopold's ministers proclaimed: "Milan, Naples, Sicily; the rest can be taken by whoever wants it."

All of these plans had been made without consulting the Spanish. If it was the aim of the European powers to partition the Spanish empire

THE SPANISH SUCCESSION

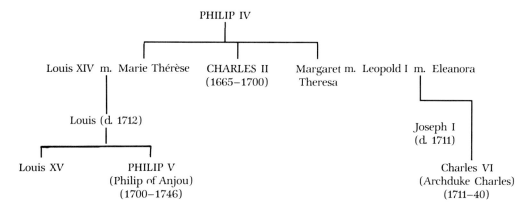

in order to prevent any one state from inheriting too much of it, it was the aim of the Spanish to maintain their empire intact. To this end, they devised a brilliant plan. Charles II bequeathed his entire empire to Philip of Anjou, the younger grandson of Louis XIV, with two stipulations. First that Philip renounce his claim to the French throne, and second that he accept the empire intact, without partition. If he—or more to the point, if his grandfather Louis XIV—did not accept these conditions then the empire would pass to Archduke Charles, the younger son of Leopold I. Such provisions virtually assured war between France and the empire unless compromise between the two powers could be reached. But before terms could even be suggested, Charles II died and Philip V (1700–1746) was proclaimed king of Spain and its empire.

Thus the eighteenth century opened with the War of the Spanish Succession (1702–14). Emperor Leopold rejected the provisions of Charles' will and sent his troops to occupy Italy. Louis XIV confirmed the worst fears of William III when he provided his grandson with French troops to "defend" the Spanish Netherlands. William III revived the Grand Alliance and initiated a massive land war against the combined might of France and Spain. The allied objectives were twofold: to prevent the unification of the French and Spanish thrones and to partition the Spanish empire so that both Italy and the Netherlands were ceded to Austria. The objective of Louis XIV was simply to preserve as much as possible of the Spanish inheritance for the house of Bourbon.

William III died in 1702 and was succeeded by Anne (1702–14). John Churchill (1650–1722), Duke of Marlborough and commander in chief of the army, continued William's policy. England and Holland again provided most of the finance and sea power, but in addition the English also provided a land army nearly seventy thousand strong. Prussia joined the Grand Alliance, and disciplined Prussian troops helped offset the addition of the Spanish army to Louis' forces. In 1704 Churchill defeated French forces at Blenheim in Germany and in 1706 at Ramillies in the Spanish Netherlands. France's military ascendancy was over.

Efforts to negotiate a peace settlement took longer than the war itself. The Austrians had taken control of Italy, the English and Dutch had secured the Spanish Netherlands, and the French had been driven back beyond the Rhine. The Allies believed that they could now enforce any treaty they pleased upon Louis XIV and along with concessions from France attempted to oust his grandson, Philip V, from the Spanish throne. This proved impossible to achieve though it took more than five years to learn the lesson. By then the European situation had taken another strange twist. Both the Emperor Leopold and his eldest son had died. Now Leopold's younger son, Archduke Charles, inherited the empire as Charles VI (1711–40) and raised the prospect of an equally dangerous combined Austrian-Spanish state. Between 1713 and 1714 a series of treaties at Utrecht settled the War of the Spanish Succession. Spanish possessions in Italy and the Netherlands were ceded to Austria; France abandoned all its territorial gains east of the Rhine and ceded its North American territories of Nova Scotia and Newfoundland to England. England also acquired from Spain Gibraltar on the southern coast of Spain and the island of Minorca in the Mediterranean. Both were strategically important to English commercial interests. English intervention in the Nine Years' War and the War of the Spanish Succession did not result in large ter-

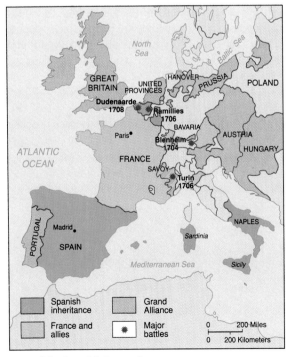

War of the Spanish Succession

ritorial gains but it did result in an enormous increase in English power and prestige. Over the next thirty years England would assert its own imperial claims.

The Colonial Wars

The Treaty of Utrecht (1713–14) ushered in almost a quarter-century of peace in western Europe. Austrian rule in the Netherlands and Italy remained a major irritant to the Spanish but Spain was too weak to do more than sulk and snarl. The death of Louis XIV in 1715 quelled French ambitions for a time and even led to an Anglo-French accord, which guaranteed the preservation of the settlement reached at Utrecht. Peace allowed Europe to rebuild its shattered economy and resume the international trade that had been so severely disrupted over the last forty years. The Treaty of Utrecht had resolved a number of important trading issues, all in favor of Great Britain, as England was known after its union with Scotland in 1707. In addition to receiving Gibraltar and Minorca from Spain, Britain was also granted the monopoly to provide slaves to the Spanish American colonies and the right to send one trading ship a year to them. In east and west, Britain was becoming the dominant commercial power in the world.

At least some of the reason for Britain's preeminence was the remarkable growth of the Atlantic colonies. By the middle of the eighteenth century tobacco and sugar were becoming staple commodities and control of their importation enriched merchants in Bristol and London as well as the British treasury. Moreover, the mainland colonies were finally beginning to show a profit, though less by production than by consumption. Over a million people now inhabited the thirteen colonies and they were awash in British goods. The colonial economy was booming and consumer goods that were in demand in London, Paris, and Amsterdam were also in demand in Boston, Philadelphia, and New York. Like every other colonial power, the British held a monopoly on their colonial trade. They were far less successful than were the Spanish and French in enforcing the notion that colonies existed only for the benefit of the parent country. But the English Parliament continued to pass legislation aimed at restricting colonial trade with other nations and

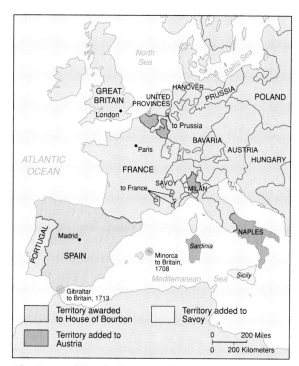

The Treaty of Utrecht, Europe 1714

other nations' colonies. Like almost all other mercantile restrictions, these efforts were stronger in theory than in practice. Tariffs on imports and customs duties on British goods provided a double incentive for smuggling—as if any incentive other than the massive profits to be made were needed.

The problem of smuggling—and its not so distant cousin, piracy—was endemic to long-distance trade. Almost every feature of the mercantile economy created conditions favorable to illegal commercial activities. Monopolies limited entry to products and markets, even though monopolists usually could not satisfy demand. Tariffs and duties raised prices. Restricted trading partnerships created artificial scarcities. Smugglers provided solutions to all of these problems. They increased the amount of commodities available, lowered the price of goods, and allowed for direct exchange between colonies controlled by different European states. Moreover, the European nations encouraged privateering—the polite term for official piracy—during times of war. Individual entrepreneurs were given license to prowl the trading lanes and to capture the ships of other nations. Cargoes were seized; the ships and crews held for ransom. Most of the goods taken found their way onto the black market despite official efforts to claim a portion for the state. Successful privateers were not always interested in the niceties of declared and undeclared wars, nor were the navies of the states themselves.

During wartime, goods that could be used directly for warfare were declared contraband, that is, articles that could not be traded at all. The ships of neutral nations could be searched and their contraband cargoes seized. The definition of what was, or was not, contraband led to much confusion. With so much unofficial interference with trade, official searches and seizures raised the political temperature among the various colonial powers. A confrontation was not long in coming, though it was perhaps surprising that it should take place first between Spain and England.

The seeds of the Anglo-Spanish conflict were sown at Utrecht. Philip V described the English occupation of Gibraltar as "a thorn in the foot of Spain." Moreover, the trading concessions that the English had received had become deeply resented. The Spanish claimed that the single English ship permitted to trade with the Spanish American colonies was constantly resupplied by a flotilla that made the journey with it. Goods smuggled from the West Indies and the mainland colonies were everywhere in Spanish America. This illicit trade grew dramatically with the establishment of English settlements in Georgia on the border of the Spanish colony of Florida. To combat what they saw as deliberate provocation, the Spanish ordered their naval vessels to stop English vessels entering Spanish colonial ports and to search their cargoes for illegal goods. The English complained that this measure turned the Spanish coast guard into officially authorized pirates. A Captain Robert Jenkins told a parliamentary committee how his ship had been ransacked and turned adrift without its navigational instruments and how he had been tied to the mast and his ear cut off. His story inflamed public opinion. In 1739 England declared war.

Though the War of Jenkins' Ear (1739–48), as it was known, settled little between Spain and Britain, it demonstrated for the first time that the English were prepared to go to war to defend their colonies and their colonial trade. During the war an invasion force landed in the Spanish West Indies, thus indicating that regular British troops would be committed to protect overseas possessions. Parliament had long resisted this policy and the change of direction was a result of the new mercantile block that was emerging as a force in British political life. Some, like Sir William Pitt the Elder (1708–78), who emerged as the leader of the House of Commons in the 1750s, saw colonial dominion as the path to national prosperity; others were protecting their own narrow interests as West Indian planters. But no matter what the motive, the new mercantile block helped shift British policy toward colonial rather than Continental affairs.

France emerged as Britain's true colonial rival. Dutch prosperity had withered as that of France and Britain had bloomed. The French established a thriving East India trade and were principally responsible for opening China to the west. In the Caribbean, the French had the largest and most profitable of the West Indian sugar

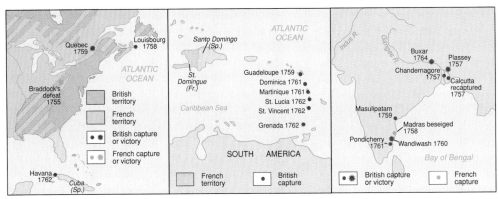

Seven Years' War

islands, Saint Domingue (modern-day Haiti), which outproduced all the British islands. In North America France held not only Canada, with its rich fishing and fur-trapping areas, but laid claim to the entire continent west of the Ohio River, a claim the English colonists hotly disputed. Nevertheless, French settlers occupied what towns there were on the Mississippi River and established an important trading port at New Orleans.

Anglo-French relations in North America had gone from bad to worse throughout the early eighteenth century. The French did not so much settle their colonial territory as occupy it. They surveyed the land, established trading relations with the Native Americans, and built forts at strategic locations. These outposts were designed to protect French commerce and to halt the westward expansion of the English settlers. The English, in contrast, had built a new society in the North American wilderness. They had developed fixed communities, which grew larger and more prosperous by the decade, and they had welcomed new immigrants from all over Europe. By 1750 there were nearly one and a quarter million settlers in British North America. There were little more than seventy-five thousand in the far larger French territories. In the face of such a disparity of numbers, France determined to defend its colonies by establishing an overseas military presence. Regular French troops were shipped to Canada and installed in Louisburg, Montreal, and Quebec. Their presence emboldened the French traders in their conflicts with the British. Ultimately, the British responded with troops of their own and sent an expeditionary force to clear the French from the Ohio River Valley. This action was the immediate cause of the Seven Years' War (1756–63).

Although the Seven Years' War had a bitter Continental phase, it was essentially a war for empire between the English and the French. There were three main theaters: the North American mainland, the West Indian sugar plantations, and the eastern coast of India. British forces also attacked French settlements in Africa in an attempt to disrupt the slave trade so essential to sugar production. All over the globe, the British won smashing victories. The British navy blockaded the water route to Canada, inflicting severe hardship on French settlers in Montreal and

War and Peace, 1648–1763

1648	Peace of Westphalia
1652–54	First Anglo-Dutch war
1665–67	Second Anglo-Dutch war
1672	Franco-Dutch war
1672–74	Third Anglo-Dutch war
1678–79	Treaty of Nijmegen
1688	Revolution of 1688; William of Orange becomes William III of England Grand Alliance formed
1688–97	Nine Years' War (France vs. Grand Alliance)
1697	Peace of Ryswick
1702–14	War of the Spanish Succession
1713–14	Treaty of Utrecht
1739–48	War of Jenkins' Ear
1756–63	Seven Years' War
1763	Peace of Paris

Quebec. British forces ultimately captured both towns. After some initial successes, the French were driven back west across the Mississippi River and their line of fortresses in the Ohio Valley fell into English hands. The English also succeeded in taking all the French sugar islands except Saint Domingue. British success in India was equally complete. The French were chased from their major trading zone and English dominance was secured.

By the end of the Seven Years' War, Britain had become a global imperial power. In the Peace of Paris (1763) France ceded all of Canada in exchange for the return of its West Indian islands. British dominion in the East Indian trade was recognized and led ultimately to British dominion of India itself. In less than a century the ascendancy of France was broken and Europe's first modern imperial power had been created.

European commercial expansion was the first step in a long process that would ultimately transform the material life of all human beings. The quest for new commodities led to the sophistication of transportation, marketing, and distribution, all vital developments for agricultural changes in the future. The ability to move large quantities of goods from place to place and to exchange them between different parts of the globe laid the foundation for organized manufacturing. The practical impact of scientific discovery, as yet only dimly glimpsed, would soon spur the transformation of handicrafts into industries. In the eighteenth century the material world was still being conquered and the most unattractive features of this conquest were all too plainly visible. Luxuries for the rich were won by the labors of the poor. The pleasures of sugar and tobacco were purchased at the price of slavery for millions of Africans. The greed of merchants and the glory of princes was an unholy alliance that resulted in warfare around the globe. But it was a shrinking globe, one whose peoples were becoming increasingly interdependent, tied together by the goods and services that they could provide to each other.

Suggestions for Further Reading

General Reading

* A. Rupert Hall, *The Revolution in Science 1500–1750* (London: Longman, 1983). The best introduction to the varieties of scientific thought in the early modern period. Detailed and complex.

* Jan de Vries, *The European Economy in an Age of Crisis* (Cambridge: Cambridge University Press, 1976). A comprehensive study of economic development, including long-distance trade and commercial change.

* K. H. D. Haley, *The Dutch in the Seventeenth Century* (London: Thames and Hudson, 1972). A well-written and illustrated history of the golden age of Holland.

* Derek McKay and H. M. Scott, *The Rise of the Great Powers 1648–1815* (London: Longman, 1983). An outstanding survey of diplomacy and warfare.

The New Science

* Margaret C. Jacob, *The Cultural Meaning of the Scientific Revolution* (New York: Knopf, 1988). Scientific thought portrayed in its social context.

* Stillman Drake, *Galileo* (New York: Hill and Wang, 1980). A short but engaging study of the great Italian scientist.

* Allen Debus, *Man and Nature in the Renaissance* (Cambridge: Cambridge University Press, 1978). An

especially good account of the intellectual roots of scientific thought.

Charles Webster, *The Great Instauration: Science, Medicine, and Reform* (London: Duckworth, 1975). A complicated but rewarding analysis of experimental science and the origins of scientific medicine.

* Frank E. Manuel, *Sir Isaac Newton: A Portrait* (Cambridge, MA: Harvard University Press, 1968). A readable account of one of the most complex intellects in European history.

Empires of Goods

* Ralph Davis, *The Rise of the Atlantic Economies* (Ithaca, NY: Cornell University Press, 1973). A nation-by-nation survey of the colonial powers.

K. N. Chaudhuri, *The Trading World of Asia and the English East India Company* (Cambridge: Cambridge University Press, 1978). A brilliant account of the impact of the Indian trade on both Europeans and Asians.

* Sidney Mintz, *Sweetness and Power* (New York: Viking Press, 1985). An anthropological examination of the lure of sugar and its impact upon Western society.

* Philip Curtin, *The Atlantic Slave Trade* (Madison, WI: University of Wisconsin Press, 1969). A study of the importation of African slaves into the New World with the best estimates of the numbers of slaves and their destinations.

* Simon Schama, *The Embarrassment of Riches* (New York: Knopf, 1987). A social history of the Dutch Republic, which explores the meaning of commerce in Dutch society.

* Holden Furber, *Rival Empires of Trade in the Orient 1600–1800* (Minneapolis: University of Minnesota Press, 1976). A comprehensive survey of the battle for control of the Asian trade in the seventeenth and eighteenth centuries.

The Wars of Commerce

A. C. Carter, *Neutrality or Commitment: The Evolution of Dutch Foreign Policy 1667–1795* (London: Edward Arnold, 1975). A tightly written study of the objectives and course of Dutch diplomacy.

Charles Wilson, *Profit and Power* (London: Longman, 1957). Still the best study of the Anglo-Dutch wars of the mid-seventeenth century.

Paul Langford, *The Eighteenth Century 1688–1815* (New York: St. Martin's Press, 1976). A reliable guide to the growth of British power.

Ragnhild Hatton, ed., *Louis XIV and Europe* (London: Macmillan, 1976). An important collection of essays on French foreign policy in its most aggressive posture.

Richard Pares, *War and Trade in the West Indies 1739–63* (Oxford: Oxford University Press, 1936). A blow-by-blow account of the struggle for colonial supremacy in the sugar islands.

---

* Indicates paperback edition available.

18

The New
European Powers

Calling the Tune

Frederick the Great loved music. During his youth it was one of his private passions that so infuriated his father. Mathematics, political economy, modern languages, even dreaded French, were the subjects that a future king of Prussia should learn. But music, never. Rather the boy should be at the hunt watching the dogs tear apart a stag, or on maneuvers with the Potsdam guards, a troop of soldiers all nearly seven feet tall. This was the regimen King Frederick William I prescribed for his son. But Frederick the Great loved music. He secretly collected all the books and manuscripts he could find on the subject, outspending his tiny allowance in the process. He had Johann Quantz (1697–1773), the great-

est flutist of the day, placed on his staff to teach him and to conspire with him against his father. At night, while the old king drank himself into a stupor—an activity he warmly recommended to his son— Frederick would powder his hair, put on a jacket of the latest French style, and regale his friends with his newest compositions. He and Quantz would take turns playing the flute, and the young spectators would do their best to imitate what they believed to be the essence of courtly manners. A lookout guarded the door in case the king wandered by unexpectedly. Once the musicians were almost discovered and Frederick's fine new jacket was tossed on the fire, but the flutes and

musical scores remained safely hidden.

After he became king, Frederick the Great could indulge his passion more openly. Yet he preferred to hold his concerts, usually small gatherings, at the Palace of San Souci, which he built in Potsdam. A special music room was designed for the king's use and he lavished attention on it. The great chandelier, lit by a circle of candles, illuminated the center of the room and highlighted the soloist. The entire palace reflected Frederick's personal taste. Unlike most great palaces of state, it was small, functional, and beautiful. Here Frederick could escape the mounting cares of governing one of the most powerful states

in Europe by reading, corresponding with eminent French intellectuals, and playing the flute. In this picture, *Das Flötenkonzert* (the Flute Concert), Frederick is portrayed performing in his great music room. Before a small audience of courtiers and intimates, he plays to the accompaniment of cello, violins, and piano.

Frederick's talent was real enough. A British visitor to Sans Souci, who had little reason to flatter the king, reported: "I was much pleased and surprised with the neatness of his execution. His performance surpassed anything I had ever heard among the dilettanti or even professors." This judgment is reinforced when one studies the expressions of the three men

in the left-hand corner of the painting. They are taking genuine pleasure in the music they are hearing, all the more genuine in that the king's back is to them. So, too, are the musicians who are accompanying the king. There is as much joy as concentration upon their faces.

Frederick's musical accomplishment was not unique among eighteenth-century monarchs. Joseph II of Austria was also a skilled flutist. But it was not so much music as accomplishment that was coming to be valued among the monarchs of the new European powers. Catherine the Great of Russia corresponded with philosophers; Frederick the Great brought the great French intellectual Voltaire (1698–1778) to

his court—though they quickly took a dislike to each other. The acquisition of culture seemed to matter more and more as the century wore on. Museums, opera houses, great art collections were established all over the Continent. The Hermitage in Saint Petersburg was stocked with the works of Dutch and English masters. The British Museum was founded in London with the support of King George II, who deposited his great library there. Whether this veneer of culture did anything to lessen the brutality of warfare and power politics is a matter of opinion. But as a veneer it was as highly polished as the flute that Frederick the Great is so delicately pressing to his mouth.

Europe in 1714

The Peace of Utrecht (1713–14) brought about a considerable reorganization of the political geography of Europe. Utrecht created a new Europe in the west, while the Treaty of Nystad (1721) created a new Europe in the east. Both agreements reflected the dynamics of change that had taken place over the previous century. The rise of France on the Continent and of Britain's colonial empire around the globe were facts that could no longer be ignored. The decline of Sweden and Poland and the emergence of Russia as a great power were the beginning of a long-term process that would continue to dominate European history.

All of this could be seen on a map of Europe in the early eighteenth century. The political divisions of the Continent in 1714 presaged the future. France's absorption of Alsace and encroachments into Lorraine would be a bone of contention between the French and Germans for two centuries and ultimately contributed to the outbreak of World Wars I and II. The political footballs of the Spanish Netherlands and Spanish Italy, now temporarily Austrian, continued to be kicked about until the nationalist movements of the nineteenth century gave birth to Belgium, Luxembourg, and a united Italy. The emergence of Brandenburg-Prussia on the north German coast and the gradual decline in the power of the Holy Roman Emperor were both vital to the process that created a unified Germany and a separate

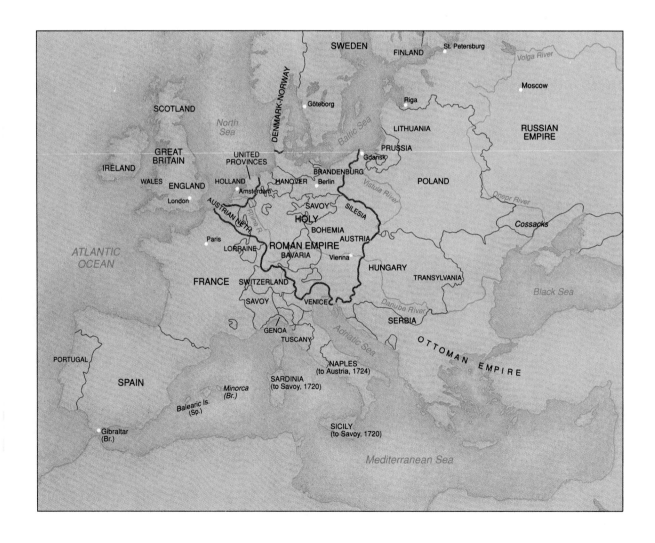

Austria. In the southeast, the slow but steady reconquest of the Balkans from Ottoman dominion restored the historic southern border of the Continent. The inexorable expansion of Russia was also already apparent.

The West

Perhaps the most obvious transformation in the political geography of western Europe was the expansion of European power around the globe. In the Atlantic, Spain remained the largest colonial power. Through its vice-royalty system it controlled all of central America, the largest and most numerous of the Caribbean islands, North America from Colorado to California (as well as Florida), and most of South America. The other major colonial power in the region was Portugal, which shared dominion over the South American continent. The Portuguese colony of Brazil, which began as a series of coastal settlements, was now expanding inland as missionaries and explorers carved a path through the jungles and millions of slaves were imported to work its fields. Brazilian production of sugar, dyestuffs, timbers, and exotic commodities amply repaid the meager investment the Portuguese had made.

In North America the French and British shared the eastern half of the continent. The French controlled most of it. They had landed first in Canada and then slowly made their way down the Saint Lawrence River. New France, as their colonial empire was called, was a trading territory and it expanded along the greatest of the waterways, the Great Lakes, and the Ohio, Missouri, and Mississippi rivers. Major settlements were on Lake Erie (near present-day Cleveland), at the base of Lake Michigan (near present-day Chicago), and at the juncture of the Missouri and Mississippi rivers (near present-day Saint Louis). French settlements had sprung up as far south as the Gulf of Mexico, where New Orleans was founded in 1718. France also claimed the territory of Louisiana, named for Louis XIV, which stretched from New Orleans to Montana, though it remained unsettled and unexplored. The British settlements were all coastal, stretching from Maine to Georgia on the Atlantic seaboard. Unlike the French, the British settled their territory and

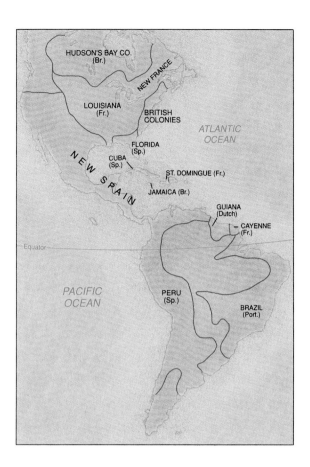

were only interested in expansion when their population, which was doubling every twenty-five years, outgrew its resources. By the early eighteenth century the ports of Boston, New York, Philadelphia, and Charleston were thriving commercial centers. Only in the British colonies had the old world been reestablished in the new.

Europeans managed their eastern colonial territories differently than they did those in the west. Initially the Portuguese and the Dutch had been satisfied with establishing trading factories—coastal fortresses that could be used as warehouses and defended against attack. But in the seventeenth century, the European states began to take control of vital ports and lucrative islands. Here the Dutch were the acknowledged leaders, replacing the Portuguese who had begun the process at the end of the sixteenth century. Holland held by force or in conjunction with local leaders all the Spice Islands in the Pacific. The Dutch also occupied both sides of the Malay Peninsula and nearly all the coastal areas of the

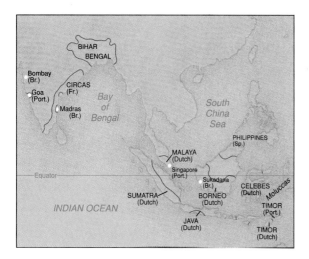

islands in the Java Sea. Dutch control of Ceylon was strategically important for its Indian trade. Compared to the Dutch Republic, all other European states had only a minor territorial presence in the East, with the exception of Spain, which still controlled the Philippines. The British had limited their eastern outposts to trading establishments. Through these they maintained a significant presence in India, especially in Bombay on the west coast, Madras on the east coast, and Calcutta in Bengal. During the eighteenth century the British began to colonize the Indian subcontinent directly.

Imperial expansion was the most obvious change in the geopolitical boundaries of Europe, but it was not the only one. A brief tour of the western states after the Treaty of Utrecht reveals some others. In 1707 England and Scotland formally joined together to form Great Britain, one of the newly emerging European powers. In addition to its eastern and western colonies, Britain had also gained control of Gibraltar at the foot of Spain, and Minorca, one of the Balearic Islands in the Mediterranean. Both territories were strategically important to British commerce. But the greatest changes in Britain's geopolitical makeup had to do with its sovereigns. After the Revolution of 1688, Britain had shared a ruler with Holland, but there had never been any attempt to integrate the two states. After William III died in 1702 the two countries went their separate ways. In 1714 Queen Anne died without a surviving heir and the British throne passed to George of Hanover, a German prince whose rich territories on the

North Sea brought Britain into Continental affairs in a new and unforeseen way.

Across the English Channel were the Low Countries, now permanently divided between the United Provinces in the north, led by Holland, and those provinces in the south that had remained loyal to the Spanish crown in the sixteenth century. By 1714 the golden age of the Dutch was over. Though the Dutch remained one of the most prosperous peoples in Europe and continued as a colonial and maritime power, their small numbers and meager natural resources eventually outweighed their abilities as innovators and managers. Gradually they lost their eastern empire to Britain, their predominance in European trade to France. What the Dutch gained at Utrecht was security, the right to maintain their forces in the towns along the border between France and the old Spanish Netherlands. The Spanish Netherlands, the original Burgundian inheritance, were now being slowly dismembered.

Since the accession of Louis XIV, France had plucked small pieces from the territories that had been contested between Habsburg and Valois since the fifteenth century. Between French aggression and the Dutch occupation of such important places as Ghent and Ypres, the ability of the southern provinces to maintain a separate identity suffered a grave blow. But not as grave as that formalized at Utrecht, when sovereignty over this territory was assigned to Austria, ostensibly because the emperor was a Habsburg, but really because the balance of power in western Europe demanded it.

To the south lay France, still the most powerful nation in Europe despite its losses in the War of the Spanish Succession. By 1714 Louis XIV had broken forever the danger of Spanish encirclement that had been the worry of every French king since Francis I in the early sixteenth century. Though Louis' Continental wars were the most spectacular aspect of his foreign policy, in fact it was his strategy of "creeping defense" that was more successful. Louis had methodically set out to occupy those territories that were strategically necessary to defend his state from invasion by the Dutch, the Spanish, the British, or the emperor. In the northeast he consolidated the imperial towns that France had acquired in 1648 by absorbing the Duchy of Bar. In the north he absorbed a healthy portion of Flanders including Dunkirk on the English Channel and the prosperous clothing town of Lille. He pushed the eastern boundary of his state to the Rhine by overrunning Alsace and parts of Lorraine. Strasbourg remained French under the settlement of 1714, testimony to the fact that it was possible to hold France only at the western banks of the Rhine. Finally, farther to the south Louis had won and held Franche-Comté, once the center of Burgundy. In 1714 France was larger, stronger, and better able to defend its borders than ever before. It was also exhausted from its efforts.

As France expanded, so Spain contracted. Less than two centuries earlier a Spanish king had

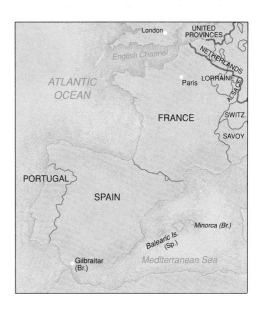

On this tapestry, Louis XIV is shown preparing for a triumphant entry into Dunkirk, which he had bought from the king of England. The city was one of Louis' first territorial acquisitions and one of the few that he obtained peacefully.

dreamed of being monarch over all of Europe. Now a Bourbon sat on the great Habsburg throne and Spain was slowly being sliced to pieces, losing an island here, a possession there. By 1714 the European territories of the Spanish empire had been reduced to Iberia itself. But the loss of its European empire was to prove a blessing in disguise for Spain, which now entered upon a new and unexpected phase of growth and influence. Under the Bourbon monarchy Spain revived.

The center of Europe remained occupied by the agglomeration of cities, bishoprics, principalities, and small states known collectively as the Holy Roman Empire, but now more accurately called the German empire. There were still over three hundred separate jurisdictions, most of them vulnerable to preying neighbors such as Louis XIV. Bavaria in the south, and Saxony, Brandenburg, and Hanover in the north were among the most important of the large states with the added twist that Hanover was now ruled by the king of Great Britain. The emperor, now officially prohibited from interference in the internal administration of the large states, was less dominant in German affairs than he had been before the Thirty Years' War. Each election of each successive Habsburg further diminished the emperor's power in the German empire.

Increasingly, Habsburg power centered on Austria, Bohemia, and Hungary. This was especially true during the reign of Leopold I (1655–1705). Withstanding threats on all sides, Leopold was able to expand his state both to the west and to the south and to bring Austria into the ranks of the great European powers. Such an outcome could hardly have been foreseen in the middle of the seventeenth century, when the Ottomans made their last great thrust into the interior of Europe. They captured more of Hungary and threatened Leopold's hereditary lands. In 1683 the Ottomans besieged Vienna itself, and only the arrival of seventy thousand Polish-led troops saved it from falling. But from that time forward, Austrian forces scored stunning victories. By 1699 almost all of Hungary had been retaken by Austria; at the Treaty of Passarowitz in 1718 Austria gained the rest of Hungary and Serbia. When the Treaty of Utrecht granted Austria control of the Netherlands, Lombardy, and Naples, the Austrian Habsburgs took the place of their Spanish cousins as rulers of a European empire.

Austria's Italian possessions included the vast southern territories of Naples (including Sicily after 1720) and the rich industrial area surrounding Milan in the north. Alongside the Austrian

territories a number of independent city-states continued to flourish on the Italian peninsula. Venice on the Adriatic and Genoa on the Mediterranean were no longer the great commercial states that they had been in the sixteenth century. But both remained prosperous and independent. The Grand Duchy of Tuscany, with its great city of Florence, and the Papal States had expanded over the course of the seventeenth century, absorbing their smaller neighbors until both were large consolidated territories. To the west of the Italian states was the Duchy of Savoy, a state which had maintained control over the vital Alpine passes that joined western and central Europe. Savoy had pursued a flexible foreign policy, pleasing whichever of its powerful neighbors was most dangerous and accepting the patronage of whichever seemed most friendly. Client of the Spanish, French, and Austrians, Savoy grew and prospered. After the War of the Spanish Succession Savoy was counted one of the victors even though it had fought on both sides. Duke Victor Amadeus II became a king when he received the island of Sicily, which he exchanged with Austria for Sardinia in 1720.

The East

This was western Europe in 1714. In the east, it was the Treaty of Nystad (1721) ending the Great Northern War (1700–1721) that fixed the political geography. Here the emerging powers were Russia and Prussia, those in decline were Sweden and Poland. The critical factor in eastern European politics remained access to the sea. Outlets to the Baltic Sea in the north and the Black Sea in the south were the vital lifeline for this part of the Continent and control of these outlets was the central motivation for the long years of war fought among the eastern states.

The expansion of Russia is one of the central events in European history, and the early eighteenth century is its pivotal period. During the long years of social and economic recovery after the death of Ivan the Terrible in 1584, Russia had been easy prey for its powerful neighbors Sweden and Poland. Through a series of wars and political pacts, Russia had ceded most of its Baltic territo-

ries to Sweden while it had relinquished land and population in the west to Poland. Peter the Great (1682–1725) set out to reclaim what had been lost. As a result of the Great Northern War, Russia regained the eastern Baltic coastline from the southeastern end of Finland to Riga in the west. Russia now occupied both sides of Lake Ladoga and controlled all of the vital Baltic ports in the east. Peter built a new Russian capital on the Gulf of Finland to be a window to the west. In this new city, named Saint Petersburg, Peter laid the foundation for the Russian navy.

What Russia gained, Sweden lost. At the height of its power in the middle of the seventeenth century, Sweden had dominated the Baltic. It occupied all of Finland—though only the southern coastal areas were actually colonized—controlled the important eastern coast of Norway, and had gained a foothold in Germany. Most importantly, Sweden had captured the southern tip of its own peninsula from the Danes, making the mainland portion of its state whole. But Sweden's century-long rise to power was followed by a rapid period of decline. The small and relatively poor population could not long succeed in governing an empire. The Great Northern War ended whatever pretensions Sweden had left. It lost all of its German territories: those on the North Sea went to Hanover, those on the Baltic to Prussia. Livonia, Estonia, and the eastern provinces were returned to Russia. Though Sweden could not maintain its position in the face of Russian and Prussian supremacy, it was able to hold on to its vital gains from the Danes. Sweden had built its own window to the west at Göteborg on the North Sea, and from there it could carry on a direct trade with Britain and the Netherlands.

The acquisition of Pomerania from Sweden was just one of the territorial gains made by Brandenburg-Prussia. Since the end of the Thirty Years' War, this strange configuration of a state had been steadily growing. Its geographical heart was in Brandenburg, one of the domains of the Holy Roman Empire. From the capital at Berlin the princes of Brandenburg directed the accumulation of small neighboring German lands: Magdeburg and Halle to the southwest, a piece of Pomerania to the northeast. But while Brandenburg expanded in every direction, it could do little to join itself to the kingdom of Prussia. A huge swath of Poland, cutting between the two, stood in the way. This division of Brandenburg-Prussia was its most important geopolitical feature. In the eighteenth century, the determination to expand to the east dominated Prussian history.

This aim meant, of course, eventual conflict with Poland. Despite its political weakness, Poland was one of the largest landmasses in Europe and one of the most pivotal. On its southern border it held back Ottoman expansion, on its eastern border it held back the Russians. Its great port of Gdansk on the Baltic dominated the grain and timber trade with northern Europe as well as local Baltic commerce between Scandinavia and the mainland. Sweden and Russia, the eastern powers, controlled Poland politically, helping nominate its elected kings and ensuring that its decentralized form of aristocratic government kept Poland weak. Poland served as a useful counterweight in the balance of power in eastern Europe. Except for its Baltic territories, Poland was not yet seen as a great prize to be fought over. But by the beginning of the eighteenth century it was already a helpless giant ready to be toppled. Not too many decades would pass before one state or another was ready to provide the push.

The Rise of Russia

In 1721 Peter I, the Great, who had been tsar in Russia since 1682, assumed the title of Emperor of All Russias. The Treaty of Nystad had confirmed the magnitude of his victory over the Swedes in the Great Northern War, both in territory and prestige. The title *tsar,* or caesar, no longer seemed enough. Emperor was more fitting. The change created consternation in the courts of Europe. Just a quarter century before, no one had cared very much what the king of Russia called himself. The Russian tsar was just another of the exotic eastern rulers whose preposterous titles Europeans were willing to recognize in order to conduct their business. In fact, little was known for sure about the Russian ruler or his state. What little mercantile contact there was between Russia and the west was conducted entirely by westerners. Foreign merchants were allowed to live in Moscow in a separate ghetto called "Germantown." Their letters were the principal source of western knowledge about the vast Muscovite empire.

Peter the Great changed all of this. Twice he visited Europe to discover the secrets of western prosperity and might. He arranged marriages between the closest heirs to his throne, including his son Alexis, and the sons and daughters of German princes and dukes. By 1721 he had established twenty-one separate foreign embassies. The sons of the Russian gentry and nobility were sent west—sometimes forcibly—to further their education and to learn to adapt to western outlooks. Peter recruited Europeans to fill the most important skilled positions in the state: foreign engineers and gunners to serve in the army; foreign architects to build the new capital at Saint Petersburg; foreign scholars to head the new state schools; foreign administrators to oversee the new departments of state. Peter borrowed freely and adapted sensibly. If necessary, he would drag his countrymen kicking and screaming into the modern world.

By 1721 Russia was recognized all over Europe as an emerging power. The military defeat of the seemingly invincible Swedes had made monarchs from Louis XIV to William III sit up and take notice. And the great Russian victory at Poltava in 1709 was no fluke. Peter's forces followed it up

This portrait of Peter the Great by his court painter Louis Caravaque pays homage to Peter's intense interest in naval matters. Ships flying English, Dutch, Danish, and Russian flags prepare for maneuvers under his command.

with several strong campaigns which proved that Russia could organize, equip, finance, and train an up-to-date military force. Moreover, Peter's absorption of Sweden's Baltic territories made Russia a power in the north. A navy, built mostly by foreigners, was now capable of protecting Russian interests and defending important ports such as Riga and Saint Petersburg. Even the Dutch, who had long plotted the decline of Swedish might, now became nervous. Thus it was unsettling that Peter wished to be recognized as emperor. Russia was now a European power, but European powers were headed by kings. There was only one emperor in Europe—the Holy Roman Emperor—and those who aspired to that title did so in the traditional way, by attempting to bribe the German electors. No one simply declared himself emperor. Rather, no one ever had before Peter the Great.

Russia Turns West

Peter the Great was not the first Russian tsar to attempt to borrow from western developments. The process had been underway for decades. The opening of the northern port of Archangel led to direct contact with British and Dutch traders, who brought with them new ideas and useful products, which were adapted to Russian needs and conditions. Russia was a vast state and Europe was only one of its neighbors. Its religion had come from Byzantium rather than Rome, thus giving Russian Christianity an eastern flavor. Its Asian territories mixed the influence of Mongols and Ottomans; its southern borders met Tartars and Cossacks. While most European states were racially and ethnically homogeneous, Russia was a loose confederation of diverse peoples. Yet it was the western states that posed the greatest threat to Russia in the seventeenth century, and it was to the west that Tsar Alexis I (1645–76) and his son Peter turned their attention.

It would be wrong to see Peter's westernizing innovation as a systematic program. System implies an organization not to be associated with the chaotic, often contradictory, policies that Peter pursued. More to the point, nearly all of what he did was done to enhance military efficiency rather than civil progress. In his thirty years of active rule there was only one year— 1724—during which he was not at war. Vital reforms like the poll tax (1724), which changed the basis of taxation from the household to the individual adult male, had enormous social consequences. The new policy of taxing individuals officially erased whole social classes. A strict census taken (and retaken) to inhibit tax evasion became the basis for further governmental encroachments on the tsar's subjects. Yet the poll tax was not designed for any of these purposes. It was instituted to increase tax revenue for war. Similarly, the establishment of compulsory, life-time military service required of the land-owning classes (the nobility and gentry) was undertaken to provide officers and state servants for an expanding military machine.

Yet if Peter's reforms were not systematic and developed from little other than military necessity, nevertheless they constituted a fundamental transformation in the life of all Russian people. The creation of a gigantic standing army and an entirely new navy meant conscription of the Russian peasantry on a grand scale. As the wars continued, those liable for military service progressed from bachelors aged sixteen to thirty to any adult male under the age of fifty. In a ten-year period of the Great Northern War the army absorbed 330,000 conscripts, most of whom never returned to their homes. Military service was not confined to the peasantry. Traditionally, the rural gentry raised and equipped the local conscript forces and gave them what training they could. Most gentry lived on estates that had been granted to them along with the resident peasants as a reward for their military contributions. Peter the Great intensified the obligations of the gentry. Not only were they to serve the state for life, but they were to accompany their regiments to the field and lead them in battle. When too old for active military service, they were to perform administrative service in the new departments of state.

The expansion of military forces necessitated an expansion of military administration as well. Peter's first innovation was the creation of the Senate, a group of nine senior administrators who were to oversee all aspects of military and civil government. The Senate became a permanent institution of government led by an entirely new official, the Procurator-General, who presided over its sessions and could propose legislation as well as oversee administration. From the Senate emanated five hundred officials known as the fiscals, who traveled throughout the state looking for irregularities in the process of tax assessment and collection. The fiscals were to locate tax evaders and to identify corrupt tax collectors. They quickly developed into a hated and feared internal police force.

Peter's efforts to reorganize his government went a step further in 1722, when he promulgated the Table of Ranks. This was an official hierarchy of the state divided into three categories—military service, civil service, and those who owned landed estates. Each category contained fourteen ranks and it was decreed that every person who entered the hierarchy did so at the bottom and worked his way up. The creation of the Table of Ranks was significant in a number of ways. It demonstrated Peter's continued commitment to merit as a criterion for advancement. This standard had been shown in the military, where officers were promoted on the basis of service and experience rather than birth or background. Equally important was Peter's decision to make the military service the highest of the three categories. This reversed the centuries-old position of the landed aristocracy and the military service class. Though the old nobility also served in the military and continued to dominate state service, the Table of Ranks opened the way for the infusion of new elements into the Russian elite.

Many of those who were able to advance in the Table of Ranks did so through attendance at the new institutions of higher learning that Peter founded. His initial educational establishments were created to further the military might of the state. The colleges of Mathematics, Engineering, and Artillery, which became the training grounds for his army officers, were all founded during the Great Northern War. But Peter was interested in liberal education as well. He had scores of western books translated into Russian. He had a press established in Moscow to print original works, including the first Russian newspaper. For a time Peter actually edited the paper himself. He decreed that a new, more westernized alphabet replace that used by the Russian Orthodox Church and that books be written in the language that the people spoke rather than in the formal literary language of religious writers. He also introduced Arabic numerals into official accounting records. His agents bought artwork and manuscripts from all over Europe, which were displayed in the public library and museum that he established. Though he did not live to see it open officially, Peter was principally responsible for the creation of a Russian Academy of Sciences (1724).

Peter's reforms of government and society were matched by his efforts to energize the economy. No state in Europe had as many natural resources as did Russia, yet manufacturing barely existed there. As with everything else he did, Peter took a direct hand in establishing factories for the production of textiles, glass, leather, and most importantly, iron and copper. The state directly owned about half of these establishments, most of them on a larger scale than any known in the west. By 1726 more than half of all Russian exports were manufactured goods and Russia had become the largest producer of iron and copper in the world.

In all of these ways and more Peter the Great transformed Russia. But the changes Peter wrought did not come without cost. The traditions of centuries were not easily broken. Intrigue against Peter led first to confrontation with the old military elite and later to conflict with his only son, Alexis. It remains unclear if the plot with which Alexis was connected existed anywhere other than in Peter's mind, but it is abundantly clear that Alexis' death from torture plunged the state into a succession crisis in 1725. Finally, the great costs of westernization were paid by the masses of people who benefited little from the improvement in Russia's international standing or from the social and economic changes that affected the elites.

Peter the Great was a precocious child. He began his education at the age of two, using a book similar to the illustrated Russian speller whose "Z" page is seen below.

Life in Rural Russia

Nearly 97 percent of the Russian people lived on the land and practiced agriculture. Farming techniques and agrarian life-styles had changed little for centuries. Although the black earth, a belt of extremely rich land, ran through southern and central Russia, most of the country's soil was poor. Harsh climate and low yields characterized Russian agriculture. Thirty-four of the one hundred Russian harvests during the eighteenth century can be termed poor or disastrous, yet throughout the century state taxation was making larger and larger demands upon the peasantry. During Peter's reign alone, direct taxation increased by 500 percent, most of it in the form of consumption taxes that struck particularly hard at the bottom levels of society.

The theory of the Russian state was one of service, and the role of Russian peasants was to serve their master. Beginning in the mid-seventeenth century, the peasantry had undergone a change in status. The law code of 1649 formalized a process that had been underway for over a century whereby peasants were turned into the property of their landlords. During the next century laws curtailed the ability of peasants to move freely from one place to another, eliminated their right to hold private property, and abolished their freedom to petition the tsar against their masters. At the same time that landlords increased their hold over peasants, the state increased its hold over landlords. They were made responsible for the payment of taxes owed by their peasants and for the military service due from them. By the middle of the eighteenth century over half of all peasants—3.2 million adult males in 1727 and 6.7 million in 1782—had thus become serfs, the property of their masters, without any significant rights or legal protection.

Private landlords reckoned their wealth in the number of serfs they owned. But in fact most owned only a small number, fewer than fifty in the middle of the eighteenth century. This resulted from the common practice whereby a father divided his estate among all of his surviving sons. Most gentry were small landholders, constantly in debt and rarely able to meet their financial and service obligations to the state. This life of poverty at the top was, of course, magnified at the bottom. Although western visitors to Russia returned home with stories of noblemen with hundreds of household serfs, and of serf orchestras and serf poets, the reality for the vast majority of serfs was far less colorful. They lived in small villages where they divided up their meager surplus to pay their taxes and drew lots to see who would be sent for military service. When the debts of their lords became too heavy, it was the serfs who were foreclosed upon. Serf families or particularly desirable individuals would be sold at auction, some to be resettled in new villages with more prosperous landowners, others to be deployed at the whim of their purchasers.

If serfs made up the bottom half of the Russian peasantry, there were few advantages to being in the top half among the state peasants. State peasants lived on lands owned by the monarchy itself. Like the serfs, they were subject to the needs of the state for soldiers and workers. The use of forced labor was a feature of each of Peter's grandiose projects. Saint Petersburg was built on the backs of peasant conscripts. From 1709, when the project began, perhaps as many as 40,000 laborers a year were forced to work on the various sites. Even skilled workers were pressed into service. In 1713, one thousand carpenters were rounded up and brought to the new city. Over half had run away by the following year. The unhealthy conditions of the swampy environment from which the new capital rose claimed the lives of thousands of these workers, as did the appalling conditions of overwork and undernourishment in which they lived.

Many Russian peasants were resigned to their fate. They developed a philosophy of submission and a rich folk culture that valued a stubborn determination to endure. For those who would no longer bend to the knout—the heavy leather whip that was the omnipresent enforcer of obedience—there was only flight or rebellion. Each proved equally fruitless. Hundreds of thousands of serfs fled to state-owned lands in hope of escaping the cruelties of individual landlords. Although severe penalties were imposed for aiding runaway serfs, in fact most state overseers and many private landlords encouraged runaways to settle on their lands. Many who escaped to either Siberia or Poland eventually found themselves re-enserfed.

The Enlightened Empress

Of all the legacies of Peter the Great, perhaps the most important was that government could go on without him. During the next thirty-seven years six tsars ruled Russia, "three women, a boy of twelve, an infant, and a mental weakling," as one commentator acidly observed. More to the point, each succession was contested as there were no direct male heirs to the throne in this period. Peter's wife, his two grandsons, his daughter, and a niece all served a turn. Nevertheless, despite turmoil at the top, government continued to function smoothly and Peter's territorial conquests were largely maintained. Russia also experienced a remarkable increase in numbers during this period. Between 1725 and 1762 population increased from 13 to 19 million, a jump of nearly one-third in a single generation. This explosion of people dramatically increased the wealth of the landholding class, who reckoned their status by the number of serfs they owned. At the beginning of the seventeenth century, a nobleman with more than five hundred serfs was considered one of the wealthiest subjects in the state. By the end of the century an owner of five hundred serfs was considered moderately well-to-do.

The expansion of the economic resources of the nobility was matched by a rise in legal status and political power. This was the period sarcastically dubbed "the emancipation of the nobility," a phrase that captures not only the irony of the growing gap between rich and poor but also the contrast between the social structures of Russia and those of western Europe. In return for their privileges and status, Peter the Great extended the duties the land-owning classes owed to the state. By granting unique rights, like the ownership of serfs, to the descendants of the old military service class, Peter the Great had forged a Russian nobility. Lifetime service, however, was the price of nobility. Women were the true estate managers in Russia, since their husbands were constantly occupied in military or administrative service.

In order to gain and hold the throne, each succeeding tsar had to make concessions to the nobility. At first it was a few simple adjustments. The sons of wealthy landowners who completed a course of education at one of the state academies were allowed to enter the Table of Ranks in the middle of the hierarchy rather than at the bottom. Then life service was commuted to a term of twenty-five years, still a long time in a world of short lives and sudden deaths. But these concessions were not enough. Twenty-five years of service did not solve the problem of estate management, especially as the tasks of management grew along with the population of serfs. Thus the next capitulation was that a single son could remain on the estate and escape service altogether. This decree opened the door more than a crack. The births of younger sons were concealed; owners of multiple estates claimed the exemption of one son for each. Most decisively, the talented remained at home to serve the family while the wastrels were sent to serve the state. Finally in 1762, the obligation for state service by the nobility was abolished entirely. If nothing else, Russia had westernized its aristocracy.

The abolition of compulsory service was not the same as the abolition of service itself. In fact the end of compulsory service enabled Catherine II, the Great (1762–96), to enact some of the most important reforms of her reign. At first, Catherine's accession seemed nothing more than a continuation of monarchical instability. She came to the throne as a result of a coup against her husband, the feeble-minded Peter III (1762), and her first two acts were to have him murdered and to lower the salt tax. Each bought her a measure of security. Catherine was a dynamic personality who alternately captivated and terrified those with whom she came into contact. A British visitor to her court reported that her gaze was like that of "a small wild animal, so piercing and full of desire that it was difficult to endure." Her policies were as complex as her personality, influenced alike by the new French ideas of social justice and the nobility of the human race and the traditional Russian ones of absolute rule over an enserfed and subhuman population. As she observed to the French writer Denis Diderot (1713–84): "You philosophers are lucky men. You write on paper and paper is patient. Unfortunate Empress that I am, I write on the susceptible skins of living beings." Catherine handled these contrasting dimensions of her rule masterfully, which gained her abroad the reputation as the most enlightened of all European monarchs and at home the sincere love and devotion of her people. Thus it was said, "Peter created Russia's body, but Catherine endowed it with a soul." (See Special Feature, "Catherine Before She Was Great," pp. 560–561.)

The most important event in the early years of Catherine's reign was the establishment of a legislative commission to review the laws of Russia. Catherine herself wrote the *Instruction* (1767) by which the elected commissioners were to operate. She borrowed her theory of law from the French jurist Baron de Montesquieu (1689–1755) and her theory of punishment from the Italian reformer Cesare Beccaria (1738–94). Among other things, Catherine advocated the abolition of capital punishment, torture, serf auctions, and the breakup of serf families by sale. Few of these radical reforms were ever put into practice. But one of the most important aspects of the legislative commission was that it drew upon the service of elected noblemen, who came to Saint Petersburg with lists of local grievances. Catherine and her advisers were able to learn firsthand about the failures of rural administration and to take steps to correct them.

With this knowledge Catherine set about, in 1775, the restructuring of local government. Russia was divided into fifty provincial districts, each with a population of between 300,000 and 400,000 inhabitants. Each district was to be governed by both a central official and elected local noblemen. This reform was modeled upon the English system of justices of the peace. The failure of all previous local reforms had stemmed from the absence of a resident local nobility. The abolition of compulsory service finally made possible the establishment of local institutions. In 1785, Catherine issued the Charter of the Nobility, a formal statement of the rights and privileges of the noble class. The Charter incorporated all the gains the nobility had made since the death of Peter the Great, but it also instituted the requirements for local service that had been the basis of Catherine's reforms. District councils with the right to petition directly to the tsar became the centerpiece of Russian provincial government.

In order to train the local nobility for government service, Catherine introduced educational reforms. Peter had established military schools for the nobility and had staffed them with foreigners. The University of Moscow had been founded in 1755, and its faculty too was dominated by European emigrants. Catherine saw the need to broaden the educational system. Borrowing from the Austrian system, she established provincial elementary schools to train the sons and daughters of the local nobility. To staff these, Catherine created teachers' colleges so that the state would have its own educators. Hostility to formal education on the part of the nobility slowed the pace of these reforms. Though the program called for the equal education of women, except in Saint Petersburg and Moscow few women attended either elementary or high schools. Some provincial schools found students only by resorting to the tactics of factory owners—that is, by forced enrollment.

Catherine's reforms did little to enhance the lives of the vast majority of her people. Though she often spoke in the terms of the French philosophers who saw the enserfment of fellow humans as a blot on civilization, Catherine effectively took no action either to end serfdom or to soften its rigors. In fact, by grants of state land Catherine gave away 800,000 state peasants, who were immediately turned into serfs. So, too, were the millions of Poles who became her subjects after the partition of Poland in 1793 and 1795. The epitaph that she wrote for herself, "when she ascended the throne of Russia she wished to do good, and tried to bring happiness, freedom and prosperity to her subjects," bore little relation to the experience of the Russian peasants.

Indeed, the most significant uprising of the century, Pugachev's revolt (1773–75), took place during her reign. Emelyan Pugachev (1726–75) was a Cossack who in his youth had been a military adventurer. Disappointed in his career, he made his way to the Ural mountains, where he recruited Asian tribesmen and laborers forced to work in the mines. By promising freedom and land ownership, he drew peasants to his cause. Pugachev declared himself to be Tsar Peter III, the murdered husband of Catherine II. He began with small raiding parties against local landlords and military outposts and soon had gained the allegiance of tens of thousands of peasants. In 1774, with an army of nearly twenty thousand, Pugachev took the city of Kazan and threatened to advance on Moscow. It was another year before state forces could effectively control the rebellion. Finally, Pugachev was betrayed by his own followers and sent to Moscow to be executed. Thousands of the rebels met similar fates. The town in

Catherine Before She Was Great

Catherine the Great wasn't always called the Empress of all the Russias. In fact, she wasn't always called Catherine. Sophie of Anhalt-Zerbst was the daughter of a petty German prince whose estates were too poor to provide for his family. He hired himself out as a military officer to the kings of Prussia and became governor of the dreary Baltic port of Stettin. Here Sophie passed her childhood. The family lived comfortably enough and Sophie was provided with a French governess, Babette Cardel. From Babette she learned not only the language of the French but also their ways. Sophie was no easy child to handle. Her natural curiosity about nearly everything led to some narrow escapes, and she was nearly killed at the age of three when she pulled a cupboard down upon herself. To curiosity was added spirit, and the shouting matches in which she and Babette engaged were long remembered. Indeed, Babette took to bribing young Sophie with sweets, which in the long run did less to soften her temper than to ruin her teeth.

By far the most significant event of Sophie's childhood was the sudden sickness that overtook her at the age of seven. She was seized by coughing, fevers, and fits that incapacitated her for weeks. For a time her life was in danger. It was not unusual for unexplained illness to appear and disappear with bewildering suddenness, and this is what happened to Sophie. One morning she awoke without fever and without the racking cough that had seared through her body. But in its place had come a physical change. Weeks of lying on her side had deformed her physique: "I had assumed the shape of a letter Z. My right shoulder was much higher than the left, the backbone running in a zigzag and the left side falling in," she later recalled. Such a result was as mysterious as the illness that occasioned it. Doctors were sought for advice. None could help until at last a veterinarian who practiced on the limbs of horses and cows was found. He prescribed a useless concoction of medicines but also built a body frame for Sophie which was designed to reshape her deformity. She wore this for four years until she regained her former posture.

Sophie's father was a strict Lutheran who prescribed a regimen for the education of his children that was to be precisely followed. At the age of seven, just after her recovery, Sophie was told that she could no longer play with her toys but must begin to behave as an adult. Tutors were brought to teach her history and geography, and a Lutheran minister was deputed to train her in religion. Sophie took delight in confounding her religion instructor and in general showed the same high spirits as she entered adolescence that she had in childhood.

Though Sophie did not have a close relationship with her mother—in later years they quarreled incessantly—it was her mother who showed her the world outside Stettin. Joanna of Holstein-Gottorp had grown up surrounded by courtly pomp rather than military rigor. Though her family, too, came from the ranks of the minor princes of the Holy Roman Empire, marriages and inclination had brought them into the circle of German aristocratic life. This was a world for which Joanna longed, and every year she visited her relations in Brunswick. Sophie began to accompany her mother on these trips, and they became for her the principal means to escape the boredom of life in Stettin. On one visit to Berlin she was introduced to Frederick William I, king of Prussia. Her relatives included a future king of Sweden and a future queen of Britain. These trips to Brunswick and Berlin opened Sophie's eyes to the possibility of a life different than the one she had expected, the possibility of life with one of the crown princes of Europe.

As it happened, Sophie had little need to wish. By a strange twist of fate, another of her mother's innumerable cousins had recently been declared heir to the throne of Russia. This was Peter, soon to be duke of Holstein-Gottorp and ultimately to be Peter III of Russia. Empress Elizabeth of Russia was childless and Peter was her nearest relative. She determined to have him married to an eligible German princess, and after much casting about, the choice fell on Sophie. In 1744 Sophie was summoned to Russia. Joanna was thrilled with

the prospect, not only because of the possibility of a successful marriage for her daughter, but also because she was to have a role in the affair. Princely marriages were matters of international diplomacy. In the case of Russia, Frederick the Great of Prussia took more than a neighborly interest. It was he who pushed the claims of a daughter of one of his own military dependents and it was he who enlisted Joanna to become an agent of Prussia at the Russian court. No one asked Sophie what she thought, since her opinion hardly mattered.

The journey to Russia was a trip that Sophie would never forget. Though Stettin was no tropical paradise, the climate there had little prepared Sophie and her mother for the rigors of the east. Carriages gave way to sleighs, and her heavy cloth clothing to sable. Sophie and Joanna huddled together for warmth, covering their faces and hands from the bitter arctic winds. It took nearly four weeks to reach Saint Petersburg, and when they arrived they were informed that they must hurry to join the royal court at Moscow. There they were received with unusual warmth as it was the sixteenth birthday of the new heir to the throne and all of Russian society was eager to see his bride-to-be.

Sophie's earliest meetings with her fiancé were not entirely satisfactory. In a strange land she might have expected strange customs, but Peter was a German like herself. Thus she was unprepared for their first interview, in which Peter professed his passionate love for one of the ladies of the court. Sophie was only fifteen and, by her own account at least, innocent in sexual matters. Peter's frank confession, which was accompanied by assurances that he would marry Sophie anyhow, caused her as much confusion as it did anger and resentment. She resolved to keep her own counsel and to attempt to please the empress if not the heir. Sophie spent the days before her marriage learning both the Russian language and the Eastern Orthodox religion. She would have to convert to the old faith before she could be betrothed. As part of her conversion, she had to take a Russian name and thus she came to be called Catherine. Whether her change of religion was sincere or not, it was required. Sophie was shrewd enough to realize the importance of the Church, and she won many admirers at court when, after being taken suddenly ill, she asked for an Orthodox priest rather than a Lutheran minister or a doctor.

Sophie's marriage took place in 1745 in one of the most magnificent ceremonies anyone could recall. By then she knew that she was alone in the world. She had fought bitterly with her mother, who had became a political liability after she bungled her role as an agent for Frederick the Great. Sophie shared nothing with her new husband—including the marriage bed. The household set up for her was composed entirely of spies for the empress and even her correspondence was monitored. She spent the next fifteen years supplementing the education that she had received as a child. She read everything that she could get hold of. Her Russian improved dramatically as she read Russian and French or German versions of the same works. She devoured the classics, especially history and philosophy, and for the first time became acquainted with the works of the new European writers whose reputations had reached as far as Russia. Sophie indulged her enthusiasm for riding, an exercise not usually taken by women. She also developed a passion for the handsome guardsmen who inhabited the palace. Perhaps in revenge for her husband's conduct, perhaps in return for his neglect, she took the first of more than twenty lovers. When she became pregnant in 1754, it was almost certainly not Peter's child. Eight years later the private life of Sophie of Anhalt-Zerbst ended. Then Empress Elizabeth died, the half-mad Peter III acceded to the throne, and Sophie, now known to the world as Catherine, began her remarkable public career.

which the rebellion began was razed to the ground and the name of the river that adjoined it was changed. No official memory of the man or the event was to be preserved, and upon pain of death, no one was to utter the name Pugachev.

The Two Germanies

The Thirty Years' War initiated a profound transformation of the Holy Roman Empire. Warfare had devastated imperial territory. It was decades before the rich imperial lands recovered and then the political consequences of the war had taken effect. There were now two empires, a German and an Austrian, though both were ruled by the same person. In the German territories, whether Catholic or Protestant, the Holy Roman Emperor was more of a constitutional than an absolute ruler. The larger states like Saxony, Bavaria, and Hanover made their own political alliances despite the jurisdictional control that the emperor claimed to exercise. Most decisively, so did Brandenburg-Prussia. By the beginning of the eighteenth century, the electors of Brandenburg had become the kings of Prussia and Prussia's military power and efficient administrative structure became the envy of its German neighbors. Prussia was becoming a player in the European balance-of-power game and a potential leader of the other German states.

The Austrian empire was composed of Austria and Bohemia, the Habsburg hereditary lands, and as much of Hungary as could be controlled. In Austria, the Habsburgs clung tightly to their power. Victories over the Turks had expanded their control in Hungary. For decades Austria was the center of the still-flourishing Counter-Reformation, and the power and influence of the Jesuits was as strong here as it was in Spain. The War of the Spanish Succession, which gave the Habsburgs control of the southern Netherlands and parts of Italy, brought Austria an enhanced role in European affairs. Austria remained one of the great powers of Europe and the leading power in the Holy Roman Empire despite the rise of Prussia. Indeed from the middle of the eighteenth century the conflict between Prussia and Austria was the defining characteristic of central European politics.

Frederick the Great painted this picture of himself surrounded by servants and members of his beloved Potsdam Grenadiers, a regiment of very tall soldiers. Frederick is third from right.

The Prussian Miracle

The transformation of Brandenburg-Prussia from a petty German principality to a great European power was one of the least expected developments of the eighteenth century. Like many other German states, Brandenburg-Prussia was important to the great European powers as a recruiting ground for their wars. Frederick William, the Great Elector (1640–88), had begun the process of forging Brandenburg-Prussia into a power in its own right by building a large and efficient military machine. At the beginning of the eighteenth century Prussia was on the winning side in both the War of the Spanish Succession and the Great Northern War. When the battlefield dust had cleared, Prussia found itself in possession of Pomerania and the Baltic port of Stettin. It was now a recognized power in eastern Europe.

Frederick William I (1713–40) and his son Frederick II, the Great (1740–86), turned this promising beginning into an astounding success. Frederick William I was a stern, humorless ruler who implanted his personality upon his policies. A devout Calvinist, Frederick William I deplored waste and display as much on moral as on fiscal grounds. The reforms he initiated were intended to subordinate both aristocracy and peasantry to the needs of the state and to subordinate the needs of the state to the demands of the military.

Because of its geographical position, Prussia's major problem was to maintain an efficient and well-trained army during peacetime. Defense of its exposed territories required a constant state of military preparedness, yet the relaxation of military discipline and the desertion of troops to their homes inevitably followed the cessation of hostilities. Frederick William I solved this problem by integrating the economic and military structures of his state. First he appointed only German officers to command his troops, eliminating the mercenaries who sold their services to the highest bidders. Then he placed these noblemen at the head of locally recruited regiments. Each adult male in every district was required to register for military service in the regiment of the local landlord.

These reforms dramatically increased the effectiveness of the army by shifting the burden of recruitment and training to the localities. But the system also had a serious drawback. It threatened

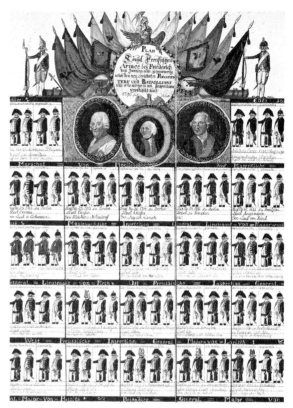

Prussian infantry officers display their uniforms in this painting from the late eighteenth century. Distinctive colorful and elaborate uniforms, different for each regiment, were common in European armies before the field-gray and khaki era of the twentieth century.

to impoverish the nobles by forcing them to take their own laborers off the land for military service. Frederick William I overcame this problem by instituting the seasonal call-up. Except in times of actual warfare, troops were called up and trained for specific periods of time and then returned to their agricultural pursuits. Thus the soldiers had the benefit of cumulative training, the nobles the benefit of their agricultural workers, and the state the benefit of both a standing army and a reserve force.

Yet despite all the attention that Frederick William I lavished on the military—by the end of his reign nearly 70 percent of state expenditures went to the army—his foreign policy was largely pacific. In fact, his greatest achievements were in civil affairs, reforming the bureaucracy, establishing a sound economy, and raising state revenues. Through generous settlement schemes and by welcoming Protestant and Jewish refugees,

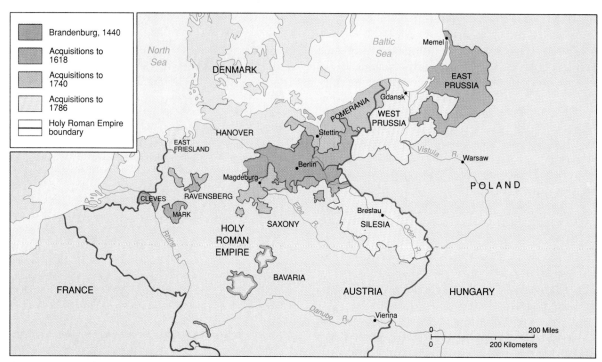

The Expansion of Prussia

Frederick William was able to expand the economic potential of these eastern territories. Unlike most other European monarchs, the king of Prussia was able to live from the rents of his own estates. Frederick William I pursued an aggressive policy of land purchase to expand the royal domain, and the addition of so many new inhabitants in Prussia further increased his wealth. While the major western European powers were discovering deficit financing and the national debt, Prussia was actually running a surplus.

Financial security was vital to the success of Frederick II, the Great (1740–86). Father and son had quarreled bitterly throughout Frederick's youth. Frederick William I treated his son as if he were a peasant on an estate rather than successor to the throne, and most observers expected that out of spite Frederick would tear down all that his father had built up. In fact father and son were cast in the same mold, with the unexpected difference that the son was the more ruthless and ambitious. With his throne, Frederick II inherited the fourth largest army in Europe and the richest treasury. He wasted no time in putting both to

use. His two objectives were to acquire the Polish corridor of West Prussia that separated his German and Prussian territories and the agriculturally and industrially rich Austrian province of Silesia to the southeast of Berlin. Just months after his coronation, Frederick invaded Silesia and by brilliant generalship, unflinching determination, and more than a little bit of luck, conquered it. The conquest of Silesia increased the size of Prussia by nearly a quarter and gave it an advanced capacity for mining and small industry. Within a decade the province dominated the Prussian economy, outproducing and outconsuming all other areas of Frederick's state.

It was Frederick's military prowess that earned him the title "the Great." But this was only a part of his achievement. More than his father, Frederick II forged an alliance with the Prussian nobility, integrating them into a unified state. A tightly organized central administration, which depended upon the cooperation of the local nobility, directed both military and bureaucratic affairs. At the center, Frederick worked tirelessly to oversee his government. Where Louis XIV had proclaimed, "I am the state," Frederick the Great announced "I am the first servant of the state." He put in place a superstructure for the training of future leaders of the state and for bettering the material lives of his subjects. He codified the laws of Prussia, abolished torture and capital punishment, and instituted agricultural techniques imported from the states of western Europe. By the end of Frederick's reign, Prussia had become a model for bureaucratic organization, military reform, and enlightened rule. Its place among the great powers was sure.

Austria Survives

Austria was the great territorial victor in the War of the Spanish Succession, acquiring both the Netherlands and parts of Italy. Austrian forces recaptured a large part of Hungary from the Turks, thereby expanding their territory to the south and the east. Hereditary ruler of Austria, Bohemia, King of Hungary, and Holy Roman Emperor of the German nation, Charles VI (1711–40) was recognized as one of Europe's most potent rulers. But appearances were deceptive. The apex of Austrian power and prestige had already passed. Austria had benefited from balance-of-power politics not so much from its own strength as from the leverage it could give to others. With the rise of Russia and Prussia there was now more than one fulcrum to power in eastern Europe.

The difficulties facing Austria ran deep. The Thirty Years' War had made the emperor more an Austrian monarch than an imperial German ruler. On the Austrian hereditary estates, the Catholic Counter-Reformation continued unabated, bringing with it the benefits of Jesuit education, cultural revival, and the religious unity necessary to motivate warfare against the Ottomans. But these benefits came at a price. Perhaps as many as two hundred thousand Protestants fled Austria and Bohemia, many resettling in Prussia and bringing with them their skills and capital. Religious intolerance was out of step with eighteenth-century political considerations, not to mention eighteenth-century ideas about freedom of thought and worship. Nor was uniformity easy to impose. For centuries the vision of empire had dominated Habsburg rule.

This meant that the Austrian monarchy was a multiethnic confederation of lands loosely tied together by loyalty to a single head. The components preserved a high degree of autonomy. As a Tyrolean nobleman wrote: "What does it concern the people of Tyrol what happens in Bohemia? They are flattered that they have a prince-protector who is a great monarch but they do not wish to pay for that honor by the loss of their fundamental laws." Such sentiments went double for Hungary, which elected the Habsburg emperor its king in a separate ceremony. Local autonomy continually restricted the imposition of central policy, and never were the localities more autonomous than in the matter of taxation.

A predominantly rural land, Austria was also predominantly agricultural. Less than 5 percent of the population lived in towns of ten thousand or more, less than 15 percent lived in towns at all. On the land the local aristocracy, whether nobility or gentry, exploited serfs to the maximum. Not only were serfs required to give labor service three days a week (and up to six during planting and harvest times), but the nobility maintained a full array of feudal privileges including the right to mill all grain and brew all beer. When they married, when they transferred property, even when they died, serfs paid taxes to their lord. As a result they had little left to give the state. In consequence, the Austrian army was among the smallest and the poorest of the major powers despite the fact that it had the most active enemies along its borders.

Lack of finance, lack of human resources, and lack of governmental control were the underlying problems of Austria, but they were not the most immediate difficulties facing Charles VI. With no sons to succeed him, Charles feared that his hereditary and elective states would go their separate ways after his death and that the great Habsburg monarchy would end. For twenty years his abiding ambition was to gain recognition for the principle that his empire would pass intact to his daughter, Maria Theresa. He expressed the principle in a document known as the Pragmatic Sanction, which stated that all Habsburg lands would pass intact to the eldest heir, male or female. Charles VI made concession after concession to gain acceptance of the Pragmatic Sanction, first from the semi-autonomous peoples of his own empire and then from the leaders of the other European powers. At every turn Austria demonstrated its inherent weakness, losing territory in Italy and Hungary during a series of bungled wars and failing to maintain a strong standing army in times of peace. Despite the Pragmatic Sanction, the leaders of Europe licked their lips at the prospect of a dismembered Austrian empire.

Maria Theresa (1740–80) quickly discovered what it was like to be a pregnant woman in a man's world. In 1740 Frederick of Prussia invaded the rich Austrian province of Silesia and attracted allies for an assault upon Vienna. Faced with Bavarian, Saxon, and Prussian armies, Maria Theresa might well have lost her inheritance had she not shown her remarkable capacities so early in her reign. She appeared before the Hungarian estates, accepted their crown, and persuaded them to provide her with an army capable of halting the allied advance. Though she was unable to reconquer Silesia, Hungarian aid helped her hold the line against her enemies, and five years of nearly continuous fighting demonstrated that Maria Theresa was every bit a Habsburg ruler.

The loss of Silesia, the most prosperous part of the Austrian domains, signaled the need for fundamental reform. The new eighteenth-century idea of building a state replaced the traditional Habsburg concern with maintaining an empire. Maria Theresa and her son Joseph II (1780–90) began the process of transformation. For Austria, state-building meant first the reorganization of the military and civil bureaucracy to clear the way for fiscal reform. As in Prussia, a central directory was created to oversee the collection of taxes and the disbursement of funds. This control was especially important in Austria, where local authorities traditionally withheld a significant portion of tax revenues for their own use. Maria Theresa personally persuaded her provincial estates both to increase taxation and to extend it to the nobles and the clergy. While her success was limited, she finally established royal control over the raising and collection of taxes. This concession was to be the basis of thoroughgoing reform in the reign of Joseph II.

The second element in Maria Theresa's reform program involved the condition of the

Maria Theresa and her family. Eleven of Maria Theresa's sixteen children are posed with the empress and her husband, Francis of Lorraine. Standing next to his mother is the future emperor Joseph II.

Austrian peasantry. Maria Theresa established the doctrine that the "peasant must be able to support himself and his family and pay his taxes in time of peace and war." She limited labor service to two days per week and abolished the most burdensome feudal dues. Joseph II ended serfdom altogether. The new Austrian law codes guaranteed peasants' legal rights and established their ability to seek redress through the law. Joseph II hoped to extend reform even further. In the last years of his life he abolished obligatory labor service and ensured that all peasants kept one-half of their income before paying local and state taxes. Such a radical reform met a storm of opposition and was ultimately abandoned at the end of the reign.

The reorganization of the bureaucracy, the increase in taxation, and the social reforms that created a more productive peasantry revitalized the Austrian state. The most ambitious plans for reorganizing the peasantry had to be abandoned, but much good came out of the reforms that were enacted, both for the peasants and for the state. The efforts of Maria Theresa and Joseph II to overcome provincial autonomy worked better in Austria and Bohemia than in Hungary. The Hungarians declined to contribute at all to state revenues, and Joseph II took the unusual step of refusing to be crowned king of Hungary so that he would not have to make any concessions to Hungarian autonomy. He even imposed a tariff on Hungarian goods sold in Austria. More seriously, parts of the empire already had been lost before the process of reform could begin. Prussia's seizure of Silesia was the hardest blow of all. Yet in 1740 when Frederick the Great and his allies swept down from the north few would have predicted that Austria would survive.

The Politics of Power

Frederick the Great's invasion of Silesia in 1740 was callous and cynical. Since the Pragmatic Sanction bound him to recognize Maria Theresa's succession, Frederick cynically offered her a defensive alliance in return for which she would simply hand over Silesia. It was an offer she should not have refused. Though Frederick's action initiated the War of the Austrian Succession, he was not alone in his desire to shake loose parts of Austria's territory. Soon nearly the entire continent became embroiled in the conflict.

The War of the Austrian Succession (1740–48) resembled nothing so much as a pack of wolves stalking its injured prey. Spain joined the fighting to recover its Italian possessions, Saxony claimed Moravia, France entered Bohemia, and the Bavarians moved into Austria from the south. With France and Prussia allied, it was vital that Britain join with Austria to maintain the balance of power. Initially the British did little more than subsidize Maria Theresa's forces, but once France renewed its efforts to conquer the Netherlands, both Britain and the Dutch Republic joined in the fray. That the British cared little about the fate of the Habsburg empire was clear from the terms of the treaty that they dictated at Aachen (Aix-la-Chapelle) in 1748. Austria was to recognize Frederick's conquest of Silesia, as well as the loss of parts of its Italian territories to Spain. France, which the British had always regarded as the real enemy, withdrew from the Netherlands in return for the restoration of a number of colonial possessions. The War of the Austrian Succession made Austria and Prussia permanent enemies and gave Maria Theresa a crash course in international diplomacy.

One of the things that she learned was that it was not always easy to distinguish friend from foe. This lesson was reinforced in 1756 when Britain and Prussia entered into a military accord at the beginning of the Seven Years' War (1756–63). Prussian expansion and duplicity had already alarmed both Russia and France, and Frederick II feared that he would be squeezed from east and west. He could hardly expect help from Maria Theresa, so he extended overtures to Britain, whose interests in protecting Hanover, the hereditary estates of their German-born king, outweighed their prior commitments to Austria. Frederick's actions drove France into the arms of both the Austrians and the Russians, and an alliance which included the German state of Saxony was formed in defense. Thus was initiated a diplomatic revolution in which France and Austria became allies after three hundred years as enemies.

Once again, Frederick the Great took the offensive and once again, he won his risk against the odds. His attack on Saxony and Austria in 1756 brought a vigorous response from the Russians, who interceded on Austria's behalf with a massive army. Three years later, at the battle of Kunersdorf, Frederick suffered the worst military defeat of his career when the Russians shattered his armies. "Of an army of 48,000 I have, as I write, less than 3,000 men left. This is a terrible mishap and I shall not survive it," he wrote after the battle. In 1760 his forces were barely a third of the size of those massed by his opponents, and it was only a matter of time before he was fighting defensively from within Prussia.

In 1762 Tsarina Elizabeth died. Her successor was the childlike Peter III, a German by birth who worshiped Frederick the Great. He had spent most of his youth marching soldiers back and forth in emulation of Frederick's innovative military maneuvers, much to the disgust of his wife, Catherine. When Peter came to the throne, he immediately negotiated peace with Frederick, abandoning not only his allies but also the substantial territorial gains that the Russian forces had made within Prussia. It was small wonder that the Russian military leadership joined in the coup d'état that brought Peter's wife, Catherine, to the throne in 1762. With Russia out of the war, Frederick was able to fend off further Austrian offensives and to emerge with his state, including Silesia, intact.

The Seven Years' War did little to change the boundaries of the German states, but it had two important political results. The first was to establish beyond doubt the status of Prussia as a major power and a counterbalance to Austria in central Europe. The existence of the dual Germanies, one led by Prussia and the other by Austria, was to have serious consequences for German unification in the nineteenth century and for the two world wars in the twentieth. The second result of the Seven Years' War was to initiate a long period of peace in eastern Europe. Both Prussia and Austria found themselves financially exhausted from two decades of fighting. Both states needed a breathing spell to initiate administrative and economic improvements, and the period following the Seven Years' War witnessed the sustained programs of internal reforms for which Frederick the Great, Maria Theresa, and Joseph II were famous.

This engraving by Le Mire is called The Cake of the Kings: First Partition of Poland, 1773. *The monarchs of Russia, Austria, and Prussia join in carving up Poland. The Polish king is clutching his tottering crown.*

Peace among the eastern European powers did not mean that they abandoned their territorial ambitions. Throughout the course of the eighteenth century one state had always swum against the tide. All over Europe absolute rulers reformed their bureaucracies, streamlined their administrations, increased their sources of revenues, and built enormous standing armies. All over Europe except in Poland. There the autonomous power of the nobility remained as strong as ever. No monarchical dynasty was ever established and each elected ruler not only confirmed the privileges of the nobility but usually was forced to extend them. In the Diet, the Polish representative assembly, small special-interest groups could bring legislative business to a halt by exercising their veto power, and rarely did the interests of one part of this vast kingdom coincide with the interests of the others. Given the size of Poland's borders its army was pathetically inadequate for the task it had to face. During the Seven Years' War Poland was used as a staging ground for Russian assaults on Prussia and for Prussian attacks on Austria. The Polish monarchy was helpless to defend its subjects from the destruction on all sides.

In 1764 Catherine the Great and Frederick the Great combined to place one of Catherine's former lovers on the Polish throne and to turn Poland into a weak dependent. Russia and Prussia had different interests in Poland's fate. For Russia, Poland represented a vast buffer state that kept the German powers at a distance from Russia's borders. It was more in Russia's interest to dominate Polish foreign policy than to conquer its territory. For Prussia, Poland looked like another helpless flower, "to be picked off leaf by leaf," as Frederick observed. Poland seemed especially appealing because Polish territory, including the Baltic port of Gdansk, separated the Prussian and Brandenburg portions of Frederick's state.

By the 1770s the idea of carving up Poland was being actively discussed in Berlin, Saint Petersburg, and Vienna. Austria, too, had an interest in a Polish partition, especially to maintain its power and status with the other two states, and perhaps to use Polish territory as a potential bargaining chip for the return of Silesia. None of the powers considered for a moment the interest of the Poles or their ability to resist. In fact, while their fate was being sealed abroad, the Poles were engaged in a series of destructive civil wars at home, wars actively encouraged by Catherine and Frederick. Finally, in 1772, the three great eastern powers struck a deal. Russia would take a large swath of the grain fields of northeast Poland, which included over one million people, while Frederick would unite his lands by seizing West Prussia. Austria gained both the largest territories, including Galicia, and the greatest number of people, nearly two million Polish subjects. Though Austrian ministers had been in on the plans from the beginning, it proved more difficult to convince Maria Theresa of the morality of the deal. After all, she knew what it was like to have her state dismembered and to be unable to do anything about it. How could she help but feel compassion for the Poles? As it was said, "she wept and wept and took and took."

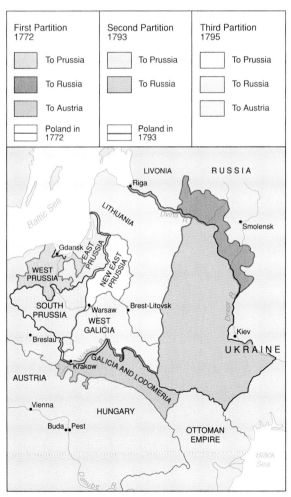

The Partition of Poland

The Greatness of Britain

By the middle of the eighteenth century, Great Britain had become the leading power of Europe. It had won its spurs in Continental and colonial wars. Britain was unsurpassed as a naval power, able to protect its far-flung trading empire and to make a show of force in almost any part of the world. Perhaps more impressively for a nation that did not support a large standing army, British soldiers had won decisive victories in the European land wars. British interests comprised one of the scales in the European balance of power and it was the one that was always favorably tipped. Until the American Revolution, Britain came up a winner in every military venture it undertook. But might was only one part of British success. Economic preeminence was every bit as important. British colonial possessions in the Atlantic and Indian oceans poured consumer products into Britain for export to the European marketplaces. Growth in overseas trade was matched by growth in home production. British advances in agricultural technique had transformed Britain from an importer to an exporter of grain. The manufacturing industries that other European states attempted to create with huge government subsidies flourished in Britain through private enterprise.

British military and economic power was supported by a unique system of government. In Britain the nobility served the state through government. The British constitutional system, devised in the seventeenth century and refined in the eighteenth, shared power between the monarchy and the ruling elite through the institution of Parliament. Central government integrated monarch and ministers with chosen representatives from the localities. Such integration not only provided the crown with the vital information necessary to formulate national policy, but it eased acceptance and enforcement of government decisions. Government was seen as the rule of law which, however imperfect, was believed to operate for the benefit of all.

The parliamentary system gave Britain some of its particular strengths, but they came at a cost. Politics was a national pastime rather than the business of an elite of administrators and state servants. Decentralization of decision making led to half-measures designed to placate competing interests. Appeals to public opinion, especially by candidates for Parliament, often played upon fears and prejudices that divided rather than united the nation. Moreover, the relative openness of the British system hindered diplomatic and colonial affairs, in which secrecy and rapid changes of direction were often the monarch's most potent weapons. These weaknesses came to light most dramatically during the struggle for independence waged by Britain's North American colonists. There the clash of principle and power was most extreme and the strengths and weaknesses of parliamentary rule were ruthlessly exposed.

The British Constitution

The British Constitution was a patchwork of laws and customs that was only gradually sewn together to form a workable system of government. Many of its greatest innovations came about through circumstance rather than design, and circumstance continued to play an essential role in its development in the eighteenth century. At the apex of the government stood the king, not an absolute monarch like his European counterparts, but not necessarily less powerful for having less arbitrary power. The British people revered monarchy and the monarch. The theory of mixed government depended upon the balance of interests represented by the monarchy in the crown, the aristocracy in the House of Lords, and the people in the House of Commons, "the most beautiful combination ever framed," as George III (1760–1820) declared. Less abstractly, the monarch was still regarded as divinely ordained and a special gift to the nation. The monarch was the actual and symbolic leader of the nation as well as the "Supreme Head" of the Church of England. Allegiance to the Anglican church, whether as a political creed among the elite or as a simple matter of devotion among the populace, intensified allegiance to the king.

The political power of the British monarch was limited by law. A series of statutes enacted after the Revolution of 1688 clearly defined the king's prerogatives and the subject's rights. The king could no longer suspend or dispense with the laws of the land, nor could he dismiss royal judges

at his pleasure. The Act of Succession (1701) established that only Protestants could wear the crown, thus bypassing the Catholic heirs of James II in favor of the princes of Hanover. More important than these general constraints were those designed to bring the crown into partnership with Parliament. No army could be raised without the consent of Parliament, just as no tax could be established or collected. At first, it was legislated that a new Parliament had to be called every three years, but the Septennial Act (1716) extended the period to seven. In reality, Parliament sat in continuous session, since most of the vital bills to fund the government and the military were passed for one year only.

The partnership between crown and representative body was best expressed in the idea that the British government was composed of King-in-Parliament. Parliament consisted of three separate organs: monarch, lords, and commons. Though each existed separately as a check upon the potential excesses of the others, it was only when the three functioned together that parliamentary government could operate. The king was charged with selecting ministers, initiating policy, and supervising administration. The two Houses of Parliament were charged with raising revenue, making laws, and presenting the grievances of subjects to the crown. Obviously there was much overlap between these responsibilities. The king could hardly initiate foreign or domestic policy without the necessary revenues, which only Parliament could grant him. Parliament's presentation of grievances was hardly practicable without the willingness of the king to redress them.

There were 558 members of the House of Commons after the union with Scotland in 1707. Most members of the lower House were nominated to their seats. The largest number of seats were located in small towns where a local oligarchy, or neighboring patron, had a customary right to make nominations that were invariably accepted by the electorate. Even in the largest cities influential citizens made arrangements for nominating members in order to avoid the cost and confusion of an actual election. Contests in which competing candidates appealed to the electorate, either on personal or political grounds, were the exception rather than the rule. Campaigns were ruinously expensive for the candidates—an election in 1754 cost the losing candidates £40,000—and potentially dangerous to the local community, where bitter social and political divisions boiled just below the surface.

The British gentry dominated the Commons, occupying over 80 percent of the seats in any session. Most of these members also served as unpaid local officials in the counties, as justices of the peace, captains of the local militias, or collectors of local taxes. They came to Parliament not only as representatives of the interests of their class, but as experienced local governors who understood the needs of both crown and subject. Most had direct connections with those who sat in the House of Lords, many through ties of blood, all through ties of service. The peerage and the gentry together formed the class that in most other European societies was labeled the nobility. Their division into the two houses of Parliament obscured similarities in background, outlook, and interest. Dozens of members of the House of Commons were the sons of members of the House of Lords. Such ties enabled the two houses of Parliament to work together in enacting legislation.

Nevertheless, the crown had to develop methods to coordinate the work of the two houses of Parliament and facilitate the passage of governmental programs. The king and his ministers began to use the deep royal pockets of offices and favors to bolster their friends in Parliament. Not only were those employed by the crown encouraged to find a place in the House of Commons, but those who had a place in Parliament were encouraged to take employment from the crown. Parliamentary patrons were eagerly solicited to nominate the king's servants, and many mutually beneficial arrangements resulted. Despite its potential for abuse, this was a political process that integrated center and locality, and at first it worked rather well. Those with local standing were brought into central offices. There they could influence central policymaking while protecting their local constituents. These officeholders, who came to be called *placemen*, never constituted a majority of the members of Parliament. They formed the core around which eighteenth-century governments operated but it was a core that needed direction and cohesion. It was such leadership and organization that was the essential contribution of eighteenth-century politics to the British Constitution.

Parties and Ministers

Though parliamentary management was vital to the crown, it was not the crown that developed the basic tools of management. Rather these techniques originated within the political community itself and their usefulness was only slowly grasped by the monarchy. The first and, in the long term, most important tool was the party system. Political parties initially developed in the late seventeenth century around the issue of the Protestant succession. Those who opposed James II because he was a Catholic attempted to exclude him from inheriting the crown. They came to be called by their opponents Whigs, which meant Scottish horse thieves. Those who supported James' hereditary rights but who also supported the Anglican church came to be called by their opponents Tories, which meant Irish cattle rustlers. The Tories cooperated in the Revolution of 1688 that placed William and Mary on the throne because James had threatened the Anglican church by tolerating Catholics and because Mary had a legitimate hereditary right to be queen. After the death of Queen Anne in 1714, the Tories supported the succession of James III, James II's Catholic son who had been raised in France, rather than of George I (1714–27), prince of Hanover and Protestant great-grandson of James I. An unsuccessful rebellion to place James III on the throne in 1715 discredited the leadership of the Tory party, but did not weaken its importance in both local and parliamentary politics.

The Whigs supported the Protestant succession and a broad-based Protestantism. They attracted the allegiance of large numbers of dissenters, those—heirs to the Puritans of the seventeenth century—who practiced forms of Protestantism different from the Anglican church. The Whigs' greatest strengths were in urban areas and among merchants, craftsmen, and shopkeepers. The Tories supported the Anglican church and the hereditary Stuart monarchy. They found their allies in the countryside and small villages, and among the landed elite. The struggle between Whigs and Tories was less a struggle for power than it was for loyalty to their opposing viewpoints. As the Tories opposed the Hanoverian succession and the Whigs supported it, it was no mystery which party would find favor with George I. Moreover, as long as there was a pretender to the British throne—another rebellion took place in Scotland in 1745 led by the grandson of James II—the Tories continued to be tarred with the brush of disloyalty.

The division of political sympathies between Whigs and Tories helped create a set of groupings to which parliamentary leadership could be applied. A national, rather than a local or regional outlook, could be used to organize support for royal policy as long as royal policy conformed to that national outlook. The ascendancy of the Whigs enabled George I and his son George II (1727–60) effectively to govern through Parliament, but at the price of dependence upon the Whig leaders. Though the monarch had the constitutional freedom to choose his ministers, realistically he could choose only Whigs, and practically none but the Whig leaders of the House of Commons. Happily for the first two Georges they found a man who was able to manage Parliament but desired only to serve the crown.

Sir Robert Walpole (1676–1745) came from a long-established gentry family in Norfolk. Walpole was an early supporter of the Hanoverian succession and an early victim of party warfare. When the Tories temporarily gained power, Walpole was impeached for financial mismanagement in 1712 and imprisoned for a time in the Tower of London. But once George I was securely on the throne, Walpole became an indispensable leader of the House of Commons. His success rested upon his extraordinary abilities: he was an excellent public speaker; he relished long working days and the details of government; and he understood better than anyone else the intricacies of state finance. Walpole became First Lord of the Treasury, a post that he transformed into first minister of state. From his treasury post, Walpole assiduously built a Whig parliamentary party. He carefully dispensed jobs and offices, using them as bait to lure parliamentary supporters. Walpole's organization paid off both in the passage of legislation desired by the crown and at the polls, where Whigs were returned to Parliament time and again.

From 1721 to 1742 Walpole was the most powerful man in the British government. He refused an offer of a peerage so that he could continue to lead the House of Commons. Walpole's long tenure in office was as much a result of his policies as of his methods of governing. He brought a measure of fiscal responsibility to government by establishing a fund to pay off the national debt. In foreign policy he pursued peace with the same fervor that both his predecessors and successors pursued war. At one point he even went so far as to form an alliance with France to ensure European tranquillity. The long years of peace brought prosperity to both the landed and merchant classes, but they also brought criticism of Walpole's methods. The way in which he used government patronage to build his parliamentary party was attacked as corruption. So too were the ways in which the pockets of Whig officeholders were lined. During his last decade in office Walpole struggled to survive. His attempt to extend the excise tax on colonial goods nearly led to his loss of office in 1733. His refusal to respond to the clamor for continued war with Spain in 1741 finally led to his downfall.

Walpole's twenty-year rule established the pattern of parliamentary government. The crown needed a "prime" minister who was able to steer legislation through the House of Commons. It also needed a patronage broker who could take control of the treasury and dispense its largess in return for parliamentary backing. Walpole's personality and talents had combined these two roles. Hereafter they were divided. Those who had grown up under Walpole had learned their lessons well. The Whig monopoly of power continued unchallenged for nearly another twenty years. The patronage network Walpole had created was vastly extended by his Whig successors. Even minor posts in the customs or the excise offices were now exchanged for political favor, and only those approved by the Whig leadership could claim them. The cries of corruption grew louder: "He admits no person to any considerable post of trust and power under him who is not either a relation, a creature, or a thorough-paced tool." The cries of opposition were taken up not only in the country houses of the long disenfranchised Tories, but in the streets of London, where a popular radicalism developed in opposition to the Whig oligarchy. They were taken up as well in the North American colonies, where two million British subjects champed at the bit of imperial rule.

America Revolts

Britain's triumph in the Seven Years' War (1756–63) had come at great financial cost to the nation. At the beginning of the eighteenth century, the national debt stood at £14 million; in 1763 it had risen to £130 million despite the fact that Walpole's government had been paying off some of it. Then, as now, the cost of world domination was staggering. George III (1760–1820) came to the throne with a desire to break the Whig stranglehold on government and a taste for reform. He was to have limited success on both counts, though not for want of trying. In 1763 the king and his ministers agreed that reform of colonial administration was long overdue. Reform of colonial administration would have the twin benefit of shifting part of the burden of taxation from Britain to North America and of making the commercial side of colonization pay.

This was sound thinking all around, and in due course Parliament passed a series of duties on goods imported into the colonies, including glass, wine, coffee, tea, and most notably sugar. The so-called Sugar Act (1764) was followed by the Stamp Act (1765), a tax on printed papers such as newspapers, deeds, and court documents. Both acts imposed taxes in the colonies similar to those that already existed in Britain. Accompanying the acts were administrative orders designed to cut into the lucrative black market trade. In 1763 it was estimated that the quantity of goods smuggled into the colonies equaled the quantity legally imported. The government instituted new rules for searching ships and transferred authority over smuggling from the local colonial courts to Britain's Admiralty courts. Though British officials could only guess at the value of the new duties imposed, it was believed that with effective enforcement £150,000 would be raised. All this would go to pay the vastly greater costs of colonial administration and security.

British officials were more than perplexed when these mild measures met with a ferocious response. Assemblies of nearly every colony officially protested the Sugar Act. They sent petitions to Parliament begging for repeal and warning of

The British Empire, ca 1763

dire economic and political consequences. Riots followed passage of the Stamp Act. Tax collectors were hounded out of office, their resignations precipitated by threats and acts of physical violence. In Massachusetts mobs that included political leaders in the colony razed the homes of the collector and the lieutenant-governor. However much the colonists might have regretted the violence that was done, they believed that an essential political principle was at stake. It was a principle of the freedom of an Englishman.

At their core, the protests of the American colonists underscored the vitality of the British political system. The Americans argued that they could not be taxed without their consent and that their consent could come only through representation in Parliament. Since there were no colonists in Parliament, Parliament had no jurisdiction over the property of the colonists. Taxation without representation was tyranny. There were a number of subtleties to this argument that were quickly lost as political rhetoric and political action heated up. In the first place, the colonists did tax themselves through their own legislatures and much of that money paid the costs of administration and defense. Secondly, as a number of pamphleteers pointed out, no one in the colonies had asked the British government to send regiments of the army into North America. The colonists had little reason to put their faith in British protection. Hard-fought colonial victories were tossed away at European negotiating tables, while the British policy of defending Indian rights in the Ohio Valley ran counter to the interests of the settlers. When defense was necessary, the colonists had proven themselves both able and cooperative in providing it. A permanent tax meant a permanent army, and a standing army was as loathed in Britain as it was in the colonies.

Colonists also tried to draw a distinction between internal and external taxation in opposing the Stamp Act. They deemed regulation of overseas commerce a legitimate power of Parliament but argued that the regulation of internal exchange was not. But this distinction was lost once the issue of parliamentary representation was raised. If the colonists had not consented to British taxation, then it made no difference whether taxation was internal or external. The

passion generated in the colonies was probably no greater than that generated in Britain. The British government also saw the confrontation as a matter of principle, but for Britain the principle was parliamentary sovereignty. This, above all, was the rock upon which the British Constitution had been built over the last century. Parliament had entered into a partnership with the crown. The crown had surrendered—willingly or not—many of its prerogatives. In return, Parliament had bound the people to obedience. There were

The New European Powers

1707	England and Scotland unite to form Great Britain
1713–14	Peace of Utrecht ends War of the Spanish Succession (1702–14)
1714	British crown passes to House of Hanover
1721	Treaty of Nystad ends Great Northern War (1700–1721)
1721–42	Sir Robert Walpole leads British House of Commons
1722	Peter the Great of Russia creates Table of Ranks
1740	Frederick the Great of Prussia invades Austrian province of Silesia
1748	Treaty of Aix-la-Chapelle ends War of the Austrian Succession (1740–48)
1756–63	Seven Years' War pits Prussia and Britain against Austria, France, and Russia
1773–75	Pugachev's Revolt in Russia
1774	Boston Tea Party
1775	American Revolution begins
1785	Catherine the Great of Russia issues Charter of the Nobility

well-established means by which British subjects could petition Parliament for redress of grievances against the monarch, but there were no channels by which they could question the sovereignty of Parliament.

Once the terms of debate had been so defined, it was difficult for either side to find a middle ground. Parliamentary moderates managed repeal of the Stamp Act and most of the clauses of the Sugar Act, but they also joined in passing the Declaratory Act (1766), which stated unequivocally that Parliament held sovereign jurisdiction over the colonies "in all cases whatsoever." This was a claim that became more and more difficult to sustain as colonial leaders began to cite the elements of resistance theory that had justified the Revolution of 1688. Then the protest had been against the tyranny of the king, now it was against the tyranny of Parliament. American writers borrowed from the rich literature of opposition that had attacked Walpole and the Whig leaders to prove that Parliament was corrupt and no longer acted as representative of the people. Propagandists claimed that a conspiracy existed to deprive the colonists of their property and rights, to enslave them for the benefit of special interests and corrupt politicians. "I love Great Britain and revere the King," wrote one colonial pamphleteer. "But it is my duty to hand down freedom to my posterity compatible with the rights of Englishmen."

The techniques of London radicals who opposed parliamentary policy were imported into the colonies. Newspapers were used to whip up public support; boycotts brought ordinary people into the political arena; public demonstrations like the Boston Tea Party (1774) were carefully designed to intimidate; mobs were occasionally given free rein. Though the government had faced down these tactics when they were used in London to support John Wilkes (1725–97), an ardent critic of royal policy, they were less successful when the crisis lay an ocean away. When, in 1770, British troops fired upon a Boston mob, American propagandists were provided with empirical evidence that Britain intended to enslave the colonies. Violence was met by violence, passion by passion. In 1775 full-scale fighting was under way. Eight years later Britain withdrew

from a war it could not win, and the American colonies were left to govern themselves.

By the end of the third quarter of the eighteenth century, Europe had a new political configuration. A continent once dominated by a single power—Spain in the sixteenth century and France in the seventeenth—was now dominated by a states system in which alliances among several great powers held the balance. Despite the loss of its American colonies, Great Britain had proved the most potent of the states. Its victories over the French in the Seven Years' War and over France and Prussia in the War of the Austrian Succession secured its position. But it was a position that could only be maintained through alliances with the German states, either with Prussia or Austria. The rise of Prussia provided a counterweight to French domination of the Continent. Though these two states found themselves allies in the middle of the century, the ambitions of their rulers made them natural enemies, and it would not be long before French and Prussian armies were again pitted against each other. France, still the wealthiest and most populous of European states, had slumbered through the eighteenth-century reorganization. The legacies of Louis XIV took a long time to reach fruition. He had claimed glory for his state, giving the French people a sense of national identity and national destiny, but making them pay an enormous price in social and economic dislocation. Thus the mid-eighteenth century was to be an age of the greatest literary and philosophical achievement for France, but the late eighteenth century was to be an age of the greatest social upheaval that Europe had ever known.

Suggestions for Further Reading

General Reading

* Olwen Hufton, *Europe: Privilege and Protest 1730–1789* (Ithaca, NY: Cornell University Press, 1980). An excellent survey of the political and social history of the mid-eighteenth century.

* Leonard Krieger, *Kings and Philosophers 1689–1789* (New York: Norton, 1970). A brilliant depiction of the personalities and ideas of eighteenth-century Europe.

* M. S. Anderson, *Europe in the Eighteenth Century 1713–1783* (London: Longman, 1976). A country-by-country survey of political developments.

Nicholas Riasanovsky, *A History of Russia* (New York: Oxford University Press, 1984). The best one-volume history of Russia.

Europe in 1714

* Derek McKay and H. M. Scott, *The Rise of the Great Powers* (London: Longman, 1983). An outstanding survey of diplomacy and warfare.

* H. C. Darby and H. Fullard, eds., *The New Cambridge Modern History*, Vol. 14, *Atlas* (Cambridge: Cambridge University Press, 1970). An invaluable collection of historical maps showing the changing boundaries of Europe over centuries.

The Rise of Russia

* Paul Dukes, *The Making of Russian Absolutism 1613–1801* (London: Longman, 1982). An extensive survey of the Russian monarchy in its greatest period.

* B. H. Sumner, *Peter the Great and the Emergence of Russia* (New York: Collier Books, 1962). A short and readable study; the best introduction.

* M. S. Anderson, *Peter the Great* (London: Thames and Hudson, 1978). A well-constructed, comprehensive biography.

* Jerome Blum, *Lord and Peasant in Russia* (New York: Columbia University Press, 1961). The best work on the social life of Russians.

John T. Alexander, *Catherine the Great: Life and Legend* (Oxford: Oxford University Press, 1989). The most up-to-date and enjoyable of many biographies.

* Dominique Maroger, ed., *The Memoirs of Catherine the Great* (New York: Collier Books, 1961). The empress' own reflections on her life.

The Two Germanies

* H. W. Koch, *A History of Prussia* (London: Longman, 1978). An up-to-date study of the factors that led to Prussian dominance of Germany.

Sidney Fay and Klaus Epstein, *The Rise of Brandenburg-Prussia to 1786* (New York: Holt, Rinehart, and Winston, 1964). The best introductory survey.

* Gerhard Ritter, *Frederick the Great* (Berkeley: University of California Press, 1974). A classic biography; short and readable.

* Walther Hubatsch, *Frederick the Great of Prussia* (London: Thames and Hudson, 1975). A full account of the reign of Prussia's greatest leader.

* Ernst Wangermann, *The Austrian Achievement* (New York: Harcourt Brace Jovanovich, 1973). The most readable study of Austrian politics, culture, and society in the eighteenth century.

* Paul Bernard, *Joseph II* (New York: Twayne, 1968). A reliable guide to the life and times of this reforming Austrian leader.

* T. C. W. Blanning, *Joseph II and Enlightened Despotism* (London: Longman, 1970). Displays the relationship between new ideas, reform policies, and the practical necessities of government.

C. A. Macartney, *Maria Theresa and the House of Austria* (Mystic, CT: Verry Inc., 1969). Still the best introductory study.

The Greatness of Britain

* J. C. D. Clark, *English Society 1688–1832* (Cambridge: Cambridge University Press, 1985). A bold reinterpretation of the most important features of English society.

* J. H. Plumb, *The Origins of Political Stability, England 1675–1725* (Boston: Houghton Mifflin, 1967). A comprehensive account of the contributions of Walpole to the establishment of the British Constitution.

Ragnhild Hatton, *George I Elector and King* (Cambridge, MA: Harvard University Press, 1978). An outstanding biography that shows the German side of a British monarch.

* John Brewer, *Party Ideology and Popular Politics at the Accession of George III* (Cambridge: Cambridge University Press, 1976). Examines the pressures on the political system in the late eighteenth century.

* Ian Christie and Benjamin W. Labaree, *Empire or Independence 1760–1777* (New York: Norton, 1977). Surveys the American troubles from the British point of view.

* Bernard Bailyn, *The Ideological Origins of the American Revolution* (Cambridge, MA: Harvard University Press, 1967). A brilliant interpretation of the underlying causes of the break between Britain and the North American colonies.

* Edward Countryman, *The American Revolution* (New York: Hill & Wang, 1985). A readable, up-to-date narrative of the events of the American Revolution.

* Indicates paperback edition available.

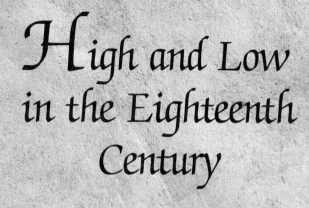

19

High and Low in the Eighteenth Century

Happy Families

"Happy families are all alike," wrote Lev Tolstoy in the nineteenth century when the idea of a happy family was already a cliché. Such an idea would never have occurred to his eighteenth-century forebears. For them the happy family was doubly new—new in the change in relationships within the family, new in the stress on happiness itself. Personal happiness was an invention of the Enlightenment, the result of novel attitudes about human aspirations and human capabilities. "Happiness is a new idea in Europe," wrote Louis de Saint-Just (1767–94). It emerged in response to the belief that what was good brought pleasure and what was evil brought pain. Happiness, both individual and collective, became the yardstick by which life was measured. This meant a reorientation in personal conduct and most of all a reorientation of family life. Especially for those with an economic cushion, a pleasurable family life was essential. Husbands and wives were to become companions, filled with romantic love for each other and devoted to domestic bliss. Children, the product of their affection, were to be doted upon, treated not as miniature adults to be lectured and beaten, but as unfilled vessels into which all that was good was to be poured.

Were ever a couple more in love than the husband and wife depicted in *A Visit to the Wet Nurse* by Jean-Honoré Fragonard (1732–1806)? The man clasps his wife's arm to his cheek, she lays her hand on his shoulder. Their sighs are almost audible! Together they admire the fruit of their love, the baby asleep in the cradle. It is hard to guess which parent dotes more, the mother with her rapturous expression or the father with his intensity. He kneels on a cushion in almost religious devotion, his hands folded as if in prayer. Who can doubt their companionship or their love for their babe? They have come together to see how the wet nurse is caring for their child. Doubtless it was they who provided the rather opulent bassinet, which makes such a contrast with the other furniture in the room, and the linens and pillows into which the baby has nestled.

At the beginning of the eighteenth century, the use of a wet nurse was still common among the families of the French bourgeoisie, the class to which this couple—judging from their clothes—undoubtedly belongs. As time moved on, however, more and more families began to keep their children at home, more and more mothers began to nurse their babies themselves. In part this change was a response to the higher mortality rate among infants sent out to wet nurses. The unsanitary environment of the towns ran a close race with the neglect that many wet nurses showed to their charges. But a wet nurse who could be supervised, that is, one who lived near enough to be visited, but far enough away from the town to enjoy wholesome air, might be the best of both worlds. This is just what the couple here has found, and today they come, with their other child (the boy in the hat), to see their baby sleeping peacefully, the wet nurse sitting attentively at the infant's side.

But there are two families in this picture, and they are hardly alike. At first glance, the wet nurse looks like an old woman, perhaps even an aging nanny. She sits with her distaff in her hand, for the arrival of her clients has interrupted her spinning. It is shocking to realize that she cannot be much older than thirty, an age beyond which wealthy families would not hire her for fear either that she would not have much milk or that it would be sour. The two younger children are undoubtedly hers, the youngest probably just weaned so that all of the milk would go to the baby. No adoring husband sits beside the wet nurse. Her husband, if he is still alive, is hard at work with no leisure time for visits to the country. Not only does the wet nurse have to sell her milk, but she also spins, to keep her family clothed and to earn a little extra to put away for hard times. The newest fads of the age have passed her family by. While the child in the cradle will be spoiled by toys manufactured especially for children— puzzles, games, rocking horses, and balls—the children of the wet nurse must make do with household objects and their own imagination. A ball of yarn thrown to the cat helps the elder child while away the hours. Like much else in the eighteenth century, the world of the family was divided between high and low.

The Nobility

At the apex of European society in the eighteenth century was the nobility. But it was far from a homogeneous group. Noble power and position differed widely from state to state. Perhaps more importantly, even within the same state there was an enormous range of wealth and power among members of the noble order. At the top, the greatest peers were also the richest of the king's subjects. Some of them were wealthy beyond description, like the Esterházy family of Hungary, who owned in excess of 10 million acres of land and controlled 700,000 peasants. But also considered part of the Hungarian nobility was the much larger number called the "sandaled nobility" because of their reputed inability to buy proper shoes. While Prince Miklós Esterházy (1714–90) built himself a palace modeled on Versailles, most of the sandaled nobility lived in houses of clay, roofed with reeds. Though the impoverished nobility were undoubtedly the more numerous of the order, it was the wealthy who set the tone of elite life in Europe.

The eighteenth-century nobility spawned a culture that was as rich as it was costly. Decorative architecture, especially interior design, reflected the increasing sociability of the aristocracy. Entertainment became a central part of aristocratic life, losing its previous formality. In this atmosphere music became one of the passions of noble culture. The string quartet made its first appearance in the eighteenth century and chamber music enjoyed unparalleled popularity. Only the wealthiest could afford to stage private operas, the other musical passion of the age. Again the Esterházys were in the forefront, employing 22 musicians and a conductor, who for most of the late eighteenth century was Joseph Haydn (1732–1809), the "father" of the modern symphony. Haydn's post was not an honorary one. In addition to hiring and managing the orchestra, he was expected to direct two operas and two concerts a week, as well as the music for Sunday services. An aristocratic patron was essential for the aspiring composer. If he could not find one or if, like Wolfgang Amadeus Mozart (1756–91), he could not bend his will to one, he could not flourish. While Haydn lived comfortably in a palace,

The seven-year-old musical prodigy Wolfgang Amadeus Mozart plays the harpsichord while his father Leopold plays the violin and his sister Nannerl sings. The boy won great ovations on concert tours throughout Europe.

Mozart, probably the greatest musical genius in Western history, lived impoverished in a garret and died at age 35 from lack of medical attention.

Musical entertainments in European country houses were matched by the literary and philosophical entertainments of the urban salons. There were to be found the most influential thinkers of the day presenting the ideas of the Enlightenment, a new European outlook on religion, society, and politics. The Enlightenment was not an aristocratic movement; indeed, many Enlightenment ideas were profoundly anti-aristocratic. But it was the nobility who had the leisure to read, write, and discuss, and many of the nobility were actively engaged in the intellectual and social changes that the Enlightenment brought in its wake. Though enlightened thinkers sought the improvement of life for the many, they pitched their appeal to the few. "Taste is thus like philosophy," Voltaire opined. "It belongs to a very small number of privileged souls."

All That Glitters

Eighteenth-century Europe was a society of orders gradually transforming itself into a society of classes. At the top, as vigorous as ever, was the nobility, the privileged order in every European state. Nobles were defined by their legal rights. They had the right to bear arms, the right to special judicial treatment, the right to tax exemptions. In Russia only nobles could own serfs; in Poland only nobles could hold government office. In France and Britain the highest court positions were always reserved for noblemen. Nobles dominated the Prussian army. In 1786 out of nearly 700 senior officers only 22 were not noblemen. The Spanish nobility claimed the right to live idly. Rich or poor, they shunned all labor as a right of their heritage. Swedish and Hungarian noblemen had their own legislative chambers, just as the British had the House of Lords. Noble privilege was as vibrant as ever.

Though all who enjoyed these special rights were noble, not all nobles were equal. In many states the noble order was subdivided into easily identifiable groups. The Spanish *grandees*, the upper nobility, were numbered in the thousands; the Spanish *hidalgos*, the lower nobility, in the hundreds of thousands. In Hungary out of 400,000 noblemen only about 15,000 belonged to the "landed" nobility who held titles and were exempt from taxes. The "landed" nobility were personally members of the upper chamber of the Hungarian Diet, while the lesser nobility sent representatives to the lower chamber. This was not unlike the situation in England where the elite class was divided between the peerage and the gentry. The peerage held titles, were members of the House of Lords, and had a limited range of judicial and fiscal privileges. In the mid-eighteenth century there were only 190 British peers. The gentry, which numbered over 20,000, dominated the House of Commons and local legal offices but were not strictly members of the nobility. The French nobility was informally distinguished among the small group of peers known as the *Grandes*, whose ancient lineage, wealth, and power set them apart from all others; a rather larger service nobility whose privileges derived in one way or another from municipal or judicial service; and what might be called the

country nobility, whose small estates and local outlook made their fiscal immunities vital to their survival.

These distinctions among the nobilities of the European states masked a more important one: wealth. As the saying went, "all who were truly noble were not wealthy, but all who were truly wealthy were noble." In the eighteenth century, despite the phenomenal increase in mercantile activity, wealth was still calculated in profits from the ownership of land. In different parts of Europe the nobility used different methods to maintain their land-based wealth. In places like Britain, Spain, Austria, and Hungary forms of entail were the rule. Simply, an entail was a restriction prohibiting the breakup of a landed estate either through sale or inheritance. The owner of the estate was merely a caretaker for his heir and while he could add land he could not easily subtract any. Entailed estates grew larger and larger and, like magnets, attracted other entailed estates through marriage. In Britain, where primogeniture—inheritance by the eldest son—accompanied entail, four hundred families owned one-quarter of the entire country. Yet this concentration of landed wealth paled into insignificance when compared to the situation in Spain, where just four families owned one-third of all the cultivatable land. In the east, where land was plentiful, the Esterházys of Hungary and the Radziwills of Poland owned millions of acres.

The second method by which the European nobility ensured that the wealthy would be noble was by absorption. There were several avenues to upward mobility, but by the eighteenth century the holding of state offices was the most common. In France, for example, a large number of offices were reserved for the nobility. Many of these were owned by their holders and passed on to their children, but occasionally an office was sold on the market and the new holder was automatically ennobled. The office of royal secretary was one of the most common routes to noble status. The number of secretaries increased from 300 to 900 during the course of the eighteenth century, yet despite this dilution the value of the offices continued to skyrocket. An office that was worth 70,000 French pounds at the beginning of the century was worth 300,000 by the 1780s. In fact, in most European societies there was more room for new nobles than there were aspiring candidates. This was because of the costs that maintaining the new status imposed. In Britain anyone who could live like a gentleman was accounted one. But the practice of entail made it very difficult for a newcomer to purchase the requisite amount of land. Philip V increased the number of Spanish *grandees* in an effort to dilute their power, yet when he placed a tax upon entrance into the lower nobility, the number of *hidalgos* dropped precipitously.

For the wealthy, aristocracy was becoming an international status. The influence of Louis XIV and the court of Versailles lasted for well over a century and spread to town and country life. Most nobles maintained multiple residences. The new style of aristocratic entertainment required more public space on the first floor, while the increasing demand for personal and familial privacy necessitated more space in the upper stories. The result was larger and more opulent homes. Here the British elite led all others. Over one hundred fifty country houses were built in the early eighteenth century alone, including Blenheim Palace, which was built for John Churchill, Duke of Marlborough, at a cost of £300,000. To the expense of architecture was added the expense of decoration. New materials, like West Indian mahogany, occasioned new styles, and both drove up costs. The high-quality woodwork and plastering made fashionable by the English Adam brothers was quickly imitated on the Continent. Only the Spanish nobility shunned country estates, preferring to reside permanently in towns.

The building of country houses was only one part of the conspicuous consumption of the privileged orders. Improvements in travel, both in transport and roads, permitted increased contact between members of the national elites. The stagecoach linked towns, and canals linked waterways. Both made travel quicker and more enjoyable. The grand tour of historical sites continued to be used as a substitute for formal education. Young men would pass from country house to country house buying up antiquities, paintings, and books along the way. The grand tour was a means of introducing the European aristocracies to each other and also a means of communicating taste and fashion among them. Whether it was a Russian noble in Germany, a Swede in Italy, or a Briton in Prussia, all spoke French and shared a cultural outlook.

Much of this was cultivated in the salons, a social institution begun by French women in the seventeenth century that gradually spread throughout the Continent. The salons, especially in Paris, blended the aristocracy and bourgeoisie with the leading intellectuals of the age. Here wit and insight replaced polite conversation. At formal meetings, papers on scientific or philosophical topics were read and discussed. At informal gatherings new ideas were examined and exchanged. The British ambassador to Spain was appalled to discover that men and women were still kept separated in the salons of Madrid and that there was no serious conversation during evenings out. It was in the salons that the impact of the Enlightenment, the great European intellectual movement of the eighteenth century, first made itself felt.

The Enlightenment

In 1734 there appeared in France a small book entitled *Philosophical Letters Concerning the English Nation*. Its author, Voltaire (1694–1778) was a well-known poet who had made a name for himself as a wit in the Parisian salons. He had spent two years in Britain and while there he made it his business to study the differences between the peoples of the two nations. In a simple but forceful style Voltaire demonstrated time and again the superiority of the British. They practiced religious toleration and were not held under the sway of a venal clergy. They valued people for their merits rather than their birth. Their political constitution was a marvel—"The English nation is the only one on earth that has succeeded in controlling the power of kings by resisting them." They made national heroes of their scientists, their poets, and their philosophers. In all of this Voltaire contrasted British virtue with French vice. He attacked the French clergy and nobility directly, the French monarchy implicitly. Not only did he praise the genius and accomplishments of Sir Isaac Newton above those of René Descartes, but he also graphically contrasted the Catholic church's persecution of Descartes with the British state's celebration of

Newton. "England, where men think free and noble thoughts," Voltaire enthused.

It is difficult now to recapture the psychological impact that the *Philosophical Letters* had on the generation of educated Frenchmen who first read them. The book went through ten editions in a decade, five in the first year of its publication. It was officially banned and publicly burned, and a warrant was issued for Voltaire's arrest. The *Letters* dropped like a bombshell upon the moribund intellectual culture of the Church and the universities and burst open the complacent, self-satisfied Cartesian world view. The book ignited in France a movement that would soon be found in nearly every corner of Europe. Though the influence of French culture was already great, the influence of French counterculture was to be even greater. Nevertheless, the Enlightenment was by no means a strictly French phenomenon. Its greatest figures included the Scottish economist Adam Smith (1723–90), the Italian legal reformer Cesare Beccaria (1738–94), and the German philosopher Immanuel Kant (1724–1804). While in France it was first composed of anti-establishment critics, in Scotland and the German states it flourished in the universities, and in Prussia, Austria, and Russia it was propagated by the monarchy. The Enlightenment began in the 1730s and was still going strong a half-century later when its attitudes had been absorbed into the mainstream of European thought.

The Enlightenment was less a set of ideas than it was a set of attitudes. At its core was criticism, a questioning of traditional institutions, customs, and morals. Some enlightened thinkers based their critical outlook on skepticism, the belief that nothing could be known for certain. When the Scottish philosopher David Hume (1711–76) was accused of being an atheist, he countered the charge by saying he was too skeptical to be certain that God did not exist. Though Hume was a systematic philosopher, most of the great figures of the Enlightenment were not so much philosophers as savants, knowledgeable popularizers whose skills were in simplifying and publicizing a hodgepodge of new views. As one Briton put it, "I shall be ambitious to have it said of me that I have brought philosophy out of libraries and schools to dwell at tea tables and in coffeehouses." In France Enlightenment

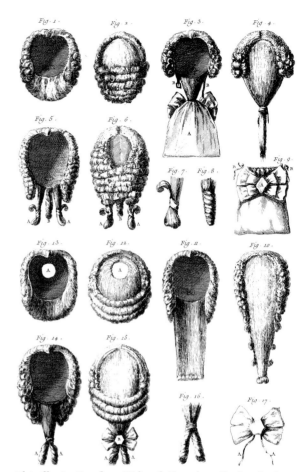

This illustration from Diderot's Encyclopedia *details the many types of wigs and tonsorial accessories worn by men in the eighteenth century. The tradition of wig-wearing lingers on in British law courts.*

intellectuals were called *philosophes* and claimed all the arts and sciences as their purview. The *Encyclopedia* (35 volumes, 1751–80), edited by Denis Diderot (1713–84), was one of the greatest achievements of the age. Entitled the *Systematic Dictionary of the Sciences, Arts, and Crafts*, it attempted to summarize all acquired knowledge and to dispel all imposed superstitions. There was no better definition of a *philosophe* than that given them by one of their enemies. "Just what is a *philosophe*? A kind of monster in society who feels under no obligation towards its manners and morals, its proprieties, its politics, or its religion. One may expect anything from men of their ilk."

Enlightened thinkers attacked established institutions, above all the Church. Most enlightened thinkers were deists who believed in the existence of God on rational grounds only. Following the materialistic ideas of the new science, deists believed that nature conformed to its own material laws and operated without divine intervention. God, in a popular Enlightenment image, was like a clockmaker who constructed the elaborate mechanism, wound it, and gave the pendulum its first swing. After that the clock worked by itself. Deists were accused of being anti-Christian and they certainly opposed the ritual forms of both Catholic and Protestant worship. They also opposed the role of the Church in education, for education was the key to an enlightened view of the future. This meant, above all, conflict with the Jesuits. "Let's eat a Jesuit," was Voltaire's half-facetious comment.

Education was crucial because the Enlightenment was dominated by the idea of the British philosopher John Locke (1632–1704) that the mind was blank at birth, a *tabula rasa*—"white paper void of all characters"—and that it was filled up by experience. Contrary to the arguments of Descartes, Locke wrote in *An Essay Concerning Human Understanding* (1690) that there were no innate ideas and no good or evil that was not conditioned by experience. For Locke, as for a host of thinkers after him, good and evil were defined as pleasure and pain. We do good because it is pleasurable and we avoid evil because it is painful. Morality was a sense experience rather than a theological one. It was also relative rather than absolute. This was an observation that derived from increased interest in non-European cultures. The *Persian Letters* (1721) of Baron Montesquieu (1689–1755) was the most popular of a genre that described non-European societies that knew nothing of Christian morality.

By the middle of the eighteenth century the pleasure/pain principle enunciated by Locke had come to be applied to the foundations of social organization. If personal good was pleasure, then social good was happiness. The object of government, in the words of the Scottish moral philosopher Francis Hutcheson (1694–1746), "was the greatest happiness of the greatest number." This principle was at the core of *Crimes and Punishments* (1764), Cesare Beccaria's pioneering

work of legal reform. Laws were instituted to promote happiness within society. They had to be formulated equitably for both criminal and victim. Punishment was to act as a deterrent to crime rather than as retribution. Therefore Beccaria advocated the abolition of torture to gain confessions, the end of capital punishment, and the rehabilitation of criminals through the improvement of penal institutions. By 1776 happiness was established as one of the basic rights of man, enshrined in the American Declaration of Independence as "life, liberty, and the pursuit of happiness."

It was in refashioning the world through education and social reform that the Enlightenment revealed its orientation toward the future. *Optimism* was a word invented in the eighteenth century to express this feeling of liberation from the weight of centuries of traditions. "This is the best of all possible worlds and all things turn out for the best," was the satirical slogan of Voltaire's *Candide* (1759). But if Voltaire believed that enlightened thinkers had taken optimism too far, others believed that it had to be taken further still. At the end of *Candide* Voltaire opines that "everyone must cultivate their own garden," and it was that cultivation that ensured human progress. Progress, an idea that not all enlightened thinkers shared, was another invention of the age. It was expressed most cogently by the French philosopher the Marquis de Condorcet (1743–94) in *The Progress of the Human Mind* (1795) in which he developed an almost evolutionary view of human development from a savage state of nature to a future of harmony and international peace.

Three Enlightenment Figures

No brief summary can do justice to the diversity of enlightened thought in eighteenth-century Europe. Because it was an attitude of mind rather than a set of shared beliefs, there are many contradictory strains to follow. In his famous essay *What Is Enlightenment?* (1784) Immanuel Kant described it simply as freedom to use one's own intelligence. "I hear people clamor on all sides: Don't argue! The officer says: Don't argue, drill! The tax collector says: Don't argue, pay. The pastor says: Don't argue, believe." To all of them Kant replied: "Dare to know! Have the courage to use your own intelligence." From this point of view, the Enlightenment was as much a movement of people as of ideas. Its outstanding figures ran the gamut from aristocrats like Condorcet and Beccaria, to university professors like Smith and Kant, to those like Diderot and Jean-Jacques Rousseau (1712–78) who lived by their pens. Rousseau authored one of the most important Enlightenment tracts on education, disguised as the romantic novel *Émile* (1762) and one of the most important works on social theory, *The Social Contract* (1762), which opened with the gripping maxim "Man is born free and everywhere he is in chains." Rousseau's own life was one of loneliness and persecution and both his ideas and experiences were better suited for the period of revolution which he did not live to see than the period of Enlightenment in which he was always so uneasy. But allowing for the variety of ideas and personalities and the conscious individualism of an era discovering the importance of the self, an examination of the lives of David Hume, Baron Montesquieu, and Voltaire will capture much of the spirit of the age.

Jean-Jacques Rousseau

David Hume was born in Scotland in 1711. He came from a prosperous legal family, but as a younger son he had no prospect of living idly on the land. At the age of twelve he and his elder brother were sent to the University of Edinburgh for three years. Despite his devotion to his mother and her devotion to Calvinism, Hume early rejected Christianity. He spent the next several years reading and contemplating, having discovered a love of moral philosophy, which was then considered to be the study of human nature. At the age of twenty-seven Hume wrote his first major philosophical work, *A Treatise of Human Nature* (1739), which made absolutely no impression upon his contemporaries and did nothing to solve the financial difficulties in which he now found himself. For a time he took a post as a merchant's clerk; then he served as a tutor; and finally he found a position as a private secretary. During the course of these various employments he continued to write, publishing a series of essays on the subject of morality and rewriting his treatise into *An Enquiry Concerning Human Understanding* (1748), his greatest philosophical work.

While his earliest writings were philosophical treatises, Hume considered himself a man of letters rather than a philosopher. Though he was extremely disappointed with the reception that his work had received—"it fell dead born from the press" was his own judgment—Hume did not engage in philosophical disputes. He twice applied for university posts and was twice rejected on the grounds of his writings against Christianity. Forced to fend for himself, Hume composed a history of England that was an immediate critical and popular success. He became the first Briton of letters to be able to live entirely on his income from writing. He visited the Continent, where he discovered that both his historical and philosophical works had achieved success. Hume's last years were occupied with his work on religion, for which he had already acquired the reputation as one of the leading skeptics and deists in Britain. He died in Edinburgh in 1776.

Hume made two seminal contributions to Enlightenment thought. In the first place, he argued that neither matter nor mind could be proved to exist with any certainty. Only perceptions existed, either as impressions of material objects or as ideas. This argument exploded the classic Cartesian synthesis of mind and matter, which dominated teaching in the schools. If human understanding was based on sensory perception rather than on reason, then there could be no certainty in the universe. Hume's second point launched a frontal attack upon established religion. If there

David Hume

could be no certainty, then the revealed truths of Christian religion could have no basis. In his historical analysis of the origins of religion Hume argued that "religion grows out of hope or fear." He attacked the core of Christian explanations based on either Providence or miracles by arguing that to anyone who understood the basis of human perception it would take a miracle to believe in miracles. Hume suppressed the publication of some of his more controversial writings on religion, which were not printed until after his death, when his work on moral philosophy and natural religion found a wide audience. He was the most penetrating of all Enlightenment thinkers and the greatest of all British philosophers.

In 1749 when Hume was in Italy and his genius was still largely unrecognized, he received in the mail a work from an admiring Frenchman, entitled *The Spirit of the Laws*. Charles-Louis de Secondat, Baron Montesquieu, was born in Bordeaux in 1689. His family were nobility of the robe, and he ultimately inherited both a large landed estate and the office of president of the Parlement of Bordeaux. He was educated first in an exclusive Catholic school and then studied law at the University of Bordeaux and in Paris. Though he was never very interested in the details of a legal career, he found the study of law intellectually challenging. After completing his education, Montesquieu settled into the routine of country life. He married a Calvinist of rather modest fortune, but a woman of unusual business skills, which were put to good effect during Montesquieu's frequent absences. The first sign of his intellectual abilities was his election to the Bordeaux Academy, a group dedicated to propagating the latest scientific and social ideas. As a member of the nobility, Montesquieu took a leading role in organizing the debates that the Academy held and even presented some of his own on topics as varied as the function of the kidneys and the causes of echoes. His satirical novel, *Persian Letters*, was published in 1721.

Persian Letters was a brilliant satire of Parisian morals, French society, and European religion all bound together by the story of a Persian despot who leaves his harem to learn about the ways of the world. The use of the Persian outsider allowed Montesquieu to comment on the absurdity of European customs in general and French practices in particular. The device of the harem allowed him to titillate his audience with exotic sexuality. The work was at once light and serious and it established Montesquieu as a new star in the literary firmament. His social standing allowed him into the very finest Parisian salons, where he cut a figure entirely different from that of the provincial magistrate of Bordeaux.

After this success, Montesquieu decided to sell his office and make the grand tour. He spent nearly two years in England for which, like Voltaire, he came to have the greatest admiration. Back in Bordeaux, Montesquieu began to assemble his thoughts for what he believed would be a great work of political theory. Though becoming progressively blind, he embarked upon a sustained program of reading in both classical and modern history. The two societies that he most admired were ancient Rome and present-day Britain, and he studied the forms of their government and the principles that animated them. *The Spirit of the Laws* was published in 1748, and despite its

The frontispiece from Montesquieu's The Spirit of the Laws *has a medallion of the author surrounded by allegorical figures, including the blind Justice. In the lower left corner are copies of the authors works.*

gargantuan size and densely packed examples, it was immediately recognized as a masterpiece. Catherine the Great of Russia kept it at her bedside, and it was the single most influential work for the framers of the United States Constitution.

In both the *Persian Letters* and *The Spirit of the Laws* Montesquieu explored how liberty could be achieved and despotism avoided. He divided all forms of government into republics, monarchies, and despotisms. Each form had its own peculiar spirit: virtue and moderation in republics, honor in monarchies, and fear in despotisms. Like each form, each spirit was prone to abuse and had to be restrained if republics were not to give way to vice and excess, monarchies to corruption, and despotisms to repression. Montesquieu classified regimes as either moderate or immoderate, and through the use of extensive historical examples attempted to demonstrate how moderation could be maintained through rules and restraints, through the spirit of the law.

For Montesquieu, a successful government was one in which powers were separated and checks and balances existed within the institutions of the state. As befit a provincial magistrate, he insisted upon the absolute separation of the judiciary from all other branches of government. The law needed to be independent and impartial and it needed to be just. Montesquieu advocated that law codes be reformed and reduced mainly to regulate crimes against persons and property. Punishment should fit the crime but should be humane. He was one of the first to advocate the abolition of torture. Like most Europeans of his age, he saw monarchy as the only realistic form of government, but he argued that for a monarchy to be successful, it needed a strong and independent aristocracy to restrain its tendency toward corruption and despotism. He based his arguments on what he believed was the case in Britain, which he praised as the only state in Europe in which liberty resided. This was one of the few points in which he was in total agreement with Voltaire, the most famous of all Enlightenment figures.

Voltaire was buried three times. It was a fitting end for a man whose career was so much larger than life. Born in Paris in 1694 into a bourgeois family with court office, François-Marie Arouet, who later took the pen name Voltaire, was educated by the Jesuits, who encouraged his

Voltaire

poetic talents and instilled in him an enduring love of literature. He was a difficult student, especially as he had already rejected the core of the Jesuits' religious doctrine. He was no less difficult as he grew and began a career as a poet and playwright. Despite his modest social background, he gained entry to the Parisian salons, where he entertained and scandalized with his irreverent wit. It was not long before he was imprisoned in the Bastille for penning verses that maligned the honor of the regent of France. Released from prison, he insulted a nobleman, who retaliated by having his servants publicly beat Voltaire. Voltaire issued a challenge for a duel, a greater insult than the first, given his low birth. Again he was sent to the Bastille and was only released on the promise that he would leave the country immediately.

Thus Voltaire found himself in Britain, where he spent two years learning English, writing plays, and enjoying his celebrity free from the dangers that celebrity entailed in France. Like Montesquieu, he identified the British with liberty, praising the ease with which the social classes met and the freedom of religion and ideas. When he returned to Paris in 1728, it was with the intention of popularizing Britain to Frenchmen.

He wrote and produced a number of plays and began writing the *Philosophical Letters* (1734), a work that not only secured his reputation but also forced him into exile, at the village of Cirey, where he moved in with the Marquise du Châtelet (1706–49). The Marquise du Châtelet, though only twenty-seven at the time of her liaison with Voltaire, was one of the leading advocates of Newtonian science in France. She built a laboratory in her home and introduced Voltaire to experimental science. While she undertook the immense challenge of translating Newton into French, Voltaire worked on innumerable projects: poems, plays, philosophical and anti-religious tracts (which she wisely kept him from publishing), and histories. It was one of the most productive periods of his life, and when the Marquise du Châtelet died in 1749, Voltaire was crushed.

Now past 50 years old, Voltaire began his travels. He was invited to Berlin by Frederick the Great, who admired him most of all the intellectuals of the age. The relationship between these two great egotists was predictably stormy and resulted in Voltaire's arrest in Frankfurt. Finally allowed to leave Prussia, Voltaire eventually settled in Geneva, where he quickly became embroiled in local politics and was none too politely asked to leave. He was tired of wandering and tired of being chased. His youthful gaiety and high spirits, which remained in Voltaire long past youth, were dealt a serious blow by the tragic earthquake in Lisbon in 1755, when thousands of people, attending church services, were killed. Optimism in the face of such a senseless tragedy was no longer possible. His black mood was revealed in *Candide* (1759), which was to become his enduring legacy. Voltaire was now a rich man and he purchased two adjacent estates on the French-Swiss border so that he could be safe from persecution on either side. In his last years, he became a social reformer, undertaking with his pen to undo the abominations of religious hatred. His motto became "abolish superstition" and his attacks upon the Church reinvigorated him for a time. He died in 1778 at the age of 84 and was buried first in Champagne.

Voltaire is remembered today for his savagely satirical *Candide*, which introduced the ivory-tower intellectual Dr. Pangloss, the overly optimistic Candide, and the very practical philosophy, "everyone must cultivate their own garden." Yet it was Voltaire's capacity to challenge all authority that was probably his greatest contribution to Enlightenment attitudes. He held nothing sacred. He questioned his own paternity and the morals of his mother; he lived openly with the Marquise du Châtelet and her husband; he once tore down a church because it obstructed his view; and he spoke as slightingly of kings and aristocrats as he did of his numerous critics. At the height of the French Revolution, Voltaire's body was removed from its resting place in Champagne and taken in great pomp to Paris, where it was interred in the Panthéon, where the heroes of the nation were put to rest. "Voltaire taught us to be free," was the slogan that the Parisian masses chanted during the funeral procession. It was an ending perhaps too solemn and conventional for one as irreverent as Voltaire. When the monarchy was restored after 1815, his bones were unceremoniously dumped in a lime pit.

The Impact of the Enlightenment

The Enlightenment was not as easily disposed of as the bones of Voltaire. A half-century of sustained critical thinking about humanity and society was bound to have its effect. As there was no single set of Enlightenment beliefs, so there was no single impact of the Enlightenment. Its general influence was felt everywhere, even seeping to the lowest strata of society. Its specific influence is harder to gauge. Paradoxically, enlightened political reform took firmer root in the east where the ideas were imported than in the west where they originated. It was absolute rulers who were most successful in borrowing Enlightenment reforms.

It is impossible to determine what part enlightened ideas and what part practical necessities played in the eastern European reform movement that began around mid-century. In at least three areas the coincidence between ideas and actions was especially strong: law, education, and the extension of religious toleration. Law was the basis of Enlightenment views of social interaction, and the influence of Montesquieu and Beccaria spread quickly. In Prussia and Russia the movement to codify and simplify the legal system did not reach fruition in the eighteenth century, but in both places it was well under way. The Prussian jurist Samuel von Cocceji (1679–1755) initiated the reform of Prussian law and legal administration. Cocceji's project was to make the enforcement of law uniform throughout the realm, to prevent judicial corruption, and to produce a single code of Prussian law. The code, finally completed in the 1790s, reflected the principles of criminal justice articulated by Beccaria. In Russia, the Law Commission summoned by Catherine the Great in 1767 never did complete its work. Nevertheless, profoundly influenced by Montesquieu, Catherine attempted to abolish tor-

Major Works of the Enlightenment

1690 *An Essay Concerning Human Understanding* (Locke)

1721 *Persian Letters* (Baron Montesquieu)

1734 *Philosophical Letters Concerning the English Nation* (Voltaire)

1739 *A Treatise of Human Nature* (Hume)

1740 *Pamela* (Richardson)

1748 *An Enquiry Concerning Human Understanding* (Hume)
The Spirit of the Laws (Baron Montesquieu)

1751–80 *Encyclopedia* (Diderot)

1759 *Candide* (Voltaire)

1762 *Émile; The Social Contract* (Rousseau)

1764 *Crimes and Punishments* (Beccaria)

1784 *What Is Enlightenment?* (Kant)

1795 *The Progress of the Human Mind* (Marquis de Condorcet)

1798 *An Essay on the Principles of Population* (Malthus)

ture and to introduce the Beccarian principle that the accused was innocent until proven guilty. In Austria, Joseph II presided over a wholesale reorganization of the legal system. Courts were centralized, laws codified, and torture and capital punishment abolished.

Enlightenment ideas also underlay the efforts to improve education in eastern Europe. The religious orders, especially the Jesuits, were the most influential educators of the age, and the Enlightenment attack upon them created a void that had to be filled by the state. Efforts at compulsory education were first undertaken in Russia under Peter the Great, but these were aimed at the compulsory education of the nobility. It was Catherine who extended the effort to the provinces, attempting to educate a generation of Russian teachers. She was especially eager that women receive primary schooling, although the prejudice against educating women was too strong to overcome. Austrian and Prussian reforms were more successful in extending the reach of primary education, even if its content remained weak.

Religious toleration was the area in which the Enlightenment had its greatest impact in Europe, though again it was in the east that this was most visible. Freedom of worship for Catholics was barely whispered about in Britain, while neither France nor Spain were moved to tolerate Protestants. Nevertheless, within these parameters there were some important changes in the religious makeup of the western European states. In Britain, Protestant dissenters were no longer persecuted for their beliefs. By the end of the eighteenth century the number of Protestants outside the Church of England was growing, and by the early nineteenth century discrimination against Protestants was all but eliminated. In France and Spain relations between the national church and the papacy were undergoing a reorientation. Both states were asserting more independence—both theologically and financially—from Rome. The shift was symbolized by disputes over the role of the Jesuits, who were finally expelled from France in 1764 and from Spain in 1767.

In the east, enlightened ideas about religious toleration did take effect. Catherine the Great abandoned persecution of a Russian Orthodox sect known as the Old Believers. Frederick the Great was a deist himself. Prussia had always tolerated various Protestant groups, and with the conquest of Silesia it acquired a large Catholic population. Catholics were guaranteed freedom of worship, and Frederick even built a Catholic church in Berlin to symbolize this policy. Austria extended furthest enlightened ideas about toleration. Maria Theresa was a devout Catholic and actually increased religious persecution in her realm. But Joseph II rejected his mother's dogmatic position. In 1781 he issued a Patent of Toleration, which granted freedom of worship to Protestants and members of the eastern Orthodox church. The following year he extended this toleration to Jews.

Joseph's attitude toward toleration was as

practical as it was enlightened. He believed that the revocation of the Edict of Nantes at the end of the seventeenth century had been an economic disaster for France, and he encouraged religious toleration as a means to economic progress. A science of economics was first articulated during the Enlightenment. A group of French thinkers known as the *physiocrats* subscribed to the view that land was wealth and thus argued that agricultural activity, especially improved means of farming and livestock breeding, should take first priority in state reforms. As wealth came from land, taxation should be based only on land ownership, a principle that was coming into increased prominence, despite the opposition of the landowning class. Physiocratic ideas combined a belief in the sanctity of private property with the need for the state to increase agricultural output. In 1774, Louis XVI appointed the physiocrat Anne-Robert-Jacques Turgot (1727–81) minister of finance, but Turgot's radical schemes, especially for tax reform, doomed his career. Ultimately the physiocrats, like the great Scottish economic theorist Adam Smith, came to believe that government should cease to interfere with private economic activity. They articulated the doctrine *laissez faire, laissez passer*—"let it be, let it go." The ideas of Adam Smith and the physiocrats ultimately formed the basis for nineteenth-century economic reform.

If the Enlightenment did not initiate a new era, it did offer a new vision. The science of the material world opened the way for a science of the human world, whether in Hume's psychology, Montesquieu's political science, Rousseau's sociology, or Smith's economic theory. All of these subjects, which have such a powerful impact on contemporary life, had their modern origins in the Enlightenment. As the British poet Alexander Pope (1688–1744) put it: "Know then thyself, presume not God to scan/ The proper study of mankind is man." A new emphasis on self and on pleasure led to a new emphasis on happiness. All three fed into the distinctively Enlightenment idea of self-interest. Happiness and self-interest were values that would inevitably corrode the old social order, which was based upon principles of self-sacrifice and corporate identity. It was only a matter of time.

The Bourgeoisie

Bourgeois is a French word, and it carried the same tone of derision in the eighteenth century that it does today. The bourgeois was a man on the make, scrambling after money or office or title. He was neither well born nor well bred, or so said the nobility. Yet the bourgeoisie served vital functions in all European societies. They dominated trade, both nationally and internationally. They made their homes in cities and did much to improve the quality of urban life. They were the civilizing influence in urban culture, for unlike the nobility they were its permanent denizens. Perhaps most importantly, the bourgeoisie provided the safety valve between the nobility and those who were acquiring wealth and power but who lacked the advantages of birth and position. By developing their own culture and class identity, the bourgeoisie provided successful individuals with their own sense of pride and achievement and eased the explosive buildup of social resentments.

In the eighteenth century the bourgeoisie was growing in both numbers and importance. An active commercial and urban life gave many members of this group new social and political opportunities and many of them passed into the nobility through the purchase of land or office. But for those whose aspirations or abilities were different, this social group began to define its own values, which centered on the family and the home. A new interest in domestic affairs touched both men and women of the European bourgeoisie. Their homes became a social center for kin and neighbors and their outlook on family life reflected new personal relationships. Marriages were made for companionship as much as for economic advantage. Romantic love between husbands and wives was newly valued. So were children, whose futures came to dominate familial concern. Childhood was recognized as a separate stage of life and the education of children as one of the most important of all parental responsibilities. The image of the affectionate father replaced that of the hard-bitten businessman; the image of the doting mother replaced that of the domestic drudge.

Urban Elites

In the society of orders, nobility was the acid test. The world was divided into the small number of those who had it and the large number of those who did not. At the apex of the non-noble pyramid was the bourgeoisie, the elites of urban Europe whose place in the society of orders was ambiguous. Bourgeois, or burgher, simply meant town dweller, but as a social group it had come to mean wealthy town dweller. The bourgeoisie was strongest where towns were strongest: in western rather than in eastern Europe, in northern rather than southern Europe, with the notable exception of Italy. Holland was the exemplar of a bourgeois republic. More than half of the Dutch population lived in towns and there was no significant aristocratic class to compete for power. The Regents of Amsterdam were the equivalent of a European court nobility in wealth, power, and prestige, though not in the way in which they had accumulated their fortunes. The size of the bourgeoisie in various European states cannot be absolutely determined. At the end of the eighteenth century the British middle classes probably constituted around 15 percent of the population, the French bourgeoisie less than 10 percent. By contrast, the Russian or Hungarian urban elites were less than 2 percent of the population in those states.

Like the nobility, the bourgeoisie constituted a diverse group. At the top were great commercial families engaged in the expanding international marketplace and reaping the profits of trade. In wealth and power they were barely distinguishable from the nobility. At the bottom were the so-called petit-bourgeois; shopkeepers, craftsmen, and industrial employers. The solid core of the bourgeoisie was employed in trade, exchange, and service. Most were engaged in local or national commerce. Trade was the lifeblood of the city, for by itself the city could neither feed nor clothe its inhabitants. Most bourgeois fortunes were first acquired in trade. Finance was the natural outgrowth of commerce and another segment of the bourgeoisie accumulated or preserved their capital through the sophisticated financial instruments of the eighteenth century. While the very wealthy loaned directly to the central government or bought shares in overseas trading companies, most bourgeois participated in government credit markets. They purchased state bonds or lifetime annuities and lived on the interest. The costs of war flooded the urban credit markets with high-yielding and generally stable financial instruments. Finally, the bourgeoisie were members of the burgeoning professions that provided services for the rich. Medicine, law, education, and the bureaucracy were all bourgeois professions, for the cost of acquiring the necessary skills could be borne only by those already wealthy.

During the course of the eighteenth century, this combination of occupational groups was expanding both in numbers and in importance all over Europe. So was the bourgeois habitat. The urbanization of Europe continued steadily throughout the eighteenth century. A greater percentage of the European population were living in towns and a greater percentage were living in large towns of over 10,000 inhabitants which, of necessity, were developing complex socioeconomic structures. In France alone there were probably over a hundred such towns, each requiring the services of the bourgeoisie and providing opportunities for their expansion. And the larger the metropolis the greater the need. In 1600 only twenty European cities contained as many as 50,000 people; in 1700 that number had risen to thirty-two; and by 1800 to forty-eight. During the course of the eighteenth century the number of cities with 75,000 inhabitants doubled. London, the largest city, had grown to 865,000, a remarkable feat considering that in 1665 over a quarter of the London population died in the Great Plague. In such cities the demand for lawyers and doctors, for merchants and shopkeepers was almost insatiable.

Besides wealth, the urban bourgeoisie shared another characteristic: mobility. The aspiration of the bourgeoisie was to become noble, either through office or by acquiring rural estates. In Britain, a gentleman was still defined by life-style. "All are accounted gentlemen in England who maintain themselves without manual labor." Many trading families left their wharves and countinghouses to acquire rural estates, live off rents, and practice the openhanded hospitality of a gentleman. In France and Spain, nobility could still be purchased, though the price was constantly going up. For the greater bourgeoisie, the transition was easy; for the lesser, the failure to move up was all the more frustrating for being just beyond their grasp. The bourgeoisie did not only imagine their discomfort, they were made to feel it at every turn. They were the butt of jokes, of theater, and of popular songs. They were the first victims in the shady financial dealings of the crown and court, the first casualties in urban riots. Despised from above, envied from below, the bourgeoisie were uncomfortable with the present yet profoundly conservative about the future. The one consolation to their perpetual misery was that as a group they got richer and richer. And as a group they began to develop a distinctive culture that reflected their qualities and aspirations.

The Charm of the Bourgeoisie

Many bourgeoisie viewed their condition as temporary and accepted the pejorative connotations of the word itself. They had little desire to defend a social group out of which they fervently longed to pass. Others, whose aspirations were lower, were nevertheless uncomfortable with the status that they had already achieved. They had no ambition to wear the silks and furs reserved for the nobility or to attend the opening night at the opera decked in jewels and finery. In fact, such ostentation was alien to their existence and to the success that they had achieved. There was a real tension between the values of noble and bourgeois. The ideal noble was idle, wasteful, and ostentatious; the ideal bourgeois was industrious, frugal, and sober. Voltaire, who made his fortune as a financial speculator rather than a man of letters, aped the life-style of the nobility. But he could never allow himself to be cheated by a tradesman, a mark of his origins. When Louis XVI tried to make household economies in the wake of a financial crisis, critics said that "he acts like a bourgeois."

Even if the bourgeoisie did not constitute a class, they did share certain attitudes that constituted a culture. The wealthy among them participated in the new world of consumption, whether they did so lavishly or frugally. For those who aspired to more than their birth allowed, there was a loosening of the strict codes of dress that reserved certain fabrics, decorative materials, and styles to the nobility. Merchants and bankers could now be seen in colored suits or with pipings made of cloth of gold; their wives could be seen in furs and silks. They might acquire silverware, even if they did not go so far as the nobility and have a coat of arms engraved upon it. Coaches and carriages were also becoming common among the bourgeoisie, to take them on the Sunday rides through the town gardens or to their weekend retreats in the suburbs. Parisian merchants, even master craftsmen like clockmakers, were now acquiring suburban homes although they could not afford to retire to them for the summer months.

But more and more, the bourgeoisie was beginning to travel. In Britain whole towns were established to cater to leisure travelers. The southwestern town of Bath, which was rebuilt in the eighteenth century, was the most popular of all European resort towns, famous since Roman times for the soothing qualities of its waters. Bath was soon a social center as notable for its marriage market as for its recreations. Brighton, a seaside resort on the south coast, quadrupled in size in the second half of the eighteenth century. Bathing—what we would call swimming—either for health or recreation, became a middle-class fad, displacing traditional fears of the sea.

The leisure that wealth bestowed on the bourgeoisie quickly became, in good bourgeois fashion, commercialized. Theater and music halls for both light and serious productions proliferated. By the 1760s an actual theater district had arisen in London and was attracting audiences of over twenty thousand a week. London was unusual, both for its size and for the number of well-to-do visitors who patronized its cultural events. The size of the London audiences enabled the German-born composer Georg Friedrich Handel (1685–1759) to earn a handsome living by performing and directing concerts. He was one of the few musicians in the eighteenth century to live without noble patronage. But it was not only in Britain that theater and music flourished. Voltaire's plays were performed before packed houses in Paris, with the author himself frequently in attendance to bask in the adulation of the largely bourgeois audiences who attended them. In Venice it was estimated that over 1,200 operas were produced in the eighteenth century.

Rome and Milan were even better known, and Naples was the center for Italian opera. Public concerts were a mark of bourgeois culture, for the court nobility was entertained at the royal palaces or great country houses. Public concerts began in Hamburg in the 1720s and Frederick the Great helped establish the Berlin Opera House some decades later.

Theater and concert going were part of the new attitude toward socializing that was one of the greatest contributions of the Enlightenment. Enlightened thinkers spread their views in the salons, and the salons soon spawned the academies, local scientific societies which, though led and patronized by provincial nobles, included large numbers of bourgeois members. The academies sponsored essay competitions, built up libraries, and became the local center for intellectual interchange. A less structured form of sociability took place in the coffeehouses and tearooms that came to be a feature of even small provincial towns. In the early eighteenth century there were over two thousand London coffee shops where men—for the coffeehouse was largely a male preserve—could talk politics, read

the latest newspapers and magazines, and indulge their taste for this still-exotic beverage. More exclusive clubs were also a form of middle-class sociability, some centering on political issues, some like the Chambers of Commerce centering on professional interests. Parisian clubs, called *sociétés*, covered a multitude of diverse interests. Literary *sociétés* were the most popular, maintaining their purpose by forbidding drinking, eating, and gambling on their premises.

Above all, bourgeois culture was literate culture. Wealth and leisure led to mental pursuits—if not always to intellectual ones. The proliferation of relatively cheap printed material had an enormous impact on the lives of those who were able to afford it. Holland and Britain were the most literate European societies and also, because of the absence of censorship, the centers of European printing. This was the first great period of the newspaper and the magazine. The first daily newspaper appeared in London in 1702; eighty years later, thirty-seven provincial towns had their own newspapers, while the London papers were read all over Britain. Then as now, the newspaper was as much a vehicle for advertise-

L'Amour au Théâtre Français (Love in the French Theatre) *(ca. 1716), by Antoine Watteau. The painting is thought to portray a scene from* Les Fêtes de l'Amour et de Bacchus, *a comic opera composed in 1672.*

ment as for news. News reports tended to be bland, avoiding controversy and concentrating on general national and international events. Advertising, on the other hand, tended to be lurid, promising cures for incurable ills, and the most exquisite commodities at the most reasonable prices. For entertainment and serious political commentary, the British reading public turned to magazines, of which there were over 150 separate titles by the 1780s. The most famous were *The Spectator*, which ran in the early part of the century and did much to set the tone for a cultured middle-class life, and the *Gentleman's Magazine*, which ran in the mid-century and was said to have had a circulation of nearly fifteen thousand. The longest-lived of all British magazines was *The Ladies Diary*, which continued in existence from 1704 to 1871 and doled out self-improvement, practical advice, and fictional romances in equal proportion.

The Ladies Diary was not the only literature aimed at the growing number of leisured and lettered bourgeois woman. Though enlightened thinkers could be ambivalent about the place of women in the new social order, they generally stressed the importance of female education and welcomed women's participation in intellectual pursuits. Whether it was new ideas about women or simply the fact that more women had leisure, a growing body of both domestic literature and light entertainment was available to them. This included a vast number of teach-yourself books aimed at instructing women how best to organize domestic life or how to navigate the perils of polite society. Moral instruction, particularly on the themes of obedience and sexual fidelity, was also popular. But the greatest output directed toward women was in the form of fanciful romances, from which a new genre emerged. The novel first appeared in its modern form in the 1740s. Samuel Richardson (1689–1761) wrote *Pamela* (1740), the story of a maid servant who successfully resisted the advances of her master until he finally married her. It was composed in long episodes, or chapters, that developed Pamela's character and told her story at the expense of the overt moral message that was Richardson's original intention. Richardson's novels were printed in installments and helped to drive up the circulation of national magazines.

Family Life

While the public life of the bourgeoisie can be measured in the sociability of the coffeehouse and the academy, private life must be measured in the home. There a remarkable transformation was under way, one that the bourgeoisie shared with the nobility. In the pursuit of happiness encouraged by the Enlightenment, one of the newest joys was domesticity. The image—and sometimes the reality—of the happy home, where love was the bond between husband and wife and care between parents and children, came to dominate both the literary and visual arts. Only those wealthy enough to afford to dispense with women's work could partake of the new domesticity, only those touched by Enlightenment ideas could attempt to make the change. But where it occurred, the transformation in the nature of family life was one of the most profound alterations in eighteenth-century culture.

The first step toward the transformation of family relationships was in centering the conjugal family in the home. In the past, the family was a less important structure for most people than the social groups to which they belonged or the neighborhood in which they lived. Marriage was an economic partnership at one end and a means to carry on lineage at the other. Individual fulfillment was not an object of marriage and this attitude could be seen among the elites in the high level of arranged marriages, the speed with which surviving spouses remarried, and the formal and often brutal personal relationships between husbands and wives.

Patriarchy was the dominant value within the family. Husbands ruled over wives and children, making all of the crucial decisions that affected both the quality of their lives and their futures. As late as the middle of the eighteenth century a British judge established the "rule of thumb," which asserted that a husband had a legal right to beat his wife with a stick, but the stick should be no thicker than a man's thumb. It was believed that children were stained with the sin of Adam at birth and that only the severest upbringing could clean some of it away. In nearly two hundred child-rearing advice books published in England before the middle of the eighteenth century, only three did not advise the beating of children. John Wesley (1703–91), the founder of Methodism, remembered his own mother's dictum that "children should learn to fear the rod and cry softly." Children were sent out first for wet-nursing, then at around the age of seven for boarding, either at school or in a trade, and finally into their own marriages.

There can be no doubt that this profile of family life began to change, especially in western Europe, during the second half of the eighteenth century. Though the economic elements of marriage remained strong—newspapers actually advertised the availability of partners and the dowries or annual income that they would bring to the marriage—other elements now appeared. Fed by an unending stream of stories and novels and a new desire for individual happiness, romantic and sexual attraction developed into a factor in marriage. Potential marriage partners were no longer kept away from each other or smothered by chaperons. The social season of polite society gave greater latitude to courtship in which prospective partners could dance, dine, and converse with each other in order to determine compatibility. Perhaps more importantly, the role of potential spouses in choosing a partner appears to have increased. This was a subtle matter, for even in earlier centuries parents did not simply assign a spouse to their children. But by the eighteenth century adolescents themselves searched for their own marriage partners and exercised a strong negative voice in identifying unsuitable ones.

The quest for compatibility, no less than the quest for romantic love, led to a change in personal relationships between spouses. The extreme formality of the past was gradually breaking down. Husbands and wives began spending more time with each other, developing common interests and pastimes. Their personal life began to change. For the first time houses were built to afford the couple privacy from their children, their servants, and their guests. Rooms were designed for specific functions and were set off by hallways. Corridors were an important innovation in creating privacy. In earlier architecture one walked through a room to the next one behind it. Now rooms were separated and doors could be closed. This new design allowed for an intimate life that earlier generations did not find necessary

The Snatched Kiss, *or* The Stolen Kiss *(1750s), by Jean-Honoré Fragonard, was one of the "series paintings" popular in the late eighteenth century. A later canvas entitled* The Marriage Contract *shows the next step in the lives of the lovers.*

and which they could not, in any case, put into practice.

Couples had more time for each other because they were beginning to limit the size of their families. There were a number of reasons for this development, which again pertained only to the upper classes. For one thing, child mortality rates were declining among wealthy social groups. Virulent epidemic diseases like the plague, which knew no class lines, were gradually disappearing. Moreover, though there were few medical breakthroughs in this period, sanitation was improving. Bearing fewer children had an enormous impact on the lives of women, reducing the danger of death and disablement in childbirth and giving them leisure time to pursue domestic tasks. This is not to say that the early part of a woman's marriage was not dominated by children; in fact, because of new attitudes toward child rearing it may have been so dominated more than ever. Many couples appear to have made a conscious decision to space births, though success was limited by the fact that the most common technique of birth control was *coitus interruptus*, or withdrawal.

The transformation in the quality of relationships between spouses was mirrored by an even greater transformation in attitudes toward children. There were many reasons why childhood now took on a new importance. Decline in mortality rates had a profound psychological impact. Parents could feel that their emotional investment in their children had a greater chance of fulfillment. But equally important were the new ideas about education, especially Locke's belief that the child enters into the world a blank slate whose personality is created through early education. This view not only placed a new responsibility upon parents but also gave them the concept of childhood as a stage through which individuals passed. This idea could be seen in the commercial sphere as well as in any other. In 1700 there was not a single shop in London that sold children's toys exclusively; by the 1780s there were toyshops everywhere, three of which sold nothing but rocking horses. Children's toys abounded: soldiers and forts; dolls and dollhouses. The jigsaw puzzle was invented in the 1760s as a way to teach children geography. There were also shops that sold nothing but clothes specifically designed for children, no longer simply adult clothes in miniature.

Most important of all was the development of materials for the education of children. This took place in two stages. At first so-called children's books were books whose purpose was to help adults teach children. Later came books directed at children themselves with large print, entertaining illustrations, and nonsensical characters, usually animals who taught moral lessons. In Britain the Little Pretty Pocket Book series, created by John Newbery (1713–67), not only encompassed educational primers but also included books for the entertainment of the child. Newbery published a Mother Goose book of nursery rhymes and created the immortal character of Miss Goody Two Shoes. Instruction and entertainment also lay behind the development of children's playing cards, in which the French specialized. Dice games, like one in which a child made a journey across Europe, combined geographical instruction with the amusement of competition.

The commercialization of childhood was, of course, directed at adults. The new books and games that were designed to enhance a child's education not only had to be purchased by parents but had to be used by them as well. More and more mothers were devoting their time to their children. Among the upper classes the practice of wet nursing began to decline. Mothers wanted to nurture their infants both literally by breast-feeding and figuratively by teaching them. Children became companions to be taken on outings to the increasing number of museums or shows of curiosities, which began to discount children's tickets by the middle of the century.

The preconditions of this transformation of family life could not be shared by the population at large. Working women could afford neither the cost of instructional materials for their children nor the time to use them. Ironically, they now began using wet nurses, once the privilege of the wealthy, for increasingly a working woman's labor was the margin of survival for her family. Working women enjoyed no privacy in the hovels in which they lived with large families in single rooms. Wives and children were still beaten by husbands and fathers and were unacquainted with enlightened ideas of the worth of the individual and the innocence of the child. By the end of the eighteenth century two distinct family cultures coexisted in Europe, one based on companionate marriage and the affective bonds of parents and children, the other based on patriarchal dominance and the family as an economic unit.

The Masses

The paradox of the eighteenth century was that for the masses life was getting better by getting worse. More Europeans were surviving than ever before, more food was available to feed them; there was more housing, better sanitation, even better charities. Yet for all of this, there was more misery. Those who would have succumbed to disease or starvation a century before now survived from day to day, beneficiaries—or victims—of increased farm production and improved agricultural marketing. The market economy organized a more effective use of land, but it created a widespread social problem. The landless agrarian laborer of the eighteenth century was the counterpart of the sixteenth-century sturdy beggar. In the cities, the plight of the poor was as desperate as ever. Men and women sold their labor or their bodies for a pittance while beggars slept at every doorway. Even the most openhearted charitable institutions were unable to cope with the massive increase in the poor. By the thousands, mothers abandoned their children to the foundling hospitals, where it was believed they would have a better chance of survival, even though hospital death rates were near 80 percent.

Not all members of the lower orders succumbed to poverty or despair. In fact, many were able to benefit from existing conditions to lead a more fulfilling life than ever before. The richness of popular culture, signified by a spread of literacy into the lower reaches of European society, was

Beggar Feeding a Child, *by Giacomo Ceruti. Every eighteenth-century European city had its legion of beggars. This man has done well enough to be able to feed himself and his little daughter for one more day.*

one indication of this change. So too were the reforms urged by enlightened thinkers to improve basic education and to improve the quality of life in the cities. For that segment of the lower orders that could keep its head above water, the eighteenth century offered new opportunities and new challenges.

Breaking the Cycle

Of all the legacies of the eighteenth century, none was more fundamental than the steady increase in European population that began around 1740. This was not the first time that Europe had experienced sustained population growth, but it was the first time that such growth was not checked by a demographic crisis. Breaking the cycle of population growth and crisis was a momentous event in European history despite the fact that it went unrecorded at the time and unappreciated for centuries after.

The figures tell one part of the story. In 1700 European population is estimated to have been 120 million. By 1800 it had grown 50 percent to over 180 million. And the aggregate hides significant regional variations. While France, Spain, and Italy expanded between 30 and 40 percent, Prussia doubled and Russia and Hungary may have tripled in number. Britain increased by 80 percent from about 5 to 9 million, but the rate of growth was accelerating. In 1695 the English population stood at 5 million. It took 62 years to add the next million and 24 years to add the million after that. In 1781 the population was 7 million, but it took only 13 years to reach 8 million and only 10 more years to reach 9 million. Steady population growth had continued without significant checks for well over half a century.

Ironically, the traditional pattern of European population found its theorist at the very moment that it was about to disappear. In 1798 Thomas Malthus (1766–1834) published *An Essay on the Principles of Population.* Reflecting on the history of European population, Malthus observed the cyclical pattern by which growth over one or two generations was checked by a crisis that significantly reduced population. From these lower levels new growth began until it was checked and the cycle repeated itself. Because people increased more quickly than did food supplies, the land could only sustain a certain level of population. When that level was near, population became prone to a demographic check. Malthus divided population checks into two categories, positive and preventive. Positive checks were war, disease, and famine, all of which Malthus believed were natural, although brutal, means of population control. Famine was the obvious result of the failure of food supplies to keep pace with demand; war was the competition for scarce resources; and disease often accompanied both. It was preventive checks that most interested Malthus. These were the means by which societies could limit their growth to avoid the devastating consequences of positive checks. Celibacy, late marriages, and sexual abstinence were among the choices of which Malthus approved, though abortion, infanticide, and contraception were also commonly practiced.

In the sixteenth and seventeenth centuries, the dominant pattern of the life cycle was high infant and child mortality, late marriages, and early death. All controlled population growth. Infant and child mortality rates were staggering: only half of all those born reached the age of ten. Late marriage was the only effective form of birth control—given the strong social taboos against sexual relations outside marriage—for a late marriage reduced a woman's childbearing years. Women in western Europe generally married between the ages of twenty-four and twenty-six; they normally ceased bearing children at the age of forty. But not all marriages lasted this fourteen- or sixteen-year span, as one or the other partner died. On average, the childbearing period for most women was between ten and twelve years, long enough to endure six pregnancies, which would result in three surviving children. (See Special Feature, "Giving Birth to the Eighteenth Century," pp. 600–601.)

Three surviving children for every two adults would, of course, have resulted in a 50 percent rise in population in every generation. Celibacy was one limiting factor, cities were another. Perhaps as much as 15 percent of the population in western Europe remained celibate either by entering religious orders that imposed celibacy or by lacking the personal or financial attributes necessary to make a match. Religious orders that enforced

celibacy were still central features of Catholic societies, and "spinsters," as unmarried women were labeled, were increasing everywhere. Cities were like sticky webs, trapping the surplus rural population for the spiders of disease, famine, and exposure to devour. Throughout the early modern period, urban areas grew through migration. Settled town dwellers might have been able to sustain their own numbers despite the unsanitary conditions of cities, but it was migrants who brought about the cities' explosive growth. Rural migrants accounted for the appallingly high urban death rates. When we remember that the largest European cities were continuously growing—London from 200,000 in 1600 to 675,000 in 1750; Paris from 220,000 to 576,000; Rome from 105,000 to 156,000; Madrid from 49,000 to 109,000; Vienna from 50,000 to 175,000—then we can appreciate how many countless thousands of immigrants perished before marriage. If urban perils were not enough, there were still the positive checks. Plagues carried away hundreds of thousands, wars halved populations of places in their path, and famine overwhelmed the weak and the poor. The worst famine in European history came as late as 1697, when one-third of the population of Finland starved to death.

The late seventeenth and early eighteenth centuries was a period of population stagnation if not actual decline. It was not until the third or fourth decade of the eighteenth century that another growth cycle began. It rapidly gained momentum throughout the Continent and showed no signs of abating after two full generations. More importantly, this upward cycle revealed unusual characteristics. In the first place fertility was increasing. This had several causes. In a few areas, most notably in Britain, women were marrying younger, thereby increasing their childbearing years. This pattern was also true in eastern Europe where women traditionally married younger. In the late eighteenth century the average age at marriage for Hungarian women had dropped to 18.6. Elsewhere, most notably in France, the practice of wet nursing was becoming more common among the masses. As working women increasingly took jobs outside the house, they were less able to nurse their own children. Finally, sexual activity outside marriage was rising. Illegitimacy rates, especially in the last decades of the century, were spurting everywhere. Over the course of the century they rose by 60 percent in France, more than doubled in England, and nearly quadrupled in Germany. So, too, were the rates of premarital pregnancy on the rise. The number of couples rushed to the altar in 1800 was nearly double that before 1750 in most of western Europe.

But increasing fertility was only part of the picture. More significant was decreasing mortality. The positive checks of the past were no longer as potent. European warfare not only diminished in scale after the middle of the century, it changed location as well. Rivalry for colonial empires removed the theater of conflict from European communities. So did the increase in naval warfare. The damage caused by war had always been more by aftershock than by actual fighting. The destruction and pillage of crops and the wholesale slaughter of livestock created food shortages that weakened local populations for the diseases that came in train with the armies. As the virulence of warfare abated, so did that of epidemic disease. The plague had all but disappeared from western Europe by the middle of the eighteenth century. The widespread practice of quarantine, especially in Hungary, which had been the crucial bridge between eastern and western epidemics, went far to eradicate the scourge of centuries.

Without severe demographic crises to maintain the cyclical pattern, the European population began a gentle but continuous rise. Urban sanitation, at least for permanent city dwellers, was becoming more effective. Clean water supplies, organized waste and sewage disposal, and strict quarantines were increasingly part of urban regulations. The use of doctors and trained midwives helped lower the incidence of stillbirth and decreased the number of women who died in childbirth. Almost everywhere levels of infant and child mortality were decreasing. More people were being born, more were surviving the first ten dangerous years, and thus more were marrying and reproducing. Increased fertility and decreased mortality could have only one result: renewed population growth. No wonder Malthus was worried.

Daily Bread

In the past, if warfare or epidemic diseases failed to check population growth, famine would have done the job. How the European economy conquered famine in the eighteenth century is a complicated story. There was no single breakthrough that accounts for the ability to feed the tens of millions of additional people who now inhabited the continent. Holland and Britain, at the cutting edge of agricultural improvement, employed dynamic new techniques that would ultimately provide the means to support continued growth, but most European agriculture was still mired in the time-honored practices that had endured for centuries. Still, not everyone could be fed or fed adequately. Widespread famine might have disappeared, but slow starvation and chronic undernourishment had not. It is certainly the case that hunger was more common at the end of the eighteenth century than at the beginning and that the nutritional content of a typical diet may have reached its lowest point in European history.

Nevertheless, the capacity to sustain rising levels of population can only be explained in terms of agricultural improvement. Quite simply, European farmers were now producing more food and marketing it better. In the most advanced societies this was a result of conscious efforts to make agriculture more efficient. In traditional open-field agriculture, communities quickly ran up against insurmountable obstacles to growth. The three-field crop rotation system left a significant proportion of land fallow each year, while the concentration on subsistence cereal crops progressively eroded the land that was in production. Common farming was only as strong as the weakest member of the community. There was little incentive for successful individuals to plow profits back into the land, either through the purchase of equipment or the increase of livestock. Livestock was a crucial variable in agricultural improvement. As long as there was only enough food for humans to eat, only essential livestock could be kept alive over the winter. Oxen, which were still the ordinary beasts of burden, and pigs and poultry, which required only minimal feed, were the most common. But

Giving Birth to the Eighteenth Century

"In sorrow thou shalt bring forth children." Such was Eve's punishment for eating of the forbidden tree, and that sorrow continued for numberless generations. Childbirth was painful, dangerous, and, all too often, deadly. Though successful childbirth needed no outside intervention whatsoever—there were no obstetricians in caves—without the accumulated wisdom of the ages, babies and mothers routinely perished. That wisdom was passed from mother to daughter and finally was accumulated by skilled women who practiced the craft of midwifery. Every village, no matter how small, had women who were capable of assisting others in childbirth. Midwives' skills ranged widely, from the use of herbal potions and strong drink to ease the pain of labor to a rudimentary understanding of how to assist a complicated delivery when the fetus was not in the proper position.

Midwives, who until the late seventeenth century were always women, were part of the support group that attended a woman during her labor. Typically, childbirth was a social occasion for women. Along with the midwife would be a wet nurse and female kin and neighbors, who would offer encouragement, bring refreshments, and tend to the ordinary chores that the pregnant woman would otherwise have performed herself. Without chemicals to induce contractions and without the ability to intervene in the delivery,

labor was usually a long-drawn-out affair. Ordinarily, it did not take place in bed, but rather in a room or a part of a room that had been set aside for the occasion. By the eighteenth century, at least in larger urban areas, poor women, who had no separate space for labor, could give birth in lying-in hospitals. Within the birthing room, the conclave of women was much like a social gathering. The pregnant woman was advised to adopt any positions that made her feel comfortable; standing and walking were favored in the belief that the effects of gravity helped the baby move downward. The woman might sit on a neighbor's lap or on a birthing stool, a chair open at the bottom, during contractions and delivery.

Most midwives subscribed to the philosophy of letting nature take its course. Because the difficulties and length of labor differed markedly from woman to woman, the midwife's most important contribution was to offer comfort and reassurance based on her long experience. By the seventeenth century manuals for midwives began to be published, some of them written by women, but most by male doctors whose surgical experiences provided them with ideas and information that were valuable to childbearing. Midwives and doctors were always at daggers drawn. Trained physicians increasingly saw childbirth as a process that could be improved by the application of

new medical knowledge, but as childbirth was a female experience, midwives jealously guarded their role in it. No matter how skilled they were, they were denied access to medical training that might have enabled them to develop lucrative practices on their own. Thus they had no intention of letting male doctors into their trade. For a time the compromise was the handbooks, which contained guides to anatomy, descriptions of the most common complications, and the direst warnings to call trained physicians when serious problems arose.

By the beginning of the eighteenth century the "man-midwife" had made his appearance in western Europe. Medically trained and usually experienced in other forms of surgery, the emergence of the man-midwife led to a number of breakthroughs in increasing the safety of childbirth. There can be no question that more mothers and children survived as a

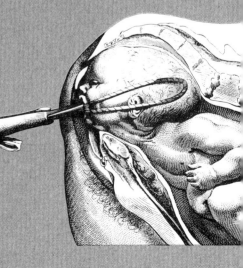

result of the man-midwives' knowledge and skills. But at the same time, the social experience of childbirth changed dramatically. What had been a female rite of passage, experienced by and with other women, now became a private event experienced by an individual woman and her male doctor. As female midwives were still excluded from medical training and licensing, their ability to practice their trade eroded in the face of new techniques and information to which they were denied access.

Though most man-midwives gained their training in hospitals where the poor came to give birth, they practiced mostly among the rich. New attitudes toward marriage and toward children made the pain and danger of childbirth less acceptable to husbands who sought every possible remedy they could afford. British and French man-midwives made large for-

tunes practicing their trade. Their first task was to ascertain that the fetus was in the proper position to descend. In order to do this, however, they had to make an examination that was socially objectionable. Though advanced thinkers could face their man-midwife with the attitude "I considered that through modesty I was not to give up my life"—as one English noblewoman reasoned—many women and more husbands were unprepared for the actual practice of a man. Thus students were taught as much about bedside manner as about medicine. They were not to examine the patient unless there was another person present in the room, they were not to ask direct questions, and they were not to face the patient during any of their procedures. They were taught to keep a linen on top of the woman's abdomen and to make the examination only by touch— incredulous students were reminded that the most famous French man-midwife was blind! If the fetus was in the correct position, nothing further would be done until the delivery itself. It was only when the fetus was in what was labeled an "unnatural" position that the skill of the physician came into play.

For the most part, a child that could not be delivered head first, face down was in serious risk of being stillborn and the mother in serious risk of dying in labor. This was the problem to which the physicians addressed themselves in the eighteenth century and for which they found remarkable solutions. Most answers came from better understanding of

female anatomy and a better visualization of the way in which the fetus moved during labor. The first advance was the realization that the fetus could be turned while still in the womb. Pressure applied on the outside of the stomach, especially in early stages of labor, could help the fetus drop down correctly. A baby who emerged feet first had to be turned face down before it was pulled through the birth canal.

For babies who could not be manually manipulated, the greatest advance of the eighteenth century was the invention of the forceps, or the *tire-tête* as the French called them. With forceps the physician could pull the baby by force when the mother was incapable of delivery. Forceps were used mostly in breech births but were also a vital tool when the baby was too large to pass through the cervix by contraction. The forceps were invented in Britain in the middle of the seventeenth century but were kept secret for more than fifty years. During that time they were used by three generations of a single family of man-midwives. In the eighteenth century they came into general use when the Scotsman William Smellie (1697–1765) developed a short, leather-covered instrument that enabled the physician to do as little damage as possible to either mother or child. Obstetrics now emerged as a specialized branch of medical practice. If neither the pain nor the sorrow of childbirth could be eliminated, its dangers could be lessened.

few animals meant little manure and without manure the soil could not easily be regenerated.

It was not until the middle of the seventeenth century that solutions to these problems began to appear. The first change was consolidation of landholdings so that traditional crop rotations could be abandoned. A second innovation was the introduction of fodder crops, some of which—like clover—added nutrients to the soil, while others—like turnips—were used to feed livestock. Better grazing and better winter feed increased the size of herds, while new techniques of animal husbandry, particularly crossbreeding, produced hardier strains. It was quite clear that the key to increased production lay in better fertilization, and by the eighteenth century some European farmers had broken through the "manure barrier." Larger herds, the introduction of clover crops, the use of human waste from towns, and even the first experiments with lime as an artificial fertilizer were all part of the new agricultural methods. The impact of new farming techniques was readily apparent. In Britain and Holland, where they were used most extensively, grain yields exceeded ten kernels harvested for

each one planted, while in eastern Europe, where they were hardly known, yields were less than five to one.

Along with the new crops that helped nourish both soil and animals came new crops that helped nourish people. Indian corn, or maize, was a staple crop for Native Americans and gradually came to be grown in most parts of western Europe. Maize not only had higher nutritional value than most other cereals, it also yielded more food per acre than traditional grains, reaching levels as high as forty to one. So, too, did the potato, which also entered the European diet from the New World. The potato grew in poor soil, required less labor, and yielded an abundant and nutritious harvest. It rapidly took hold in Ireland and parts of Prussia, from which it spread into eastern Europe. French and Spanish peasants reluctantly introduced it into their diet. Wherever it took root, the potato quickly established itself as survival food. It allowed families to subsist on smaller amounts of land and with less capital outlay. As a result, potato cultivation enabled people in some parts of Europe to marry younger and thus to produce more children.

It must be stressed, however, that these new developments involved only a very narrow range of producers. The new techniques were expensive and knowledge of the new crops spread slowly. Change had to overcome both inertia and intransigence. With more mouths to feed, profits from agriculture soared without landowners having to lift a finger. Only the most ambitious were interested in improvement. At the other end, peasant farmers were more concerned with failure than success. An experiment that did not work could devastate a community; one that did only meant higher taxes. Thus the most important improvements in agricultural production were more traditional ones. Basically, there was an increase in the amount of land that was utilized for growing. In most of western Europe there was little room for agricultural expansion, but in the east there remained great tracts of uncultivated land. In Russia, Prussia, and Hungary hundreds of thousands of new acres came under the plow, though it must be admitted that some of it simply went to replace land that had been wastefully exhausted in previous generations. In one German province, nearly 75 percent more land was in cultivation at

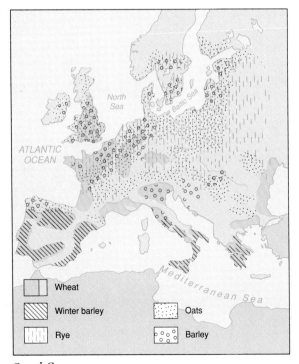

Cereal Crops

Agricultural techniques are illustrated in this plate from Diderot's *Encyclopedia.* In the foreground, a man steers a high-wheeled, horse-drawn plow while a woman operates a hopper device to sow seeds.

the end of the eighteenth century than had been at the beginning. Even in the west, drainage schemes and forest clearance expanded productive capacity.

There was also an upswing in the efficiency with which agricultural products were marketed. From the seventeenth century onward, market agriculture was gradually replacing subsistence agriculture in most parts of Europe. Market agriculture had the advantage of allowing specialization on farms. Single-crop farming enabled farmers to benefit from the peculiarities of their own soil and climate. They could then exchange their surplus for the range of crops they needed to subsist. Market exchange was facilitated by improved transportation and communication and above all by the increase in the population of towns, which provided demand. On a larger scale, market agriculture was able to respond to regional harvest failures in a way that subsistence agriculture could not. The most hated figure in the eighteenth century was the "grain engrosser,"

a middleman who bought up local surplus and shipped it away. Engrossers were accused of driving up prices—which they did—and of creating famines—which they did not. In fact, the national and international trade in large quantities of grain evened out regional variations in harvests and went a long way toward reducing local grain shortages. The upkeep of roads, the building of canals, and the clearing of waterways created a national lifeline for the movement of grain.

Finally, it is believed that the increase in agricultural productivity owed something to a change in climate that took place in the late eighteenth century. This is very difficult to substantiate and impossible to explain. It is thought that the annual ring of growth inside trees is an indicator of changes in climate. Hot years produce markedly different rings than cold ones; wet years are etched differently than dry ones. Examination of trees that are centuries old seems to indicate that the European climate was unusually cold and wet during the seventeenth century—some have even called it a little ice age—and that it gradually warmed during the eighteenth century. Even moderate climatic change, when combined with new techniques, new crops, expanded cultivation, and improved marketing, would go a long way toward explaining how so many more people were being fed at the end of the eighteenth century.

The Plight of the Poor

"Of every ten men one is a beggar, five are too poor to give him alms, three more are ill at ease, embarrassed by debts and lawsuits, and the tenth does not represent a hundred thousand families." So observed an eighteenth-century Frenchman about the distribution of wealth in his country. There can be no doubt that the most serious social problem of the eighteenth century centered on the explosion of poor people throughout Europe. There was grim irony in the fact that advances in the production and distribution of food and the retreat of war and plague allowed more people to survive from hand to mouth than ever before. Where their ancestors had succumbed to quick death from disease or starvation, they eked out a miserable existence of constant hunger and chronic pain with death at the end of a seemingly endless corridor.

It is impossible to gauge the number of European poor or to separate them into categories of greater and greatest misery. The truly indigent, the starving poor, probably composed 10 to 15 percent of most societies, perhaps as many as 20 million people throughout the Continent. They were most prevalent in towns but were an increasing burden on the countryside, where they wandered in search of agricultural employment. The wandering poor had no counterpart in the east, where serfdom kept everyone tied to the land, but the hungry and unsheltered certainly did. Yet the problem of poverty was not only to be seen among the destitute. In fact, the uniqueness of the poor in the eighteenth century is that they were drawn from social groups that even in the hungry times of the early seventeenth century had been successful subsistence producers. Perhaps another 40 percent of the population in western Europe was described by contemporaries as those without a fixed interest: in the country, those without land; in the towns, those without steady jobs.

It was easy to see why poverty was increasing. The relentless advance of population drove up the price of food and drove down the price of wages. In the second half of the eighteenth century, the cost of living in France rose by over 60 percent while wages rose only by 25 percent. In Spain the cost of living increased by 100 percent while wages rose only 20 percent. Only in Britain did wages nearly keep pace with prices. Rising prices made land more valuable. At the beginning of the eighteenth century, as the first wave of population expansion hit western Europe, smallholdings began to decrease in size. The custom of partible inheritance, by which each son received a share of land, shrank the average size of a peasant holding below that necessary to sustain an average-size family, let alone one that was growing larger. In one part of France it was estimated that thirty acres was a survival plot of land in good times. At the end of the seventeenth century 80 percent of the peasants there owned less than twenty-five acres.

As holdings contracted, the portion of the family income derived from wage labor expanded. In such circumstances males were more valuable than females, either as farmers or laborers, and there is incontrovertible evidence that European rural communities practiced female infanticide. In the end, however, it became increasingly difficult for the peasant family to remain on the land. Mediterranean sharecroppers fell further and further into debt until they finally lost their land entirely. Small freeholders were forced to borrow against future crops until a bad harvest led to foreclosure. Many were allowed to lease back their own lands, on short terms and at high rents, but most swelled the ranks of agricultural laborers, migrating during the planting and harvest seasons, suffering cruelly during winter and summer. In Britain the rural landless outnumbered the landed by two to one. In France there were as many as 8 million peasants who no longer owned their own land.

Emigration was the first logical consequence of poverty. In places where rural misery was greatest, like Ireland, whole communities pulled up stakes and moved to America. Frederick the Great attracted hundreds of thousands of emigrants to Prussia by offering them land. But most rural migrants did not move to new rural environments. Rather they followed the well-trodden paths to the cities. Many traditional domestic crafts were evolving into industrial activities. In the past, peasants supplemented their family income by processing raw materials in the home. Spinning, weaving, and sewing were common cottage industries in which the workers took in the work, supplied their own equipment, and were paid by the piece. Now, especially in the cloth trades, a new form of industrial activity was being organized. Factories, usually located in towns or larger villages, assembled workers together, set them at larger and more efficient machines, and paid them for their time rather than for their output. Families unable to support themselves from the land had no choice but to follow the movement of jobs.

Urban poverty seemed more extreme to observers because there were more poor to observe. They crowded into towns in search of work or charity, though they were unlikely to find much of either. It was certainly true that urban areas were better equipped to assist the poor than were the rural communities from which they came. But likelihood of finding aid only attracted more and more poor, straining and finally breaking the capacities of urban institutions. The death rate of these migrants and their children was staggering. It is perhaps best typified by the dramatic increase in the numbers of abandoned babies throughout western European cities. The existence of foundling hospitals in cities meant that unwed or poor mothers could leave their children in hopes that they would receive better care than the mother herself could provide. In fact, this was rarely the case. In the largest foundling hospital in Paris, only 15 percent of the children survived their first year of "care." But this did little to deter abandonment. In 1772, over 7,500 babies were left in this charnel house, representing 40 percent of all the children born in Paris that year. The normal rates of abandonment of between 10 and 15 percent of all children born in such diverse cities as Madrid and Brussels were little better.

Neither state nor private charities could cope with the flood of poor immigrants. Though the English pundit Samuel Johnson (1709–84) opined that "a decent provision for the poor is the true test of civilization," what he meant was provision for the deserving poor, those unfortunates who were physically or mentally unable to support themselves. The distinction between the worthy and unworthy poor was one involved with changing definitions of charity itself. In earlier times, charity was believed to benefit the soul of the giver as much as the body of the recipient. Thus the poor were socially useful, providing the rich with opportunity to do good works. But now the poor were coming to be viewed as a problem of social administration. Hospitals, workhouses, and more ominously, prisons were established or expanded to deal with them.

Hospitals were residential asylums rather than places for health care. They took in the old, the incapacitated, and increasingly, the orphaned young. Those in France were aptly named "Hotels of God," considering their staggering death rates. "There children dwell who know no parents' care/ Parents who know no children's care dwell there," one poet lamented. Workhouses existed for those who were capable of work but incapable of finding it. They were supposed to improve the values of the idle by keeping them busy, though in most places they served only to improve the profits of the industrialists, who rented out workhouse inmates at below-market wages. Prisons grew with crime. There were spectacular increases in crimes against property in all eighteenth-century cities and despite severe penalties that could include hanging for petty theft, more criminals were incarcerated than executed. Enlightened arguments for the reform of prisons and punishment tacitly acknowledged the social basis of most crime. As always, the victims of crime were mostly drawn from the same social backgrounds as the perpetrators. Along with all of their other troubles, it was the poor who were most commonly robbed, beaten, and abused.

Popular Culture

However depressing is this story of the unrelieved misery of the poor, we should not think of the masses of eighteenth-century society only as the downtrodden victims of social and economic forces beyond their control. For the peasant farmer about to lose his land or the urban artisan without a job, security was an overwhelming concern. While many were to endure such fates, many others lived comfortably by the standards of the age and almost everyone believed that things were better now than they had ever been before. Popular culture was a rich mixture of family and community activities that provided outlets from the pressures of work and the vagaries of fortune. It was no less sustaining to the population at large than was the purely literate culture of the elite, no less vital as a means of explanation for everyday events than the theories of the philosophers or the programs of the *philosophes*.

In fact, the line between elite and popular culture in the eighteenth century is a thin one. For one thing, there was still much mixing of social classes in both rural and urban environments. Occasions of display, like festivals, village fairs, or religious holidays, brought entire communities together and reinforced their collective identities. Moreover, there were many shared elements between the two cultures. All over Europe, literacy was increasing, the result of primary education, of new business techniques, and of the millions of books that were available in editions tailored to even the most modest purse. Nearly half of the inhabitants of France were literate by the end of the eighteenth century, perhaps 60 percent of those in Britain. Men were more likely to have learned to read than women, as were those who lived in urban areas. More than a quarter of French women could read, a number that had doubled over the century. As the rates of female literacy rose, so did overall rates, for women took the lead in teaching children.

Popular literacy spawned popular literature in remarkable variety. Religious works remained the most important, but they were followed by almanacs, romances, and, perhaps surprisingly, chivalric fiction. Religious tracts aimed at the populace were found throughout Europe. They contained stories of the saints in Catholic countries or of the martyrs in Protestant ones, proverbs intended to increase spirituality, and prayers to be offered for all occasions. Almanacs combined prophecies, home remedies, astrological tables, predictions about the weather, and advice on all varieties of agricultural and industrial activities. In the middle of the century just one of the dozens of British almanacs was selling over eighty thousand copies a year. Romances were the staple of lending libraries, which were also becoming a common feature of even small towns. These books were usually published in inexpensive installments spaced according to the time working families needed to save the pennies to purchase them. Written by middle-class authors, popular romances had a strong moral streak, promoting chastity for women and sobriety for men. Yet the best-selling popular fiction, at least in western Europe, was melodramatic tales of knights and ladies from the age of chivalry. These themes seeped into popular consciousness after having fallen out of favor among the elites. But cultural tastes did not only trickle down. The masses kept the chivalric tradition alive during the eighteenth century; it would percolate up into elite culture in the nineteenth.

Nevertheless, literate culture was not the dominant form of popular culture. Traditional social activities continued to reflect the violent and even brutal nature of day-to-day existence. Village festivals were still the safety valve of youth gangs who enforced sexual morals by shaming husbands whose wives were unfaithful or women whose reputations were sullied. Many holidays were celebrated by sporting events that pitted inhabitants of one village against those of another. These almost always turned into free-for-alls in which broken bones were common and deaths not unknown. In fact, the frequent breakdown of sporting activities into gang wars was the principal cause for the development of rules for soccer as well as more esoteric games like cricket in Britain. Well-organized matches soon became forms of popular entertainment. Over twenty thousand spectators attended one eighteenth-century cricket match, and soccer and cricket soon became as popular for gambling as was horse racing among the wealthy.

Even more popular were the so-called blood sports, which continued to be the most common form of popular recreation. These were brutal competitions in which, in one way or another, animals were maimed or slaughtered. Dog- and cock-fighting were among those that still survive today. Less attractive to the modern mind were blood sports like bearbaiting or bullrunning, in which the object was the slaughter of a large beast over a prolonged period of time. Blood sports were certainly not confined to the masses—foxhunting and bullfighting were pastimes for the very rich—but they formed a significant part of local social activity.

So too did the tavern or alehouse, which in town or country was the site for local communication and recreation. There women and men gossiped and gambled to while away the hours between sundown and bedtime. Discussions and games became animated as the evening wore on, for staggering amounts of alcohol were consumed. "Drunk for a penny, dead drunk for two pennies, straw for nothing," advertised one of the thousands of British gin mills that dominated the poorer quarters of towns. The increased use of spirits—gin, brandy, rum, and vodka—changed the nature of alcohol consumption in Europe. Wine and beer had always been drunk in quantities that we would find astounding, but these beverages were also an important part of diet. The nutritional content of spirits was negligible. People drank spirits to get drunk. The British reformer Francis Place (1771–1854), who grew up in a working-class family, commented that the British masses had only two pleasures, "sex and drinking. And drunkenness is by far the most

The Cockpit *(ca. 1759),
by William Hogarth. The
central figure is a blind
nobleman who was said
never to have missed an
important cockfight. The
steel spurs on the birds'
legs enabled them to
inflict serious damage in
the heat of the battle.*

desired." The level to which it rose in the eighteenth century speaks volumes about the changes in social and economic life that the masses of European society were now experiencing.

Eighteenth-century society was a hybrid of old and new. It remained highly stratified. Birth and occupation determined wealth, privilege, and quality of life as much as they had in the past, but there were now more paths toward the middle and upper classes, more wealth to be distributed among those above the level of subsistence. Opulence and poverty increased in step as the fruits of commerce and land enriched the upper orders while rising population impoverished the lower ones. Enlightenment ideas highlighted the contradictions. The attack on traditional authority, especially the Roman Catholic church, was an attack on a conservative, static world view. Enlightenment thinkers looked to the future, to a new world shaped by reason and knowledge, a world ruled benevolently for the benefit of all human beings. Government, society, the individual—all could be improved if only the rubble of the past was cleared away. They could hardly imagine how potent their vision would become.

Suggestions for Further Reading

General Reading

* Olwen Hufton, *Europe: Privilege and Protest 1730–1789* (Ithaca, NY: Cornell University Press, 1980). An excellent survey of the political and social history of the mid-eighteenth century.

* Leonard Krieger, *Kings and Philosophers 1689–1789* (New York: Norton, 1970). A brilliant depiction of the personalities and ideas of eighteenth-century Europe.

* Isser Woloch, *Eighteenth Century Europe, Tradition and Progress, 1715–89* (New York: Norton, 1982). Especially strong on social movements and popular culture.

* William Doyle, *The Old European Order 1660–1800* (Oxford: Oxford University Press, 1978). An important essay on the structure of European societies and the ways in which they held together.

* Raymond Birn, *Crisis, Absolutism, Revolution: Europe 1648–1789/91* (New York: Dryden Press, 1977). A reliable survey with especially good chapters on the Enlightenment.

The Nobility

Michael Bush, *Noble Privilege* (New York: Holmes & Meier, 1983). A good analytic survey of the rights of European nobles.

J. V. Beckett, *The Aristocracy in England* (London: Basil Blackwell, 1986). A comprehensive study of a tightly knit national aristocracy.

* Albert Goodwin, ed., *The European Nobility in the Eighteenth Century* (New York: Harper & Row, 1967). Separate essays on national nobilities, including those of Sweden, Poland, and Spain.

* Norman Hampson, *The Enlightenment* (London: Penguin Books, 1982). The best one-volume survey.

* Peter Gay, *The Enlightenment: An Interpretation*, 2 vols. (New York: Knopf, 1966–69). A difficult but rewarding study by one of the leading historians of the subject.

Carolyn Lougee, *Le Paradis des Femmes: Women, Salons, and Social Stratification* (Princeton, NJ: Princeton University Press, 1976). A study of the foundation of the French salons and the role of women in it.

* Judith Sklar, *Montesquieu* (Oxford: Oxford University Press, 1987). A concise, readable study of the man and his work.

Theodore Besterman, *Voltaire* (Chicago: University of Chicago Press, 1976). The best of many biographies of an all-too-full life.

* John G. Gagliardo, *Enlightened Despotism* (New York: Thomas Y. Crowell, 1967). A sound exploration of the impact of Enlightenment ideas on the rulers of Europe, with most emphasis on the east.

The Bourgeoisie

Jan de Vries, *European Urbanization 1500–1800* (Cambridge, MA: Harvard University Press, 1984). An important, though difficult study of the transformation of towns into cities with the most reliable estimates of size and rates of growth.

* P. J. Corfield, *The Impact of English Towns 1700–1800* (Oxford: Oxford University Press, 1982). A thorough survey of the role of towns in English social and economic life.

* Elinor Barber, *The Bourgeoisie in Eighteenth Century France* (Princeton, NJ: Princeton University Press, 1955). Still the best study of the French bourgeoisie.

* Simon Shama, *The Embarrassment of Riches* (Berkeley: University of California Press, 1987). The social life of Dutch burghers richly portrayed.

* Ian Watt, *The Rise of the Novel* (Berkeley: University of California Press, 1957). An important essay on the relationship between literature and society in the eighteenth century.

David Garrioch, *Neighborhood and Community in Paris, 1740–90* (Cambridge: Cambridge University Press, 1986). A good microstudy of Parisian neighborhoods and of the people who inhabited them.

George Sussman, *Selling Mothers' Milk: The Wet-Nursing Business* (Bloomington: Indiana University Press, 1982). A study of buyers and sellers in this important social marketplace.

Samia Spencer, *French Women and the Age of Enlightenment* (Bloomington, IN: Indiana University Press, 1984). A survey of the role of women in French high culture.

* Lawrence Stone, *The Family, Sex and Marriage in England 1500–1800* (New York: Harper & Row, 1979). A controversial but extremely important argument about the changing nature of family life.

* Jean Louis Flandrin, *Families in Former Times* (Cambridge: Cambridge University Press, 1979). Strong on family and household organization.

The Masses

* Michael W. Flinn, *The European Demographic System* (Baltimore: Johns Hopkins University Press, 1981). The best single-volume study, especially for the nonspecialist reader.

E. A. Wrigley and R. S. Schofield, *The Population History of England* (Cambridge, MA: Harvard University Press, 1981). The most important reconstruction of a national population by a team of researchers.

Olwen Hufton, *The Poor in Eighteenth Century France* (Oxford: Oxford University Press, 1974). A compelling study of the life of the poor.

* Roy Porter, *English Society in the Eighteenth Century* (London: Penguin Books, 1982). A breezy, entertaining survey of English social life.

* J. M. Beattie, *Crime and the Courts in England* (Princeton, NJ: Princeton University Press, 1986). A difficult but sensitive analysis of crime and criminal justice.

* Peter Burke, *Popular Culture in Early Modern Europe* (New York: Harper & Row, 1978). A wide survey of practices throughout the Continent.

Robert Muchembled, *Popular Culture and Elite Culture in France, 1400–1750* (Baton Rouge, LA: Louisiana State University Press, 1985). A complex but richly textured argument about the relationship between two cultures.

* Robert Malcolmson, *Popular Recreation in English Society, 1700–1850* (Cambridge: Cambridge University Press, 1973). Sport and its role in society.

* Indicates paperback edition available.

20

The French Revolution and the Napoleonic Era, 1789–1815

"Let Them Eat Cake"

The Queen of France was bored. Try as she might, Marie Antoinette (1755–93) found insufficient diversion in her life at the great court of Versailles. When she was fourteen, she had married the heir to the French throne, the future Louis XVI. By the age of nineteen, she was queen of the most prosperous state in continental Europe. Still she was bored. Her life, she complained to her mother, Empress Maria Theresa of Austria, was futile and meaningless. Maria Theresa advised the unhappy queen to suffer in silence or risk unpleasant consequences.

Sometimes mothers know best. As head of the Habsburg Empire, Maria Theresa understood more about politics than her youngest child. She understood that people have little sympathy with the boredom of a monarch, especially a foreign-born queen. But Marie Antoinette chose to ignore maternal advice and pursued amusements and intrigues that had unpleasant consequences indeed.

Unpopular as a foreigner from the time she arrived in France, Marie Antoinette suffered a further decline in her reputation as gossip spread about her gambling and affairs

at court. The public heard exaggerated accounts of the fortunes she spent on clothing and jewelry. In 1785 she was linked to a cardinal in a nasty scandal over a gift of a diamond necklace. In spite of her innocence, rumors of corruption and infidelity surrounded her name. Dubbed "Madame Deficit," she came to represent all that was considered decadent in royal rule.

She continued to insist, "I am

afraid of being bored." To amuse herself, she ordered a life-size play village built on the grounds of Versailles, complete with cottages, a chapel, a mill, and a running stream. Then, dressed in the silks and muslins intended as the royal approximation of a milkmaid's garb, she whiled away whole days with her friends and children, all pretending they were inhabitants of this picturesque "Hamlet." Her romantic view of country life helped pass the time, but it did little to bring her closer to the struggling peasants who made up the majority of French subjects.

Marie Antoinette's problems need not have mattered much. Monarchs before her had been considered weak and extravagant. The difference was that her foibles became public in an age when the opinion of the people affected political life. Rulers, even those believed to be divinely appointed, were subjected to a public scrutiny all the more powerful because of the growth of the popular press. Kings, their ministers, and their spouses were held accountable—a dangerous phenomenon for an absolute monarchy.

This Austrian-born queen may not have been more shallow or spendthrift than other queens, but it mattered that people came to see her that way. The queen's reputation sank to its nadir when it was reported that she dismissed the suffering of her starving subjects with the haughty retort: "Let them eat cake." What better evidence could there be of the queen's insensitivity than this heartless remark?

Marie Antoinette never said, "Let them eat cake," but everyone thought she did. This was the kind of callousness that people expected from the monarchy in 1789. Marie Antoinette understood the plight of her starving subjects, as her correspondence indicates. Probably a courtier at Versailles was the real source of the brutal retort, but the truth didn't matter. Marie Antoinette and her husband were being indicted by the public for all the political, social, and fiscal crises that plagued France.

In October 1793, Marie Antoinette was put on trial by the Revolutionary Tribunal and found guilty of treason. She was stripped of all the trappings of monarchy and forced to don another costume. Dressed as a poor working woman, her hair shorn, the former queen mounted the guillotine, following in the footsteps of her husband, who had been executed earlier that year. The monarchy did not fall because of a spendthrift queen with too much time on her hands. Nor did it fall because of the mistakes of the well-meaning but inept king. The monarchy had ceased to be responsive to the profound changes that shook France. It fell because of a new concern in the land for royal accountability in words and deeds. A rising democratic tide carried with it ideas about political representation, participation, and equality. If a queen could change places with a milkmaid, why should not a milkmaid be able to change places with a queen?

The Crisis of the Old Regime in France, 1715–88

France in the eighteenth century, the age of the Enlightenment, was a state invigorated by new ideas. It was also a world dominated by tradition. The traditional institutions of monarchy, Church, and aristocracy defined power and status. Talk of reform, progress, and perfectibility coexisted with the social realities of privileges and obligations determined by birth. The eighteenth century was a time when old ways prevailed even as a new view of the world was taking shape.

At the end of the eighteenth century, a number of foreign visitors to France commented on the disparities that characterized French social and political life. One English visitor in particular, Arthur Young (1741–1820), an agronomist writing on his travels in France in the 1780s, observed that although a prosperous land, France was pocked with extreme poverty; although a land of high culture and great art, it was riddled with ignorance, illiteracy, and superstition; although a land with a centralized bureaucracy, it was also saddled with local interests and obsolete practices. The French nation presented a great challenge to any observer attempting to make sense of its diversity.

Charles Dickens (1812–70), a British novelist of the next century, captured well the contradictions of the age:

It was the best of times, it was the worst of times, it was the age of wisdom, it was the age of foolishness, it was the epoch of belief, it was the epoch of incredulity, it was the season of Light, it was the season of Darkness, it was the spring of hope, it was the winter of despair, we had everything before us, we had nothing before us, we were all going direct to Heaven, we were all going direct the other way.

Dickens recognized that the tensions generated by the clash of continuity and change made this an exciting and complex period in both Britain and France. In France, reformers talked of progress while peasants still used wooden plows. The *philosophes* glorified reason in a world of violence, superstition, and fear. The great crisis of eighteenth-century France, the French Revolution, destroyed what we now know as the old regime. But the Revolution was as much a product of continuities and traditions as it was a product of change and the challenge of new ideas.

Louis XV's France

When Louis XV (1715–74) died, he was a hated man. In his fifty-nine-year reign, he managed to turn the public against him. He was denounced as a tyrant who was trying to starve his people, a slave to the mistresses who ruled his court, and an indecisive sybarite dominated by evil ministers. Louis XV's apathy and ineptitude contributed to his poor image. The declining fortunes and the damaged prestige of the monarchy, however, reflected more than the personality traits of an ineffectual king: they reflected structural challenges to fiscal solvency and absolutist rule that the monarchy was unable to meet.

Louis XV, like his great-grandfather Louis XIV, laid claim to rule as an absolute monarch. He insisted that "the rights and interests of the nation . . . are of necessity one with my own, and lie in my hands only." Such claims failed to mask the weaknesses of royal rule. Louis XV lacked a sufficiently developed bureaucracy to administer and tax the nation in an evenhanded fashion. By the beginning of the eighteenth century, the absolute monarchy had extended royal influence into the new areas of policing, administration, law-making, and taxation. But none of this proved sufficient to meet the growing needs of the state.

The growing tensions between the monarch and the aristocracy found expression in various institutions, especially the *parlements*, the thirteen sovereign courts in the French judicial system with their seats in Paris and a dozen provincial centers. The magistrates of each parlement were members of the nobility, some of them nobles of recent origin and others of long standing, depending on the locale. The king needed the parlements to record royal decrees before they could become law. This recording process conferred real political power on the parlements, which could withhold approval for the king's policies by refusing to register his decrees. When the king attempted to make new laws, the magistrates could refuse to endorse them. When decrees involved taxation, they often did. Because magistrates purchased their offices in the parlements, the king found it difficult to control the courts. His fiscal difficulties prevented him from buying up the increasingly valuable offices in order to appoint his own men. Stripping magistrates of their positions was considered tantamount to the theft of property. By successfully challenging the king, the parlements became a battleground between the elite, who claimed that they represented the nation, and the king, who said the nation was himself.

The king repeatedly attempted to neutralize the power of the parlements by relying instead on his own state bureaucracy. His agents in the provinces, called *intendants*, were accountable directly to the central government. The intendants, as the king's men, and the magistrates who presided in the parlements represented contradictory claims to power. As the king's needs increased in the second half of the eighteenth century, the situation was becoming intolerable for those exercising power and those aspiring to rule in the name and for the good of the nation.

The nadir of Louis XV's reign came in 1763 with the French defeat in the Seven Years' War both on the Continent and in the colonies. In the Treaty of Paris, France ceded territory, including its Canadian holdings, to Great Britain. France lost more than lands; it lost its footing in the competition with its chief rival Great Britain, which had been pulling ahead of France in international affairs since the mid-eighteenth century. The war was also a financial debacle, paid for by loans secured against the guarantee of victory. The defeat not only left France barren of funds; it also promoted further expenditures for strengthening the French navy against the superior British fleet. New taxation was the way out of the financial trap in which the king now found himself.

Louis XV's revenue problem was not easily solved. In order to raise taxes, the king had to turn to the recording function of the parlements. Following the costly Seven Years' War, the parlements chose to exercise the power of refusal by blocking a proportional tax to be imposed on nobles and commoners alike. The magistrates resisted taxation with an argument that confused liberty with privilege: the king, the magistrates asserted, was attacking the liberty of his subjects by attempting to tax those who were exempt by virtue of their privileged status.

René Nicolas Charles Augustin de Maupeou (1714–92), Louis XV's chancellor from 1768 to 1774, decided that the political power of the parlements had to be curbed. In 1770, in an attempt to coerce the magistrates into compliance with the king's wishes, he engineered the overthrow of the Parlement of Paris, the most important of the high courts. Those magistrates who remained obdurate were sent into exile. New courts whose membership was based on appointment instead of the sale of offices took their place amid much public criticism. Ultimately, Maupeou's attempt failed. His action did nothing to improve the monarch's image and it did less to solve the fiscal problems of the regime. The conflict between Louis XV and the parlements revealed the dependent nature of the monarchy that claimed to be absolute and accountable only to God.

The dignity and prestige of the monarchy were seriously damaged in the course of Louis XV's long reign. His legacy was well captured in the expression erroneously attributed to him, *après moi le déluge*—"after me, the flood." Continuing to live the good life at the court, he failed dismally to offset rising state expenditures—caused primarily by military needs—with new sources of revenue. In 1774 Louis XV died suddenly of smallpox. His unprepared twenty-year-old grandson, Louis XVI (1774–92), a young man who amused himself by hunting and pursuing his hobby as an amateur locksmith, was left to try to stanch the flood.

The End of the Old Regime

Louis XV left to his heir Louis XVI the legacy of a disastrous deficit. Deficits were not unknown to the monarchs of France, who had centuries of experience in spending more than they had, but this debt promised to be worse than most. From the beginning of his reign, Louis XVI was caught in the vicious circle of excessive state spending—above all, military spending—followed by bouts of heavy borrowing. Borrowing at high rates required the government to pay out huge sums in interest and service fees on the loans that were keeping it afloat. These outlays in turn piled the state's indebtedness ever higher, requiring more loans, and threatening to topple the whole financial structure and the regime itself.

In inheriting this trouble-ridden fiscal structure, Louis XVI made his own contribution to it.

Following in the footsteps of his grandfather, Louis XVI involved France in a costly war, the War of American Independence (1775–83), by supporting the thirteen colonies in their revolt against Great Britain. The involvement brought the French monarchy to the brink of bankruptcy. Contrary to public opinion, most of the state's expenditures did not go toward lavishing luxuries on the royal court and the royal family at Versailles. They went to pay off loans. More than half of the state budget in the 1780s represented interest on loans taken to pay for foreign military ventures.

The king needed money and he needed it fast. To those who could afford to purchase them, the king continued to sell offices that carried with them titles, revenues, and privileges. He also relied on the sale of annuities that paid high interest rates and that attracted speculators, large and small. The crown had leased out its rights to collect the salt tax in return for large lump-sum advances from the Royal General Farms, a syndicate of about one hundred wealthy financier families. The Royal General Farms reaped healthy profits on their annual transactions at the state's expense. The combined revenues collected by the king through these various stratagems were little more than a drop compared to the vast ocean of debt that threatened to engulf the state.

The existing tax structure proved hopelessly inadequate to meet the state's needs. The *taille*, a direct tax, was levied, either on persons or on land, according to region. Except for those locales where the *taille* was attached to land, the nobility was always exempt from direct taxation. Members of the bourgeoisie could also avoid the direct tax as citizens of towns enjoying exemption. That meant that the wealthy, those best able to pay, were often exempt. Indirect taxes, like those on salt (the *gabelle*) and on food and drink (the *aide*), and internal and external customs taxes were regressive taxes that hit hardest those least able to pay. The peasantry bore the brunt of the nation's tax burden, as the drawing of a simple farmer carrying on his back a noble and a priest conveyed. Louis XVI knew all too well that he could not squeeze blood from a stone by increasing indirect taxes. A peasantry too weighted down would collapse—or rebel.

The privileged elite persisted in rejecting the crown's attempts to tax them. As one of the first acts of his reign, in 1775 Louis XVI had restored the magistrates to their posts in the parlements, treating their offices as a form of property of which they had been deprived. In his conciliatory act, Louis XVI nevertheless stressed that the self-interest of the aristocracy was at odds with the common good of the nation and urged the approval of his programs. By 1776 the Parlement of Paris was again obstructing royal decrees.

Louis XVI appointed Anne Robert Jacques Turgot (1727–1781) as his first controller-general. Turgot's reformist economic ideas were influenced by Enlightenment *philosophes*. In order to generate revenues, Turgot reasoned, France needed to prosper economically. The government was in a position to stimulate economic growth by eliminating regulations, by economizing at court, and by improving the network of roads through a tax on landowners. Each of Turgot's reforms offended established interests, thereby ensuring his early defeat. Emphasis on a laissez-faire economy outraged the guilds; doing away with the forced labor of peasants on the roads (the *corvée*) threatened privileged groups who had never before been taxed. As the king was discovering, divine right did not bring with it absolute authority or fiscal solvency.

As he floundered about for a solution to his economic difficulties, the king turned to a new adviser, Jacques Necker (1732–1804), a Swiss-born Protestant banker. The king and the public expected great things from Necker, whose international business experience was counted on to save the day. Necker, a prudent man, applied his accounting skills to measuring—for the first time—the total income and expenditures of the French state. The budget he produced and widely circulated allayed everyone's fears of certain doom and assured the nation that no new taxes were necessary—an assurance based on disastrous miscalculations.

Instead of raising taxes, Necker committed his ministry to eliminating costly inefficiencies. He promised to abolish venal offices that drained revenues from the crown. He next set his sights on contracts of the farmers-general, collectors of the indirect salt taxes, whom he likened to weeds sprouting in a swamp. Necker's aim was to reduce ordinary expenses of the realm in order to be ready for the extraordinary ones associated with waging a war. Such policies made him enemies in high places and numbered his days in office.

Necker and those who preceded him in controlling and directing the finances of the state under Louis XV and Louis XVI were committed to reforming the system. All the advisers recognized that the state's fiscal problems were structural and required enlightened solutions, but no two of them agreed on the same program of reforms. Necker had somehow captivated popular opinion and there was widespread regret expressed over his forced resignation.

Charles Alexandre de Calonne (1734–1802), appointed controller-general in 1783, had his own ideas of how to bail out the ship of state. He authored a program of reforms that would have shifted the tax burden off those least able to pay and onto those best able to support the state. Such a move would have minimized the differences between nobles and commoners. He proposed a tax on land proportional to land values, a measure that would have most seriously affected the land-rich nobility. In addition, taxes that affected the peasantry were to be lightened or eliminated. Finally, Calonne proposed the sale of Church lands for revenues. In an attempt to bypass the recalcitrant parlements, Calonne advised the crown in 1787 to convene an Assembly of Notables made up of 150 individuals from the magistracy, the Church hierarchy, the titled nobility, and municipal bodies, for the purpose of enlisting their support for reforms. Louis listened to Calonne, who was denounced by the Assembly of Notables for attacking the rights of the privileged. He too was forced to resign.

All of Louis XVI's attempts to persuade the nobility to agree to tax reforms had failed. Considered by his courtiers to be well-meaning but weak and ineffectual, Louis was incapable of the effort required either to inspire or to manipulate the privileged classes to support his plans. Aristocratic magistrates insisted on a constitution, in which their own right to govern would be safeguarded and the accountability of the king would be defined. In opposing the royal reforms, nobles spoke of the "rights of man" and used the term *citizen*. They rebuffed the monarch with the cry, "No taxation without consent." The nobility had no sympathy for tax programs that would have resulted in a loss of privilege and what some nobles were beginning to consider an attack on individual freedom. Louis XVI was met with passivity from the Assembly of Notables and resistance from the Parlement of Paris and the provincial parlements.

In the 1780s, almost 50 percent of annual expenditures went to servicing the accumulated national debt of 4 billion livres and paying interest. The new controller-general, Archbishop Loménie de Brienne (1727–94) recommended emergency loans. The crown once again disbanded the Paris Parlement, which was now threatening to block loans as well as taxes. The aristocracy seemed on the verge of its own revolt against royal authority.

Louis XVI was a desperate man in 1788, so desperate that he yielded to the condition placed on him by the Paris Parlement: he agreed to convene the Estates-General, a medieval body that had not met since 1614 and that had been considered obsolete with the rise of a centralized bureaucratic government. The Estates-General included representatives from the three "estates" of the clergy, nobility, and commoners. About two hundred thousand subjects belonged to the first two estates. The Third Estate was composed of all those members of the realm who enjoyed a common identity only in their lack of privilege—over 23 million French people. In the 1614 voting of the Estates-General, each of the three orders was equally weighted. This arrangement favored the nobility, who controlled the first two estates. The nobility was understandably not worried by the prospect of the Estates-General deciding the tax-reform program. Many were sure that a new age of liberty was at hand.

The Three Estates

French society, to which the king and the noble elite turned in 1788, was divided by law and custom into a pyramid of three tiers called orders or estates. At the top were those who prayed— the clergy, followed by those who fought—the nobility. The base of the pyramid was formed by the largest of the three orders, those who worked—the bourgeoisie, the peasantry, and urban and rural workers. In the second half of the eighteenth century, these traditional groups no

This cartoon depicts the plight of the French peasants. An old farmer is bowed down under the weight of the privileged aristocracy and clergy while birds and rabbits, protected by unfair game laws, eat his crops.

longer reflected social realities—a situation that proved to be a source of serious problems for the Estates-General. The piety of the first order had been called into doubt as religious leaders were criticized for using the vast wealth of the Church for personal benefit instead of public worship. The protective military function of the second order had ceased to exist with the rise of the state and the changing nature of war. The bourgeoisie, those who worked with their heads, not their hands, shared privileges with the nobility and aspired to a noble life-style, in spite of their legal and customary presence in the ranks of the Third Estate.

The vast majority of French subjects who constituted the Third Estate certainly were identified by work, but the vast array of mental and physical labor—and lack of work—splintered the estate into a myriad of occupations, aspirations, and identities. All power flowed upward in this arrangement, with the First and Second Estates dominating the social and political universe. Women and men accepted this hierarchy as the natural organization of society in eighteenth-

century France. But it was a hierarchy whose rationale was under attack.

The king continued to stand at the pinnacle of the eighteenth-century social pyramid. Traditionally revered as the "father" of his subjects, he claimed to be divinely appointed by God. Kingship in this era had a dual nature. The king was both supreme overlord from feudal times, and he was absolute monarch. As supreme overlord he stood dominant over the aristocracy and the court. As absolute monarch he stood at the head of the state and society. When the king equated himself with the state—"L'état, c'est moi," as Louis XIV boasted—all problems—economic, social, and political—also came to be identified with the king. Absolutism required a weakened nobility and a bureaucracy strong enough to help the monarchy to adjust to changes. After the death of Louis XIV in 1715, Louis XV and Louis XVI faced a resurgent aristocracy without the support of a state bureaucracy capable of successfully challenging aristocratic privilege or of solving fiscal problems.

"To live nobly," that is, to live as a noble, was the social ideal to which one could aspire in the eighteenth century. While the system of orders set clear boundaries of social status, distinctions within estates created new hierarchies. The clergy, a privileged order, contained both commoners and nobles, but leadership in the Church depended on social rank. The aristocracy retained control of the bishoprics, even as an activist element among the lower clergy agitated for reforms and better salaries. In a state in which the king claimed to rule by God's will, Catholicism, virtually enshrined as the state religion, was important in legitimizing the divine claims of the monarchy.

The nobility experienced its own internal tensions, generated by two groups: the older nobility of the sword, who claimed descent from medieval times; and the more recent nobility of the robe, who had acquired their position through the purchase of offices that conferred noble status. By increasing the numbers of the nobility of the robe, Louis XIV hoped to undermine the power of the aristocracy as a whole and to decrease its political influence. But aristocrats rallied and closed ranks against the dilution of their power. As a result, both Louis XV and Louis XVI faced a reviving rather than a declining aristocracy. One in four nobles had moved from the bourgeoisie to the aristocratic ranks in the eighteenth century; two out of every three had been ennobled during the seventeenth and eighteenth centuries. Nobles had succeeded in restoring their economic and social power. A growing segment of the aristocracy, influenced by Enlightenment ideas and the example of English institutions, was intent on increasing the political dominance of the aristocracy too.

The nobility strengthened their powers in two ways. First, they monopolized high offices and closed access to nonnobles. They took over posts in ministries, the Church, and the army. Second, the nobility benefited greatly from the doubling in land values brought on by the increase in the value of crops. Nobles enjoyed privileges, the greatest being, in most cases, exemption from taxes. Seeking ever higher returns from the land, some members of the aristocracy adopted new agricultural techniques to achieve greater crop yields. There were certainly poor aristocrats who lacked the lands to benefit from this trend, but those who did control sizable holdings profited greatly from higher dues paid to them, as they reaped increased incomes from crops. In addition, many aristocrats revived their feudal claims to ancient seigneurial, or lordly, privileges. They hired lawyers to unearth old claims and hired agents to collect dues. This was merely good business.

A spirit of innovation characterized the values of certain members of the nobility. Although technically prevented from participating in trade by virtue of their titles and privileges, an active group among the nobility succeeded in making fortunes in metallurgy, glassmaking, and mining. Others participated in trade. These nobles were an economically dynamic and innovative segment of the aristocracy. In spite of the obsolete aspect of their privileges, aristocrats were often responsible for the introduction of modern ideas and techniques in the management of estates and in the bookkeeping involved with collection of rents. Capitalist techniques were not unknown to nobles adapting to the marketplace. These nobles formed an elite partnership with forward-looking members of the bourgeoisie.

Common people, that is, those who did not enjoy the privileges of the nobility, embraced a broad range of the French populace. The peasantry was by far the largest group, joined in the designation as "commoners" by the middle class, or bourgeoisie, and by workers in both cities and rural areas. Most French peasants were free, no longer attached to the soil as serfs were in a feudal system. Yet all peasants endured common obligations placed on them by the crown and the privileged classes. Peasants owed the tithe to the Church, land taxes to the state, and seigneurial dues and rents to the landlord. A bewildering array of taxes afflicted peasants. In some areas peasants repaired roads and drew lots for military service. Dues affected almost every aspect of rural life, including harvests and the sale of property. In addition, indirect taxes like that on salt (the hated *gabelle*) were a serious burden for the peasantry. As if all this were not enough, peasants who were forced to take loans to survive from one harvest to another paid exorbitant interest rates. No matter how bad conditions were, peasants had to be sure to save the seed for next year's crop.

The peasants who staggered and collapsed under all these obligations were forced to leave the land. The precariousness of rural life and the increase in population in the countryside contributed to the permanent displacement and destitution of a growing sector of rural society. Without savings and destroyed by poor harvests, impoverished rural inhabitants wandered the countryside looking for odd jobs and eventually begging to survive. Many peasants with small plots were able to work for wages. The labor of women was essential to the survival of the rural family. Peasant women sought employment in towns and cities as seamstresses and servants in order to send money back home to struggling relatives. Children, too, added their earnings to the family pot. In spite of various strategies for survival, more and more families were disrupted by the end of the eighteenth century.

The bourgeoisie—as the term was used in the eighteenth century—meant those members of the middle class who lived on income from investments. Yet the term really embraced within it a whole hierarchy of professions from bankers and financiers to businessmen, merchants, entrepreneurs, lawyers, shopkeepers, and craftsmen. Along with the nobility, wealthy bourgeois formed the urban elites that administered cities and towns. Prestigious service to the state or the purchase of offices that carried with them noble status enabled the wealthiest members of the bourgeoisie to move into the ranks of the nobility.

Many bourgeois served as middlemen for the nobility by running estates and collecting dues.

Like the rest of the social universe, the world of artisans and workers was shaded with various gradations of wealth and status. Those who owned their own shops and perhaps employed other workers stood as an elite among the working class. In spite of their physical proximity, there was a vast difference between those who owned their own shops and those who earned wages or were paid by the piece. Wage earners represented about 30 percent of the population of cities and towns. And their numbers were swelling, as craftsmen were pushed out of their guilds and peasants were pushed off their land.

In 1775, the king in an attempt to promote free trade temporarily abolished the guilds. Those who worked in crafts were a labor elite, and guilds were intended to protect the corporations of masters, journeymen, and apprentices through monopolistic measures. Guilds insisted that they were best able to ensure the quality of goods. But the emphasis on free trade and the expansion of markets in the eighteenth century weakened the hold of the guilds. Merchants often took them over and paid workers by the piece. The effect was a reduction in the wages of skilled workers. By the 1780s, most journeymen who hoped to be masters knew that their dream would never be realized. Frustration and discontent touched workers in towns and cities who may not have shared a common work experience. But they did share a common anger about the high cost of food—especially bread.

In August 1788 Louis XVI announced that the Estates-General would meet at Versailles in May 1789. He directed each of the three estates—clergy, nobility, and commoners—to elect their representatives, who would come together to discuss the fiscal and political problems plaguing the nation. Every social group, from the nobles to the poorest laborers, had its own grievances and concerns, but all greeted the news with fireworks, parades, and toasts to the best of all kings.

The French Revolution and the End of the Old Regime

Those who lived through it were sure that there had never been a time like it before. The French Revolution, or the Great Revolution, as it was known to contemporaries, was a time of creation and discovery. The ten years from 1789 to 1799 were punctuated by genuine euphoria and democratic transformations. The Revolution achieved most in the area of politics. Revolutionary slogans and songs reflected people's hopes and a new expectation for the future. From the privileged elites who initiated the overthrow of the existing order to peasants and workers, women and men, who united against tyranny, the Revolution touched every segment of society.

The overthrow of absolutist monarchy brought with it new social theories, new symbols, and new behavior. The excitement of anarchy was matched by the terror of repression. Revolutionary France had to contend with a Europe-wide

Revolutionary France

war. The Revolution had its dark side of violence and instability. In the Revolution's wake came internal discord, civil war, and violent repression. In the search for a new order, political forms followed one upon the other in rapid succession: constitutional monarchy, republic, oligarchy. The creation of Napoleon's dictatorship at the end of the century was the act that signified that the Revolution had come to an end.

Similar revolutionary incidents flared up throughout Europe in the second half of the eighteenth century—in the Netherlands, Belgium, and Ireland. Absolute authority was challenged and sometimes modified. Across the Atlantic, American colonists concerned with the principle of self-rule had thrown off the yoke of the British in the War of Independence. But none of these events, including the American Revolution, was so violent in breaking with the old order, so extensive in involving millions of men and women in political action, and so consequential for the political futures of other European states, as was the French Revolution.

Many people alive for these events were sure that they had crossed the threshold of a new era. Succeeding generations agreed. The triumphs and contradictions of the revolutionary experiment in democracy mark the end of the old order and the beginning of modern history. Politics would never be the same again.

Taking Politics to the People

Choosing representatives for the Estates-General in March and April 1789 stirred up hope and excitement in every corner of France. From the very beginning, there were warning signs that a more astute monarch might have noticed. The call for national elections set in motion a politicizing process the king could not control. Members of the Third Estate, traditionally excluded from political and social power, were presented with the opportunity of expressing their opinions on the state of government and society. In an increasingly literate age, pamphlets, broadsides, and political tracts representing every political persuasion blanketed France. Those who could not read stood in marketplaces and city squares or sat around evening fires and had the political literature read to them. Farmhands and urban laborers realized that they were participating in the same process as their social betters. And they believed they had a right to speak and be heard.

This was a time of great hope, especially for people who had been buffeted by the rise in prices, decline in real wages, and the hunger that followed crop failures and poor harvests. Although probably better able than their grandparents to endure periodic hardships, most Frenchmen and women were sure that things were getting worse. Now there was the promise of a respite and a solution. Taxes could be discussed and changed, the state bureaucracy could be reformed—or better, abolished.

Intellectuals discussed political alternatives in the salons of the wealthy. Nobles and bourgeois met in philosophical societies dedicated to enlightened thought. Commoners gathered in cafes to drink and debate. The poor fell outside of this network of communication, but they were not immune to the ideas that emerged. In the end, people of all classes had opinions and they were more certain than ever of their right to express their ideas. Absolutism was in trouble, although Louis XVI did not know it, as people began to forge a collectively shared idea of politics. People now had a forum—the Estates-General—and a focus—the politics of taxation. But most important, they had the elections. The message of the elections and the representative principle on which they were based was that one could compete for power.

In competing for power, some members of the Third Estate were well aware of their vast numerical superiority over the nobility. Because of it, they demanded greater representation than the three hundred members per estate defined according to the practices of 1614. At the very least, they argued, the number of representatives of the Third Estate should be doubled to six hundred members, giving commoners equality in numbers with nobles and priests together. Necker, recalled as director-general of finance in August 1788, agreed to the doubling in the size of the Third Estate as a compromise but left unresolved the additional demand of vote by head rather than by order. If voting was to be left as it was, in accordance with the procedures of 1614, the nobility who controlled the First and Second Estates would determine all outcomes. With a voting procedure by head instead of by order, however, the deputies of the Third Estate could easily dominate the Estates-General, confident that they could count on liberal nobles, like the Marquis de Lafayette, and parish priests to defect from voting with the First and Second Estates and join their cause.

In conjunction with this political activity and in scheduled meetings, members of all three estates drew up statements of their problems. This took place in a variety of forums, including guilds and village and town meetings. The people of France set down their grievances in note-books—known as *cahiers de doléances*—that were then carried to Versailles by the deputies elected to the Estates-General. This was the first national poll of opinion commissioned by the crown, and it involved every level of society. It was a tool of political education as the mass of French people were being given the impression for the first time that they were part of the policy-making process.

"If only the king knew!" In this phrase, French men and women expressed their belief in the inevitability of their fate and the benevolence of their king. They saw the king as a loving and wise father who would not tolerate the injustices visited upon his subjects, if only he knew what was really happening. In 1789 peasants and workers were questioning why their lives could not be better, but they continued to express their trust in the king. Combined with their old faith was a new hope. The peasants in the little town of Saintes recorded their expectations in their *cahier*:

> Our king, the best of kings and father of a great and wise family, will soon know everything. All vices will be destroyed. All the great virtues of industriousness, honesty, modesty, honor, patriotism, meekness, friendliness, equality, concord, pity, and thrift will prevail and wisdom will rule supreme.

The *cahiers* expressed the particular grievances of each estate. These notebooks contained a collective outpouring of problems and are important for two major reasons. First, they made clear the similarity of grievances shared throughout France. Second, they indicated the extent to which a common political culture, based on a concern with political reform, had permeated different levels of French society. Both the privileged and the nonprivileged identified a common enemy in the system of state bureaucracy to which the

monarch was so strongly tied. Although the king was still addressed with respect, new concerns with liberty, equality, property, and the rule of law were voiced.

Those who opposed the Revolution later alleged that these notebooks proved the existence of a highly coordinated plot on the part of secret societies out to destroy the regime. They were wrong. Similarities in complaints, similarities in demands, similarities in language proved, not a conspiracy, but the forging of a new political consciousness. Societies and clubs circulated "model" *cahiers* among themselves, resulting in the use of similar forms and vocabulary. People were questioning their traditional roles and now had elected deputies who would represent them before the king. In the spring of 1789 a severe economic crisis that heightened political uncertainty swept through France. For a king expected to save the situation, time was running out.

Convening the Estates-General

The elected deputies arrived at Versailles at the beginning of May 1789, carrying in their valises and trunks the grievances of their estates. The opening session of the Estates-General took place in a great hall especially constructed for the event. The 1,248 deputies presented a grand spectacle as they filed to their assigned places to hear speeches by the king and his ministers. Contrasts among the participants were immediately apparent. Seated on a raised throne under a canopy at one end of the hall, Louis XVI was vested in full kingly regalia. On his right sat the archbishops and cardinals of the First Estate, dramatically clad in the pinks and purples of their offices. On his left were the richly and decorously attired nobility. Facing the stage sat the 648 deputies of the Third Estate, dressed in plain black suits, stark against the colorful and costly costumes of the privileged. It was clear, in the most visual terms, that "clothes make the man." Members of the Third Estate had announced beforehand that they would not follow the ancient custom for commoners of kneeling at the king's entrance. Fired by the hope of equal treatment and an equal share of power, they had come to Versailles to make a constitution. The opening ceremony degenerated into a moment of confusion over whether members of the Third Estate should be able to don their hats

This painting of the Oath of the Tennis Court is by the Revolution's leading artist, Jacques Louis David. Sieyès sits at a table on which Bailly stands reading the oath. Robespierre is seen clutching his breast in the group behind Sieyès.

in the presence of the king. Many saw in the politics of clothing a tense beginning to their task.

The tension between commoners and privileged was further aggravated by the unresolved issue of how the voting was to proceed. The Third Estate was adamant in its demand for vote by head. The privileged orders were equally adamant in insisting on vote by order. Paralysis set in, as days dragged into weeks and the Estates were unable to act. The body that was to save France from fiscal collapse was hopelessly deadlocked.

Two men in particular whose backgrounds made them unlikely heroes emerged as leaders of the Third Estate. One, the Abbé Emmanuel Joseph Sieyès (1748–1836), was a member of the clergy who frequented Parisian salons. The other, the comte Honoré Gabriel Victor de Mirabeau (1749–91), a black sheep among the nobility, had spent time in prison because of his father's charges that he was a defiant son who led a misspent, debauched, and profligate youth. In spite of his nobility, Mirabeau appeared at Versailles as a deputy for Aix and Marseilles to the Third Estate. His oratory and presence commanded attention from the start. As a consummate politician, Mirabeau combined forces with Sieyès, who had already established his reputation as a firebrand reformer with his eloquent pamphlet, "What Is the Third Estate?" published in January 1789. To the question posed in the title, Sieyès answered, "What is the Third Estate? Everything! What has it been in the political order up to the present? Nothing!"

Sieyès and Mirabeau reminded members of the Third Estate of the reformist consensus that characterized their ranks. Under their influence, the Third Estate decided to proceed with its own meetings. On 17 June 1789, the Third Estate, joined by some sympathetic clergy, changed its name to the National Assembly as an assertion of its true representation of the French nation. Three days later, members of the new National Assembly found themselves locked out of their regular meeting room by the king's guard. Outraged by this insult, they moved to a nearby indoor tennis court, where they vowed to stay together for the purpose of writing a constitution. This event, known as the Oath of the Tennis Court, marked the end of the absolutist monarchy and the beginning of a new concept of the state that power resided in the people. The Revolution had begun.

The drama of Versailles, a staged play of gestures, manners, oaths, and attire, also marked the beginning of a far-reaching political revolution. Although it was a drama that took place behind closed doors, it was not one unknown to the general public. Throughout May and June 1789, Parisians trekked to Versailles to watch the deliberations. Then they brought news back to the capital. Deputies wrote home to their constituents to keep them abreast of events. Newspapers that reported daily on these wranglings and pamphleteers who analyzed them spread the news throughout the nation. Information, often conflicting, stirred up anxiety; news of conflict encouraged action.

The frustration and the stalemate of the Estates-General threatened to put the spark to the kindling of urban unrest. The people of Paris had suffered through a harsh winter and spring under the burdens of high prices (especially of bread), limited supplies, and relentless tax demands. The

This lively amateur painting of the fall of the Bastille is by Claude Cholat, one of the attackers. Tradition has it that Cholat is manning the cannon in the background. The inscription proclaims that the painting is by one of the "Conquerors of the Bastille."

rioting of the spring had for the moment ceased, as people waited for their problems to be solved by the deputies of the Estates-General. The suffering of the urban poor was not new, but their ability to connect economic hardships with the politics at Versailles and to blame the government was. As hopes began to dim with the news of political stalemate, news broke of the creation of the National Assembly. It was greeted with new anticipation.

The Storming of the Bastille

The king, who had temporarily withdrawn from sight following the death of his son at the beginning of June, reemerged to meet with the representatives of each of the three estates and propose reforms, including a constitutional monarchy. But Louis XVI refused to accept the now popularly supported National Assembly as a legitimate body, choosing instead to rely on the three estates for advice. He simply did not understand that the choice was no longer his to make. He summoned troops to Versailles and began concentrating soldiers in Paris. Civilians constantly clashed with members of the military, whom they jostled and jeered. The urban crowds recognized the threat of repression that the troops represented. People decided to meet force with force. To do so, they needed arms themselves and they knew where to get them.

On 14 July 1789, the irate citizens of Paris stormed the Bastille, a royal armory that also served as a prison for a handful of debtors. The storming of the Bastille has become the great

symbol in the revolutionary legend of the overthrow of the tyranny and oppression of the old regime. But it is significant for another reason. It was an expression of the power of the people to take politics into their own hands. Parisians were following the lead of their deputies in Versailles. They had formed a citizen militia, known as the National Guard, and were prepared to defend their concept of justice and law.

The people who stormed the Bastille were not the poor, the unemployed, the criminals, or the urban rabble, as they were portrayed by their detractors. They were bourgeois and petit bourgeois, shopkeepers, guild members, family men and women, who considered it their right to seize arms to protect their interests. The Marquis de Lafayette (1757–1834), a noble beloved of the people because of his participation in the American Revolution, helped organize the National Guard. Under his direction, the militia adopted the tricolor flag as their standard. The tricolor combined the red and blue colors of the city of Paris with the white of the Bourbon royal family. It became the flag of the Revolution, replacing the fleur-de-lis of the Bourbons. It is the national flag of France today.

The king could no longer dictate the terms of the constitution. By their actions, the people in arms had ratified the National Assembly. Louis XVI was forced to yield. The events in Paris set off similar uprisings in cities and towns throughout France. National guards in provincial cities modeled themselves after the Parisian militia. Government officials fled their posts and abandoned their responsibilities. Commoners stood ready to fill the power vacuum that now existed. But the Revolution was not just an urban phenomenon. The peasantry had their own grievances and their own way of making a revolution.

The Revolution of the Peasantry

In the spring and early summer of 1789, food shortages drove bands of armed peasants to attack manor houses throughout France. In the areas surrounding Paris and Versailles, peasants destroyed game and devastated the forests where the king and his nobles hunted. The anger reflected in these seemingly isolated events was suspended as the hope grew that the proceedings at Versailles would produce results. Remote as peasant involvement in the drawing up of the *cahiers* might have been, peasants everywhere expected that aid was at hand.

News of the events of Versailles and then of the revolutionary action in Paris did not reassure rural inhabitants. By the end of June the hope of deliverance from crippling taxes and dues was rapidly fading. The news of the Oath of the Tennis Court and the storming of the Bastille terrified country folk, who saw the actions as evidence of an aristocratic plot that threatened sorely needed reforms. As information moved along postal routes in letters from delegates to their supporters, or news was repeated in the Sunday market gatherings, distortions and exaggerations crept in. It seemed to rural inhabitants that their world was falling apart. Some peasants believed that Paris was in the hands of brigands and that the king and the Estates-General were victims of an aristocratic plot. Rural vision, fueled by empty stomachs, was apocalyptic.

This state of affairs was aggravated as increasing numbers of peasants had been pushed off the land to seek employment as transient farm laborers, moving from one area to another with the cycles of sowing and harvesting. Throughout the 1780s the number of peasants without land was increasing steadily. Filthy, poorly dressed, and starving men, women, and children were frightening figures to villagers who feared that the same fate would befall them with the next bad harvest. As one landowner lamented, "We cannot lie down without fear, the nighttime paupers have tormented us greatly, to say nothing of the daytime ones, whose numbers are considerable."

Most peasants had lived in the same place for generations and knew only the confines of their own villages. They were uneasy about what existed beyond the horizon. Transients, often speaking strange dialects, disrupted and threatened the social universe of the village. In order to survive, wanderers often resorted to petty theft, stealing fruit from trees or food from unwatched hearths. Traveling often in groups, hordes of vagabonds struck fear into the hearts of farmworkers, trampling crops and sleeping in open fields. Peasants were sure that these unfortunate souls were brigands paid by the local aristocracy to persecute a peasantry already stretched to the breaking point.

Hope gave way to fear. Beginning on 20 July 1789, peasants in different areas of France reacted with a kind of collective hysteria, spreading false rumors of a great conspiracy. Fear gripped whole villages, and in some areas spawned revolt. Just as urban workers had connected their economic hardships to politics, so too did desperate peasants see their plight in political terms. They banded together and marched to the residences of the local nobility, breaking into the chateaus with

This engraving from the late eighteenth century shows French country houses ablaze while speeding carriages carry their frightened owners to safety. The peasants attacked and looted the houses of the gentry and burned the rolls of feudal duties.

a single mission in mind: to destroy all legal documents by which nobles claimed payments, dues, and services from local peasants. They drove out the lords and in some cases burned their chateaus, putting an end to the tyranny of the privileged over the countryside. The peasants had taken matters into their own hands. In the bonfires of aristocratic documents, peasants intended to consign the last vestiges of aristocratic privilege to the flames.

The overthrow of privileges rooted in a feudal past was not as easy as that. Members of the National Assembly were aghast at the eruption of rural violence. They knew that to stay in power they had to maintain peace. They also knew that to be credible they had to protect property. Peasant destruction of seigneurial claims posed a real dilemma for the bourgeois deputies directing the Revolution. If they gave in to peasant demands, they risked losing aristocratic support and undermining their own ability to control events. If they gave in to the aristocracy, they risked a social revolution in the countryside, which they could not police or repress. Liberal members of the aristocracy cooperated with the bourgeois leaders in finding a solution.

In a dramatic meeting that lasted through the night of 4–5 August 1789, the National Assembly agreed to abolish the principle of privilege. The peasants had won—or thought they had. In the weeks and months ahead, rural people learned they had lost their own prerogatives—the rights to common grazing and gathering—and were expected to buy their way out of their feudal services. In the meantime, parliamentary action had saved the day, as the deputies stabilized the situation through legislating compromise.

Women's Actions

Women participated with men in both urban and rural revolutionary actions. Acting on their own, women were responsible for the most dramatic event of the early years of the Revolution: in October 1789 they forced the king and the royal family to leave Versailles for Paris to deal in person with the problems of bread supply, high prices, and starvation. Women milling about in the marketplaces of Paris on the morning of 5 October were complaining bitterly about the high cost and shortages of bread. The National Assembly was in session and the National Guards were patrolling the streets of Paris. But these trappings of political change had no impact on the brutal realities of the marketplace.

Women were in charge of buying the food for their families. Every morning they stood in lines with their neighbors reenacting the familiar ritual. Some mornings they were turned away, told by the baker or his assistants that there was no

A contemporary print of the women of Paris advancing on Versailles. The determined marchers are shown waving pikes and dragging an artillery piece. The women were hailed as heroines of the Revolution.

bread. On other days they did not have enough coins in their purses to buy this staple of their diet. Women, who were responsible for managing the consumption of the household, were most directly in touch with the state of provisioning the capital. When they were unable to feed their families, the situation became intolerable.

So it was on the morning of 5 October 1789, that six thousand Parisian women marched out of the city and toward Versailles. They were taking their problem to the king with the demand that he solve it. Later in the day, Lafayette, sympathetic to the women's cause, led the Parisian National Guard to Versailles to mediate events. The women were armed with pikes, the simple weapon available to the poorest defender of the Revolution, and they were prepared to use them. The battle came early the next morning, when the women, tired and cold from waiting all night at the gates of the palace, invaded the royal apartments and chased Marie Antoinette from her bedroom. Several members of the royal guards, hated by the people of Paris for alleged insults against the tricolor cockade, were killed by the angry women, who decapitated them and mounted their heads on pikes. A shocked Louis XVI agreed to return with the crowd to Paris. The crowd cheered Louis' decision, which briefly reestablished his personal popularity. But as monarch, he had been humiliated at the hands of women of the capital. "The baker, the baker's wife, and the baker's son" were forced to return to Paris that very day. Louis XVI was now captive to the Revolution, whose efforts to form a constitutional monarchy he purported to support.

The Revolution Threatened

The disciplined deliberations of committees intent on fashioning a constitutional monarchy replaced the passion and fervor of revolutionary oratory. The National, or Constituent, Assembly divided France into new administrative units for the purpose of establishing better control over municipal governments. The administrative reformers intended that by the creation of *départements* the central government would have greater control over local interests and that anarchy would be avoided.

In addition to new administrative trappings, the government promoted its own rituals. On 14 July 1790, militias from each of the newly created eighty-three *départements* of France came together in Paris to celebrate the first anniversary of the storming of the Bastille. A new national holiday was born and with it a sense of devotion and patriotism for the new France liberated by the Revolution. In spite of these unifying elements, however, the newly achieved revolutionary consensus showed signs of breaking down.

In February 1790 legislation dissolved all monasteries and convents, except for those that provided aid to the poor or that served as educational institutions. As the French church was stripped of its lands, Pope Pius VI (1775–99) denounced the principles of the Revolution. In July 1790 the government approved the Civil Constitution of the Clergy: priests now became the equivalent of paid agents of the state. By requiring an oath of loyalty to the state from all practicing priests, the National Assembly created a new arena for dissent: Catholics were forced to choose to embrace or reject the Revolution. Many "nonjuring" priests who refused to take the oath went into hiding. The wedge driven between the Catholic church and revolutionary France allowed a mass-based counterrevolution to emerge. Aristocratic émigrés who had fled the country because of their opposition to the Revolution were languishing because of lack of a popular base. From his headquarters in Turin, the king's younger brother, the comte d'Artois, was attempting to incite a civil war in France. When the revolutionaries decided to attack the Church not just as a landed and privileged institution but also as a religious one, the counterrevolution rapidly expanded.

The Constitution of 1791, completed after over two years of deliberations, established a constitutional monarchy with a ministerial executive power answerable to a legislative assembly. Louis XVI, formerly the divinely anointed ruler of France, was now "Louis, by the grace of God and the constitutional law of the state, King of the French." In proclaiming his acceptance of the constitution, Louis expressed the sentiments of many when he said, "The end of the revolution is come. It is time that order be reestablished so that the constitution may receive the support now most necessary to it; it is time to settle the opinion of Europe concerning the destiny of France, and to show that French men are worthy of being free."

Louis, who had been wrong often enough in the past, could not have been more mistaken when he declared that the end of the Revolution was at hand.

The Constitution of 1791 marked the triumph of the principles of the Revolution. But it was at best a precarious political compromise. Months before the ink was dry on the final document, the actions of the king doomed the new constitution to failure. To be successful, constitutional monarchy required a king worthy of honor and respect. Louis XVI seemed to be giving the revolutionaries what they wanted by cooperating with the framers of the constitution. Yet late one night in June 1791, Louis XVI, Marie Antoinette, and their children disguised themselves as commoners, crept out of the royal apartments in the Tuileries Palace, and fled Paris. Louis intended to leave France to join foreign forces opposing the Revolution at Metz. He got as far as Varennes, where he was captured by soldiers of the National Guards and brought back to a shocked Paris. The king had abandoned the Revolution. Although he was not put to death for another year and a half, he was more than ever a prisoner of the Revolution. The monarchy was effectively finished as part of a political solution and with its demise went liberal hopes for a constitutional settlement.

The defection of the king was certainly serious, but it was not the only problem facing the revolutionaries. Other problems plagued the revolutionary government, notably the fiscal crisis coupled with inflation, and foreign war.

In order to establish its seriousness and legitimacy, the National Assembly had been willing in 1789 to absorb the debts of the old regime. The new government could not sell titles and offices, as the king had done to deal with financial problems, but it did confiscate Church property. In addition, it issued treasury bonds in the form of *assignats* in order to raise money. The assignats soon assumed the status of banknotes. By spring 1790, in spite of growing public suspicion, the assignats became compulsory legal tender. Initially they were to be backed by land confiscated from the Church and now being sold by the state. But the need for money soon outran the value of the land available and the government continued to print assignats according to its needs. De-preciation of French currency in international markets and inflation at home resulted. The revolutionary government found itself in a situation which in certain respects was worse than that experienced by Louis XVI before the calling of the Estates-General. Assignat-induced inflation produced a sharp decline in fortunes of bourgeois investors living on fixed incomes. Rising prices meant increased misery for workers and peasants.

New counter revolutionary groups were becoming frustrated with revolutionary policies. Throughout the winter and spring of 1791–92 people rioted and demanded that prices be fixed, as the assignat dropped to less than half of its face value. Peasants refused to sell their crops for the worthless paper. Hoarding further drove up prices. The situation was becoming desperate, caused now not by crop failures or the weather but by government policy. Angry crowds turned to pillaging, rioting, and murders, which became more frequent as the value of the currency declined and prices rose.

Foreign war beginning in the fall of 1791 also challenged stability. Some moderate political leaders welcomed war as a blessing in disguise, since it could divert the attention of the masses away from problems at home and could promote loyalty to the Revolution. Others envisioned war as a great crusade to bring revolutionary principles to oppressed peoples throughout Europe. The king and queen, trapped by the Revolution, saw war as their only hope of liberation. Louis XVI could be rightfully restored as the leader of a France defeated by the sovereigns of Europe. Others opposed the war, believing it would destabilize the Revolution. France must solve its problems at home, they argued, before fighting a foreign enemy. Louis, however, encouraged those ministers and advisers eager for battle. In April 1792, France declared war against Austria.

Individuals, events, economic realities, and the nature of politics conspired against the success of the first constitutional experiment. The king's attempt to flee France and the Revolution in the summer of 1791 seriously wounded the attempt at compromise. Many feared that the goals of the Revolution could not be preserved in a country at war and with a king of dubious loyalties.

Experimenting with Democracy

A political universe populated by individual citizens replaced the eighteenth-century world of subjects loyal to their king. This new construction of politics in which all individuals were equal ran counter to prevailing ideas about collective identities defined in guilds and orders. Before the Revolution, public opinion was being voiced outside of traditional institutions—in cafes, salons, and philosophical societies. French provincial academies sponsored a dynamic intellectual life as centers for debate over capital punishment, civic virtue, and the best form of government. Nobles and bourgeois met in these provincial academies to talk about government, power, and the means of social improvement.

New forms of social intercourse fostered the growth of democratic ideas and the emergence of a new political culture that was both progressive and democratic, and that considered individuals as perfectible. Political documents, like the Constitution of 1791, reflected these changes to some extent. But the revolutionaries intended to do more than reallocate political power: they aimed to change the ways people thought, talked, and lived. People needed new symbols to replace those that had been repudiated. They needed new words to talk about new political realities. The Revolution created its own calendar, setting the beginning of accounted time in the revolutionary era. The first day of the first year of the rest of history was 22 September 1792—the beginning of the Year I. New patterns of speech that were developed during the Revolution fostered a new way of looking at the world. People now addressed each other familiarly as "tu" instead of the more formal "vous," as the vague concepts of liberty, equality, and fraternity took root in people's lives.

The French Revolution was a school for the French nation. People on all levels of society learned politics by doing it. In the beginning, experience helped. The elites, both noble and bourgeois, had served in government and administration. But the rules of the game under the old regime had been very different, with birth determining power. After 1789, all men were declared free and equal, in opportunity if not in rights. Men of ability and talent, who had served as middlemen for the privileged elite under the old regime, now claimed power as their due. Many of them were lawyers, educated in the rules and regulations of the society of orders. They experienced firsthand the problems of the exercise of power in the old regime and had their own ideas about reform. But the school of the Revolution did not remain the domain of a special class. Women demanded their places. Workers seized their rights. And because of the inherent contradictions of representation and participation, experimenting with democracy led to outcomes that did not look very democratic at all.

Declaring Political Rights

"Liberty consists in the ability to do whatever does not harm another." So wrote the revolutionary deputies of 1789. Sounding a refrain similar to that of the American Declaration of Independence, the *Declaration of the Rights of Man and Citizen* appeared on 26 August 1789. The document amalgamated a variety of Enlightenment ideas drawn from the works of political philosophy, including those of Locke and Montesquieu. "Men are born and remain free and equal in rights. Social distinctions may be based only on common utility." Perhaps most significant of all was the attention given to property, which was declared a "sacred and inviolable," "natural," and "imprescriptible" right of man.

In the year of tranquillity that followed the violent summer of 1789, the new politicians set themselves the task of creating institutions based on the principle of liberty and others embodied in the *Declaration of the Rights of Man and Citizen.* The result was the Constitution of 1791, a documentary monument to the belief in a progressive constitutional monarchy. A king accountable to an elected parliamentary body would lead France into a prosperous and just age. The constitution acknowledged the people's sovereignty as the source of political power. It also enshrined the principle of property by making voting rights dependent on property ownership. All men might be equal before the law, but by the Constitution of 1791 only wealthy men had the right to vote for

Slaves revolting against the French in Saint Domingue in 1791. Napoleon sent an army to restore colonial rule in 1799, but yellow fever decimated the French soldiers and the rebels defeated the weakened French army in 1803.

representatives and hold office. A new male elite, those who owned property and controlled wealth, was emerging within the Revolution.

All titles of nobility were abolished. In the early period of the Revolution, civil liberties were extended to Protestants and Jews, who had been persecuted under the old regime. Previously excluded groups were granted freedom of thought and worship and full civil liberties. More reluctantly, slavery in the colonies was outlawed in 1794. Slave unrest in Saint Domingue (modern-day Haiti) had coincided with the political conflicts of the Revolution and exploded in rebellion in 1791, driving the revolutionaries in Paris to support black independence although it was at odds with French colonial interests. Led by Toussaint L'Ouverture (1743–1803), black rebels worked to found an independent Haitian state, which was declared in 1804. But the concept of equality with regard to race remained incompletely integrated with revolutionary principles, and slavery was reestablished in the French colonies in 1802.

Men were the subject of these newly defined rights. No references to women or their rights appear in the constitutions or the official Declarations of Rights. Women's organizations agitated for an equitable divorce law, and divorce was legalized in September 1792. Women were critical

actors in the Revolution from its very inception and their presence shaped and directed the outcome of events, as the women's march to Versailles in 1789 made clear. The Marquis de Condorcet (1743–94), elected to the Legislative Assembly in 1791, was one of the first to chastise the revolutionaries for overlooking the political rights of women who, he pointedly observed, were half of the human race. "Either no individual of the human race has genuine rights, or else all have the same; and he who votes against the right of another, whatever the religion, color, or sex of that other, has henceforth abjured his own." Condorcet argued forcefully but unsuccessfully for the right of women to be educated and for state support of this right. Women's talents, he warned, were slumbering under the ignorance of neglect.

"Woman, wake up!" In such a manner did Olympe de Gouges (d. 1793), a self-educated playwright and the daughter of a butcher, address French women in 1791. Aware that women were being denied the new rights of liberty and property extended to all men by the *Declaration of the Rights of Man and Citizen*, Gouges composed a *Declaration of the Rights of Woman and Citizen*, modeled on the 1789 document. "Article One. Woman is born free and remains equal in rights to man." Women are equal to men before the law in citizenship, duties, and property rights. "The right of property is inviolable and sacred to both sexes, jointly or separately." Gouges spoke out for the freedom of slaves and for women's political rights. She foreshadowed her own demise for her political beliefs at the mercy of revolutionary justice when she wrote, "Woman has the right to mount the scaffold; she must equally have the right to mount the rostrum."

The Second Revolution: The Revolution of the People

The first revolution of 1789 through the beginning of 1792 was based on liberty—the liberty to compete, to own, and to succeed. The second revolution that began in 1792 took equality as its rallying cry. This was the revolution of the working people of French cities. The popular movement that spearheaded political action in 1792 was committed to equality of rights in a way not characteristic of the leaders of the Revolution of 1789. Urban workers were not benefiting from the Revolution, but they had come to believe in their own power as political beings. Organized on the local level into sections, craftsmen in cities identified themselves as *sans-culottes*, literally those who did not wear knee breeches, to distinguish themselves from the privileged elite.

On 10 August 1792, the people of Paris stormed the Tuileries, chanting their demands for "Equality!" and "Nation!" The people tramped across the silk sheets of the king's bed and broke his fine furniture, reveling in the private chambers of the royal family. Love and respect for the king had vanished. What the people of Paris demanded now was universal manhood suffrage and participation in a popular democracy. Working people were now acting independently of other factions, and the bourgeois political leadership became quickly aware of the need to scramble.

Who constituted the popular movement? The self-designated *sans-culottes* were the working men and women of Paris. Some were wealthier than others, some were wage earners, but all shared a common identity as consumers in the marketplace. They hated the privileged (*les gros*), who appeared to be profiting at the expense of the people. The *sans-culottes* wanted government power to be decentralized, with neighborhoods ruling themselves through sectional organizations. As the have-nots, they were increasingly intent on pulling down the haves, and they translated this sense of vengeance into a new revolutionary justice. When they invaded the Tuileries Palace on the morning of 10 August, the *sans-culottes* did so in the name of the people. They saw themselves as patriots whose duty it was to brush the monarchy aside. The people were now a force to be reckoned with and feared.

"Terror is the Order of the Day"

Political factions characterized revolutionary politics from the start. The terms *Left* and *Right*, which came to represent opposite ends of the political spectrum, originated in a description of where people sat in the Assembly in relation to the podium. The arrest and trial of Louis XVI for treason, followed by his execution on the guillotine in January 1793, irrevocably polarized politics. As the royalist Right was weakened and eliminated, political factions within the new legislative body, the National Convention, were described in terms borrowed from geography. The Mountain, sitting in the upper benches on the left, was made up of members of the Jacobin Club (named for its meeting place in an abandoned monastery). The Jacobins were the most radical element in the National Convention, supporting democratic solutions and speaking in favor of the cause of people in the streets. The Plain held the moderates, who were concerned with maintaining public order against popular unrest. Many members of the Plain came to be called Girondins in the mistaken belief that they originated in the Gironde *département* of France.

Both Girondins and Jacobins were from the middle ranks of the bourgeoisie and both groups were dedicated to the principles of the Revolution. At first the two groups were more similar than different. Although controlling the ministries, the Girondins began to lose their hold on the Revolution and the war. The renewed European war fragmented the democratic movement, and the Girondins, unable to control violence at home, saw political control slipping away. They became prisoners of the Revolution when eighty thousand armed Parisians surrounded the National Convention in June 1793.

Girondin power had been eroding in the critical months between August 1792 and June 1793. A new leader was working quietly and effectively behind the scenes to weld a partnership between the popular movement of *sans-culottes* and the Jacobins. He was Maximilien Robespierre (1758–94), leader of the Mountain and the Jacobin Club. Robespierre was typical of the new breed of revolutionary politician. Only 31 years old in 1789, he wrote mediocre poems and attended the local provincial academy to discuss the new ideas, when he was not practicing law in his hometown of Arras. Elected to the Estates-General, Robespierre began to make his mark as a bright young man with a promising political future. He joined the Jacobin Club and quickly rose to become its leader. He was willing to take controversial stands on issues: unlike most of his fellow members of the Mountain, he opposed the war in 1792. Although neither an original thinker nor a compelling orator, Robespierre discovered with the Revolution that he was a stunning political

The Guillotine and Revolutionary Justice

In the sultry summer days of 1792, Parisians found a new way to entertain themselves. They attended executions. French men, women, and children were long accustomed to watching criminals being tortured and put to death in public view. During the old regime, spectators could enjoy the variety of a number of methods: drawing and quartering, strangling, or hanging. Decapitation, reputedly a less painful death, was a privilege reserved for nobles sentenced for capital crimes. The Revolution extended this formerly aristocratic privilege to all criminals condemned to death. What especially attracted people into public squares in the third year of the Revolution was the introduction of a novel method of decapitation. In 1792 the new instrument of death, the guillotine, became the center of the spectacle of revolutionary justice.

The guillotine promised to eliminate the suffering of its victims. Axes, swords, and sabers—the traditional tools of decapitation and dismemberment—were messy and undependable, producing slow and bloody ordeals when inept and drunken executioners missed their mark or victims flinched at the fatal moment. The design of the guillotine took all of this into account. On its easel-like wooden structure, victims, lying on their stomachs, were held in place with straps and a kind of pillory. Heavy pulleys guaranteed that the sharp blade would fall efficiently from its great height. A basket was placed at the base of the blade to catch the severed head, another was used to slide the headless body for removal through the base of the scaffolding. In place of unintended torture and gore, the guillotine was devised as a humanitarian instrument to guarantee swift and painless death.

It should have been called the Louisette, after its inventor, Dr. Antoine Louis. In what now seems a dubious honor, the new machine was named instead after its greatest supporter, Dr. Joseph Ignace Guillotin, a delegate to the National Assembly. Both Guillotin and Louis were medical doctors, men of science influenced by Enlightenment ideas and committed to the Revolution's elimination of the cruelty of older forms of punishment. In the spirit of scientific experimentation, Louis' invention was tested on sheep, cadavers, and then convicted thieves. In 1792 it was used for the first time against another class of offenders, political prisoners.

Early in the Revolution, the Marquis de Condorcet, *philosophe* and mathematician, had opposed capital punishment with the argument that the state did not have the right to take life. Ironically, Maximilien Robespierre, future architect of the Reign of Terror, was one of the few revolutionaries who agreed with Condorcet. Those who favored justice by execution of the state's enemies prevailed. The revolutionary hero and associate of the radical Jacobins, Jean Paul Marat (1743–93), who was himself stabbed to death in his bathtub, advocated the state's use of violence against its enemies: "In order to ensure public tranquillity, 200,000 heads must be cut off." By the end of 1792, as revolution and civil war swept over France, eighty-three identical guillotines were constructed and installed in each of the *départements* of France. For the next two years, the guillotine's great blade was rhythmically raised and lowered daily in public squares all over France. In the name of the Revolution, the "axe of the people" dispatched over 50,000 victims.

Although intended as a humanitarian instrument, the guillotine became the symbol of all that was arbitrary and repressive about a revolution run amok. Day and night in Paris, the Revolutionary Tribunal delivered the death sentence to the "enemies of the people." Most of those executed were members of what had been the Third Estate: members of the bourgeoisie, workers, peasants. Only 15 percent of the condemned were nobles and priests. During the Terror, the

guillotine could be used to settle old scores. *Sans-culottes* turned in their neighbors, sometimes over long-standing grievances that owed more to spite than politics. The most fanatical revolutionaries had fantasies that guillotines were about to be erected on every street corner to dispense with hoarders and traitors. Others suggested that guillotines be made portable so that by putting justice on wheels, it could be taken directly to the people.

As usual, Paris set the style. The most famous of the guillotines stood on the Place du Carrousel, deliberately placed in front of the royal palace of the Tuileries. It was eventually moved to the larger Place de la Révolution in order to accommodate the growing numbers of spectators. Famous victims drew especially large crowds. The revolutionary drama took on the trappings of a spectacle, as hawkers sold toy guillotines, miniature pikes, and liberty caps as souvenirs, along with the usual food and drink. Troops attended these events but not to control the crowd. Members of the National Guard in formation, their backs to the people, faced the stage of the scaffold. They, like the citizenry, were there to witness the birth of a new nation and, by their presence, to give legitimacy to the event. The crowd entered into the ritual, cheering the victim's last words and demanding that the executioner hold high the severed head. In the new political culture death was a festival.

For two centuries, Western societies have debated the legitimacy of the death sentence and have periodically considered the relative merits of the guillotine, the gas chamber, and the electric chair. For the French, the controversy temporarily ceased in 1794, when people were convinced that justice had gotten out of hand and that they had had enough. For the time being, the government put an end to capital punishment. The guillotine would return. But at the height of its use between 1792 and 1794, it had played a unique role in forging a new system of justice: the guillotine had been the great leveler. In the ideology of democracy, people were equal—in death as well as in life. The guillotine came to be popularly known as the "scythe of equality." It killed king and commoner alike.

tactician. He gained a following and learned how to manipulate it. It was he who engineered the Jacobins' replacement of the Girondins as leaders of the government.

Robespierre's chance for real power came when he assumed leadership of the Committee of Public Safety in July 1793. Due to the threat of internal anarchy and external war, the elected body, the National Convention, yielded political control to the twelve-man Committee of Public Safety that ruled dictatorially under Robespierre's direction. The Great Committee, as it was known at the time, orchestrated the Reign of Terror (1793–94), a period of systematic state repression that meted out justice in the people's name. Summary trials by specially created revolutionary tribunals were followed by the swift execution of the guilty under the blade of the guillotine.

Influenced by the *Social Contract* (1762) and other writings of Jean-Jacques Rousseau, Robespierre believed that sovereignty resided with the people. For him individual wills and even individual rights did not matter when faced with the will of the nation. The king was dead; the people were the new source of political power. Robespierre saw himself in the all-important role of interpreting and shaping the people's will. His own task was to guide the people "to the summit of its destinies." As he explained to his critics, "I am defending not my own cause but the public cause." As head of the Great Committee, Robespierre oversaw a revolutionary machinery dedicated to economic regulation, massive military mobilization, and a punitive system of revolutionary justice characterized by the slogan, "Terror is the Order of the Day." Militant revolutionary committees and revolutionary tribunals were established in the *départements* to identify traitors and to mete out the harsh justice that struck hardest against those members of the bourgeoisie who were perceived as opponents of the government.

The guillotine became the symbol of revolutionary justice, but it was not the only means of execution. In Lyon, officials of the Reign of Terror had prisoners tied to stakes in open fields and fired on them with cannon. In Nantes, a Parisian administrator of the new justice had enemies of the Revolution chained to barges and drowned in the estuary of the Loire. The civil war, which raged most violently in the Vendée in the west of France,

consisted often of primitive massacres that sent probably a quarter of a million people to their deaths. The bureaucratized Reign of Terror was responsible for about forty thousand executions in a nine-month period, resulting in the image of the republicans as "drinkers of blood." (See Special Feature, "The Guillotine and Revolutionary Justice," pp. 630–631.)

The Cult of the Supreme Being, a civic religion influenced by Rousseau's ideas about nature, followed dechristianization. The cathedral of Notre Dame de Paris was turned into the Temple of Reason, and the new religion established its own festivals to undermine the persistence of Catholicism. The cult was one indication of the Reign of Terror's attempt to create a new moral universe of revolutionary values.

Conspicuously absent from the summit of political power were women. After 1793 Jacobin revolutionaries, who were willing to empower the popular movement of workers, turned against women's participation and denounced it. Women's associations were outlawed and the Society of Revolutionary Republican Women was disbanded. Olympe de Gouges was guillotined. Women were made unfit for political participation, the Jacobins declared, by their biological functions of reproduction and child-rearing. Rousseau's ideas about family policy were probably more influential than his political doctrines. His best-selling books, *La Nouvelle Héloïse* (1761) and *Emile* (1762), which combined went into seventy-two editions before 1789, were moral works that transformed people's ideas about family life. Under his influence, the reading public came to value a separate and private sphere of domestic and conjugal values. Rousseau's own relations with women and the fact that he put his five illegitimate children in foundling hospitals contradicted his ideas about familial virtues. Following Rousseau's lead, Robespierre and the Jacobins insisted that the role of women as mothers was incompatible with women's participation in the political realm.

Robespierre attacked his critics to the Left and to the Right, thereby undermining the support he needed to stay in power. He abandoned the alliance with the popular movement that had been so important in bringing him to power. Robespierre's enemies—and he had many—were able to break the identification between political

The French Revolution

August 1788	Louis XVI announces meeting of Estates-General to be held May 1789
5 May 1789	Estates-General convenes
17 June 1789	Third Estate declares itself the National Assembly
20 June 1789	Oath of the Tennis Court
14 July 1789	Storming of the Bastille
20 July 1789	Revolution of peasantry begins
26 August 1789	*Declaration of the Rights of Man and Citizen*
5 October 1789	Parisian women march to Versailles; force Louis XVI to return to Paris
February 1790	Monasteries, convents dissolved
July 1790	Civil Constitution of the Clergy
June 1791	Louis XVI and family attempt to flee Paris; are captured and returned
April 1792	France declares war on Austria
10 August 1792	Storming of the Tuileries
22 September 1792	Revolutionary calendar implemented
January 1793	Louis XVI executed
July 1793	Robespierre assumes leadership of Committee of Public Safety
1793–94	Reign of Terror
1794	Robespierre guillotined
1799	Napoleon overthrows the Directory and seizes power

power and the will of the people that Robespierre had established. As a result, he was branded a traitor by the same process that he had enforced against many of his own enemies and friends. He saved France from foreign occupation and internal collapse but he could not save democracy through terror. If the will of the people legitimated new political forms, how could one be sure that the will of the people was being interpreted correctly? In the summer of 1794, Robespierre was guillotined. The Reign of Terror ceased with his death.

The Revolution did not end with the fall of Robespierre, but his execution initiated a new phase. For some, democracy lost its legitimacy. The popular movement was reviled and *sans-culotte* became a term of derision. Jacobins were forced underground. Price controls were abolished, resulting in extreme hardship for most urban residents. Out of desperation in April 1795, the Jacobins and the *sans-culottes* renewed their alliance, united in a dying revolutionary gasp to demand, "Bread and the Constitution of 1793." The politics of bread had never been more accurately captured in slogan. People saw the universal manhood suffrage of the unimplemented 1793 constitution as the way to solve their economic problems. But the popular revolution had failed. People had no bread and they had no power.

The End of the Revolution

The Revolution that had begun with a bang ended with a whimper. In the four years after Robespierre's fall, a new government by committee called the Directory appeared to offer mediocrity, caution, and opportunism, in place of the idealism and action of the early years of the Revolution. No successor to Robespierre stepped forward to command center stage; there were no heroes like Lafayette or the great Jacobin orator Georges-Jacques Danton (1759–94) to inspire patriotic fervor. Nor were there women like Olympe de Gouges to demand in the public arena equal rights for women. Most people, numbed after years of change, barely noticed that the Revolution was over. Ordinary men in parliamentary institutions effectively did the day-to-day job of running the government. They tried to steer a middle path between royalist resurgence and popular insurrection. This nearly forgotten period in the history of the French Revolution was the fulfillment of the liberal hopes of 1789 for a stable, constitutional rule.

The Directory, however, continued to be dogged by European war. A mass army of conscripts and volunteers had successfully extended France's power and frontiers. France expelled foreign invaders and annexed territories, including

Belgium, while increasing its control in Holland, Switzerland, and Italy. But the expansion of revolutionary France was expensive and increasingly unpopular. Military defeats and the corruption of the Directory undermined government control. The Directory might have succeeded in the slow accretion of a parliamentary tradition. But reinstatement of conscription in 1798 met with widespread protest and resistance. No matter what their political leanings, people were weary. The people turned to those who promised stability and peace. Ironically, the savior that they found was a military man who plunged France into sixteen more years of intermittent war.

The Reign of Napoleon, 1799–1815

Napoleon is one of those individuals about whom one can say that if he had not lived, history would have been different. He left his mark on an age and on a continent. The great debate that rages to this day about Napoleon revolves around the question of whether he fulfilled the aims of the Revolution or perverted them. In his return to a monarchical model, Napoleon resembled the enlightened despots of eighteenth-century Europe. In a modern sense, he was also a dictator, manipulating the French people through a highly centralized administrative apparatus. He locked French society into a program of military expansionism that depleted its human and material resources. Yet, in spite of destruction and war, he dedicated his reign to building a French state according to the principles of the Revolution.

Bonaparte Seizes Power

In Paris in 1795 a young, penniless, and unknown military officer moved among the wealthy and the beautiful of Parisian society and longed for fame. Already nicknamed at school "the Little Corporal" on account of his short stature, he was snubbed because of his background and ridiculed for his foreign accent. His story is typical of all stories of thwarted ambition. Yet the outcome of this story is unique. Within four years this young man had become ruler of France. The

story of his ascent to power is also a story of both the demise and the legacy of the Revolution.

Napoleon Bonaparte (1769–1821) was a true child of the eighteenth century. He shared the *philosophes'* belief in a rational and progressive world. Born in Corsica, which until a few months before his birth was part of the Republic of Genoa, he received his training in French military schools. Even as a youth, he was arrogant and ambitious. But he could have never hoped to rise to a position of leadership in the army during the old regime because he lacked the noble birth necessary for advancement. The highest rank Napoleon could hope to achieve was that of captain or major.

The Revolution changed everything for him. First, it opened up careers previously restricted by birth, including those in the military, to talent. Second, the Revolution made new posts available when aristocratic generals defected and crossed over to the enemy side both before and after the execution of the king. Finally, the Revolution created great opportunities for military men to test their mettle. Foreign war and civil war required military leaders devoted to the Revolution.

Bonaparte's early career seemed a web of contradictions. Forced to flee Corsica because he had

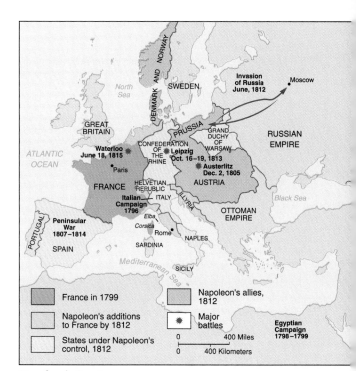

Napoleon's Empire

The 1804 coronation of Napoleon by Jacques Louis David. Pope Pius VII is seated behind the emperor, who is about to place a crown on the head of Josephine. Napoleon later ordered David to alter the painting to show the pope's hand raised in blessing.

sided with the Jacobins, he coolly crushed Parisian protesters who rioted against the Directory in 1795. His highly publicized campaigns in Egypt and Syria made him a hero at home as a defender of the government. Above all, his victories in the Italian campaign in 1796–97 launched his political career. As he extended French rule into central Italy, he became the embodiment of revolutionary values and energy. In 1799 he readily joined a conspiracy the pulled down the Directory, the government he had earlier preserved, and became the First Consul of a triumvirate of consuls.

Napoleon set out to secure his position of power by eliminating his enemies on the Left and weakening those on the Right. He guaranteed the security of property acquired in the Revolution, a move guaranteed to undercut royalists who wanted to return property to its original owners. Through policing forces and special criminal courts, law and order prevailed and civil war subsided. The First Consul promised a balanced budget and appeared to deliver it. Bonaparte spoke of healing the nation's wounds, especially those opened by religious grievances caused by dechristianization during the Revolution. Realizing the importance of religion in maintaining domestic peace, Napoleon reestablished relations with the pope in 1801 in the Concordat, which recognized Catholicism as the religion of the French and restored the Roman Catholic hierarchy.

Napoleon's popularity as First Consul flowed from his military and political successes and his religious reconciliation. He had come to power in 1799 by appealing for the support of the army. In 1802 Napoleon decided to extend his power by calling for a plebiscite in which he asked the electorate to vote him First Consul for life. Public support was overwhelming. An electoral landslide gave Napoleon greater political power than any of his Bourbon predecessors. Using revolutionary mechanisms, Napoleon laid the foundation for a new dynasty.

War and More War

Napoleon was at war or preparing for war during his entire reign. He certainly seemed up to the task of defeating the European powers. His military successes, real and apparent, before 1799 had been crucial in his bid for political power. By 1802, he had signed favorable treaties with both Austria and Great Britain. He appeared to deliver a lasting peace and to establish France as the dominant power in Europe. But the peace was

This engraving from the series Disasters of War by Francisco Goya depicts the horrors of war. The series was inspired by Napoleon's invasion and occupation of Spain from 1808 to 1813.

short-lived. In 1803 France embarked on an eleven-year period of continuous war. Under Napoleon's command, the French army delivered defeat after defeat to the European powers. Austria fell in 1805, Prussia in 1806, and the Russian armies of Alexander I were defeated at Friedland in 1807. In 1808 Napoleon invaded Spain in order to drive out British expeditionary forces intent on invading France. The great painter of the Spanish court, Francisco Goya (1746–1828), produced a series of etchings, *The Disasters of War,* that depicted the atrocities accompanying the Napoleonic invasion. Spain became a satellite kingdom in the French Empire, although the conflict continued.

Britain was the one exception to the string of Napoleonic victories. Napoleon initially considered sending a French fleet to invade the island nation. Lacking the strength necessary to achieve this, he turned to economic warfare and blockaded European ports against British trade. Beginning in 1806, the Continental System, as the blockade was known, erected a structure of protection for French manufactures in all continental European markets. The British responded to the tariff walls and boycotts with a naval blockade that succeeded in cutting French commerce off from its Atlantic markets. The Continental System did not prove to be the decisive policy that Napoleon had planned: the British economy was not broken and the French economy did not flourish when faced with restricted resources and the persistence of a black market in smuggled goods.

Still by 1810, the French leader was master of the Continent. French armies had extended revolutionary reforms and legal codes outside France and brought with them civil equality and religious toleration. They had also drained defeated countries of their resources and had inflicted the horrors of war with armies of occupation, forced billeting, and pillage. Napoleon's empire extended across Europe, with only a diminished Austria, Prussia, and Russia remaining independent. He placed his relatives and friends on the thrones of the new satellite kingdoms of Italy, Naples, Westphalia, Holland, and Spain. It was a fine empire, Napoleon later recalled in the loneliness of exile. Napoleon's empire did not endure, but at its acme, it seemed as though it would never fall.

Peace at Home

Napoleon measured domestic prosperity in terms of the stability of his reign. Through the

1802 plebiscite that voted him First Consul for life, he maintained the charade of constitutional rule, while he ruled as virtual dictator. In 1804, he abandoned all pretense and had himself proclaimed emperor of the French. Mimicking the rituals of kingship, he staged his own coronation and that of his wife Josephine at the cathedral of Notre Dame de Paris. Breaking the tradition set by Charlemagne, Napoleon took the crown from the hands of Pope Pius VII (1800–1823) and placed it on his own head.

Secure in his regime, surrounded by a new nobility that he created based on military achievement and talent, and that he rewarded with honors, Napoleon set about implementing sweeping reforms in every area of government. Like many of the men of the revolutionary assemblies who had received scientific educations in their youth, he recognized the importance of science for both industry and war. The Revolution had removed an impediment to the development of a national market by creating a uniform system of weights and measures. The metric system was established by 1799. But Napoleon felt the need to go further. France must be first in scientific research and application. To assure French predominance, Napoleon became a patron of science, supporting important work in the areas of physics and chemistry. Building for the future, Napoleon made science a pillar in the new structure of higher education.

The Directory had restored French prosperity through stabilization of the currency, fiscal reform, and support of industry. Napoleon's contribution to the French economy was the much needed reform of the tax system. He authorized the creation of a central banking system. French industries flourished under the protection of the state. The blockade forced the development of new domestic crops like beet-sugar and indigo, which became substitutes for colonial products. Napoleon extended the infrastructure of roads so necessary for the expansion of national and European markets.

Perhaps his greatest achievement was the codification of law, a task begun under the Revolution. Many of the new articles of the code were hammered out in Napoleon's presence, as he presided regularly over meetings with legal reformers. Combined with economic reforms, the code facilitated trade and the development of commerce by regularizing contractual relations and protecting property rights and equality before the law.

The civil laws of the new Napoleonic Code carved out a family policy characterized by hierarchy and subordination. Married women were neither independent nor equal to men in ownership of property, custody of children, and access to divorce. Women also lacked political rights. In the Napoleonic code, women, like children, were subjected to paternal authority. The Napoleonic philosophy of woman's place is well captured in an anecdote told by Madame Germaine de Staël (1766–1817), a leading intellectual of her day. As the daughter of Jacques Necker, the Swiss financier and adviser to Louis XVI at the time of the Revolution, she had been educated in Enlightenment ideas from an early age. On finding herself seated next to Napoleon at a dinner party, she asked him what was very likely a self-interested question: whom did he consider the greatest woman, alive or dead? Napoleon had no name to give her but he responded without pausing, "The one who has had the most children."

Napoleon turned his prodigious energies to every aspect of French life. He encouraged the arts, while creating a police force. He had monuments built but did not forget about sewers. He organized French administrative life in a fashion that has endured. In place of the popular democratic movement, he offered his own singular authority. In place of elections, clubs, and free associations, he gave France plebiscites and army service. To be sure, Napoleon believed in constitutions but he thought they should be "short and obscure." For Napoleon the great problem of democracy was its unpredictability. His regime solved that problem by eliminating choices.

Decline and Fall

Militarily, Napoleon went too far. The first cracks in the French facade began to show in the Peninsular War (1808–14) with Spain as Spanish guerrilla tactics proved costly for French troops. Napoleon's biggest mistake, the one that shattered the myth of his invincibility, occurred when he decided to invade Russia in June 1812. Having decisively defeated Russian forces in 1807, Napoleon entered into a peace treaty with Tsar Alexander I that guaranteed Russian allegiance to French policies. Alexander repudiated the Conti-

This 1835 painting by De Boisdenier depicts the suffering of Napoleon's Grand Army on the retreat from Moscow. The Germans were to meet a similar fate over one hundred years later when they invaded Russia without adequate winter clothing.

nental System in 1810 and appeared to be preparing for his own war against France. Napoleon seized the initiative, sure that he could defeat Russian forces once again. With an army of 500,000 men, Napoleon moved deep into Russia in the summer of 1812. The tsar's troops fell back in retreat. It was a strange war, one that pulled the French army to Moscow like a bird following breadcrumbs. When Napoleon and his men entered Moscow in September, they found a city in flames. The people of Moscow had destroyed their own city to deprive the French troops of winter quarters.

Winter comes early in Moscow, Napoleon's men discovered. They had left France basking in the warmth of summer and of certain and early victory. They now found themselves facing a severe Russian winter without overcoats, without supplies, and without food. The Russian strategy has become legendary. The Russians destroyed grain and shelter that might be of use to the French. Napoleon and his starving and frostbitten troops were forced into retreat. The horses of the French cavalry died because they were not properly shod for cold weather. The French army was

decimated. Fewer than 100,000 men made it back to France.

The empire began to crumble. Britain, unbowed by the Continental System, remained Napoleon's sworn enemy. Prussia joined Great Britain, Sweden, Russia, and Austria in opposing France anew. In the Battle of Nations at Leipzig in October 1813, France was forced to retreat. Napoleon refused a negotiated peace and fought on until the following March, when the victorious allies marched down the streets of Paris and occupied the French capital. Only then did Napoleon abdicate in favor of his young son, François, the titular king of Rome (1811–32).

Still it was not quite the end for Napoleon. While the European heads of state sat in Vienna trying to determine the future of Europe and France's place in it, Napoleon returned from his exile on the Mediterranean island of Elba. On 15 June 1815, Napoleon once again and for the final time confronted the European powers in one of the most famous military campaigns in history. With 125,000 loyal French forces, Napoleon seemed within hours of reestablishing the French Empire in Europe.

He had underestimated his opponents. The defeat of Napoleon's forces at Waterloo was decisive. Napoleon later explained, "Everything failed me just when everything had succeeded!" He had met his Waterloo, and with his defeat a new expression entered the language to describe devastating and permanent and irreversible downfall. Napoleon's return proved brief—it lasted only one hundred days. An era had come to an end. Napoleon was exiled to the less hospitable island of Saint Helena in the South Atlantic. For the next six years, Napoleon wrote his memoirs under the watchful eyes of his British jailors. He died a painful death from cancer on 5 May 1821.

The period of Revolution and Empire from 1789 to 1815 radically changed the face of France. A new, more cohesive elite of bourgeois and nobles emerged, sharing power based on wealth and status. Ownership of land remained a defining characteristic of both old and new elites. A new state bureaucracy, built on the foundations of the old, expanded and centralized state power.

The people as sovereign now legitimated political power. Napoleon at his most imperial never doubted that he owed his existence to the people. In this sense, Napoleon was the king of the Revolution—an apparently contradictory fusion of old forms and new ideology. Napoleon channeled democratic forces into enthusiasm for empire. He learned his lessons from the failure of the Bourbon monarchy and the politicians of the Revolution. For sixteen years Napoleon successfully reconciled the old regime with the new France. Yet he could not resolve the essential problem of democracy: the relationship between the will of the people and the exercise of political power. The picture in 1815 was not dramatically different from the situation in 1789. The Revolution might be over, but changes fueled by the revolutionary tradition were just beginning. The struggle for a workable democratic culture recurred in France for another century and elsewhere in Europe through the twentieth century.

The Reign of Napoleon

1799	Napoleon establishes consulate, becomes First Consul
1802	Plebiscite declares Napoleon First Consul for life
1801	Napoleon reestablishes relations with pope, restores Roman Catholic hierarchy
1804	Napoleon proclaims himself Emperor of the French
1806	Continental System implemented
1808–14	France engaged in Peninsular War with Spain
June 1812	Napoleon invades Russia
September 1812	French army reaches Moscow, is trapped by Russian winter
1813	Napoleon defeated at Battle of Nations at Leipzig
March 1814	Napoleon abdicates and goes into exile on island of Elba
March 1815	Napoleon escapes Elba and attempts to reclaim power
15 June 1815	Napoleon is defeated at Waterloo and exiled to island of Saint Helena

Suggestions for Further Reading

The Crisis of the Old Regime in France, 1715–88

C. B. A. Behrens, *Society, Government, and the Enlightenment* (New York: Harper & Row, 1985). A comparative study of eighteenth-century France and Prussia, focusing on the relationship between government and the ruling classes, that explains how pressures for change in both countries led to different outcomes, revolution in France, and reform in Prussia.

Olwen Hufton, *The Poor in Eighteenth-Century France, 1750–1789* (Oxford: Clarendon, 1974). Examines the lives of the poor before the Revolution and the institutions that attempted to deal with the problem of poverty.

Olwen Hufton, *Europe: Privilege and Protest, 1730–1789* (Sussex: The Harvester Press, 1980). An overview of the impact of rapid social, ideological, and economic changes on the concept and exercise of privilege.

* Daniel Roche, *The People of Paris* (Berkeley, CA: University of California Press, 1987). An essay on popular culture in the eighteenth century, in which the author surveys the lives of the Parisian popular classes—servants,

laborers, and artisans—and examines their housing, furnishing, dress, and leisure activities.

Isser Woloch, *Eighteenth-Century Europe: Tradition and Progress, 1715–1789* (New York: Norton, 1982). A discussion of eighteenth-century Europe, comparing social, economic, political, and intellectual developments elsewhere in Europe to the French experience, with special attention to cultural aspects, such as popular beliefs and religion.

The French Revolution and the End of the Old Regime

* Georges Lefebvre, *The Great Fear of 1789* (New York: Pantheon Books, 1973). This classic study analyzes the rural panic that swept through parts of France in the summer of 1789. The Great Fear is presented as a distinct episode in the opening months of the Revolution, with its own internal logic.

François Furet and Denis Richet, *The French Revolution* (New York: Macmillan, 1970). Two experts on the French Revolution present a detailed overview of the period from 1789 to 1798 when Bonaparte returned to Paris.

* Simon Schama, *Citizens* (New York: Knopf, 1989). A synthetic view that stresses the dynamic aspects of pre-revolutionary France, focussing on the nature of the social and cultural environment within which the Revolution occurred. The author argues that the violence of the Revolution was fueled by hostility to modernization.

* D. M. G. Sutherland, *France, 1789–1815: Revolution and Counter-Revolution* (New York: Oxford University Press, 1986). An interpretation of the revolutionary period which stresses the struggle against counterrevolution and presents the Revolution as a complex and contradictory process of social and political conflict over incompatible rights and privileges enjoyed by significant portions of the population.

* Michel Vovelle, *The Fall of the French Monarchy* (Cambridge: Cambridge University Press, 1984). A social history of the origins and early years of the Revolution beginning with a brief examination of the old regime and paying special attention to social and economic changes initiated by the Revolution, the role of the popular classes, and the creation of revolutionary culture.

Experimenting with Democracy

* François Furet, *Interpreting the French Revolution* (Cambridge: Cambridge University Press, 1981). A series of essays challenging many of the assumptions concerning the causes and outcome of the Revolution and reviewing the historiography of the Revolution. The author argues that political crisis, not class conflict, was the Revolution's primary cause and that revolutionary ideas concerning democracy are central to an understanding of the Terror.

* Lynn Hunt, *Politics, Culture, and Class in the French Revolution* (Berkeley, CA: University of California Press, 1984). A study of the Revolution as the locus of the creation of modern political culture. The second half of the book examines the social composition and cultural experiences of the new political class that merged in the Revolution.

* Joan B. Landes, *Women and the Public Sphere* (Ithaca, NY: Cornell University Press, 1988). Landes examines the genesis of the modern notion of the public sphere from a feminist perspective and argues that within the revolutionary process women were relegated to the private sphere of the domestic world.

Dorinda Outram, *The Body of the French Revolution: Sex, Class and Political Culture* (New Haven, CT: Yale University Press, 1989). Examines how images of the body in the late eighteenth century differed from class to class and how bourgeois attitudes toward physicality resulted in a gendered political discourse in which the hero replaced the king.

* Albert Soboul, *The Sans-Culottes* (New York: Anchor, 1972). An exhaustive study of the artisans who composed the core of popular political activism in revolutionary Paris. The political demands and ideology of the *sans-culottes* are examined with the composition, culture, and actions of the popular movement during the Revolution.

The Reign of Napoleon, 1799–1815

* Louis Bergeron, *France Under Napoleon* (Princeton, NJ: Princeton University Press, 1981). An analysis of the structure of Napoleon's regime, its social bases of support, and its opponents.

* Felix Markham, *Napoleon* (New York: New American Library, 1963). This classic study treats both Napoleon's life and legend, while giving a balanced account of the social and intellectual life of the period and the impact of the Empire on Europe.

Jean Tulard, *Napoleon: The Myth of the Saviour* (London: Weidenfeld and Nicolson, 1984). This biography of Napoleon situates his rise to power within the crisis of legitimacy created by the destruction of the monarchy during the Revolution. The Empire is presented as a creation of the bourgeoisie who desired to end the Revolution and consolidate their gains and control over the lower classes.

Isser Woloch, *The French Veteran From the Revolution to the Restoration* (Chapel Hill, NC: University of North Carolina Press, 1979). Examines the social impact of revolutionary and Napoleonic policies by concentrating on the changing fortunes of war veterans.

* Indicates paperback edition available.

MAP CREDITS

PHOTOGRAPH CREDITS

INDEX